POLITICAL AND SOCIAL UPHEAVAL

1832–1852

BY

WILLIAM L. LANGER

Harvard University

ILLUSTRATED

1817

HARPER & ROW, PUBLISHERS

New York, Evanston, and London

FIRST EDITION

LIBRARY OF CONGRESS CATALOG CARD NUMBER: 69–17284

To the Memory

of

Archibald Cary Coolidge

CONTENTS

CONTENTS

CONTENTS

ILLUSTRATIONS

These photographs, grouped in a separate section, will be found following page 140.

MAPS AND CHARTS

INTRODUCTION

Our age of specialization produces an almost incredible amount of monographic research in all fields of human knowledge. So great is the mass of this material that even the professional scholar cannot keep abreast of the contributions in anything but a restricted part of his general subject. In all branches of learning the need for intelligent synthesis is now more urgent than ever before, and this need is felt by the layman even more acutely than by the scholar. He cannot hope to read the products of microscopic research or to keep up with the changing interpretations of experts, unless new knowledge and new viewpoints are made accessible to him by those who make it their business to be informed and who are competent to speak with authority.

These volumes, published under the general title of *The Rise of Modern Europe,* are designed primarily to give the general reader and student a reliable survey of European history written by experts in various branches of that vast subject. In consonance with the current broad conception of the scope of history, they attempt to go beyond the merely political-military narrative, and to lay stress upon social, economic, religious, scientific and artistic developments. The minutely detailed, chronological approach is to some extent sacrificed in the effort to emphasize the dominant factors and to set forth their interrelationships. At the same time the division of European history into national histories has been abandoned and wherever possible attention has been focused upon larger forces common to the whole of European civilization. These are the broad lines on which this history as a whole has been laid out. The individual volumes are integral parts of the larger scheme, but they are intended also to stand as independent units, each the work of a scholar well qualified to treat the period covered by his book. Each volume contains about fifty illustrations selected from the mass of contemporary pictorial material. All noncontemporary illustrations have been excluded on principle. The bibliographical note appended to each volume is designed to facilitate further study of special aspects touched upon in the text. In general every effort has been made to give the reader a clear idea of the main movements in European history, to embody the monographic contributions of research workers, and to present the material in a forceful and vivid manner.

The foregoing two paragraphs have prefaced each of the volumes of the present series which have appeared since 1934. In view of the developments in historical work during the past generation they seem more appropriate than ever before. Over the intervening years the number of scholars trained and working in the field has increased greatly, the publication of source materials of all kinds has assumed formidable proportions, and the outpouring of monographs and articles has become all but unmanageable. It would now be impossible to master, in any one professional lifetime, any twenty years of European history if one were to work directly from the sources. Perhaps the greatest task now confronting the historian is less the search for new information than the organization and integration of the specialized literature produced by an ever-growing number of researchers. If this literature is to have any bearing on our historical understanding, it must be meshed with our existing knowledge and with other contributions in the field. This in turn means that historians, most of whom are admirably trained in the methods of research, must devote greater attention and effort to the larger task of historical synthesis and understanding.

The present book is the product of many years of study and reflection, frequently interrupted by government service and by the demands made by other commitments. Imperfect though it be, it represents a valiant attempt to draw together the vast, almost terrifying mass of literature and to establish a generally valid pattern of European development in a rather crucial period. It would be presumptuous and misleading to suggest that everything of importance has been taken into account. The fact that nowadays all countries, even the smallest, are actively engaged in the study and writing of their history confronts the historian with insuperable language difficulties. I cannot pretend to have studied the eastern European materials in as great detail as the western. Without command of such languages as Polish, Czech and Hungarian I have been obliged to deal with recent studies at second hand. Nonetheless, I have every hope of having done them justice or at least no injustice. I have tried also to take account of the Marxist slant which characterizes most of the recent eastern European historical work, to say nothing of some notable products of the western countries.

It has been rightly said that every historical period is a transitional one, and that the panorama of constant change in human affairs may be justly described as permanent revolution. Yet the idea and the reality of change are more characteristic of the period since the French Revolution than of preceding ages, and it can be argued with some cogency that the two decades analyzed in this volume mark the onset and spread of one of the truly major, epoch-making changes in the human condition. I refer, of course, to the accelerating industrialization of European society. Even in Britain, which in methods of production was still well in advance of the Continent, the full impact of industrial change came only with the dawn of the railway age. On the Continent the years 1832–1852 were marked by the first, often painful shock of economic and social innovation.

To trace the process of gradual social transformation and to recapture what Wordsworth called "the still, sad music of humanity" is far more difficult than to narrate the story of court intrigue, or trace the evolutions of political struggle, or recapture the history of military exploits. My studies of the early nineteenth century have impressed upon me the similarity between many of the problems of that time and those confronting European and world society more than a century later. Then as now the world was faced with tremendous population pressures, with all-too-rapid urbanization, with the menace of growing pauperism, and with rural as well as urban disturbances culminating in the cycle of revolutions at the end of the period. Governments, faced with novel problems and harassed by conflicting pressures, dreaded reform as the possible prelude to more drastic change and for the most part resorted to repression, so running the risk of mass violence and possible chaos. I have tried to analyze these and other forces, such as nationalism and socialism, as phenomena of European civilization as a whole, yet with due reference to the varying conditions in different countries. The lot of the common man is a major concern of my account. I strongly suspect that in these years the state of the lower classes sank lower than it had ever been before.

In pursuance of my studies I benefited greatly from a year as fellow of the Center for Advanced Study in the Behavioral Sciences at

Stanford, California, which is a veritable haven for scholars in need of consecutive months of undistracted work on some major project. I am glad, too, to acknowledge the work of my former assistants, Mrs. Edward W. Fox and the late Mrs. Miller Chapman, who in the initial phases of the project blocked out basic bibliographical data. Mrs. Edward B. Shannon typed the manuscript most competently. Needless to say, I have profited greatly not only from the splendid resources of the Harvard College Library but from the devotion of its staff. Miss Y. T. Feng, presently on the staff of the Boston Public Library, was unfailing in her helpfulness. And, in conclusion, I have to thank my good wife for her unflagging patience and generous understanding, to say nothing of her aid in proofreading and index-making.

POLITICAL AND SOCIAL UPHEAVAL

1832–1852

Chapter One

TWILIGHT OF THE OLD SOCIETY

1. THE RULING CLASS

THE two or three decades preceding the European revolutions of 1848 are commonly thought of as the period when the so-called Industrial Revolution came into full swing and quickly transformed the very bases of the social structure. This interpretation of developments is generally acceptable, but it should not obscure the fact that even in the midcentury the traditional society and its institutions continued to exist and indeed to function. It is truly astonishing how much of the old regime survived the upheavals of the French Revolution and the Napoleonic period, and how great was the continued resistance to change even in the face of fundamental alterations in the conditions of human living.

The institution of monarchy was one of those that most successfully weathered the storm. In the mid-nineteenth century there was but little disposition to question it, for the republicans constituted but a small and irreconcilable faction. The rulers, most of whom still claimed absolute power, took a more serious view of their responsibilities than they had in the past. Indeed, in Britain the young queen, Victoria, and her prince consort, Albert, set an example of almost painful respectability and sober devotion to public affairs.

The age-old antagonism between the nobility and the monarchy had worked itself out as community of interest in opposing the new forces became apparent. There was, one might say, a gentlemen's agreement by which the aristocracy recognized the unquestionable authority of the crown in return for preference in appointment to the desirable and lucrative positions in the administration, the army and the established church. Friction and intrigue there was at every court, but basically the alliance of throne and aristocracy was unshakable.

In most of Europe landed property continued throughout the nineteenth century to be the most important form of wealth. In England and France and even in more eastern parts of the Continent, commoners were increasingly investing the profits of trade and industry in the purchase of large landed estates, but it was the aristocracy that was the landholding class *par excellence* and in many areas still exercised substantial feudal rights.

France and the adjacent parts of the Low Countries, Germany, Switzerland and Italy were exceptional, in as much as they constituted an area of small landholdings. Even before the great Revolution serfdom had largely disappeared and peasant land tenure had made substantial progress. During the Revolution this process had been accelerated by the sale of the properties of the church and of the *émigré* nobility. Some aristocrats were able, through subterfuge, to retain or regain a substantial part of their holdings after 1815, but politicians, businessmen and the more prosperous peasants managed to acquire the lion's share of the confiscated lands. Nevertheless France was decidedly a country of small proprietors. There were over six million landowners, of whom the vast majority had diminutive holdings of less than five acres, often divided into disconnected strips. In the western part of France large estates of 500 to 1,000 acres were still fairly common, but after the Revolution of July, 1830, the high aristocracy (ultraroyalists and legitimists) were ruled out of political life. Still, the new, supposedly "bourgeois" regime of Louis Philippe was controlled not by bankers and businessmen, but by liberal elements of the nobility (many of them officials ennobled during the Napoleonic regime), by the gentry and by well-to-do peasants. The men elected to Parliament by the 200,000 French electors (paying 200 francs or more per year in direct taxes) were mostly landowners influential in their localities, while the members of the French cabinets were mostly judges, officials and professional politicians. In novels such as *Eugénie Grandet* (1833), *The Peasants* (1844) and *The Deputy for Arcis* (1847), Balzac has provided unforgettable examples of provincial notables, in many cases well-to-do peasants, who held much of the best land, gave mortgages, lent money at usurious rates, engaged in trade and local industry, and reckoned their resources in hundreds of thousands of francs.[1]

[1] Arthur Girault: "L'évolution de la propriété rurale en France depuis un siècle" (*Economiste français*, Oct. 4, 1924); Gérard Walter: *Histoire des paysans de France* (Paris, 1963), 393 ff., 405; E. Beau de Loménie: *Les responsabilités des dynasties bourgeoises* (Paris, 1943), I, 96; Jean Lhomme: *La grande bourgeoisie au pouvoir, 1830–1880* (Paris, 1960), 51 ff.; André-Jean Tudesq: "Les listes électorales de la Monarchie Censitaire" (*Annales*, XIII, 1958, 277–288) and his exhaustive study *Les*

With respect to land tenure, the British Isles were the very antithesis to France. In England and Wales about 500 members of the peerage (dukes, marquesses, earls, viscounts and barons) owned almost half of the total acreage (15 million acres), while roughly 1,300 members of the gentry and landed commoners possessed most of the remainder. The nobility, composed largely of families which had amassed wealth in the eighteenth century through the East India trade or in the West Indian sugar industry, enjoyed enormous incomes, the more so as many peers possessed Irish as well as British estates. The Duke of Bedford, with 86,000 acres in the agriculturally valuable counties of Bedford, Cambridge and Devon, with mines in Devon and 119 acres of London real estate, had an annual income of some £150,000; while the Earl of Derby, with some 70,000 acres, mostly in industrial Lancashire, had an income of £163,000; and the Marquess of Westminster, with large London properties, had about £100,000. These men, with palatial town houses and often several country "seats" situated in extensive parks, represented the ultimate in luxurious living (see Illustrations 1 and 2). Their estates were self-sufficient establishments with hundreds of rooms and sometimes a hundred or more servants, catering to droves of guests who were entertained for extended stays.[2]

The British nobility was distinguished by its active interest in public affairs. Among the most prominent and wealthy were the "governing families," members of which were constantly in high office. But the gentry and squirearchy also played an active role in public affairs, as justices of the peace or simply as local notables. Even contemporaries were impressed by the fact that after the great reform bill of 1832, which gave the franchise to the more well-to-do middle class, the aristocracy retained its political position essentially unchanged. The House of Lords was the special preserve of the peerage, but the House of Commons, as elected in December, 1832, also contained a hundred sons of peers and some two hundred placemen. Actually, there were fewer representatives of trade and industry than there had been in the

---

grande notables de France, 1840–1849 (Paris, 1964); Charles H. Pouthas: "Les ministres de Louis Philippe" (Revue d'histoire moderne et contemporaine, I, 1954, 102–130).

[2] John Bateman: The Great Landowners of Great Britain and Ireland (4 ed., London, 1883); David Spring, "English Landownership in the 19th Century" (Economic History Review, Ser. 2, Vol. IX, 1957, 472–484), and The English Landed Estate in the Nineteenth Century (Baltimore, 1963), 41; F. M. L. Thompson: English Landed Society in the Nineteenth Century (London, 1963), chaps. iv, v.

unreformed house. The position of the landed aristocracy was unshaken. In the cabinets of the period 1832 to 1866 no less than sixty-four ministers were aristocrats, as against twelve who were lawyers and only five primarily businessmen.[3]

In Central and Eastern Europe, still almost entirely agrarian in structure, the same situation existed. Naturally conditions varied somewhat from area to area. In the Scandinavian and Low Countries, as well as in regions adjacent to France, there was a substantial landholding peasantry, but even in these countries the nobility monopolized political power. Farther to the east, the dominance of the feudal elements was undiminished. In Prussia the Junkers (i.e., the East-Elbian landlords, some six to seven thousand noble families) had increased substantially the moderately large holdings they had had in the eighteenth century. In Silesia almost half of the total area was in the hands of fifty-four proprietors, each with holdings of more than 2,500 acres. These great landlords might own twenty or even more estates, totaling tens of thousands of acres. The Prince of Pückler-Muskau, well-known in his day as a *bon vivant,* traveler and writer, had several large estates of which one (Muskau) comprised 470 square kilometers, with forty-one villages and 16,000 inhabitants. These *grands seigneurs* lived much like their British cousins, and appropriated the best positions in the army, the church and the administration. In 1842 nine out of eleven Prussian ministers, twenty-nine out of thirty diplomats, twenty out of twenty-eight provincial governors and 7,264 out of 9,434 army officers belonged to the Junker caste.[4]

The situation in the Hapsburg Monarchy was comparable to that in Silesia. In the entire German-Slavic section of the monarchy there were probably fewer than a thousand families belonging to the nobility, of

[3] J. A. Thomas: *The House of Commons* (Cardiff, 1939), 4 ff.; S. F. Woolley: "The Personnel of the Parliament of 1833" (*English Historical Review*, LIII, 1938, 240–262); Harold J. Laski: "Le personnel du cabinet en Angleterre, 1801–1924" (*Revue du droit public*, L, 1933, 94–116).

[4] Otto E. Schüddekopf: *Die deutsche Innenpolitik im letzten Jahrhundert und der konservative Gedanke* (Brunswick, 1951), 22–23. On the number and size of the Prussian estates, see the data in Emile Jacquemin: *L'Allemagne agricole, industrielle et politique* (Paris, 1842), 23; J. Conrad: "Agrarstatistische Untersuchungen: die Latifundien im preussischen Osten" (*Jahrbücher für Nationalökonomie*, L, 1888, 121–170); Joseph Partsch: *Schlesien* (Breslau, 1911), II, 8 ff., 197 ff.; Walter Görlitz: *Die Junker* (Glücksburg, 1956), 171, 221 ff.; For an excellent survey of the agrarian situation in Germany, see Theodore S. Hamerow: *Restoration, Revolution, Reaction* (Princeton, 1958), chap. iii.

which several owned enormous properties. The Schwarzenbergs had almost 450,000 acres in Bohemia alone. In the Kingdom of Hungary only a few hundred aristocrats were classed as "magnates." Five of the leading families together owned 550 square miles of land. Prince Esterhazy alone had twenty-nine properties, with sixty market towns and 414 villages, a total of ninety-three square miles, which netted him an annual income of one million florins.[5]

In the vast Russian Empire it was customary to reckon landed property in terms of the number of male peasant-serfs ("souls") attached to the land. There were about 1,500 extremely wealthy families having more than a thousand "souls" each. Count Sheremetev, decidedly the richest landowner in Russia, is reputed to have had 2 million acres with 38,000 souls, Prince Yussupov 800,000 acres with 33,000 souls and Count Vorontsov 750,000 acres with 47,000 souls.[6] The Russian nobility was, as a class, certainly the most privileged in Europe, for it had been officially relieved of any obligation to serve the state, yet continued to enjoy exemption from personal taxes and, through the Charter of the Nobility (1785), exercised extensive control in local government. In national affairs its position was analogous to that of the aristocracy in neighboring countries, although Nicholas I tended to appoint commoners to many responsible positions.

It must not be supposed, however, that all nobles were wealthy, in terms either of land or money. Indeed, in countries like Hungary, Poland and Russia there was a substantial number of impoverished, landless nobles living on the level of the peasantry. Yet even they enjoyed tax exemption and preference in government employment. In a word, the aristocracy was still well entrenched in all parts of Europe. The storms of the French Revolution and of the Napoleonic period, which had destroyed so much of the old regime and had remade so many states, had failed to demolish the position of the traditional aristocracy which, allied with the monarchs, was able, as of yore, to use its wealth, position and prestige to retain control over government and administration.

[5] Heinrich Ditz: *Die ungarische Landwirtschaft* (Leipzig, 1867), 98 ff.; Jerome Blum: *Noble Landowners and Agriculture in Austria, 1815–1848* (Baltimore, 1948), 25 ff., 33 ff.

[6] Bertrand Gille: *Histoire économique et sociale de la Russie* (Paris, 1949), 144; Jerome Blum: *Lord and Peasant in Russia* (Princeton, 1961), chap. xviii; Michel Laran: "Nobles et paysans en Russie, 1762–1861" (*Annales*, XXI, 1966, 111–140).

2. THE POLITICS OF REPRESSION

It was probably inevitable that so one-sided a system as the European agrarian society should be challenged from time to time by the "black masses" which were exploited for the benefit of the few. Not only the Russian but the entire European landlord class lived in constant remembrance of the great uprising of 1773–1774 known as Pugachev's Revolt, during which the Russian nobility had been murdered wholesale, and its estates burned down. But even greater and more immediate was the fear of French revolutionary ideas; for while the peasantry was ignorant and dispersed and therefore hard to organize, the French Revolution was the work of educated men, inspired by the rationalist philosophy of the eighteenth century and intent on the destruction not only of the absolute monarchy but also of the whole system of aristocratic privilege (see Illustration 3). The Revolution had shown how the lands of the nobility and the church could be confiscated, and how the rising middle class could take its revenge on those who claimed a divine right to the good things of this world.

The European powers banded together to defeat the forces of the Revolution and of its heir, Napoleon. But the final defeat of France in 1815 did not exorcize the specter of social upheaval. The preceding volume of the present series has reviewed in some detail the consistent and determined efforts made during the so-called Restoration to suppress all expression of opposition to the old regime.[7] The Austrian chancellor, Prince Metternich, had a better appreciation of the issues involved than most statesmen. He recognized the rise of the middle class and was not opposed to all change. But such change could be only gradual unless the entire social fabric was to be rent asunder. Meanwhile the governments should really govern. Under his guidance the states of Central Europe tried systematically to choke liberal movements in the universities, and to muzzle the press. But in France, the very hearth of revolution, the returning nobility would hear nothing of gradualism or compromise. It made every effort to recover its properties and to restore the conservative influence of the church. It was a purblind and indeed hopeless effort, as other governments recognized, and was so provocative that in July, 1830, the Paris populace rose in revolt, drove out the Bourbon dynasty and chose a suitable ruler, Louis

[7] Frederick B. Artz: *Reaction and Revolution, 1814–1832* (New York, 1934).

Philippe, to assume the crown. The diehard ultraroyalist elements were driven from office and the more progressive groups took over. The landholding class was still in the saddle, but the new men had no thought of undoing the work of the great Revolution and were quite prepared to operate the constitutional, representative regime introduced in 1814.[8]

In Britain, where the middle class was more numerous than in France and the agitation for reform was of long standing, the crisis precipitated by the July Revolution threatened to end in insurrection, both in the cities and in the countryside. The situation was saved when the Parliament, though dominated by the landed interest, finally passed the Reform Bill, which admitted to political life the well-to-do elements of the middle class. By the strategy of concession the ruling caste, less hidebound than the French Ultras, enlisted the support of the most influential sector of the opposition, thus forestalling a real alliance between the upper middle class and the lower strata of the population in town and country.

This compromise was more possible and more natural in Britain than it would have been in France, for the dividing line between classes was less rigid. Although there were in Britain true-blue peers who looked down on the "shopkeepers" and "calico printers" with as great disdain as did their compeers across the Channel, they were definitely in the minority. Most British peerages went no farther back than the eighteenth or early nineteenth centuries and were based on fortunes made in business or in the military or diplomatic service.[9] There was therefore no great obstacle to the admission to the political "club" of men who had many of the required qualifications, including the ownership of landed property. The basic community of interest was reflected at once in the readiness of the newly enfranchised voters to elect the same type of landed aristocrat who had theretofore dominated the House of Commons. Conversely, the ruling class came more and

---

[8] As a result of the July Revolution 52 Legitimist deputies resigned their seats and another 68 had their seats invalidated. In addition 165 peers were excluded from the upper house, and 76 prefects and 196 subprefects either resigned or were discharged. See E. Beau de Loménie: *Les responsabilités des dynasties bourgeoises* (Paris, 1943), I, 96; René Rémond: *La Droite en France de 1815 à nos jours* (Paris, 1954), 55.

[9] Rudolf Gneist: *Adel und Ritterschaft in England* (Berlin, 1853), 24–25; John L. Sanford and Meredith Townsend: *The Great Governing Families of England* (London, 1865), passim; A. S. Turberville: *The House of Lords in the Age of Reform* (London, 1958), 366 f.

more to see the need for progressive reform and, in fact, came to identify itself with the new bourgeoisie. Of the aristocratic members of the house which sat from 1841–1847, fully 15 per cent were also active businessmen, while 35 per cent had at least such business connections as directorships of banks, insurance companies or railroad enterprises.[10]

In Central Europe, where industrialization was only just beginning to undermine the traditional social structure, the well-to-do middle class, that is, the business class, was still weak and unorganized. The liberals and radicals were for the most part academic people, along with writers, lawyers and other professional men. The July Revolution in Paris led to disturbances in various German states and resulted in some constitutional gains, which will be discussed in a later context (Chapter IV). But efforts to stage a revolutionary movement failed lamentably, their sole effect being to provide the governments further excuse for repressive measures. Under Metternich's guidance the federal Diet forbade all unauthorized popular meetings and associations, as well as petitions and appeals. Above all, the press was subjected to even more stringent supervision and censorship.

If repression was the order of the day in the Germanies and in Italy, it was even more so in the Russian Empire of Nicholas I. No ruler in Europe had a greater fear of revolution than he, nor a stronger determination to stamp out subversion. Nicholas had come to the throne in 1825 in the midst of the Decembrist insurrection, which was clearly inspired by foreign revolutionary doctrines. Having meted out the most severe punishment to the conspirators, the czar established a secret police, the chief function of which was to watch all foreigners and arrest all suspicious persons. Every effort was made to check the influx of subversive literature from abroad and to hold foreign travel on the part of Russians to a minimum. A rigorous system of censorship went almost without saying, as did police supervision of the universities.[11]

Although the czar did not succeed in stamping out disaffection, especially among the younger members of the educated class, he at least managed to forestall further organized revolt. The insurrection in

[10] W. O. Aydelotte: "The House of Commons in the 1840's" (*History*, XXXIX, 1954, 249, 262), and the same author's appendix to George Kitson Clark's *The Making of Victorian England* (Cambridge, 1962).

[11] Sidney Monas: *The Third Section: Police and Society in Russia under Nicholas I* (Cambridge, 1961).

Poland in 1830–1831 was more an attempt to win independence from Russian rule than a struggle for political or social reform. It was, in brief, a movement initiated by patriotic cadets at the military academy, supported by a group of intellectuals. As it progressed, some members of the aristocracy were drawn in, more or less reluctantly, while at the other end of the social spectrum the populace of Warsaw and other cities drove the provisional government in a radical direction. At no time did the revolution touch the peasant masses. On the contrary, all parties were alike averse to anything like land reform. No doubt this was one of the prime reasons for the failure of the war against Russia. In any event, the collapse of Polish resistance (September, 1831) was the prelude to ferocious revenge on the part of Nicholas. Such autonomy as Poland had enjoyed under the Treaty of Vienna was abolished and the country was incorporated with Russia. Martial law was maintained for twenty-four years and all the machinery of repression was put into operation. Insurgents who had failed to make their escape to the West were tried by courts-martial and their properties confiscated. Their children were in many cases seized as vagabonds or orphans, and sent off to the hated military colonies (see Illustration 6).[12]

In Poland as in Russia the autocratic czar spared no effort and shirked no methods to stamp out disaffection. He was convinced of the existence of a great international conspiracy to overturn the divinely appointed political and social order, and regarded himself as a gendarme defending the state and society. Though perhaps not cruel by nature, he held that order could be maintained only through constant vigilance, through energetic action and through quick and merciless punishment. Since at that time Russia and indeed all Eastern Europe was still untouched by the technological changes which were transforming Western Europe, there was no substantial, influential middle class clamoring for change. Opposition elements, inspired by the advanced ideas of the West, were few in number and without popular support. Under these conditions it was quite possible, with sufficient determination and ruthlessness, to choke off protest. Absolutely convinced of his own superior wisdom, Nicholas demanded of his subjects unqualified obedience. To have one's own ideas and above all to

[12] R. F. Leslie: *Polish Politics and the Revolution of November, 1830* (London, 1956).

express them, was tantamount to rebellion. The czar desired his subordinates to keep their peace even to the extent of abstaining from praise of the autocratic system.[13]

3. THE BLACK MASSES

The agitation for reform and the impetus to revolution centered largely if not wholly in the nonprivileged middle classes of the towns, but the unrest in the countryside must not be overlooked or underrated. For both the ruling class and the revolutionary elements kept the peasant problem constantly in mind. Occasional large-scale insurrections, such as the revolt of the Silesian handloom workers in 1844 or the large-scale uprising of the peasantry in Galicia in 1846, highlighted the agrarian problem, but tended to obscure the chronic peasant unrest as reflected in the so-called Tithe War in Ireland during the 1830's, the "Rebecca Riots" in Wales in 1842–1843 and the repeated rural outrages in Russia and elsewhere which made many remote estates almost uninhabitable for their owners.[14]

This particular problem warrants closer examination, for in 1850 the population of Europe was still overwhelmingly a peasant population and it was a matter of great concern what the role of the peasantry would be if ever the ideas of equality should materialize.

We may safely assume that the standard of living of the peasantry had been miserably low ever since the dawn of sedentary society. In the eighteenth century the "common herd," the "black masses," were generally rated as not much higher in the social scale than the cows and pigs which shared their hovels. Yet the evidence leaves little doubt that in many parts of Europe their lot had become harder by the early nineteenth century. It is dangerous to generalize, because of the multiplicity of systems of land tenure and the varying conditions in different countries. But so much seems clear: that with the rapidly increasing population, the demand for food and clothing became urgent. Farming

---

[13] Alexandre Koyré: *La philosophie et le problème national en Russie* (Paris, 1929), 154. See also Theodor Schiemann: *Geschichte Russlands unter Kaiser Nikolaus I* (Berlin, 1904–1919), I, chap. vii; Nicholas V. Riasanowsky: *Nicholas I and Official Nationality in Russia* (Berkeley, 1959); Hugh Seton-Watson: *The Russian Empire, 1801–1917* (Oxford, 1967), chap. vi.

[14] Geroid T. Robinson: *Rural Russia under the Old Regime* (New York, 1932), 60 ff.; Blum: *Lord and Peasant in Russia,* 551 ff.; J. I. Linkor: *Ocherki istorii krest' yanskogo dvisheniia v Rossii v 1825–1861* (Moscow, 1952).

and grazing were increasingly profitable and it was perhaps inevitable that changes should take place. Improved breeds of cattle and sheep were introduced; the methods of agriculture were modernized; waste lands were drained. Above all, the larger landowners everywhere attempted to enlarge and consolidate their holdings, if only to increase efficiency of operation. The result was the abolition of the open fields and common lands by legal procedure, by chicanery or by pressure. In England this was the process of "enclosure"; in Scotland of "clearance"; in eastern Germany of "regulation." The details might differ widely, but the result was in all instances much the same. By 1830 the rural scene had been profoundly altered. The poorer people had lost the right to glean the fields, to gather faggots in the forests, to run their cow or pig on the common. In return they had received small allotments of land, frequently so meager in size as to be unprofitable. In such cases there was no alternative to selling the land to the nearest landowner and becoming a landless farm laborer.

The results in most countries were strikingly similar. By the mid-nineteenth century there were in England and Wales some 700,000 families of landless agricultural laborers, representing about a fifth of the total population.[15] In Scotland many Highland lairds showed little compunction in "clearing" the cotters from the land so as to run sheep. The heiress of Sutherland, who owned almost the entire county, established a record by expelling 15,000 people from her estates and burning their cottages, while "generously" providing them with a couple of acres per family on which to eke out a living on the coast.[16]

In Ireland the condition of the peasants was perhaps worse than anywhere else in Europe. Some 6,000–7,000 English landlords, the "Protestant Ascendancy," held 90 per cent of the land, in estates running to tens of thousands of acres. The natives rack-rented small farms or one- or two-acre potato patches in return for payment in

---

[15] James Caird: *English Agriculture in 1850–1851* (London, 1851), 389; Pierre Flavigny: *Le régime agraire en Angleterre au XIXe siècle* (Paris, 1932), 138 ff., 173 ff.; H. G. Hunt, "Landownership and Enclosure, 1750–1830" (*Economic History Review*, Ser. 2, XI, 1959, 497–505); J. D. Chambers and G. E. Mingay: *The Agricultural Revolution, 1750–1880* (London, 1966), chap. iv; Barrington Moore, Jr.: *Social Origins of Dictatorship and Democracy* (Boston, 1966), 20 ff.

[16] John Prebble: *The Highland Clearances* (London, 1963) is rather journalistic. See also Ian Grimble: *The Trial of Peter Sellar* (London, 1962) for the Sutherland clearance, and in general R. H. Campbell: *Scotland since 1707* (New York, 1965), 173 ff.

"duty labor." Yet here, too, many landlords undertook "clearing" of their properties so as to run cattle for the British market (see Illustration 8).[17]

On the Continent the same process was under way in all countries except France, where small holdings appear to have actually increased in number, though the peasants progressively lost some of their traditional rights. In Scandinavia the consolidation of landholdings was virtually complete by the midcentury. It left a fifth of the population of Sweden and Norway and two-fifths of the Finnish population landless.[18] Similarly, the great estates of the Po valley and of central Sicily were gradually taking over the small holdings and reducing numerous peasant families to the status of day laborers.[19] With regard to Germany there is still some controversy as to how many peasants were made landless through the laws of 1807 emancipating the serfs and "regulating" the peasantry. So much, however, is agreed upon: in return for abolition of feudal dues the peasants paid with one-third to one-half of their land, while in the enclosure of the common lands they received only 14 per cent, mostly wasteland. Large numbers of small holdings were completely liquidated and absorbed in the large estates.[20] Yet farther east, where the feudal system was still in operation, the peasants owned little if any land, and were completely at the mercy of the landowners. In Hungary, for example, the landowners, by hook or crook, appropriated the common pastures. By 1846 there were 825,000

[17] John E. Pomfret: *The Struggle for Land in Ireland, 1800–1923* (Princeton, 1930); Thomas W. Freeman: *Pre-Famine Ireland* (Manchester, 1957).

[18] Robert Baird: *A Visit to Northern Europe* (New York, 1842), 322 ff.; B. J. Hovde: *The Scandinavian Countries, 1720–1865* (Boston, 1943), I, chap. viii; Eli F. Heckscher: *An Economic History of Sweden* (Cambridge, 1954), 215 ff.; Florence E. Janson: *The Background of Swedish Emigration, 1840–1930* (Chicago, 1931), chaps. iii and iv.

[19] Giorgio Candeloro: *Storia dell'Italia moderna* (Milan, 1958), I, 246 ff., 322 f.; Domenico Demarco: "L'economia degli Stati italiani prima dell'unità" (*Rassegna Storica del Risorgimento*, XLIV, 1957, 191–258); Rosario Villari: "L'economia degli Stati Italiani dal 1815 al 1848" (in *Nuove Questioni di Storia del Risorgimento*, Milan, 1961, 607–648); Luigi Bulferetti and Raimondo Luraghi: *Agricoltura, industria, e commercio in Piemonte dal 1814 al 1848* (Turin, 1966), chap. i; Pasquale Vacchini: *Mezzogiorno tra riforme e rivoluzione* (Bari, 1962), 322 ff.

[20] Kurt Hanefeld: *Geschichte des deutschen Nährstandes* (Leipzig, 1935), 228 ff.; Werner Conze: "L'émancipation des paysans d'après de récents travaux allemands" (*Journal of World History*, I, 1953, 179–194); Friedrich Lütge: "Über die Auswirkungen der Bauernbefreiung in Deutschland" (*Jahrbücher für Nationalökonomie und Statistik*, CLVII, 1943, 353–404); Dietrich Saalfeld: "Zur Frage des bäuerlichen Landverlustes in Zusammenhang mit den preussischen Agrarreformen" (*Zeitschrift für Agrargeschichte und Agrarsoziologie*, XI, 1963, 163–171).

peasant families without land as against 550,000 who still had small holdings.[21]

Where they could, the peasants rented or leased land in return for labor and produce. The systems of tenure varied enormously and in Italy usually took the form of sharecropping. Elsewhere in Central Europe the peasants contributed a substantial part of their time to domestic or field work for their landlords. Sometimes the law specified the maximum amount, but such restrictions were always circumvented. In the Danubian Principalities (modern Rumania), where the legal limit was twelve days a year, peasants were devoting forty to sixty days to the service of their voracious lords; in Russia, the classic land of forced labor, the law specified three days a week of work for the lord, while in practice the peasants, especially at harvest time, were left only Sundays and moonlit nights to cultivate their own little holdings. In addition to labor, the peasants almost everywhere had to pay taxes and make contributions to the lord in grain or other produce. Furthermore, they were required to supply the needed tools, carts and draft animals.[22]

The condition of the peasantry in the midcentury was such as to appall many observers. Henry Colman, the American, saw the landless workers as condemned to labor without any prospect whatever of betterment: "They are not slaves, but they are not free. . . . They have no chains on their hands, but the iron enters into their souls. Their limbs may be unshackled, but their spirits are bound. . . . They are used, and thrown aside, as occasion may require, like mere implements upon the farm."[23] This was said with reference to the agricultural laborers who were hired by the week or the day and consequently

[21] B. G. Ivanyi: "From Feudalism to Capitalism: the Economic Background to Szé-chenyi's Reform in Hungary" (*Journal of Central European Affairs*, XX, 268–288).

[22] On Rumania: David Mitrany: *The Land and the Peasant in Rumania* (New Haven, 1930), 22 ff.; Marcel Emérit: *Les paysans roumains dupuis le traité d'Andrinople* (Paris, 1937), 251–258; André Oţeţea: "Le second servage dans les Principautés, Danubiennes, 1831–1864" (*Nouvelles Etudes d'Histoire*, II, 1960, 325–346). The literature on Russian serfdom is almost endless. Outstanding are the comments of the eminent German scholars Johann G. Kohl: *Reisen in Südrussland* (Leipzig, 1847), III, 311 ff., and Baron August von Haxthausen: *The Russian Empire* (London, 1856). See also the references in an earlier footnote and, in addition, Peter I. Lyashchenko: *History of the National Economy of Russia* (New York, 1949), chap. xvii; Pierre Pascal: "Le paysan dans l'histoire russe" (*Revue historique*, CLXXIII, 1934, 32–79); Olga Crisp: "The State Peasants under Nicholas I" (*Slavonic and East European Review*, XXXVII, 1959, 387–412).

[23] Henry Colman: *European Agriculture and Rural Economy* (2 ed., Boston, 1849), II, 65, 140.

suffered long winter months of unemployment. Their wages in England were between eight and eleven shillings a week, which was not sufficient to support a family. Even with the addition of the woman's or children's work it was barely possible to stay alive. Traditionally the peasants had turned to home industry, especially spinning and weaving, as winter occupations to supplement their incomes. But increasingly as the century advanced the machine was taking over these functions and depriving the peasants of this last resource. The fate of the handloom workers was everywhere incredibly hard, leading in 1844 to the insurrection in Silesia during which factories were gutted and their owners beaten or murdered.

It takes but little imagination to envision the living conditions of the poorer peasants and rural laborers. Many of them lived in half-buried hovels of mud or wattle, with next to no furniture or bedding (see Illustration 7). Their food consisted largely of potatoes, the culture of which had become universal in the late eighteenth century and provided at least good food value. Potatoes might be supplemented by a little milk or cheese and, in the autumn, when the pig was slaughtered, with occasional pork or bacon. The time between potato planting and harvesting was the "summer famine," when in many parts of Europe droves of half-starved, half-naked men, women and children plodded along the roads begging for food and rags. As for the winter, that was made hideous not only by unemployment but by want of fuel.[24]

Hunger and cold led to a great increase in the consumption of hard liquor by the lower classes of both country and town. In Ireland the production of distilled liquor doubled between 1820 and 1830, while in 1830 Sweden produced 35 million gallons of *branvin* and *akvavit*, consumption reaching ten gallons per capita in that year. In the northern countries it was, one might say, the golden age of inebriation, so much so that heroic countermeasures became imperative. Agents of American temperance societies were warmly received in Europe even

---

[24] In my opinion the classic account of J. L. Hammond and Barbara Hammond: *The Village Labourer* (London, 1911) calls for but little correction. See, more recently, Norman Gash: "Rural Unemployment, 1815–1834" (*Economic History Review*, VI, 1935, 90–93); G. E. Fussell: *The English Rural Labourer* (London, 1949). On conditions in Germany see C. F. G.: "Der Pauperismus und seine Bekämpfung" (*Deutsche Vierteljahrschrift*, 1844, Heft 3, 315–340); on Italy, Domenico Demarco: *Il Crollo del Regno delle Due Sicilie* (Naples, 1960), 123 ff.; on Russia, Ronald Hingley: *Russian Writers and Society, 1825–1904* (London, 1967), 114 ff.

by monarchs and princes. By 1840 Europe was covered by local and national temperance organizations and that amazing Irishman, Father Theobald Mathew, was inspiring hundreds of thousands of people to take the oath of total abstinence. Mathew was undoubtedly one of the truly charismatic leaders of his day, a man whose deep concern for the suffering poor struck a responsive chord. Maria Edgeworth, the Irish novelist, called him "the greatest benefactor of his country," and the Boston Unitarian leader, William Ellery Channing, suggested that his name be inserted in the calendar of saints just below those of the apostles. For a time at least, in the 1840's, Mathew's efforts led to a marked reduction in liquor consumption in the British Isles.[25]

4. POPULATION PRESSURES

The plight of the European masses was due in large measure to the phenomenal increase of the European population which set in about 1760 and continued through the nineteenth century. Following a slow growth over millennia, that population suddenly took a great spurt, rising from 140 million in 1750 to 188 million in 1800 and 266 million in 1850, increasing by about 40 per cent in the first half of the nineteenth century. During that period it rose from 11 million to 22 million in Great Britain, from 5 million to 8½ million in Ireland, and, at the other end of the Continent, from 39 million to 60 million in European Russia.[26] So striking and revolutionary was the change that it can justly be called an "explosion."

As yet this all-important phenomenon awaits an adequate explanation. Earlier efforts (based largely on the British experience) to tie the population increase to the industrialization of the same period have had to be abandoned, since what happened in Britain happened everywhere in Europe, even in places where there was no suggestion of industrialization. Neither can it be attributed to advances in medical

[25] Rev. Patrick Rogers: *Father Theobald Mathew* (Dublin, 1943). Of great interest is the account of the American emissary, Robert Baird: *Visit to Northern Europe* (New York, 1842), II, 332 ff., and the contemporary review by P. S. White and H. R. Pleasants: *The War of Four Thousand Years* (Philadelphia, 1846), 240 ff. See also John C. Woolley and William E. Johnson: *Temperance Progress of the Century* (Philadelphia, 1905), chap. xv; Johann Bergmann: *Geschichte der Anti-Alkoholbestrebungen* (Hamburg, 1907), chap. xii.

[26] For most recent estimates, see John D. Durand: "The Modern Expansion of World Population" (*Proceedings of the American Philosophical Society*, CXI, 1967, 137–159).

knowledge and sanitation, for even though some progress had been made in these directions, they were far too modest to account for a drastic reduction in the death rate. It was only after the second great cholera epidemic of 1849 that European countries came to grips with problems of urban sanitation. Meanwhile the Continent continued to suffer heavy losses through cholera, smallpox, typhus and especially tuberculosis. In any case, the population increase came in the rural areas, where medical services were all but unknown and where the problems of sanitation were less acute. The cities continued to have a very high mortality rate and would have lost rather than gained population had it not been for the steady influx of newcomers from the surrounding countryside.

It seems more likely that the population explosion was due first to a higher marriage rate resulting from the relaxation or abolition of the controls of the seigneurial and guild systems, and second to a marked increase in the available food supply. It was here that the potato, the "miracle vegetable," appears to have played a crucial role. It would grow in rather poor soil, it could easily be cultivated with the spade, on very small parcels of land, and would yield in food value four times as much as wheat (see Illustration 10). Incredible though it may seem, a peasant could raise enough potatoes on one acre of land to support a family of eight, along with a cow and a pig, for an entire year. Peasants in many places were at first reluctant to give up wheaten bread for potatoes, but by 1800 the great value of the vegetable had been generally recognized and by 1830 it had become the main item in the diet of the poor throughout most of the Continent. During the whole nineteenth century the potato was to play a key role in social history. It meant that a young man with only a scrap of land could marry and have children. It meant also that girls could and did marry earlier and so prolong the period of their childbearing.[27]

The growing pressure for more food led to a great drive for more efficient agriculture. England was far in the lead. Great estates such as those of the Dukes of Bedford at Woburn were famous showplaces,

---

[27] On this entire problem, see the present author's article: "Europe's Initial Population Explosion" (*American Historical Review*, LXIX, 1963, 1–17). The excellent book by Redcliffe N. Salaman: *The History and Social Influence of the Potato* (Cambridge, 1949) deals largely with the British Isles. See also William Stuart: *The Potato; its Culture, Uses, History and Classification* (4 ed., Philadelphia, 1937).

visited by "improving" landlords from all over the Continent. In all countries agricultural societies were founded and trade journals published. Behind the enclosure movement and the gradual disappearance of peasant rights was the desire for large and more workable units. Furthermore, a great deal was accomplished in the way of drainage of old and clearing of new lands. There was even some improvement in the use of fertilizers (bone meal, guano). Actually there was no important increase in the yield of wheat per acre until after 1840, when the use of machinery became increasingly common in agriculture. But as late as 1850 much farming was still done by spade. Plows were heavy and ill-designed. Harvesting was done with sickle or scythe and threshing with the flail. It is an error to suppose that the improvements in agronomy which had been achieved in the eighteenth century were of much importance, except on certain large estates, prior to the mid-nineteenth century. The increased food production, which in general kept pace with the growth of population until 1840, was due primarily to the opening of additional arable land and to the consolidation of holdings. And, not to be forgotten, the inestimable value of the potato crop.[28]

By 1840 a good many areas of Europe were definitely overpopulated in the sense that there was not enough food available at prices consonant with the income of the common man, and that there was not enough employment to ensure even a subsistence wage. Ireland, with its large stagnant pool of surplus labor, was a glaring example that sent shudders through many contemporary observers. In the 1840's government investigators reported that 585,000 men (with families totaling 2,400,000) out of a population of 8 million were unemployed for more than a third of the year. Each year tens of thousands of Irishmen crossed the sea to Scotland and England to find work during the harvest or to settle in the cities as unskilled laborers or scavengers. "Nothing can exceed the destitution and squalidness in which they are seen," reported Henry Colman, after observing them in the south of England; "starved, ragged and dirty beyond all description, with tatters

---

[28] For the state of agriculture in England, admittedly the most advanced country in Europe, see the contemporary account of James Caird: *English Agriculture in 1850–1851* (2 ed., London, 1852), 474 ff., and standard histories of Lord Ernle: *English Farming Past and Present* (6 ed., Chicago, 1961), 357 ff.; Chambers and Mingay: *Agricultural Revolution*, 2 ff. On productivity see M. J. R. Healy and E. L. Jones: "Wheat Yields in England, 1815–1859" (*Journal of the Royal Statistical Society*, Ser. A, CXXV, 1962).

hanging about them like a few remaining feathers on a plucked goose."
At the same time some 75,000 Irishmen of at least some means were
emigrating to the New World.[29]

Conditions were not much better in parts of Scotland, England and
Wales. One parliamentary report revealed that in southern England
many men could not find employment for as much as nine months of
the year, while another reported two million people who used to subsist
on wheaten bread being reduced to a potato diet. More and more
people were being driven, albeit reluctantly, to seek salvation abroad.[30]
On the Continent it was Flanders and especially southwestern Germany that suffered from population pressure. In France, on the other
hand, the population was becoming stabilized by 1850. The evidence
indicates that there, alone among the European countries, even the
peasantry had concluded that for property reasons if for no other it was
undesirable to have too many children, and had therefore resorted to
elementary methods of birth control as early as the late eighteenth
century.[31] But in the overcrowded sections of Germany the men frequently had to move to other areas in search of seasonal employment,
and after 1840 the flow of emigration abroad became formidable. Even
in the vast Russian Empire some of the old central provinces were so
overpopulated that the landlords were constantly faced by the threat of
large-scale flight of serfs to the sparsely settled southeastern provinces.
Eventually the government and the landlords had to undertake the
systematic resettlement of the most destitute peasantry. In the critical
year 1843 not fewer than 171,000 were so moved.[32]

---

[29] K. H. Connell: *The Population of Ireland, 1750–1845* (Oxford, 1950), 24–25;
Barbara Kerr: "Irish Seasonal Migration to Great Britain, 1800–1838" (*Irish Historical
Studies*, III, 1942, 365–380); William F. Adams: *Ireland and Irish Migration to the New
World from 1815 to the Famine* (New Haven, 1932); Colman: *European Agriculture* (2
ed., Boston, 1849), II, 50.

[30] There is a wealth of information in William T. Thornton: *Over-Population and its
Remedy* (London, 1846), chaps. i to iii. See also G. E. Fussell: *The English Rural
Labourer* (London, 1949); E. L. Jones: "The Agricultural Labour Market in England,
1793–1872" (*Economic History Review*, Ser. 2, XVII, 1964, 322–338); Wilbur S.
Shepperson: "The Agrarian Aspects of Early Victorian Emigration to North America"
(*Canadian Historical Review*, XXXIII, 1952, 254–264).

[31] Charles H. Pouthas: *La population française pendant la première moitié du XIXe
siècle* (Paris, 1956); Hélène Bergues: *La prévention des naissances dans la famille* (Paris,
1960); Erich Keyser: *Bevölkerungsgeschichte Deutschlands* (3 ed., Berlin, 1943).

[32] François-Xavier Coquin: "Faim et migrations paysannes en Russie au XIXe siècle"
(*Revue d'histoire moderne et contemporaine*, XI, 1964, 127–144).

5. THE RULERS AND THE WORKERS

The European masses had no political rights and sent no deputies to Parliament. They were, for the most part, inarticulate and far too ignorant to have any clear conception of their relation to the rest of society. But they were hungry and cold and, despite the limitations of their intelligence, had an ingrained conviction that the land should belong to those who work it; that furthermore, a man willing to work should be able to feed and house his family. The European peasantry might appear to some as being resigned to their fate, but their resignation was a sullen one, easily fanned into revolt. The upper classes were only too well aware of this, though in different countries they approached the problem in different ways. In England, for example, humanitarianism was running strong and there was a growing feeling of responsibility for alleviating suffering. From their bounty English landlords would occasionally organize a feast for their tenants and workers. Lord Egremont in 1834 fed 6,000 people on roast beef, plum pudding and other delicacies. Others built decent cottages for the workers and opened schools for their children. Lord Spencer's cottages were provided each "with a pump, and with a kitchen to every five cottages, fitted up with oven, copper, iron-board, etc." The Duke of Bedford built 288 cottages on his Devon estate and 374 on his Bedford estate, and rented them at uneconomic rates in order to secure the good will of his peasants. The Duke of Devonshire, in turn, built a village at Edensor, complete with church and school, and with most attractive cottages "constructed substantially of white freestone, with variegated roofs, and interspersed with pretty green slopes and shrubs; their pointed gables, Italian towers, and snug picturesque little porches show that the labourer has both a comfortable and elegant home," wrote a visitor.[33]

The English example of progressive farming and enlightened social relations made a deep impression on foreign aristocrats, such as the Italian Count Cavour and the Hungarian Count Széchenyi. Returning home, they became advocates of social reform and particularly of the

---

[33] Caird: *English Agriculture in 1850–1851*, 401 ff., 431 ff.; Arthur J. Turberville: *The House of Lords in the Age of Reform* (London, 1958), 377 ff., quoting the Greville *Diaries;* David Owen: *English Philanthropy, 1660–1960* (Cambridge, 1964); David Spring: *The English Landed Estate in the Nineteenth Century* (Baltimore, 1963), 52.

extinction of all remaining remnants of feudalism. Among the Junkers of East Elbia there were many pietists who for religious if for no other reasons felt an obligation to the impoverished lower classes. Even in Russia, where ruthless exploitation and callous brutality were the order of the day, there emerged young aristocrats who were moved by idealism as well as by the progressive ideas of the West. Alexander Herzen deeply resented his father's maltreatment of his household serfs and denounced the lesser landlords, who were the most heartless, as tyrants, gamblers and drunkards. The great novelist, Ivan Turgenev, was haunted throughout life by memories of his mother's abominable abuse of her five thousand "souls," while another great writer, Fedor Dostoievsky, had reason to remember the murder of his father by his outraged serfs.[34]

The efforts of the good landlords were at best palliatives. The question what to do about surplus ("redundant") population and the all-pervading pauperism remained pressing. The Austrian Emperor Francis I saw that the problem of serfdom was "a red-hot poker," but for that very reason thought it had best be let alone. Czar Nicholas admitted that something would eventually have to be done and even appointed commissions to study the question. In the 1840's some rather fundamental reforms were introduced in behalf of the crown serfs, but the czar was never prepared to arouse the ire of private landowners, who insisted that serfdom was a divine institution, not to be tinkered with.

With respect to Western and Central Europe the teachings of Thomas Malthus had far-reaching effects. His famous *Essay on the Principles of Population* (1798, greatly expanded in 1803) was at once translated and much discussed in Germany. Faced with the doctrine that population tended to increase faster than the means of subsistence and that there was, therefore, a real and present danger of overpopulation, several South and West German states, as well as the Hapsburg Monarchy, introduced legislation to check population growth by restricting the right to marry. In some cases the marriage age for men

---

34 Nikolai I. Tourguénieff: *La Russie et les Russes* (Paris, 1847), II, 120 ff.; Jerome Blum: *Lord and Peasant in Russia*, 299 ff. Karl Stählin: *Geschichte Russlands* (Berlin, 1935), III, 438 ff., quotes secret Russian police reports on the sexual abuses committed by the landlords on their helpless household serfs. It was said that most of them maintained a veritable harem of peasant girls (see Illustration 11). See also Bernhard Stern: *Geschichte der öffentlichen Sittlichkeit in Russland* (Berlin, 1920), II, 1–56.

was set at thirty, and was made subject to evidence submitted to the local authorities that the applicant was of good character, had learned a trade, possessed at least some property, had not recently been on the relief roles, and had assurance of employment. In a sense this meant a return to the restrictions formerly exercised by the feudal lords and city guilds. Though a serious infringement of personal freedom, these laws were approved by eminent jurists, and even by economists such as Sismondi and John Stuart Mill, as being one of the few promising methods for dealing with the increasingly desperate population problem. In actual fact they seem to have produced only a higher rate of illegitimacy and a stronger current of emigration.[35]

In Britain, where a major agrarian uprising had threatened in 1830–1831, the situation was such that drastic action seemed indicated. Malthus had argued that the plight of the poor was due in large measure to their own indolence and improvidence. Public relief, especially the system of supplementing wages through contributions from the poor rates, served only to protect them against their own folly and delinquency, in as much as the existing poor laws encouraged early marriage and large families. Malthus would have preferred no poor law whatever, but Parliament in 1832 appointed a commission to study the entire problem of poverty and make recommendations for reform. The most active and influential member of the commission, the man who drafted the voluminous report and formulated the principles of the new poor law, was Edwin Chadwick, an ardent disciple of Jeremy Bentham and a convinced utilitarian, whose main objective was to reduce costs and improve efficiency. The system of allowances to supplement wages tended, he believed, to keep the worker from the labor market rather than to drive him into it. Hence he proposed an end to outdoor or home relief. Paupers were to be housed in workhouses, where on principle life was to be made less desirable than even the most precarious existence outside. To this end the aged and infirm, the children, the men and women were to be housed separately, kept in healthy though drab surroundings and fed on minimum rations. English parishes were to be combined for poor-law purposes in

[35] Franz Herzog: *Systematische Darstellung der Gesetze über den politischen Ehe-Consens in Kaiserthume Oesterreich* (Vienna, 1829); Friedrich Thudichum: *Ueber unzulässige Beschränkungen des Rechts der Verehelichung* (Tübingen, 1866); David V. Glass: *Introduction to Malthus* (London, 1953), 39 ff.

"unions," each with its workhouse and its locally elected guardians. At the top, three poor-law commissioners were to exercise supervision and control.

The new poor law passed through Parliament without meeting serious opposition. There was much objection to the powers of the proposed commissioners, which interfered with traditional local authority, but even the diehard ("pigtail") Tories were lured by the prospect of substantial savings in the poor rates.[36] These were, in fact, greatly reduced as workhouses were built and laborers forced to work or take the consequences. Outside Parliament, however, there was much and violent opposition to the new system, chiefly on humanitarian grounds. The London *Times* was filled for years with stories of abuses and was reinforced by the account of workhouse life and poor-law administration in Dickens' famous novel *Oliver Twist* (1836). Modern research has, however, revealed other aspects of the situation. For example, the system of allowances, Chadwick's great bugbear, is now seen as an effort to tie wages to the cost of living and to provide unemployment relief: "basically a humanitarian policy which helped keep alive a swelling rural proletariat at the expense of the farmers' profits and the landlords' rent."[37] Evidently Chadwick, to prove his case, greatly exaggerated the situation as he found it. Furthermore, the workhouse system appears to have been not nearly as bad as many maintained. No doubt workhouse life was unspeakably drab and the effort to reduce the birth rate among the poor by separating husbands and wives can hardly be described as anything but inhumane. But the food was as good as the outside average and such abuses as there were stemmed mostly from guardians and supervisors, not from the provisions of the law.[38] However, the workers objected so violently to the workhouses (the "Bastilles") and in some areas the living standards of the rural workers were so low that it was impossible to make the workhouse less desirable, so that the new poor law could not be en-

---

[36] On the importance of the administrative innovation, see David Roberts: *Origins of the British Welfare State* (New Haven, 1960), 38 ff.

[37] Chambers and Mingay: *Agricultural Revolution,* 119 ff.; Mark Blaug: "The Myth of the Old Poor Law and the Making of the New" (*Journal of Economic History,* XXIII, 1963, 151–184), and "The Poor Law Report Re-examined" (*ibid.,* XXIV, 1964, 229–245).

[38] David Roberts: "How Cruel was the Victorian Poor Law?" (*Historical Journal,* VI, 1963, 97–107).

forced, especially in the northern counties. The system of outdoor relief was resumed and in 1840 about 85 per cent of poor relief was of this character. The new poor law, then, was interesting as an experiment and certainly as a revolutionary step in administration, but it did not fundamentally alter the structure of relief and it did not affect the rate of population growth. In the last analysis it is clear that Chadwick and his associates did not see or did not want to see what French critics were constantly emphasizing: that at bottom the problem of rural poverty and unemployment derived from the system of land tenure. The commissioners' inquiries revealed an insistent demand for allotments of land sufficient to support a family. But this demand was ignored, in the interests of economy and efficiency, if for no others. Alexis de Tocqueville, who, as a Frenchman, knew all about the land hunger of the peasantry, was amazed to find that in England "the thought of even a gradual sharing of the land has not in the least occurred to the public imagination."[39]

In reviewing the condition of the vast majority of the European population in this period, one cannot fail to be impressed by the tensions generated by the precipitous increase in people, aggravated by the dislocations of the Revolutionary and Napoleonic period and, in Western Europe, the adjustments to a new system of production. Many members of the upper classes felt that they were living on a volcano, and so they were, for even though organized revolt on the part of the peasantry was difficult, there could be no question of their latent hostility and it was impossible to ignore the significance of their periodic outbursts. In Ireland the so-called Tithe War of the 1830's was actually a social insurrection. In Central Europe there was the revolt of the Silesian weavers and the bloodcurdling massacre of the landlords in Galicia, while in Russia peasant outbreaks were chronic. Many of them were hushed up, yet it was officially admitted that between 1826 and 1854 there were over 500 "serious" disturbances and 132 occasions when troops had to be called in to restore order. A contemporary German observer, Johann Kohl, estimated that each year about sixty landlords

[39] Tocqueville: *Journeys to England and Ireland*, 72. Of recent literature on the poor laws, see the excellent biography of Chadwick by S. E. Finer (London, 1952); S. Maccoby: *English Radicalism, 1832–1852* (London, 1935), chap. vii; H. L. Beales: "The New Poor Law" (*History*, XV, 1931, 308–319), and "The Passing of the Poor Law" (*Political Science Quarterly*, XIX, 1948. 312–322); Oliver MacDonagh: "The Nineteenth Century Revolution in Government" (*Historical Journal*, I, 1953, 52–57).

were beaten to death or otherwise murdered by their serfs. The peasant problem was indeed a red-hot poker, but its very magnitude defied solution. It was perhaps unreasonable to suppose that the upper classes should repeat the night of August 4, 1789, in the French National Assembly. But when the revolutions of 1848 broke out, the threat of agrarian insurrection became so great and so immediate that everywhere serfdom and the vestiges of feudalism were swept away as the prelude to a newer and brighter period of European agriculture and general welfare.

Chapter Two

THE MARCH OF MODERN INDUSTRY

I. BRITAIN: WORKSHOP OF THE WORLD

By 1832 the Industrial Revolution, that is, the progressive mechanization and concentration of the processes of production and the substitution of mechanical power for human effort, had been changing British society for upward of fifty years. Britain was well on the way to becoming the first truly industrialized state. The national product was growing at something like 3 per cent per annum, a hitherto undreamed-of rate, and the national income was already being derived largely from manufacturing (35 per cent) and trade (17 per cent).[1] Clearly the British people had by this time accumulated a substantial amount of capital, much of which was being constantly plowed back into business. The financial and banking system was being geared to the new requirements and presently measures would be taken to adapt company structure to the changed conditions.

In the field of technology all the basic inventions had already been made and were being constantly improved and refined.[2] In smelting, coke had replaced charcoal, and the puddling process was being commonly employed in casting iron. The steam engine had been brought to a high degree of efficiency and was in widespread use not only in coal and iron mines but in the new textile factories, where spinning and weaving and presently many other processes were being mechanized. Thomas Carlyle, writing in 1831 of the Age of Machinery, commented that

nothing is done now directly, or by hand; all is by rule and calculated contrivance. For the simplest operation, some helps and accompaniments, some

---

[1] Walt W. Rostow: *British Economy in the Nineteenth Century* (Oxford, 1948), 8; Phyllis Deane and W. A. Cole: *British Economic Growth, 1688–1959* (Cambridge, 1962), 170: Phyllis Deane: *The First Industrial Revolution* (Cambridge, 1965), chap. xiv.

[2] G. B. L. Wilson: "Technical Gains during the Nineteenth Century" (*Journal of World History*, VI, 1960, 517–558); T. Kingston Derry and Trevor I. Williams: *A Short History of Technology* (Oxford, 1960), Part II.

cunning abbreviating process is in readiness. Our old modes of exertion are all discredited and thrown aside. On every hand, the living artisan is driven from his workshop, to make room for a speedier, inanimate one.[3]

This was something of an exaggeration, but the stamp of industrialism had certainly been put upon British life. Modern industrial cities, such as Manchester, Leeds and Glasgow, were rapidly crowding out the earlier industrial villages. They were linked to the sources of coal and iron and to the seaports through an extensive system of canals and turnpikes. Steam carriages, true automobiles, were already running from the City to the outlying parts of London and from the capital to Bath. On the navigable rivers and in the coastal trade hundreds of small steamboats and packets were providing speedy transportation for passengers and goods.[4]

It was at this juncture that a new and all-important phase of industrialization was inaugurated by the coming of the railway or, perhaps more accurately, the steam locomotive. Roads of wooden or iron rails had been known for some time, and years were yet to pass before the use of horse-drawn vehicles on railways was to be abandoned, at least on the Continent. The steam locomotive, built by George Stephenson, had been first introduced on the Stockton-Darlington Railway in 1825. It was used primarily for the haulage of coal, but the railway was available also to the coach companies, which, as on any toll road, could run their horse-drawn coaches on payment of a fee. The Liverpool-Manchester line, which was opened in 1830, was quite different and was, in fact, the first modern railway. Built and equipped by Stephenson and his son Robert, it was designed more for passenger traffic than for freight and was from the start powered exclusively by steam locomotives. Stephenson's famous engines, the *Rocket* and especially the *Planet,* established the steam locomotive as the pre-eminent instrument of land transportation. The promising steam automobile soon disappeared when faced by the hostility of the coaching companies. But the railway was quite another matter. Its capacity, speed and cheapness were at once recognized. It answered an immense unsatisfied demand for passenger travel and was at once amazingly successful (see Illustra-

---

[3] Carlyle: "Characteristics" (*Edinburgh Review,* 1831), quoted in David Daiches: *Carlyle and the Victorian Dilemma,* Edinburgh, 1963.

[4] C. S. Davison: *History of Steam Vehicles* (London, 1953); George Chandler: *Liverpool Shipping* (London, 1960), 50 ff., 111 ff.

tion 17). In 1831 the Liverpool-Manchester line was already transporting hundreds of passengers a day, covering the thirty-two miles in seventy-five minutes at the cost of five shillings. Contemporaries were duly impressed. In the words of Henry Booth, the secretary of the company,

It was altogether a new spectacle, to behold a carriage crowded with company, attached to a self-moving machine, and whirled along at the speed of thirty miles per hour. . . . The railway has brought a sudden and marvellous change . . . in our ideas of time and space. . . . Speed, despatch, distance are still relative terms, but their meaning has been totally changed within a few months: what was quick is slow; what was distant is now near; and this change in our ideas will not be limited to the environs of Liverpool and Manchester—it will pervade society at large.[5]

Industrial Britain was a marvel the like of which had never been seen. Visitors came in ever greater numbers to booming Lancashire, where the population rose from 1,335,000 in 1831 to 2,031,000 in 1851 and where the clustered factory towns could be distinguished by the forests of smokestacks shrouded in smog, "an inky canopy which seemed to embrace and involve the entire place." The chief city and the industrial center par excellence was Manchester-Salford. Its population grew from 271,000 in 1831 to 455,000 in 1851 and its dozens of cotton mills each employed from 300 to 1,500 workers. The sight of it was both thrilling and frightening.[6]

The further industrialization of Britain in the 1830's and 1840's was greatly stimulated by the development of the steamship and the railway, the former opening up the avenues of international trade and the other of the domestic market. The introduction of the screw propeller in 1838 made possible the construction of larger hulls with greater fuel capacity, and so paved the way for the iron steamship. The Cunard Line (1840) operated at first with wooden ships, but the iron, screw-propelled steamer gradually came into its own. In 1838 the *Great Western,* designed by I. K. Brunel, had crossed the Atlantic in two

[5] Henry Booth: *An Account of the Liverpool and Manchester Railway* (Liverpool, 1830), 74, 89; Michael Robbins: *The Railway Age in Britain and its Impact on the World* (Baltimore, 1965), 15.

[6] Sir George Head: *A Home Tour through the Manufacturing Districts of England in the Summer of 1835* (New York, 1836), 145 ff., 279; W. Cooke Taylor: *Notes of a Tour in the Manufacturing Districts of Lancashire* (2 ed., London, 1842), 2; A. J. Taylor: "Concentration and Specialization in the Lancashire Cotton Industry, 1825–1850" (*Economic History Review,* 2 Series, I, 1948 114–122).

weeks. Presently the Peninsular and Oriental Steam Navigation Company (the P. and O.) inaugurated mail service from England to Alexandria (1840) and then from Suez to Calcutta (1843). To be sure, the British merchant fleet in 1852 was still predominantly a sailing fleet and the great days of the clippers were only beginning. Nonetheless, oceanic steam shipping was being rapidly developed.[7]

The railway proved itself more immediately popular and profitable. Within a couple of years the Liverpool-Manchester line was carrying 1,100 persons per day on the average, and when it paid a dividend of 10 per cent the value of its shares quickly doubled. More companies were organized and more lines were chartered, eighty-eight during the first railway boom of 1834–1836 alone. In 1837 the important London-Birmingham line was opened and work was progressing on the Grand Junction line that was to connect it with the Liverpool-Manchester. By 1843 some seventy companies were operating 2,000 miles of railway and carrying 25 million passengers a year. There followed the second and greatest railway boom (1844–1845), when people from all walks of life invested frantically in several hundred new companies chartered by Parliament. Though the bubble soon burst, with the usual tragic results, a vast amount of capital had been subscribed and the work of construction went on. Iron foundries worked desperately to supply the 300 tons of rail needed for every mile of new line, and tens of thousands of workers (navvies) labored with pick and shovel to bore tunnels, excavate cuts, and build bridges or viaducts.[8]

The years 1846–1849 were the golden age of George Hudson, a self-made Yorkshireman, a great organizer and a man of vision, who managed to amalgamate many competing lines and lay the foundation for a national network. Hudson's business eventually collapsed when it became clear that he had misappropriated funds and had otherwise engaged in financial wizardry, but his achievement in consolidation remained.[9] By 1851 there were about 7,000 miles of railway in operation and over 47 million passengers traveled by rail.

[7] C. R. Vernon-Gibbs: *British Passenger Liners of the Five Oceans* (London, 1963), 31 ff., 173 ff.

[8] Cuthbert H. Ellis: *British Railway History* (London, 1954, 1959), I, 31; O. S. Nock: *The Railways of Britain* (London, 1949), 10 ff.; Jack Simmons: *The Railways of Britain* (London, 1961), chap. i; Robbins: *Railway Age*, 33 ff.; Henry G. Lewin: *The Railway Mania and its Aftermath, 1845–1852* (London, 1936); L. T. C. Holt: *George and Robert Stephenson: the Railway Revolution* (London, 1960).

[9] Richard S. Lambert: *The Railway King: a Study of George Hudson and the Business Morals of His Time* (London, 1934).

The railway companies were opposed by the canal and turnpike interests, as well as by landowners who resented the invasion of their privacy and the interference with their hunting. But the companies had many devoted investors and enjoyed immense popularity, despite numerous accidents. Efforts were made by the Board of Trade to introduce some measure of government control, but the opposition was too great. All that eventuated (1844) was provision for at least one third-class train daily on each line, with benches in the coaches and some overhead protection (see Illustration 17). By 1850 the upper classes were able to travel in luxurious carriages, at speeds up to sixty miles per hour, and to any one of the important towns of the kingdom. The railway age had indeed arrived (see Illustration 19).

In connection with the development of the railways note must be taken of an important invention of the period, the electric telegraph, though only its beginnings fall within this period. As the tempo of travel increased and the volume of trade expanded, the need for faster and more reliable communications made itself felt. On the Continent the system devised by the Chappe brothers in 1804 was being more and more widely adopted. This system involved the use of specially constructed towers at intervals of ten miles, equipped with semaphore arms for signaling. In daylight when the weather was clear the Chappe system was remarkably efficient. For instance, when in 1829 it took a courier five days to carry news of the papal election from Rome to Toulon, the same news was telegraphed from Toulon to Paris in four hours. The French government continued to expand its network until in 1844 it had 5,000 kilometers in operation, connecting Paris with twenty-nine cities. In 1833 the Prussian government had constructed connections between Berlin and the cities of the Rhineland, and in 1838 the Russian government opened a line from St. Petersburg to Warsaw.

But the dream cherished by scientists since the eighteenth century centered on the possible use of electric current for the transmission of messages. The way was finally opened by the discoveries of Oersted (1820) and Faraday (1830), and in 1833 the great mathematician Johann K. F. Gauss and his Göttingen colleague Wilhelm Weber built a line over a mile long which worked very well and was presently simplified by C. A. Steinheil. A few years later Charles Wheatstone, a well-known scientist at the University of London, together with William Cooke, an ex-army officer and promoter, pooled their experience

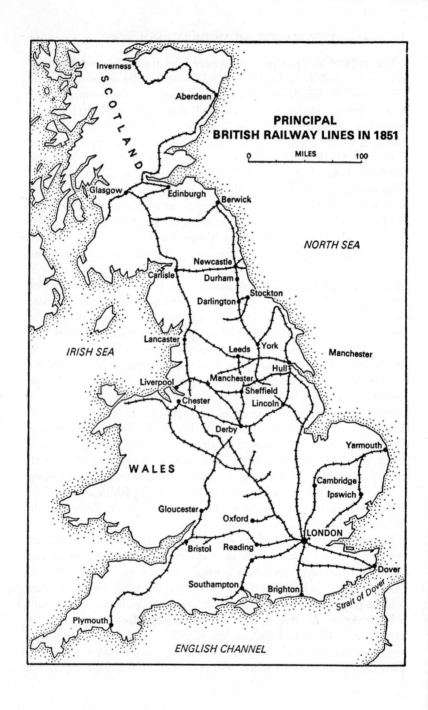

**PRINCIPAL
BRITISH RAILWAY LINES IN 1851**

0   MILES   100

Inverness

S C O T L A N D

Aberdeen

Glasgow   Edinburgh   Berwick

NORTH SEA

Newcastle

Carlisle   Durham

Darlington   Stockton

Lancaster

IRISH SEA

Leeds   York

Manchester

Liverpool   Manchester   Hull

Sheffield

Chester   Lincoln

Derby

Yarmouth

WALES

Cambridge

Ipswich

Gloucester

Oxford

LONDON

Bristol   Reading

Dover

Southampton   Brighton

Strait of Dover

Plymouth

ENGLISH CHANNEL

and patented the first really successful system. In the very same year the Americans Samuel F. B. Morse and his associates devised an even better system, employing the "Morse" code for transmitting actual words. But it was 1843 before Morse succeeded in persuading Congress to appropriate money for construction of the Washington-Baltimore line, which was put into operation in 1844.

Developments in Britain were somewhat faster. In 1839 the Great Western Railway installed a thirteen-mile line from Paddington to West Drayton, which was then slowly expanded. Even with the use of the railway right of way, construction of telegraph lines was extremely expensive, which accounts for the reluctance of the companies to exploit the invention. However, a new Electric Telegraph Company, based on the Wheatstone-Cooke patents, was organized and financed in 1846, after which the electric communications system was quickly and widely adopted. By 1852 the British railways had installed 4,000 miles of line and London had been hooked up with Paris by a cable under the Channel. Governments all over the Continent, chastened by the revolutions of 1848-1849, were hastily connecting up major cities and garrisons. Cooke had long since tried to point out to government authorities that the telegraph would permit them "to transmit their orders to the local authorities and, if necessary, send troops for their support; while all dangerous excitement of the public might be avoided." He and Morse had also stressed the potential use of the new system for transmission of commercial information. But prior to 1852 the electric telegraph was still essentially an instrument for railway signaling, where its immense value was quickly demonstrated.[10]

To review the progress of British industry in this period would make a long story. Only a few points need be made here. The cotton trade remained in the forefront. Between 1830 and 1850 the importation of raw cotton, mostly from the United States, rose from 250 million to 620 million pounds. Sixty per cent of the yarns, threads and finished goods were exported, the United States being one of the chief customers.[11]

[10] Charles Singer et al.: A History of Technology (Oxford, 1958), Vol. IV, chap. xxii; Derry and Williams: Short History of Technology, 621 ff.; George Hubbard: Cooke and Wheatstone and the Invention of the Electric Telegraph (London, 1965); Carleton Mabee: The American Leonardo: the Life of Samuel F. B. Morse (New York, 1943), esp. 189 ff., 258 ff.

[11] J. Potter: "Atlantic Economy, 1815-1860: The United States and the Industrial Revolution in Britain" (in L. S. Presnell, ed.: Studies in the Industrial Revolution, presented to T. S. Ashton, London, 1960, 236-280).

The cotton-spinning industry was almost completely mechanized, and the weaving process was rapidly becoming so (see Illustration 24). The cotton industry so dominated the industrial scene that discussions of factory conditions referred almost invariably to the cotton mills. Nonetheless other textile industries—woolens, linens, silks—also grew substantially, as shown by the rate of increase of raw-materials imports, which amounted to 60 to 100 per cent, though in these lines handwork and the putting-out system persisted in a much larger degree than in cottons.

The demands of industry and especially the rapid development of the railways provided the coal and iron industries with a powerful stimulus. The production of coal more than doubled in this period, while that of pig iron just about quadrupled yet even so was hardly able to keep up with the demand for rails, cables, tubes and shafts. At one of the largest plants—Sir John Guest's at Doulais, Wales—there were eighteen blast furnaces. Seven thousand workers produced 74,888 tons of finished iron annually. Small wonder that visitors were impressed with the four-ton steam hammers, the huge rollers and the towering chimneys. By 1848 Britain was producing almost two million tons of iron, more than the rest of the world combined. The prohibition on the export of machines was lifted in 1843, after which contrivances of every sort, as well as rails, were exported to all parts of the world.[12]

In reviewing the amazing growth of British industry, one should avoid the impression that the process of economic change was even or steady. Exactly the reverse was true. The period was one punctuated by booms and recessions which at the time were not understood and therefore provoked much discussion and inspired much uneasiness. A century later their origins and character were still the subject of speculation.[13] Modern studies reveal a strong upward trend in the

[12] David Spring: "The Earls of Durham and the Great Northern Coalfield, 1830–1880" (*Canadian Historical Review*, XXXIII, 1952, 237–253); G. W. Allen: *The Industrial Development of Birmingham and the Black Country, 1860–1927* (London, 1929), Part I, chap. ii; Henry Hamilton: *The Industrial Revolution in Scotland* (Oxford, 1932); W. H. Marwick: *Economic Developments in Victorian Scotland* (London, 1936), 17 ff.; R. H. Campbell: *Scotland since 1707* (New York, 1965), chap. vii; Evan J. Jones: *Some Contributions to the Economic History of Wales* (London, 1928), 53 ff., 66 ff.

[13] Walt W. Rostow: *British Economy in the Nineteenth Century* (Oxford, 1948); Arthur D. Gayer, Walt W. Rostow and A. J. Schwartz: *The Growth and Fluctuation of British Economy, 1790–1850* (2 vols., Oxford, 1953); Robert C. O. Matthews: *A Study in Trade-Cycle History: Economic Fluctuations in Great Britain, 1833–1842* (London,

years 1833–1836, followed by a sudden depression and slow recovery to 1839, and then another period of hard times to 1842. There was a short period of real prosperity which ended with the bursting of the railway bubble in 1845 and was followed by the famine and crisis years 1845–1849. The final few years marked a slow recovery from the turmoil of the 1848 revolutions. It is clear that the accelerated tempo of economic life and the greatly enhanced rate of production presented the business world with problems of which previously it had had only the barest inkling. In the days before the telegraph it was impossible to predict or even know the demand for various goods in distant parts, and so to adjust production to changing market requirements. The industrial scene was as unpredictable as the harvests. People at the time were keenly aware that they were living in a new and rapidly changing world, a world that was marvelous, not to say fantastic, but at the same time unstable and distressingly uncertain.

2. THE CONTINENT: ON THE THRESHOLD OF THE NEW ECONOMY

In the summer of 1851 there opened in London the first great international exhibition, intended, in the words of Prince Consort Albert, its sponsor, to provide "a living picture of the point of development at which the whole of mankind has arrived." It was a truly impressive affair, housed in the immense Crystal Palace, a structure of glass on iron supports which covered an area of nineteen acres (see Illustration 18). One-half the space was devoted to British exhibits, the remainder to foreign contributions. The former completely overshadowed the latter. Over six million people, mostly Britishers, were brought to London by the new railways and all marveled at the examples of British machinery and British products. These were convincing evidence of Britain's primacy in the fields of production and transportation. They left little doubt that Britain was in fact a full generation in advance of Continental competitors.

The exhibits of other European nations were also impressive, but they were traditional. There were beautiful examples of French and Italian *objets d'art,* fine furniture and specialized handicrafts in textiles and leather and metal. German states submitted fine chinaware, musi-

1954); Phyllis Deane and W. A. Cole: *British Economic Growth, 1688–1959* (Cambridge, 1962); Sydney G. Checkland: *The Rise of Industrial Society in England, 1815–1885* (London, 1965).

cal and other instruments and weapons. It was clear that the Continental nations were easily holding their own in items of the traditional, artisanal economy, but that they were far from being able to compete in the fields of mechanization, mass production or the application of inanimate power to industry and transportation.[14]

In the late eighteenth century it had seemed that some of the nations of the Continent might follow close behind Britain in matters of industrialization, but the turmoil of the Revolutionary and Napoleonic periods had proved highly detrimental. It had disrupted the traditional economy by liquidating the guild system, had destroyed large amounts of capital and, through the Continental blockade, had upset normal trade relationships. It is true that Napoleon's economic policies encouraged the development of the beet-sugar industry and provided a stimulus for the armaments and textile trades, but these industries, along with others, were to feel the severe impact of British competition after 1815. Europe was then flooded with the cheap products of British industry and governments, large and small, hastily resorted to high protective tariffs which, in turn, served further to obstruct international trade and prevent the exploitation of a large market.[15]

The Continent remained, during the first half of the nineteenth century, a predominantly agricultural area, which exported not only grain and cattle but many raw materials such as iron (from Sweden and Spain), wool, flax and raw silk for processing in British factories. Industry there was, of course, but of the traditional type. Major cities such as Paris, Berlin, Vienna and Milan and also lesser centers were beehives of industry, producing clothes, shoes, cutlery, jewelry, saddlery, furniture and housing of every kind.[16] Even in the countryside there was much manufacturing under the home-industry and putting-out systems. Peasants commonly spent part of their time, especially in winter, in spinning and weaving and in other handicrafts.

[14] Christopher Hobhouse: *1851 and the Crystal Palace* (rev. ed., London, 1950); C. H. Gibbs-Smith: *The Great Exhibition of 1851* (London, 1950); Charles R. Fay: *The Palace of Industry, 1851: a Study of the Great Exhibition and its Fruits* (Cambridge, 1951).

[15] John U. Nef: "The Industrial Revolution Reconsidered" (*Journal of Economic History*, III, 1943, 1–31); David S. Landes: "Technological Change and Development in Western Europe, 1750–1918" (in H. J. Habakkuk and M. Postan: *"The Cambridge Economic History of Europe*, Cambridge, 1965, VI, Part I, 353 ff.).

[16] There is an interesting tabulation of the innumerable industries of Paris in Charles Dupin: *Les forces productives et commerciales de la France* (Paris, 1827), II, 196 ff.

Merchants of putters-out would supply the raw material and then purchase the finished product (see Illustration 23). The great silk industry of Lyons was an excellent example of this system in operation. There were about 50,000 persons (men, women and children) engaged in weaving the silk thread, most of which was produced and exported from northern Italy. Of the total number about 800 were merchants (*marchands-fabricants*) who bought the raw material and distributed it to the weavers, from whom they then bought the finished goods. The actual workers were divided into loom owners (*chefs d'atelier*), about 8,000 in number, who owned from four to eight looms, set up in their lodgings in the crowded hill suburb of Croix-Rousse (see Illustration 28). The rest were the journeymen, women and children, who lived with their masters, sleeping in hammocks over the looms or over the family table. Even after the advent of the factory, this system continued to operate in other textiles as well as in the silk trade. Factory owners at times employed hundreds and even thousands of homeworkers in the tasks of spinning and weaving. It was the cheapest form of labor and therefore continued to be profitable.[17]

The industrialization of the Continent was hampered not only by the tendency of the propertied classes to invest capital in land but also by lack of the resources in which Britain was so rich. There were large coal and iron deposits in close conjunction in western Germany, but the immense potentialities of the Ruhr Basin were only just being recognized and exploited in 1850. In France coal was mined chiefly in the central areas, far from the centers of population and production. The valuable iron ores of Sweden were mostly exported to Britain, and the minerals of the Urals were floated down the rivers to the Moscow area. Spain had rich deposits of copper, lead and quicksilver on which European industry was dependent. But only in Belgium were the coal and iron industries on a modern basis. In 1850 several hundred Belgian collieries produced twice as much coal as the rest of the Continent combined, and of this about half was exported, chiefly to France. The

---

[17] Most accounts of the Lyons industry go back to Louis R. Villermé: *Tableau de l'état physique et morale des ouvriers* (Paris, 1840), I, 358 ff., but see also A. Audiganne: *Les populations ouvrières et les industries de la France* (2 ed., Paris, 1860), Book VI, chap. i, and the excellent modern studies of E. Pariset: *Histoire de la fabrique lyonnaise* (Lyons, 1901), 297 ff.; A. Kleinclausz: *Histoire de Lyon* (Lyons, 1952), III, 82 ff.; Claude Lévy: "La fabrique de soie lyonnaise, 1830–1848" (*1848 et les révolutions du XIXe siècle*, 1947, 20–48).

production of pig iron was also far in excess of that of other countries, and the great centers at Liège and Verviers were replacing charcoal with coke for smelting and applying steam power to a large extent. The great firm of John Cockerill and Company, near Liège, was a great engineering plant which could compete on even terms with British interests in machine making and the construction of all types of engines and locomotives.[18]

In France the production of coal and pig iron, protected against British competition by high tariffs, just about tripled between 1830 and 1848, and there was a constantly increasing use of coke and steam power in the heavy industries. There were a few large concerns, such as the coal mines at Anzin and the iron works at Saint-Étienne and Le Creusot, but most heavy industry was conducted in small shops, even at the end of the period. In Spain the lack of communications permitted only the exploitation of the most valuable mineral deposits. Even these remained on a primitive basis. A foreign visitor in 1843 found the quicksilver mines at Almadén del Azogue using one of the original Watt steam engines (1790 vintage), and another reported the iron foundry at Pedroso still doing its hauling in 1848 with seventy pairs of bullocks, while employing water power for its blast.[19]

The German scene was hardly different. Innumerable small foundries in the wooded hill districts operated with charcoal and water power. There was no substantial change until after 1840, when larger plants began to spring up near the Ruhr and Saar coal fields and were thus able to use coke in the smelting process (see Illustration 15). By 1848 Germany had made noteworthy progress in the metallurgical trades and particularly in machine building. The great Borsig plant outside Berlin in 1841 built the first German locomotive. Nonetheless, the heavy industries as a whole were only just emerging, in 1850, from the old traditional forms. For instance, in 1850 there were some two hundred coal mines in the Ruhr Basin, but the great majority of them

---

[18] Laurent Duchesne: *Histoire économique et sociale de la Belgique* (Paris, 1932), chaps. xiii and xiv; Richard M. Westebbe. "State Entrepreneurship: King Willem I, John Cockerill and the Seraing Engineering Works, 1814–1844" (*Explorations in Entrepreneurial History*, VIII, 1956, 205–232); E. A. Wrigley: *Industrial Growth and Population Change* (Cambridge, 1961), 12 ff.

[19] S. E. Widdington: *Spain and the Spaniards* (London, 1844), 166, 208 ff.; Friedrich Heinzelmann: *Reisebilder und Skizzen aus der pyrenäischen Halbinsel* (Leipzig, 1851), 170 ff.; Jaime Vincenz Vives: *Manual de historia economica de España* (Barcelona, 1959), 589 ff.

produced less than 10,000 tons of coal per annum.[20] As for Russia, where the iron industry was long-established, there was no substantial rise in production or alteration in method. There were a few large enterprises such as the Gubin works at Serginsk in the Urals, but the industry rested almost entirely on serf labor and made almost no use of machinery.[21]

The railways, which in Britain gave so great a stimulus to the heavy industries, on the Continent made their appearance but hesitatingly and usually in the midst of controversy and obstruction. Only progressive Belgium was an exception. There the government took the matter in hand. The first line (Brussels to Malines) was opened in 1835 and by 1845 a carefully planned national network was substantially complete. Belgian ironworks and engineering plants not only produced rails and locomotives but did a thriving business in the export of all railway equipment. In France, on the other hand, there was endless debate. The followers of Saint-Simon, particularly Michel Chevalier, were enthusiastic over the new means of communication, which were to bring the European peoples into closer contact and strengthen the bonds of peace. As early as 1831 Chevalier was dreaming of trunk lines from Cadiz on the Spanish coast to St. Petersburg, from the various Mediterranean ports into the heartland of the Continent, and from Paris through the Germanies and the Balkans to Constantinople (the later Orient Express route). Alexis Legrand, the director of the government Bureau of Bridges and Roads, in 1832 projected a rail network for France not unlike the one that was eventually constructed. There was no lack of vision, but the government was committed to a further program of canal building and private interests felt unable to

[20] Maurice Baumont: *La grosse industrie allemande et le charbon* (Paris, 1928); Pierre Benaerts: *Les origines de la grande industrie allemande* (Paris, 1934), chaps. xi and xii; Kurt Wiedenfeld: "Die Montanindustrie" (in Joseph Hansen, ed.: *Die Rheinprovinz, 1815–1915*, Bonn, 1917, I, chap. vii); Norman J. G. Pounds: *the Ruhr: a Study in Historical and Economic Geography* (Bloomington, 1952), chaps. ii and iii; Conrad Matschoss: *Ein Jahrhundert Maschinenbau* (2 ed., Berlin, 1922); Fritz Redlich: "Leaders of the German Steam Engine Industry during the First Hundred Years" (*Journal of Economic History*, IV, 1944, 121–148); Richard Tilly: "The Political Economy and the Industrialization of Prussia, 1815–1866" (*ibid.*, December, 1966).

[21] Peter I. Lyashchenko: *History of the National Economy of Russia* (New York, 1949), 329 ff.; M. V. Nechkina: *Russia in the Nineteenth Century* (Ann Arbor, 1953), 216 ff.; Michael Confino: "Maîtres des forges et ouvriers dans les usines metallurgiques de l'Oural aux XVIIIe et XIXe siècles" (*Cahiers du monde russe et soviétique*, I, 1959, 239–284).

finance any but short lines designed for specific purposes. Such a line had been opened from the iron center of Saint-Étienne to Lyons in 1832, but little more was done while the great debate went on from 1836 to 1842. The desirability of a trunk line from Marseilles to Le Havre, to capture the Mediterranean trade, was generally recognized and eventually two lines, from Paris to Rouen and from Paris to Orléans, were authorized. But it was only in 1842 that Parliament adopted the program for six major lines to radiate from Paris to the various frontiers and to major seaports. The dispute as to government or private ownership was settled by compromise: the government was to buy the land; build the roadbed, bridges and tunnels; and to reserve to itself the right to purchase the lines. Private enterprise was to provide the rails, rolling stock and stations. The Paris-Rouen line, largely financed and constructed by British interests, was opened to traffic in 1843 and extended to Le Havre in 1847, but the Paris-Marseilles line was not completed until 1853. In 1844–1845 France, like Britain, went through a railway boom, which led to much disillusionment. Progress was therefore slow. In 1848 there were some thirty different companies, but only 1,931 kilometers of railway in actual operation. This was not even a third of the British mileage and hardly more than a half of the Prussian.[22]

The Spaniards did nothing about railways until 1848, when the short line from Barcelona to Mataró was completed. The Italian states were hardly more progressive. Two short noncommercial lines were built from Naples in 1839 and 1843, but even in the more developed north little was accomplished, despite much discussion of a trunk line from Brindisi which would capture the Oriental trade. Lines were opened from Venice to Padua and Vicenza and from Milan to Treviglio in 1846, but Venice and Milan were not to be connected until

---

[22] Ernest Charles: *Les chemins de fer en France pendant le règne de Louis-Philippe* (Paris, 1896), 1–38; Maurice Wallon: *Les Saint-Simoniens et les chemins de fer* (Paris, 1908), 35 ff.; G. Lefranc: "Les chemins de fer devant le parlement français, 1835–1842" (*Revue d'histoire moderne,* V, 1930, 337–364); Henri Peyret: *Histoire des chemins de fer en France et dans le monde* (Paris, 1949); L. M. Jouffroy: *L'ère du rail* (Paris, 1953), 80 ff.; Louis L. Dunham: *The Industrial Revolution in France* (New York, 1955), 51 ff.; Rondo E. Cameron: *France and the Economic Development of Europe, 1800–1914* (Princeton, 1961), 204 ff.; W. O. Henderson: *The Industrial Revolution on the Continent* (London, 1961), 108 ff.; Bertrand Gille: *Histoire de la Maison Rothschild* (Paris, 1965), Vol. I, contains a wealth of material on the financing of the early French railways.

1857. Piedmont's first line (Turin to Moncalieri) dated only from 1848.[23]

The German states, on the other hand, proceeded to improve communications during these years. There was much road and canal

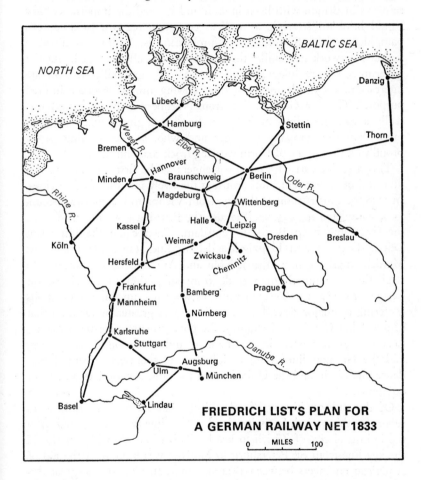

FRIEDRICH LIST'S PLAN FOR A GERMAN RAILWAY NET 1833

0   MILES   100

[23] Corrado de Biase: *Il problema delle ferrovie nel Risorgimento* (Modena, 1940); Candeloro: *Storio dell'Italia Moderna*, II, chap. iv; Kent R. Greenfield: *Economics and Liberalism in the Risorgimento* (Baltimore, 1934, 1966); Domenico Demarco: "L'economia degli Stati Italiani prima dell'unità" (*Rassegna Storica del Risorgimento*, XLIV, 1957, 191–258).

building and much dredging and regulating of important rivers so as to facilitate the steamboat traffic, which had quickly become important, especially for upstream trade. Industrialists and economists such as Friedrich Harkort and Friedrich List followed the development of the railways in Britain with keen interest and stressed the importance they would have for strategic as well as economic reasons. In a famous pamphlet on the Saxon railway problem, List in 1833 outlined a national network not unlike the one that eventually emerged. But the governments were lukewarm and it was only gradually that private interests raised funds for local lines serving mines or other limited purposes. The first German line, from Nürnberg to Fürth (1835) was really a consumer line, built by an English engineer who was paid more than the company manager and who, at the opening, stood proudly on the engine platform wearing frock coat and silk hat.[24]

This first line carried 500,000 passengers in the first year and paid a dividend of 20 per cent, thus arousing the lively interest of other cities. In 1838 the construction of the line from Vienna to Prague was begun, to be completed in 1845. In 1838 also the Prussian government opened the short line from Berlin to Potsdam. Then came the important Leipzig-Dresden and Leipzig-Magdeburg lines (1839–1840) and the Munich-Augsburg line (1840). Köln and Antwerp were connected in 1843, thus freeing German trade from subjection to Dutch transit charges. By 1850 the German railways were still unconnected systems centering on major cities, but the mileage was greater by far than that of any other Continental country, the governments were participating to an ever greater extent in the financing and regulation of the systems, and the German lines were rapidly freeing themselves from dependence on Britain and the United States for rails, locomotives and other equipment.[25]

Of the railway history of other European states there is little to report for this period. In Switzerland a short line was constructed from the industrial city of Zürich to nearby Baden in 1848, while in Russia the key line from St. Petersburg to Moscow was built with the aid of American engineers between 1842 and 1851. In view of the great dis-

---

[24] *Hundert Jahre deutscher Eisenbahnen* (2 ed., Berlin, 1938), 17.

[25] Max Hoeltzel: *Aus der Frühzeit der Eisenbahnen* (Berlin, 1935); Benaerts: *Origines de la grande industrie allemande,* chap. viii; William O. Henderson: *The State and the Industrial Revolution in Prussia* (Liverpool, 1958), chap. viii; Jerome Blum: "Transportation and Industry in Austria, 1815–1848" (*Journal of Modern History,* XV, 1943, 24–38).

tances in the Russian Empire, one might have expected the railway to make a great appeal. Nicholas I was, in fact, favorable to the development of industry, and had a railway built from St. Petersburg to the imperial seat at Tsarkoe Selo (1837), but Count Kankrin, the minister of finance, on whom the czar relied for economic advice, regarded railways as too expensive and at bottom unnecessary.[26]

CONTINENTAL RAILWAYS COMPLETED BY 1851

The construction of the railways and indeed the entire industrial development of the Continent were matters of international action. British finance, British engineering and management, even British

26 Nechkina: *Russia in the Nineteenth Century,* 215 ff.; Bertrand Gille: *Histoire économique et sociale de la Russie* (Paris, 1949), 152; Walter M. Pintner: "Government and Industry during the Ministry of Count Kankrin, 1827–1844" (*Slavic Review,* XXIII, 1964, 45–62).

technicians and construction crews, played a large role in all countries, just as British machines and equipment proved indispensable. But by the 1830's many other interests were in the field. Belgian, French, Swiss and German entrepreneurs were active in Spain, Italy, Scandinavia, Russia and even in the Balkans and the Near East. It would be difficult indeed to exaggerate the importance of this give and take in the dispersal of capital and the dissemination of technological knowledge and managerial skills throughout the entire European Continent. Thus the British, who had initially forbidden the migration of technicians to foreign countries and had maintained the prohibition of the export of machinery until 1843, actually contributed in many ways to the generalization of the new industry.[27]

A detailed review of the growth and changes in the textile industries may be dispensed with, since the history of these trades was much the same all over the Continent. Raw wool and flax were produced in many localities. Spinning the yarn was done mostly by women, during the winter months, in the home, while the finished cloth was manufactured by the men on handlooms, also in the home. By the late eighteenth century the putting-out system was widespread on the Continent and continued to function for many years. The expansion of production in these trades was due in part to the ever-growing demand for British yarn which, being prepared by mechanized spinning methods, was far cheaper than any prepared by hand. Most governments attempted to protect their industries by erecting tariff walls. At the same time, however, everything possible had to be done to keep up with modern methods of production.

Woolen and linen clothing was being superseded by cotton garments and this in itself reacted unfavorably on these old-established industries. The linen trade languished everywhere, since the Continental manufacturers were unable to compete with the machine-made products of Britain and Ireland. As for wool, the production continued to increase,

[27] This aspect of the Industrial Revolution has been much studied of late. See W. O. Henderson: *Britain and Industrial Europe, 1750–1870* (Liverpool, 1954); Rondo E. Cameron: *France and the Economic Development of Europe, 1800–1914* (Princeton, 1961); E. A. Wrigley: *Industrial Growth and Population Change* (Cambridge, 1961); Erik Amburger: "Der fremde Unternehmer in Russland" (*Tradition*, IV, 1957, 337–356); Peter Stearns: "British Industry through the Eyes of French Industrialists, 1820–1848" (*Journal of Modern History*, XXXVII, 1965, 50–61); Maurice Lévy-Leboyer: *Les banques européennes et l'industrialisation internationale dans la première moitié du XIXe siècle* (Paris, 1964).

but in a modest way. In France the industry was widely dispersed, with important centers at Reims, Elbeuf, Sedan and Lodève, and in Germany there was a concentration at Aachen, in the Vogtland, and in Augsburg. But technologically there was little progress. Spinning mills run by water power were established in the 1830's and in the course of the following decade a certain number of power looms, sometimes driven by steam engines, were introduced. In a word, the linen industry was generally in eclipse and the wool industry, while still important, was only slowly catching up with the new technology.

Silk was in great demand by the upper classes and was a thriving industry in a number of countries, notably in England, France and Switzerland, and to a lesser extent in Germany and Russia. The raw silk came largely from Italy, particularly from Lombardy, where in season women were gathered in "factories," that is, in large sheds, to unwind the silk from the cocoons. Originally the silk was exported in the raw state, but more and more the spinning was done before export. In centers such as London and Lyons silk fabrics were then woven, either by the putting-out system, as in Lyons, or in modern mills driven either by water power, as in Switzerland, or by steam. But it was only in the 1840's that power looms began to replace the traditional hand-looms.

It was the relatively new cotton trade that set a standard for the development of modern industry on the Continent. Since all the raw material had to be imported from overseas, the cotton industry provided a particularly good measure for comparison. Between 1832 and 1850 the British consumption of raw cotton rose from roughly 125,000 to 220,000 tons, the French from 33,000 to 60,000, the Belgian from 2,500 to 7,200, and the German from 2,500 to 17,000. It has been estimated that in 1840 the consumption per inhabitant was 7.3 kilograms in Britain, 3.7 in Switzerland, 2.8 in Belgium, 1.5 in France, and 0.9 in Germany.[28]

Initially the mechanical spinning of cotton took place in small factories, commonly located, as in Saxony, Bohemia and Lombardy, in the foothills of mountain ranges, where there was ample water power available. By 1830 the spinning process had been generally mechanized and there were cotton mills everywhere in Europe, with the possible

---

[28] Landes, in *Cambridge Economic History*, VI, 394; P. Bairoch: "Niveaux de developpement économique de 1810 à 1910" (*Annales*, XX, 1965, 1091–1117).

exception of the Scandinavian countries. In 1828 there were sixty-nine of them, water powered, in the Bohemian mountain areas alone. By that time larger textile centers had also appeared.[29] In the generally unindustrialized Netherlands, British and Belgian interests had built larger mills in Twente, Haarlem and Leiden, using to some extent the available wind power. In Belgium, Ghent became a great center and one of the first to make extensive use of steam power and eventually to introduce the power loom. French interests were chiefly responsible for developing Barcelona as a major textile center and they were active also in Lombardy and Piedmont.[30]

Switzerland was literally covered with small cotton factories, using the abundant water power. Zürich presently became a major center. In Germany the industry was best established in the Rhineland, Saxony, Upper Silesia, Bohemia and Upper Austria, with cities such as Chemnitz and Krefeld becoming increasingly important. Here, too, water power was widely used, and steam power gradually replaced it only in the larger centers.[31] Russia presented a somewhat different picture, for there the cotton industry, alone among others, was being operated with free rather than with serf labor. That is to say, in the region around Moscow, Vladimir and Ivanovo, there grew up huge cotton mills whose workers, while serfs, had been allowed by their masters to seek work in the cities and who paid their masters only a relatively small annual fee or tax (*obrok*) for this privilege. In some of these mills even

---

[29] Hans Raupach: *Der tschechische Frühnationalismus* (Halle, 1939), 49 ff.; Bernard Michel: "La Révolution Industrielle dans les pays tchèques au XIXe siècle" (*Annales*, XX, 1965, 984–1005).

[30] P. Romeva Ferrer: *Historia de la Industria Catalana* (Barcelona, 1952), II, 258 ff.; Jaime Carrera Pujol: *La Economía de Cataluña en el siglo XIX* (Barcelona, 1961), II, chaps. ii and iii; Greenfield: *Economics and Liberalism in the Risorgimento*, chaps. iii to v; Shepard B. Clough: *The Economic History of Modern Italy* (New York, 1964), 60 ff.; Antonio Fossati: *Lavoro e produzione in Italia* (Turin, 1951), 99 ff.; Roberto Tremelloni: *Storia dell'industria italiana contemporanea* (Turin, 1947), I, chap. iv; Rosario Villari: "L'economia degli Stati Italiani dal 1815 al 1848" (in *Nuove Questioni di Storia del Risorgimento*, Milan, 1961, 607–648).

[31] William E. Rappard: *La Révolution Industrielle et les origines de la protection légale du travail en Suisse* (Bern, 1914), 157 ff.; Ernst Gagliardi: *Geschichte der Schweiz* (3 ed., Zurich, 1938), III, 1270 ff.; Friedrich Lütge: *Deutsche Sozial- und Wirtschaftsgeschichte* (Berlin, 1952), 358 ff.; Theodore S. Hamerow: *Restoration, Revolution, Reaction* (Princeton, 1958), 3 ff.; Hermann Lehmann: "Die Textilindustrie" (in Joseph Hansen, ed.: *Die Rheinprovinz*, Bonn, 1917, I, chap. viii); Johann Slokar: *Geschichte der oesterreichischen Industrie* (Vienna, 1914), 279 ff.; H. Benedikt: "Die Anfänge der Industrie in Niederoesterreich" (*Der Donauraum*, II, 1957).

the managers belonged to the serf category and at times became wealthy owners in the names of their masters.[32]

France in 1840 used only one quarter the amount of raw cotton consumed by Britain, yet was by far the leading Continental country in this branch of industrialism. Large cotton mills grew up around Rouen, in the area around Lille and Roubaix, and in Alsace at Mulhouse and Colmar. In addition there were countless small mills, often with fewer than a thousand spindles, scattered over the country, even in the more backward western areas. In one of his charming early paintings Corot has pictured one of these modest enterprises, with the owner's home adjacent to the factory.[33] The spinning process was almost completely mechanized by 1830, but power looms were slow in establishing themselves in the 1840's. Water was still the predominant source of power in 1848, though the steam engine was making headway, especially in the Lille area.[34]

In reviewing the general economic development of the Continental nations in this period, certain features appear as of prime importance. First, it is obvious that the entire Continent, with the possible exception of Belgium, was a full generation behind Britain, even in 1848. Second, that traditional industrial activities were still not only widespread but also predominant. Nowhere outside a few great textile centers was there a sizable population of the new factory proletariat, which in fact did not as yet play a leading political role. But, third, the decisive fact was this: that in this "take-off" period the traditional industrial system of Europe was already being severely shaken; the

---

[32] Valentin Gitermann: *Geschichte Russlands* (Zürich, 1949), III, 86; Henry Rosovsky: "The Serf Entrepreneur in Russia" (*Explorations in Entrepreneurial History,* VI, 1954, 207–233); Valentine T. Bill: *The Forgotten Class: Russian Bourgeoisie from the Earliest Beginnings to 1900* (New York, 1959), 103 ff.; Roger Portal: "The Industrialization of Russia" (in *Cambridge Economic History,* VI, 801–874).

[33] See Illustration 14.

[34] F. V. Potemkine: "Les industries cotonnières en France avant la Révolution de 1848" (*Questions d'histoire,* II, 1954, 39–56). There appears to be no recent study of the Rouen center, but the progressive Mulhouse industry has been carefully analyzed in Marie-Madeleine Kahan-Rabecq: *L'Alsace économique et sociale sous le règne de Louis-Philippe* (Paris, 1939) and Paul Leuillot: *L'Alsace au début du XIXe siècle* (Paris, 1959–1960). On the Lille-Roubaix complex, see the chapter "Aspects industriels de la crise: le Départment du Nord" (in Ernest Labrousse, ed.: *Aspects de la crise et de la dépression de l'économie française, 1846–1851,* Paris, 1956). Audiganne: *Les populations ouvrières et les industries de la France* provides a detailed contemporary description of all the industrial centers.

peasantry was being deprived of important sources of supplementary income, such as spinning and weaving. Countless artisans, if they were not already the victims of the new machines, were in imminent danger of seeing their crafts disappear. When to these considerations is added the overriding threat of overpopulation, one can understand that industrialism, which was to bring so many blessings to humanity, was at first regarded by many artisans as a threat of the first order. The great historian, Jules Michelet, himself of worker origin, declared that "man, weak and pale, is now the humble servant of these steel giants."[35] Industrialism had gone far enough to upset the social equilibrium, yet not far enough to have produced notable benefits.

3. BUSINESS AND THE SOCIAL STRUCTURE

The process of industrialization entailed inevitably a redistribution of wealth and consequently of influence and power. The Industrial Revolution strengthened the social position of the traditional middle or bourgeois class and at the same time created an urban, factory labor force which was roughly the equivalent of the landless, rural worker. It has become fashionable in our day to question the validity of so simple a classification. The concept of social class has become a favorite subject for dissection and analysis. But the highly sophisticated categories that emerge are not very helpful to the historian. He must of necessity hold to the thinking of the period he is describing. In 1830 or 1840 people knew perfectly well what they meant by the various classes. Class distinctions had existed since time immemorial, but it was only in the late eighteenth century that class consciousness and class antagonism in the modern sense emerged.

The term "middle classes" came into use only about 1800 and the term "working classes" about 1815. Originally the middle class was thought of simply as that stratum of society which lay between the privileged, usually landed, upper class and the unpropertied, generally illiterate, lower or wage-earning class. But the use of the plural suggests that contemporaries sensed the differentiation that was taking place. Stendhal, writing in 1824, distinguished between the aristocracy of birth, the aristocracy of wealth, the industrial and commercial bourgeoisie, the bourgeoisie of investments, and the propertied shopkeepers

---

[35] Jules Michelet: *Le peuple* (1846). For the expression of apprehension by French poets, see Elliott M. Grant: *French Poetry and Modern Industry, 1830–1870* (Cambridge, 1927), 21–29, 44.

and rich peasants. Although he omitted the emerging urban proletariat, his classification quite accurately reflects the opinion of his time. His aristocracy of wealth was known in France as the *haute* or *grande bourgeoisie,* consisting essentially of the rich merchants and bankers, many of whom bought landed estates and presently secured a title to nobility. Stendhal's industrial and commercial bourgeoisie was the newly rising element which in many respects was quite different from the foregoing class. The bourgeoisie of investments was probably a peculiarly French group, the people (*rentiers*) who lived from the rents of their lands or from investments in government securities, without having any particular profession. As for the fifth category, it would include the urban craftsmen, the lower clergy, professional men and shopkeepers, together with small landholders. The lowest class, ignored by Stendhal, would comprise urban journeymen, apprentices, factory workers and rural laborers—all those who depended almost entirely on the work of their hands to gain a living.[36]

It cannot be said that the European upper classes were altogether averse to business enterprise. Enlightened monarchs of the eighteenth century, notably Frederick the Great, made concerted efforts to raise the standard of living by encouraging and supporting trade and manufacture. The Hapsburgs went so far as to appoint nobles and prelates to manage mines and factories. In the nineteenth century one finds such rulers as William I of the Netherlands, who, for all his political conservatism, was a keen businessman and an active promoter. Or Louis Philippe of France, who had amassed a huge fortune before ascending the throne, and was quite at home in the company of Parisian bankers. Leopold I of Belgium was a man of the same stamp and his nephew, Prince Consort Albert, was alert to the problems as well as the possibilities of the new industrial order. It was he who provided much of the motive force behind the great exhibition of 1851.[37]

In Britain the aristocracy had been and continued to be recruited

[36] Stendhal in the *London Magazine,* 1824, quoted by Lucien Jansse: "Stendhal et les classes sociales" (*Stendhal Club,* VI, 1963, 35–45). See further, G. D. H. Cole: "The Conception of the Middle Classes" (*British Journal of Sociology,* I, 1950, 275–290); Raymond Williams: *Culture and Society, 1780–1950* (New York, 1958), xiii; Asa Briggs: "The Language of 'Class' in Early 19th Century England" (in Asa Briggs and John Saville, eds.: *Essays in Labour History,* London 1960, 43–74).

[37] Fritz Redlich: "European Aristocracy and Economic Development" (*Explorations in Entrepreneurial History,* VI, 1953, 78–91); Heinrich Bechtel: *Der Wirtschaftsstil des deutschen Unternehmers in der Vergangenheit* (Dortmund, 1955).

from the ranks of successful merchants and bankers, whose interests and attitudes reacted on at least some members of the nobility. Several peers (such as the Duke of Devonshire, the Marquess of Londonderry, the Earl of Durham, the Earl of Crawford, Earl Fitzwilliam) found themselves the owners of huge coal or iron deposits and engaged actively in the exploitation of their resources. They became involved in foundries, railways and shipping. Some, such as Lord Fitzwilliam, became spokesmen in Parliament in behalf of progressive economic and social policies. In the Parliament in 1841–1847 at least a third of the aristocratic members were engaged in business, if only as directors of banks, insurance companies, railways or public utilities.[38]

The role of the French aristocracy in business enterprise has been less studied than that of the British or German, but it seems likely that, despite the social exclusiveness of the French nobility, some members of that caste were involved in the heavy industries. Judging by the results of recent researches, it would seem that the most affluent stratum of French society, the "notables," were men of landed property who, however, frequently engaged in business, at least of the traditional kind. On the other hand, the German entrepreneurs were frequently members of the nobility. Certain of the Silesian magnates (Prince Henckel von Donnersmarck, Count Pückler-Muskau, Count Dohna) owned large mines and did much to develop the iron and machine-building industries, to say nothing of their role in the linen manufacture. In Bohemia it was the nobility that seems to have played the leading part in the furtherance of the heavy industries, the sugar refineries and eventually the glass and textile industries.[39]

It may well be that the European aristocracy has been given insufficient credit for the economic advances of the early nineteenth century, but it certainly remains true that the makers of the new industry—as distinct from banking, trade and even transportation—were predominantly men of the middle class. The inventors were frequently lock-

---

[38] David Spring: "Earl Fitzwilliam and the Corn Laws" (*American Historical Review*, LIX, 1954, 287–304); W. O. Aydelotte: "The House of Commons in the 1840's" (*History*, XXXIX, 1954, 249–262), and the same author's appendix to George Kitson Clark: *The Making of Victorian England* (London, 1961).

[39] Wilhelm Treue: "Deutsche Wirtschaftsführer im 19 Jahrhundert" (*Historische Zeitschrift*, CLXVII, 1943, 548–566); Wolfgang Zorn. "Typen und Entwicklungskräfte deutschen Unternehmertums im 19 Jahrhundert" (*Vierteljahrschrift für Sozial- und Wirtschaftsgeschichte*, XLIV, 1957 57–76); Hans Raupach: *Der tschechische Frühnationalismus* (Halle, 1939), 49 ff., 57 ff.

smiths by trade or clockmakers, carpenters or artisans capable of dealing with the new technology. The second and third generation of entrepreneurs in the textile industries were no longer self-made men who had risen from the dunghill to the chariot, as Cobbett claimed. Many captains of industry came from merchant and banking circles, were men trained to watch and gauge the market and were accustomed to taking risks. Others were petty tradesmen in the putting-out business, who started by setting up a few spinning machines in a farmhouse by a stream and, by reinvesting their profits, were able to build up large mills. On the Continent particularly, the relatively small, family-owned mill was the prevalent form of business organization.[40]

The influence of Protestantism, especially of Calvinism, in the evolution of the modern business ethic has long been recognized. Many of the new industrialists were, in fact, Calvinists or other nonconformists, imbued with a sense of mission, hard-working, sober, self-reliant, reserved, yet at the same time proud and even arrogant (see Illustration 67). Parisian satirists ridiculed those who, as officers of the National Guard, liked to appear on horseback and in full accouterment. Their counterpart could be found in Germany in the banker Johann Schickler, who engaged no less prominent an artist than Horace Vernet to paint his portrait as colonel of the Basel militia riding a prancing black charger and waving his naked blade.[41] The great industrialists of Alsace, Calvinists in the midst of a Catholic population, formed something like a closed caste, intermarrying and collaborating in various enterprises. The same exclusiveness was characteristic even of Catholic industrial interests. In the Rouen and Lille centers, as in Barcelona, there was a tendency for a few clans to dominate the scene.[42]

[40] Kurt Wiedenfeld: "Die Herkunft der Unternehmer und Kapitalisten im Aufbau der kapitalistischen Zeit" (*Weltwirtschaftliches Archiv*, LXXII, 1954, 254–279); Heinz Wutzmer: "Die Herkunft der industriellen Bourgeoisie Preussens in den vierziger Jahren des 19 Jahrhunderts" (in Hans Mottek, ed.: *Studien zur Geschichte der Industriellen Revolution in Deutschland*, Berlin, 1960, 145–163).

[41] Wolfgang Zorn: "Das deutsche Unternehmerporträt in sozialgeschichtlicher Betrachtung" (*Tradition*, Nos. 2–3, 1962, 78–92).

[42] Charles Wilson: "The Entrepreneur in the Industrial Revolution in Britain" (*History*, XLII, 1957, 101–117); J. Lambert-Dansette: *Quelques familles du patronat de Lille-Armentières, 1789–1914* (Lille, 1954); Jean Schlumberger, ed.: *La bourgeoisie alsacienne* (Strasbourg, 1954); André-Jean Tudesq: "La bourgeoisie du Nord au milieu de la Monarchie de Juillet" (*Revue du Nord*, XLI, 1959, 277–285); Walther Dabritz: *Unternehmergestalten aus dem rheinischwestfälischen Industriebezirk* (Jena, 1929);

The early industrialist has often been pictured as something of a monster, as a money-mad fiend ruthlessly exploiting female and child labor in pursuit of his selfish interests. This was certainly not true of businessmen generally. Many of them were ambitious; even more were adventurous. One can hardly withhold admiration from those promoters who, in foreign countries and under strange conditions, opened mills and engineering works and took great chances in developing foreign markets. Your Manchester man, wrote a contemporary, "will undertake to supply all the markets between Lima and Pekin and he will be exceedingly vexed if, by any oversight, he has omitted a petty village which could purchase a yard of cloth or a hank of yarn."[43] But they were not all selfish. As Dissenters many of them felt a responsibility for the welfare of their workers. Like the Strutts and the Owens in England, they built cottages for their employees and provided religious and educational opportunities. Some called on prominent architects to design well-ventilated and well-heated mills, fireproofed and equipped with personnel elevators to enable employees to pass from one floor to another of the mill without exhaustion (see Illustration 16).[44]

The industrialists, unlike the bankers, made little effort to break into the circles of the aristocracy. They had but little regard for the idle rich, whom their spokesman, Brougham, described as "a few persons of overgrown wealth, laughable folly, and considerable profligacy," and whom Dickens put down as "Noodle and Doodle." Mr. Millbank, in Disraeli's novel, *Coningsby,* is a successful mill owner who will have nothing to do with his neighbor, the Duke, and will not hear of his daughter's marrying into the nobility; while in Dickens' *Dombey and Son,* Mr. Dombey is quite above aristocratic aspirations. Like other successful businessmen, he maintains a large and elegant house in

---

Walter Serlo: *Bergmannsfamilien in Rheinland und Westfalen* (Münster, 1936); Jaime Vincens Vives: "La mentalidad de la burguesía catalana en el primera mitad del siglo XIX" (*X Congresso Internazionale di Scienze Storiche,* Rome, 1955, VII, 323–327).

[43] W. Cooke Taylor: *Notes of a Tour in the Manufacturing Districts of Lancashire* (2 ed., London, 1842), ii.

[44] R. S. Fitton and A. P. Wadsworth: *The Strutts and the Arkwrights* (Manchester, 1958), 192 ff., and the contemporary accounts of Ure and Taylor. On the French side, Marie-Joseph Bopp: "L'oeuvre sociale de la haute bourgeoisie haut-rhinois au XIXe siècle" (in *La bourgeoisie alsacienne,* 387–402); on the Germans, Heinrich Bechtel: *Der Wirtschaftsstil des deutschen Unternehmers* (Dortmund, 1955).

London and leads a self-assured existence. In France, too, men of the new business class looked with contempt on the old aristocracy and established their own salons. They might buy a hunting lodge, but showed less interest in acquiring landed estates than had the bankers of a preceding generation. In the Rhineland it seems to have been only the representatives of heavy industry who courted the aristocracy and promoted intermarriage of their daughters with impecunious nobles.[45]

The new business class appears nowhere to have been interested in securing political office. In Britain not many more businessmen were Whigs than Tories, and there were no more of them in the House of Commons after the Reform Bill of 1832 than before. Even in 1847 only about 200 members of the house in a total membership of over 800 could be classified as businessmen. The point is that these men were too engrossed in their own activities to have time for political careers. But the Reform Bill signified their victory and ensured their influence. They could and did insist on continuing reform, that is, on the modernization of the government, with due reference to the interests of the business community. The Anti-Corn Law League of the 1840's demonstrated the fact that industrialists could and would organize to impose their demands on a reluctant Parliament with its preponderantly landed membership. They did not, however, resort to revolutionary action. On the contrary, they relied on peaceful agitation and sustained pressure to attain their ends. Nowhere in Europe was this upper middle class in any sense subversive. It must be emphasized, however, that it was middle-class agitation that inspired the lower and far more revolutionary elements to assert their demands, not only against the conservative privileged order, but against the new employing class as well.[46]

The role of the middle class in the political life of the July Monarchy in France is more obscure than that of its British counterpart. This may well be because in France the terms *bourgeois* and *middle class*

[45] O. F. Christie: *The Transition from Aristocracy, 1832–1867* (New York, 1928), 88 f.; Etienne Juillard: "Indifférence de la bourgeoisie alsacienne à l'égard de la propriété rurale aux XVIIIe et XIXe siècles" (in *La bourgeoisie alsacienne*, 377–386); Marcel Chaminade: *La Monarchie et les puissances d'argent* (Paris, 1933), 195; F. Zunkel: *Der rheinisch-westfälische Unternehmer, 1834–1879* (Köln, 1962).

[46] On the British side, see S. F. Woolley: "The Personnel of the Parliament of 1833" (*English Historical Review*, LIII, 1938, 240–262); J. A. Thomas: *The House of Commons, 1832–1901* (Cardiff, 1939), 4 ff.

were used far more loosely than across the Channel. They were often applied to that fairly numerous class of notables, mostly provincials— owners of landed property who engaged in local banking and business enterprises and, like the father in Balzac's *Eugénie Grandet* (1833), amassed a considerable fortune and often controlled the political life of their community. The expansion of the electorate in 1830 gave the vote to about 166,000 men in a population of 33 million. After 1830 as before, the French electors chose men of substance to represent them in Parliament. Of the ten deputies elected in the Département du Nord, each one paid at least 500 francs annually in direct taxes, and six paid more than 1,000 francs.

It is true that the July Revolution of 1830, which was started by Paris printers and fought out by craftsmen and artisans, was taken over by a group of adroit bankers, of whom Lafitte, Casimir-Périer and Dellessert were the most prominent. But when the excitement was over, it turned out that for the next eighteen years France was to be ruled not by bankers and industrialists but by provincial notables, by lawyers and by bureaucrats, many of whom were officers or officials of the Napoleonic regime. In 1837 there were hardly more than forty deputies who could be fairly described as members of the new industrial class. More representative of the ruling caste was Marshal Soult, who served repeatedly as a cabinet minister. He had accumulated a large fortune during the Napoleonic Wars and this he invested in coal and iron mines, as well as in other business ventures.[47]

In most other countries of Continental Europe constitutional government was nonexistent and there was therefore but little opportunity for the middle class to exercise influence or power. As aforesaid, some of the early German industrialists curried favor with the aristocracy and adopted essentially conservative views. But a constantly growing group of intellectuals—academic personnel, lawyers, physicians and journalists—agitated against the absolutism of the princes and the

[47] Régime Pernoud: *Histoire de la bourgeoisie en France* (Paris, 1962) II, 428, 438 ff.; Jean Lhomme: *La grande bourgeoisie au pouvoir, 1830–1880* (Paris, 1960), 51 ff.; Sherman Kent: *Electoral Procedures under Louis-Philippe* (New Haven, 1937), 28 ff., 50 ff.; André-Jean Tudesq: "Les listes electorales de la Monarchie Censitaire" (*Annales* XIII, 1958, 277–288); David H. Pinkney: "The Myth of the French Revolution of 1830" (*Essays in Honor of Frederick B. Artz*, Durham, 1964, 52–71); Lenore O'Boyle: "The Middle Class in Western Europe, 1815–1848" (*American Historical Review*, LXXI, 1966, 826–845); Alfred Cobban: "The 'Middle Class' in France, 1815–1848" (*French Historical Studies*, V, 1967, 41–52).

privileges of the aristocracy, demanding a voice in government for the middle class and a more businesslike administration. By the 1840's this liberal movement had converted a number of the Rhineland industrialists, who presently assumed the leadership. But here again one must note the fact that these business interests were not revolutionary. Close students of Cobden's Anti-Corn Law League, they aimed at reform by peaceful means. But in this instance, too, lower strata of society soon transformed the situation.[48]

[48] Jacques Droz: *Le libéralisme rhénan, 1815–1848* (Paris, 1940); Wolfgang Hock: *Liberales Denken im Zeitalter der Paulskirche* (Münster: 1957); Karl Eder: *Der Liberalismus in Altoesterreich* (Vienna, 1955); Georg Franz: *Liberalismus: die deutsch-liberale Bewegung in der habsburgischen Monarchie* (Munich, 1956).

Chapter Three

LIBERALISM: THEORY AND PRACTICE

THE political and social upheaval involved in the French Revolution and in the Industrial Revolution served to crystallize class consciousness and define the doctrines of the old and the new order. On the one hand the theories of Burke, Bonald and Maistre championed the traditional society based on custom and privilege, and vindicated the claims of the landed interests. On the other hand the rising business class, that is, the upper middle class, could draw inspiration from the eighteenth-century Enlightenment, from the practitioners of the French Revolution, and from specific theorists such as Bentham and Constant. Businessmen, with a high opinion of their economic and intellectual importance, insisted that property in industry was or should be on a par with landed property, that it, too, provided "respectability," and that therefore its possessors were entitled to an appropriate share in the conduct of public affairs. They were therefore opposed to arbitrary government in any form, to any kind of privilege, to all corruption and inefficiency. They advocated constitutional, representative government, equality of all before the law, and the right of every individual to the utmost possible measure of freedom in thought, speech, association and contract.

These men were in no sense extremists and certainly not revolutionaries. In the words of R. H. Tawney: "Men do not burn down the house which they intend to occupy, even though they regard its existing tenant as a public nuisance."[1] They were determined to abolish all restrictions favoring one type of wealth at the expense of another. Inequality of wealth did not trouble them, but they wanted equal opportunities of becoming unequal. Like the landed upper class, they feared the growing numbers of the dark, illiterate, unpropertied masses which, under a democratic system, might overthrow the existing social order and confiscate private property of all kinds. The "populace,"

[1] R. H. Tawney: *Equality* (4 ed., London, 1952), 99.

according to Macaulay, might well use political power "to plunder every man in the kingdom who had a good coat on his back and a good roof over his head." It was the function, then, of the middle class to serve as buffer between "a narrow oligarchy above and an infuriated multitude below."[2]

Actually the democratic and republican elements, though feared, were neither numerous nor formidable. In Britain there were, among the Philosophical Radicals, a few doctrinaires who on principle insisted on carrying the logic of politics to its ultimate conclusion. On the Continent, where, excepting for Belgium and France, the political and economic development lagged far behind the British, the entire liberal movement continued for some time to be primarily intellectual, drawing its strength from academic circles and the liberal professions. The radical, democratic movement was, in a sense, the left wing of liberalism, if anything even more intellectual. Harking back to Rousseau and more directly to the Jacobins of the French Revolution, the democrats were so exposed to government persecution that they reverted to secret organization and conspiratorial methods. Drawing their strength largely from writers and from the educated stratum of the urban, artisan class, they were almost invariably revolutionary, hostile to the upper middle class as well as to the aristocracy, aiming at universal suffrage and a democratic republic and, in some instances, going beyond the program of political democracy to advocate theories of socialism.

The counterpart of political liberalism was *laissez faire,* or the doctrine of economic freedom, which was directed at the abolition of the restrictions and regulations associated with the mercantilist system. Government was, in the early nineteenth century, in ill repute, being generally regarded as both corrupt and inefficient. Its constant interference with economic activity was therefore most undesirable. In the words of the liberal spokesman, Lord Macaulay, in 1830:

Our rulers will best promote the improvement of the nation by strictly confining themselves to their own legitimate duties, by leaving capital to

[2] Walter E. Houghton: *The Victorian Frame of Mind, 1830–1870* (New Haven, 1957), 54 ff.; S. G. Checkland: *The Rise of Industrial Society in England, 1815–1885* (London, 1964), 391 ff. On the general history of liberalism, see Guido de Ruggiero: *The History of European Liberalism* (London, 1927); Harold J. Laski: *The Rise of Liberalism* (New York, 1936); and the succinct survey in J. Salwyn Shapiro: *Liberalism, its Meaning and History* (New York, 1958).

find its most lucrative course, commodities their fair price, industry and intelligence their natural reward, idleness and folly their natural punishment, by maintaining peace, by defending property, by diminishing the price of law, and by observing strict economy in every department of the State.[3]

In short, if the businessman be master in his own house and follow his own interest, then society in general will benefit. Government interference in economic matters should be held to an absolute minimum.

The phrase *laissez faire* was not used by the British classical economists, all of whom recognized the need for state action in cases touching social welfare and exceeding the capabilities of private enterprise. *Laissez faire*, it has been aptly said, "was not a passport given by an indifferent state to ruthless enterprise,"[4] but rather a demand for the removal of obstructions to the new economic forces. Nonetheless, it soon came to mean, throughout Europe, the system of free competition, with particular reference to nonintervention by government in the relations of employer to employees, that is, to any infringement of the freedom of contract. As such it was bound to arouse the utmost hostility of the lower classes and to become a chief point of attack by socialist writers.[5]

2. THE VICTORIAN COMPROMISE

In Britain the passing of the great Reform Bill in 1832 ensured the position and established the influence of the new business class. Yet the elections to the reformed House of Commons in 1833 indicated almost no change in the political structure. The upper house remained the preserve of the landed aristocracy, while the lower house continued as before to be an assembly of younger sons of the nobility and placemen of influential magnates. As for the cabinet, it was more solidly aristocratic than ever before. Evidently the business class had little interest in actual participation in the government. Either it was too much occupied with its own concerns or else it was ready to leave government to

[3] Quoted by David Daiches: *Carlyle and the Victorian Dilemma* (Edinburgh, 1963).
[4] George N. Clark: "The Idea of the Industrial Revolution" (*Glasgow University Publications*, XCV, 1953).
[5] John M. Keynes: *The End of Laissez Faire* (London, 1926), esp. 17 ff.; J. Bartlett Brebner: "Laissez Faire and State Intervention in Nineteenth Century Britain" (*Journal of Economic History*, VIII, 1948, Suppl., 59–73); Jacob Viner: "The Intellectual History of Laissez Faire" (*Journal of Law and Economics*, III, 1960, 45–69).

that class which by its traditional social position was best suited to conduct the affairs of state. Both major parties, the Tories like the Whigs, represented the landed interest and tended to regard the Reform Bill as a generous but conclusive concession. They were divided only by political animosity and were at times tempted to form a coalition so as to present a common front to movements for further reform. They had been willing, in 1832, to grant the business class representation in Parliament, partly because this new "interest" by its wealth and education had become too important to ignore, but also because this upper middle class had shown that in order to attain its objective it was prepared to ally itself with the lower classes. There may be differences of opinion as to the gravity of the revolutionary threat in 1831–1832, but there can be no doubt that Lord Grey and his Whig cabinet were fearful of political and social upheaval, at least in the long run. Their policy was to enlist the support of the new interest so as to forestall an alliance of the upper middle class with the lower classes. They could coalesce with the upper middle class because that class was itself an aristocracy, unprivileged to be sure, but wealthy and essential to the public good. From the standpoint of the ruling classes the Reform Bill was indeed "one of those transactions of which history does not present many examples, when the right thing was done in exactly the right way at exactly the right time."[6]

The gist of the so-called Victorian Compromise was this: that the upper classes, landed and business, made an unwritten gentlemen's agreement that the interests of the landholders should be respected on condition that the requirements of business receive due consideration. Both wings of the propertied class were united in the determination to defend the institution of private property and to resist the pressure of the lower classes for a democratic system and a new society. But the transformation of English society had already progressed to the point where further reforms were imperative. The Evangelicals, within and without the Established Church, had already for some time staged

[6] George M. Young: *Victorian Essays,* ed. W. D. Handcock (London, 1962), 40–41. On the general political situation, see O. F. Christie: *The Transition from Aristocracy, 1832–1867* (New York, 1928), 114, 162, 180; Norman Gash: *Politics in the Age of Peel* (London, 1953), 14 ff.; Donald Southgate: *The Passing of the Whigs, 1832–1886* (London, 1962), 23 ff.; W. L. Guttsman: *The British Political Elite* (London, 1963), 34 ff., 60 ff.; Joseph Hamburger, *James Mill and the Art of Revolution* (New Haven, 1963), 199 ff., 277 ff.

impressive crusades of a humanitarian nature. In the years immediately following the Reform Bill they drove through reforms in the Established Church and forced through the abolition of slavery in the colonies, albeit with generous compensation to the slaveholders. By 1840 the Evangelical movement had begun to lose impetus, but its influence on the British ethic was to prove a lasting one.[7]

Another influential group pressing for further reform was the utilitarian Radical element in Parliament consisting of seventy-five or eighty members. It was by no means a homogeneous group, for it included many landowners as well as merchants, manufacturers, lawyers and writers. With different backgrounds they had also different interests and were therefore never able to organize under a recognized leadership or an agreed program. They were intellectual free lances, each of whom followed a more or less independent course. Nonetheless they were an extremely influential group, particularly prior to the election of 1837, when many of them were defeated. For they had at least a political philosophy in common. Disciples of Jeremy Bentham and James Mill, they approached problems of government from the standpoint of utility and efficiency and never tired of attacking the illogicality, corruption and ineffectiveness of many traditional institutions. They were by no means radical in a revolutionary sense. Indeed, their objective was reform of government and administration within the framework of the system of free competition. As the only group that had a clear notion of strong government and efficient administration, they prepared the way for the future welfare state. Their immediate role was to see to it that the government, whether in the hands of Whigs or Tories, should not overlook the need for modernization or sink into smug inactivity. In the early 1830's the Whig government was dependent on the support of the Radicals and was therefore obliged, however reluctantly, to accept further reform measures. The new poor law of 1834; the reform of municipal government in 1835, which replaced the old privileged town corporations by town councils elected by all householders; and various items of labor legislation, to be considered in a later context, were all due to Radical pressure. Sharp

---

[7] The importance of the religious factor was heavily stressed in the classic account of Élie Halévy: *A History of the English People in the Nineteenth Century* (rev. ed., London, 1950), III, chaps. i and ii. See also Raymond G. Cowherd: *The Politics of English Dissent, 1815–1848* (London, 1959).

criticism and inexorable logic prepared the way for constant and progressive change to meet the requirements of the modern world.[8]

The larger part of British history in the nineteenth century, from 1837 on, is generally termed the Victorian Age, from the long reign of the queen, who, as a girl of eighteen, ascended the throne in 1837 and continued to reign until her death in 1901. There was, at the time, an understandable interest in a young woman called suddenly to high estate, the more so as Portugal and Spain also had girl queens. But as a matter of politics the monarchy no longer played a decisive role. Under Victoria's immediate predecessors royalty had sacrificed the respect of the public, while the Reform crisis had demonstrated that, in the last resort, the House of Commons could force its will on the crown. When, in 1834, William IV attempted to replace the Whig cabinet by a more congenial Tory ministry, the elections proved conclusively that a government, to operate, must have the support of a majority in the Commons. Yet in the course of years Victoria was to exert a growing personal influence on affairs. Though she was small and homely, she impressed contemporary statesmen at the very outset with her self-assurance and firmness, to say nothing of her grace and high purpose.

Victoria had received no special training for her high position, but found a congenial mentor in her prime minister. Melbourne was three times her age, an erudite, sagacious, cynical man of the world, yet charming, witty and mischievous. He became altogether devoted to his young sovereign and taught her the ways of statecraft, continuing in the role of private secretary until the queen's marriage to Prince Albert of Saxe-Coburg. The latter, a most attractive and intelligent young man of Victoria's age, was a nephew of Leopold I of Belgium and so a cousin of the queen. Victoria was for some time loath to marry and in any event was determined not to share her authority. But eventually she fell deeply in love with Albert and they were married in 1840. Thenceforth the prince consort exercised an ever-increasing influence. Although initially more interested in art and science than in politics, he studied English constitutional law under his

---

[8] S. Maccoby: *English Radicalism, 1832–1852* (London, 1935), chaps. vii, viii, xxi, xxvi; John Plamenatz: *The English Utilitarians* (2 ed., London, 1958), and the corrective writings of Oliver MacDonagh: "The Nineteenth Century Revolution in Government" (*Historical Journal*, I, 1958, 52–67); David Roberts: *Victorian Origins of the British Welfare State* (New Haven, 1960), 28 ff.

former tutor, the learned, solemnly earnest and altogether discreet Baron Christian von Stockmar. Albert passed along what he learned to the queen, taught her to observe impartiality with respect to political parties, and to direct the influence of the crown toward liberal, progressive government. The prince was disliked by the aristocracy because he was a foreigner and because he was a strait-laced stickler for morality. Nonetheless, he made his mark and proved himself an enlightened, up-to-date leader. His active interest in the working classes was indicative of his social awareness. By the time of the great exhibition (1851), of which he was the chief sponsor, he had not only overcome earlier prejudices but had done much to dispel the "dry, bleak and critical" atmosphere that surrounded the monarchy in 1837 and to win for it renewed respect and popularity.[9]

The first five years of Victoria's reign were among the worst of modern English history, years of bad harvests, economic depression and widespread unemployment. Out of them sprang two important movements, the first the agitation against the corn laws, the other the democratic movement known as Chartism. Although the latter came to a head as early as 1839, it will be more convenient to consider first the movement for abolition of the corn laws, because its fruition, in 1846, marked the complete and definitive triumph of economic liberalism through the active intervention of the middle classes in politics.

The British corn laws of 1815 and 1828 had established a graduated tariff on the importation of foreign grain whenever the price of domestic grain remained below a certain high level. In effect, foreign wheat in the period 1831–1841 was subject to a duty of thirty shillings per quarter (ton), which meant that in normal times foreign wheat was virtually excluded from the British market. Similar legislation had been introduced in other Western European states in the understandable attempt to protect agriculture against the cheap wheat available for

[9] Lytton Strachey's *Queen Victoria* (London, 1921) is a literary as well as a historical classic. The latest and most detailed biography is Elizabeth Longford's *Victoria R. I.* (London, 1964). On the prince consort, see Hector Bolitho: *Albert, Prince Consort* (London, 1964); Frank Eyck: *The Prince Consort. A Political Biography* (Boston, 1959), which is based largely on the royal archives. On Melbourne, see David Cecil: *The Young Melbourne* (London, 1939), 250 ff.; John A. R. Marriott: *Queen Victoria and Her Prime Ministers* (New York, 1934), chap. ii. Among special studies may be mentioned Charles K. Webster: "The Accession of Queen Victoria" (*History*, XXII, 1937, 14–33); John P. MacKintosh: "The Early Political Influence of Queen Victoria" (*Parliamentary Affairs*, XII, 1958, 174–188).

export in countries such as Germany and Poland.[10] As such it had fulfilled its purpose, ensuring the country an adequate food supply in time of war. It had, however, at the same time given the landed interest a practical monopoly of the home market and so enabled the landlords to enrich themselves at the expense of the general population. Ricardo, Malthus and other economists never tired of stressing the conflict of interest between the landed and the industrial segments of society. "The interest of the landlord is always opposed to that of the consumer and manufacturer," argued Ricardo, whose sentiments were echoed in such influential writings as the anonymous pamphlet *The Iniquity of the Landlords* (1826) and Thompson's *Catechism of the Corn Laws* (1828). It is perhaps not too much to say that the conflict of interest inherent in the corn laws contributed mightily to popularizing the notion of the class struggle and so provided the ammunition needed by Karl Marx and the socialists.[11]

What brought the issue to a head was the growing population pressure and the increasing difficulty in providing adequate food for the nation. Britain in the 1840's was already obliged to import from 10 per cent to 15 per cent of the required grain supply, which meant that prices were kept at the top level. The new industrialists became increasingly irked and more and more determined to put an end to the economic privileges of the landed class. The agitation for repeal of the corn laws was, in the words of John Morley, not "a battle about a customs duty, but a struggle for political influence and social equality between the landed aristocracy and the great industrialists," or, according to a more recent authority, "an outpouring of social emotion" using the corn laws as a symbol.[12]

This feeling of social grievance was reinforced by the growing conviction that the progressive industrialization of Britain called for greater freedom of trade. The notion of a tight, self-sufficient empire was becoming quite untenable. Indeed, the manufacturing interest was

10 S. Fairlie: "The Nineteenth Century Corn Law Reconsidered" (*Economic History Review*, Ser. 2, XVIII, 1965, 562–575).

11 Mark Blaug: *Ricardian Economics* (New Haven, 1958), 6 ff., 28; Donald G. Barnes: *A History of the English Corn Laws from 1660 to 1846* (London, 1930), 148, 210 ff. Some economists favored a moderate fixed duty on grain in the interest of national security (William D. Grampp: *The Manchester School of Economics*, Stanford, 1960, 16 ff.).

12 George Kitson Clark: "The Repeal of the Corn Laws and the Politics of the Forties" (*Economic History Review*, Ser. 2, IV, 1951, 1–13).

quite indifferent if not hostile to the idea of colonial expansion or even colonial rule. Most colonies were low-consumption areas which held little promise as markets for finished products. Among the British Radicals it was argued that colonies were a liability rather than an asset, that they were essentially a preserve for aristocratic patronage and corruption, and that, furthermore, they were a continuing source of international friction. There were but few who advocated scrapping the empire, but many thought that the colonies should, as soon as possible, be given local self-government, in the hope that eventually they could be amicably separated from the mother country. In hard, business terms, what the new Britain needed was not overseas territories but free access to raw materials and markets everywhere. The world would not be able to buy British manufactures unless it could pay in terms of food and raw materials. In a word, the development of trade depended not on "the miserable foundation of bounties and prohibitions, but on the gratification of real wants and desires."[13]

Agitation in behalf of greater freedom of trade and more particularly for repeal of the corn laws rose and fell as the British economy was depressed or prosperous. In the difficult years 1837–1842, when the Manchester merchants were living in a perpetual "nightmare of uncertainty," terrified by the growing competition of the United States, France and Switzerland in the Latin American markets, it was inevitable that a new drive for repeal should be launched. In the closing months of 1838 a number of Manchester Radicals organized the Anti-Corn Law League, which was definitely a middle-class venture. The president was an unusually gifted organizer, George Wilson, while the intellectual drive came from two cotton manufacturers, Richard Cobden and John Bright, who denounced the landlords as "a bread-taxing oligarchy," "power-proud plunderers" and "blood-sucking vampires," and publicly proclaimed their intention to break the power of the landed aristocracy and ensure the dominance of the middle class. Both Cobden and Bright were pacifists, convinced that free trade would underline the reciprocal interests of nations, reduce the need for

---

[13] Klaus E. Knorr: *British Colonial Theories, 1570–1850* (Toronto, 1944), chap. viii; Robert L. Schuyler: *The Fall of the Old Colonial System* (New York, 1945), 70 ff.; Paul Knaplund: *James Stephen and the British Colonial System, 1813–1847* (Madison, 1953), 253; Helen T. Manning: "The Colonial Policy of the Whig Ministers, 1830, 1837" (*Canadian Historical Review*, XXXIII, 1952, 203–236, 341–368).

government intervention and so end the pointless conflicts of dynastic days.[14]

The Anti-Corn Law League was undoubtedly the most effective propaganda machine that Britain had yet seen. It was never influential in London and the agricultural south, nor was it ever successful in overcoming the suspicions of industrial workers that the employers were intent on lowering the price of food so that they might correspondingly reduce wages. But the Leaguers were able to mobilize the entire middle class in the crusade against aristocratic privilege and to raise ample funds to set up local branches, publish newspapers and pamphlets, organize meetings and campaign in elections. "The great capitalist class formed an excellent basis for the Anti-Corn Law movement," wrote Cobben after the repeal, "for they had inexhaustible purses, which they opened freely in a contest where not only their pecuniary interests, but their pride as 'an order' was at stake."[15]

Cobden was elected to Parliament in 1841 and, along with Radical free-traders and contributors to the brilliant new journal *The Economist* (founded 1843), did much to convince political circles of the pressing need for reform. But the restlessness and discontent in the country were probably just as important, and the role of Sir Robert Peel, who headed the Tory cabinet of 1841, was probably decisive. Peel was a strange chief for what was increasingly called the Conservative Party and he was, in fact, unpopular with the diehard landlord element. But he was one of the greatest parliamentarians of modern Britain and one of the men who best represented the outlook of the progressive upper middle class. Peel belonged to one of the great cotton dynasties and was a man of more than adequate private income. He could therefore serve the country selflessly and, when necessary, override the interests of party for the sake of larger national interests. Not a great creative mind, he was keenly aware of current problems and

---

[14] John A. Hobson: *Richard Cobden, the International Man* (London, 1919); F. H. Hinsley: *Power and the Pursuit of Peace* (Cambridge, 1963) 96 ff. See also Arthur Redford: *Manchester Merchants and Foreign Trade, 1794–1858* (Manchester, 1934), 80 ff.; Albert Imlah: *Economic Elements in the Pax Britannica* (New York, 1958), 14, 38, 40, 145.

[15] Quoted by Grampp: *Manchester School of Economics,* 63. See also Norman McCord: *The Anti-Corn Law League* (London, 1958); J. D. Chambers and G. E. Mingay: *The Agricultural Revolution, 1750–1850* (London, 1966), chap. vi.

prepared to tackle them in an intelligent, systematic way. In his electoral program of 1834 (the *Tamworth Manifesto*) he had first advanced a coherent program of gradual reform and modernization, and he helped to organize the Conservatives as a well-defined party. He was what Walter Bagehot called "a business gentleman," who had nothing but scorn for the aristocrats "who spend their time in eating and drinking, and hunting, shooting, gambling and horse-racing." These people would have to be saved despite themselves. The social transformation of Britain through industrialization could not be halted or reversed: "Our lot is cast; we cannot change it and we cannot recede." Therefore, adjustments would have to be made, for reform could be obstructed only at the peril of the governing class. Widely read in the literature of the French Revolution, Peel was "afraid of catching revolution, as old women are of catching cold." He lived in constant fear lest drastic change produce a chain reaction and end in class struggle and social upheaval. Therefore, necessary reforms must be carried through at all costs and without delay.[16]

Peel was the first representative of the business class to become prime minister. In the years 1841–1846 he dominated not only his party but the exceptionally able men who composed his cabinet. With a strong majority in the House of Commons and with the support of the Radicals, Peel undertook reforms on many fronts: the Bank Charter Act (1844), restricting note issue to the Bank of England; the Companies Act (1844), requiring companies to register and publish their balance sheets; the Factory Act (1844), restricting the hours of work for women and children; the Coal Mines Act, regulating the employment of women and children in mines. Most important in the present context, however, were the financial reforms: the restoration of a modest income tax and the revision of the tariff—in 1842, 750 items out of 1,200 were reduced and, in 1845, 430 items were struck from the tariff entirely; taxes on exports were abolished, as was also the import duty on raw cotton. But the overriding issue was that of the corn laws. Discontent in the country and the unremitting agitation of the Anti-Corn Law League were making more and more converts to the

---

[16] Walter Bagehot: "The Character of Sir Robert Peel" (1856), now reprinted in Norman St. John-Stevas: *Walter Bagehot* (Bloomington, 1959); George Kitson Clark: *Peel* (London, 1936), 70 ff.; Sir Llewellyn Woodward: *The Age of Reform* (2 ed., Oxford 1962), 109 ff.

principles of free trade. By 1846 the great majority of the Whigs (now becoming known as Liberals) was in favor of repeal of the corn laws and many conservatives had come over to the same side.[17]

Peel himself had become convinced of the need for repeal even before the onset of the Irish famine in 1845 made action imperative. The required legislation was enacted in June, 1846, repeal to become fully effective in three years. A majority of the conservatives, led by Lord George Bentinck and Benjamin Disraeli, voted against the measure and presently defeated Peel on an Irish coercion bill, thus forcing the resignation of the government. But the Whig leader, Lord John Russell, took up the work of reform where Peel had left off. In 1849 the navigation laws, a tremendous conglomeration of antiquated regulations, were wiped out, throwing open British trade to the shipping of all nations, except for British and colonial coastal trade. Thus, by 1850 the system of free trade had been adopted. The business class had won its point. Once again, as in 1832, the landed interest, seeing the writing on the wall, had given way on an important issue and accepted economic as before it had accepted political liberalism. "Saving common sense had again saved the British upper classes," in the words of Mr. Kitson Clark. In 1848, while revolutions were raging on the Continent, Peel remarked that by abolition of the corn laws he had spared Britain a major upheaval. He had also saved the aristocratic elements from the gathering social revolution. "We have not seen the last of the Barons," wrote Bright to Wilson after repeal, "but we have taught them which way the world is turning."[18]

The legislation of 1846 and 1849 did much to allay the class antagonism in British society, which by the 1840's had become acute. Furthermore, it ushered in a period of great business expansion and prosperity. Foodstuffs could now be brought in freely even from the New World, and the shipping of all nations could be drawn upon to supply the workshop of the world with the needed sustenance. British imports,

---

[17] George Kitson Clark: "The Electorate and the Repeal of the Corn Laws" (*Transactions of the Royal Historical Society*, Ser. 5, I, 1951, 109–126); William O. Aydelotte: "Voting Patterns in the British House of Commons in the 1840's" (*Comparative Studies in Society and History*, V, 1963, 134–163). For the parliamentary history of the issue, see Maccoby: *English Radicalism*, chap. xv; Southgate: *Passing of the Whigs*, chap. v; Norman Gash: *Reaction and Reconstruction in English Politics, 1832–1852* (Oxford, 1965), chaps. v and vi.

[18] Quoted by McCord: *Anti-Corn Law League*, 204.

which had averaged in value about £80 million per annum in the years 1841–1845, rose to over £122 million per annum in the years 1851–1853. The value of exports rose correspondingly from £54 million to £84 million. The boom was reflected also in shipping reports. Vessels entering in cargo in 1842 totaled 3.65 million tons, and in 1848, 5.58 million. Ships clearing in cargo totaled 3.69 million tons in 1842, and 5.05 million in 1848. This increased business activity on the part of Britain was then soon reflected in the favorable turn of the entire world economy.[19]

That the repeal of the corn and navigation laws was of more than national importance is shown by the keen interest with which the campaign for repeal was followed throughout the Continent. Its success demonstrated that the old order could be reformed by nonviolent, constitutional methods. Liberals everywhere took heart and when, in 1847, Cobden embarked on a grand tour of the Continent, he was hailed everywhere with wild enthusiasm, like a St. George who had destroyed the dragon of privilege. At imposing banquets he explained the techniques of modern propaganda pressure, which were carefully noted by his hosts and were to influence liberal policies and procedures in the eventful year to come.

The Chartist movement, concurrent with the campaign for repeal of the corn laws, was basically a workers' movement, the ultimate though ill-defined objective of which was drastic social reform. Its leaders were convinced, however, that the working class must first secure political power and they therefore drafted a purely political program. It would be logical enough to discuss Chartism in the larger framework of the social problem and the organization of labor, but it makes even more sense to view it as a left-wing political movement going beyond the program of liberalism and aiming at a genuinely democratic system.

Though agitation for democracy and republicanism went back to the late eighteenth century, it emerged as a formidable factor only in the years 1831–1832, when the urban workers took an active part in the campaign for the Reform Bill, only to discover that that measure held nothing for the lower classes: far from being democratic, it was actually antidemocratic, designed to rally the upper middle class to support of the existing order. In their disillusionment a number of London artisans, led by William Lovett, founded in 1836 the Workingmen's Association for Benefitting Politically, Socially and Morally the Useful

[19] Imlah: *Economic Elements in the Pax Britannica,* 38, 114, 156, 173.

Classes. This organization, with monthly dues of one shilling, never had a membership of more than a hundred or two. But it represented the literate upper crust of London craftsmen and enjoyed great prestige. Far from being revolutionary, it aimed at the conquest of political power by suasion and moral force. In 1838 Lovett, assisted by that amazing ex-tailor and labor leader, Francis Place, and by a few Radical members of Parliament, drew up the famous Charter which gave its name to the burgeoning movement. There was nothing novel about it. The Charter was simply a restatement of familiar democratic demands: universal suffrage, secret ballot, salaries for members of Parliament, abolition of tax requirements for political candidates, and annual elections. Workers were to secure the vote, and also the opportunity to stand for office. In the words of an eminent British historian, the Chartist movement was "the first political attack upon the social order which had emerged from the growth of capitalist industry," the essence of which was "an attempt to make possible social reconstruction by the overthrow of the political oligarchy."[20]

The activities of the London artisans were quite innocuous compared to the agitation that arose simultaneously in the industrial cities of the Midlands and the North, where the efforts of the government to enforce the new poor law of 1834 met with desperate resistance. The "sullen, revengeful humour of revolt" (Carlyle) led to the organization of Anti-Poor Law Associations, led by Richard Oastler, a Tory Radical, and J. R. Stephens, a Methodist preacher. So formidable was the opposition that the poor-law commissioners were obliged to abandon the effort to extend the workhouse system to the industrial areas.

The distress and privations of the working class prepared the ground for popular agitators, of whom the two well-educated Irishmen, Bronterre O'Brien and Feargus O'Connor, were soon dominant. These two men had broken away from the London Workingmen's Association and now called for a more revolutionary line. O'Brien was well versed in the history of the French Revolution, considered Robespierre "one of the purest and most enlightened reformers that ever lived," and greatly admired Buonarroti's recently published account of Babeuf's con-

---

[20] R. H. Tawney: *The British Labor Movement* (New Haven, 1925), 15. *Similarly* Edouard Dolléans: *Le Chartisme, 1831–1848* (new ed., Paris, 1949), Introd. On the origins of the Charter, see Graham Wallas: *The Life of Francis Place* (3 ed., New York, 1919), chap. xiii; Maccoby: *English Radicalism,* chap. ix.

spiracy for equality in 1796. A big man with a big voice and a breezy manner, O'Brien could easily sway the largest crowds through his violent denunciations of "the big-bellied, little-brained, numbskull aristocracy," and with his humor and pathos. O'Connor, for his part, founded the newspaper *Northern Star* in November, 1837, and used it as his mouthpiece to attack the poor law and the factory system.[21]

Chartism does not lend itself well to summary treatment, for it was not a single, organized movement. In different places it meant different things and relied for support on different elements. In London it drew its strength from the skilled traditional workers, such as printers, tailors, shoemakers, coachbuilders, and was a relatively conservative movement, closely linked to the Radicals and intent primarily on further political reform. In the North, where Chartism was most widespread and powerful, it was essentially an outgrowth of provincial radicalism, with many variations from place to place. Its supporters were mainly those suffering from the transformation of industry, such as the handloom weavers and framework knitters, several hundred thousands in number, including large numbers of impoverished Irish immigrants. In the new industrial areas Chartism reflected the class struggle through marked hostility to the upper middle class or employers. The leaders were often flamboyant agitators, "wild leaders of hungry men," whose ideas might be nebulous but whose purpose was to provoke an armed uprising if necessary. There was throughout a marked variation between these "physical force" men of Lancashire and the "moral force" men of London. They all subscribed to the Charter, but beneath this cover the welter of conflicting drives persisted.[22]

Countless Chartist meetings, processions, torchlight parades and petitions, accompanied by ever-increasing talk of revolution, finally culminated in a grand Convention of the Industrious Classes which met in London in February, 1839. This informal workers' parliament, consisting of fifty-three members, held sessions five times a week

[21] Donald Read and Eric Glasgow: *Feargus O'Connor* (London, 1961).

[22] Among many studies of the Chartist movement may be mentioned Mark Hovell: *The Chartist Movement* (Manchester, 1918); Julius West: *A History of the Chartist Movement* (Boston, 1920); Dolléans: *Chartisme;* and the admirable pamphlet of F. C. Mather: *Chartism* (London, 1965). *Chartist Studies,* edited by Asa Briggs (London, 1959), consists of essays by various authors stressing particularly the local aspects of the movement.

between February and May, debated the terms of a projected petition to Parliament and discussed what should be done in the event of the petition's being rejected. The "physical force" men were led by George J. Harney, a brilliant twenty-year-old member of the London Democratic Association and the would-be Marat of the coming revolution.[23] O'Connor and other Northerners backed him up and urged a "collision with the tyrants." This wild language led many moderates and representatives of the trade unions to withdraw from the convention, but by May 1,280,000 signatures had been collected and the famous petition was presented to Parliament.[24]

The negative reaction of the House of Commons was a foregone conclusion, for the membership, liberal as well as conservative, was unalterably opposed to universal suffrage and democracy, which were thought to be the inevitable prelude to communism. The fear of revolution which hung over the propertied classes had already led the government to prepare for the worst. London, where the sentiment for violence was but feeble, presented no serious problem, for the city was protected by an efficient police force, established in 1829. But in the North, where the danger was greatest, none of the big cities had such police protection. It was therefore necessary to rely on the troops. Sir Charles Napier, in command, was the ideal man for the emergency. While sympathizing with the workers, he made it clear that he would take drastic action if necessary to maintain order. He posted his troops in strategic locations and brought over a regiment from Ireland as insurance against defection on the part of the English soldiers. He even pioneered the use of the new railway lines to move his forces quickly from one place to another.[25]

Under the circumstances even the most rabid revolutionary had to recognize the futility of an uprising, and none took place, even when Parliament on July 12 rejected the petition by a vote of 235–46. A few extremists formed an insurrectionary committee and organized scattered disorders, but these only gave the authorities the desired

[23] A. R. Schoyen: *The Chartist Challenge* (New York, 1958) is essentially a study of Harney and his role.

[24] A vivid description of a meeting of the convention, by a French labor leader, is included in Flora Tristan's *Promenades in London* (Paris, 1840), chap. v. The convention is treated also in Disraeli's novel *Sybil* (1845).

[25] See the exhaustive study of Frederick C. Mather: *Public Order in the Age of the Chartists* (London, 1959).

excuse for progressively arresting some five hundred Chartist leaders. The one serious incident was the attempt of Welsh miners on November 3-4 to seize the town of Newport. Plans went awry, the troops intervened and a dozen insurgents were killed, after which the remainder retreated. John Frost and other leaders were captured, tried and convicted. Sentenced to be hanged and quartered, in barbaric medieval fashion, they finally had their sentences commuted to transportation for life.[26]

Revolutionary Chartism had clearly shot its bolt, but Chartist agitation continued. In July, 1840, the National Charter Association was founded in Manchester along the lines of the rival Anti-Corn Law League, with regular dues and many local branches. Another petition was gotten up, this time with 3,300,000 signatures. It was carried to Parliament on the shoulders of sixteen men and had to be cut in pieces so as to pass the door of the house. It, too, was rejected by a heavy vote (287-49). There followed an outbreak of strikes and turnouts in the North, but these were more pathetic than formidable and were easily dealt with. John Bright described one at Rochdale in August:

We had an invasion of the town at eleven by 2,000 women and girls who passed through the streets singing hymns—it was a very singular and striking spectacle—approaching the sublime—they are dreadfully hungry—a loaf is devoured with greediness indescribable, and if the bread is nearly covered with mud, it is eagerly devoured.[27]

After this second failure the Chartists showed a greater disposition to co-operate with trade unionists and even with the middle-class anti-corn-law agitators. O'Connor, with his *Northern Star,* became more and more enamored of schemes of land settlement for workers, though he continued to talk in subversive terms.[28] There was a final flare-up of Chartism in April, 1848, when news of the revolutions on the Continent led to serious riots in Glasgow and London. O'Connor, supported by Ernest Jones, planned for a monster demonstration of London

[26] David Williams: *John Frost: a Study in Chartism* (London, 1939); Evan J. Jones: *Some Contributions to the Economic History of Wales* (London, 1928); Alexander Cordell's *The Rape of the Fair Country* (New York, 1959), though fictional, provides an authentic account of life in the mining country and the insurrection of 1839.

[27] Quoted in McCord: *Anti-Corn Law League,* 127. See also George Kitson Clark: "Hunger and Politics in 1842" (*Journal of Modern History,* XXV, 1953, 355-374).

[28] Joy MacAskill: "The Chartist Land Plan" (in Asa Briggs, ed.: *Chartist Studies,* chap. x.).

workers on Kennington Common on April 10, after which another petition was to be taken to Parliament. This time the government took even greater precautions than before. The aged Duke of Wellington was entrusted with the defense of the city and all strategic points were protected with sandbags, while 150,000 special constables were enrolled for the occasion. These volunteers were drawn from all levels of the propertied classes and even from the ranks of skilled labor. They symbolized unity of purpose in suppressing radicalism and revolution. Even O'Connor quailed and, at the behest of the police, counseled the 25,000 workers who braved the rain to foregather on the Common to disperse in orderly fashion, while the petition was taken to Parliament in several hackney cabs. It was a pathetic ending to the story of lower-class efforts to attain political power and effect a social revolution. "From that day it was a settled matter that England was safe from revolution," wrote Harriet Martineau triumphantly after the Kennington Common fiasco. There were, to be sure, disturbances in the industrial North for several more months, but these only gave the authorities a pretext for arresting most of the leaders of Chartism. The lesson was unmistakable. Whereas the middle classes were strong and influential enough to impose the will of the business elements on a Parliament consisting largely of landed proprietors, the lower middle class and the workers were as yet too undeveloped and too heterogeneous to be welded into a unified political movement or to make their weight felt. "All they had in common was that they were the losers in the great distribution of incomes that was involved in the Industrial Revolution." Democracy, the wave of the future, was as yet hardly more than a ripple.[29]

3. FRANCE OF THE GOLDEN MEAN

The regime which, in France, derived from the July Revolution of 1830 was roughly the counterpart of the British system following the passage of the Reform Bill. Revisions of the Charter of 1815 increased the number of electors from 90,000 to about 166,000 by reducing the tax

---

[29] The quotation is from Phyllis Deane: *The First Industrial Revolution* (Cambridge, 1965), 195. On the closing phase of Chartism, see John Saville: *Ernest Jones, Chartist* (London, 1932), and "Chartism in the Year of Revolution" (*Modern Quarterly*, VIII, 1952–1953, 23–33); Preston W. Slosson: *The Decline of the Chartist Movement* (New York, 1916), 94 ff.; West: *History of the Chartist Movement*, chap. viii; Schoyen: *The Chartist Challenge*, 160 ff.

requirement to the payment of 200 francs per annum. The regime was commonly described at the time and afterward as one of bankers and speculators, but, as pointed out in the preceding chapter, it remained essentially what it had been under the Bourbons, a regime of the notables, most of whom were owners of landed property even though they may also have engaged in business. Balzac's characterization of the regime as a "democracy of the rich" was reasonably accurate and there is no reason to doubt that it was one of "soulless commercialism," to borrow a phrase of R. H. Tawney. It would almost seem as though mankind had discovered all the things that could be done with money and how easily it could be obtained. Balzac's novels, like those of Stendhal, are full of financial schemes and manipulations and all emphasize the mad passion for gain. Numerous companies, many of them fraudulent, were being floated and all levels of the population gathered each afternoon at the Paris Bourse to speculate in stocks and bonds of governments and private enterprises. What the Parisian populace saw and read about were the great and wealthy banking families, French, British and Swiss, such as the Rothschilds, Laffitte, Hottinguer, Mallet, Hope, who lived in palatial houses and entertained on a lavish scale. These bankers were certainly very influential and their salons were crowded with ministers and politicians, but they were not the entire establishment by any means, though they were the most obvious element.

Louis Philippe, the "King of the French," was a man of late middle age whose experiences went back to the French Revolution. Though a highly successful businessman and a real plutocrat, he was chronically worried to provide richly for his five sons and three daughters, to establish effective control over government policy and to secure recognition from his fellow sovereigns. The king's powers were not clearly defined, but he had the recognized right to appoint the members of the Senate, or upper house, who held office only for life and were, to a large extent, former officials of the Napoleonic regime. The king could also dissolve the lower Chamber, but that Chamber (of Deputies) now elected its own presiding officer and could insist that the cabinet command the support of a majority in Parliament. Since the powers of the king and the Parliament were precariously balanced, the regime was at no time stable. There were fourteen cabinets between 1830 and 1840 and not a single session of the Chamber of Deputies fulfilled its legal term of five years. Only after 1840, during the Guizot regime, was the king in effective control.[30]

The traditional aristocracy was now in eclipse. In 1831 the hereditary nobility as an institution was declared abolished and the Legitimist elements for the most part withdrew to their estates and boycotted the new regime. In his novel *Lucien Leuwen* Stendhal has drawn an amusing picture of life in a French garrison town about 1835 where the prefect and the regimental commander, as officials of the government, were mercilessly snubbed by the local aristocracy, which paraded its opposition to the new monarchy by wearing the Bourbon colors in their cravats and by demonstrating on every occasion their devotion to the pretender, "Henry V." How harmless their opposition actually was appeared from the adventure of the Duchesse de Berry, the mother of "Henry V," who in the spring of 1832 landed in southern France with a small filibustering force. She eventually reached western France, the traditional Legitimist stronghold, but her efforts to provoke an insurrection fell flat. Eventually she was betrayed by one of her own agents and arrested, only to be released soon after by the authorities, who wisely avoided making a martyr of her.[31]

In the abstract one might suppose that the regime of the *grande bourgeoisie* was the appropriate one for France at a time when the old order was in dissolution and the country had not yet progressed socially to the point where full democracy was indicated. François Guizot, the eminent historian who played so large a political part in this period, was as much convinced as his English fellow-historian Macaulay that the middle class represented the golden mean between despotism and mob rule. All men were entitled to certain civil rights, but political rights could not be equal because of the "natural inequalities it pleases Providence to establish among men." Only those were entitled to political rights who had the wealth, education and independence to

---

[30] On the nature and institutions of the regime, see Paul Bastid: *Les institutions politiques de la Monarchie parlementaire française, 1814–1848* (Paris, 1954); Félix Ponteil: *Les institutions de la France de 1814 à 1870* (Paris, 1966), Book II, chap. i; Jean Lhomme: *La grande bourgeoisie au pouvoir, 1830–1880* (Paris, 1960), 51 ff.; Marcel Chaminade: *La Monarchie et les puissances d'argent* (Paris, 1937).

[31] G. Bertier de Sauvigny: *La conspiration des légitimistes et de la duchesse de Berry contre Louis Philippe, 1830–1832* (Paris, 1950); Charlotte T. Muret: *French Royalist Doctrines since the Revolution* (New York, 1933); René Rémond: *La Droite en France de 1815 à nos jours* (Paris, 1954), 55 ff.

exercise them, and these same qualifications would enable them to represent also the interests of those elements of the population who lacked them. This did not mean that the regime should be exclusive. Everyone was free, even the lowliest, to rise to middle-class status. Only the "dull, lazy and licentious" would remain excluded. Hence Guizot's famous reply to his opponents: "enrich yourselves," which was what the ruling class had done. And indeed, many did so, for the number that met the tax requirement rose from 166,000 in 1831 to 200,000 in 1837 and to 250,000 in 1846. Given time, more and more could enter the ranks of the privileged and eventually there would emerge a classless, bourgeois society.[32]

For the time being, however, only about 3 per cent of the adult male population was deemed qualified to represent the national interest. Parliament was, so to speak, a rich man's club. During the eighteen years of the July Monarchy, only a thousand persons served as deputies, and only sixty held cabinet office. Political parties were more or less a fiction. There was talk of a party of resistance and a party of movement, and later of a left center and a dynastic left. But none of these groupings were organized or stable. There was certainly no more difference between resistance and movement than between Tory and Whig in Britain. At bottom these two "parties" reflected the rivalry between Guizot and Adolphe Thiers, the young Marseillais journalist who had played so prominent a role in setting up the new regime in 1830. For Guizot the system was just about perfect and nothing but the gradual change envisaged by his theory was required. Thiers for his part was less compliant than Guizot where the royal influence was concerned and more eager to espouse a foreign policy less pacifist than what appealed to the king and Guizot. In the large the regime was more exclusive than the British after 1832 and decidedly less disposed to undertake reforms looking toward modernization of the political and administrative system. By the mid-forties it had become hardened and

[32] Roger Soltau: *French Political Thought in the Nineteenth Century* (New Haven, 1931), 43 ff.; Douglas Johnson: *Guizot: Aspects of French History, 1787–1874* (Toronto, 1963); Vincent E. Starzinger: *Middlingness: Juste Milieu Political Theory in France and England, 1815–1848* (Charlottesville, 1965), 57 ff.; Richard Fossaert: "La théorie des classes chez Guizot et Thierry" (*La Pensée*, January–February, 1955); Dietrich Gerhard: "Guizot, Thierry und die Rolle des Tiers Etat in der französischen Geschichte" (*Historische Zeitschrift*, CXC, 1960, 290–310).

corrupt, even the ministers at times becoming involved in scandalous graft transactions.[33]

Louis Philippe was probably as good a king as could be found anywhere, sane and sober, well-informed and widely experienced, basically bourgeois in his attitude and habits. Yet from the very outset he and the new regime were intensely unpopular, at least in the larger cities and especially in Paris. The reasons for this were many and complicated. In a general account they can hardly be more than tabulated.

In the first place, Paris was a veritable hive of industry. Some 300,000 workers, mostly in highly skilled specialist trades and many of them literate, were politically interested and alert. They had hated the aristocratic-clerical regime of Charles X and had seized the opportunity in July, 1830, for staging an insurrection. The printers started it; the artisans joined in; the students, journalists and former Napoleonic officers provided leadership. The "Three Glorious Days" were definitely the work, not of the lowest classes, but of the lower middle class. Those who manned the barricades were mostly carpenters, masons, shoemakers, locksmiths, tailors and other craftsmen. Among the dead there was not a single banker, nor lawyer, nor deputy.[34]

Now these young men (they were mostly twenty to thirty-five) had only foggy notions of the French Revolution and the Napoleonic Empire, but they yearned for those "good old days" and wanted a democratic republic that would do something for the working classes. Their revolutionary fervor had been recently kindled by the publication, in 1828, of *The Conspiracy for Equality,* a vivid account of Gracchus Babeuf's socialist movement (1796) by his companion and associate Filippo Buonarroti. This book made a profound impression on radical circles throughout Europe and Buonarroti himself, on his arrival in Paris from Brussels in 1830, quickly became the grand old man of the revolution, the inspiration of younger men and more particularly of Auguste Blanqui, who soon became the leader of the activist elements.[35]

[33] Roger A. Priouret: *Le République des députés* (Paris, 1959), 70 ff.

[34] See the valuable study of David H. Pinkney: "The Crowd in the French Revolution of 1830" (*American Historical Review* LXX, 1964, 1–17).

[35] Armando Saitta: *Filippo Buonarroti* (Rome, 1950); Alessandro Galante Garrone: *Filippo Buonarroti e i rivoluzionari dell' Ottocento* (Milan, 1951); Arthur Lehning:

If the revolutionary crowds in 1830 shouted both *Vive la République* and *Vive l'Empereur,* they may not have known just what they wanted, but they did not want another Bourbon king, even of a younger line. They wanted liberty and democracy for France and they wanted France to assume the leadership of a crusade to free all peoples from the tyranny of the old order. When disorders broke out in Belgium, Germany and Italy, they clamored for intervention and envisaged the recovery by France of her hallowed "natural frontiers" on the Rhine and the Alps. Influential popular writers such as the Abbé Lamennais and Armand Carrel, the editor of the *National,* were passionate advocates of a crusade of liberation and foreign visitors were impressed and even shocked by the ardor of public opinion on this issue. It stands to reason that Louis Philippe and his ministers, determined to avoid war at all costs, should appear as craven toadies of the Holy Alliance and traitors to the national mission.

The notion of crusade against the oppressors of the peoples naturally refreshed the memory of Napoleon, whose thrilling victories were still vivid in the minds of many. The heavy taxation, the heartless conscription, the rigid discipline of the imperial regime appear to have been already forgotten, while the common man heard the veterans—the *grognards* who, while perpetually grousing, carried the standards of France from one victory to another—tell of past glories. Napoleon's comrades on the rocky island of his exile, notably Las Cases (*Mémorial de Sainte-Hélène,* 1823), had already floated the Napoleonic legend, according to which the emperor was the defender of the fruits of the Revolution, the champion of nationality, the restorer of religion, the misunderstood idealist whose generous objectives had been shattered by a cruel destiny in the form of hostile rulers. Pictures of the "little corporal" were everywhere, poems were written and songs were sung in his praise, and in the popular theaters no plays were so enthusiastically received as those dealing with his exploits.

Balzac, in his novel *The Country Doctor* (1833), conveyed vividly the adulation of Napoleon among the peasants. Gathered in a barn,

"Buonarroti and His Secret Societies" (*International Review of Social History,* I, 1956, 112–140); Elizabeth L. Eisenstein: *The First Professional Revolutionist: Filippo Michele Buonarrotti* (Cambridge, 1959); and on Blanqui, Neil Stewart: *Blanqui* (London, 1939) and the analytical studies of Alan B. Spitzer: *The Revolutionary Theories of Louis Auguste Blanqui* (New York, 1957); Maurice Dommanget: *Les idées politiques et sociales d'Auguste Blanqui* (Paris, 1958).

they call on the local veteran, Goguelat, to tell them not about any specific battle, but just about the emperor. He was always referred to as "the man," says Goguelat, but he was clearly more than human: "He had a star of his own; he was the child of God, created to be the soldier's father, for no one ever saw him as a lieutenant or a captain; he was a major from the very start." Then, carried away by his subject, Goguelat exclaims: "What fine times they were! Colonels became generals before your very eyes; generals became marshals of France, and marshals became kings." Those who say the emperor is dead "do not know him, that is plain! They go on telling this fib to deceive the people, and to keep things quiet for their tumble-down government."[36]

This adulation was by no means confined to the gullible masses. Many of the great writers and artists of the Romantic period, such as Stendhal, Quinet, Musset, Vigny, Hugo, Béranger among the literary men and Charlet, Raffet, Daumier and Horace Vernet among the artists, were unrestrained in their admiration. Stendhal in the *Life of Napoleon* (1835) called him "the greatest man who had appeared in the world since Caesar . . . the most amazing man who had appeared since Alexander." Quinet, in a long poem *Napoléon* (1836), saw in him a new Prometheus, a man of the people and at the same time a universal, divine figure. Musset, in his *Confessions,* recalled the stirring days when warrior fathers returned home bedecked with medals and covered with glory, while Vigny declared that the dream of his generation was to make war, win the *Croix de guerre* at twenty, become a colonel at thirty, or die gloriously in the interval. And finally Victor Hugo, in his address to the French Academy in 1841, outdid all his colleagues in the lavishness of his praise:

His military reputation was immense, his conquests colossal. Each year he pushed the frontiers of his empire beyond even the majestic and essential limits which God gave to France. He wiped out the Alps as did Charlemagne, and the Pyrenees as did Louis XIV; he crossed the Rhine as did

---

36 This little twenty-page masterpiece was first published as a magazine article and then as a pamphlet before being incorporated in the novel. See André-Jean Tudesq: "La légende napoléonienne en 1848" (*Revue historique,* CCXVIII, 1957, 64–68). On the general subject, see Jean Skerlitch: *L'opinion publique en France d'après la poésie politique et sociale de 1830 à 1848* (Lausanne, 1901), 56 ff.; Philippe Gonnard: *Les origines de la légende napoléonienne* (Paris, 1906), 334 ff.; Albert L. Guerard: *Réflections on the Napoleonic Legend* (New York, 1924); Jean Lucas-Dubreton: *Le culte de Napoléon 1815–1848* (Paris, 1960), chaps. xiii *et seq.*

Caesar. . . . He was the ruler of forty-four million Frenchmen and the protector of a hundred million Europeans. . . . Everything about this man was grand and splendid. He hovered over Europe like an extraordinary vision.[37]

The historians and artists contributed mightily to the growth of the legend. Year after year biographies of the emperor or narratives of his deeds came from the presses, many of them richly illustrated, as, for example, the 350 vignettes by Raffet in J. de Norvin's *History of Napoleon* (1839) or Horace Vernet's glowing pictures in Laurent d'Ardèche's biography. Vernet was the Napoleonic painter *par excellence*. Louis Philippe gave him a commission for three huge Napoleonic battle scenes for the new museum at Versailles and Czar Nicholas of all men, paid him 25,000 francs for a painting showing Napoleon reviewing the Imperial Guard.[38]

The restlessness, the longing for glory and the thirst for revenge were perhaps the most prominent features of the French mentality in the 1830's, and found their best expression in the cult of Napoleon.[39] But while dreaming of the great emperor, the Frenchman found himself confronted by Louis Philippe, an aging gentleman, portly and heavy of jowl, walking demurely with his green umbrella, like any proper bourgeois, and stopping to talk with the shopkeeper or to shake hands with a worker. According to current gossip, as reported by the German poet Heinrich Heine, the king wore for this purpose a dirty glove "which he always drew off and replaced with a new, clean 'kid' when he climbed again into the higher regions inhabited by his ancient nobility, bankers, ministers, intriguers and scarlet lackies."[40]

This malicious story serves at least to reflect the contempt with

---

[37] Quoted in Jean Bourguignon: *Napoléon Bonaparte* (Paris, 1936), I, xii–xiii; see also Elliott M. Grant: *The Career of Victor Hugo* (Cambridge, 1945), 128, and for the other quotations the valuable study of Georges Lote: "Napoléon et le romantisme" (*Romanische Forschungen*, XXXIII, 1913, 247–304).

[38] On the histories of Napoleon, see Gonnard: *Origines*, 334 ff; Pieter Geyl: *Napoleon, for and against* (New Haven, 1949), 37 f.; Peter Stadler: *Geschichtsschreibung und historisches Denken in Frankreich, 1789–1871* (Zürich, 1958), chap. xiii. On the artists, Armand Dayot: *Les peintres militaires: Charlet et Raffet* (Paris, n.d.) and *Les Vernet* (Paris, 1898), 138 ff., 189 ff.

[39] Jules Bertaut: *Le roi bourgeois* (Paris, 1936), 288 ff.; Karl Epting: *Das französische Sendungsbewusstsein im 19 und 20 Jahrhundert* (Heidelberg, 1952), 41 ff., 68 ff., 105 ff.

[40] Heinrich Heine: *French Affairs* (Eng. trans., London, 1893), I, 41.

which the new ruler was regarded. Whatever Louis Philippe's virtues, he was certainly not colorful. The average Parisian craftsman or shopkeeper, exulting in the victory of July, 1830, felt that the fruits of the Revolution had been stolen from him, that he had been betrayed. Such exactly was the feeling of the English lower classes on the morrow of the Reform Bill, but the Frenchman had a stronger revolutionary tradition and a more excitable temperament. He was not willing to accept the new regime without protest or opposition. Barricade fighting had given him a perhaps exaggerated notion of how much could be accomplished. It had certainly given him a taste for rioting and disorder, for a life of adventure and heroism. The young people, reported Heine, "yearned for great deeds and scorned the stingy small-mindedness and huckstering selfishness of the powers that be." In no time they had built up an aversion to the "king of the speculators" as well as to the deputies and officials and in fact to all the flashy bourgeois rich who paraded in elegant coaches drawn by four or even six well-groomed and well-fed horses.[41]

The Parisian malcontents, true to the revolutionary tradition, presently organized the Society of the Friends of the People, which included just about all of the revolutionary elite. Many of the names are still deeply revered in France, such as Godefroy Cavaignac, hero of the July barricades, a charismatic man of action; Ulysse Trélat, saintly physician and friend of the poor; Armand Marrast, Lycée professor and editor of *La Tribune;* François Raspail, eminent scientist and advocate of social reform; Armand Carrel, former military officer and now editor of *Le National;* and finally Auguste Blanqui, son of a university professor and brother of a leading economist, one of the outstanding revolutionary leaders of modern times. As yet the program of the society was rather vague but definitely moderate. In fact, those who pressed for revolutionary action were periodically purged.[42]

Perhaps because of its moderation the Friends of the People was soon overshadowed by the Society of the Rights of Man, which made a greater effort at organization and discipline. Meeting secretly in small

---

[41] Heine: *French Affairs;* see also Théophile Lavallée: *Histoire de Paris* (Paris, 1852), 188.

[42] I. Tchernoff: *Le parti républicain sous la Monarchie de Juillet* (Paris, 1901), 52 ff., 90 ff.; Georges Weill: *Histoire du parti républicain en France de 1814 à 1870* (new ed., Paris, 1928), 31 ff., 60 ff.; Gabriel Perreux: *Au temps des sociétés secrètes* (Paris, 1931), 8 ff.

sections, each with a provocative name such as Robespierre, Tocsin or Army of the Bastille, it made a real drive to enlist skilled workers and tradesmen, and to found branches in other cities. It is said to have had 4,000 members in Paris alone. Even yet, however, the program was essentially moderate, calling for a single-chamber Parliament elected by universal suffrage, freedom of association and other civil rights.

While these societies were basically debating clubs and propaganda organizations, the populace in Paris and other large cities took matters into its own hands. The years following 1830 were marked by economic depression and widespread unemployment, which further aggravated the unrest. There were strikes and efforts at the formation of trade unions, to say nothing of food riots and workers' demonstrations of all kinds. In addition, ominous crowds were on the streets on the slightest provocation. In November and December, 1830, the trial of the ministers of Charles X brought thousands to the Place de la Concorde and threatened another insurrection unless the ministers were given the death sentence. In February, 1831, mobs broke up a memorial service for the Duc de Berry (assassinated in 1820), sacked the convent of Saint Germain l'Auxerrois and then destroyed the palace of the archbishop. Later that year the collapse of the Polish resistance to Russia led to much clamor for intervention against Russian tyranny. The outbreak of cholera in the spring of 1832 raised popular suspicion that the fountains were being poisoned by the upper classes so as to get rid of superfluous proletarians. Then, in June, 1832, just as the Reform Bill was being passed in England, a monster demonstration of some 25,000 took place on the occasion of the funeral of the republican General Lamarque. The crowds shouted "Down with Louis Philippe" and "Long Live Poland." Barricades went up in the workers' sections. But the movement lacked leadership and soon petered out, leaving several hundred dead on the pavements.

The record shows plainly that the forces of radicalism and republicanism were as yet too amorphous to carry through any concerted action. But of the bitterness of sentiment among the lower classes there can be no doubt. Every disturbance, every suppression, every conviction of ringleaders aroused further animosity. Some of the radical newspapers, such as *La Tribune,* knew no bounds in their attacks on the king and his ministers or in their charges of deception and ineptitude, to say nothing of incitement to revolt. Under the July Monarchy there were literally hundreds of convictions for press offenses, and many editors served prison sentences.[43]

Along with this virulent press campaign went a phenomenal development of political caricature. In November, 1830, Charles Philipon founded *La Caricature,* a weekly consisting of two pages of text and two pictures, and two years later *Charivari,* a daily of three pages with one picture. Philipon had a vivid satirical imagination and at the same time unusual organizational ability. He soon enlisted for his publications a brilliant band of artists—Grandville, Gavarni, Decamps and above all others Charles Traviès and the greatest satirist of the century, Honoré Daumier, at that time in his mid-twenties. It was Philipon himself who first pictured Louis Philippe's head as a pear, a word which in popular French parlance may also mean a nitwit. The pear then became the symbol for the entire regime (see Illustration 44). In a long series of lithographs and other engravings Daumier, for example, in the years 1831–1835 lampooned the king, his ministers and the deputies, almost all of whom appeared as heavy, homely, potbellied figures. Never, perhaps, had a monarch and his advisers been so mercilessly, so scurrilously attacked. Great art though many of these prints undoubtedly were, it is hard to condone the unsparing contempt and hatred that breathes from them. Small wonder that both Philipon and Daumier spent months in prison, as a result of which their hostility seems to have become even more intense.[44]

The government could meet the ideological attack by prosecutions, fines and imprisonment, but was at a loss how to deal with the chronic disorder on the streets. Casimir-Périer, the well-known banker who was prime minister in 1831–1832 until carried off by cholera, had initiated a policy of firmness and repression, but had by no means mastered the problem, as shown by the Lamarque demonstrations which took place shortly after his demise. One of the major difficulties was the fact that the Paris police (*garde municipale*), though tough, numbered only

---

[43] Irene Collins: *The Government and the Newspaper Press in France, 1814–1881* (Oxford, 1959), chap. viii; Charles Ledré: *La presse à l'assaut de la Monarchie, 1815–1848* (Paris, 1960), 128 ff.

[44] Wolfgang Balzer: *Der junge Daumier und seine Kampfgefährten, 1830–1835* (Dresden, 1965) provides a splendid selection of this material, with valuable text. See also Armand Dayot: *Les maîtres de la caricature française au XIXe siècle* (Paris, n.d.), iii ff.; and the excellent biographical study by Oliver W. Larkin: *Daumier, Man of His Time* (New York, 1966).

some 1,500 men and was therefore quite inadequate for preserving order in a city of almost a million. There was, of course, the garrison of the capital, consisting of about 30,000 troops housed in numerous barracks scattered about the city. But the army was a conscript army, with a term of service of seven years. It was always doubtful whether soldiers taken from the common people could be relied upon to shoot on the populace. In July, 1830, two regiments had defected on the Place Vendôme and others had had to be moved before they could follow suit. So the government was almost obliged to rely on a citizen militia, the National Guard (*Garde nationale*), which existed in most of the cities and was reconstituted by the law of March 22, 1831. Technically, all men between twenty and sixty were liable for service, but actually only taxpayers were enrolled and the Guard was, frankly, intended as a bourgeois force to protect property and defend the regime: "maintain obedience to the laws, preserve or re-establish order or public peace," according to the text of the law.

In Paris the National Guard consisted of some 80,000 men (one legion for each arrondissement, plus an elite cavalry legion). It was to support the police in case of disorder, and in the event of foreign war to serve as a reserve for the army. In domestic crises the troops were not to act until the National Guard had been put in motion. The system worked well enough at first, for it was the National Guard that was most instrumental in preventing the disorders of the first few years from ending in open insurrection. In reliance upon it the government then attempted to suppress radicalism by progressively introducing repressive legislation.[45]

The law of April 10, 1834, engineered by Adolphe Thiers as minister of the interior, declared political organizations of even less than twenty members illegal and made individual members responsible for any violation. It was the debates on this law that provoked a major uprising in Lyons, which was followed by an insurrection in Paris. For two days (April 13-14) national guards and troops literally massacred the ill-prepared insurgents. In the Rue Transnonain they invaded a house

---

[45] J. Monteilhet: *Les institutions militaires de la France, 1814-1924* (Paris, 1926), 21 ff.; Adeline Daumard: *La bourgeoisie parisienne de 1815 à 1848* (Paris, 1963), 584, 595 ff.; Louis Girard: *La garde nationale, 1814-1871* (Paris, 1964), the basic treatment; Jean Vidalenc: "L'institution fondamentale de la France bourgeoise: la garde nationale" (*Revue d'histoire économique et sociale*, XLIII, 1965, 240-255).

from which they thought there had been shooting and slew fourteen of the inhabitants indiscriminately. This was the subject of Daumier's masterpiece, one of the most moving prints of all time (see Illustration 41). When all was over, some 2,000 persons, including most of the republican leaders, had been arrested. Their trial, before the House of Peers in May, 1835, produced much oratory and tumult. Some of the accused managed to escape, but most were sentenced to imprisonment or deportation.[46]

The crowning step in the government's policy of repression, the September Laws of 1835, followed the most atrocious and bloody, though abortive, of the eight attempts to assassinate the king. As Louis Philippe and his sons and ministers rode along the boulevards to review the troops on the anniversary of the July Revolution, a fanatic named Fieschi exploded an infernal machine which, though it spared the royal family, left many dead on the pavement. The new press laws now required newspapers to deposit 100,000 francs as a guarantee of good behavior and doubled the scale of fines for press offenses. Henceforth no drawing, engraving or emblem was to be published without official permission. Any incitement to attack the king or overthrow the government, any article designed to inspire contempt or hatred of the king, was made a treasonable offense to be tried by the House of Peers. Indeed, it became a criminal offense even to introduce the name of the king into a discussion of the acts of the government, or to express the wish, hope or threat to overthrow the regime and restore the Bourbon dynasty.[47]

These harsh laws, a sad commentary on the "liberalism" of the French bourgeoisie and the July Monarchy, obliged the radical societies to dissolve and many of the newspapers to close down. Philipon, Daumier and their associates had to turn their satire to more general social problems. A few irreconcilable revolutionaries, such as Blanqui, Armand Barbès and Martin Bernard, ran the risk of organizing secret societies, first the Society of the Families and then the Society of the Seasons (1837–1839). In May, 1839, at the very time of the great

---

[46] The Lyons rising was one of the earliest social insurrections, and will be dealt with in Chapter VI. For the rest, see Jean Jaurès: *Histoire socialiste* (Paris, 1900) II, chaps. xi and xii; Octave Festy: *Le mouvement ouvrier au début de la Monarchie de Juillet* (Paris, 1908); John M. S. Allison: *Thiers and the French Monarchy* (London, 1926), chap. x.

[47] Collins: *Government and the Newspaper Press,* chap. viii.

Chartist demonstrations in England, they staged another insurrection in Paris, but only to be promptly captured, convicted and imprisoned.[48]

In the effort to counteract the prevalent discontent, the government, under Guizot's direction, passed a primary-education law in 1833, and tried to compensate for its pacifist foreign policy by catering to the popular interest in Napoleon. Both of these programs deserve at least brief consideration.

The conviction was widespread among liberals in all countries that one remedy for popular unrest was more education, through which the poor might be enabled to improve their position. In France as in England there was much interest in schooling and societies to promote elementary education were extremely active. The key to the situation seemed to lie in the monitorial or Bell-Lancastrian system, by which the shortage of teachers could be overcome by having the older pupils or monitors teach the younger, with only one adult pedagogue in supervision of as many as a thousand children (see Illustration 31). The government of Louis Philippe gave its approval to these schools, of which there were some 2,000 in 1831. But much more needed to be done. Most primary-school teachers were village priests or war veterans, whose intellectual efforts inspired many lampoons. The new law of 1833 made modest provision for improving the situation. Every commune (village) was thenceforth to maintain a private school and pay a teacher at least 200 francs per year plus adequate lodgings. Children of indigent parents were to be taught free of charge, but others were required to pay a modest fee. Communes of over 6,000 population were to provide training schools for trade and industry, and the *départements* were obliged to have normal schools for teacher training. Provision was made for supervision at all levels, committees consisting of the mayor, the curé and a local notable passing on the qualifications of both lay and clerical instructors.

Though the Guizot law did not make primary education compulsory, it did make basic education available and ensured more satisfactory facilities. The number of pupils increased from about two million in 1831 to three and a quarter million in 1846. In 1847 almost two-thirds of the recruits for the army were found to be literate. But whether this spread of popular education served the intended purposes is a debatable

---

[48] Alexandre Zevaès: *Une révolution manquée: l'insurrection du 12 mai, 1839* (Paris, 1933).

question. The evidence would indicate that many who learned to read soon forgot the "sound" principles which were inculcated and made use of their new capability to devour the radical and even socialist literature against which they were supposed to have received immunity.[49]

As for the cult of Napoleon, the government was ready to provide a solatium for the people. The statue of the "little corporal" was replaced on the Vendôme Column in 1833 and three years later the Arc de Triomphe was completed and dedicated, with the famous bas-relief by François Rude depicting the departure of the volunteers in 1792, one of the finest pieces of sculpture of the period and an ardent expression of republican patriotism (see Illustration 68).[50] Then, in December, 1840, came the great event, engineered by Thiers, the return of Napoleon's remains from St. Helena and their enshrinement in the Hôtel des Invalides. Brought by barge up the Seine from Le Havre, the imperial bones were taken in grand procession down the Champs Elysées and across the river. Despite the severity of the winter weather, huge crowds turned out to pay tribute (see Illustration 48).[51]

The government's notion that the adulation for the late emperor was an innocent thing that might provide vicarious satisfaction to a restless populace seemed to be vindicated by the almost complete lack of interest shown in the efforts of Napoleon's heir, Prince Louis Napoleon, to exploit the legend and upset the regime. This is another way of saying that Frenchmen looked back nostalgically to the days of the glorious empire, but had little use for Bonapartism in the abstract.

Louis Napoleon was the son of the emperor's brother Louis, the king of Holland. After the death of Napoleon's son, the Duke of Reichstadt (1832), Louis Napoleon assumed the role of pretender. In October, 1836, he managed to subvert an artillery regiment at Strasbourg, which

[49] Maurice Gontard: *L'enseignement primaire en France, de la Révolution à la loi Guizot* (Paris, 1959); Patience Hunkin: *Enseignement et politique en France et en Angleterre* (Paris, 1962), 69 ff.; Felix Ponteil: *Histoire de l'enseignement en France, 1789–1964* (Paris, 1966), 189 ff.; Elizabeth P. Brush: *Guizot in the Early Years of the Orleans Monarchy* (Urbana, 1929), chap. iv; Douglas Johnson: *Guizot* (Toronto, 1963), chap. iii.

[50] Louis Allard: *Esquisses parisiennes en des temps heureux, 1830–1848* (Montreal, 1943), 135 ff.; Lucas-Dubreton: *Le culte de Napoléon*, 316 ff.; Louis de Fourcaud: *François Rude* (Paris, 1904), chaps. xix and xx.

[51] Jean Bourguignon: *Le retour des cendres* (Paris, 1941); Lucas-Dubreton: *Le culte de Napoléon*, 353 ff., 375 ff.

he hoped would inspire other troops to join in a triumphal march on Paris. When the coup was attempted (October 30), it took the Strasbourgers by surprise. Most of the garrison remained loyal and the pretender, unwilling to countenance bloodshed, surrendered. The government, determined not to make a martyr of him, shipped him off to the United States, while a jury acquitted his accomplices.

Within a year Louis Napoleon was back in Switzerland, whence he took refuge in England after severe pressure on the Swiss authorities by the French government. In exile he devoted himself to serious study as well as to high life. In 1839 he published a little book, *Napoleonic Ideas,* which was a competent and persuasive restatement of the Napoleonic legend, as well as an attempt to harmonize it with the forces and aspirations of the new age. The Napoleonic idea, argued the prince, "is not an idea of war, but a social, industrial, commercial, humanitarian idea."

In August, 1840, in the midst of an acute international crisis and an outburst of chauvinism in France, Louis Napoleon tried once more to provoke insurrection. With fifty followers he landed near Boulogne, accompanied by a trained eagle as symbol of imperial power. Once again the local troops failed to respond. After a few hours the filibusters re-embarked, while loyal soldiers shot at them like sitting ducks. The prince himself was captured, tried by the House of Peers and sentenced to imprisonment in the fortress of Ham, near the Belgian frontier. From this conveniently located prison he managed to escape in due time and returned to England.[52]

The year 1840 marks a turning point in the history of the July Monarchy, introducing the period during which Guizot was the dominant figure and during which the regime became stabilized. The great historian never wavered in his political conviction that the golden mean had been attained and that further reform was not only unnecessary but dangerous. In contrast to most other political leaders, he held

---

[52] All biographies of the later Napoleon III discuss these escapades in perhaps undue detail. F. A. Simpson: *The Rise of Louis Napoleon* (London, 1909), chap. vi, is still one of the best, but see more recent studies such as Paul Guériot: *Napoléon III* (Paris, 1933), I, chap. ii; Maurice La Fuye and Emile A. Babeau: *Louis Napoléon Bonaparte avant l'Empire* (Amsterdam, 1951), chaps. vi, x–xi; Adrien Dansette: *Louis Napoléon et la conquête du pouvoir, 1808–1851* (Paris, 1961); and the very solid, detailed study of Heinrich Euler: *Napoleon III in seiner Zeit: der Aufstieg* (Würzburg, 1961), chaps. xxiv ff.

that the throne should not be an empty chair, in other words, that the king should exercise authority and formulate policy. The function of the ministry should be to ensure that there was, in the Chamber, the majority needed to support the royal program. An obvious and time-honored method of doing so was to have the prefects and sub-prefects see to it that the proper candidates were nominated; that local newspapers, when friendly, should be subsidized; that dependable electors should be duly registered; and that undesirables should be kept from voting by chicanery of one sort or another. Another device, equally familiar, was to reward loyal deputies with remunerative positions and to encourage officials and army officers to stand for election. Balzac, in his *Deputy for Arcis* (1847), has given a vivid account of the skulduggery that marked the 1839 election. The winning candidate was exactly the type desired by the government: a successful bonnet manufacturer, the perfect bourgeois, "a model of inanity, with his fixed smile and string of clichés, punctuated by imbecile cackles—a man completely devoid of ideas outside business."[53]

Under Guizot's guidance the government became firmly entrenched. The Chamber of 1846 consisted of 185 officials, 142 landowners and rentiers, 48 lawyers, 34 merchants and manufacturers, 16 men of letters, 11 bankers and 7 doctors. We have the testimony of the great political theorist, Alexis de Tocqueville, himself a deputy, that political life became utterly dull. Even the finest oratorical talents were wasted in empty declamations: "These great orators were bored to death listening to one another and, what was worse, the whole country was bored with listening to them." Everyone understood that affairs turned on the interests of one and the same class and that a capitalist oligarchy was running the country as an industrial enterprise. Public works, such as the modernization of Paris, the extension of the canal system, the development of the railway net, provided ample oppportunities for logrolling and graft. The principles of economic liberalism demanded that trade should gradually be freed, and efforts were made by prominent economists in 1845 to found a free-trade association along the lines

[53] Sherman Kent: *Electoral Procedures under Louis Philippe* (New Haven, 1937), chaps. iv, vi, viii, ix; Peter Campbell: *French Electoral Systems and Elections, 1789–1957* (London, 1958), 61 ff.; A. Roubaud: "Les élections de 1842 et de 1846 sous le ministère de Guizot" (*Revue d'histoire moderne*, XIV, 1939, 261–287); André-Jean Tudesq: "Les listes électorales de la Monarchie Censitaire" (*Annales*, XIII, 1958, 277–288); Lhomme: *La grande bourgeoisie au pouvoir*, 51 ff.

of the British Anti-Corn Law League. But agriculturists, iron and steel manufacturers, and sugar interests banded together in a Committee for the Defense of National Work to block all efforts at liberalizing the tariff.[54]

It stands to reason that the more progressive minority in Parliament not only resented its exclusion from the good things of political life but also feared lest the rigid policy of the government build up too great popular pressure for change. Men such as Thiers (Guizot's confirmed rival) and Odilon Barrot (leader of the "dynastic left") were sincerely convinced that the whole regime was being jeopardized. They called for reduction of the tax requirement for the franchise from 200 francs to 100, and especially for the admittance to the vote of the professional men, the writers, doctors, lawyers, professors, without any tax requirement whatever. These men formed the highly articulate element which had every qualification except wealth and which was already spearheading the attack on the regime. In retrospect it is hard to escape the conclusion that it was indeed an egregious error to shut out the professional class from political life.

One particularly ominous development, perhaps not recognized at the time, was the progressive disintegration of the National Guard. By 1835 the wealthier elements were already getting themselves excused from active service on one pretext or another and by 1840 most of the Paris legions were disaffected. They saw less and less reason to support a regime which required their services yet denied them the vote. In the eastern sections of Paris the legions were known to be favorable not only to reform but to the republican program. The king, aware of their disgruntlement, no longer dared review them. Instead, the municipal guard was more than doubled in number and the regime for the future had to rely on the police and the troops rather than on the National Guard. By 1848 it had definitely lost its main prop.[55]

---

[54] Shepard B. Clough: *France: a History of National Economics, 1789–1939* (New York, 1939), chap. v. On Tocqueville, see especially his own *Recollections* (New York, 1959), 3 ff.; J. Salwyn Shapiro: "Alexis de Tocqueville: Pioneer of Democratic Liberalism in France" (*Political Science Quarterly*, LVII, 1942, 545–563); Raymond Aron: "Idées politiques et vision historique de Tocqueville" (*Revue française de science politique*, September, 1960); J. P. Mayer: *Alexis de Tocqueville* (New York, 1960), 32 ff.; Jack Lively: *The Social and Political Thought of Alexis de Tocqueville* (New York, 1962).

[55] Charles Simond: *Les centennales parisiennes* (Paris, 1903), 23 ff.; Daumard: *La bourgeoisie parisienne*, 595 ff.; Girard: *La garde nationale*, 249 ff.

Guizot, however, was unmoved by this *"fronde bourgeoise,"* which to him was but "a superficial, artificial, deceptive movement, stirred up by newspapers and committees."[56] The result was a growing tendency for the parliamentary opposition to draw closer to the democratic, republican, socialist elements, which by the 1840's were becoming better organized. In 1843 Alexandre Ledru-Rollin, a prosperous Paris lawyer, joined with the scientist François Arago and the journalist Louis Blanc to found the newspaper *La Réforme,* which became the mouthpiece not only of the republicans but of the democrats throughout Europe. Ledru-Rollin became the great champion of universal suffrage, through which the lower middle class and the workers could then transform the social order by political action. *La Réforme* was certainly not the advocate of a social revolution, but it did call for social reforms, for recognition of the right to work, and for state intervention in the interests of social security.[57]

Taking a leaf from Cobden's book, various leaders of the opposition in 1847 undertook a grand campaign of agitation and education in the form of political banquets. The first was held on July 9, 1847, at Château-Rouge, a suburb of Paris. Here some 1,200 electors dined at ten francs per person and then listened to toasts and speeches denouncing the government, demanding reform and ending in the rousing singing of the "Marseillaise." Many more banquets were held in the ensuing months throughout France, with Odilon Barrot, the poet Lamartine, Louis Blanc and eventually Ledru-Rollin emerging as the principal speakers. The main promoters were republicans and the meetings became progressively more radical, attracting large numbers of non-dining spectators. Such was the situation when, in the closing days of December, 1847, the Parliament met to hear the king's address from the throne.[58]

By this time the campaign of the opposition had been reinforced by the writings of eminent authors which revived interest in the

[56] Guizot: *Histoire parlementaire,* III, 557.

[57] Weill: *Histoire du parti républicain,* 138 ff.; Alvin R. Calman: *Ledru-Rollin and the Second French Republic* (New York, 1922), 23 ff.; Robert Schnerb: *Ledru-Rollin* (Paris, 1948); Stanislas Mitard: *Les origines du radicalisme démocratique: l'affaire Ledru-Rollin* (Paris, 1952), chap. iii.

[58] H. Monim: *Le banquet du Château-Rouge* (Paris, 1897); John J. Baughman: "The French Banquet Campaign of 1847–1848" (*Journal of Modern History,* XXXI, 1959, 1–15).

French Revolution and in France's mission. The parliamentary history of the Revolution, by Buchez and Roux, was completed in many volumes in 1848, and the writings of Robespierre had been edited by Laponneraye in 1842. There followed in rapid succession the sympathetic histories of the Revolution by Blanc, Cabet and others, and finally the works which exercised a major influence. In 1845 Thiers, temporarily in political eclipse, published the first three volumes of his *History of the Consulate and the Empire.* In 1847 came the first two volumes of Jules Michelet's *History of the French Revolution* and all eight volumes of the poet Lamartine's *History of the Girondists.*

Michelet, truly a man of the people and one of the greatest of French historians, wrote with romantic ardor of the great days of 1789–1790, when the spirit of the people shone in all its splendor. The period of the Terror he regarded as an interlude of brutal minority rule, a blot on what was otherwise the national epic of liberty and democracy. It was inevitable that Michelet's stirring narrative should have aroused Frenchmen to take up once more the role of Messiah among the nations. By contrast Lamartine's history was little more than a brilliantly written romance, with little reference to historical truth. The author, disgusted with the regime, had turned republican in 1843 and aimed to make himself the guide of popular forces. "France," he declared, "is revolutionary or it is nothing. The Revolution of 1789 is her political religion." His *Girondists,* written under great pressure, was careless and obviously propagandistic, but it made excellent reading and achieved its purpose. Within three months 25,000 copies of the eight-volume set had been sold and the needy author received royalties of 240,000 francs.

Thiers' history, of which six volumes had appeared by 1848, was a conscientious piece of scholarship based on much unpublished material and on careful study of battlefields and other historic localities. Written in lively style, always clear, it quickly became favorite reading throughout the Continent. Its effect was to recapture again the drama of the past and stimulate national pride. Napoleon's early conquests were described almost as the work of Providence. The contrast to the colorlessness and stagnation of the July Monarchy hardly needed emphasis.[59]

[59] These writings are discussed at length in such works as George P. Gooch: *History and Historians of the Nineteenth Century* (London, 1913, 1959), chap. ix, but see also Leo Gershoy: "Three French Historians and the Revolution of 1848" (*Journal of the History of Ideas,* XII, 1951, 131–146); A. Aulard: "Michelet, historien de la Révolution

Granting that Guizot underestimated the extent and strength of the agitation, it is true nevertheless that neither the parliamentary opposition nor the *Réforme* group was revolutionary. The organizers of the banquets were inspired by the resounding victory scored by Cobden in England by strictly peaceful methods. They hoped in the same way to force Guizot to loosen his control, to liberalize the franchise, to check the corruption and to make his following less exclusive. But those who engaged in this "family row" were fully as blind as Guizot. They did not realize that in stirring up passions they were encouraging far more radical popular forces, especially the lower middle class of craftsmen and shopkeepers who had mounted the barricades in July, 1830, and had felt so deeply betrayed by the regime they had helped bring into being. These popular forces were disorganized because after their rampancy in the early 1830's they had been so effectively repressed by the September laws of 1835. But they were still there and more ready than ever to explode whenever the lid was lifted. The years 1845–1847 were years of famine and economic depression, years of unemployment and misery, and by 1848 the industrial changes had more and more deeply shaken the traditional social structure. The Revolution of 1848 in France was not inevitable, but it took very little indeed to provoke it.

As a matter of theory there was no important difference between the liberalism of Britain and that of France. But in France the enfranchised propertied classes were proportionately less numerous than in Britain after 1832. Furthermore, the politically active elements in France (the *pays légal*) showed little of the flexibility and adaptability of their British counterparts, nor did the French lower classes evidence much of the deference characteristic of the British. The political settlement following the July Revolution was simply too narrow and too rigid to satisfy the articulate segment of the population. As a result, when trouble came in 1848 there was almost no support for the regime—a striking contrast to the situation in Britain, where the propertied classes closed ranks to foil any Chartist effort at insurrection.

Française" (*Revue française*, 1928, 136–150); J. Salwyn Shapiro: "Lamartine: a Study of the Poetic Temperament in Politics" (*Political Science Quarterly* XXXIV, 1919, 632–643); Louis Saurel: "Lamartine, promoteur de la Révolution de 1848" (*Europe*, XXVI, 1948/1/, 130–139); and in general, Peter Stadler: *Geschichtsschreibung und historisches Denken in Frankreich, 1789–1871* (Zürich, 1958), 256 ff.

4. THE BELGIAN MODEL

The newly independent state of Belgium, which soon became the most industrialized country of the Continent, provided perhaps the best example of adjustment. Its 1830 Revolution, much like the French, was an uprising of the urban populace, which was skillfully channeled by the upper middle classes. For practical reasons the national assembly in 1831 decided for the monarchical form of government, while intending to reserve most power to the Chamber of Deputies. ("All powers come from the nation.") The Chamber, in turn, was to be elected by "the people," which meant, as in Britain and France, those whose wealth qualified them for the conduct of public business. But in Belgium the electorate, numbering perhaps 50,000, was decidedly more numerous proportionately than in France. In the 1830's and 1840's the government was in the hands of two "parties," the Catholics, who were particularly strong in the rural areas, and the Liberals, whose strength lay chiefly in the cities. However, the differences between them were by no means as great as their names would suggest. At bottom they were both upper-middle-class groupings, divided chiefly on the question of clerical control of education. Even this issue was settled in 1842 by a compromise which provided that all communes should have primary schools and that there should be compulsory religious instruction for Catholic children. Since the numerous existing Catholic schools were included in the new system, the church controlled about half the primary and most of the secondary schools.[60]

The Belgians were particularly fortunate in the king they finally chose. Leopold I was a man of middle age, the widowed husband of Princess Charlotte of Britain and the uncle of the future Queen Victoria. Though basically conservative and scornful of constitutions and popular pretensions, Leopold was better able than Louis Philippe (whose daughter, Louise Marie, he presently married) to adjust to the regime of the *bourgeoisie*. He had spent many years in England and

[60] John Gilissen: *Le régime représentatif en Belgique depuis 1790* (Brussels, 1958); René Hislaire: "Parties" (in Jan-Albert Goris, ed.: *Belgium*, Berkeley, 1945, 93–102); G. Guyot de Mishaegen: *Le parti catholique belge de 1830 à 1884* (Brussels, 1946); and the excellent chapters, by various authors, in Jean de Harveng, ed.: *Histoire de la Belgique contemporaine* (Brussels, 1928–1930) and in J. A. van Houtte: *Algemene Geschiedenis de Nederlanden* (Brussels, 1956).

understood the complexities of party politics. Through his international connections he was able to exercise a decisive influence on foreign policy and through his position as commander-in-chief of the army he built up a personal following to counteract the pressures of the politicians. Furthermore, he fitted well into the business milieu and worked closely with the Chamber to develop mining and metallurgy, to improve the credit system and to construct the canal and railway net.[61]

The close and effective collaboration between parties and between the king and the Parliament was certainly facilitated by the ignorance and lack of organization of the lower classes, both rural and urban. Illiteracy ran to about 85 per cent and was much higher in cities such as Brussels and Antwerp than, for example, in Paris or Lyons. The workers in Belgium suffered the same hardships as in other industrializing countries, but they were inarticulate and helpless. It was therefore only in the 1840's that more democratic tendencies began to appear. Adelson Castiau's book *What Is Liberalism?* (1843) first called for expansion of the franchise, revision of the tax structure, extension of public education and legislation in behalf of the workers. Thereafter the crop failures and depression of 1845–1847, by aggravating the social problem, increased the pressure for reform. A Liberal congress in Brussels (June, 1846) drew up a program along the lines of Castiau's book and a year later the Liberal Party for the first time won a majority of the seats in the Chamber.

Charles Rogier, one of the "heroes" of 1830, and Hubert Frère-Orban, a successful lawyer, eloquent orator and forceful political leader, became the dominant figures in a new Liberal cabinet, which was soon overtaken by the February Revolution of 1848 in France. Shocked and badly frightened, the Belgian parties at once closed ranks in defense against radical upheaval. A considerable number of foreign democrats and republicans resident in Brussels were arrested, while others fled. Recognizing that the key to the situation was maintenance of employ-

[61] B. S. Chlepner: *Cent ans d'histoire sociale en Belgique* (Brussels, 1956), chap. i. On the position and influence of the king, Egon C. Corti: *Leopold I von Belgien* (Vienna, 1922) deals primarily with international affairs, while Comte Louis de Lichtervelde: *Leopold I* (New York, 1930) is fullest on domestic problems. Carlo Bronne: *Leopold Ier et son temps* (Brussels, 1947) is well-informed but does not supersede the masterly appreciation in Henri Pirenne: *Histoire de Belgique*, VII (Brussels, 1932), 47 ff.

ment, the government organized public works along with relief. On March 12, 1848, it reduced the tax requirement for the franchise and thereby raised the electorate from 59,000 to 79,000. There followed legislation prohibiting officeholding by deputies, abolishing the tax on newspapers, and so on. These timely concessions, together with the support of hastily organized bourgeois guards, enabled the authorities to suppress all disturbances and defeat an attempted invasion of French revolutionaries. Once again the solidarity of the upper and middle classes and their readiness to yield under pressure enabled the new state to weather the storm that swept most of the Continent.[62]

5. PORTUGAL AND SPAIN: THE IDEOLOGICAL WARS

The history of the Iberian countries is generally given short shrift in studies of the nineteenth century, because, in the words of one Spanish historian, it seems like "an endless list of ministers and cabinets, of generals and ringleaders, of proclamations, riots and disorders, of incomprehensible and unedifying revolutions, of parties and intrigues, a confused chaos of events with no connection beyond their succession in time." To an American historian the political history of Spain in the midcentury appeared like "a comic opera in which every scene ends in tragedy."[63] Yet much can be learned from the developments in these countries, for there the forces of the old regime met those of liberalism in open battle, and the so-called Carlist War highlighted the division of Europe by aligning the major powers on one side or the other of the conflict in the peninsula.

Both Portugal and Spain were, at the dawn of the century, impoverished, illiterate and priest-ridden. Nonetheless, they had not escaped the impact of the Enlightenment. In Spain Charles III and in Portugal the Marquis de Pombal had undertaken important reforms of a religious, social and administrative kind, while the Napoleonic occupation had provoked not only a popular resistance to the invading

---

[62] The most informative account is still the rather diffuse book by Louis Bertrand: *Histoire de la démocratie et du socialisme en Belgique depuis 1830* (Paris, 1906), 214 ff., but see also Harry Isay: *Liberalismus und Arbeiterfrage in Belgien, 1830–1852* (Berlin, 1915), 39 ff., 51 ff., and especially Brison D. Gooch: *Belgium and the February Revolution* (The Hague, 1963).

[63] Federico Suarez Verdaguer: "Plantamiento ideológico del siglo XIX español" (reprinted in his *La crisis política del antiguo regimen en España,* Madrid, 1950, chap. i); John B. Trend: *The Origins of Modern Spain* (New York, 1934), 15.

foreigner but also a new drive for modernization. The famous Cortes at Cadiz (1810–1812) had deprived the nobility of political privileges and of seigneurial jurisdiction, and had embarked upon the liquidation of the huge church properties. Ferdinand VII attempted, in the years after 1815, to reverse the tide, but the revolutions of 1820–1823 in both Spain and Portugal were well on the way toward drastic reforms when they were snuffed out by military intervention.

It must be emphasized, then, that in 1830 there was, in the Iberian countries, a genuine and indeed an aggressive liberal movement, which drew additional inspiration after 1823 through the emigration in France and England. Though the two Iberian countries were still backward and deeply devoted to tradition, many government officials were convinced of the urgent need for change and many army officers, discharged after 1815 or put on half pay, in any case unpaid, had come to believe that fundamental changes were imperative. Above all, the towns of the coastal areas, of which the largest, Barcelona, had a population of some 150,000, had become hotbeds of liberalism. The commercial middle class, the professional men and the newly emerging industrial bourgeoisie, were all committed to the ideas which had triumphed in France, Belgium and Britain in 1830–1832. As in those countries, there were two varieties of liberalism, known at different times under various names, but emerging eventually as Moderates (*Moderados*) and Radicals (*Progresistas*), of whom the latter represented the lower middle classes of the towns and constituted the revolutionary, democratic wing of the opposition to the absolutism of Ferdinand VII.[64]

The crisis of the 1830's actually began in Portugal, where in 1826 Pedro VI had succeeded to the crown, but, preferring his imperial throne in Brazil had abdicated in favor of his seven-year-old daughter, Maria II da Gloria, who was betrothed to Pedro's younger brother, Dom Miguel. Miguel, evidently with much popular support,

[64] Suarez Verdaguer: "Genesis del liberalismo politico español" (in his *Crisis politica*); Jaime Vicens Vives: *Historia social y economica de España y America* (Barcelona, 1957–1959), Vol. V; *Aproximación a la historia de España* (2 ed., Barcelona, 1960), 185 ff., and "L'Espagne" (in Max Beloff *et al.*, eds.: *L'Europe du XIXe et du XXe siècle*, Milan, 1959), II, 729–764. Vicente Llorens Castillo: *Liberales y Romanticos* (México, 1954) is an interesting study of the Spanish emigration in France and England, and of the evolution of liberal doctrine. A stimulating contemporary analysis is S. T. Wallis: *Spain, Her Institutions, Politics and Public Men* (Boston, 1853), 250 ff.

ignored the constitution of 1826, harried the Liberals out of the country and in 1828 had himself declared king, while the little queen took refuge with her father in Brazil. Miguel was recognized by the conservative governments of Europe and enjoyed also the sympathy of Tory circles in England. But in 1831 Pedro abdicated the Brazilian throne, appeared in England, and proceeded to organize an expedition to recover the Portuguese throne for his daughter. In this project he was warmly supported by the Whig foreign secretary, Lord Palmerston, who regarded Miguel as a member of the reactionary syndicate of which Nicholas I of Russia was the patron, and who took it for granted that the Portuguese eagerly desired the return of Maria and the restoration of the Constitution. Holding that intervention by all means short of open war was perfectly compatible with the vaunted principle of nonintervention, he permitted Pedro to recruit thousands of British, Belgian and Polish volunteers and authorized Sir Charles Napier, masquerading as Admiral Carlos Ponza, to assume command of Pedro's armada. In June, 1832, the expedition arrived off Oporto, the very center of Portuguese trade and Portuguese liberalism.[65]

Miguel, expecting an attack on Lisbon, had neglected the defenses of Oporto, which was easily taken by Pedro's forces. Then, while the Miguelists were attempting to recapture the city, Napier's squadrons defeated the Miguelist fleet off Cape St. Vincent (July 5, 1833) and so enabled a force under the Duke of Terceira to land and capture Lisbon, which in turn Miguel tried in vain to reconquer. He appears to have had the widespread support of the Portuguese peasantry, and certainly of the nobility and church. He received increasing aid also from Don Carlos, the younger brother of Ferdinand of Spain, who arrived in person with a considerable force. But the Miguelists proved no match for Pedro's better-equipped, better-financed, and better-led troops. The war dragged on for another nine months, by which time it had become enmeshed in the disputed succession in Spain.[66]

The Spanish king, Ferdinand, despite three marriages had no heir, and it was generally assumed that his brother, Don Carlos, the darling

[65] On British policy, see Charles K. Webster: *The Foreign Policy of Palmerston, 1830–1841* (London, 1951), I, 237 ff.; Donald Southgate: *'The Most English Minister'* (New York, 1966), 13 ff., 47 ff.

[66] Harold V. Livermore: *A New History of Portugal* (Cambridge, 1966), 265 ff.; Carlos de Passos: *D. Pedro VI e D. Miguel I, 1826–1834* (Oporto, 1936); Denyse Dalbian: *Dom Pedro, empereur du Brésil, roi de Portugal* (Paris, 1959).

of the ultraconservative clerical elements (*Apostólicos*) would succeed
to the throne. But in 1829 the king took as his fourth wife one of his
nieces, Maria Cristina of Naples, who soon presented him with
daughters, Isabella (1830) and Luisa Fernanda (1832). Maria Cristina

**THE IBERIAN COUNTRIES
TO ILLUSTRATE THE MIGUELIST AND CARLIST WARS**

was an attractive young woman, practical-minded and courageous. She
induced the king to revoke the Salic Law, which forbade succession in
the female line, and thereby destroyed Carlos' hopes. He, however,
refused to accept his brother's action and presently took refuge in
Portugal, where he rejoined Dom Miguel.

To protect the rights of her daugher, Maria Cristina was prepared to make a pact even with the devil. This proved unnecessary, for she readily found support among the liberals, especially among the enlightened officialdom and the army. While abhorring liberal principles, she made a direct bid for liberal aid against the Carlist faction. She persuaded Ferdinand to reopen the universities and proclaim an amnesty which enabled thousands of exiles, many of them prominent intellectuals, to return to Spain.[67]

Ferdinand died on September 29, 1833, and Maria Cristina became regent for her little daughter. She appointed a new ministry under Don Francisco Martínez de la Rosa, an eminent writer and leading liberal who had spent years of his life in prison or exile. The new government son promulgated a constitution (the *Estatuto Real* of April 10, 1834), which was closely modeled on the French Charter. It provided for a two-chamber Parliament (Cortes) of which the upper chamber was to be appointed by the crown and the lower elected by the taxpaying classes. The crown retained the right to summon and dissolve the Cortes, which, in any event, had little more than deliberative power. All in all, this was an example of "respectable liberalism" which, while safeguarding the monarchical principle, permitted the participation of the wealthy classes and excluded the radical elements. At the same time, in imitation of the French, urban militias or national guards consisting of property owners were established in the towns to ensure order and protect the regime.[68]

Isabella II was at once recognized by the liberal governments of Britain and France. Palmerston, indeed, was determined to block any action by Don Carlos and regarded the Spanish problem as only another aspect of the conflict that had already broken out in Portugal. He therefore negotiated the Quadruple Alliance of April 22, 1834, between Britain, France, Spain and Portugal, which was designed to ensure the

[67] F. Soldevila: *Historia de España* (Barcelona, 1959), VII, 58; Suarez Verdaguer: *La crisis política,* chaps. v and vi; Edmund B. D'Auvergne: *A Queen at Bay* (London, 1910); Robert Sencourt: *The Spanish Crown* (New York, 1932), 130 ff. On Cristina's cultivation of the army, see Eric Christiansen: *The Origins of Military Power in Spain, 1800–1854* (Oxford, 1967), 44 ff.

[68] Jean Sarrailh: *Un homme d'état espagnol: Martínez de la Rosa* (Paris, 1930); F. G. Bruguera: *Histoire contemporaine d'Espagne* (Paris, 1933), 171 ff.; Raymond Carr: *Spain, 1808–1939* (New York, 1966), 157 ff.; Stanley G. Payne: *Politics and the Military in Modern Spain* (Stanford, 1967), 21; and, on the constitution especially, Luis Sanchez Agesta: *Historia del constitucionalismo español* (Madrid, 1955), 211 ff.

victory of liberalism in the Peninsula and at the same time provide a counterblast to the Holy Alliance, which had been resuscitated by the Münchengrätz agreement of September, 1833 (see Chapter IX). The Quadruple Alliance specified that a Spanish army should aid Pedro in driving Miguelists and Carlists from Portugal, while the British navy should lend its support and the French government should supply as yet undefined assistance. Under these circumstances the Portuguese problem was quickly liquidated. Miguel was defeated near Lisbon on May 16, 1834, and gave up the fight. By the Convention of Évora Monte both he and Carlos agreed to leave Portugal permanently. Their supporters were amnestied and given an opportunity to enter the service of the Portuguese queen. Pedro died soon after (September), whereupon the young queen arrived from abroad to assume her royal functions.[69]

The Carlist War in Spain may be said to have begun when, in July, 1834, Don Carlos arrived surreptitiously from exile in England. He set up his headquarters in the Basque country, where, as in Navarre and Aragon, the mountain-dwelling peasantry was deeply religious and always ready to defend its local privileges against the centralizing tendencies and anticlericalism of the liberals. Carlos, who had declared himself the rightful king, was a man of high principle and deep piety, but not very intelligent or attractive and above all quite inept in political and military matters. In the first year of the war he was fortunate to have an outstanding commander in General Tomás Zumalacárregui, a veritable modern Cid, devoted to his faith, his prince and his troops. Zumalacárregui managed to organize a disciplined force of 30,000 and, operating in the difficult mountain terrain of the north, was able to defeat one after another the Cristino generals sent against him. In the southeast Ramón Cabrera, a young soldier, rose from the ranks to become one of the most dashing as he was one of the most brutal guerrilla leaders on the Carlist side.

Carlism, though hard to defeat, never had much chance of success, for the bureaucracy, the army and the urban centers all stood by the

<hr>

69 On the Spanish side, see Jerónimo Becker: *Historia de las relaciones exteriores de España durante el siglo XIX* (Madrid, 1924), I; Federico Suarez: "La intervención extranjera en los cominezos del regimen liberal español" (*Revista de estudios políticos,* VII, 1944, 409–471); on the British-French side, John Hall: *England and the Orleans Monarchy* (London, 1912), chap. vi; Raymond Guyot: *La première entente cordiale* (Paris, 1927), chap. iii; Webster: *Foreign Policy of Palmerston,* I, 386 ff.; Southgate, *'Most English Minister,'* 75.

government, which was actively supported also by the British and halfheartedly by the French, while the conservative powers (including the pope) had such grave doubts of Carlos' chances that they pursued a shrewd policy and never gave more than feeble financial aid. Carlos hoped that, if he were able to capture a seaport such as Bilbao, he could open more efficient communications with the outside world, but the siege of that town brought the pretender nothing but the loss of Zumalacárregui, who died of wounds in June, 1835.

The government should by all odds have mastered the rebellion in short order, but was so racked by dissension and so plagued by financial crisis that little could be accomplished. The army, above all, was completely overstaffed with officers, all contending for rank and power. British observers lost all confidence in Spanish constitutionalism. They reported army officers lounging in the cafés, arguing politics and leaving their commands to brutal subordinates. They thought the upper classes generally "corrupt, selfish, ignorant, brutally and despotically tyrannical when in power, servile and intriguing till they got there." "There is no probity or patriotism or public spirit," moaned the British ambassador, "no confidence between man and man, no object but money, no means which are not justifiable to obtain it."[70]

The general hopelessness of the situation led Cristina to the conviction that success depended on outright military aid from France. She appealed for an army to occupy the Carlist areas, but Louis Philippe, fearing an attack by the powers of the Holy Alliance, rejected formal intervention unless the British guaranteed France against attack. The French government went no further than to permit 4,000 men of the Foreign Legion to volunteer for service in Spain. This figure was later doubled. Meanwhile the British government, having a great stake in the success of the liberal cause, lent Spain three million pounds sterling, without interest, to finance the purchase of munitions. It also encouraged the Rothschild bank to lend three million in return for the concession of Spain's valuable mercury mines. Lastly, it suspended the foreign enlistment act and furthered the recruitment of some 10,000 British,

[70] Sir Herbert Maxwell: *The Life of Clarendon* (London, 1913), I, 102 ff.; George Villiers: *A Vanished Victorian* (London, 1938), 88. On Carlism the account of Charles F. Henningsen: *The Most Striking Events of a Twelve-Month's Campaign with Zumalacárregui* (London, 1836) is still of great interest, but see also Benjamin Jarnès: *Zumalacárregui, el caudillo romántico* (Madrid, 1931); Gaston Capdupuy: *Don Carlos* (Paris, 1938); Roman de Oyarzún: *Historia del Carlismo* (2 ed., Madrid, 1944).

Irish, Belgian and Polish volunteers to form the British Legion under command of Colonel George de Lacy Evans, veteran of the Peninsular War and Radical member of Parliament. The British navy, too, continued to shield the northern coastal towns.[71]

The British Legion arrived in Spain in July, 1835, but was so ill-equipped and untrained that a full year had to be devoted to preparation. Meanwhile the severe winter of 1835–1836 decimated the Legion and resulted in many defections to the Carlist side. The year 1836 was still the year of the Carlists, for they were able to hold their mountain bases while Cabrera carried his operations into upper Aragon and another daring general, Miguel Gómez, evaded the Cristino generals and raided as far as southern Spain. Indeed, in the summer of 1836 Don Carlos appeared before Madrid with 16,000 men, evidently expecting to take the city without fighting. When the populace showed its determination to defend the city, Carlos eventually withdrew. His one great chance had been lost. Thenceforth even the conservative powers lost faith in his cause.[72]

During these years the situation was so precarious that the moderate liberal government was in real danger of being overwhelmed by the forces of radicalism. In the cities, notably in Barcelona, the National Guard fell more and more into the hands of the lower classes. Local juntas took control and agitated for re-establishment of the democratic constitution of 1812, while mobs attacked churches and monasteries and massacred their inmates. The government was obliged to expel the Jesuits and close down hundreds of small religious houses. In desperation the queen-regent turned over the ministry to Don Juan Alvarez Mendizábal, a Radical (*Progresista*) leader who, while in English exile, had amassed a fortune by financing Pedro's expedition to Portugal. The new minister was an able, energetic, self-confident Jew, who undertook to solve the overriding financial crisis by implementing the

[71] Francis Duncan: *The English in Spain* (London, 1877); Edgar Holt: *The Carlist Wars in Spain* (London, 1967), chap. viii; Paul Azan: *La Légion Etrangère en Espagne* (Paris, 1907); Suarez: *La crisis política;* Philip E. Mosely: "Intervention and Non-Intervention in Spain" (*Journal of Modern History,* XIII, 1941, 195–217); Egon C. Corti: *The Reign of the House of Rothschild* (New York, 1928), chap. iv; Heinz Gollwitzer: "Der erste Karlistenkrieg und das Problem der internationalen Parteigängerschaft" (*Historische Zeitschrift,* CLXXVI, 1953, 479–520).

[72] Holt: *Carlist Wars* is a well-informed though undocumented account of the operations. For the shady negotiations connected with Carlos' expedition, see Pierre de Luz: *Isabelle II* (Paris, 1934), 38 ff.

long-standing program to wipe out the national debt by confiscating and selling the property of the church, after which he hoped to float a victory loan in London.

But Mendizábal, too, met only with disappointment and failure. Sale of church property netted the government but little return, for the lands had to be sold quickly and at fantastically low prices. The peasants, who were supposed to acquire the lands, derived no benefit from the transaction, for the wealthy classes, along with speculators of all types, snapped up the bargain. The government was no better off than before and the unrest in the cities continued unabated. There was not even money to pay the foreign legionnaires. In the summer of 1837 the British Legion, which had seen but little active service, reached the end of its contract and was discharged.[73]

Politically the crisis came to a head when the rank and file of the army became disaffected. In August, 1836, the palace guard at the summer palace of La Granja rose in revolt. Led by two aggressive sergeants, a delegation of soldiers forced their way into the queen-regent's presence and demanded restoration of the constitution of 1812. Cristina courageously held them off with palaver until three in the morning, when she finally agreed to the constitution of 1812 pending the time when "the nation, as represented by the Cortes, shall have manifested its will or adopted another constitution." Since the Moderate majority in the Cortes had no desire whatever to adopt a democratic system, the new constitution voted on April 27, 1837 fell far short of what the soldiers had aimed at. While proclaiming the sovereignty of the people, it retained the tax requirement for the franchise and the royal veto. In short, it was hardly more than a mild liberalization of the *Estatuto* of 1834.[74]

With the year 1837 the military initiative finally passed to the government forces. General Baldomero Espartero, a man of humble birth who had risen to high rank in the South American campaigns of the 1820's, was given command and, because of his strong personality, his

[73] Soldevila: *Historia de España*, VII, 102 ff.; Carr: *Spain*, 165 ff.; E. Allison Peers: *Spain, the Church and the Orders* (London, 1939), chap. iii; A. Ramón Oliveira: *Politics, Economics and Men of Modern Spain* (London, 1946), 50 ff.

[74] Sanchez Agesta: *Historia del constitucionalismo español*, 229 ff.; H. Butler Clarke: *Modern Spain* (Cambridge, 1906), 135; Carr: *Spain*, 162.

known devotion to the *Progresista* cause and his sincere concern for the common soldier, was soon able to restore order and authority.[75]

In 1838 Espartero staged the first systematic drive against the Carlists, who had become increasingly demoralized and divided between the extreme clerical elements and the more moderate royalists. General Rafael Maroto, a Carlist general disgusted with the reactionaries at the pretender's court and strongly suspecting a plot against himself, in the spring of 1839 entered into secret negotiations with Espartero and, with the aid of the British ambassador, concluded the Convention of Vergara (August 31). This provided that Carlist officers might transfer to government service without loss of rank and that the northern provinces should retain their traditional local rights. Carlos promptly denounced Maroto's "treason," but in the end had no choice but to cross the Pyrenees and seek refuge in France. In 1840 the last Carlist commander, Cabrera, was obliged to abandon the struggle, thus ending the war.

Spain emerged from the Carlist War as a liberal, constitutional state, indeed a state in which the more radical (*Progresista*) elements and their general, Espartero, were for the time being in the ascendant. This represented a victory of the commercial towns over the rural interior of the country. But this victory would never have been possible had not the queen-regent been obliged to enlist the support of the business class as well as the army to ensure the succession of her infant daughter. The years 1833–1836 were to show that the liberal elements were not strong enough either to master the Carlist threat or to prevent the lower working classes of cities such as Barcelona from overturning the regime. The lower classes, on their part, were illiterate and leaderless, even more unorganized than the liberals. The main effect of their numerous outbreaks was to alarm the propertied middle class as well as the upper classes and so strengthen the trend toward a more conservative regime.[76]

---

[75] See the contemporary appraisal by Karl Marx (reprinted in his *Revolution in Spain*, New York, 1939); further, Conde de Romanones: *Espartero, el general del pueblo* (Madrid, 1932), and Payne: *Politics and the Military in Modern Spain*, 21 ff.

[76] The best studies of the rise of the middle class and the emergence of the workers center on Barcelona, e.g., Jaime Vicens Vives: "La mentalidad de la burguesía catalana en la primera mitad del siglo XIX" (*X Congresso Internazionale di Scienze Storiche*, Rome, 1955, VII, 323–327), *Industrials i polítics del siglo XIX* (Barcelona, 1958), and

In 1838 the Moderates regained a majority in the Cortes and made desperate efforts to break the power of the city juntas and national guards by depriving the municipalities of the right to elect their own mayors and by reorganizing the local militias on a national basis. But the immediate result was armed insurrection in Madrid and an open challenge to the government from Espartero, himself a *Progresista*. Cristina was obliged to name the general to head the government, while she herself left the country to live in exile in France. Espartero became sole regent in May, 1841, but soon estranged even the *Progresistas* and the army by his dictatorial pose and political ineptitude. In July, 1843, he was driven into flight by an insurrectionary movement that swept the country, precipitated by what Karl Marx described as "a hurricane of pronunciamentoes" against "the tyrant." He was succeeded by his rival, General Ramón Narváez, darling of the *Moderados* though a soldier of aristocratic background. The liberals in the Cortes were soon overawed by the vehement language and fierce glance of this energetic and unscrupulous soldier. He had Isabella declared of age, though she was only thirteen, and invited Maria Cristina to return (1844). In 1845 he had the Cortes vote the adoption of a new constitution which restricted the suffrage to a small oligarchy and circumscribed civil liberties. Thenceforth the regime became increasingly corrupt and unpopular. The upper chamber was packed with compliant generals and the elections to the lower chamber were controlled through flagrant manipulation.[77]

One of the chief concerns of the Narváez period was the marriage of Queen Isabella, which culminated in a major international crisis and as such must be reserved for later treatment (see Chapter IX). For the rest, liberalism was soon in eclipse. Dissident movements were ruthlessly suppressed, so that the European upheavals of 1848–1849 left Spain almost untouched. Spasmodic outbreaks in some cities were short-lived. The British ambassador, alleged to have encouraged liberal

---

Cataluña en el siglo XIX (Madrid, 1961), 188 f., 217 ff.; Rosa Ortega Canadell: "La crisis política española de 1832–1833" (*Estudios de historia moderna,* V, 1957, 349–384); Jaime Carrera Pujol: *La economía de Cataluña en el siglo XIX* (Barcelona, 1961).

[77] S. T. Wallis: *Spain, Her Institutions, Politics and Public Men* (Boston, 1853) provides a vivid contemporary account of the Narváez regime. See also Sanchez Agesta: *Historia del constitucionalismo,* 249 ff.; Carr: *Spain,* 227 ff.; Payne, *Politics and the Military,* 23 ff.

agitation, was unceremoniously expelled. Cabrera's effort to rekindle Carlism in the north proved altogether abortive.[78]

By 1850 the propertied classes were so frightened by the specter of revolution and social upheaval that they were all too ready to return to the alliance of throne and altar. Eminent writers such as Jaime Balmes were preaching that royal power should be firmly grounded on Christian teaching, while Juan Donoso Cortés had, by the end of the Carlist War, turned against the liberal middle class with its endless arguments (*una clasa discutador*) and espoused a conservatism based on Christian faith. In a famous speech of January 4, 1849, Donoso Cortés defended dictatorship as a necessary bulwark against revolution and mass domination. Finally, in his main work, the *Essay on Catholicism, Liberalism and Socialism* (Madrid and Paris, 1851), he emerged as the prophet of the decline of European culture. The decisive battle of Catholicism against the corroding, demonic forces of atheistic socialism he saw drawing nigh. Only divine intervention could save mankind from a horrible fate.[79] It was in keeping with such doctrines that the Spanish government in 1851 concluded a concordat with the Papacy by which the sale of church property was suspended and the clergy restored to its former estate.

The events of these stormy years were reflected also in the history of Portugal. Violent outbursts of anticlericalism were followed, in September, 1836, by a flare-up of radicalism inspired by the "sergeants' revolt" at La Granja. The "Septembrists," led by Sa da Baniera, forced the queen, Maria II, to promise the restoration of the radical constitution of 1822. But what eventually emerged, as in Spain, was a compromise charter.

Like its Iberian neighbor, Portugal continued to suffer from financial stringency and political strife. When, in 1841, the Septembrist leader,

---

[78] J. Quero Molares: "Spain in 1848" (in Francois Fejtö, ed.: *The Opening of an Era, 1848*, London, 1948).

[79] Charles de Mazade: *L'Espagne moderne* (Paris, 1855), chaps. iii and iv, gives an excellent analysis of this conservative thought without the overlay of later totalitarian doctrine. See also Alois Dempf: *Christliche Staatsphilosophie in Spanien* (Salzburg, 1937), 128 ff.; Carl Schmitt: *Donoso Cortés in gesamteuropäischer Interpretation* (Köln, 1950); Federico Suarez: *Evolución política de Donoso Cortés* (Santiago, 1949); Jules Ciax-Ruy: *Donoso Cortés, théologien de l'histoire et prophète* (Paris, 1956); Joachim Fernandez: *Spanisches Erbe und Revolution* (Münster, 1957), 34 ff.

Antonio da Costa Cabral, defected from his party to join the Chartists (moderates), the latter were able to restore the moderate constitution of 1826. But in a few years Costa Cabral was driven from power (1845) as a result of the so-called Maria da Fonte riots, provoked by a government decree forbidding further burials in the overcrowded churchyards. These disturbances marked a recrudescence of radicalism and a renewed threat of civil war. The government was able to master the situation only with the aid of the British. Costa Cabral returned to office and with the year 1850 a more stable and generally more conservative period began. Like Spain, Portugal emerged from a chaotic period as a constitutional state, but the moderate liberal elements which had defeated the archconservative forces remained a distinct minority which in the long run could maintain itself only with the occasional intervention and support of the British.[80]

---

[80] Harold V. Livermore: *A New History of Portugal* (Cambridge, 1966), chap. xi.

Chapter Four

CENTRAL EUROPE: LIBERALISM OF
THE INTELLECTUALS

1. REPERCUSSIONS OF THE JULY REVOLUTION

CENTRAL EUROPE, in contrast to the unified national states of the West, was in 1830 still fragmented, a medley of large and small, important and insignificant principalities. The "Germanies" were loosely connected in a federation that included only half of the Hapsburg Empire and was in fact little more than a defensive alliance. The twenty-odd cantons of the Swiss Confederation were even less tenuously bound to each other, while the states of Italy, two of the most important of which were ruled by Austria, were completely independent. This meant that in the entire area, with its varying traditions and conditions, there were bound to be many individual movements and little if anything in the way of organization or plan. In addition it must be recalled that in the heart of the Continent the impact of industrialism was only just making itself felt. There were only a few cities, such as Vienna, Berlin, Milan and Naples, that had a population beyond 100,000 and none of these enjoyed the pre-eminence that was London's or Paris'. The upper-middle or business class was still very small and generally inarticulate prior to 1840, and the pressure for change came chiefly from the intellectuals (professors, writers, lawyers and other professional men) who staffed the many universities established over the centuries by prestige-seeking princes. This largely academic liberalism had been effectively suppressed in 1819–1820, but broke out again with renewed force after 1830.

News of the July Revolution in Paris evoked enormous excitement throughout Central Europe. The notion of a spontaneous rising of "the people," of its defiance of the troops and its ultimate success in driving out a detested ruler, was highly intoxicating. Within a few weeks the unrest sparked not only the revolution in Brussels but similar upheavals farther to the east. These outbreaks were so numerous and so varied that details must be eschewed. In Germany there were serious urban outbreaks in Saxony, Brunswick, Hesse-Cassel and Hanover, accompanied in some places by peasant attacks on estates and burning of records. In Brunswick the crowds stoned the detestable Duke Charles as he returned from the theater, burned down his palace, and eventually forced him to abandon the throne. In Göttingen the students took the lead in an insurrection that had to be suppressed by the military. In all these states the governments were obliged to permit the formation of national or civic guards and to grant constitutions comparable to those of France and Belgium.

Similar movements took place in Switzerland and Italy. In Switzerland popular demonstrations led the urban patriciates to yield. In the economically and socially more highly developed cantons of the north and west, the work of "regeneration" produced popular forms of government. Discrimination between the urban and rural population was ended, the remnants of feudal obligations were abolished, while civil rights were recognized and secular free education provided for. In a short time all but five of the cantons had been "regenerated" and efforts were made to strengthen the federal system, if only to get rid of the hundreds of transit and tariff dues that still encumbered trade. But these projects had to be abandoned in the face of conservative opposition and the warnings of Austria and other powers which claimed the right to intervene in all matters touching the federal system established in 1815.[1]

In Italy the famous secret society, the Carbonari, took advantage of the situation to organize insurrections in Modena and Parma that obliged the rulers to flee to Lombardy for protection. Thereupon revolution broke out in Bologna (February, 1831) and, as many of the papal troops defected, soon engulfed most of the States of the Church. The various papal provinces then sent delegates to an assembly at Bologna which declared the temporal power of the pope at an end and proclaimed national union in a federal republic. The newly elected pope, Gregory XVI, saw no alternative but to call on Austria for aid, whereupon Hapsburg troops in March, 1831, occupied Ferrara and Bologna. France, on whose support the insurgents had counted, had

[1] Ernst Gagliardi: *Geschichte der Schweiz* (3 ed., Zürich, 1938), III, 1307 ff.; Anton von Muralt: *Die Juli-Revolution und die Regeneration in der Schweiz* (Zürich, 1948), 12 ff.; Walter Rüpli: *Zollreform und Bundesreform in der Schweiz, 1815–1848* (Zürich, 1949); Werner Näf: *Die Schweiz und Europa* (Berne, 1938), 55 f.

avoided trouble by proclaiming nonintervention but now felt impelled to counter the Austrian action. A conference of ambassadors assembled under French auspices and worked out a program of "indispensable" reforms which was submitted to the pope. Gregory, however, refused to countenance foreign interference with his government and rejected the note. Thereupon the French government abandoned the policy of nonintervention and occupied Ancona, on the Adriatic coast. Not until 1838 did the Austrians and French, under continuing pressure from the pope, finally evacuate his territories.[2]

As it turned out, the movements of 1830-1831 were only the prelude to more organized and far-reaching attacks on the existing order. The crisis over the Reform Bill in England, the danger of war over the Belgian question and the struggle of the Poles for independence from Russia all kept popular excitement at fever heat and encouraged the more radical elements to redouble their efforts. In southwest Germany, the headquarters of German liberalism and radicalism, two journalists, Philipp Siebenpfeiffer and Johann Wirth, launched radical newspapers in the Bavarian Palatinate, which was adjacent to France and much under French influence. In February, 1832, they founded the Press and Fatherland Society for the purpose of disseminating radical publications and aiding the defense of incriminated editors. They made no secret of their program, which aimed at national unity on a democratic, republican basis. Small wonder the Bavarian government suppressed their newspapers and forbade their serving as editors for a period of five years.

By the spring of 1832 the unrest in Germany had been further fanned by the migration of several thousand Polish refugees, officers and men, who had escaped capture by the Russians following their defeat and the collapse of the war of independence. The liberalism of the Poles was certainly qualified if measured by western standards, but they were hailed by the German populace as champions of liberty and defenders of humanity against Russian barbarism (see Illustration 39). German

---

[2] Josef Schmidlin: *Papstgeschichte der neuesten Zeit* (2 ed., Munich, 1933), I, 520 ff.; Jean Leflon: *Histoire de l'Eglise: la crise révolutionnaire, 1789–1846* (Paris, 1951), 432 ff.; H. Daniel-Rops: *The Church in an Age of Revolution, 1789–1870* (New York, 1965), 186 ff.; R. John Rath: "The Carbonari, Their Origin, Initiation Rites and Aims" (*American Historical Review*, LXIX, 1964, 353-370); and, in general, Giorgio Candeloro: *Storia dell'Italia moderna* (2 ed., Milan, 1959), II; F. Catalano, R. Moscati and F. Valsecchi: *L'Italia nel Risorgimento* (Milan, 1964), 348 ff.

poets produced *Polenlieder* in quantity; there were official receptions and banquets; substantial sums were raised for relief; and, most importantly, the Polish cause served to cloak the aspirations of the Germans themselves.[3]

The chiefs of the Press and Fatherland Society made the most of the situation to organize a great protest meeting, which took place on May 27, 1832, at the castle ruins of Hambach, in the Palatinate. Some 30,000 people, mostly townspeople and workers, participated, among them Polish refugees, members of the Strasbourg branch of the French society Friends of the People and, above all, students from nearby universities, such as Heidelberg. The national colors—black, red and gold—were everywhere in evidence, while bands played patriotic songs. But the main feature was the series of speeches, of which those by Siebenpfeiffer, Wirth and the student leader Karl Brüggemann were most noteworthy. They first denounced the repressive policies of the federal Diet and rejected the South German constitutions as altogether inadequate. His demand was for full democracy and a unitary republic. Wirth in turn called for deposition of the princes, for the liberation not only of Germany but also of Poland, Hungary and Italy, and for the federation of all countries in a new European Republic. Brüggemann, finally, urged revolutionary action if necessary to attain the desired ends.

It is easy to ridicule the Hambach Festival as a demonstration of Romantic oratory, of "agitated somnambulism," to borrow the words of a French commentator. Yet it was the first great mass demonstration in German history and has its importance as reflecting both the aspirations and the conflicts in the nascent liberal movement. In the days immediately following the festival, efforts were made by Siebenpfeiffer to set up a National Assembly to serve as a popular counterpart to the federal Diet, but most of the leaders were unwilling to follow up words with action. They were not really revolutionary. Their purpose was to protest, not to fight.[4]

[3] Gunter Weber: *Die polnische Emigration im 19 Jahrhundert* (Essen, 1937), 22 ff.; R. F. Leslie: *Polish Politics and the Revolution of November, 1830* (London, 1956), 258 ff.; J. Müller: *Die Polen in der öffentlichen Meinung Deutschlands, 1830–1832* (Marburg, 1923); H. Delbrück: *Deutsche Polenlieder* (Berlin, 1927); Wolfgang Hallgarten: *Studien über die deutsche Polenfreundschaft* (Munich, 1928), 10 ff.
[4] Kurt Baumann: *Das Hambacher Fest: Männer und Ideen* (Speyer, 1957) is a valuable collection of biographical studies by various authors. See also Veit Valentin: *Das*

In any event, the mass demonstration in the Palatinate gave the Austrian and Prussian governments ample excuse to redouble federal efforts at repression. The Bavarian government was obliged to arrest and try such leaders as Wirth, who had not succeeded in escaping to Switzerland or France. Martial law was proclaimed in the Palatinate and a large military force was sent to maintain it. Meanwhile Metternich, constantly stressing the connections of German radicalism with French Jacobinism, piloted through the federal Diet new regulations restricting the powers of the state parliaments, stiffening the censorship, forbidding political societies and popular demonstrations, and banning the wearing of national badges or colors. The state governments agreed to extradite political offenders on request.[5]

Before these repressive measures could take effect, another attempt was made to stage a German revolution. A band of about fifty radicals, mostly instructors and students from Heidelberg and neighboring universities, planned to overrun the city guard of Frankfurt-am-Main, the seat of the federal Diet. This move, it was thought, would spark a general upheaval throughout the country. The leader, Ernst von Rauschenplatt, former instructor in law, had led the insurrection in Brunswick in September, 1830, and had played a prominent part at Hambach. He was evidently convinced that one determined move would crystallize the unrest which was certainly prevalent. After all, a strike of printers had sufficed to set off the July Revolution in Paris, the singing of revolutionary songs had sparked the uprising in Brussels in August, and a coup by the cadets of the military school had initiated the Polish revolution in November, 1830. As a matter of fact, the conspirators did succeed in overpowering the guard (April 3, 1833), though the plot had been revealed to the police. But neither the population of Frankfurt nor of any other town responded. The insurgents had no choice but to flee or surrender. Austrian and Prussian troops promptly occupied the city while the Diet resurrected the Central Investigating Commission to watch revolutionaries and foreigners.

Hambacher Nationalfest (Berlin, 1932); Johann Bühler: *Das Hambacher Fest: Deutsche Sehnsucht vor Hundert Jahren* (Berlin, 1932); and the excellent synthesis by Fritz Trautz: "Das Hambacher Fest und der südwestdeutsche Frühliberalismus" (*Heidelberger Jahrbücher*, II, 1958, 14–52).

[5] This complicated legislation is analyzed in some detail in Ernst R. Huber: *Deutsche Verfassungsgeschichte seit 1789* (Stuttgart, 1960), II, 152 ff.

Of the Frankfurt revolutionaries eleven were given life terms and others six- to ten-year sentences. In addition the Prussian government arrested hundreds of students as members of the "treasonable" *Burschenschaft* and of these 39 were sentenced to death and another 150 to life or long-term prison detention. It is true that these death sentences were commuted to life imprisonment and that most of the offenders were amnestied in 1840. Nonetheless the secret interrogations, the solitary confinement, the prolonged starvation, the deprivation of sleep and the physical punishment made political persecution a terrible and unforgettable experience and brought the governments, especially the Prussian, into deepest ill repute.[6]

In Italy as in Germany, the failure of the radicals to precipitate a general revolution in 1831 led to renewed efforts in the years that followed. Meanwhile Paris became the center for revolutionary organization and planning. Among others there were some 5,000 Poles in France, whom the historian Joachim Lelewel attempted to rally to a democratic program. He was convinced that the original downfall of the Polish state had been due chiefly to social inequality that culminated in aristocratic anarchy, and that the eventual restoration of Poland could be achieved only by enlisting the support of the people, that is, by complete emancipation of the peasantry and partition of the land without compensation to the nobles. In March, 1832, Lelewel founded the Polish Democratic Society, with an executive committee (called "Centralization") which was to prepare for armed insurrection against Russia and was also to support the revolutionary efforts of other peoples. Led by Josef Zaliwski, Polish exiles in 1833 tried to invade Russian Poland from Galicia, but only to be rounded up and captured by Russian forces. Other Poles participated in the attack of German radicals on the Frankfurt guard and in Mazzini's ill-starred attempt to invade Savoy in 1834. Louis Philippe and his ministers saw the dangers inherent in the Society. Lelewel was expelled from France and the formation of a Polish Legion was forbidden. The government decreed that, in return for subsistence support, the Polish refugees should settle in the provinces. Eventually small groups of ten or twelve were assigned to about 180 towns and villages, and every

[6] H. Gerber: "Der Frankfurter Wachensturm vom 3 April, 1833" (*Quellen und Darstellungen zur Geschichte der Burschenschaft*, XIV, 1934, 172–212); Huber: *Deutsche Verfassungsgeschichte*, 164 ff.; 177 ff.

effort was made to keep them from coming to Paris. "They were kept in honorable semi-confinement," says an English historian, "on meager allowances, with no duties to perform, regimented yet undisciplined and idle."[7]

The Italian refugees in France, of whom there were 1,000 to 1,500 after the collapse of the revolutions of 1831, experienced much the same fate. In return for a modest allowance, the French government insisted on their taking residence in one of about thirty designated places, so that co-ordination became extremely difficult. Filippo Buonarroti, the eminent Jacobin leader, tried to bring the various factions together by founding an Italian Junta of Liberation (*Giunta liberatrice italiana*), the members of which took the name True Italians. The objective of the organization was independence and unity, but its methods were the traditional ones of conspiracy and subversion. Its history is still obscure, but there is no evidence that it ever played an effective role.[8]

Efforts to continue work along these traditional lines were soon overshadowed by the activity and organization of Giuseppe Mazzini, the perfect example of the Romantic radical and, as he was to prove himself, the most influential revolutionary of his century. Mazzini was the son of a Genoese professor and his highly intelligent but puritanical wife. Educated for the law, he turned to journalism and at the age of twenty-one joined the Carbonaro lodge. He appears to have been from the outset a successful propagandist and was soon arrested for his activities. Soon released from detention, he left Italy to settle at Marseilles, where there was an Italian colony of several hundred. He soon attracted the attention of Austrian secret agents, one of whom reported in May, 1831, that the young enthusiast was a dangerous

---

[7] Lewis B. Namier: *1848: the Revolution of the Intellectuals* (London, 1944), 43 ff. See also Michel Sokolniki: *Les origines de l'émigration polonaise en France, 1831–1832* (Paris, 1910); A. P. Coleman: "The Great Emigration" (in *Cambridge History of Poland*, Cambridge, 1941, II, chap. xivA); W. Feldman: *Geschichte der politischen Ideen in Polen seit dessen Teilungen* (Munich, 1917), 103 ff.; R. F. Leslie: "Politics and Economics in Congress Poland, 1815–1864" (*Past and Present*, No. 8, 1955, 43–63).

[8] Alessandro Galante Garrone: *Filippo Buonarroti e i rivoluzionari dell'Ottocento, 1828–1837* (Turin, 1951); Elizabeth L. Eisenstein: *The First Professional Revolutionist: Filippo Michele Buonarroti* (Cambridge, 1959); Salvo Mastellone: *Mazzini e la 'Giovine Italia'* (Pisa, 1965), I, chaps. iii and viii; Carlo Francovich: "Filippo Buonarroti e la Società dei 'Veri Italiani'" (*Il Ponte*, 1951, 136–145, 261–269); Arthur M. Lehning: "Buonarroti and His International Secret Societies" (*International Review of Social History*, I, 1956, 112–140).

character because he was free of all self-interest. He thought of nothing but the regeneration of Italy, for which he was prepared to face any danger and to sacrifice all, even his life, and to resort even to assassination if this was to the interest of Italy.[9]

While Buonarroti was trying to organize the True Italians, Mazzini took a different tack. He seems to have known Buonarroti's pamphlet *Reflections on Federative Government as Applied to Italy* (March, 1831) and to have borrowed several ideas from it. But he was impatient of the "old guard," resented the tradition that France must have the lead in the European revolution, and objected to the notion that the revolution must be social, in the interests of the lowest classes. He wanted also to get away from the Carbonaro movement, which seemed to him too aristocratic, too regional in character and too much given to secrecy, ceremonial and useless hocus-pocus. His readings had convinced him that revolutions, to be successful, must have the support of all the people and that the people must be moved by a truly ardent faith. Through co-ordinated insurrections the princes were to be driven from their thrones, after which the Italians could unite in an offensive to expel the Austrians from the peninsula. Twenty million Italians, if properly motivated and led, could defeat Austria without foreign aid: "Italy in revolution would be strong enough to defeat three Austrias."[10]

Mazzini's ideas represented a complete amalgam of radicalism and nationalism, even more so than those of the German radicals. All Central Europe was still smarting under the recent French domination and felt helpless in the face of possible further French aggression. National pride as well as security called for the union of the many states in a centralized national state, such as France, which would be able to overcome internal differences and present a strong front toward

---

[9] Alessandro Luzio: *Giuseppe Mazzini, Carbonaro* (Turin, 1920), 106.

[10] Mazzini: *Faith and the Future*, in his *Life and Writings* (London, 1890), III, 79–144. Among the many biographies of Mazzini, Gwilyn O. Griffith: *Mazzini, Prophet of Modern Europe* (New York, 1932) and Arturo Codignola: *Mazzini* (Turin, 1946) are thoroughly satisfactory. On his thought, Gaetano Salvemini: *Mazzini* (1905, Eng. trans., Stanford, 1957) is excellent. See also Otto Vossler: *Mazzinis politisches Denken und Wollen* (Berlin, 1927), 32 ff.; Francesco De Sanctis: "Le basi teoretiche de 'La Giovine Italia' " (in Arturo Codignola, ed.: *Pensiero e azione in Giuseppe Mazzini*, Genoa, 1955, 29–34); Walter Maturi: "Partiti politici e correnti di pensiero nel Risorgimento" (in *Nuove questioni di storia del Risorgimento e dell'unità d'Italia*, Milan, 1961, 39–130).

the outer world. But Mazzini, like Wirth and others in Germany, thought not in combative terms. On the contrary, he envisaged a fraternal union of independent, democratic republics in a grand European federation. Deeply influenced by the teachings of Herder and Saint-Simon, Mazzini was devoted to the ideas of evolution and progress and believed that nations had a mission to contribute to the cause of humanity: "Nationality is the role assigned by God to a people in the work of humanity. It is its mission, its task on earth, to the end that God's thought may be realized in the world."[11]

Mazzini's basic ideas were all enshrined in the Statutes of his new society, Young Italy (*La giovine Italia*), founded at Marseilles in July, 1831. Its membership was to consist of men under forty years of age, and was to be kept secret. But in contrast to the Carbonari, its program was to be proclaimed to all the world: expulsion of the princes, establishment of a unitary, democratic republic, and a war of independence against Austria. Beyond that, Italy was to assume the initiative in the European revolutionary movement that was envisaged to end in a federation of national republics. A journal, *Young Italy,* of which six numbers appeared between 1832 and 1834, was to be the organ of propaganda for the new ideas, and branches of the society were to be founded in as many cities as possible.

Mazzini possessed undoubted charismatic qualities and his efforts seem to have met with enthusiastic response. Branches of Young Italy were opened at Genoa, Livorno, Milan and other centers and before long the organization is said to have had 50,000 to 60,000 members. Buonarrotti, who looked upon Mazzini as a presumptuous young fellow, nevertheless had to recognize the success of the new star, and in September, 1832, proposed cooperation, to which Mazzini agreed. The two were to work out a new constitution for Italy. Actually, nothing came of the plan. The ideas of the two men were too different, the tension between generations too great, the personal rivalry too deep-seated. Within a year the agreement had broken down.[12]

In Mazzini's plan to set off an insurrection that would engulf all

---

[11] Renato Treves: *La dottrina sansimoniana nel pensiero italiano del Risorgimento* (Turin, 1931); Guido Bozzoni: *La critica del federalismo in Giuseppe Mazzini* (Pisa, 1941); Maurice Vaussard: *De Pétrarque à Mussolini: évolution du sentiment nationaliste italien* (Paris, 1961), 44 ff.

[12] See footnote 8 above, and Franco Della Peruta: "Per la storia dei rapporti fra Giovine Italia e Buonarrottismo" (*Critica Storica*, III, 1964, 342–363).

Italy, Piedmont was the crucial state, for it alone had a substantial, well-trained army that could spearhead a national assault on Austria. Preparations were therefore made for a large-scale mutiny in the Piedmontese land and naval forces. Unfortunately the plot was revealed by two soldiers engaged in a brawl. Many of the conspirators were arrested, tried and convicted. Indeed, the government went even beyond the Prussian in its repressive measures. Mazzini was sentenced to death *in absentia,* but fourteen other leaders were executed and sixty-seven were sentenced to long prison terms.[13]

Although the French government, at the request of Turin, had ordered Mazzini expelled (July, 1832), he managed to elude the police for almost a year, after which he removed to Switzerland. During this time he laid plans for an even larger operation, namely, an invasion of Piedmont both from Switzerland (Geneva) and from France (Lyons-Grenoble). Success, he reckoned, might provoke intervention by Austria and counterintervention by France and so set the entire Continent aflame. The first step would be an attack on Savoy, a province of Piedmont on the French side of the Alps and claimed by French radicals and other nationalists as French territory. Mazzini counted on enlisting Italian refugees in France, and also on French and Polish revolutionaries. Several hundred Poles had left France in the spring of 1833 to settle in Switzerland, hoping that soon a revolution would break out in Germany. They were given a warm welcome by Swiss radicals and German refugees, and there was every indication that Mazzini's plan would unite republican, revolutionary elements of all these countries. Funds were provided by a few patriotic aristocrats, who insisted, however, that a professional soldier be put in command of the filibusters. Eventually the choice fell on General Girolamo Ramorino, like Mazzini a Genoese by birth, a man who had fought in the Napoleonic armies, who had taken an active part in the Polish war against Russia, and who was presently engaged in recruiting men for Dom Pedro of Portugal. He was given 40,000 francs with which to recruit a thousand revolutionaries in France and with these he was to lead the invasion of Savoy from Lyons to Annecy. Mazzini, meanwhile, recruited several hundred Poles in Switzerland and planned to

13 César Vidal: *Louis-Philippe, Mazzini et la Jeune Italie, 1832–1834* (Paris, 1934), 26, 30 ff.: Jean C. Biaudet: *La Suisse et la Monarchie de Juillet, 1830–1838* (Lausanne, 1941), 115 ff.; Edward E. Y. Hales: *Mazzini and the Secret Societies* (New York, 1956), 79 ff.; Mastellone: *Mazzini e la Giovine Italia,* II, chaps. x and xi.

lead a column from Geneva to St.-Julien, after which he hoped to unite with Ramorino's main force. Concurrently a young naval officer, the later famous Giuseppe Garibaldi, was to provoke a mutiny among the sailors at Genoa and if possible stir revolution in central Italy. The Savoy expedition was ill-fated from the start. The French government obstructed recruitment in every possible way, so that Ramorino was obliged to admit that the Lyons column could not be organized. Given then command of the Geneva column, he repeatedly deferred his arrival till Mazzini came to suspect him of being in French pay. Furthermore, Buonarrotti refused all support, arguing that success was unthinkable without French aid and that in general the situation was unfavorable, since France as well as Austria were opposed to any such venture. Further details may well be omitted, for by the time that Ramorino reached Geneva (January 31, 1834) the Piedmontese government had learned of the project and had taken adequate measures to foil it. The Geneva government, too, obstructed the movement of the Polish and German contingents from Berne to Geneva. All was therefore in confusion when Ramorino on February 1 led about 300 men over the frontier into Savoy. For unknown reasons he did not attack St.-Julien but quickly recrossed the border into Switzerland, where for a while he marched and countermarched before declaring the expedition dissolved. The local population helped most of the participants to escape, but the Swiss authorities, under heavy pressure from the Austrian and Piedmontese governments, presently ordered all refugees who had engaged in revolutionary activities to leave the country. Mazzini was able, by constantly changing his abode, to remain in Switzerland until 1836, when he took refuge in England.[14]

The Savoy expedition was a fiasco as complete as any coup previously attempted by other conspiratorial elements. The bonfires on the hilltops, which were to signal the spread of insurrection throughout Italy and all Europe, were never lit. The "people" remained unmoved. Mazzini blamed Ramorino and he blamed Buonarrotti, but he presently recovered from a near nervous collapse and, still convinced of the

---

[14] The basic account is still Wilhelm Prechner: "Der Savoyerzug" (*Zeitschrift für schweizerische Geschichte*, IV, 1924, 459–507), but must now be supplemented by the works of Vidal, Biaudet, Hales and especially Mastellone, who adduces much evidence from archives and police reports. On international aspects, see Marguerite Mauerhofer: "Mazzini et les refugiés italiens en Suisse" (*Zeitschrift für schweizerische Geschichte*, XII, 1932, 45–100); Giovanni Perretti: *Esuli del Risorgimento in Svizzera* (Bologna, 1948).

rightness of his course, proceeded to further planning. Probably in response to Buonarrotti's effort to found a Universal Democratic Carbonari (*Charbonnerie démocratique universelle*) in the autumn of 1833, Mazzini in the spring of 1834 floated a new international society to be known as Young Europe. On April 15 various refugees in Switzerland (six Italians, five Germans and five Poles) signed the Act of Brotherhood to underwrite the new "Holy Alliance of the Peoples" and ensure mutual support in the fight for freedom. In the ensuing few years national branches were founded in Switzerland, France, Spain and Hungary. But Young Europe remained largely a paper organization. Far from merging their interests in the cause of humanity, the various national contingents soon fell to disputing about aims and tactics. Most were unwilling to recognize the primacy of the Italian movement, so dear to Mazzini. Even in 1835 Young Europe was little more than a symbol of solidarity in the revolutionary struggle.[15]

2. MODERATE LIBERALISM: THE GERMANIES

By 1835 the governments of Central Europe, like that of France, had introduced repressive measures which seriously trammeled the revolutionary movement through police supervision, through restrictions on liberty of the press, and through the prohibition of political societies and public demonstrations. The radical movement was therefore driven underground. In Paris, the traditional hearth of revolution, there were the secret societies of the Seasons and of the Families, to which many of the foreign refugees belonged. In addition there were the separate organizations of Poles, Italians and Germans, the latter being especially numerous because so many German journeymen worked in Paris for a couple of years as part of their artisanal training. The Germans had a League of Outlaws (*Bund der Geächteten*) and then a League of the Just (*Bund der Gerechten*), both of which have been much studied because of their bearing on the development of the

[15] According to the German federal police, which had little difficulty in penetrating the organization, Young Italy in 1835 consisted of eighty-six clubs, of which seventy-four, with 693 members, were in Italy itself. Young Germany had only fourteen clubs, mostly in Switzerland and France; Young Poland numbered fifty clubs, of which nineteen were in Poland; Young Switzerland counted sixty-two clubs with 480 members, most of them in Italian Switzerland. The best account is Hans Keller; *Das 'Junge Europa,' 1834–1836* (Zürich, 1938), but see also Hales: *Mazzini and the Secret Societies,* chaps. vii and ix; and Gunther F. Eyck: "Mazzini's Young Europe" (*Journal of Central European Affairs,* XVII, 1958, 331–355).

German labor movement and Marxian socialism. All these organizations were more or less interconnected. There was in fact a European revolutionary movement, as the governments contended. But as yet it operated on the lines of the former Carbonari and thereby proved once again the futility of conspiracy and insurrection by an elite minority.[16]

The interest shifts, then, from the outright revolutionary elements, heirs of the French Jacobins, to the more "respectable," sober advocates of reform and modernization, to the people who, far from glorifying the French Revolution, were impressed more by the British system and by the successes of reform agitation in England. It is difficult, without getting into detail, to do these currents of liberalism full justice, for they were not only numerous but also different. This is most clearly revealed by the developments in the Germanic Confederation. First of all, attention should be directed to Austria, the dominant power at that time in Central Europe and, under Francis I and Prince Metternich, the pace setter in repressive policy.

The Emperor Francis I was a man not only fearful by nature and pedantic by temperament but also suspicious of all innovation and hence deaf to all proposals, even of modest reform. So intent was he on upholding the existing order that, before his death in 1835, he named as his successor his son Ferdinand, known to be feeble-minded and epileptic. Then, instead of appointing either of his two brothers, the Archdukes Charles and John, both of them reasonably progressive in outlook, as mentor for his infirm successor, he turned to his youngest brother, Louis, who was known to be even more reactionary, procrastinating and narrow-minded than Francis himself. Louis, together with Prince Metternich and Count Franz von Kolowrat, constituted the State Conference (*Staatskonferenz*) which, because of the struggle for influence between Metternich and Kolowrat, soon proved itself altogether ineffectual. Policy formation and execution became all but impossible. The Austrian government became paralyzed and, in the period before 1848, could justly be described as stagnant and immobile.

---

[16] All earlier studies of the German organizations abroad have been superseded by the superb monograph by Wolfgang Schieder: *Anfänge der deutschen Arbeiterbewegung: die Auslandsvereine im Jahrzehnt nach der Juli Revolution* (Stuttgart, 1963); see also, on the refugee organizations in Switzerland, Ernst Schraepler: "Geheimbündelei und soziale Bewegung: zur Geschichte des 'Jungen Deutschland' in der Schweiz" (*International Review of Social History*, VII, Part II, 1962).

Well before the outbreak of the revolution in 1848, the existing regime had begun to arouse opposition in the empire. Within court circles there was much criticism of Metternich on the part of the archdukes, while in the provincial diets the dominant aristocracy and officialdom became so irked by the interference and inefficiency of the Vienna authorities that there was increasing pressure for reform of central as well as local government. More important still was the critical attitude of the lesser bureaucracy (consisting in considerable part of recently ennobled bourgeois officials), which held fast to the tradition of eighteenth-century enlightened rule and insisted on the need for modernizing reform. And finally, closely related to the foregoing, was the pressure for change on the part of the rising *bourgeoisie* of Vienna and other cities. This consisted largely of merchants and bankers (mostly settlers from Switzerland and from other German states), but with a sprinkling of the new business, that is, industrial, class. The leadership of this element came, as in Germany proper, from writers and journalists, together with a few university professors and members of other professions. Their aspirations were directed to abolition of the remnants of feudalism and establishment of representative government with a voice for the propertied classes.[17]

Strange though it may seem, the *Vormärz,* that is, the period before the revolution of March, 1848, was culturally a particularly rich and varied one in Viennese life. The many poets, dramatists and storytellers all chafed under the system of preliminary censorship to which all books, pamphlets, articles and newspapers were subjected. The regulations were strictly enforced by the chief of police, Count Josef Sedlnitzky, but Metternich's chancellery also played an active role. The aging prince was more firmly convinced than ever that the international revolutionary movement presented an immediate and serious threat to governments and society, and that everything possible must be done to obstruct radical activities and propaganda.[18]

[17] Fritz Valjavec: *Der Josefinismus* (Munich, 1945); Karl Eder: *Der Liberalismus in Altoesterreich* (Vienna, 1955); Georg Franz: *Liberalismus: die deutschliberale Bewegung in der habsburgischen Monarchie* (Munich, 1956), 18, 25; Otto Brunner: "Staat und Gesellschaft im vormärzlichen Oesterreich" (in Werner Conze, ed.: *Staat und Gesellschaft im deutschen Vormärz,* Stuttgart, 1962, 39–78); Ernst R. Huber: *Deutsche Verfassungsgeschichte seit 1789* (Stuttgart, 1960), II, 7 ff., 451 ff.

[18] On Metternich's role, see the concluding estimate in the classical biography of Heinrich von Srbik: *Metternich, der Staatsmann und der Mensch* (Munich, 1954), III, 13 ff. See also R. W. Seton-Watson: "Metternich and Internal Austrian Policy" (*Slavonic and East European Review,* XVII, 1939, 539–555; XVIII, 1939, 129–141); Werner

Irritation and resentment with the regime showed through many of the thinly veiled references in the literature of the period. In 1831 Anastasius Grün (pen name of a liberal nobleman) published his *Rambles of a Viennese Poet,* full of nostalgia for the enlightened, reforming days of Joseph II. Other poets, too, criticized the humiliating restrictions under which they worked and expressed their yearnings for a more liberal regime. The greatest of them all and a dramatist of European standing, Franz Grillparzer, was a confirmed Josefinian, who went so far as to criticize Metternich personally.[19]

In the 1840's, as other nations were forging ahead toward a new industrial society, Austrians became more and more irked by the stagnation of their affairs. Even aristocratic circles began to raise their voices in protest. Explicitly critical writing could, of course, not be published in the empire, but was often printed in Leipzig or Hamburg and then smuggled in. Outstanding among works of this kind was Baron Victor von Andrian-Werburg's *Austria and Her Future* (1841), published anonymously by an official of the imperial chancellery. Andrian made much of the progress enjoyed by other German states and declared the Hapsburg Empire a "lifeless mummy." He denounced the policy of repression and called for freedom of the press, judicial reform and liberalization of the educational system. A special object of his attack was the financial administration with its superfluous personnel and its habit of solving problems by raising loans from private bankers who then battened on the proceeds. Constructively Andrian looked to the provincial estates (*Stände*) to develop self-government and introduce reforms. The estates should be strengthened by giving the townsmen and peasants representation. Furthermore, the provincial diets should be crowned by an imperial Diet (*Reichsstände*) consisting of delegates from the local assemblies and members chosen by the government. This central Parliament should be given some control

---

Meyer: *Vormärz: die Ära Metternichs* (Potsdam, 1948); Alfred Schweder: *Politische Polizei* (Berlin, 1937); Julius Marx: *Die oesterreichische Zensur im Vormärz* (Vienna, 1959), 31 ff.

[19] In addition to his two prose essays on Metternich, Grillparzer wrote the impressive poem *Der kranke Feldherr.* See P. Kuranda: "Grillparzer und die Politik des Vormärzes" *(Jahrbuch der Grillparzer Gesellschaft,* XXVIII, 1926, 11 ff.). On the literature of the period in general, see Josef Nadler: *Literaturgeschichte Oesterreichs* (2 ed., Salzburg, 1951), 335; Otto Rommel: *Der oesterreichische Vormärz* (Leipzig, 1931), 83 ff.; Heinz Rieder: *Wiener Vormärz: das Theater, das literarische Leben, die Zensur* (Vienna, 1959).

over expenditures and at least a limited right to vote taxes and debate legislation. Like so many German liberals, Andrian was enamored of the British constitution, which he once described as "the model, the pride of Germanic institutions and of the Germanic spirit."[20]

It will be seen that Andrian's proposals were anything but radical or revolutionary. His dream was a return to the progressive, modernizing policies of Joseph II, expanding the traditional diets and adding a central Parliament. In the years just before 1848 some of the provincial diets, notably that of Lower Austria, embarked upon lively agitation for reform, thus demonstrating at least the prevalent discontent of even the upper classes with the general stagnation.[21]

In the light of the growing opposition, special interest attaches to various societies which Count Kolowrat, as minister of the interior, sanctioned and protected so as to quiet the restlessness of upper circles or, as some say, to spite his rival, Metternich. The first was the Lower Austrian Trade Association (1839), which consisted chiefly of merchants and industrialists, but included also some progressive nobles and academics. In 1840 a group of writers was permitted to found the Concordia Society, the members of which in 1845 drew up an impressive petition asking abolition of censorship. There followed, in 1841, the most important of these organizations, the Juridical-Political Reading Society, the purpose of which was to enable university people and officials to keep abreast of foreign writings on government matters. The membership consisted of professors, lawyers, officials and military men, and the meetings were markedly Josefinian in tone. French and British books and periodicals were carefully scanned and the reform campaigns in France and Britain followed with keen interest. The organization was in no sense radical. There was not a trace of hostility either to the dynasty or the state, and in fact there was no agreement on any specific program of reform. The society was basically a discussion group, a clearinghouse for news and ideas, but as such an important school for those who were called on to deal with the revolutions of 1848.[22]

---

[20] His book, still anonymous, soon ran through three editions and was enlarged in 1847 by addition of a second part.

[21] Hanns Schlitter: *Aus Oesterreichs Vormärz,* Part IV, *Niederoesterreich* (Vienna, 1920); Josef Redlich: *Das oesterreichische Staats- und Reichsproblem* (Leipzig, 1920), I, 175 ff.

[22] The basic study is Friedrich Engel-Janosi: "Der Wiener juridisch-politische Leseverein" (*Mitteilungen des Vereins für Geschichte der Stadt Wien,* IV, 1923, 58–66).

In the other German states liberalism, of the moderate as well as the radical variety, continued to be a movement of intellectuals, reinforced by elements of the bureaucracy and increasingly by the business interests which emerged from the progressive economic changes. Because of the widely differing conditions and the many different governments, it is hard to present an adequate picture of these opposition movements. Nothing more can be attempted here than to indicate some of the larger trends and the more significant happenings.

The extent to which the repression of thought could go was best shown by the fate of the Young German movement, a strictly literary movement which bore no relation to the Mazzinian organization of the same name. The Young Germans were a group of prose writers who had in common their reaction against classicism, idealism and romanticism and their devotion to the attitude and thought of the Enlightenment. Greatly concerned with the questions of the day, they aimed to reach a large public through effective, journalistic writing. The group was greatly influenced by two eminent expatriate writers, Ludwig Börne and Heinrich Heine. Börne, sometimes described as the father of German political journalism, was a thoroughgoing democrat, an admirer of Robespierre as the incarnation of republican virtue. He had hurried to Paris on the morrow of the July Revolution and during the years 1831–1833 sent to Germany 112 *Letters from Paris* in which he described French conditions in glowing terms and compared the fighting French democrats with the humble and subservient Germans.[23] Heine, one of the greatest of German writers and a satirist *sans pareil,* arrived in Paris in the spring of 1831 and in 1832 published his reports under the title *French Conditions,* in which, again, he rhapsodized about the land of liberty and laughed heartily over his benighted and submissive countrymen. In France, he declared, even one-tenth of the sufferings borne by the Germans would have provoked thirty-six revolutions and have cost thirty-six German princes their heads as well as their thrones.[24]

In their ardor the Young German writers attacked all tendency

---

[23] Gerard Ras: *Börne und Heine als politische Schriftsteller* (The Hague, 1926), and especially Helmut Bock: *Ludwig Börne* (Berlin, 1962), a Marxist study.

[24] The reference, of course, is to the thirty-six German states of the Confederation. The passage, from Heine's *Salon,* is quoted in Georg Eckert: *Das Junge Deutschland und die Revolutionsdichtung des Vormärz* (Brunswick, 1949), 32. Among the countless biographies of Heine, that by E. M. Butler: *Heinrich Heine* (London, 1956) is particularly strong on the Paris period.

toward resignation. Rejecting bourgeois morality, they called for the emancipation of women, easier divorce, greater sexual freedom. Bitterly opposed to Catholicism and its superstitions, they were inclined to reject all religion as an opiate of the people. They were not great writers, but their novels and dramas did "let in the fresh air," to quote the great critic, George Brandes. The upshot was that they outraged all "proper" people and in 1835 were violently attacked for their godless, French immorality by the historian Wolfgang Menzel. The federal Diet thereupon seized the opportunity to forbid the dissemination of the works of Heine, Börne, Gutzkow and other leaders of the school.[25]

In Germany proper as in Austria there was a marked strain of liberalism in the ranks of the bureaucracy, military as well as civilian. The tradition of the Enlightenment and the reform era persisted in Prussia, especially among university-trained officials, many of whom were of middle-class origin. Through their efforts the economic and social policies of the Prussian government remained progressive, but in the political sphere there was no advance, despite the fact that a Parliament for the entire monarchy to supplement the provincial diets would have done much to weld the disparate parts of the kingdom together.[26]

In the states of southwest Germany, which already had constitutions, the struggle for more modern institutions went on unabated. The rulers, supported by the landholding nobility, and aided by the federal Diet, were constantly trying to restrict the powers of the parliaments or at least to break the strength of the opposition by rigging the elections. On the other hand, the members of the lower chamber, many of whom, as in Baden, were liberal-minded officials, continued their attacks on feudal dues, princely extravagance and military appropriations. Since the officials were irremovable, the gov-

[25] Fritz Martini: *Deutsche Literaturgeschichte* (2 ed., Stuttgart, 1950), 348 ff.; and the excellent introduction to Jost Hermand's anthology: *Das Junge Deutschland* (Stuttgart, 1966). Heinrich von Treitschke's *Deutsche Geschichte im 19 Jahrhundert*, IV, 419 ff., and George Brandes: *Main Currents in Nineteenth Century Literature*, VI, are still well worth reading.

[26] Wilhelm Treue: *Wirtschaftszustände und Wirtschaftspolitik in Preussen, 1815–1852* (Stuttgart, 1937); Adam Simonson: *Die Anfänge des Liberalismus in Preussen* (Berlin, 1933), 20 ff.; Reinhart Koselleck: "Staat und Gesellschaft in Preussen" (in Werner Conze, ed.: *Staat und Gesellschaft im deutschen Vormärz*, Stuttgart, 1962, 79–112).

ernment could rid itself of their opposition only by refusing them leave of absence from their duties to attend the sessions of Parliament.[27]

Among the many figures of South German liberalism, Karl von Rotteck and Karl Theodor Welcker, both professors at the University of Freiburg and both members of the Baden Parliament, are best known. Rotteck, the older of the two, was the author of a nine-volume *General History* which, by 1854, had run through nineteen editions and provided the standard middle-class, liberal interpretation of the past. Rotteck believed firmly in natural rights and paid tribute to the aims of the French Revolution and, like other liberals, extolled the American system of liberty, equality and respect for civil rights.[28]

Together Rotteck and Welcker edited a famous *Political Encyclopedia (Staatslexikon)* in fifteen volumes (1834–1844), covering the entire field of the social sciences in articles by experts who provided not only facts but good, sound liberal doctrine. In this great work, still valuable, the influence of British institutions and thought was very evident. Friedrich Dahlmann, the northern counterpart of Rotteck and Welcker, wrote histories of both the English and the French Revolutions in which he glorified the constitutional monarchy and rejected the French Rights of Man as dangerously extravagant.[29]

These German scholars were not simple-minded idealists, but men deeply engrossed in political problems and exponents of sane, moderate ideas, for which some of them at least were willing to suffer hardship, as shown by the "Göttingen Seven" in 1837. In that year Ernest Augustus an uncle of Queen Victoria succeeded to the throne of Hanover and Hanover became independent of England. The new king, known as an archconservative, promptly abrogated the constitution which in 1833 had been wrung from his predecessor. Seven eminent professors

[27] Friedrich C. Sell: *Die Tragödie des deutschen Liberalismus* (Stuttgart, 1933), chap. iv; and the essays by Wolfram Fischer and Wolfgang Zorn in Conze: *Staat und Gesellschaft*.

[28] Robert von Mohl, an eminent South German professor of law, had in 1824 published the first systematic study of the United States Constitution. See the admirable biography by Erich Angermann (Neuwied, 1962); and Hildegarde Meyer: *Nord-Amerika im Urteil des deutschen Schrifttums bis zur Mitte des 19 Jahrhunderts* (Hamburg, 1929), 39 ff.; Ernst Fränkel: *Amerika im Spiegel des deutschen politischen Denkens* (Köln, 1959), 26 ff., 88 ff.

[29] Hans Zehnter: *Das Staatslexikon von Rotteck und Welcker* (Jena, 1929); T. Wilhelm: *Die englische Verfassung und der vormärzliche deutsche Liberalismus* (Stuttgart, 1928); F. Gunther Eyck: "English and French Influences on German Liberalism before 1848" (*Journal of the History of Ideas*, XVIII, 1957, 313–341).

at the university protested and were dismissed from their posts. The historians Dahlmann and Gervinus, along with the philologist Jakob Grimm were expelled from the realm for having circulated their protest. The incident evoked a storm of indignation throughout Germany. At Göttingen the student demonstrations became so formidable that the king called out the military, thereby making matters worse. Presently Germans in Switzerland, England and even the United States organized Göttingen Societies to raise funds for the seven and help them find new positions. Some were offered appointments at Swiss universities and, after the accession of Frederick William in 1840, the others were named to Prussian faculties.[30]

German liberalism was reinforced in this period by growing dissatisfaction with the strict orthodoxy and archconservatism of the churches, both Catholic and Protestant. This matter will be discussed in a later chapter dealing with religious issues, but mention should here be made of the fact that Biblical criticism did much to undermine faith in traditional beliefs. David Strauss' *Life of Jesus* (1835), Bruno Bauer's studies of the Gospels and Ludwig Feuerbach's *The Nature of Christianity* (1841), all of them among the most influential books of the nineteenth century, did much to drain accepted faiths of their authority and to weaken the support which princes had derived from the church.[31]

One result of this destructive criticism was the effort made to organize Christian churches along more liberal lines. On the Protestant side there emerged the Friends of Light (*Lichtfreunde*, 1841), who rejected obscurantist orthodoxy and called for a return to simple Christianity. The movement was outlawed by the Prussian government in 1845. Its counterpart, the German Catholic movement (1844), originated in a protest against the exhibition, at Trier, of the Holy Cloak, which attracted more than a million pilgrims. Johannes Ronge denounced this as a "modern indulgence racket" and was at once

---

30 Herbert Van Thal: *Ernest Augustus, Duke of Cumberland and King of Hanover* (London, 1936); Hans Kück: *Die Göttinger Sieben: ihre Protestation und ihre Entlassung* (Berlin, 1934); Wilhelm Schoof: "Der Protest der Göttinger Sieben" (*Geschichte in Wissenschaft und Unterricht*, XIII, 1962, 333–345). On constitutional aspects, see Huber: *Deutsche Verfassungsgeschichte*, II, 96 ff.

31 Walter Nigg: *Geschichte des religiösen Liberalismus* (Zürich, 1937), 143 ff.; Franz Schnabel: *Deutsche Geschichte in 19 Jahrhundert* (2 ed., Freiburg, 1950), IV, 493 ff.; Adolf Rapp: "David Friedrich Strauss; seine Lebensleitung und sein Schicksal" (*Die Welt als Geschichte*, XVII, 1957, 213–220); Karl Löwith: *From Hegel to Nietzsche* (New York, 1964), 62 ff.

excommunicated. But in 1845 he succeeded in founding a number of free congregations, using a German liturgy and rejecting confession, celibacy of the clergy, fasting, indulgences and pilgrimages. The movement was closely watched by the governments but, lacking aggressive leadership, was permitted to exist until after 1848.[32]

During the 1840's the liberal and also the radical movements were transformed and strengthened through the increasing tempo of economic change. The organization of the Customs Union (*Zollverein*) under Prussian leadership in 1834 brought a great improvement in communications and trade, while the advent of the railroad had begun to alter basically the terms of economic life. Furthermore, the process of industrialization was setting in in earnest. The Prussian Rhineland and Westphalia and the Kingdom of Saxony became major centers of the textile and metallurgical trades, in which both business interests and the new industrial proletariat began to play an influential role. Leading Rhineland entrepreneurs such as David Hansemann, Ludolf Camphausen, August von der Heyd, Hermann von Beckerath and Gustav Mevissen were men educated in England or France, or at least widely traveled in those countries. They were practical men, interested in many phases of business development, not much given to theorizing but convinced, like the great teachers of liberalism, that the middle class was "the center of gravity of the state," to which every government should give heed. They were not in any sense hostile to the rulers or to the state; all they asked was that remnants of the restrictive feudal system be swept away and that well-to-do, educated elements of the population be given some voice in decisions affecting their welfare. Hansemann had, as early as 1830, memorialized the Prussian king on these matters, and in 1840 had tried to persuade the new ruler that only through constitutional, representative government could the dangers of revolution and democracy be forestalled. In 1842 these liberals banded together to found the *Rhenish Gazette* (*Rheinische Zeitung*) in which the most progressive economic and political doctrines were expounded.[33]

---

[32] Nigg: *Geschichte des religiösen Liberalismus*, 176 ff., 188 ff.; Jacques Droz: *Les révolutions allemandes de 1848* (Paris, 1957), 60 ff., 127 ff.

[33] The basic account is that of Jacques Droz: *Le libéralisme rhénan, 1815–1848* (Paris, 1940), esp. 217 ff., 425 ff.; but see also Joseph Hansen: *Geschichte des Rheinlandes von den ältesten Zeiten bis zur Gegenwart* (Essen, 1922); Pierre Benaerts: *Les origines de la grande industrie allemande* (Paris, n.d.), chap. ix; Wolfgang Hock: *Liberales Denken im Zeitalter der Paulskirche* (Münster, 1957), 34 ff., 154 ff.; Leonard Krieger: *The German Idea of Freedom* (Boston, 1957), 303 ff.

The accession of Frederick William IV to the Prussian throne in 1840 proved to be a landmark, for it raised high hopes followed by deep despair. The new king was a man in his mid-forties, of fine presence and real charm, well-educated and genuinely interested in science and art. He at once proclaimed an amnesty for political offenders and presently ordered restrictions on the press and on civil rights to be relaxed. There was every reason to think that he would initiate a more enlightened, more modern regime. Unfortunately he soon proved himself anything but a friend of the liberal program. Though well-intentioned, he was vague, weak-willed and unaccountable. A devout Christian, he dreamed of establishing a Christian state on an aristocratic, patriarchal basis. Words such as freedom, constitution and unity came easily to his lips, but they did not mean to him what they meant to other people. The king thought entirely in medieval terms and before long revealed himself to the disillusioned public as an incurable romantic, a man utterly out of step with his times.[34]

Though not willing to be bound by his father's promises of a constitution, Frederick William did plan some type of representative body for the entire kingdom. In 1842 he convoked a meeting of delegates from the eight provincial assemblies (diets), which were organized on a traditional class basis. But this solution was far from meeting the desires for a national Parliament elected on a limited franchise, like the French or Belgian parliaments. The delegations refused to vote the funds required by the king and the latter, outraged by the presumption of his subjects, began to abandon his earlier, supposedly friendly attitude. Johann Jacoby, a distinguished Königsberg physician, was charged with high treason for publishing his *Four Questions of an East Prussian,* in which he argued the need for a representative constitution and recalled earlier royal promises. The *Rhenish Gazette,* at that time edited by the young Karl Marx and much more radical than its sponsors had intended it to be, was suppressed in 1843 and the *Königsberg Journal* was effectively shackled.[35]

The king, in dire need of funds and unable to levy new taxes with-

[34] Ernst Lewalter: *Friedrich Wilhelm IV, das Schicksal eines Geistes* (Berlin, 1938). Not many biographers have been tempted by this enigmatic subject. For one of the best-balanced analyses of the king's personality, see Erich Marcks: *Der Aufstieg des Reiches* (Berlin, 1936), I, 221ff.

[35] An outstanding study of this period is Gustav Mayer: "Die Anfänge des politischen Radikalismus im vormärzlichen Preussen" (*Zeitschrift für Politik,* VI, 1913, 1–113).

out consent of the diets, finally yielded to the extent of summoning them all to Berlin as a United Diet (*Vereinigter Landtag*), which was still far from being a popularly elected Parliament, the more so as the United Diet was to have only consultative powers. Nonetheless, the businessmen took the realistic view that it was at least a step in the direction of participation in government and so decided to attend, albeit reluctantly. The United Diet met in Berlin in April, 1847, when the king in his opening address once more deflated all popular hopes. The Diet, he said, would be summoned only at his own discretion and, he warned, he would never permit a written constitution to be inserted between himself and his people. It was clear now that the king and his liberal subjects were talking entirely different languages. The Rhineland leaders therefore restated their demand for constitutional government in quite unvarnished terms, and in this they were supported by some liberal aristocrats from the east. In June the Diet refused (by a vote of 360–179) to approve the loan desired by the government, and was promptly dissolved. Though its session ended in deadlock, it was of great importance as being the first Prussian Parliament. It achieved, if nothing else, a clear definition of both the position of the king and that of the liberal opposition. Though of course its members could not know it, the Diet sounded the upbeat to the Revolution of March, 1848, much as the reform banquets in France sounded the death knell of the July Monarchy.[36]

It cannot be stated too strongly, however, that the liberals were not in any sense revolutionary. On the contrary, they hoped and expected to attain their ends by continuing pressure. They were heartened by the resounding success of Cobden's Anti-Corn Law League and by the rising tide of liberalism in France, Switzerland and Italy. It must be remembered, however, that the years 1846 and 1847 were years of famine and depression everywhere in Europe and that the widespread misery was bound to spawn new radical movements. Many of these were directly concerned with the social question and can therefore be most advantageously discussed in connection with the doctrines of socialism. But Marx and other members of the so-called Young

---

[36] Eduard Hemmerle: *Beiträge zur Geschichte des ersten Vereinigten Landtages* (Langensalza, 1912), 30 ff.; Droz: *Le libéralisme rhénan*, 314 ff.; Veit Valentin: *Geschichte der deutschen Revolution von 1848–1849* (Berlin, 1930), I, 63 ff.; Huber: *Deutsche Verfassungsgeschichte*, II, 491 ff.

Hegelian school, such as Arnold Ruge, were starting their careers at this time primarily as philosophical radicals. Ruge in 1838 had founded the *Halle Yearbooks,* in which he called for the application of the Hegelian dialectic to the political and social problems of the day. He was obliged to move from Halle to Dresden in 1841 and to Paris in 1843, by which time his journal, renamed the *German-French Year-books,* had become the forum for the most advanced democratic and socialist ideas. Marx and his associate, Friedrich Engels, as well as Heine and Jacoby, were contributors to this publication.[37]

Ruge and Marx criticized Hegel for implying that the world was coming to an end with his own all-inclusive philosophical structure. They parted company also with the Young Hegelian school, which, they asserted, thought a great revolution could be effected by successive attacks on the Hegelian system. The new philosophy must be grounded on understanding of the realities of modern life; mere criticism of institutions was futile unless it led to political and social action. And so the scene was set for revolutionary socialism or communism, the philosophy of which was to be expounded in the *Communist Manifesto* of 1848. Meanwhile the revived activism found expression in the works of German poets. In his *Germany, a Winter's Tale* (1844) Heine poured scorn on German complacency and acceptance, challenging his countrymen to do something about their grievances. Even before this Georg Herwegh had made a great reputation with his *Poems of a Live Man* (1841), which ran through six editions in two years and brought the author a triumphant ovation when he toured Germany. Herwegh joined the German exiles in Paris in 1843 and was there lionized by revolutionary circles. The other outstanding revolutionary poet of the period was Ferdinand Freiligrath, whose *Confessions* appeared in 1844 and his collection of poems, *Ça Ira,* in 1846. A sincere democrat and republican, Freiligrath was obliged to flee Germany, first to Brussels and then to London, where he soon became associated with Marx.[38]

Interesting though these writers are as forerunners of the radical

---

[37] See especially Fritz Schlawe: "Die junghegelische Publizistik" (*Die Welt als Geschichte,* XX, 1960, 30–50), and the well-balanced Marxist account in Karl Obermann: *Deutsche Geschichte* (Berlin, 1965), II, 198 ff.

[38] Valentin Pollak: *Die politische Lyrik und die Parteien des deutschen Vormärz* (Vienna, 1911); Georg Eckert: *Das Junge Deutschland und die Revolutionsdichtung des Vormärz* (Brunswick, 1949).

trends in the revolutions of 1848, it must not be supposed that they represented anything more than a minority of the politically minded intellectual and business classes. The majority was still opposed to revolution and staked its hopes on peaceful reform. But the majority was under increasing pressure from the activist elements. In September, 1847, two of the more radical members of the Baden Parliament, Friedrich Hecker and Gustav von Struve, convoked a meeting at Offenburg, near Frankfurt, where demands were formulated not only for a popularly elected federal Parliament but for a militia to replace the regular army; a progressive income tax; free education at all levels; freedom of the press, of conscience and of instruction; the abolition of all privileges; and even measures to regulate the relations between capital and labor. This democratic program had at least this effect, that it induced the moderate liberals to formulate their own demands. In October, 1847, liberals from many German states met at Heppenheim (in Hesse) and agreed on demands for active participation in government, abolition of remaining feudal obligations, abrogation of all repressive measures, and above all the guarantee of free discussion of public affairs. Thus the two wings of German liberalism defined their positions. The great issue was whether change could be brought about by British methods of agitation and pressure, or whether the new order could be brought into existence only by revolution.[39]

3. SPOTLIGHT ON SWITZERLAND: THE SONDERBUND WAR

The growing pressure for reform and for broader participation of the nonprivileged classes in government manifested itself in other countries, such as the Scandinavian, though there the Industrial Revolution had as yet made no significant impress. The conservative governments of Denmark and Sweden (Norway was joined to Sweden in a personal union) relied heavily for support on the Lutheran Church, which had become rigid and formalistic. Consequently the first stirrings of opposition were directed against the established church. Bible and

[39] Johanna Köster: *Der rheinische Frühliberalismus und die soziale Frage* (Berlin, 1938), 111; Karl Griewank: "Vulgärer Radikalismus und demokratische Bewegung in Berlin, 1842–1848" (*Forschungen zur brandenburgischen und preussischen Geschichte,* XXXVI, 1924, 14–38); Walter Bussmann: "Zur Geschichte des deutschen Liberalismus im 19 Jahrhundert" (*Historische Zeitschrift,* CLXXXVI, 1958, 527–557); Lenore O'Boyle: "The Democratic Left in Germany, 1848" (*Journal of Modern History,* XXXIII, 1961, 374–383).

reading societies sprang up and Nicholas Grundtvig, perhaps the most eminent Scandinavian intellectual of the period, eventually became the advocate of a simple, apostolic Christianity, organized as a People's Church. In Sweden the Reverend George Scott, minister of the Wesleyan congregation in Stockholm, attracted such large audiences by his destructive preaching that the government obliged him to leave the country (1842). However, men such as Henrik Schartau and Carl Rosenius followed the same line and brought about a veritable "preaching sickness" in both Sweden and Norway. The extent and depth of discontent with the conservative church and government was so great that it induced many Scandinavians to emigrate.[40]

Although the business class was of small account in Scandinavia, intellectuals played an important role, as in Germany. The universities of Kiel, Copenhagen and Uppsala were outstanding institutions in close contact with foreign scholars. Many members of their faculties visited England as well as Germany and became impressed by the restless energy and intellectual vigor of British life. They returned home converted to the ideas of political and economic liberalism and began to agitate for greater freedom of the press and more liberal education, as well as for free trade.[41] Furthermore, here as in Germany the French influence, more specifically the French Revolutionary influence, made itself felt. The Norwegian poet Henrik Wergeland returned from a visit to Paris in 1831 a confirmed democrat and republican, a champion of human dignity and liberty. He was no politician, but in his poetry he denounced Russian tyranny in Poland, English exploitation of the Irish, the Carlist challenge in Spain. His short life was devoted to the cause of free education, free libraries and adequate relief for the poor.[42]

[40] E. L. Allen: *Bishop Grundtvig* (London, n.d.), 56 ff.; Hal Koch: *Grundtvig* (Yellow Springs, Ohio, 1952), chap. x; Theodore E. Blegen: *Norwegian Migration to America* (Northfield, 1931), chap. vii; George M. Stephenson: *The Religious Aspects of Swedish Immigration* (Minneapolis, 1932), chaps. i–iv; Franklin D. Scott: "The Causes and Consequences of Swedish Emigration in Sweden" (*The Chronicle*, 1955, 2–11); Gunnar Westlin: "Emigration and Scandinavian Church Life" (*Swedish Pioneer Historical Quarterly*, VIII, 1957, 35–49).

[41] Grundtvig is the best example. See Kaj Baagö: "Grundtvig of den engelske liberalisme" (*Grundtvig Studier*, 1955, 7–37); Koch: *Grundtvig*, 102 ff.

[42] For a vivid contemporary impression of Wergeland and his work, see Robert G. Latham: *Norway and the Norwegians* (London, 1840), II chap. xiv; further, Skard's essay in Halvdan Koht and Sigmund Skard: *The Voice of Norway* (New York, 1944), 194 ff.; Harold Beyer: *A History of Norwegian Literature* (New York, 1956), 124 ff.

Politically more important was the career of the Dane, Orla Lehmann, an ardent student of French affairs and the organizer of the
National Liberal Party, with a typical program of constitutional government. Lehmann became the leader of the Danish nationalists in the
struggle with the Germans in Schleswig-Holstein, but that is a matter
best reserved for later treatment. The important thing in the present
context is that Lehmann, while making no original contribution to
liberalism, provided a striking example of the infiltration of western
ideas into even economically undeveloped countries.[43]

It was Switzerland, however, that became the great testing ground of
liberalism in the years preceding the revolutions of 1848. There the
moderate liberal elements had secured control of most of the cantonal
governments through the "regeneration" of 1830–1831, and there many
German professors and revolutionaries had found refuge.[44] But the
very liberalism of the Swiss cantons exposed them to radical pressures.
At Geneva, for example, there was a democratic group headed by
James Fazy, an ex-Carbonaro in close touch with Buonarroti, and a
man who had taken part in the July Revolution in Paris. Among the
refugees, too, were extremists who carried on an active propaganda.
Julius Fröbel in 1840 opened a publishing house which printed radical
books and pamphlets, while the Snell brothers became Swiss citizens
and edited the leading radical journal, the *Schweizerischer Republi-
kaner*.[45]

Liberals and radicals were as one at least in their opposition to the
Catholic Church, which here as elsewhere was regarded as the bulwark
of reaction. In 1841 the canton of Aargau ordered four monasteries and
four nunneries closed, confiscated their property and obliged the inmates to evacuate in midwinter. Other cantonal governments protested
and the Austrian government brought pressure sufficient to effect the
restoration of the nunneries, but the episode produced a sharp cleavage

---

[43] Christian Degn: *Orla Lehmann und der nationale Gedanke* (Neumünster, 1936),
36 ff., 48 ff., 69 ff.
[44] Johannes Dierauer: *Geschichte der schweizerischen Eidgenossenschaft* (2 ed., Gotha,
1922), V, 647 ff.; Thomas Velin: "Die Rolle der deutschen Emigration" (*Schweizer
Rundschau*, XLVII, 1947–1948, 338–343).
[45] Heinrich Schmidt: *Die deutschen Flüchtlinge in der Schweiz* (Zürich, 1899)
57 ff.; Hans G. Keller: *Die politischen Verlagsanstalten und Druckereien in der Schweiz*
(Berne, 1935); Werner Näf: *Die Schweiz in der deutschen Revolution* (Leipzig, 1929),
46 ff.

between conservatives on the one hand and liberals and radicals on the other. Several of the Catholic cantons, led by Lucerne, began to take counsel and even to consider secession from the Confederation. Passions were aroused to the point where in 1844 the Lucerne Diet defiantly recalled the Jesuit order and turned over the theological seminary to it. It was a dangerous move, against which not only the pope and Prince Metternich but even the head of the Jesuit order had warned the government, though in vain. As it was, the radicals now had in hand a perfect weapon for attack.[46]

In the federal Diet the radicals now demanded the expulsion of the Jesuits as a national menace. At the same time Lucerne liberals and radicals, supported by volunteers from other cantons, on two occasions (December, 1844; March, 1845) staged filibustering expeditions designed to overthrow the Lucerne government and forestall the arrival of the Jesuits. The first attempt was easily defeated and led only to repressive measures. The second, in which 3,500 men participated, reached the outskirts of the town but failed when part of the force was ambushed and captured. Hundreds were tried and sentenced to prison terms, with the result that feelings became highly exacerbated. The Catholic cantons, elated by their success, then committed a second serious blunder. On December 11, 1845, seven of them formed a separate league (Sonderbund), ostensibly for common defense, but actually to forestall liberal-radical action for federal reform at the expense of cantonal sovereignty. The agreement called for establishment of a war council with full military powers.

The formation of the Sonderbund was incompatible with the spirit and also with the letter of the federal pact, which forbade alliances "prejudicial to the federal pact." It was, in the words of a Jesuit historian, "a stupidity of the first order."[47] It inevitably led the liberals and radicals to redouble their efforts. In the summer of 1846 they staged insurrections in Berne and Geneva which gained them control of those cantons. When, in the spring of 1847, they took over the

[46] Even the Jesuit historian Ferdinand Strobel: *Die Jesuiten und die Schweiz im 19 Jahrhundert* (Freiburg, 1955), 452 ff., deprecates the move. See further Ernst Staehelin: *Die Jesuitenfrage* (Basel, 1935), chap. v; Hubert Becher: *Die Jesuiten* (Munich, 1951), 346 ff.

[47] Strobel: *Die Jesuiten*, 459; Marc Paschoud: "Le Sonderbund était-il incompatible avec le Pacte fédéral de 1815?" (*Zeitschrift für schweizerische Geschichte*, XVII, 1947, 456–504).

cantonal government of St. Gall, they were able to command a majority of votes in the federal Diet. On July 20 the Diet voted to dissolve the Sonderbund and on August 16 set up a commission to "study" the question of federal reform. On September 3 the Diet called on the Catholic cantons to expel the Jesuits and, when they refused, voted to call up 50,000 troops. Thus the religious issue was exploited by the dominant party to veil larger plans for reorganizing the Confederation so as to form an integrated, national state on a democratic basis.

The Sonderbund War, which broke out on November 4, after the Catholic cantons had withdrawn from the federal Diet, was a most unequal struggle and lasted only four weeks. The dissident cantons had only one-fifth of the population and could muster only 37,000 men as against the 100,000 available to the federal government. Furthermore, the commander, Johann von Salis-Soglio, proved no match for Wilhelm Heinrich Dufour, the federal general, a man who enjoyed a European reputation as a military engineer. Dufour quickly enclosed the garrison of Freiburg and forced its capitulation. There followed some fighting in the environs of Lucerne (battles of Gislikon and Meyerskappel, November 23) before the Sonderbund capital surrendered. The leaders fled to Italy. In the final reckoning this civil war had cost the dissidents only fifty dead, while the federalists had lost seventy-eight.[48]

It must not be supposed, however, that the conflict in Switzerland was an unimportant sideshow. The victors made every effort to overcome resentments and invited the defeated cantons to participate in the work of federal reform. In the course of 1848 the commission drafted a new constitution along American lines. Authority in all matters of national concern was to be vested in the federal government, which was to consist of a two-chamber Parliament: a national council elected by popular vote, and a council of states consisting of two representatives of each canton. The two houses together were to elect an executive of seven members and provide for a federal court. Cantonal governments were to be subordinated to the federal authorities. Protection was to be withdrawn from the Catholic monasteries,

---

[48] Recent literature includes Fritz Rieter: *Der Sonderbundkrieg* (Zürich, 1948); Ollivier Reverdin: *La guerre du Sonderbund vue par le Général Dufour* (Geneva, 1948); and the authoritative biography by Edouard Chapuisat: *Général Dufour* (Zürich, 1940).

while the expulsion of the Jesuits was confirmed. The new constitution, when submitted to popular vote (see Illustration 52), was approved by almost two million against 300,000. When the new Parliament met it turned out that the liberals and radicals had ninety seats, while the conservatives commanded only eighteen. The liberals and radicals were now in secure control. The long-drawn contest between the economically and socially more advanced parts of the country (the northern, German-speaking, Protestant cantons) and the conservative section (the central, mountain, Catholic cantons) had been resolved not only in favor of political liberty but also in favor of national unity.[49]

But the outcome of the crisis was of great importance for Europe as well as for Switzerland. Though Palmerston made no secret of his sympathy for the liberals, other governments saw the danger involved in a liberal-radical victory. Because they anticipated such a victory they did their best, even Metternich, to deter the Catholic cantons from provocative action. "For Germany the saving of Switzerland from the hands of the radicals is simply a vital question," wrote Frederick William of Prussia to Queen Victoria; "if they are victorious there, in Germany likewise torrents of blood will flow . . . thousands of emigrated malefactors wait only for a sign . . . to pour forth beyond the German frontier." The question whether the great powers would intervene in the Swiss crisis was for a time an acute one, but this question must be reserved for treatment in a later chapter. In any event, the war was brought to so speedy a close that the Swiss were able to settle their problems by themselves. But the victory of the Swiss liberals had the effect of heartening the liberals everywhere. From Germany more than fifty addresses of congratulations were showered on the federal Diet. Some were signed by prominent liberals and radicals, while others stemmed from simple people: artisans, workers, even peasants. Most of them expressed the belief that the stage was now set for a general European revolution; some even voiced the hope that a Swiss people's army might invade Germany and precipitate an insurrection. People everywhere sensed that events in little Switzerland reflected

[49] Among the best constitutional studies are Eduard His: *Geschichte des neueren schweizerischen Staatsrechts* (Basel, 1938), III, 6–30; William E. Rappard: *La constitution fédérale de la Suisse: ses origines, son élaboration, son évolution* (Neuchâtel, 1948), chaps. vii and viii; Edgar Bonjour: *Die Gründung des schweizerischen Bundesstaates* (Basel, 1948), chap. vii.

larger European problems and that the victory of liberalism and nationalism in Switzerland presaged major changes in European life.[50]

4. LIBERALISM AND REFORM: ITALY

From his exile in London Mazzini was unable to exert much direct influence on the affairs of Italy. No doubt the Young Italy movement continued to exist and it may well have instigated the isolated outbreaks that occurred from time to time in central and south Italy. The best-known episode was the attempt of the Bandiera brothers in 1844 to land on the coast of Calabria and initiate an uprising in the Kingdom of Naples. The two young men were officers in the Austrian navy, but, inspired by Mazzini's teaching, they defected and fled to Corfu, at that time under British rule. Their correspondence with Mazzini was intercepted and read by the British postal officials and their plans (which Mazzini discouraged) were revealed to the Neapolitan government by the British. When, with a handful of followers, they landed in June, 1844, they were promptly ambushed and captured. Their trial, conviction and execution followed soon after, adding their names to the roster of idealistic heroes and national martyrs.[51]

Mazzini, naturally, did his utmost to keep alive the program of revolution. He published a *Memoir of the Bandiera Brothers* and also a *Scheme of 1844* projecting a plan for an uprising in the Papal States which, he hoped, might spread to all Italy and even to Central Europe. But Mazzini, who had never traveled in Italy beyond Livorno and had no personal knowledge of popular sentiment, fell more and more out of step with the leaders of Italian thought.[52] By 1840 the tides of liberalism were running strong in the direction of moderation, that is,

---

[50] On the international aspects of the Sonderbund War, see Chapter IX. For the rest, see Werner Näf: *Die Schweiz in der deutschen Revolution,* 18 ff., 107 ff.; Jean Halperin: "The Transformation of Switzerland" (in Francois Fejtö, ed.: *The Opening of an Era: 1848,* London, 1948, 50–68).

[51] R. Pierantoni: *Storia dei Fratelli Bandiera* (Milan, 1909). The interference with Mazzini's mail, when it became known, called forth Carlyle's eloquent protest and defense of his Italian friend, but it was not until long after that Lord Aberdeen's communications to the Neapolitan government became known. See Bolton King: *A History of Italian Unity* (London 1912), I, 148 ff., and in general Alberto Ghisalberti: *Conspirazioni del Risorgimento* (Palermo, 1938).

[52] On his ignorance of Italian conditions see Gaetano Salvemini: *Mazzini* (Stanford, 1957), 85, 155, 178.

of reform rather than revolution. This had all along been the line of the enlightened aristocracy of northern Italy, of whom Count Cavour was perhaps the best example. It was also the approach of the landed *bourgeoisie,* which was relatively far more numerous in Italy than in other countries. These were sober, realistic people, interested in modernizing the methods of agriculture, encouraging trade, expanding education and in general working toward conditions as they existed in France and Britain. Utterly opposed to insurrection, they were convinced that violence resulted only in driving the governments further in the direction of repression and reaction. And such Mazzinian ideas as the establishment of a unitary republic were positively anathema to them, for they dreaded democracy as a threat to private property. Nothing could be more dangerous than to arouse the "people," to stir the embers of peasant discontent. Cavour made no bones about stating that the upper and middle classes had far too many interests to defend to contemplate revolution. Only a minute minority was seriously disposed to put into effect "the principles of an embittered and adventurous sect."[53]

What is generally regarded as the programmatic work of the moderate liberal school was Abbé Vincenzo Gioberti's book *Concerning the Moral and Civil Primacy of the Italians (Del Primato morale e civile degli Italiani* [1843]). Gioberti, after being closely associated with Mazzini, was obliged to seek refuge in Brussels, where he taught and wrote on philosophical subjects. Like Mazzini he was much concerned to restore the self-respect of the Italians, which led him to denigrate French culture and discover that over the centuries the Italians had been pre-eminent in all fields of endeavor. The *Primato* was a book of great importance in the history of Italian nationalism, which must be left for later discussion. It had relatively little to say of the principles

---

[53] Cavour: *Des chemins de fer en Italie* (1846), quoted by Walter Maturi: "Partiti politici e correnti di pensiero nel Risorgimento" (in *Nuove questioni di storia del Risorgimento,* Milan, 1961, 39–130). See also Corrado Raimone: "Liberisti e Liberali: pensiero economico e pensiero politico in Italia avanti il 1861" (*ibid.,* 513–564); and the important essay of Franco Valsecchi: "Le classi popolari e il Risorgimento" (*Cultura e Scuola,* No. 15, 1965, 82–93). For the development of liberalism in Piedmont, see Rosario Romeo: *Dal Piemonte sabaudo all'Italia liberale* (Turin, 1963); in Lombardy, Raffaele Ciasca: *L'origini del 'Programma per l'opinione nazionale italiana' del 1847–1848* (Milan, 1916); Kent R. Greenfield: *Economics and Liberalism in the Risorgimento* (Baltimore, 1934); in Naples, Domenico Demarco: "La nuova borghesia industriale e commerciale del Regno di Napoli" (in *Orientamenti per la storia d'Italia nel Risorgimento,* Bari, 1932, 89–139).

and prospects of liberalism, though Gioberti rejected the philosophy of the French Revolution and insisted on peaceful reform as the only sensible solution to the Italian problem. Mazzini's notion of a centralized republic he discarded as "a solemn utopia."[54]

In many ways more illuminating was the pamphlet of Massimo d'Azeglio, *On the Recent Events in the Romagna* (1845), discussing the serious disorders that had broken out in the Papal States. D'Azeglio was much impressed by O'Connell's Irish Repeal agitation and by the propaganda methods of Cobden's Anti-Corn Law League, which led him to condemn all forms of insurrection and emphasize the possibilities of peaceful reform. This was also the line taken by Cobden himself, when in 1847 he toured Italy. After many talks with intellectuals and businessmen he recommended concentration on reform and the foundation of a customs union which would further economic development.[55]

The liberals looked to King Charles Albert of Piedmont to take the lead in the work of modernization. The king was anything but a liberal, but he was obsessed with the idea of driving the Austrians out of Italy and acquiring the rich provinces of Lombardy and Venetia for Piedmont. He was therefore intent on any proposals for strengthening his state, especially if such proposals made for his popularity in other Italian states as well. In the years before 1848 he therefore built up his army and navy, reformed the finances, encouraged trade by reducing the tariff and negotiating trade treaties with foreign countries, promulgated new law codes, and constructed railroads and port facilities. The moderate liberals had every reason to suppose that before long these economic measures would be followed by political reforms and the introduction of constitutional government.[56]

[54] Giovanni Saitta: *Il pensiero di Gioberti* (2 ed., Florence, 1927); Tullio Vecchietti: *Il pensiero politico di Vincenzo Gioberti* (Milan, 1941), Introd.; and the stimulating discussion in Adolfo Omodeo: *Vincenzo Gioberti e la sua evoluzione politica* (Turin, 1941); also Maurice Vaussard: *De Pétrarque à Mussolini* (Paris, 1961), 50 ff.

[55] Cobden's letter to Marco Minghetti, cited in the latter's *Ricordi* (Turin, 1889), IV, 259–260; Palo Santangelo: *Massimo d'Azeglio, politico e moralista* (Turin, 1937), chap. i; A. Gustarelli: *Massimo d'Azeglio* (Milan, 1938).

[56] The controversial literature on Charles Albert is reviewed by George F. H. Berkeley: "Some Fresh Documents concerning the Italian Risorgimento" (*Proceedings of the British Academy*, XXVI, 1940); Ettore Rota: "Carlo Alberto nel contrastato giudizio della storiografia" (in his *Questioni di storia del Risorgimento e dell'unità d'Italia*, Milan, 1951, 907–932). The interesting observations of the United States minister have been published by Howard R. Marraro: "An American Diplomat Views the Dawn of Liberalism in Piedmont" (*Journal of Central European Affairs*, VI, 1946, 167–192).

Moderate liberalism was given unexpected impetus by the election of Pius IX as pope (June, 1846), which seemed to vindicate Gioberti's hope for the modernization of the church and the renewal of papal leadership in Italy and Europe. Pius was a relatively young man (he was fifty-four) who was known not only for his piety and generosity but also for his progressive attitude and live interest in problems of the day. The fact that he was selected by a cardinalate largely appointed by his conservative predecessor, Gregory XVI, can only mean that a majority of the highest officials of the church had convinced itself that the existing regime was no longer tenable and that reforms were imperative. Pius was elected in the unprecedented time of forty-eight hours, on the fourth ballot, which suggests that the Italian cardinals, concerned for the future of the pope's temporal power, hastened the election so as to avoid contrary pressures from foreign churchmen and more particularly from the Austrian government.[57]

Actually, even the Austrian government welcomed the election of a pontiff who might make much-needed changes in the antiquated government of the Papal States. It may well be imagined, then, with what enthusiasm Pius' elevation was hailed by liberals throughout Italy and indeed throughout Europe. The election of a "liberal pope," hitherto regarded as an impossibility, was indeed an event of European importance.

In retrospect one can only conclude that the hopes placed on the new pope were definitely exaggerated. He did at once proclaim an amnesty for political prisoners and soon set about reforms in the Papal States despite opposition from the papal bureaucracy. Though it is more than doubtful whether he ever intended political reforms such as the admission of laymen to important positions or the establishment of representative government, his administrative reforms, while not revolutionary, were by no means negligible. There was the announcement of plans for four key railway lines, there were reductions in the tariff, there were

[57] Basic treatments are those of Josef Schmidlin: *Papstgeschichte der neuesten Zeit* (Munich, 1934), II, 6 ff., and Roger Aubert: *Histoire de l'Église: le pontificat de Pie IX* (Paris, 1952). Edward E. Y. Hales: *Pio Nono* (New York, 1954) is a competent general biography, while Alberto Serafini: *Pio Nono* (Vatican City, 1958) is a vast collection of documents bearing on Pius' career prior to 1846. On the election of 1846, a fundamental study is Antonio Monti: *Pio IX nel Risorgimento Italiano* (Bari, 1928), which may be supplemented by monographic works such as Alberto Ghisalberti: *Nuove ricerche sugli inizi del pontifico di Pio IX e sulla Consulta di Stato* (Rome, 1939) and Friedrich Engel-Janosi: *Oesterreich und der Vatikan, 1846–1918* (Graz, 1958).

1. Shugborough Park, Staffordshire. Imposing seat of Viscount Anson, built in the classical style.

2. Toddington, Gloucestershire, seat of Lord Sudeley, in strict Gothic style.

3. An estate of the Russian gentry, near Pinsk. (From A. K. Dzhivelegov: *Velikaiia Reforma*, V)

4. A typical French château. Lithograph after Lami.

5. Peasant life. A Russian village near Moscow. (From A. K. Dzhivelegov: *Velikaia Reforma,* II)

6. A Russian military colony. (From A. K. Dzhivelegov: *Velikaia Reforma,* III)

7. An Irish peasant family. Sally throwing potato peels to the pigs. Lithograph by Sibson, from William Carleton: *Traits and Stories of the Irish Peasantry.*

8. The ejectment of Irish peasants, 1848. (*Illustrated London News,* December 16, 1848)

9. French peasants going to work. Etching by J. F. Millet.

10. Planting potatoes. Painting by J. F. Millet. (Courtesy, Museum of Fine Arts, Boston. Shaw Collection)

11. The Landlord's Harem. (Reprinted by permission of The Macmillan Company from *Rural Russia under the Old Regime,* by G. T. Robinson)

12. Rural Dances. (Reprinted by permission of The Macmillan Company from *Rural Russia under the Old Regime* by G. T. Robinson)

13. Russian peasants making rope. (From A.K. Dzhivelegov: *Velikaia Reforma,* III)

14. Residence and factory of M. Henry, near Soissons. Painting by J. B. C. Corot, 1833. (Courtesy of the Philadelphia Museum of Art. W. P. Wilstach Collection)

15. The Harkort Machine Works, in the ruins of Wetter Castle. Painting by Alfred Rethel, 1834. (Courtesy of Demag Aktiengesellschaft, Duisburg)

16. Mr. Orrell's New Cotton Factory at Stockport, 1834. (From Andrew Ure: *The Philosophy of Manufactures*)

17. Early railway coaches, first and second class. (From O. S. Nock: *The Railways of Britain*)

18. The Crystal Palace, 1851, the "Aeronautic View." Built by Joseph Paxton. (From C. H. Gibbs-Smith: *The Great Exhibition of* 1851)

19. King Louis Philippe entertained aboard the Royal Railway Coach by Queen Victoria and Prince Albert. A contemporary print.

20. Discovery of chloroform as an anesthetic, by Sir James Simpson and his staff, 1847. Drawing in the Wellcome Museum.

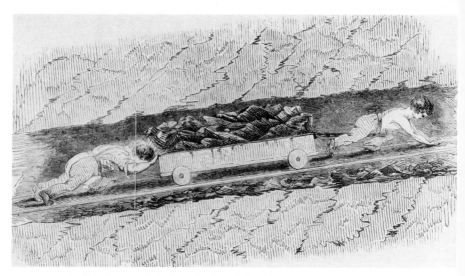

21. Child labor in a British coal mine. "The child in front is harnessed by his belt and chain to the waggon; the two boys behind are assisting in pushing it forward." (From *Children's Employment Commission*: First Report, Mines. 1842)

22. Female labor in a British coal mine. Testimony of Betty Harris, age 37: "I have a belt around my waist, and a chain passing between my legs, and I go on my hands and feet. The road is very steep, and we have to hold by a rope, and when there is no rope, by anything we can catch hold of." (From *Children's Employment Commission*: First Report, Mines. 1842)

23. Spitalfield weavers. The entire family and the loom in one room. (From George Godwin: *London Shadows*, 1854)

24. Power-loom weaving. Drawing by Allom, engraving by Tingle. (From Edward Baines: *History of the Cotton Manufacture*, 1835)

25. Unemployed French workers, with a bourgeois national guard. Print by C. J. Traviès, in *La Caricature,* January 5, 1832)

26. The Drunkard's Children, in the gin-shop. By Cruikshank, 1848.

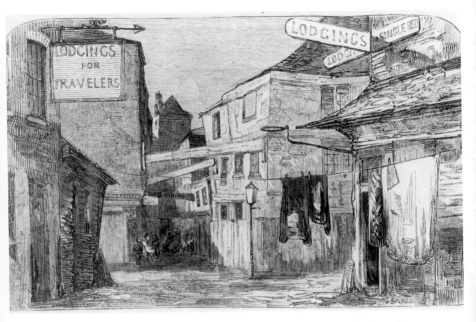

27. Duke Street, Southwark, a cheap London lodging-house district. (From George Godwin: *London Shadows,* 1854)

28. The Croix-Rousse, center of the Lyons silk-weaving industry. Etching by Drevet. (Bibliothèque de Lyon)

29. and 30. French factory children. (From Louis Halphen and Roger Doncet: *Histoire de la société française*)

31. A monitorial school in the 1830's. (From Brian Simon: *Studies in the History of Education*, 1780-1870)

32. Factory children snatching food from a pigsty. (Illustration from Frances Trollope: *Michael Armstrong, The Factory Boy*, 1840, Vol. II)

33. Factory children called to Sunday school by a "serious" factory owner. (Frontispiece of Vol. II of Frances Trollope: *Michael Armstrong, The Factory Boy*)

VOYAGE EN ICARIE

PAR

M. CABET.

FRATERNITÉ.

Tous pour chacun.   Chacun pour tous

☉

SOLIDARITÉ   AMOUR
ÉGALITÉ—LIBERTÉ   JUSTICE   ÉDUCATION
ÉLIGIBILITÉ   SECOURS MUTUEL   INTELLIGENCE—RAISON
UNITÉ   ASSURANCE UNIVERSELLE   MORALITÉ
PAIX.   ORGANISATION DU TRAVAIL   ORDRE
          MACHINES AU PROFIT DE TOUS   UNION.
          AUGMENTATION DE LA PRODUCTION
          RÉPARTITION ÉQUITABLE DES PRODUITS
          SUPPRESSION DE LA MISÈRE
          AMÉLIORATIONS CROISSANTES
          MARIAGE ET FAMILLE
Premier droit,   PROGRÈS CONTINUEL   Premier devoir,
Vivre.   ABONDANCE   Travailler.
          ARTS.
          ☉
À chacun   De chacun
suivant ses besoins.   suivant ses forces.

BONHEUR COMMUN.

PARIS

AU BUREAU DU POPULAIRE, RUE JEAN-JACQUES-ROUSSEAU, 14.

Dans les Départements et à l'Étranger, chez les Correspondants du Populaire

1848

34. Title page of Etienne Cabet's *Voyage en Icarie*, with an appropriate place for every conceivable virtue.

Manifest

DER

Kommunistischen Partei.

Veröffentlicht im Februar 1848.

———

———

Proletarier aller Länder vereinigt euch.

London.

Gedruckt in der Office der "Bildungs-Gesellschaft für Arbeiter"
von J. E. Burghard.
46, Liverpool Street, Bishopsgate.

35. Title page of the original edition of the *Communist Manifesto*, 1848. (From Karl Marx–Friedrich Engels:

36. Irish Famine: Old Chapel Lane, Skibbereen, County Cork. "Not a single house out of 500 could boast of being free from death and fever...." (*Illustrated London News*, February 13, 1847)

37. Exodus of people from Milan on the eve of the Austrian reoccupation, August 5, 1848. (Museo Risorgimento dell'Instituto Mazziano, Genoa)

38. Specter of 1793. Good constitutional bourgeois shocked by the apparition. Woodcut by Daumier, 1834

39. Barbarism and cholera sweeping over Europe, as the Poles resist and the Powers draft protocols. Lithograph by Raffet, 1831.

40. The National Workshops on the Champs-de-Mars, Paris, 1848.

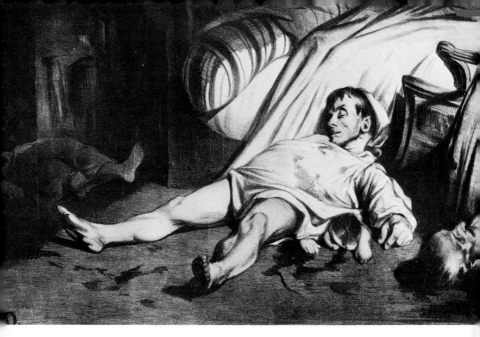

41. Rue Transnonain, April 15, 1834, on the morrow of brutal police action. Lithograph by Daumier, 1834.

42. Cholera. Etching by Daumier.

43. Paris, February, 1848. Hoodlums on the throne of Louis Philippe. Lithograph by Daumier.

44. Louis Philippe: Past, Present, Future. Caricature by Daumier, 1834.

46. Paganini. Painting by Delacroix, 1832. (The Phillips Collection, Washington)

45. Guizot. Caricature by Daumier

47. Napoleon: The Nocturnal Review. Lithograph by Raffet.

48. The remains of Napoleon I en route to the Hôtel des Invalides, December, 1840. Engraving by Raffet.

49. The Four Horsemen of the Apocalypse. Drawing by Cornelius, 1846. (East Berlin: Staatliches Museum)

50. Every Man for Himself. The bourgeois hurrying through a group of starving people to deposit his money in the bank. Lithograph by Charlet, 1840.

51. Rent Day. "Tell your husband to pay up and to stop having so many children. Do I have them? No, yet I have the means to support them." Lithograph by Raffet.

52. Swiss town meeting voting for reform, Appenzell, 1833. Aquatint by Bühler.

53. Bread riots at Stettin, April 24, 1847. "The military, not being able to quell the riot, and the soldiers, officers and general being pelted with mud and stones, it was at length necessary to fire, by which several persons were wounded and two killed." (*Illustrated London News,* May 15, 1847)

54. The Bosporus, looking to the Black Sea from the landing place of the Russians in 1833. (Drawing by Bartlett in Julia Pardoe: *The Beauties of the Bosporus*, 1838)

55. Buda (*Ofen*) and Pest connected by the new Danube suspension bridge. (From Ungarischer Offizier: *Ungarn*, 1850)

56. Pope Pius IX blessing Italian Confederation, 1847. At top level, Charles Albert of Piedmont and Ferdinand II of Naples. At lower right, lesser Italian princes. At lower left, Italia showing Metternich that in unity is strength. (Museo di San Martino, Naples)

57. Battle of St. Jean d'Acre, November 3, 1840. Steamships in action along with frigates. Drawing by J. K. Wilson. (Bibliothèque Nationale, Paris)

58. Paris: "Massacre" on the Boulevard des Capucines, February 23, 1848. Lithograph by Arnout and Adam.

59. Huge barricade at the entrance to the Rue du Faubourg Saint-Antoine, Paris, June, 1848. (*Illustrated London News,* July 1, 1848)

60. Hall of the French National Assembly, May, 1848. (*Illustrated London News,* May 13, 1848)

61. The Frankfurt Parliament in session in the Paulskirche, 1848. (From Paul Wentzke: 1848, *Die unvollendete deutsche Revolution*)

63. A series of barricades in Naples, May 15, 1848. (Drawing by Metania in F. Bertolini: *Storia del Risorgimento*)

62. One of sixty Vienna barricades, May 26, 1848. Lithograph by Pettenkofer. (From Hans Tietze: *Das vormärzliche Wien in Wort und Bild*)

64. Dragoons charging the demonstrators at the Royal Palace in Berlin, March 18, 1848. (*Illustrated London News,* April 1, 1848)

65. Frederick William IV saluting the insurgent dead. Lithograph by Anton Menzel.

66. Madame d'Haussonville, a superb drawing by Ingres. (Fogg Museum, Cambridge)

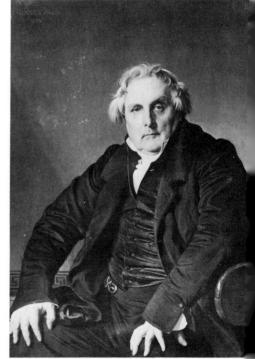

67. M. Bertin, painting by Ingres (1832) of a successful businessman, director of the influential *Journal des Débats*. (Louvre)

Departure of the Volunteers, 1792.
Triomphe, Paris. Sculpture by Rude,
ng by Brun.

69. Giaour and Slave. Painting by Delacroix.
(Fogg Museum, Cambridge)

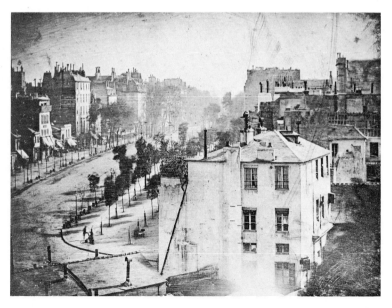

70. The Boulevard du Temple, Paris. One of the earliest daguerreotypes, a present from Daguerre to King Louis I of Bavaria, 1839. (Courtesy of George Eastman House)

71. Crossing the Elbe at Shreckenstein. Painting by Richter, 1837.
(Dresden: Gemälde Galerie)

72. Chopin. Painting by Delacroix, 1837.
(Louvre)

73. Jenny Lind in Meyerbeer's opera
le Diable. (*Illustrated London News,*
1847)

efforts to regulate the price of wheat during the famine years, there was alleviation of the censorship, and finally there were some halting steps in the direction of political innovation. In April, 1847, Pius proclaimed his intention of convoking a consultative assembly, and in July he authorized the formation of civic guards (restricted to members of the propertied class). Then, in October, he appointed a state council (the *Consulta*) and in December named nine responsible ministers, of whom several were laymen. These were welcome measures, and represented real improvements, but they were unsystematic and incomplete and certainly not fundamental enough to warrant the wild enthusiasm with which they were greeted.[58]

Pius, a man of fine presence and much charm, with a beautiful, resonant voice, was received with thunderous applause on his every appearance in public. He seems to have enjoyed popularity and allowed himself to be carried along from one measure to another, each one raising even higher the expectations of his subjects. People began to take things into their own hands. Clubs and newspapers sprang up and added to the confusion of voices. Presently radical elements made their appearance, inspiring much uneasiness on the part of the propertied classes. By the end of 1847, foreign ambassadors in Rome were reporting the situation as getting out of hand, the well-intentioned pope being carried along by popular pressure which he could no longer resist.[59]

[58] Alfonso Ventrone: *L'administrazione dello Stato Pontificio, 1814–1870* (Rome, 1942). There are excellent summaries of the reforms in George F. H. Berkeley: *Italy in the Making* (Cambridge, 1934), II, chap. iv; Domenico Demarco: *Pio IX e la rivoluzione romana del 1848* (Modena, 1947), 11 ff.; R. M. Johnston: *The Roman Theocracy and the Republic, 1846–1849* (New York, 1901) is still well worth reading.

[59] Friedrich Engel-Janosi: "French and Austrian Political Advice to Pius IX, 1846–1848" (*Catholic Historical Review*, XXXVIII, 1952, 1–20); Berkeley: *Italy in the Making*, II, chap. v; Luigi Salvatorelli: *Prima e dopo il Quarantotto* (Turin, 1948), 108 ff.

Chapter Five

STIRRINGS OF LIBERALISM IN THE EAST

I. HUNGARY: LIBERALISM OF THE ARISTOCRATS

To THE east of the German states, Europe in 1830 was still almost exclusively an agrarian area. Roads were few and abominably bad, hence each community lived its own existence and, except for the export of grain and raw materials such as flax, wool, hides, timber and iron, the entire region had no economic ties with the West. Society, then, was strictly traditional. The narrow upper stratum consisted of the aristocracy, a handful of higher nobility and the much larger number of lesser landowners or gentry. Eighty-five or 90 per cent of the population was rural, consisting of serfs or "free" peasants who, though legally liberated, were economically entirely dependent on their lords. Towns were few and small, and almost everywhere had a substantial element of German craftsmen, working independently or in small shops, while a merchant class operated chiefly on the putting-out system. Here and there, notably in Russia, larger cotton mills, using modern spinning equipment, had made their appearance, but they were still so few in number as to be utterly exceptional. In these preindustrial societies the middle class was diminutive and, except for the nascent professional element in the larger towns, as yet without significant influence.

All these countries had suffered an acute economic crisis following the end of the Napoleonic Wars and the collapse of the demand for foodstuffs. The landowning classes became impoverished and, by their efforts to recoup their losses through more intense exploitation of the peasantry, extended the crisis to the lowest strata of the population. When, in 1830–1831, cholera ravaged Eastern Europe, the peasantry in many places turned on the landowners, burned their estates and not infrequently murdered their masters. The situation had in fact become so tense that at least some members of the upper, exclusively literate, class saw the need for reform. These were often nobles who, either as military men or as tourists, had visited England or France, had observed the new industrial society and had come to realize that, without modernization, there was little hope for their own peoples. These enlightened aristocrats introduced improved methods of agriculture on their estates, began to advocate abolition of remaining feudal institutions and the creation of free labor, and presently found themselves enmeshed in the related problems of political change. As far as Eastern Europe is concerned, one can speak as confidently of the liberalism of the aristocrats as, with reference to Central Europe, one can speak of the liberalism of the intellectuals. For in Eastern Europe the intellectuals, with few exceptions, belonged to the upper, landowning classes.

Hungary, which, though part of the Hapsburg Empire, was a separate kingdom ruled by a viceroy (palatine) under the direction of a special Hungarian chancellery in Vienna, provides a clear example of the dawn of liberalism and nationalism in these agrarian societies. The upper classes were almost exclusively Magyar by race, while the majority of the population consisted of Slavs (Croats, Serbs, Slovaks) and Rumanians. There were a few hundred great "magnates," some 30,000 untitled families of the "middle nobility," and perhaps 100,000 families of the "lower nobility," many of whom possessed little or no land and were hardly distinguishable from the peasantry, except in terms of privilege. The vast majority of the population, which, with Transylvania and Croatia, totaled about thirteen million, consisted of landless serfs, though in the towns there were some professional men (lawyers, doctors, teachers and writers) classed as *honoratiores,* that is, men more honorable than peasants but, like the peasants, enjoying no political rights.

The venerable Kingdom of St. Stephen operated on the basis of a hoary "constitution" which gave all the nobility (including the higher clergy) the same prerogatives, the same exemption from taxation, the same "liberty," whatever its particular rank, while the non-noble elements were lumped together as the miserable taxpayers (*misera plebs contribuens,* in the corrupt Latin which still served as the official language). Baron Joseph Eötvös, in a great novel of Hungarian life entitled *The Village Notary,*[1] pictured vividly the great gulf which separated the nobility, however poor and ignorant, from the non-privileged classes, which had no rights and no redress. One of the chief characters of the story is a peasant who was arrested for failure to obey an order of his master and who, in desperation, killed one of his

[1] English translation, in three volumes, published in London, 1850.

tormentors. Forced to become an outlaw, he was captured and tried by "court-martial," that is, by an assembly of the local gentry, who expected to hang him within a couple of hours, without much nonsense about evidence and defense. When, happily, he manages to escape, he presently murders the gentry lawyer who was his chief persecutor.

Hungary was divided into some fifty counties (*Komitat*), each of which had an assembly of the nobility to manage local affairs and send representatives to the national Diet (*Landtag*), meeting periodically at Pressburg (modern Bratislava). The Diet sat as two houses: the Table of Magnates, in which every titled noble had a seat, and the Table of Estates, consisting of the hundred-odd delegates from the county assemblies and voting under instructions from them. Traditionally the Hungarian Diet was the locus of opposition to the efforts of the Vienna government to integrate the Hungarian Kingdom with the rest of the empire. It was the organ of what has been called "feudal nationalism," resistance of the Magyar nobility to all attacks on its sacred privileges.[2]

The story of Hungarian liberalism begins properly with the emergence of Count Stephen (István) Széchenyi, one of the greatest of the Hungarian landowners. As an officer, Széchenyi had spent much of his life abroad and as a result was fluent in German, French, Italian and English, while having only an imperfect acquaintance with the Magyar language and literature. In the course of two visits to England he had been impressed with the progressiveness of the English upper classes and their readiness to engage in trade and industry. He read extensively in British economic literature, from Arthur Young and Adam Smith on, and convinced himself that if Hungary was to survive in the modern world it must abandon the system of privilege, adopt modern methods and undertake fundamental social changes.

Széchenyi was instrumental in founding the Academy of Sciences (1825) and also the Casino, which was intended to be a forum in which the upper classes could discuss the problems of the country. On

---

[2] C. M. Knatchbull-Hugessen: *The Political Evolution of the Hungarian Nation* (London, 1908) is an excellent analysis. See also Zsombor Szász: "The Constitution and the Holy Crown" (in *A Companion to Hungarian Studies*, Budapest, 1943, 305–338). On the social structure, Jerome Blum: *Noble Landowners and Agriculture in Austria, 1815–1848* (Baltimore, 1948), 33 ff.; Gustave Heckenast: "Les roturiers intellectuels en Hongrie, 1780–1848" (*Revue d'histoire comparée*, n.s. VII, 1948, 53–76); B. G. Ivanyi: "From Feudalism to Capitalism: the Economic Background to Széchenyi's Reform in Hungary" (*Journal of Central European Affairs*, XX, 1960, 268–288).

his own estates he turned over the better half of the land to his peasantry, developed the system of crop rotation, drained large areas of land and introduced improved farm implements. He wrote books on the scientific breeding of livestock, and personally supervised the culture of silkworms. Among his basic writings were *Credit* (*Hitel*), a comprehensive critique of the political and social system; *Light* (*Világ*), largely a reply to his critics; and *Stage* (*Stadium*), outlining a program of progressive reform. There was real danger, argued Széchenyi, that the oppressed peasantry might rise in revolt. To lighten their burden all feudal obligations should be liquidated and the peasants should be given land. The upper classes should give up their cherished exemption from taxation and all members of the population should enjoy equality. "Let us open our eyes," exclaimed Széchenyi in his *Credit*. "Let us use our brains! We have got to bestir ourselves, whether we like it or not; and lest we be pushed backward, let us stride forward."[3]

When Széchenyi spoke of the danger of a peasant uprising, he was thinking also of a possible insurrection of the non-Magyar peoples against the Magyar upper classes. His reforms were intended to forestall an upheaval that might destroy the Hungarian state. Therefore he deprecated the age-old struggle against the Vienna authorities and advocated co-operation with them, holding that Hungary by itself was too weak to stand alone, exposed as it was to so many pressures. Unfortunately he got little support for this policy even from Vienna, where his ideas were regarded as visionary and dangerous.[4]

In Hungary itself Széchenyi soon gained influence, especially among the gentry in the county assemblies. He undertook a number of major projects of national interest: inauguration of steamboat traffic on the Danube (1831); blasting of the Danube narrows (the Iron Gates) so as to make the river navigable throughout its course (1834); the building of a suspension bridge from Buda to Pest (see Illustration 55) on opposite sides of the Danube (1832); the importation of machinery and technicians for steam-driven mills; the regulation of the Tisza River and

---

[3] There is an excellent brief appreciation of Széchenyi in English by I. Barta: "István Széchenyi" (*Acta Historica*, VII, 1960, 63–101). The extensive recent literature is reviewed in Fritz Valjavec: "Die neue Széchenyi-Literatur und ihre Probleme" (*Jahrbücher für die Geschichte Osteuropas*, IV, 1939, 90–110).

[4] Julius Miskolczy: *Ungarn in der Habsburger-Monarchie* (Vienna, 1959); George Barányi: "The Széchenyi Problem" (*Journal of Central European Affairs*, XX, 1960, 249–269).

drainage of large areas of inundated land; and finally the construction of the first railway line, from Budapest to Vienna (1838).[5]

Politically, the Diet of 1832–1836 formed a watershed. Széchenyi won an important victory when the Diet reluctantly agreed that nobles like commoners should pay toll on the projected Danube bridge, thus accepting the first breach in the system of privilege. There was also much discussion of the peasant problem, but the upper house was firmly opposed to Széchenyi's program and obstructed progress in the direction of social reform.[6] Nonetheless, some significant steps were taken; peasants were given the right to migrate in search of work, and were given the right to appeal to the courts for the redress of grievances. Feudal dues were more clearly defined and, in 1840, peasants were authorized to own land and, in agreement with their lords, to commute labor dues into rental payments.[7]

The struggle for reform against the entrenched upper classes received added impetus in the 1840's from the appearance on the scene of Louis (Lajos) Kossuth, who presently eclipsed Széchenyi as a political leader. Kossuth was a member of the untitled nobility of northern Hungary and a lawyer by profession. As proxy for one of the great landowners in the Diet of 1832–1836, he had undertaken the publication, in lithograph form, of the debates in the Diet, so as to show up the obstructionist attitude of the upper house. When this practice was prohibited, he arranged with some of his young friends to have abstracts copied by hand and sent to the local assemblies.[8] Kossuth, a brilliant writer as well as an eloquent orator, soon became the spokes-

---

[5] R. W. Seton-Watson: "The Era of Reform in Hungary" (*Slavonic and East European Review*, XXI, 1943, 145–166); Miklos S. Nicolson: "Count István Széchenyi: His Role in the Economic Development of the Danube Basin" (*Explorations in Entrepreneurial History*, VI, 1954, 163–180).

[6] In Eötvös' novel there is a fanatically Anglophile character who, ignoring the brutal exploitation of the peasantry, founded a Society for the Prevention of Cruelty to Animals. But his gentry friends reserved not only the right to flog their own horses but also to inflict physical punishment on peasants when engaged on estate labor.

[7] For the opposition to Széchenyi's proposals, see Erzsébet Andiés: "Der Widerstand der feudalen Kräfte in Ungarn am Vorabend der bürgerlichen Revolution des Jahres 1848" (*Acta Historica*, IV, 1955, 151–210), valuable despite its communist slant.

[8] It was customary for the county assemblies to send to the Diet fifteen or twenty young men as part of their political training. This meant that a large number of eager aspirants crowded the galleries and expressed their sentiments through cheers and boos. It was from among their ranks that Kossuth recruited his collaborators. See Knatchbull-Hugessen: *Political Evolution*, I, 289; George Barányi: "The Hungarian Diet of 1839–1840" (*Slavic Review*, XXII, 1963, 285–303).

man for the reformers. But presently the government interfered. Kossuth was convicted of seditious activity and spent four years in prison, during which time he learned English and read extensively in the English, French and American political and economic literature. He was to demonstrate in the sequel a truly impressive grasp of modern theories and practices.[9]

Kossuth's program, like that of his predecessor, was pronouncedly nationalistic as well as liberal. He was as much intent on strengthening the position of the Magyars and their state as he was on redressing social grievances. But this important aspect of his policy can be better treated in a later context and is therefore reserved for discussion in Chapter VIII. We return, then, to domestic issues in the 1840's, when Kossuth, having served his sentence, became editor of the *Budapest Gazette* (*Pesti Hirlap*). Through this influential political journal he was able to propagate the advanced ideas of western liberalism, including the principles of American democracy. Lardner's *History of the United States* had appeared in Magyar translation in 1836 and Sparks' *Life of Washington* in 1841. To this must be added the Hungarian translation (1841–1843) of Tocqueville's famous and influential *Democracy in America*. Where Széchenyi had drawn his inspiration from aristocratic England, Kossuth looked more and more across the Atlantic for his ideal of good government and a free society.[10]

Széchenyi was much concerned lest Kossuth force the issue of reform to the point of revolution. In his own journal, *The Present* (*Jelenkor*), he criticized and warned. Soon the press conflict destroyed the united front of the liberal elements and fanned class antagonisms. Kossuth declared that if reform could not be effected with the support of the aristocracy, it would be carried through without the aristocracy or even in opposition to it. Hungary, he insisted, must have economic

[9] Dénes A. Jánossy: "Great Britain and Kossuth" (*Archivum Europae centro-orientalis*, III, 1937, 53–190); Michel Bariska: "Les lectures françaises de Louis Kossuth" (*Nouvelle revue de Hongrie*, XXVIII, 1935, 167–173); Otto Zareck: *Kossuth* (London, 1937), 68 ff.

[10] T. Baráth: "Histoire de la presse hongroise" (*Bulletin of the International Committee of the Historical Sciences*, VII, 1935, 243–266); Walter Raichel: *Das ungarische Zeitungswesen* (Berlin, 1939), 18 ff.; Eugene Pivány: *Hungarian-American Historical Connections* (Budapest, 1927), 32 ff.; Imre Lukinich: "American Democracy as Seen by the Hungarians of the Age of Reform, 1830–1848" (*Journal of Central European Affairs*, VIII, 1948, 270–281); Louis J. Lekai: "Historiography in Hungary, 1790–1848" (*ibid.*, XIV, 1954, 3–18).

as well as political independence. He followed closely O'Connell's masterly campaign for repeal of the union of Britain and Ireland, and reported at length in his newspaper on the organization and progress of Cobden's Anti-Corn Law League. His critical articles reveal an amazing understanding of British politics and of the inwardness of the free-trade movement. Castigating "the cowardly selfishness of the landowner class," he urged his countrymen to learn their lesson, warning that the lower classes would fight against starvation and in their desperation would show no respect for property rights. Inspired by Friedrich List's *National System of Political Economy* (Hungarian translation, 1843), he agitated for the development of industry and in 1844 founded the Protective Association, the members of which undertook to buy and use only Hungarian products, to work for the introduction of new industries, for the development of Fiume as a Hungarian national port, and for the construction of key railway lines.[11]

In Hungary as in other countries the more radical reformers tended to gain at the expense of the moderates in the years before 1848. Baron Eötvös, himself a member of the upper house but a confirmed advocate of drastic reform, had traveled in the West and had met Lamartine, Hugo and other French intellectuals. In 1840 he had published well-informed articles on poverty in Ireland and on the emancipation of the Jews. Again and again he inveighed against oppression and warned that it could not succeed in the long term. His novel *Hungary in 1514* (1847) was inspired by the peasant rising in Galicia in 1846 and recounted the great Peasants' War in Hungary in 1514, again an admonition to the diehard conservative elements.[12] Eötvös did his utmost to prevent the break between Széchenyi and Kossuth but, having failed, lined up with the more advanced group, as did the influential politician Francis Deák. By 1848 Széchenyi had definitely seen his day. To many activists he appeared a somewhat pompous, garrulous old gentleman, hoping against hope to remake his country without serious ructions.

---

[11] See the interesting "Reports on the Hungarian Parliament of 1843–1844" (*South Eastern Affairs,* I, 1931) by J. A. Blackwell, who, married to a Hungarian lady and fully conversant with the Magyar language, was in close touch with political figures in both camps. See also the illuminating quotations from Kossuth's articles in E. H. Haraszti: "Contemporary Hungarian Reaction to the Anti-Corn Law Movement" (*Acta Historica,* VIII, 1961, 381–403); Gottfried Fittbogen: *Friedrich List in Ungarn* (Berlin, 1942).

[12] D. Mervyn Jones: *Five Hungarian Writers* (Oxford, 1966), 160 ff.

Kossuth, as the representative of the impoverished gentry and the intellectuals, was from the nature of things in the better position to rally popular support. But, having imbibed the advanced ideas of England, France and the New World, he was carried far beyond what the circumstances and developments of Hungary warranted. There was, after all, small chance that the government would seriously entertain a program in Hungary which for years it had been actively combating in Austria. On the eve of 1848 the situation was fraught with danger. The Hungarian Diet was defiant while the Vienna government was adamant. An explosion was all but inevitable. Small wonder that Széchenyi was appalled by the genii he had conjured up.[13]

2. RUSSIA: ORIGINS OF THE INTELLIGENTSIA

Czar Nicholas I (1825–1855) was one of the dominant figures of the period spanned by this volume. Described by the American minister, Andrew D. White, as "the most majestic being ever created," tall, handsome, energetic and courageous, he was much admired by his fellow rulers for his firmness, devotion to duty and insistence on unquestioning obedience. Convinced of his own superior wisdom, he demanded of his subjects, high as well as low, acceptance of his decisions. To have one's own ideas, much less to express them, he regarded as tantamount to rebellion.[14]

Nicholas was by training a soldier and by nature a martinet. He loved nothing better than to prescribe the uniforms and the manuals of his army, or to watch the parade of his splendid guard regiments. But despite his troops (some 800,000 in number) and his cavalry and infantry guards (over 50,000), he spent his life in constant dread of social and political upheaval. On the one hand was the threat of another

---

[13] The liberal program of 1847 is well summarized in Knatchbull-Hugessen: *Political Evolution*, I, 306. On the position of the Vienna government, see Hanns Schlitter: *Aus Oesterreichs Vormärz*, III, *Ungarn* (Vienna, 1920), 49 ff.; Miskolczy: *Ungarn in der Habsburger-Monarchie*. The intellectual trends are well treated in Julius von Farkas: *Die ungarische Romantik* (Berlin, 1931) and *Der ungarische Vormärz: Petöfi's Zeitalter* (Berlin, 1943).

[14] Among Russian biographies, Mikhail A. Polievktov: *Nikolai I* (Moscow, 1918) and A. E. Presnyakov: *Apogei Samoderzhaviia: Nikolai I* (Leningrad, 1925) rate high. Leonid Strakhovsky: *L'Empéreur Nicolas I et l'esprit national russe* (Louvain, 1928) is generally favorable. Interesting also is Constantin de Grunwald: *Tsar Nicholas I* (New York, 1955). Theodor Schiemann: *Geschichte Russlands unter Kaiser Nikolaus I* (Berlin, 4 vols., 1904–1919) is a basic scholarly study of the entire reign.

major peasant insurrection. The great revolt of Pugachev, with all its horrors, was hardly fifty years in the past, the discontent of the serfs was well known, and the secret police was continually reporting the peasants as expecting a new Pugachev. So great was the latent social tension that Nicholas not only recognized the urgent need for reform but on one occasion warned the landowners against discussing social questions during meals, lest the domestic serf servants hear too much and develop dangerous ideas. That the czar's fears were justified was demonstrated by the great uprising of the crown serfs in the military colony at Novgorod in July, 1831, which required major troop action for its suppression, or the peasant insurrection in Kazan province in 1842, which involved some 130,000 serfs.[15]

Nicholas' fear of popular insurrection was matched by his dread of revolutionary ideas from the West. His succession to the throne had been endangered by the Decembrist Insurrection, an attempt by young noblemen to introduce constitutional government along western lines and so end the autocratic rule of the czars. Furthermore, Nicholas was confronted in 1830–1831 with the formidable revolution in Poland, which was suppressed only at the cost of large-scale campaigns. He was convinced that there was on foot a vast international conspiracy designed to subvert the existing political and social order. He regarded it as his foremost duty to frustrate such designs and therefore bent every effort to prevent the infiltration of dangerous literature from the West and to suppress all potential opposition movements.

To ensure against an uprising of the masses, Nicholas had all malcontents, all potential peasant leaders, drafted into the army. There the men were drilled till they all but sank in their tracks. Even minor breaches of discipline were punished by merciless floggings, so severe as to be not infrequently fatal. True, inhumane treatment was at this time still normal in all European armies, but the Russians were notorious for their brutality and certainly their practices went far beyond anything known in the West. In any case, Russian troops were so beaten into submission that they could be used regularly to stamp out

15 On the police reports, see Karl Stählin: *Geschichte Russlands* (Berlin, 1935), III, 308 ff. For the rest, Alan D. Ferguson: "The Russian Military Settlements" (in Alan D. Ferguson and Alfred Lewin, eds.: *Essays in Russian History . . . Dedicated to George Vernadsky,* Hamden 1964, 107–128).

peasant revolts, as a result of which, again, hundreds to thousands of offenders were whipped before being sent in chains to Siberia. During Nicholas' reign, unrest in the country became endemic, but no uprising was allowed to attain dangerous proportions. There was no new Pugachev terror.[16]

The problem of forestalling organized revolution was far more complex, the more so as the czar, as a sequel to the Decembrist uprising, felt unable to trust the nobility, on which his predecessors had relied for the administration of the country. Nicholas, himself by blood a German, therefore appointed Germans (mostly landowners from the Baltic provinces) to key positions, and looked to his personal friends and trustworthy generals to serve on special commissions or staff his own chancellery. The imperial chancellery was constantly enlarged and was encouraged to take over many of the functions of the traditional ministries. The most notorious section soon came to be the Third, the primary mission of which was to supervise foreigners traveling in Russia and to watch, arrest and send into exile all suspicious persons. Each year some 8,000 to 10,000 persons were shipped off to Siberia, often without knowledge of their alleged offense, to spend their lives in the mines or as colonists.[17]

The Third Section also played a prominent role in literary censorship, an activity in which the czar took a personal interest. Because of his concern the censors felt obliged to err, if at all, on the side of harshness, lest they find themselves, along with the offending author, in the guardhouse. The records of the censorship show that not only the writings of western liberals and socialists were banned but that books about the United States were excluded on principle, while even presumably innocent foreign literature, such as *Peter Paley's Juvenile Tales for Boys and Girls,* met with disfavor. As for Russian authors,

---

16 Hugh Seton-Watson: *The Russian Empire, 1801–1917* (Oxford, 1967), 230 ff. On the use of the army, see John S. Curtiss: *The Russian Army under Nicholas I* (Durham, 1965), chap. xiv, and the informative but all-but-forgotten book by Charles F. Henningsen (published anonymously): *Revelations of Russia in 1846* (London, 3 ed., 1846) which is exceptionally full on military affairs.

17 August Freiherr von Haxthausen: *Studien über die inneren Zustände . . . Russlands* (3 vols., Berlin, 1847–1852). I use the somewhat abridged English edition (*The Russian Empire,* London, 1856), I, 240 ff., 311; II, 24, because it brings the study of the land reform down to 1850.

there was hardly one, even among the greatest or most conservative, who did not suffer at the hands of the censors.[18]

Like Prince Metternich, Czar Nicholas was soured on the schools and universities, which he thought should be devoted to the training of officials but which he suspected of being hotbeds of subversive thought. Education in the western sense was still new in Russia, being chiefly an innovation of Alexander I. In 1825 there were six universities, some sixty high schools (gymnasia) and about 370 county schools, in addition to 360 private schools and 600 parish schools. There was no thought of educating the lower classes, which was regarded as suicidal. The peasantry was, in fact, excluded even from the county schools, which were reserved for children of the gentry and civil servants. The universities, it is true, were open to all classes, but were naturally a preserve of the nobility.

In the matter of education the czar was confronted by a serious dilemma. The need for competent officials at the higher grades was a crying one and this meant that the universities must provide high-grade instruction. Hence there was no alternative to permitting young professors to complete their training abroad, mostly at German universities, and to allowing them to import from the West the books and materials required for proper instruction. Considering his distrust of the traditional nobility, one might have thought that Nicholas would have encouraged the enrollment and training of non-noble students. But the danger of thus raising up a "university Pugachev" (the phrase was Maistre's), that is, an educated peasant leader, appeared too great. Actually, systematic efforts were made to restrict the number of non-noble students and eventually even to hold the total enrollment of each university to about three hundred.[19]

Highly influential in the formulation of educational policy and indeed of the entire official philosophy was Count S. S. Uvarov, who in 1833 was appointed minister of public instruction, a post which he

[18] Avram Yarmolinsky: "A Note on the Censorship of Foreign Books under Nicholas I" (*N.Y. Public Library Bulletin*, XXXVIII, 1934, 907–910). The classic account is Mikhail K. Lemke: *Nikolaievskie Zhandarmy i Literatura*, 1826–1855. (St. Petersburg, 1908), and in English, Sidney Monas: *The Third Section: Police and Society under Nicholas I* (Cambridge, 1961), particularly chap. iv.

[19] Seton-Watson: *Russian Empire*, 19 ff.; William H. E. Johnson: *Russia's Educational Heritage* (Pittsburgh, 1950), chap. vi; Nicholas Hans: *The Russian Tradition in Education* (London, 1963), 20 ff.

retained until 1849. Uvarov was a scholar and writer of international standing, an enlightened cosmopolitan and a free thinker, but a man convinced of the need for "dams to hold up the flow of new ideas into Russia." In a famous memorandum which earned him his appointment, he argued thus:

Our common obligation consists in this, that the education of the people be conducted according to the supreme intention of our August Monarch in the joint spirit of Orthodoxy, Autocracy and Nationality. I am convinced that every professor and teacher, being permeated by one and the same feeling of devotion to throne and fatherland, will use all his resources to become a worthy instrument of the government and to earn its complete confidence.[20]

Uvarov's formula was to become the slogan of the Russian autocracy to the end of its days and was to provoke considerable difference of opinion as to exactly what was meant by "nationality" (*narodnost*), which Russian historians speak of as "official nationality" and others have translated as "national principle." It would appear that Uvarov had in mind the Russian national genius, as expressed in language and literature and social institutions. In later writings he explained that autocracy and serfdom were "two parallel forces which had developed simultaneously and which reposed on the same historic principle and therefore had the same legality." Russian society was clearly different from that of the West. It was Uvarov's contention, fully supported by Nicholas, that Russians should be loyal to their own institutions and maintain their faith in Russia's mission.[21]

Under Uvarov's direction a new statute for the universities was issued in 1835. The appointment of professors was henceforth vested in the ministry of education. Inspectors were appointed to supervise both professors and students. Eventually, under the impact of the revolutions of 1848, further restrictions were imposed. The curricula were purged of philosophy and the social sciences, and more weight was given to the classics and to vocational training. Students were obliged to wear uniforms for easier identification, and to have their hair cut in a certain style. They were forbidden to frequent coffeehouses or read

[20] Michael T. Florinsky: *Russia* (New York 1953), II, 797 ff.; Nicholas V. Riasanowsky: *Nicholas I and Official Nationality in Russia* (Berkeley, 1959), 64 ff.

[21] Paul Milioukov, Charles Seignobos and Louis Eisenmann: *Histoire de Russie* (Paris, 1932), II, 777 ff.; Riasanowsky: *Nicholas I*, 124 ff., 140, 168 ff.

foreign newspapers. In each university there was to be an inspector of morals. Eventually the regulation and supervision were carried to such extremes that Uvarov himself requested permission to resign.[22]

Nicholas' determined efforts to forestall a peasant upheaval, his attempts to stifle revolutionary ideas and influences, and his role in 1848–1849 as the "gendarme of Europe" have certainly tended to obscure the constructive aspects of his reign. The czar was an admirer of Peter the Great and aimed to carry on, albeit gradually, the work of modernizing Russia. A man of great energy, he slaved away at the stupendous task of governing the largest and most populous as well as one of the most backward countries in Europe. He was forever traveling, at breakneck speeds, from one end of his domains to another, forever investigating, reprimanding, correcting. He held before him, as an ideal, the integrity and efficiency of the Prussian bureaucracy, but all his efforts foundered on the ineptitude and depravity of his own officialdom. The educated nobility, distrusted by the czar, tended more and more to shirk government service, with its inefficiency and endless red tape. This meant that the bureaucracy fell more and more into the hands of the impoverished gentry and the lower clergy. Being miserably paid (as we are told over and over again by Russian writers), they resorted to systematic bribery and corruption, far beyond what was known in other countries, with the possible exception of the Danubian Principalities. "Public corruption is so great," wrote A. V. Nikitenko, a famous diarist and himself a bureaucrat, "that concepts of honor and justice are considered a sign of pusillanimity or romantic exaltation." Russian literature of the period is replete with stories of official incompetence, chicanery and graft, while the travel accounts of foreigners provide mountains of further evidence.[23]

It so happens that the great novelist Nicholas Gogol more or less unintentially provided a most vivid picture of Russian officialdom and its place in society. Gogol lived in the bureaucratic world, for he was a subordinate clerk in a government office, earning hardly enough

---

[22] A. S. Nifontow: *Russland im Jahre 1848* (Berlin, 1954), 258, 266 ff., 311 ff.

[23] A classic account of the bureaucracy is in V. O. Kliuchevsky: *A History of Russia* (London, 1931), V, chap. xx. See also Florinsky: *Russia*, II, chaps. xxix and xxx on local administration, and Samuel Kutscheroff: "Administration of Justice under Nicholas I" (*American Slavic and East European Review*, VII, 1948, 125–138); Marc Raeff: "The Russian Autocracy and Its Officials" (*Harvard Slavic Studies*, IV, 1957, 77–92); Simone Blanc: "La pratique de l'administration russe dans la première moitié du XIXe siècle" (*Revue d'histoire moderne et contemporarine*, January–March, 1963).

to meet his most pressing needs. He was a frustrated, introverted person, constantly in conflict with censors and embittered with life in general. His stories (e.g., "The Diary of a Madman" or "The Overcoat") lampoon the red tape of the system and reveal the abuse of poor pen-pushing underlings by their superiors. His masterpieces, the comedy *The Inspector-General* (1836) and the novel *Dead Souls* (1843), are even more eloquent testimony to the sordid scheming and cynical corruption of officialdom. Gogol wrote both the play and the novel as studies in human nature, but they were taken at once as brilliant satires on Russian society and made a deep impression. The author was so shocked by the reaction to his play that he left Russia and but rarely returned home on visits.[24]

Nicholas was furious whenever a case of bribery or other misconduct came to his attention. He would make an example of offenders, but the battle was an all but hopeless one. The czar does deserve credit, how-ever, for sponsoring the codification of the laws, about which little or nothing had been done since 1649. Count Michael Speransky as chief of the Second Section of the imperial chancellery was entrusted with the project. His plan was to supplement the collection of the laws by a digest of those laws still in force and, finally, to draft a new code, based on the digest but allowing for new concepts derived from the require-ments of modern life. This last item was vetoed by the czar, but the collection of laws was published in forty-five volumes in 1830 and the digest in 1833. The latter was of particular importance because Speran-sky managed to introduce new definitions and concepts which to some extent met the need for a new code. Thus he laid the foundation for improved administration of justice. How badly this was needed is suggested by the fact that in 1842 over three million cases were still pending in various tribunals of the empire.[25]

Nicholas saw that sooner or later even the problem of serfdom would have to be tackled. He was aware of the fact, as he said, that there were very few good and conscientious landowners, but many

[24] Among recent studies are Janko Lavrin: *Nikolai Gogol* (London, 1951); V. Setschkareff: *N. V. Gogol* (Wiesbaden, 1953); David Magarshak: *Gogol* (London, 1957), 88, 132 ff. See also Adolf Stender-Petersen: *Geschichte der russischen Literatur* (Munich, 1957), II, 164 ff.; Ettore Lo Gatto: *Storia della Letteratura Russa* (5 ed., Florence, 1964), 294 ff.; Ronald Hingley: *Russian Writers and Society* (London, 1967), 185 ff.

[25] Kliuchevsky: *History of Russia,* IV, 180; Kutscheroff: "Administration of Justice"; Marc Raeff: *Michael Speransky* (The Hague, 1957), chap. xi.

who were only average and even more who were bad. He also admitted that serfdom in its existing state was an evil felt by all and evident to everyone. But he had to acknowledge that to touch it would prove even more disastrous. The landowners were overwhelmingly opposed to emancipation, or at least to emancipation linked to a land settlement. They foresaw nothing but chaos in the countryside. It was, of course, a fact that there was for the time being no administrative system to deal with the problems that would be created by so fundamental a reform. Nicholas appointed numerous secret committees to study various aspects of the problem, but felt unequal to attacking the question of privately owned serfs. However, almost half of the peasant population consisted of crown or state serfs and in their regard reform was possible without touching the rights of the landowner.

In 1833 Nicholas appointed to the Fifth Section of his chancellery Count Paul D. Kiselev, a man known for his organizing ability, his incorruptibility and his breadth of view. In 1837 Kiselev was made chief of a new Ministry of Imperial Domains and was given a free hand to work out reforms that became all the more urgent with the severe crop failures of 1839–1840 and the warnings of the secret police that "the unbelievable fury" of the population might at any time burst into flames.

For twenty million crown peasants Kiselev introduced what can only be called revolutionary changes. These peasants were declared "free inhabitants residing on crown lands," and the lands were redistributed so as to provide about thirty acres for each family. The poll tax was changed to a land tax, and recruitment for the army was henceforth to be by lot. An entirely new system of local administration was set up: standard village communities of fifteen hundred souls were organized; village assemblies and tribunals were given charge of peasant affairs; schools were opened; model farms, warehouses and savings banks were established; free vaccination for smallpox and free instruction in midwifery provided for. Despite many obstacles, substantial progress was made in the implementation of these drastic changes. In 1850 the eminent German agronomist, Baron Haxthausen, could declare that the program was "the greatest event which has occurred in Russia since the time of Peter the Great."[26]

Kiselev hoped that private serfs, too, might be given their personal

---

[26] Haxthausen: *Russian Empire.* The basic account was written by Kiselev's collaborator A. Zablotskii-Desyatovskii: *Graf Kiselev i ego vremia* (4 vols., St. Petersburg,

freedom and in addition an allotment of land for which they could pay the landowner in cash or labor. But the opposition of the nobility was such that nothing was achieved beyond the law of 1842, which authorized landowners to make agreements with their serfs along the lines of Kiselev's proposals. It stands to reason that but few nobles availed themselves of this authorization. The situation of the private serfs remained substantially unchanged and when, in 1848–1849, crop failures and a new cholera epidemic threatened a major crisis, Nicholas ordered all disturbances ruthlessly suppressed and issued instructions to all governors to see that the established relations between owners and serfs should be rigorously upheld.[27]

Under Nicholas' system of surveillance and repression, no opposition movement such as the Decembrist was even remotely possible. Members of the nobility and writers such as Pushkin resented deeply the harsh treatment meted out to the idealistic revolutionaries of 1825, but could not hope to avenge them. Enlightened circles were discouraged and depressed. Pushkin himself felt harassed by the censorship and disgusted with the whole atmosphere of repression. "We must admit," he wrote in 1836, "that our social life is a sad affair, that the absence of public opinion, the indifference toward everything that spells *duty, justice,* and *truth,* the cynical disdain for thought and for the dignity of man, are truly desolating."[28] The great writer, after completing his masterpiece *Eugene Onegin* in 1832, devoted himself to a history of the great Pugachev insurrection of 1774. His fine novel, *The Captain's Daughter* (1836), was a by-product of his history and provided a vivid and realistic picture of Russian provincial life in the eighteenth century, as well as a truly impressive account of the great peasant upheaval.[29]

1882), and there is a wealth of information in A. K. Dzhivelegov, ed.: *Velikaiia Reforme: russkoe obshchestvo i krestianskii v proshlom i nastoiashchem* (6 vols., Moscow, 1911). Standard modern treatments are Nikolai M. Druzhinin: *Gosudarstvennie krestiae i reforma P. D. Kiseleva* (2 vols., Moscow, 1946 1958) and Ia. Linkov: *Ockerki istorii krestianskogo dvizheniia v Rossii v 1825–1861* (Moscow, 1952). See also Olga Crisp: "The State Peasants under Nicholas I" (*Slavonic and East European Review,* XXXVII, 387–412).

[27] Geroid T. Robinson: *Rural Russia under the Old Regime* (New York, 1932), 62; Jerome Blum: *Lord and Peasant in Russia* (Princeton, 1961), 545 ff.; Nifontov: *Russland im Jahre 1848,* chap. iii.

[28] Ernest J. Simmons: *Pushkin* (Cambridge, 1937), 382.

[29] Michael Karpovich: "Pushkin as an Historian" (in Samuel H. Cross and Ernest J. Simmons, eds.: *Centennial Essays for Pushkin,* Cambridge, 1937, 181–200).

Pushkin was mortally wounded (1837) in a duel with a Frenchman who had persisted in paying attention to his wife. Lest his funeral lead to popular demonstrations, the government had his body hurried off for secret burial in a monastery. This mean procedure inspired Pushkin's great contemporary, the poet Michael Lermontov, to circulate in manuscript a scathing poem; "The Death of a Poet," for which he was exiled to the Caucasus. This did not prevent him from becoming an ever more outspoken opponent of the regime. His *Sashka* (1836) satirized the demoralized provincial gentry, while his prose masterpiece, *A Hero of Our Time* (1839), depicted the tragic failure of Pechorin, a man of strong nature and great ability, completely frustrated by lack of any appropriate outlet for his creativity.[30]

Lermontov, like Pushkin, was a victim of the duel (1841). Both great writers expressed the prevalent malaise and discontent with Nicholas' repressive regime. So also did the "circles" which flourished in the 1830's and 1840's, especially in Moscow. These were informal groups, largely academic, resting on personal friendship and common interest in ideas and problems. In the 1830's they met to discuss the French and German literature brought back by those who had lived or studied in the West. The all-absorbing interest was in German Romantic literature and especially in the idealist philosophy of Schelling.

In any country other than Russia these "circles" would have had hardly more significance than similar gatherings for an evening of chamber music. But in Russia the educated elite was so small and the background of intellectual achievement so thin that the "circles" loom as bright centers in a world of intellectual repression. They are the more important because they presaged the rise of the intelligentsia. This word in the thirties was used simply to express "intelligence" or "culture," but in the 1860's came to mean a small, self-conscious elite which, because of its deep attachment to Russia, found intolerable the backwardness and barbarism in which it lived.[31]

30 Leonid I. Strakhovsky: "Pushkin and the Emperors Alexander I and Nicholas I" (*Canadian Slavonic Studies*, I, 1956, 16–30); Simmons: *Pushkin*, chap. xviii; Henri Troyat: *Pushkin* (New York, 1950), 374 ff. On Lermontov, see Janko Lavrin: *Russian Writers* (New York, 1954), chap. vi. Also Stender-Petersen: *Geschichte der russischen Literatur*, II, 130 ff.; Lo Gatto: *Storia della Letteratura Russa*, 216 ff., 284 ff.
31 On the difficult concept of intelligentsia, see Martin Malia: "What Is the Intelligentsia?" (in Richard E. Pipes, ed.: *The Russian Intelligentsia*, New York, 1961, 1–18); Alan P. Pollard: "The Russian Intelligentsia: the Mind of Russia" (*California Slavic*

In the 1860's and 1870's the intelligentsia was indeed a rootless and alienated group, consisting to a considerable extent of non-noble elements (*raznochintsi*) that had only just begun to emerge in the 1830's and eventually became leaders of the intellectual opposition on both political and social grounds. But it would doubtless be a mistake to carry the above notions back into the reign of Nicholas. The early circles consisted, with very few exceptions, of young noblemen who were unwilling to serve in either the army or the bureaucracy. They were, most of them, "superfluous men," holding no positions of responsibility, living from the proceeds of serf labor and rarely concerning themselves even with the management of their estates. They were agreed that serfdom was the root evil of their society, but only very few were prepared to liberate their serfs. For the most part they were content to meet in their comfortable Moscow homes, discuss Schelling's cosmic philosophy or search for the eternal harmony underlying the chaos of the empirical world.[32]

Three members of the early circles were of such importance for the development of the revolutionary movement that they call for at least brief special mention. Alexander I. Herzen, possibly the most eminent Russian intellectual of the nineteenth century and a literary figure of European stature, was the illegitimate son of a wealthy aristocrat and his German housekeeper. His father was devoted to him and surrounded him with tutors and books. Widely read in French and German literature, Herzen entered the University of Moscow in 1829 and soon became imbued with the ideas of Saint-Simon. He fell a prey to the secret police, who stamped him "a daring free-thinker, extremely

---

Studies, III, 1964, 1–32). Marc Raeff: *Origins of the Russian Intelligentsia: the Eighteenth Century Nobility* (New York, 1966) attempts to establish a direct line of descent from the Enlightenment through the Decembrists to the midcentury. For a detailed, critical analysis of this thesis, see Michael Confino: "Histoire et psychologie: à propos de la noblesse russe au XVIIIe siècle" (*Annales*, XXII, 1967, 1163–1205).

[32] The classic account is Mikhail O. Gershenzon: *Istoriia molodoi Rossii* (Moscow, 1908, 1923), chap. iii. See further the brilliant essay by Isaiah Berlin: "A Marvellous Decade" (*Encounter*, IV, 1955, 27–39); Peter Scheibert: *Von Bakunin zu Lenin* (Leiden, 1956), 3 ff.; E. Lambert: *Studies in Rebellion* (New York, 1957), 30 ff., and the specialized studies of Edmund Kostka: "At the Roots of Russian Westernism: N. V. Stankevitch and His Circle" (*Slavic and East European Studies*, VI, 1961, 158–176); Vladimir C. Nahirny: "The Russian Intelligentsia" (*Comparative Studies in Society and History*, IV, 1962, 403–435); Edward J. Brown: *Stankevich and His Moscow Circle, 1830–1840* (Stanford, 1966).

dangerous to society." In 1834 he was banished to a remote provincial town, where he spent the next six years as a minor official.[33]

On his return to Moscow, Herzen became a devoted student of the Hegelian philosophy, but continued also his studies of French socialist thought. Going gradually beyond purely philosophical questions, he became engrossed in the problems of individual rights and liberty, and soon adopted the contempt for bourgeois society characteristic of western radicals. What was needed, he now argued, was an entirely new social order based on liberty and justice. Thus Herzen illustrates the gradual transition from interest in philosophical abstractions to concern for concrete political and social problems. In 1847 he finally secured permission to travel abroad, whence his *Letters from France and Italy* (1847) and his essays *From the Other Shore* (1848–1849) reflect his dislike of bourgeois society and his rejection of ideas of gradual reform. The failure of the radical movements of 1848–1849 then led him to develop the notion of Russia's mission to lead in the total revolution which would usher in the new society.[34]

The most important phase of Herzen's career was to come in the 1850's and 1860's, when, from his exile in London, he served as spokesman for the revolutionary elements in Russia. At that same time his friend, Michael Bakunin, became a European figure and the founder of modern anarchism. Bakunin was a man of keen critical mind and inexorable logic, but at the same time undisciplined, turbulent and unscrupulous. Like Herzen the son of well-to-do aristocrats, he was a member of the Moscow circles in the 1830's. In 1840 he went to Berlin to study the Hegelian philosophy and, like the Young Hegelians, soon drifted into extreme radicalism. With an insatiable thirst for influence and power, he became a revolutionist almost for the sake of revolution. "He wanted to set on fire as much as possible," says one

[33] The standard biography is by Iakov E. Elsberg: *A. I. Gertsen, zhizn i tvorchestvo* (3 ed., Moscow, 1956). Raoul Labry: *Alexander Ivanovich Herzen* (Paris, 1928) is an admirable study of Herzen's thought, to which the chapter in Alexandre Koyré: *Etudes sur l'histoire de la pensée philosophique en Russie* (Paris, 1950) is intended as a critical supplement. Of recent studies, see Jan Kucharzewski: *The Origins of Modern Russia* (New York, 1948), chap. iv; Richard Hare: *Pioneers of Russian Social Thought* (Oxford, 1951), chap. vii; and above all, Martin Malia: *Alexander Herzen and the Birth of Russian Socialism, 1812–1855* (Cambridge, 1961).

[34] Isaiah Berlin: "Herzen and Bakunin on Individual Liberty" (in Ernest J. Simmons, ed.: *Continuity and Change in Russian Soviet Thought*, Cambridge, 1955, 473–499); Henri Granjard: "Alexandre Herzen à la croisée des chemins, 1842–1846" (*Revue des études slaves*, XXXV, 1958, 57–76).

commentator. "The thought of any kind of chaos, violence, upheaval he found boundlessly exhilarating." In one of his most closely reasoned essays, *Reaction in Germany,* which appeared pseudonymously in the Neo-Hegelian *German Yearbooks* (1842), he called on democratic forces to destroy the existing order and create a new life. Denouncing mere reforms and compromise solutions, he exalted destruction: "The passion for destruction is also a creative passion."[35]

In some ways more interesting for this period than either Herzen or Bakunin was Vissarion Belinski, the son of a poor army doctor, a man who grew up in want and illness and in 1848 succumbed to tuberculosis at the age of thirty-seven. As a non-noble, dependent on his writings for a living, Belinski was the forerunner of the *raznochintsi* (the "classless people") who were to become the leaders of the intelligentsia. Expelled from the University of Moscow for writing a drama about serfdom, Belinski joined one of the Moscow circles and devoted himself to philosophical studies until, in 1840, he moved to St. Petersburg and began to write on social conditions and problems. The time had not yet come to talk of politics and constitutions, he argued, for the immediate problems are injustice and oppression and the most urgent needs are education and social regeneration. Coming more and more under the influence of western socialist thought, Belinski violently attacked those who remained attached to a despicable past. Only a new Peter the Great, only a social cataclysm, could clear the air and usher in the new age of equality and fraternity.

Belinski's last outburst was in reply to Gogol's *Selections from a Correspondence with Friends* (1847), in which the great novelist apologized for his earlier "thoughtless and immature" works, reasserted the divine character of the autocracy and defended the Orthodox Church. His solution for the peasant problem was to have the landowners explain to the serfs that it was God's decree that they should labor; that the masters were acting solely as God's agents. To this Belinski replied in a scathing letter, widely circulated in manuscript, but published only years later. Russia, he declared,

Needs no sermons—she has heard enough of them—nor prayers—she has repeated them too often. She needs the awakening in the people of a sense

[35] Edward H. Carr: *Michael Bakunin* (London, 1937), 24, 107; Benoît P. Hepner: *Bakounine et le panslavisme révolutionnaire* (Paris, 1950), 152 ff.; Thomas Masaryk: *The Spirit of Russia* (London, 1919), chap. xiii; Scheibert: *Von Bakunin zu Lenin,* chap. viii.

of their human dignity, lost for so many centuries amidst the dirt and the refuse. She needs rights and laws conforming not with the preaching of the Church, but with common sense and justice; and she needs their strictest possible observance.[36]

As disciples of the German Romantic thinkers and of Saint-Simon, the members of the Russian circles were much interested in historical evolution and in the philosophy of history. They were fascinated by the questions of Russia's past, of Russia's current place among the nations, and of Russia's future mission. Of the utmost importance, therefore, was the anonymous publication in 1836 of the first and most influential of Peter J. Chaadaev's *Philosophical Letters,* of which the last five were published only in 1935. The author, an unassuming scholar, had spent many years in Western Europe and, far from becoming infected by liberal or radical doctrines, had convinced himself that the greatness of England and France rested chiefly on the depth of religious feeling and the role of the churches. Guizot's emphasis on the Christian basis of European civilization made a deep impression upon him. In his first *Letter,* written in 1829 and circulated in manuscript before publication in 1836, he castigated the Russians for their backwardness:

Leading an isolated life in the world, we have given nothing to the world; we have taught it nothing; we have not contributed a single idea to the sum total of human ideas; we have not in any way taken a share in promoting the progress of human thought, and every element of that progress which has come our way, we have marred and distorted.

Russia, he continued, is falling rapidly behind: "The world is undergoing a transformation, while we vegetate in our hovels of wood and clay." The trouble was that Russia lacked the tradition and unifying influence of the Roman Catholic Church. If the country was to save itself, it must imitate the West and go through the same cycle of development.

Herzen wrote later that this *Letter* was like a shot ringing out on a dark night and, again, that it had broken the ice after the freeze brought on by the failure of the Decembrists.[37] Whether Chaadaev's

---

[36] For excerpts of Belinski's letter, see Hans Kohn: *The Mind of Modern Russia* (New Brunswick, 1955), 135 ff. On Belinski's thought, the appreciation in Masaryk: *Spirit of Russia,* chap. x, is still outstanding, but see also Hare: *Pioneers of Russian Social Thought,* 35 ff.; Herbert E. Bowman: *Vissarion Belinski* (Cambridge, 1954).

[37] Herzen: *Du développement des idées révolutionnaires en Russie* (Paris, 1851), 109 ff.

assertions were exaggerated or not, his thesis was provocative to the last degree. Czar Nicholas and all conservatively minded people were profoundly shocked and concluded that the *Letter* was worthy only of a lunatic. The negligent censors, who had permitted publication, were punished and Chaadaev himself declared insane. Confined for some months to his home, he then wrote *The Apology of a Madman,* which again circulated only in manuscript. In this he reiterated his earlier contentions and castigated those who held that Russia should stand by its past and its institutions. However, he now introduced a note of wry optimism: the West had fulfilled its historic role; it might well be reserved for Russia to point the way to a new and higher Christian spirituality.[38]

Though Chaadaev was unable to enlist much support for his advocacy of Roman Catholicism, he certainly focused attention on the problems of Russia's cultural future. While throughout the period prior to 1848 the "Westerners," those who saw salvation only in the adoption of western ideas and institutions, in continuance of the policy initiated by Peter the Great, rallied many followers, there emerged in the Moscow salons and circles a group of "Slavophiles," who regarded the West, for all its achievements, as in decline—"wrapped in the mantle of death." The future, they believed, belonged to young and vigorous Russia. It therefore behooved Russians to stand fast by their own institutions.

The leader of this group and a well-known figure in the Moscow circles was Alexis Khomiakov, a wealthy landowner who had traveled widely in Western Europe and commanded the English, French and to a less extent the German language. Khomiakov was a man of immense erudition and far-ranging interests, a poet, an artist, an inventor, but above all a brilliant and formidable controversialist. He soon gathered about him a number of able intellectuals, such as the

---

[38] Excerpts of the *Letter* and the *Apology* are given in Kohn: *Mind of Modern Russia,* 38 ff. The basic study of Chaadaev is by Mikhail O. Gershenzon: *P. J. Chaadaev, zhizn i myshlenie* (St. Petersburg, 1908). There is an exhaustive later study by Charles Quénet: *Tchaadaev et les "Lettres Philosophiques"* (Paris, 1931), and readable biographical studies by Martin Winkler: *Peter Jakovlevic Caadaev* (Berlin, 1927), and E. Moskoff: *The Russian Philosopher Chaadaev: His Life and His Epoch* (New York, 1937). The recently published letters are analyzed in Heinrich Falk, S.J.: *Das Weltbild Peter J. Tschaadajews nach seinen acht "Philosophische Briefe"* (Munich, 1954). See further Masaryk: *Spirit of Russia,* II, chap. viii; Koyré: *Etudes sur l'histoire de la pensée philosophique,* 19–102; Alexander von Schelting: *Russland und Europa* (Berne, 1948), 26 ff.

Kireevski brothers and the Aksakov brothers. Building on the Romantic nationalism that had made its appearance in literature during the 1820's, they idealized the items of Uvarov's formula (Orthodoxy, Autocracy and Nationality) and more particularly those two most peculiarly Russian institutions, the Orthodox Church and the peasant village community (*mir*). They were not hostile to the West, which in fact they knew better than most "Westerners," but they firmly believed in Russia's mission and were convinced that it could be realized only through its own institutions.[39]

Neither the Westerners nor the Slavophiles had a single agreed program. Nor was there at first any basic antagonism between them. Both groups came from the same social milieu, both had the same education, both were devoted to Russia and had faith in Russia's mission, both were critical of the existing regime and hostile to the bureaucracy, both were convinced of the need for social reform. For a time at least, members of the two groups continued to meet in the same gatherings and debate their differences in a friendly way. But with the 1840's came much greater journalistic activity and often the written word hurt more than the spoken. By the mid-forties there began personal attacks and ridicule. Thereafter reconciliation was all but impossible.

The dispute about Russia and its place in the modern world was fanned by the appearance, in Western Europe, of a spate of books highly critical of the Russian people and the regime. Best known, though based on only a short visit, was the well-written, disillusioned work of the Marquis de Custine, *La Russie en 1839* (5 vols., Paris, 1843).[40] It ran through many editions and was translated at once into English and German. Everywhere in the West it was taken at face value, for Russophobia—fear of the northern colossus—had been de-

---

[39] Albert Gratieux: *A. S. Khomiakov et le mouvement slavophile* (2 vols., Paris, 1939) and Peter K. Christoff: *An Introduction to Nineteenth Century Russian Slavophilism*, I, *A. S. Xomjakov* (The Hague, 1961) are both first-rate scholarly treatments, which may be supplemented by the more specialized studies of Nicholas V. Riasanowsky: *Russia and the West in the Teaching of the Slavophiles* (Cambridge, 1952) and Edward C. Thaden: *Conservative Nationalism in Nineteenth Century Russia* (Seattle, 1964), Part I.

[40] Others, of equal or even greater interest, were Charles F. Henningsen's anonymous *Revelations of Russia, or the Emperor Nicholas and his Empire* (2 vols., London, 1844); La Croix's *Les mystères de la Russie* (5 vols., Paris, 1844); Ivan Golovin's *La Russie sous Nicholas I* (Paris, 1845); Nicholas I. Turgenev's *La Russie et les Russes* (3 vols., Paris, 1847).

veloping rapidly, fanned as it was by the Polish *émigrés* and by the march of Russian power in the Near East. Custine reinforced the idea that the Russians were "regimented Tatars," that "nowhere in the world do people enjoy less real happiness than in Russia," and that Nicholas' regime, riddled by corruption, had reduced the country to lifelessness.

Naturally the Custine book and its successors outraged the czar, who had government scribes prepare one blast after another in the effort to discredit foreign critics. Above all, Slavophiles and Westerners were bound to part company on the issue. Khomiakov was on the verge of opening up with his heaviest literary artillery, but Herzen praised Custine's book, despite some of its errors: the essence of his views were correct: "that terrible society and that country are Russia."[41]

In the years approaching 1848 two incidents occurred that reflected new trends in the opposition. In the spring of 1847 the secret police at Kiev arrested and sent to St. Petersburg the members of a secret Society of Saints Cyril and Methodius. This group, founded in 1845 by a young professor, Nicholas Kostamariv, was devoted to the cultivation of Ukrainian history and literature, but in addition formulated a political, national program. Hostile to Russian rule, it was opposed to autocratic government and favored the abolition of all class distinctions. The ideal was a republican government based on complete equality, providing for the abolition of serfdom and the development of popular education. Beyond that came the national program: Russia was to be divided into a number of independent republics, of which the Ukraine should be one. These republics were then to be united with other Slav peoples in a federated republic in which a congress (*rada*) and an elected president should manage the affairs of the union. Obviously this national program was of major importance in the history of later Pan-Slavism,

41 Labry: *Herzen*, 269; Kucharzewski: *Origins of Modern Russia*, 23 ff., 35 ff.; Oscar Hammen: "Free Europe against Russia, 1830–1854" (*American Slavic and East European Review*, XI, 1952, 27–41); John H. Gleason: *The Genesis of Russophobia in Great Britain* (Cambridge, 1950); Heinrich Stammler: "Wandlungen des deutschen Bildes vom russischen Menschen" (*Jahrbücher für Geschichte Osteuropas*, n.s., V, 1957, 271–305); Raymond T. McNally: "Das Russlandbild der Publizistik Frankreichs zwischen 1814 und 1843" (*Forschungen zur osteuropäischen Geschichte*, VI, 1958, 82–169); Roger Portal: "Russia as Seen by the French in the 18th and First Half of the 19th Centuries" (in Evelyn Acomb and Marvin L. Brown, Jr., eds.: *French Society and Culture since the Old Regime*, New York, 1966, 177–203).

but it should not, as it frequently has, obscure the political radicalism of the Society.[42]

Most outstanding among those associated with Kostomariv was Taras Shevchenko, greatest of Ukrainian poets, at that time a young man of thirty who had already made a reputation as a Ukrainian Robert Burns. Shevchenko was a former serf who had seen and experienced systematic oppression and humiliation at first hand. His poetry was stamped by intense love of his native country and its stirring Cossack past, but also by profound pity for the sufferings of the common people and hatred for the oppressive Russian czarism. Shevchenko was unusually well read in the literature of the western nations and from early years could be described as a thoroughgoing democrat and revolutionary. In his poems he even went so far as to attack the imperial family specifically and to criticize Russian policy in the Caucasus and elsewhere.[43]

The members of the Society were tried in the capital under the personal supervision of the czar. Many of them were sentenced to prison terms, to be followed by exile. Among them Shevchenko was considered the most objectionable. He was condemned to indefinite military service as a private soldier, without right of promotion. Nicholas added in his own hand "with express prohibition of all writing and drawing." The misery of the great poet under this regime may well be imagined. Not until 1857 was he pardoned by Nicholas' successor.[44]

Even harsher was the treatment meted out to the members of the Petrashevski circle in St. Petersburg. Michael V. Petrashevski was an official of the foreign office, a man of broad interests and education and by nature a propagandist. Deeply imbued with the doctrines of French socialism (see Chapter VII), he convinced himself that the Russian village community or *mir* could be transformed into something like

[42] Omeljan Pritsak and John S. Reshetar, Jr.: "The Ukraine and the Dialectics of Nation-Building" (*Slavic Review*, XXII, 1963, 224–255) stress the political side. See further W. E. D. Allen: *The Ukraine, a History* (Cambridge, 1940), 240 ff.; Dmytro Doroshenko: *History of the Ukraine* (Edmonton, 1939), 544 ff.; Clarence A. Manning: *The Story of the Ukraine* (New York, 1947), chap. xiii; Ivan Mirtschuk: *Geschichte der ukrainischen Kultur* (Munich, 1957), 47 ff., 158 ff.

[43] H. Koch: *Die ukrainische Lyrik, 1840–1940* (Wiesbaden, 1955); C. H. Andrusyshen and Watson Kirkconnell: *The Poetical Works of Taras Shevchenko* (Toronto, 1964), with an excellent introduction; Alfred Jensen: *Taras Schewtschenko* (Vienna, 1916), a solid literary study; Dmytro Doroshenko: *Taras Shevchenko* (Winnipeg, 1936); Clarence A. Manning: *Ukrainian Literature* (Jersey City, 1944), chap. v.

[44] Sidney Monas: *Third Section*, 260 ff.

Fourier's phalanstery and that, through a network of such communities, a new social order could be founded. Hostile to the autocracy and the church, Petrashevski dreamed of an eventual federation of democratic republics. From 1845 onward a fluctuating group of officials, officers and intellectuals met weekly at his home, where there was a large collection of western political and socialist literature and where there was always lively discussion not only of the host's favorite Fourierism but of the emancipation of the serfs and other current problems.

The Petrashevski group was essentially, like other circles, a debating club to which many notables, such as the budding novelist Fedor Dostoievski, resorted from time to time. The European revolutions of 1848 inspired a few members to strike a revolutionary note, but all plans for propaganda in the army or among the peasants were nipped by the intervention of the police, which considered this "intoxication with visionary utopias" as so dangerous that anything might be expected of these people.[45] On the night of April 22, 1849, the police arrested all those present at Petrashevski's soirée. Over two hundred other suspects were apprehended during the next months. After prolonged examination seventy-two were convicted, of whom twenty-one were sentenced to death for "intent to subvert the existing laws of the fatherland and the state order." One of these was Dostoievski, whose offense was having read aloud to the group Belinski's famous reply to Gogol.

As it turned out, the death sentences were intended chiefly as a warning. On December 22, 1849, the convicted men were prepared for execution and marched to the scaffold. Then, by prearrangement, a messenger arrived with news of the czar's clemency: the death sentences were commuted to prison terms in Siberia. It was a grim farce that was to leave a deep mark on the victims, and indeed to color the attitude of the ensuing revolutionary movement.[46]

And so Nicholas I managed to suppress all conceivably dangerous

[45] Report of one police agent, quoted by Kucharzewski: *Origins of Modern Russia*, 95 ff.

[46] On Dostoievski, see Edward H. Carr: *Dostoevsky* (Boston, 1931), chap. iv. On the larger problem, see Vasilii I. Semevskii: *M. V. Butashevich–Petrashevskii i Petrashevtsi* (Moscow, 1922); Georges Sourine: *Le Fourierisme en Russie* (Paris, 1936), chaps. ii–vi; Iogenson I. Zilberfarb: *Sotsialnaia filosofiia Sharlia Fure i ee mesto v istoriia sotsialisticheskoi mysli* (Moscow, 1964); Nicholas V. Riasanowski: "Fourierism in Russia; an Estimate of the Petrasevcy" (*American Slavic and East European Review*, XIII, 1953, 289–302); Frederick I. Kaplan: "Russian Fourierism of the 1840's" (*ibid.*, XVII, 1958, 161–172); Monas: *Third Section*, 248 ff.

movements and to escape the revolutionary storm that swept over Europe. Russia, wrote the poet Fedor Tyuchev, stood like a great rock in the sea, unmoved by the tempest that raged about. But it was only by a miracle that Russia escaped, for by 1848 the problem of serfdom had become truly acute and the country was on the verge of upheaval. Furthermore, the opposition was no longer strictly aristocratic. The "unclassified men" such as Belinski were coming to the fore, and the circles, which originally had concerned themselves chiefly with the ultimate problems of nature and man, had begun to come to grips with immediate problems of political and social life. Westerners and Slavophiles alike hated the autocracy and recognized the urgent need for a settlement of the peasant problem. The Society of Saints Cyril and Methodius introduced the theme of reorganization along national, republican lines, while the Petrashevtsy went all the way, condemning western liberalism and free competition (which hardly existed in Russia), and reaching out for a new society along communist lines. This increasingly formidable opposition Nicholas managed still to master with the help of his troops and secret police, but he was only postponing the Russian crisis. He had settled nothing.

3. THE DAWN OF LIBERALISM IN THE BALKANS

The Balkan area, with the exception of the newborn Greek Kingdom, was in 1830 still under the direct or indirect rule of the Turks but was, at the same time, the theater of conflicting interests of the great powers, Russia, Britain, Austria and France. Following Russia's defeat of the Turks in the war of 1828–1829, the czar's troops remained until 1834 in occupation of the Danubian Principalities—Moldavia in the north and Wallachia in the south—which lay on the left bank of the lower Danube. Though technically still part of the Ottoman Empire, the two provinces were self-governing under Turkish and Russian protection. The two principalities, the nucleus of the later Rumanian state, were fertile territory, traditionally devoted to the herding of cattle and sheep but becoming increasingly cultivated and grain-growing. Under the enlightened governorship of Count Paul Kiselev, order was restored and some progress made in overcoming the devastations of the armies and the ravages of plague and cholera.

The czar felt unable to annex the two principalities, as his predecessor had annexed Bessarabia, because of the certain opposition of

Austria and Britain. He therefore arranged to ensure his authority by endowing each principality, separately, with a constitution which, in order to avoid a hated word, was to be called an Organic Statute. These statutes were drafted by small commissions of notables and eventually approved by general assemblies of revision composed of the great landowners and high ecclesiastics. The great landowners or nobles (great boyars) were, as elsewhere in Eastern Europe, a small minority of the population. In Moldavia, out of a population of 1,500,000, they numbered only 880, while in Wallachia, with a population of 2,500,000, they counted about 1,200.[47] There were a few thousand other persons exempt from taxation (priests, monks, soldiers, officials, etc.), while the mass of the population were serfs, working the land which they did not own.

It was the Russian policy to work with the high nobility, whom Kiselev described as "an avid and fanatical oligarchy."[48] Provision was therefore made, in the organic statutes, for each principality to have an assembly of boyars with extensive legislative and administrative power. The membership of these assemblies was heavily weighted in favor of the great boyars as against the more numerous lesser boyars or gentry. The assemblies, in turn, were to elect one of their number to be prince (hospodar) for life. The prince was empowered to dissolve the assembly (with Russian and Turkish approval) and, through his control of appointments, could force compliance from the boyars. There was, then, a precarious balance between the boyar assembly and the elected prince. In practice the last word was with the Russian consul general.[49]

The first princes, Michael Sturdza in Moldavia and Alexander Ghika in Wallachia, were Russian nominees and throughout were careful not to offend the czar. Ghika proved himself less adroit than Sturdza and was replaced in 1843 by George Bibescu. The latter, like Sturdza, had received part of his education in the West. Both used their position to amass enormous wealth, but also launched various progressive under-

[47] Felix Colson: *De l'état présent et de l'avenir des Principautés de Moldavie et de Valachie* (Paris, 1839), chap. iv.

[48] Pompiliu Eliade: *Histoire de l'esprit public en Roumanie au XIXe siècle* (Paris, 1905), I, 127 ff.

[49] R. W. Seton-Watson: *History of the Roumanians* (Cambridge, 1934); Barbara Jelavich: *Russia and the Rumanian National Cause* (Bloomington, 1959), chap. i; and for analysis of the statutes: Crisan T. Axente: *Essai sur le régime répresentatif en Roumanie* (Paris, 1937).

takings to improve administration, develop foreign trade and encourage education. But in the large the Principalities remained the preserve of a few thousand landed families. The boyars spent much if not most of their time in Bucharest, at that time a sprawling collection of hovels intersected by a few avenues on which were located the residences of the rich and the shops which catered to them by importing the latest fashions and luxuries from the West. Like the Russian nobility, the boyars had taken on a veneer of French culture, but only a few of them were really educated and fewer yet showed even a rudimentary sense of civic virtue. As a class they were notoriously corrupt, immoral, extravagant and irresponsible; so much so that even the Russian representatives were shocked.[50] As for the peasants, their lot had been fixed in the statutes. Their right to the use of the land was carefully restricted and they were obliged to work on the estates of the boyars far more days per year than ever before.[51]

Yet even this unregenerate society was not immune to the infiltration of western ideas. In 1824–1826 Constantine Golescu, a wealthy boyar, had traveled extensively in the Germanies and France and left a record of his impressions.[52] He was amazed by the prosperity of the West and marveled at the honesty and efficiency of the administration, as well as the energy and orderliness of the people. All of which led him to plead with his countrymen in behalf of the illiterate, exploited, utterly wretched Rumanian peasantry. On his return home Golescu became a patron of literature and an advocate of popular education.[53]

The elementary schools, such as they existed at that time, were of the

[50] Charles and Barbara Jelavich: *The Education of a Russian Statesman* (Berkeley, 1962), being the memoirs of the later Russian foreign minister, de Giers. Vivid accounts of Bucharest life in the midcentury are in Edouard Thouvenel: "La Valachie en 1839" (*Revue des Deux Mondes*, XVIII, 1839); A. Bally: "Le voyage de Cochelet dans les Principautés roumaines, 1834–1835" (*Revue historique du Sud-Est européen*, VIII, 1931, 276–294); Anatol N. Demidoff: *Voyage dans la Russie méridionale . . . par la Hongrie, la Valachie et la Moldavie* (Paris, 1840–1842), I, 116 ff., 131, 144, 184–185; Lord de Ros: *Journal of a Tour in the Principalities . . . in the Years 1835–1836* (London, 1855), 126 ff.

[51] Colson: *De l'état présent*, II, chap. i, paints a vivid picture of peasant misery under the statutes. There are several excellent modern studies: Ifor L. Evans: *The Agrarian Revolution in Roumania* (Cambridge, 1924); David Mitrany: *The Land and the Peasant in Roumania* (New Haven, 1930); and especially Marcel Emérit: *Les paysans roumains depuis le traité d'Andrinople, 1829–1864* (Paris, 1937).

[52] Published in 1826 in Budapest.

[53] Eliade: *Histoire*, 171 ff.; Nicolas Iorga: *Idées et formes littéraires françaises dans le Sud-Est de l'Europe* (Paris, 1924), 87 ff.

most primitive type, meeting in barns, without benches or books, sadly lacking not only in teachers but in pupils. The boyars, as a class, held that education of the lower classes was pure folly. For some time to come any movement for reform would have to come from the upper classes, from men such as Golescu. There was, in Bucharest, a school founded earlier in the century by French refugees and in this College of Saint Sava a good many boyar children were given a French education, whence they were called *Bonjourists*. The French influence, in turn, found further expression through the works of poets such as Lamartine and Hugo and through liberal and democratic ideas that gradually took hold among the rising generation.[54]

The program and activity of Széchenyi in Hungary also played a role in stimulating Rumanian liberalism and nationalism. As the Hungarians resented the domination of Vienna, so the Rumanians chafed under the despotic methods of the princes, who were regarded as mere tools of the Russians. One of the liberal leaders, Ion Campineanu, actually went to Paris and London to enlist foreign aid in revising the statutes, but on his return home in 1840 was thrown into prison for his pains. His associate, the historian Nicolas Balcescu, who was more radical than most of the opposition group, tried to organize a revolutionary movement aiming at abolition of the boyar privileges, at distribution of the land among the peasants, and establishment of a democratic republic. But he was unable to rally much support for so extreme a program and, besides, the princes soon drove the opposition underground.[55]

In 1843 the liberals founded a secret society, Fraternity, which operated under the cloak of local literary societies and engaged in negotiations with Polish emissaries who were working for a Polish-Rumanian alliance against Russia. Somewhat later, in 1845, a group of Rumanian students in Paris, inspired by the lectures of Michelet, Quinet and Mickiewicz, organized a Society of Rumanian Students in

[54] Eliade: *Histoire,* 220 ff.; Nicolas Iorga: *Histoire des relations entre la France et les Roumains* (Paris, 1918), chap. viii; Petre V. Hanes: *Histoire de la littérature roumaine* (Paris, 1934), 78 ff.; John C. Campbell: "The Influence of Western Political Thought in the Rumanian Principalities, 1821–1848" (*Journal of Central European Affairs,* IV, 1944, 262–273).

[55] Vasile Maciu: "De la conception sociale et politique de Nicolae Balcescu" (*Nouvelles études d'histoire,* I, 1955, 373–389); M. Losano: "Nicolae Balcescu" (*Rivista storica italiana,* LXXVIII, 1966); Cornelia Bodea: "Actions prérévolutionnaires roumaines avant 1848" (*ibid.,* III, 1965, 271–284).

Paris, of which Lamartine became the patron. Thoroughly imbued with the radical doctrines of democracy and nationality, some of these young men took an active part in the Paris barricade fighting of February, 1848.[56]

Outwardly the forces of opposition at that time presented a united front. But the further developments of the revolutionary year (to be taken up in a later chapter) were to reveal here, as in Hungary and elsewhere, the fundamental divergence of view between the moderate, liberal and the radical, democratic elements. In the first place it must be emphasized that only relatively few boyars were involved in the movement. Those that were had a common objective: to put an end to Russian influence and to break the power of the princes, the puppets of the Russians. They all dreamed, too, of a Rumanian national state which would unite the two principalities and join to them the province of Transylvania, which was under Hapsburg rule, was claimed by the Hungarians as part of the crown of St. Stephen, but was actually inhabited largely by Rumanians. Beyond that point agreement ceased. A radical minority, of which Nicolas Balcescu, C. A. Rosetti and Ion Bratianu were prominent members, had become converted not only to the principles of democracy and republicanism but also to the ideas of socialism. As in other countries it was this left wing that was the activist element. The question remained whether, conditions being as primitive as they were in the Principalities, such drastic changes could be attempted without running into the powerful opposition of conservative vested interests.

The Principality of Serbia was, like the Danubian Principalities, tributary to the Ottoman Empire, but completely self-governing and, after 1829, under Russian protection. It was a remote, mountainous territory, without a native aristocracy and with little social differentiation. The notables were village chieftains engaged for the most part in the raising of pigs, which were herded by the peasantry in the vast oak forests and eventually exported to Budapest or Vienna.[57]

---

[56] Marceli Handelsman: *Czartoryski, Nicolas I et la question du Proche-Orient* (Paris, 1934), chap. iv; Hélène Vacaresco: "La mystique nationale roumaine aux environs de 1848" (*Revue d'histoire diplomatique*, XLII, 1929, 8–19); Vasile Maciu: "Un centre révolutionnaire roumain dans les années 1845–1848: la Société des Etudiants Roumains à Paris" (*Nouvelles études d'histoire*, III, 1965, 243–270).

[57] Milorad Stanojevich: *Die Landwirtschaft in Serbien* (Halle, 1913), 78 ff.; Jozo Tomasevich: *Peasants, Politics and Economic Change in Yugoslavia* (Stanford, 1955), 28 ff.

By an imperial rescript of August 29, 1830, the Turkish sultan recognized, as hereditary prince of Serbia, Milosh Obrenovich, the leader of the Serbian insurrection of 1815, who had already been chosen prince by a Serbian assembly. In accordance with the czar's desire, the prince was to rule with the assistance of a senate or council of notables, appointed for life, much as in the Danubian Principalities. But Milosh was not the man to dance to the tune of the Russians, and at the same time the czar took less interest in Serbia than in the Danube provinces. Milosh was able to ignore instructions from Constantinople or St. Petersburg and to rule like a Turkish pasha. He brooked no insubordination, treated all officials as though they were slaves and subjected even the highest to punishment of the most humiliating kind. Those who defied him were harried from the land and their property confiscated. Even the high clergy were treated as subalterns, mere agents of the prince's desires. Milosh arranged and dissolved marriages and arbitrarily disposed of inheritances. He thought nothing of interrupting divine service, of ordering the church choir to end its cacophonous efforts, or of upbraiding the priest for his long-winded sermon. For the rest he exploited his position for personal gain by enclosing the choicest forests for his swine and setting up what amounted to a monopoly of the export trade in hogs as well as of the salt trade. It was common knowledge that Milosh was the wealthiest man in the Balkans and that he had acquired huge estates in neighboring Wallachia as a hedge against the future.[58]

What happened in Serbia in the 1830's and 1840's had nothing to do with western liberalism. It was simply a duel between Milosh and the notables, who considered themselves in no way inferior to the prince and resented his monopoly of power and trade. By 1835 a group of them forced Milosh, by threat of insurrection, to call an assembly and agree to the establishment of a senate with extensive executive and

---

[58] Important contemporary accounts of Milosh's rule are those of his Italian physician Barthélemy S. Cunibert: *Essai historique sur les révolutions et l'indépendance de la Serbie, 1804–1850* (Leipzig, 1855), II; Wilhelm Richter: *Serbiens Zustände unter dem Fürsten Milosch* (Leipzig, 1840), 66 ff.; Leopold von Ranke: *A History of Servia and the Servian Revolution* (London, 1847), 391 ff.; Andrew A. Paton: *Servia, the Youngest Member of the European Family* (London, 1845), 264 ff., 320 ff. Among more modern treatments, see Saint-René Taillandier: *La Serbie au XIXe siècle* (2 ed., Paris, 1875), 291 ff.; Harold W. V. Temperley: *History of Serbia* (London, 1917), 209 ff.; Emile Haumant: *La formation de la Yougoslavie* (Paris, 1930), chap. xxv; Jean Mousset: *Le Serbie et son église* (Paris, 1938), 107 ff.; Dragutin P. Subotić: "The Serbia of Prince Milos" (*Slavonic Review*, III, 1924, 156–165).

legislative power and control. Milosh, however, induced the sultan to protest against this "French" constitution and the project had to be shelved.[59]

Presently the "constitutional" issue in Serbia became a matter of international import. Palmerston, the British foreign secretary, obsessed with the determination to counter Russian influence wherever possible, had in May, 1837, sent Colonel George L. Hodges to Belgrade as consul, with instructions to induce Milosh to undertake necessary reforms so as to strengthen his position with respect to the oligarchs. Hodges had been chosen, not because of his knowledge of the country, for he had none, but because he was "firm, resolute and bold in character." He and Milosh soon became friends, which naturally roiled the opposition. Some of the "patriots" fled to Bucharest and thence appealed to the czar for support. Nicholas, troubled by the activities of Hodges, decided to send to Belgrade one of his young adjutants, Prince Vasili Dolgoruki, who arrived on the scene in October and had several secret interviews with Milosh. The details are still obscure, but Dolgoruki insisted that Milosh agree to the appointment of the senate envisaged in the Turkish rescript of 1830.

While the European public was amused by the spectacle of Britain supporting the despot while Russia was pressing him to accept a "constitution" which would deliver him into the hands of his enemies, Milosh had no alternative but to yield to Russian demands, for he could not put much faith in British assurances of "powerful support" in the event of his resisting. To console Hodges and the British he promulgated decrees declaring the person and property of all citizens inviolable, abolishing all forced labor and declaring all trade freely open to all. Before long he was then obliged to accept a new Turkish rescript establishing a system like that in the Danubian Principalities. A senate, consisting of high clergy and "persons of the greatest consideration among the Servians," was to afford the (unwilling) prince its aid and incidentally to exercise extensive power over the administration and budget.[60]

59 Milan Vladissavlievich: "Développement constitutionnel de la Serbie" (*Revue d'histoire politique et constitutionnelle*, II, 1938, 529–550); Traian Stoianovich: "The Pattern of Serbian Intellectual Evolution, 1830–1880" (*Comparative Studies in Society and History*, I, 1959, 242–272).

60 See the basic, archival study by Stevan K. Pavlowitch: *Anglo-Russian Rivalry in Serbia, 1837–1839* (Paris, 1961), which brings out the futility of British efforts to compete with Russia for influence in Serbia.

Milosh, finding the new system intolerable, abdicated on July 13, 1839, in favor of his son Milan, who was almost immediately succeeded by his brother Michael, a boy of sixteen. Though it should have been easy for the "Defenders of the Constitution" to manage the young prince, they were not satisfied until they had driven him into exile. They then chose as his successor Alexander Karageorge, son of the hero of the initial Serbian revolt against the Turks in 1804. Alexander was a man to their taste—easygoing and generally uninterested in politics—but his election met at first with protests from Czar Nicholas, who objected to the unceremonious way in which one dynasty was replaced by another and, besides, suspected the leaders of the oligarchs to be working with Polish *émigré* revolutionaries. The czar insisted on new elections, by a new national assembly which operated under the guidance of a Russian-Turkish commission. Alexander's election was ratified, but he was not given hereditary right to the throne or even a specified term of office.[61]

Alexander made no attempt to undo the system of oligarchical dominance which thenceforth prevailed in Serbia as in the Danubian Principalities. Like its counterparts, the Serbian regime was soon discredited by corruption and factional strife. The evidence suggests that among the populace there was much sentiment for the return of Milosh, who, though oppressive, seemed preferable to the new bosses. But Russia stood firmly by the "Defenders of the Constitution" and opposed all efforts at change.

In all this there was not, it is clear, even a scintilla of liberalism in the western sense. Yet in the 1840's Serbia began to experience some western influence. Some progress was made in modernizing the administrative and judicial institutions and there was a marked expansion of agriculture. Elementary education made considerable advances and there was at least a modest development of higher education. The University of Belgrade was founded in 1838; agricultural and commercial high schools followed in the 1840's. Even in the field of politics there were interesting stirrings before 1848. A number of young men who had studied at German universities in 1847 founded a Young Serbia Society which revealed the existence of liberal and even demo-

[61] Marceli Handelsman: *Czartoryski, Nicolas I et la question du Proche-Orient* (Paris, 1934), chap. ii; Paul N. Hehn: "Prince Adam Czartoryski and the South Slavs" (*Polish Review*, VIII, 1963, 76–86). On Russian policy, see Theodor Schiemann: *Geschichte Russlands unter Kaiser Nikolaus I* (Berlin, 1913), IV, 31 ff.

cratic ideas among those of the rising generation. In retrospect it would seem that the opponents of Milosh, by breaking his almost Oriental despotism, had at least prepared the way for the rooting of progressive ideas.

Despite great differences in environment, history and conditions, the political development of Greece in this period was not unlike that of the other Balkan countries. The Greeks were both an agricultural and a seafaring people. Those who stayed at home were for the most part tillers of the soil in behalf of local notables or chieftains, or of the Orthodox Church hierarchy. Those who engaged in trade moved about widely in the Mediterranean region and beyond. Some of them acquired great wealth and many of them absorbed western ideas. The revolution which broke out in 1821 against Turkish rule was inspired by an organization of merchants and intellectuals who hoped to secure the support of Russia, but in a short time the insurrection turned into a series of "civil wars" or, better, factional struggles between powerful local bosses. The highbrow element attempted to establish some form of western constitutional government, but was increasingly overshadowed by the *Kapitani* (captains). Without a doubt the rebellion would have been suppressed by the Turks, had it not been for the intervention of Britain, France and Russia, the governments of which were under heavy pressure from the sentimentally pro-Greek educated classes. After the Russian-Turkish War of 1828–1829 the three powers reluctantly agreed that Greece should be an independent state within very restricted boundaries (hardly more than the Peloponnesus, with Attica and a strip of territory on the north side of the Gulf of Corinth together with many of the Aegean Islands). The new Greek state included only about a fourth of the Greek population and it was therefore natural that in the sequel Greek patriots should clamor for a more national boundary. As a matter of fact they went much further, cherishing the "grand idea" of reviving the Byzantine Empire with Constantinople as the capital.[62]

In the hope of overcoming the factional disorder in Greece the powers decided that the new state should be a monarchy, and they eventually chose Otho, the second son of King Louis of Bavaria, as

[62] The vicissitudes of the "grand idea" are the basic theme of the magistral study of Edouard Driault and Michel Lhéritier: *Histoire diplomatique de la Grèce* (Paris, 1925), especially Vol. II, which is far more than mere diplomatic history.

king. Otho was only seventeen and could hardly be expected to govern effectively for some years, so four regents were named to assist him. The entire Bavarian party arrived at Nauplia on February 6, 1833, amid wild rejoicing on the part of the long-suffering populace. To get the new regime started, the three protecting powers guaranteed a loan of 60 million francs and permitted the dispatch of 3,000 Bavarian troops, pending the recruitment of an even larger number of volunteers.

The regents were convinced that order and prosperity could be restored only through strong government. Nothing was done, therefore, to draw up yet another constitution. The monarchy was an absolute one, though devoted and benevolent in its intentions.[63] Unfortunately the regents had had no previous experience of Greek conditions and were by no means always of one mind. Their feverish activity was often misdirected. Since the most pressing need was to establish government authority, they built up a bureaucracy of some 500 reliable Bavarian officials, reducing even the most prominent native politicians to the status of secretaries who were to take orders rather than make policies. With equal impetuosity they disbanded the Greek forces, mostly irregulars (*Pallikares*) and gradually replaced them with some 5,400 German volunteers.

Yet the regency must be credited with real and important achievements: it established a centralized administrative system; declared the Greek Church independent of the Constantinople patriarchate; suppressed over three hundred small monasteries; introduced law codes and judicial procedures; established strict quarantines against plague and cholera; made vaccination for smallpox compulsory; furthered primary education; and, lastly, began the reconstruction of Athens, which in 1833 was little more than a heap of ruins. Many streets were laid out and a royal palace built. In 1837 the University of Athens was opened and in the same year steamship service to Trieste was inaugurated.[64]

[63] On the constitutional issue, see Alexander P. Couclelis: *Les régimes gouvernementaux de la Grèce de 1821 à nos jours* (Paris, 1921), 29 ff.; Nicholas Kaltchas: *Introduction to the Constitutional History of Modern Greece* (New York, 1940), 82–93.

[64] William Miller: *The Early Years of Modern Athens* (London, 1926). A wealth of information can be derived from the contemporary works of Frederick Strong: *Greece as a Kingdom* (London, 1842) and Henry M. Baird: *Modern Greece* (New York, 1856), as also from the classic accounts of Karl Mendelssohn-Bartholdy: *Geschichte Griechenlands*

But the accomplishments of the "foreigners" netted them more resentment than gratitude. The irregulars found it difficult to adjust to the strict discipline of the new army, while the Greek leaders were disgruntled by their exclusion from the best posts and infuriated by the all-too-obvious contempt of the Germans for the unpolished Greeks. Count Josef von Armansperg, the chief regent, is said to have urged the young king to enlist popular support by promulgating a constitution, but Otho, who had reached his majority in 1835, was undecided and under heavy pressure from his father not to embark on a policy of concessions. As discontent became more and more pronounced, the king eventually dismissed Armansperg and, in 1837, appointed a few Greek notables to cabinet rank. Even then he continued to govern without considering their views.

The situation was further complicated by the fact that the opposition elements looked to the representatives of the protecting powers for support. In the Armansperg period the British "party," the chief proponent of a constitutional regime, was in the ascendant. The dismissal of Armansperg was regarded as a victory for the Russian or Nappist "party," which was undoubtedly the largest faction. This group was, one might say, the party of the oligarchs or local bosses, hostile to the absolute rule of the king, the more so as he was a Roman Catholic and the oligarchs were champions of the Orthodox faith. The French "party," though most sympathetic to the program of Greek expansion, was at first in eclipse, and only in the 1840's rose to prominence. It would be a mistake, however, to suppose that the aims and activities of these factions necessarily reflected those of the governments whose patronage they claimed. Thus, when the Greek government in 1839 discovered the existence of a secret society bent on an uprising against the Turks and conquest of Thessaly and Epirus, as well as replacement of Otho by an Orthodox prince, the whole affair was condemned by Czar Nicholas, despite its implied Russian support. The czar, though much offended by Otho's refusal to adopt the Orthodox faith or even promise that his heirs should be brought up in that faith, nevertheless

---

(Leipzig, 1874), II, 426–511; George Finlay: *A History of Greece* (rev. ed., Oxford, 1877), VII, chap. iv; Gustav F. Hertzberg: *Neueste Geschichte Griechenlands* (Gotha, 1879), 589–639. More directly concerned with the German contribution are the readable and well-informed books of Siegfried Mackroth: *Das Deutschtum in Griechenland* (Tübingen, 1930); and Wolf Seidl: *Bayern in Griechenland* (Munich, 1965).

supported the king's absolute rule and rejected entirely all programs of further expansion at the expense of the Ottoman Empire. Like the British, the Russian government was at this time committed to maintenance of the Turkish Empire.[65]

Greek hopes of expansion, aroused by the collapse of the Turks in the crisis of 1839–1841, were completely blasted by the co-operation of the British and Russian governments in support of the sultan. Discontent with the foreign regime grew apace and culminated (September 14–15, 1843) in a bloodless coup led by Colonel Demetrios Kallergis, commander of the Athens garrison and leader of the Orthodox, Nappist party. Otho barely escaped deposition and was obliged to dismiss his Bavarian advisers, appoint a new ministry and convoke a national assembly. When the latter met, in November, it was dominated by the native oligarchs or notables, who then drew up the constitution of March 30, 1844, a document modeled rather closely on the French Charter of 1830. Here again the British and Russian influence was pooled, this time in behalf of moderation. Czar Nicholas was far from pleased by the tactics of the Russian party. He made known his opposition to any attempt to replace Otho or even seriously diminish his authority. Under the circumstances the British party was able to gain ground or assume a prominent role in formulation of the constitution. The king retained the right to name his ministers, to nominate the members of the upper chamber of the Parliament (the Senate or Gerousia), and to dissolve the lower chamber (the Boulé).[66]

Under the constitutional system the Greek oligarchs were able to resume their factional strife in the parliamentary arena. Presently the leader of the French party, John Kolettis, popular because of his frank

[65] A vivid analysis of the diplomatic conflict was given in the report of a special French envoy, M. Piscatory, dated August 20, 1841 (see Jean Poulos: "La Grèce d'Othon vue par l'homme d'état et diplomate français Piscatory," in L'Hellénisme contemporain, Ser. II, IX, 1955, 321–351, 408–447). On British policy, see A. W. Ward: "Greece and the Ionian Islands, 1832–1864" (in Cambridge History of British Foreign Policy, New York, 1923, II, 583–622); Charles K. Webster: The Foreign Policy of Lord Palmerston (London, 1951), I, 272, 503 ff. Russian policy is well analyzed on the basis of important documents by Barbara Jelavich: Russia and Greece during the Regency of King Othon, 1832–1835 (Thessaloniki, 1962), and Russia and the Greek Revolution of 1843 (Munich, 1966). The same author's article "The Philorthodox Conspiracy of 1839" (Balkan Studies, 1966, 89–102) is also illuminating.

[66] For detailed analyses, see Couclelis: Les régimes gouvernementaux, 34; Kaltchas: Constitutional History, 96 ff.; Nicholas Svoronos: Histoire de la Grèce moderne (Paris, 1953), 55.

espousal of the "grand idea," rose to power and remained in control, through personal influence, unabashed corruption and political maneuvering, until his death in 1847. His successors, the revolutionary heroes Kondouriottis and Kanaris, adopted the same methods, though less successfully.[67]

The western institutions adopted in 1844 were, then, little more than a façade, behind which the Greek notables took over from the monarchy the effective control of affairs. This in itself was a disappointment for Lord Palmerston, a disappointment much aggravated by the success of the French party at a time when London and Paris were more than ever at loggerheads (see Chapter IX). The Greek government was chronically in financial straits and the British had various claims for which they demanded satisfaction with ever greater insistence. Once the international upheavals of 1848–1849 were over, Palmerston suddenly submitted an ultimatum demanding settlement of seven major claims, failing which the British threatened to blockade Greek ports. When the Greek government rejected this ultimatum, Admiral Parker blockaded the Piraeus and seized over two hundred Greek ships. The Athens government had no choice but to yield (April 27, 1850).

Of this famous demonstration of British sea power one can only say that never before had so formidable a force been deployed in so trivial a cause. One of the chief claimants was Don Pacifico, a Portuguese Jew born in Gibraltar and therefore a British citizen. His Athens home had been sacked during an Easter demonstration and he demanded $100,000 as compensation for the loss of alleged vouchers of high value. Since he was later willing to settle for $750, one can only conclude that his claim was really a minor one. Yet the "Don Pacifico" affair has gone down in all textbooks because of Palmerston's valiant defense of the rights of Englishmen and because of his grandiloquent apology for his bullying policy when attacked by his opponents in Parliament. In the last analysis the episode is of mild interest as a demonstration of exaggerated national pride rather than as a revelation of Greek weakness.[68]

67 John Mavrogordato: *Modern Greece* (London, 1931), 41 ff.; Michael Sakellariou: "Hellenism and 1848" (in François Fejtö, ed.: *1848, the Opening of an Era*, London, 1948, 377–393).

68 Herbert C. Bell: *Lord Palmerston* (New York, 1936), II, 22 ff.; Donald Southgate: *"The Most English Minister"* (New York, 1966), 263 ff.; and the detailed and highly critical account in Driault and Lhéritier: *Histoire diplomatique de la Grèce*, II, 327 ff.

Chapter Six

THE SOCIAL QUESTION

I. THE STANDARD OF LIVING

In the decades preceding 1848 Europe was deluged with literature discussing the "social question" or, as it was called in Britain, the "condition of England question." Everywhere thoughtful people were appalled not so much by the existence of poverty, hunger and disease, for they had been familiar social afflictions since the beginning of time, as by the alarming increase of what came to be known as "pauperism" and by what seemed like the further deterioration of the lower classes. "Such is now the accumulation of misery endured by thousands of skilled and industrious labourers, that no conceivable alteration for the worse can take place," wrote an English journal in 1826, while Thomas Carlyle, in his *Past and Present* (1843), could declare: "I venture to believe that in no time since the beginnings of society, was the lot of those same dumb millions of toilers so entirely unbearable as it is even in the days now passing over us."[1]

Since the deterioration in the condition of the working classes was most striking in the cities, it was natural that it should have been linked by many contemporary writers to the concurrent progress of industrialization. The question was often raised whether the price being paid for greater and cheaper production of goods was not, in terms of human suffering, disproportionately high. Goethe, among others, saw industrialization as a slowly gathering storm, soon to break over the land, bringing with it, along with obvious benefits, social calamity.[2]

Actually it was a mistake to attribute the greater woes of mankind to the coming of the machine, for the frightening growth of pauperism was fully as great in nonindustrialized areas as in the new manufactur-

[1] Sidney Pollard: "Nineteenth Century Coöperation" (in Asa Briggs and John Saville, eds.: *Essays in Labour History*, London, 1960, 74–112); David Daiches: *Carlyle and the Victorian Dilemma* (Edinburgh, 1963).
[2] *Wilhelm Meisters Wanderjahre* (1829).

ing centers. The basic fact, increasingly so recognized by modern scholars, was the unprecedented growth of the European population after 1760, already discussed in Chapter I. This led to overpopulation, "that condition of a country in which part of the inhabitants, although able-bodied and capable of labour, are permanently unable to earn a sufficiency of the necessaries of life."[3] There were, according to Edward Gibbon Wakefield, simply "too many competitors for a limited fund of enjoyment."[4] Everywhere, on the Continent as in Britain, there were just too many people for the available jobs, and the surplus (or "redundant") population was the great ulcer of European nations, "the master evil," to borrow Francis Place's description.[5]

It was inevitable that so great and sudden an increase in the population should have entailed major dislocations in European society. Agrarian laborers unable to find work were reduced to utmost destitution or forced to migrate to the nearest towns in the hope of finding employment, if possible in the new factories, or at any rate in some menial occupation. In the cities many of them were no better off than they had been before, to put it mildly. The new machine industry provided a precarious existence for some, but at the same time proved ruinous for many engaged in the traditional home industries, which were unable to compete with the new methods of production. Taken all in all, it would seem that in Europe the lowest classes, the "poor," those who lived on the brink of starvation and who in the sixteenth century had comprised about one-fifth of the population, had come in the nineteenth to number a third or more.[6]

Among present-day British writers there has existed for some time a school of so-called "optimists," who hold that industrialization brought at least some rise in the standard of living; in other words, that the workers shared to some extent, however modest, in the benefits of the new economy. This was certainly not the impression of contemporary

---

[3] William A. Thornton: *Overpopulation and its Remedy* (London, 1846), 1.

[4] *A View of the Art of Colonization* (London, 1848), 66.

[5] Quoted by James A. Field: *Essays on Population* (Chicago, 1931), chap. iii.

[6] Wolfram Fischer: "Soziale Unterschichten im Zeitalter der Frühindustrialisierung" (*International Review of Social History*, VIII, 1963, 414–435). In 1844 Friedrich Harkort estimated that one-third of the Prussian population was hardly able to earn a living, and it has been asserted that in the 1840's fully a third of the Paris population lived in a "precarious condition." See Max Quarck: *Die erste deutsche Arbeiterbewegung* (Leipzig, 1924), 11; Adeline Daumard: *La bourgeoisie parisienne de 1815 à 1848* (Paris, 1963), 8–9.

writers and indeed it is a view that has been vigorously challenged by adherents of the "pessimist" school, who think that the lower classes were for a time worse off than they had ever been. The question is obviously one of prime importance, but unfortunately one that can never be "solved," for lack of adequate statistical data. The debate has been complicated by the fact that different students have taken different periods for their analyses, and that the term *workingman* has frequently been loosely used. In the cities as in the country there were endless gradations of labor, from skilled technicians and specialized craftsmen, through artisans, journeymen and apprentices, to the home-workers of the putting-out system and factory workers, among whom again there were gradations from foremen to the younger child workers. Lowest of all was what Karl Marx was to term the *Lumpenproletariat,* the riffraff consisting of nondescript workers, mostly unemployed and often driven by desperation to vice and crime.

Although the standard-of-living debate has proved inconclusive, it has brought at least some measure of agreement. There was undoubtedly an aggregate rise in real wages, but this benefited the skilled, well-paid worker rather than the lowest class. It may be that even the poorest element experienced some improvement, for while wages remained fairly unchanged, prices declined. However, all seem to be agreed that if there was a change in the standard of living, it was not a significant one. Furthermore, the actual condition of the poorest class depended at any time largely on the availability of work, about which reliable data are meager and unsystematic.[7]

While it is true that aggregate prices declined in this period, food prices remained high, reflecting the pressure of population,

[7] The literature on the standard of living in England is so rich that it cannot be listed here. Among important recent items are the debate between R. M. Hartwell and E. J. Hobsbawm: "The Standard of Living during the Industrial Revolution" (*Economic History Review,* Ser. 2, XVI, 1963, 119–149); E. J. Hobsbawm: "The Standard of Living Debate: a Postscript" (in his *Labouring Men,* London, 1964, 120–125); J. E. Williams: "The British Standard of Living, 1750–1850" (*Economic History Review,* Ser. 2, XIX, 1966, 581–589); Phyllis Deane: *The First Industrial Revolution* (Cambridge, 1965), chap. xv; E. P. Thompson: *The Making of the English Working Class* (London, 1963); Sydney G. Checkland: *The Rise of Industrial Society in England, 1815–1885* (London, 1965), 225 ff.; and, on the general problem: W. Woodruff: "Capitalism and the Historians" (*Journal of Economic History,* XVI, 1956, 1–17); A. J. Taylor: "Progress and Poverty in Britain, 1780–1850" (*History,* XLV, 1960, 16–31); J. Potter: " 'Optimism' and 'Pessimism' in Interpreting the Industrial Revolution" (*Scandinavian Economic History Review,* X, 1962, 245–261).

and fluctuated greatly according to the state of the harvest and the general economic situation. Meanwhile, wages certainly did not rise substantially, if at all, until after the depression of 1841–1842. The matter is one difficult to generalize about, for the data, which are abundant, are often contradictory or at least widely divergent. Regional differences were important. Wages were markedly higher in Britain than on the Continent and might vary greatly within any country. Furthermore, wages differed according to the type of work and might fluctuate significantly according to the supply and demand for labor. Finally, any discussion of actual wages must take account of the changing values of money, of the fact that family income was more important than that of the individual male worker, and that the extent of unemployment was often the crucial factor in deciding the fate of the worker and his family.

Certain general statements can, however, be ventured. Everywhere in Europe workers in the traditional skilled handicrafts and trades, as also foundrymen and the new mechanics, ordinarily earned a wage that enabled them to live in relative comfort, with decent lodgings and an adequate diet that might include meat two or three times a week. In England such workers might earn thirty shillings to two pounds a week, and in France twenty-five to thirty francs. British coal miners could earn fifteen to twenty shillings and so could the average cotton mill "operative." The French journeymen or factory workers had about the same wage, but the rate was distinctly lower in Belgium, Switzerland and Italy. In Germany the average worker had a money wage of about nine to ten marks a week, which was somewhat more than he could earn in Austria. Everywhere in Europe, in Britain as on the Continent, the hardest hit were the handloom weavers, particularly in the cotton industry. In their case the population pressure made itself keenly felt, for the handloom weavers were not exposed to the competition of the machine until the 1830's in Britain and the 1840's elsewhere. Their problem derived from the fact that ever more unskilled and unwanted laborers resorted to the handloom in the hope of earning at least a pittance, with the result that they achieved that and nothing more. While in 1815 they were still earning thirteen shillings and sixpence a week, their wages had fallen to six shillings in 1833 and never again rose much above that figure. In Germany, where handloom weaving was still the most important industry, the wages had fallen to two and a half marks per week and in Silesia even to one and a half marks. The position of framework knitters and ribbon makers was hardly better.[8] The figures in themselves are fairly meaningless unless taken in conjunction with the cost of living. The evidence is quite conclusive that the average worker (for example, the millhand) could barely earn enough to support a family with three children when he was fully employed. It was estimated that in London in 1841 a family could live in reasonable comfort on thirty shillings a week; that it led a tight existence on twenty-one shillings; and that it could barely survive on fifteen shillings. Another study demonstrates that in Switzerland a textile worker could earn only a little more than half of what was required to support a family, while in the mountainous region of Saxony, one of the poorest sections of home industry in Europe, most families could not make a living and were therefore dependent on relief or charity.[9]

This consideration if no other explains the widespread employment of women and children, who were welcomed in the textile mills because they could do the work as well as men, were far more tractable, and required respectively only one-half or one-quarter of the man's wage. To be sure, women and children had always been employed in home industries, but now they were subjected, even at tender ages, to the long unbroken hours and strict discipline of the factories (see Illustrations 21, 22). Besides, during the first half of the nineteenth cen-

[8] The movement of wages is, of course, discussed in all economic histories. Thornton: *Overpopulation*, 26 ff., gives a useful contemporary survey, based largely on government reports. For the Continent, see Carl von Tyska: *Löhne und Lebenskosten in West Europa im 19 Jahrhundert* (Munich, 1914); Paul Louis: *Histoire de la classe ouvrière en France* (Paris, 1927), 58 ff.; Ernest Labrousse: *Aspects de la crise de l'économie française, 1846–1851* (Paris, 1956), 93–141; Jürgen Kuczynski: *Darstellung der Lage der Arbeiter in Deutschland von 1800 bis in die Gegenwart* (6 ed., Berlin, 1954); P. H. Noyes: *Organization and Revolution* (Princeton, 1966), chaps. i and ii; M. Peeters: "L'évolution des salaires en Belgique de 1831 à 1913" (*Bulletin de l'Institut de Recherches Economiques et Sociales*, X, 1939, 389–420); Antonio Fossati: *Lavoro e produzione in Italia* (Turin, 1951), 135 ff.; Luigi Bulferetti and Raimondo Luraghi: *Agricoltura, Industria e Commercio in Piemonte dal 1814 al 1848* (Turin, 1966), 118 ff.; and in general, John Burnett: *Plenty and Want* (London, 1966), chap. iii.

[9] Burnett: *Plenty and Want*, 45; Jürg Siegenthaler: "Zum Lebensstandart schweizerischer Arbeiter im 19 Jahrhundert" (*Schweizerische Zeitschrift für Volkswirtschaft und Statistik*, CI, 1965, 423–444); Heinrich Bodemer: *Die industrielle Revolution mit besonderer Berücksichtigung der Erzgebirgischen Erwerbsverhältnisse* (Dresden, 1856), 99.

tury there was a vast increase in this type of labor, so that in most mills less than half the employees (sometimes only one-quarter) were adult men, while another half consisted of boys and girls under eighteen. The same was true of the industrial labor force in France, Belgium and Germany.[10]

European workers had been accustomed, long before the Industrial Revolution, to stay at their tasks from dawn till dusk. This traditional workday, long in summer and shorter in winter, was taken over by the factories, though there was soon a tendency to extend it as gaslighting became available. Everywhere in Europe the normal workday was twelve to fourteen or fifteen hours, with about an hour and a half out for lunch and afternoon refreshment. This stiff regimen applied not only to women as well as men but also to the children, many of whom tended to doze off unless prodded to continue at their task. The factory system, unlike that of home industry, did not permit variations in the work tempo. The inexorable demands of the machine therefore taxed the endurance of mankind to the very utmost.

The worst feature of the new industrial system was its instability, no doubt natural under the circumstances but nonetheless puzzling, even to the economists. Good and bad times alternated every four or five years, the depressions coming with great suddenness and the periods of recovery tending to be long and unsteady. This meant that the factory workers were liable at any time and without warning to find themselves without work, while the home-industry workers likewise could not dispose of their product. If the crisis continued for several years, like that of 1838–1842, all business would stagnate to the point where even skilled workers were obliged to accept any kind of work, with miserably low wages. At Bolton in 1842 the earnings of handloom

[10] For contemporary accounts, see Peter Gaskell: *The Manufacturing Population of England* (London, 1833), chap. vii; John Fielden: *The Curse of the Factory System* (London, 1836), 2 ff., 40; Edouard Ducpétiaux: *De la condition physique et morale des jeunes ouvriers, etc.* (Brussels, 1843). Further, I. Pinchbeck: *Women Workers in the Industrial Revolution* (Chicago, 1959); Jürgen Kuczynski: *Geschichte der Kinderarbeit in Deutschland* (Berlin, 1958); Gustav Otruba: "Zur Geschichte der Frauen und Kinderarbeit im Gewerbe . . . von Niederoesterreich" (*Jahrbücher für Landeskunde von Niederoesterreich*, n.s. XXXIV, 1958–1960); Karl-Heinz Ludwig: "Die Fabrikarbeit von Kindern im 19 Jahrhundert" (*Vierteljahrschrift für Sozial- und Wirtschaftsgeschichte*, LII, 1965, 63–85); Valerie Castronovo: *L'Industria cotoniera in Piemonte nel secolo XIX* (Turin, 1965), chap. iv.

weavers were down to three shillings and sevenpence hapenny a week. Masons, who ordinarily made thirty-four shillings a week, were lucky to earn ten shillings and sixpence. In Bath 150 skilled workers were obliged to content themselves with five shillings and eightpence per week.[11]

It is unfortunate that statistics on unemployment in this period are lacking in all countries, but British government reports and private analyses provide enough evidence to indicate that it was extensive and that its consequences were often disastrous. Karl Marx estimated in 1845 that one in ten of the European population was a pauper, that is, dependent on relief. This figure was probably too high for the Continent and too low for Britain, where at times one in six was destitute. Reliable investigations showed that in Manchester 50 to 75 per cent of all workers were idle in 1841–1842. In Stockport, out of a population of 15,823, only 4,070 were even partially employed, while the remainder were totally unemployed or unemployable.[12]

On the Continent as many as 60 or 70 per cent of the workers might be idle at certain periods. In the large cities they made a pathetic sight as in winter they stood around in the public squares, shivering and hungry, hoping for something to turn up (see Illustration 25). Many were dependent on public relief (which was meager) or on private charity (which was hard to come by). In Paris 85,000 were on relief in 1840; in all Belgium 400,000, the figure rising to 530,000 in 1845 and to 691,000 in 1847. In one district of Silesia, where destitution reached unprecedented dimensions, 30,000 were in need for relief in 1844 out of a population of 40,000. In many parts of Europe the problem of relief had become so formidable that local authorities were unable to cope with it.[13]

Under the circumstances, the food consumption of the workers was

[11] Thornton: *Overpopulation*, 30 ff.; R. S. Neale: "The Standard of Living, 1780–1844: a Regional and Class Study" (*Economic History Review*, Ser. 2, XIX, 1966, 590–606).

[12] W. Cooke Taylor: *Tour in the Manufacturing Districts of Lancashire* (2 ed., London 1842), 38, 113, 220; Friedrich Engels: *The Condition of the Working Class in England* (1845, new ed. by W. O. Henderson and W. H. Chaloner, Oxford, 1958), chap. iv; Thornton: *Overpopulation*, 30 ff.; Hans Stein: "Pauperismus und Assoziation" (*International Review for Social History*, I, 1936, 1–120).

[13] Ferdinand Dreyfus: *L'assistance sous la Séconde République* (Paris, 1907), 13 ff.; Ernest Labrousse: *Aspects de la crise . . . de l'économie française, 1846–1851* (Paris, 1956), 104 ff.; Laurent Dechesne: *Histoire économique et sociale de la Belgique* (Paris,

absolutely minimal. Their diet consisted of bread, potatoes, a little milk or cheese, an occasional turnip or cabbage, and very rarely a bit of bacon or meat. In some places bread was reported to be a luxury, the population subsisting almost entirely on potatoes, like the Irish peasants. The evidence is conclusive that the lower classes were obliged to spend 60 to 70 per cent of their income on food and drink, this in itself an indication of a very low standard of living. Careful studies leave little doubt that the worker in 1850 could buy far less food for his wages than he could in the year 1500. The decline was most striking in the item of meat consumption. In 1500 the per capita meat consumption in Germany was in the neighborhood of 200 pounds per annum; in the early nineteenth century, in both Germany and England, it was thirty-five to forty pounds.

Budgets of workers' families are hard to come by. In 1825 an English family of five required per week twenty-four pounds of grain stuffs (at three shillings and sixpence); roughly two pecks of potatoes (one shilling and twopence); six pounds of animal food (two shillings and threepence); and coal (one shilling and ninepence). Three shillings and sixpence were spent on clothing and two shillings and threepence on rent. In Paris a carpenter's family of four, of which the father could earn 1,200 francs a year if he had 300 days of work, required 1,050 to 1,300 francs to live decently. In Belgium a poor linen weaver, together with his wife and two children, could earn only 12.90 francs a week, while his living expenses (including two younger children) required 14.20 francs. Fortunately, in this case the deficit could be met by cultivating a little home garden.[14] Obviously, wages and cost of living were such as to leave the worker without a margin even in good times. When out of work he was reduced to relief and even to starvation. It

---

1932), 411 ff.; J. Dhondt: "De sociale kwestie in Belgie" (in *Algemene Geschiedenis de Nederlanden,* Utrecht, 1955, X, 314–349); Kuczynski: *Lage der deutschen Arbeiter,* 233 ff.; Karl Obermann: *Die deutschen Arbeiter in der Revolution von 1848* (2 ed., Berlin, 1953), 40.

14 There is some discussion of workers' budgets in Gaskell: *Manufacturing Population,* chaps. iv and v, and in Edouard Ducpétiaux: *Budgets économiques des classes ouvrières en Belgique* (Brussels, 1855). See also Frances Collier: *The Family Economy of the Working Classes in the Cotton Industry, 1784–1833* (Manchester, 1964), 49 ff.; Burnett: *Plenty and Want,* 42; E. H. P. Brown and Sheila V. Hopkins: "Seven Centuries of Prices of Consumables compared with Builders' Wage-rates" (*Economica,* n.s., XXIII, 1956, 296–314); Wilhelm Abel: *Der Pauperismus in Deutschland am Vorabend der industriellen Revolution* (Dortmund, 1966), 17 ff.

was the plight of the urban workers that inspired Thomas Carlyle to write his impassioned *Past and Present* (1843) and produced throughout Europe a landslide of literature on the shocking social question.[15]

2. THE ROOKERIES OF THE POOR

The problems of modern city life appear to be unending, for two centuries after the onset of the Industrial Revolution the great cities of Europe and America are still grappling with the problems of unemployment, poverty, congestion and sanitation. But so much is certain: that in no European city of the late twentieth century are conditions comparable to those of the first half of the nineteenth, when the importance of sanitation was little recognized and almost nothing was known of the causes of disease. The surplus population was streaming into the cities—into the old centers as well as into the new industrial towns—and creating conditions of unprecedented complexity. A large part of the European population was being uprooted. Society was in a state of disruption.

Some idea of the magnitude of the changes can be derived from a few representative figures. In the decade 1831–1841 London's population grew by 130,000, Manchester's by almost 70,000, Birmingham's by 40,000. The rate of increase in the British industrial centers was of the order of 40 to 70 per cent in each decade.[16] The statistics for Continental cities are much the same. Paris gained about 120,000 souls between 1841 and 1846 and reached one million population before 1848. Vienna grew by 125,000 in the years 1827–1847 and became a city of 400,000. Berlin, which in 1848 had a comparable population, had grown from 180,000 in 1815, chiefly through immigration from the eastern provinces.[17]

[15] On the voluminous German literature, see Jürgen Kuczynski: *Bürgerliche und halbfeudale Literatur aus den Jahren 1840 bis 1847 zur Lage der Arbeiter* (Berlin, 1960). Carl Jantke and Dietrich Hilger: *Die Eigentumslosen* (Munich, 1965) is an admirable anthology of these writings.

[16] Arthur Redford: *Labour Migration in England, 1800–1850* (London, 1926), chap. iv; H. A. Shannon: "Migration and the Growth of London, 1841–1891" (*Economic History Review*, Ser. 2, V, 1935, 79–86); Leon S. Marshall: "The Emergence of the First Industrial City: Manchester, 1780–1850" (in Caroline F. Ware, ed.: *The Cultural Approach to History*, New York, 1940, 140–161).

[17] On Paris, Louis Chevalier: *La formation de la population parisienne au XIXe siècle* (Paris, 1949), 45, 48, 183; on Vienna, Friedrich Walter: *Wien: die Geschichte einer*

It was hardly to be expected that adequate housing could be found for this influx of new people. On the contrary, new construction lagged far behind the population increase. In Vienna, for example, where the population rose by 42 per cent between 1827 and 1847, the increase in housing was only 11½ per cent (900 new houses). The newcomers were therefore obliged to crowd into the old, already congested central sections of the cities, while the more well-to-do inhabitants moved into new sections on the outskirts. "The difficulty of finding lodgings," wrote a contemporary historian of Paris[18] "is for the worker a constant ordeal and a perpetual cause of misery." In Paris some 30,000 workers (mostly unmarried men and women immigrants) lived in lodging-houses, where they were housed eight and nine to a room, without discrimination of sex.[19]

Sources describing the living conditions of the lowest classes in the midcentury are legion. Most workers lived in single rooms, not infrequently two or three families in one room, with a few ragged curtains for partitions. The Irish laborer of Manchester or Glasgow was, according to Carlyle, "the sorest evil" the country had to contend with, for "he lodges in any pig hutch or doghutch, roosts in outhouses, and wears a suit of tatters the getting off and on of which is said to be a difficult operation, transacted only in festivals and the high tides of the calendar." The Irish immigrant was apt to add a pig, a goat or a donkey to the family circle. In St. Giles, the Irish quarter of London, 461 persons were living in twelve houses in 1847, each having only 175 cubic feet of space. In Liverpool and Manchester the lowest class, chiefly Irish, lived in cellars, which were a popular abode in Continental as well as British cities because they were less leaky than the garrets and warmer in winter. Few of the workingman dwellings

---

Gross-stadt an der Grenze (Vienna, 1944), III, 105 ff.; on Berlin, Richard Dietrich: "Berlins Weg zur Industrie- und Handelsstadt" (in Berlin: *Neun Kapitel seiner Geschichte,* Berlin, 1960, 159–198).

18 Théophile Lavallée: *Histoire de Paris* (Paris, 1852), 205.

19 Etienne Laspeyres: *Der Einfluss der Wohnung auf die Sittlichkeit* (Berlin, 1869); Honoré-Antoine Frégier: *Des classes dangereuses de la population dans les grandes villes* (Paris, 1840), I, 22; Louis Chevalier: *Classes laborieuses et classes dangereuses à Paris pendant la première moitié du XIXe siècle* (Paris, 1958), 216 ff., 271 ff. On the German cities, see Ernst Dronke: *Berlin* (Frankfurt, 1846), chap. vi. The situation in England was discussed in the famous report by Edwin Chadwick on *The Sanitary Condition of the Labouring Population of Great Britain* (London, 1842; new ed. with intro. by M. W. Flinn, Edinburgh, 1963), 411 ff.

had heat, for fuel was expensive. In cold weather six or more individuals of both sexes and all ages would lie huddled on a pile of dank straw or rotting potato peels with nothing but a ragged hanging for a cover. In her novel *Mary Barton* (1848) Mrs. Gaskell, who lived for years in "dull, ugly, smoky, grim, gray Manchester" as a parson's wife, has left a heart-rending account of lowest-class life.[20]

The problem of congestion was aggravated by the hopelessly inadequate sanitation. The great cholera epidemic of 1832 had struck particularly in the slum areas and had convinced many physicians that the incidence of disease depended largely on filth and polluted air. In France much attention was given to studies of public as well as private hygiene. Boards of public health were established in most large cities and important books were published on the relations of indigence and disease.[21] Chadwick, in planning and drafting his famous report on sanitary conditions among the working class, was much influenced by these studies. His painstaking investigations constitute one of the most important public documents of the nineteenth century, for they prepared the way for the passage of the Public Health Act of 1848.

The evidence collected by Chadwick was fully corroborated by contemporary writers such as Engels, Gaskell, Beames and others, to say nothing of those great pioneers, James Kay, Neil Arnott and Southwood Smith, all of them devoted physicians and humanitarians. They pictured the main streets of the cities as paved, cleaned and frequently lined with trees as well as with elegant shops and imposing residences,

[20] The Chadwick report, cited in the previous footnote, is the most important single source for working-class conditions. Its record is well borne out by the classic account of Friedrich Engels: *The Condition of the Working Class in England in 1844* and by such contemporary studies as Gaskell: *The Manufacturing Population of England*, chap. v; Taylor: *Tour in the Manufacturing Districts*, 13. The classic French account is that of Louis R. Villermé: *Tableau de l'état physique et morale des ouvriers* (Paris, 1840), 361 ff., which may be supplemented by Chevalier: *Classes laborieuses*, 216 ff. Conditions in the Belgian cities are recounted in Armand Julien: "La condition des classes laborieuses en Belgique, 1830–1930" (*Annales de la Société Scientique de Bruxelles*, LV, 1935, Ser. D, 247–302). For the German cities, see Johannes Scheer: *Deutsche Kultur- und Sittengeschichte* (1860, new ed., 1938), 586; Alfons Fischer: *Geschichte des deutschen Gesundheitswesens* (Berlin, 1933), II, 500 ff. An excellent anthology of English source materials is E. Royston Pike's *Hard Times: Human Documents of the Industrial Revolution* (New York, 1966).

[21] Such as A. J. P. Parent-Duchâtelet: *Hygiène publique* (Paris, 1836) and Michel Lévy: *Traité d'hygiène publique et privée* (Paris, 1844–1845). See Erwin H. Ackerknecht: "Hygiene in France, 1815–1848" (*Bulletin of the History of Medicine*, XXII, 1948, 117–155).

while behind or near them were often slums—narrow lanes and courts, many with alluring names such as Angel Court or Paradise Court, but unpaved, littered with garbage and other refuse, and invariably so noisome as to offend even those whose olfactory sense had already been dulled. Add to this the smog and smoke, the "inky panoply" that hung over the cities (see Illustration 27). Flora Tristan, the French labor leader, visiting the St. Giles district of London in 1840, was appalled by the sight of women in tatters, of children playing naked in the filth, lean and feverish, with looks of stupid ferocity: "The dreams of a delirious imagination would fall short of this frightful reality," she exclaimed.[22]

No city in Europe had at this time an adequate or sanitary water supply. In England water was supplied by private companies which, in the poorer sections, turned on the local pumps or standpipes only for a few hours on three days a week (never on Sundays). Workers were obliged to store water, which had at least the advantage of allowing the dirt to settle. For the water was taken mostly from rivers which received the street drainage. Paris had better water than London, for Napoleon had constructed a purification plant on the Seine above the city, and had begun to bring in water from the Ourcq River. In 1823 the opening of the Ourcq-Marne Canal had made possible the tapping of Marne water also. Furthermore, a great deal was done during the July Monarchy. The number of street fountains and standpipes was increased from about 500 to 1,850. Yet even in Paris the water supply was inadequate, being sufficient only for two baths per capita per annum.

Worse even than the water supply was the sewage system, for the existing sewers were intended only for drainage of the surface water and were, therefore, not connected with the houses. In all but the best sections of the city the refuse was thrown into the streets or courts, while human excrement went into cesspools under the houses. In London there were still 250,000 of these cesspools in 1850. At best they were emptied only once or twice a year. What is more, there were far too few of them for the requirements of the burgeoning population. In Manchester in 1832 a third of the houses had no privy. In many cities

22 Flora Tristan: *Promenades à Londres* (Paris, 1840), chap. x. Thomas Beames: *The Rookeries of London* (London, 1851), 48 ff., describes the same area in much the same terms.

there was only one convenience for several hundred people. It stands to reason that in the congested areas the streets were full of "stagnant pools, ordure and heaps of refuse." In 1838 Chadwick could report from London on the "pondings of ordurous liquids as made one universal atmosphere of filth and stink." Much of this waste was ultimately washed into the sewers and carried to the rivers from which the water supply was taken. Friedrich Engels, in his classic account of the condition of the working classes, has left an all too vivid description of the River Irk, which, flowing through Manchester, gave off such a miasmic stench that it was all but impossible to cross the bridge. Even the great Thames was, at London, little more than a vast pool in which millions of tons of sewage were washed to and fro with the changing tides. In London, Paris and other cities the work of extending and modernizing the sewer system had gotten under way by 1850, but the task was a Herculean one, requiring years of effort.[23]

The great manufacturing towns, "reeking with lean misery and hungry wretchedness" (Dickens), were perfect breeding grounds for disease, as the medical profession was coming to realize. The rate of mortality was much higher than in the rural areas; indeed the cities would have become depopulated except for the constant influx of immigrants. Half the children born failed to survive the fifth year and the general expectancy of life was at birth still less than forty years. The horrible cholera epidemic of 1832 aroused interest in public health, but in terms of mortality the chronic illnesses, mostly pulmonary or dietary, were far more important than this novel affliction. Tuberculosis (consumption) was endemic, and was accepted as inevitable. It accounted for about 30 per cent of all deaths and seems to have been at its worst in the decade from 1837 to 1847. In Paris 42,614 people died of it between 1839 and 1848. Typhus, loosely classed as one of the many "fevers" (asthma, catarrh, etc.), was epidemic as well as endemic, serious outbreaks occurring every five to ten years. By 1840 it was recognized as a disease of destitution, a product of slum conditions.

---

[23] Chadwick's classic *Report* puts all other studies in the shade, but see also S. E. Finer: *The Life and Times of Sir Edwin Chadwick* (London, 1952), especially Book V, chap. i. On Paris there is a wealth of information in Henri Meding: *Essai sur la topographie médicale de Paris* (Paris, 1852). 250 ff., and in David H. Pinkney: *Napoleon III and the Rebuilding of Paris* (Princeton, 1958), 8 ff. On the German cities, the authoritative treatment is that of Alfons Fischer: *Geschichte des deutschen Gesundheitswesens* (Berlin, 1933), II, 500 ff.

Smallpox had been brought under a fair measure of control through the introduction of vaccination, but its place as a fatal disease of children was being taken by measles. Add to these afflictions rheumatism, constipation and dysentery and one can readily understand the weakness and apathy of many workers. Dr. Southwood Smith kept preaching that what was needed was not more charity but a better water supply, good drainage and pure air. The work of the physicians, like that of administrators such as Chadwick, was to culminate in the Public Health Act of 1848 and the inauguration of serious sanitary reform.[24]

Considering the appalling conditions under which the proletarian elements lived, it is not at all surprising that they should have become demoralized. Whenever they had a little pay they were apt to escape from the discipline of the factory and spend "blue" Monday at some popular amusement place, whence they would return dead drunk and penniless. Or more likely the entire family would resort to the café or pub, in winter about the only refuge from the cold and the dark (see Illustration 26). All cities were well supplied with pubs. In 1836 there were 8,659 in London and 1,200 in Manchester. In Whitecross Street (London) there were twenty-three in 300 yards. That they were prosperous is beyond doubt. In one large London establishment 3,146 men, 2,189 women and 686 children entered in one day, by actual count. In Manchester one pub was entered by 412 persons within the space of an hour. In Glasgow, where conditions were at their very worst, it is recorded that nearly 30,000 persons would be in a "state of brutal intoxication" on a Saturday night.[25]

Extreme want also drove many into crime. In times of unemploy-

---

[24] M. W. Flinn, in the introduction to the new edition of the Chadwick *Report*, 8 ff.; Meding, *Essai*, 122 ff. There is rich material in Charles Creighton: *A History of Epidemics in Britain* (Cambridge, 1894), II, 598 ff. On cholera, see R. E. McGrew: "The First Cholera Epidemic and Social History" (*Bulletin of the History of Medicine*, XXXIV, 1960, 61–73); Asa Briggs: "Cholera and Society in the 19th Century" (*Past and Present*, July 1961, 76–96). On tuberculosis, S. L. Cummins: *Tuberculosis in History* (Baltimore, 1949); René and Jean Dubos: *The White Plague* (Boston, 1952). In general, B. L. Hutchins: *The Public Health Agitation, 1833–1848* (London, 1909), chap. iv; M. C. Buer: *Health, Wealth and Population in the Early Days of the Industrial Revolution* (London, 1926), chaps. vii and viii; Richard A. Lewis: *Edwin Chadwick and the Public Health Movement, 1832–1854* (London, 1952); William M. Frazer: *A History of English Public Health, 1834–1919* (London, 1950).

[25] The contemporary accounts of Gaskell, chap. iv; Engels, 142; Taylor, 256 ff. Further, Wade: *A Treatise on the Police and Crimes of the Metropolis* (London, 1829), 223 ff., 305; James S. Buckingham: *History and Progress of the Temperance Reformation* (London, 1854), 28 ff.; Meding: *Essai*, 97 ff.; A. Baer: *Der Alcoholismus* (Berlin, 1878), *passim*.

ment juvenile delinquency, as depicted in Dickens' *Oliver Twist* or
Eugène Sue's *Mysteries of Paris,* became alarmingly widespread. A
London police official estimated the number of thieves in London alone
at 70,000. In all large cities organized gangs prowled the streets at
night, breaking into bakers' and grocers' shops, attacking pedestrians
and generally terrorizing the well-to-do.[26]
Especially ominous was the rapid spread of prostitution and the
growing rate of illegitimacy. "We verily believe," wrote a London
police commissioner in 1829, "that there are fewer conscientious scru-
ples entertained respecting sexual intercourse than at any former
period."[27] There was apparently no marked increase in the number of
registered prostitutes, of whom there were about 9,000 in London and
3,600 in Paris, lodged either in brothels or in private rooms of varying
degrees of elegance. These professionals were not the problem. It was
the unknown number of poor women—factory workers, laundresses,
seamstresses, domestics,—who were driven to supplement their meager
earnings through at least occasional prostitution. It was thought at
the time that in London there were some 80,000 regular and occasional prostitutes. In the Waterloo Road district a French visitor
was shocked to see them sitting in doorways or at the windows, nude
to the waist and in most provocative postures. At night they would
invade the West End in groups, as starving girls did in Vienna also,
some of them carrying old mats as an added inducement to prospective
customers. Recent researches leave little doubt that Victorian sexual
morality was largely a myth. Immorality was everywhere prevalent,
but was not discussed in polite society.[28]
In the days when advocacy of contraceptive methods was just begin-

26 Wade: *Treatise,* 158 ff.; Beames: *The Rookeries of London,* 119 ff.; Chevalier,
Classes Laborieuses, introd. and Book I; Scheer: *Deutsche Kultur- und Sittengeschichte,*
587 ff.
27 Wade: *Treatise,* 148.
28 The pioneer classic of the subject, A. J. G. Parent-Duchâtelet: *De la prostitution
dans la ville de Paris* (Paris, 1836), falls squarely into this period. On the situation in
England, see Wade: *Treatise,* 152 ff.; Flora Tristan: *Promenades à Londres* (Paris,
1840), chap. viii; Michael Ryan: *Prostitution in London* (London, 1839); Gordon R.
Taylor: *The Angel-Makers* (London, 1958), chap, iv; Steven Marcus: *The Other
Victorians* (New York, 1966), 6 ff. On France, see also Frégier: *Des classes dangereuses,*
49, 97, and chap. iv; Meding: *Topographie médicale,* 94 ff.; Chevalier: *Classes
laborieuses,* 334; on Vienna, Adolf Schmidl: *Wien und seine nächsten Umgebungen*
(Vienna, 1847), 141; Ernst Violand: *Die sociale Geschichte der Revolution in Oesterreich* (Leipzig, 1850), 45 ff.; and on Berlin Scheer: *Deutsche Kultur- und Sittengeschichte,* 587.

ning, widespread prostitution inevitably resulted in a high rate of illegitimacy, especially among the lower classes. In the large cities a third to a half of all babies born were illegitimate. Since their mothers were unwilling or unable to support them, they were quietly disposed of by smothering or simple neglect. Dr. Edwin R. Lankester, the biologist, is reputed to have stated that in London alone there were 16,000 mothers who had murdered their offspring.[29] Certain it is that infanticide was widely practiced everywhere and that the abandonment of newborn children in doorways and on the streets had reached alarming proportions. In France and other Latin countries foundling hospitals accepted infants without asking questions, with the result that large numbers of children were so disposed of, many of them through professional *sages femmes*. In France not fewer than 127,507 children were so abandoned in the year 1833 alone. Since many of the babies were already in poor condition and the hospitals were unable to care for such large numbers, the majority of the children died within a few weeks or en route to the provinces, where they were sent to be nursed. Small wonder that the entire system was denounced as "legalized infanticide."[30]

The "barbarians" or "savages," as the Parisians called them, were utterly ignorant and brutalized. Gaskell was shocked by the profanity and obscenity of their language, even within the family. Disraeli, in turn, thought them different from the brutes only in their inferior morality.[31] Certainly religion played no part in the lives of the vast majority. The construction of churches was far from keeping pace with the population increase, and in any case the workers would hardly have been welcome in the houses of the Lord, dirty and ragged as they were. Many of them admitted to investigators that they never prayed and in fact had never heard of Jesus. A census of church attendance taken in England in 1851 revealed that the working people of the cotton and coal towns were "as utter strangers to religious ordinances as the people of a heathen country." Few of them attended church or chapel; indeed,

[29] Quoted by Annie Besant: *The Law of Population* (London, 1878), 25 ff.

[30] See the two excellent articles by Alphonse Esquiros: "Les enfants trouvés" (*Revue des Deux Mondes*, XIII, 1846, 211–242, 1007–1044). Further, Alexander von Oettingen: *Die Moralstatistik* (3 ed., Erlangen, 1882), 236 ff.; F. S. Hügel: *Die Findelhäuser und das Findelwesen Europas* (Vienna, 1863), 137 ff.; Léon Allemand: *Histoire des enfants trouvés* (Paris, 1885), 205, 276; Arthur Keller and C. J. Klumper: *Säuglingsfürsorge und Kinderschutz in den europäischen Staaten* (Berlin, 1912), I, 441 ff.

[31] Gaskell: *Manufacturing Population of England*, chap. v; Disraeli: *Sybil*.

in one of the poorest sections of London, only about 6,000 out of a population of 90,000. The workers made no secret of the fact that they regarded religion as a luxury of the upper classes, that they thought the churches indifferent to the sufferings of the poor, that they were excluded from the pews rented by the rich, and that, besides, they had no decent clothing to appear for public worship.[32]

The situation in France was much the same. The urban laborers were indifferent if not actively hostile to religion. In many districts of Paris only about one in ten of the men observed Easter Communion. According to prominent churchmen, there were in Paris only about 50,000 to 100,000 practicing Catholics in a population of almost a million, and of these most were women.[33] In religion as in other respects the workingman had become socially alienated, degraded, ostracized. Eugène Sue compared his famous *Mysteries of Paris* to James Fenimore Cooper's Indian tales: respectable Parisians were likened to the American settlers, living among dangerous savages. European society was indeed, as Disraeli asserted, becoming divided into two nations, one of which was increasingly moved by resentment and hatred, while the other was becoming more and more frightened by the sight of its sullen and at times ferocious neighbors. Carlyle, writing in his *Chartism* (1839) of the "wild, inarticulate souls," spoke emphatically of their sense of social injustice, which was harder to bear than even material want. Mrs. Gaskell, too, in her novel *Mary Barton* (1848), noted the rising antagonism of the workers to the propertied classes and had one of them say: "They'n screwed us down to the lowest peg in order to make their great fortunes and build their great big houses." In Ger-

32 J. L. and B. Hammond: *The Age of the Chartists* (London, 1930), chaps. xii and xiii; George Kitson Clark: *The Making of Victorian England* (London, 1962), chap. vi; Kenneth S. Inglis: *Churches and the Working Classes in Victorian England* (London, 1963), 1 ff.; Owen Chadwick: *The Victorian Church* (New York, 1966), I, 332 ff., 363 ff. Thomas Cooper's *Wise Saws and Modern Instances* (London, 1845) is a collection of stories by a self-educated worker which throw light on the attitude of the workers toward the churches.

33 Thomas W. Allies: *Journal in France in 1845 and 1848* (London, 1849), 41, 112 ff., 257, 278; M. H. Vicaire: "Les ouvriers parisiens en face du catholicisme de 1830 à 1870" (*Schweizerische Zeitschrift für Geschichte,* I, 1951, 226–244); Monique Vincienne and Hélène Courtois: "Notes sur la situation religieuse en France en 1848" (*Archives de sociologie des religions,* No. 6, 1958, 104–118); François A. Isambert: *Christianisme et classe ouvrière* (Tournai, 1961); 180 ff.; Yver-Marie Hilaire: "La pratique religieuse en France de 1815 à 1878" (*Information historique,* XXV, 1963, 57–69).

many eminent writers such as Franz Baader and Robert von Mohl warned of the coming crisis, while the Swiss pastor-novelist Jeremias Gotthelf declared: "A new spirit has arisen among the workers. Their hearts seethe with hatred of the well-to-do; their eyes lust for a share of the wealth about them; their mouths speak unblushingly of a coming day of retribution. . . ."[34]

3. THE GATHERING STORM

In the period before 1848 the workers were still too ignorant and physically too decrepit to undertake large-scale, concerted action. In the early days of the Industrial Revolution they had expressed their feelings by smashing machines, burning down factories and even attacking their employers. In England there were only sporadic outbreaks of this kind after 1830, but on the Continent there were a number of violent clashes, especially among the home weavers, but also among the factory workers. The uprisings of the silk workers in Lyons in 1831 and 1834, discussed in a previous chapter, and of the Silesian weavers in 1844 belong in this category. Both had to be suppressed by armed force. Even more ominous was the strike of the textile workers in Prague in June, 1844, which was soon joined by the railway construction crews operating in the vicinity. The immediate reason for this outbreak was the introduction of new cotton printing machines, which the workers feared would throw them out of work. There was wholesale destruction of machinery and for a time real danger that the workers might take control of the city. Eventually they were driven back to the factories by troops hastily assembled from the neighborhood. Finally, during the famine years 1846–1847 there was much unrest, of which the "potato war" in Berlin in April, 1847, was perhaps the most spectacular example (see Illustration 53).[35]

34 Franz Baader: *Ueber das Missverhältnis der Vermögenslosen oder Proletairs zu den Vermögenbesitzenden Klassen der Sozietät* (Munich, 1835); Robert Mohl: *Ueber die Nachteile der fabrikmässigen Industrie* (1835); Jeremias Gotthelf: *Die Armennot* (1841). These writers are all excerpted in Carl Jantke and Dietrich Hilger: *Die Eigentumslosen* (Munich, 1965).

35 Wilhelm Wolff: "Das Elend und der Aufruhr in Schlesien" (1845); Alfred Zimmermann: *Blüthe und Verfall des Leinengewerbes in Schlesien* (2 ed., Oldenburg, 1892); Herbert Kisch: "The Textile Industries of Silesia and the Rhineland" (*Journal of Economic History*, XIX, 1959, 541–564); Horst Blumberg: "Ein Beitrag zur Geschichte der Leinenindustrie von 1834 bis 1870" (in Hans Mottek, ed.: *Studien zur Geschichte der industriellen Revolution in Deutschland*, Berlin, 1960, 65–143). On the Bohemian

In Britain, where the strike had been legalized, it was the instrument usually employed by the workers to secure better pay or, more often, to protest against reduction of wages or work force. But most strikes were not backed by strike funds; they usually lasted only a few days, the more so as mill owners would commonly band together for a lockout of the entire local industry. The story of a major (illegal) strike in the woolen center of Lodève, in southern France, was typical of many others. In 1845 the workers of one mill struck in protest against the extension of the workday without corresponding pay increases. Thereupon the owners of other plants closed down and refused all negotiation: "Let the workers submit and an agreement will be possible; without submission there is no hope for them," wrote the local newspaper. The workers, trying to live on five centimes worth of potatoes a day, along with what charity could provide, were forced within a month to submit. But thereafter, when opportunity offered, they would throw stones at their employers and otherwise give vent to their hostility.[36]

Effective action by the workers could come only from the better-educated craftsmen and artisans, many of whom, in the skilled trades, were threatened less by the competition of the machine than by the pressure of population, which made work harder and harder to obtain. On the Continent these elements played an important role in political disturbances supporting, as they usually did, the activities of the bourgeois radicals. But labor organizations and economic strikes were illegal and, whenever attempted, met with stern repressive measures. The uprisings in Lyons and Paris were put down by the military, and so was the strike of Paris tailors in 1840, which had been quickly joined by workers in other trades and had begun to spread to the provinces. Hundreds of leaders were arrested, tried and transported.[37]

Only in Britain, then, was labor organization and action possible. The background was provided by the Friendly Societies, which, origi-

---

troubles, Friedrich Walter: "Die böhmischen Arbeiterunruhen des Jahres 1844" (*Mitteilungen des oesterreichischen Instituts für Geschichtsforschung*, Suppl. XI, 1929, 717–734).

[36] Frank E. Manuel: "La grève des tisserands de Lodève" (*Revue d'histoire moderne*, 1935, 1–38); Peter N. Stearns: "Patterns of Industrial Strike Activity in France during the July Monarchy" (*American Historical Review*, LXX, 1965, 371–394).

[37] Octave Festy: "Le mouvement ouvrier à Paris en 1840" (*Revue des sciences politiques*, XXX, 1913, 67–79, 226–274, 333–361).

nally designed for entertainment and mutual aid, soon became the favorite form of organization among the workers, especially of Lancashire and Yorkshire. By 1850 they had a total membership of 1,500,000 and had their own newspapers (for instance, *The Poor Man's Guardian*) and their own coffeehouses and reading rooms, of which there were some 1,600 in London alone.[38]

During the political crisis of 1831–1832 William Lovett, a London cabinetmaker, founded the National Union of the Working Classes, based on the proposition that the workers must secure universal suffrage as a prelude to control of Parliament and to the inauguration of a system of social democracy which would "justly distribute the blessings of plenty, which the sons of industry have gathered." In famous meetings at the London Rotunda speeches became so radical as to alarm not only the propertied classes but moderate labor leaders such as Francis Place. Yet in the end Lovett's movement was doomed to disappointment. The middle classes secured parliamentary reform, but the program of the workers was soon forgotten.[39]

The failure of political action shifted the interest of the workers toward methods of self-help and for some years attention was focused on the co-operative and trade-union movements. Robert Owen, the successful mill owner and social reformer, had for years been preaching *A New View of Society* (1812–1814), which was to be based not on competition but on co-operation. In the mid-1820's a group of brilliant theorists lent him support by demonstrating that the laborer was receiving only about one-fifth of the product of his labor, whereas he was entitled to all of it. If he were given an adequate return he would have a greater purchasing power and thus would help to prevent economic crises and unemployment.[40] Under these influences workers began to open co-operative stores in the hope of making the money needed to found their own, communal shops. The movement spread so rapidly to all large cities that in 1831 there were about 500 societies with some 20,000 members. Although these co-operatives were not exactly what

38 Hammond: *Age of the Chartists,* chap. xvii; Brian Simon: *Studies in the History of Education, 1780–1870* (London, 1960), 226 ff.; J. H. Gordon: *The Friendly Societies in England, 1815–1875* (Manchester, 1961), 2 ff.

39 R. W. Postgate: *The Builders' History* (London, n.d.), 58 ff.

40 John Gray: *Lecture on Human Happiness* (1825); Thomas Hodgskin: *Labour Defended against the Claims of Capital* (1825); William Thompson: *Labour Rewarded* (1827).

Owen had in mind, he became converted to the movement and lent it the prestige of his name.[41]

Closely related to the co-operative movement was the trade-union movement and more particularly the effort to combine unions in various trades so as to bring the full force of labor to bear on relations with employers. In 1830 John Doherty, who had already tried to organize the cotton operatives, founded the National Association for the Protection of Labour, which soon comprised some 150 unions in the textile, coal and mining industries of Lancashire and the north. Two years later the Operative Builders' Union united some 30,000 workers of Manchester and Liverpool, and finally in 1834 Robert Owen accepted the presidency of the Grand National Consolidated Trades Union of Great Britain and Ireland. This pretentious organization was prepared to take in all workers, including agricultural laborers and women. Actually it was a creation of London artisans, the membership of which consisted largely of skilled laborers, with tailors playing a leading role. At first it evoked an enthusiastic response throughout the country, yet it lasted only some six months and, historically speaking, is far more interesting for the ideas it embodied than for any real achievement. Its weakness was, from the outset, in a conflict of ideologies. Owen hoped that within a few years the union would be able, through co-operative production, to effect social changes that would come upon the world "like a thief in the night." But other leaders, notably the journalists James Morrison and James E. Smith, were imbued with class consciousness and favored an avowed class struggle. The workers, they held, should organize without reference to Parliament or capitalists. They must secure control of society as a prelude to command of politics. It was in this spirit that William Benbow in 1832 published his book *A Grand National Holiday and a Congress of the Productive Classes,* advocating a general strike, that is, a complete stoppage of work for a month to enforce the rights of the workers. During this "sacred month" they should simply seize whatever they needed. Again, there was great enthusiasm for "a long strike, a strong strike, and a

---

41 Margaret Cole: *Robert Owen of New Lanark* (London, 1953), 163 ff.; Asa Briggs: *Robert Owen in Retrospect* (London, 1959); Max Beer: *A History of British Socialism* (London, 1919), I, 160 ff., 211 ff.; H. L. Beales: *The Early English Socialists* (London, 1934); Sidney Pollard: "Nineteenth Century Coöperation: from Community-Building to Shop-keeping" in Asa Briggs and John Saville, eds.: *Essays in Labour History,* London, 1960, 74–112).

strike all together." But the obstacles confronting the organizers of labor soon blasted these high hopes.[42]

In retrospect it becomes clear that the effort of 1834 was premature. Very few unions were effectively organized, least of all on a national basis. Furthermore, some important trades, such as the builders and clothiers, held aloof, and many factory workers were lukewarm. The whole project, as we now see it, was too hasty and overambitious. It did, however, have the important effect of frightening the upper classes. "The trades unions are, we have no doubt," wrote the influential *Morning Post* on March 29, 1834, "the most dangerous institutions that were ever permitted to take root, under the shelter of the law, in any country." When in that same month George Loveless and five companions were arrested at Tolpuddle (Dorsetshire), charged with organizing agricultural workers in a union to be affiliated with the Grand Consolidated, the government took prompt and drastic action. The men were convicted of administering secret oaths and were sentenced to deportation. This episode, which evoked loud protests from the workers and precipitated an orgy of strikes, was a real body blow to the labor movement. Thenceforth employers insisted that workers, before being employed, sign the "document," that is, a statement renouncing the union and promising not to support its members. For some years unionism, while it continued to develop, found the going difficult. Before long it was to be overshadowed by the great agitation known as Chartism.[43]

The Chartist movement has been discussed in considerable detail in Chapter III because, while it was a movement supported primarily by workingmen, it was designed for political action in the hope that political democracy, once attained, would make social democracy possible. As a political movement it was therefore part and parcel of the

[42] Sidney and Beatrice Webb: *A History of Trade Unionism* (new ed., London, 1920); A. L. Morton and G. Tate: *The British Labour Movement, 1770–1920* (London, 1956); Henry Pelling: *A History of British Trade Unionism* (New York, 1963); G. D. H. Cole: *Attempts at General Union, 1818–1834* (London, 1953); Neil F. Smelser: *Social Change in the Industrial Revolution* (Chicago, 1959), chap. xii; Herbert A. Turner: *Trade Union Growth, Structure and Policy* (Toronto, 1962), 73 ff.; W. H. Oliver: "The Consolidated Trades Union of 1834" (*Economic History Review*, Ser. 2, XVII, 1964, 77–95).

[43] On the Tolpuddle affair, see especially the contribution of Walter Citrine to the centenary volume *The Book of the Martyrs of Tolpuddle* (London, 1934); also Bertram Newman: *Lord Melbourne* (London, 1930), 113 ff.

radicalism which aimed at extending the program of reform. Chartism had relatively little to do with the lowest stratum of society. Like the unionist movement, it was essentially an affair of artisans and skilled workers, who were apt to be literate and have the drive necessary to stage a campaign. Like the unionist movement, too, it was rent by the conflict between the "moral force" and the "physical force" men. Nonetheless, it rallied the support of the working classes and made a deep impression not only on British but on Continental opinion.

4. EARLY SOCIAL LEGISLATION

The attitude of the propertied classes toward the social question derived largely from the teachings of the economists, notably Malthus, Ricardo, James Mill and Nassau Senior. Since, according to Malthus, population tended to outrun available subsistence, a considerable in-crement of the population must at any time live on the very verge of starvation. Poverty, while hideous and deplorable, was nonetheless in-evitable. Efforts to alleviate it through state action would be harmful as well as futile, and private charity, while commendable, would run the danger of prolonging the misery of its recipients. The only hope for the lowest class lay in better understanding of their plight, in realization that improvement of their situation depended on restriction of their numbers. Through the exercise of "moral restraint," that is, through postponement of marriage and complete sexual continence before mar-riage, they themselves must effectuate a decline in the birth rate. Un-intentionally Malthus thus relieved the well-to-do of any responsibility for the prevalence of pauperism and excused them from attempting any amelioration. "The doctrine that poverty was inevitable and in-curable put a soft pillow under the conscience of the ruling class."[44]

The writings of the British economists were quickly translated into other languages and provided the framework for Continental thought on social problems. Charles Dunoyer, author of an exhaustive treatise on the *Freedom of Labor* (*De la liberté du travail*, 3 vols., Paris, 1845), never tired of the theme that the tribulations of the workers were due chiefly to their own intemperance, lack of foresight, and general

---

[44] John L. and Barbara Hammond: *The Town Labourer, 1760–1832* (new ed., London, 1925), II, 34. See also David V. Glass: *Introduction to Malthus* (London, 1953) and the excellent discussion of economic theories in S. G. Checkland: *The Rise of Industrial Society in England, 1815–1885* (London, 1964), chap. x.

depravity. He argued, furthermore, that a certain amount of want and misery was socially beneficial, since it served as a warning to the more sober elements of the working class. Dunoyer objected to any state action and, like many others, pointed out that popular education could lead only to greater discontent on the part of the workers, without in any way changing the inexorable march of history.[45]

Yet the threat of overpopulation was so great and the danger of social upheaval so pressing that more and more voices were raised in opposition to a simple policy of laissez faire. The eminent Swiss historian-economist Sismondi had in 1819 challenged the Malthusian teaching and stamped Britain a shocking example of free competition, resulting in the concentration of enormous wealth in the hands of a few while at least a tenth of the population was dependent on charity for its mere existence. Then, badly frightened like many other propertied people by the turmoil of the years 1830–1832, Sismondi conjured up the prospect of a proletarian threat to existing civilization. The state, he argued, had a moral, Christian responsibility for the workers. The important thing was to protect men, not industries; goods are of no value if they do not promote the general welfare.[46]

Sismondi's ideas were reflected in the writings of French social critics such as Alban de Villeneuve-Bargement, Louis Villermé and Eugène Buret, and probably influenced also the British physicians and investigators who pioneered the early social legislation. These men were well acquainted with the condition of the working class. One and all they argued the need for welfare legislation such as a minimum wage, increased relief, establishment of savings banks and agricultural colonies as refuges for the unemployed.[47] In Germany, too, there was

[45] Charles Gide and Charles Rist: *Histoire des doctrines économiques* (7 ed., Paris, 1947), I, 359 ff., 387 ff.; René Gonnard: *Histoire des doctrines économiques* (Paris, 1947), 200 ff.; Ernest Labrousse: *Le mouvement ouvrier et les idées sociales en France* (Paris, 1948), 59, 63, 124 ff.; Guy P. Palmade: *Capitalisme et capitalistes français au XIXe siècle* (Paris, 1961), 104 ff.

[46] Sismonde de Sismondi: *Nouveaux principes d'économie politique, ou de la richesse dans ses rapports avec la population* (Paris, 1819), especially II, 260 ff., and "Du sort des ouvriers dans les manufactures" (*Revue mensuelle d'économie politique*, III, July, 1834). See also Octave Festy: "Sismondi et la condition des ouvriers français à son temps" (*Revue d'économie politique*, XXXII, 1918, 46–72, 118–136); Jean R. De Salis: *Sismondi* (Paris, 1932), chap. xv.

[47] Alban de Villeneuve-Bargement: *Economie politique chrétienne* (Paris, 1834); Louis Villermé: *Tableau de l'état physique et moral des ouvriers employés dans les manufactures de coton, de laine et de soie* (Paris, 1840); Eugène Buret: *De la misère des*

growing concern with the plight of the lower classes. Hegel considered the problem of the worker the overriding question of modern society. Economists such as Karl Heinrich Rau and Robert von Mohl urged state support for workers' associations, co-operatives, banks, and so on. In the rapidly industrializing Rhineland two prominent businessmen, Friedrich Harkort and Gustav Mevissen, called for state action to regulate the hours of labor, check the abuses of the truck system, and provide education for the lower classes.[48]

In England more and more attention was paid in literature to the laboring masses, reflecting the rising tide of humanitarianism deriving from the eighteenth century. Charles Dickens in *Oliver Twist* (1836) had his little hero born in a workhouse and then farmed out to an elderly female who pocketed most of the parish allowance and practically starved the twenty or thirty infants entrusted to her care. At least eight out of ten of the children sickened from hunger and cold, or fell into the fire from neglect, or were simply half smothered (by accident). Later, when apprenticed to an undertaker, Oliver was fed on the dog's meal of scraps from the table, which he tore asunder "with horrible avidity . . . with all the ferocity of famine." In the 1840's came a succession of "social novels," beginning with Frances Trollope's *Michael Armstrong, the Factory Boy* (1840), with illustrations of half-grown lads disputing with the pigs for the food in the trough (see Illustration 32). In 1845 came Benjamin Disraeli's *Sybil,* perhaps most influential of these novels, reflecting not only the data provided by government reports but also personal observation in the factory towns. Charlotte Brontë's *Jane Eyre* (1847) reverted again to the miseries of

---

classes laborieuses en France et en Angleterre (Paris, 1842). Maurice Deslandres and Alfred Michelin: *Il y a cent ans: état physique et moral des ouvriers au temps du libéralisme* (Paris, n.d.) is a useful digest of Villermé's two volumes. For an illuminating discussion, see Jean-Baptiste Duroselle: *Les débuts du catholicisme social en France, 1822–1870* (Paris, 1951), 60 ff.

48 Hanns E. Jansen: *Das Proletariat im Vormärz in den Anschauungen deutscher Denker* (Kiel, 1928), 19 ff.; Johanna Köster: *Der rheinische Frühliberalismus und die soziale Frage* (Berlin, 1938), 34 ff., 53 ff., 94 ff.; Jacques Droz: *Le libéralisme rhénan* (Paris, 1940), 242, 248 ff.; William O. Shanahan: *German Protestants Face the Social Question* (Notre Dame, 1954), chap. i; Donald G. Rohr: *The Origins of Social Liberalism in Germany* (Chicago, 1963), 78 ff., 136 ff. There are two valuable anthologies of the German literature on the social question: Jürgen Kuczynski: *Bürgerliche und halbfeudale Literatur aus den Jahren 1840–1847 zur Lage der Arbeiter* (Berlin, 1960), which includes an exhaustive bibliography; and Carl Jantke and Dietrich Hilger: *Die Eigentumslosen* (Munich, 1965).

poor orphan children. Jane at the age of ten was sent to a charitable orphanage where discipline was Draconian while food and clothing were exceedingly scant. The children, perpetually hungry, suffered agony at night under their meager bedding. However, their religious welfare was kept in mind, for even in winter they had to trudge miles through slush and sleet to attend church services. Charlotte Brontë had personal experience of such institutions and of life in factory towns, as reflected in her later novel *Shirley* (1849). But of greatest authenticity and interest was Elizabeth Gaskell's *Mary Barton* (1848), an admirable story of workingmen's lives in Manchester based on long personal observation.[49]

The problems of overpopulation, unemployment and pauperism were of such a magnitude that many minds grappled with them and advanced possible solutions. One pseudonymous writer, "Marcus," in an essay *On the Possibility of Limiting Populousness* (1838), described proletarian populousness as "the great ulcer of modern nations" and recommended that unwanted newborn babies be painlessly put to permanent sleep by asphyxiation, an idea that so enraged the workers that the Chartists, suspecting poor-law officials of the authorship, re-published the essay in 1839 as *The Book of Murder*.[50]

Marcus' proposition, though extreme, was by no means the only drastic proposal put forward at the time. Far more important, though hardly less acceptable to Victorian society, was the doctrine of contraception, first propounded by Francis Place, Richard Carlile and others in the 1820's with the avowed purpose of inducing the workers to restrict their numbers and so improve their position. The *Diabolical Handbills* (1822–) and Carlile's *What is Love, or Every Woman's Book* (1826) were widely distributed in London and the industrial North and may well have had a significant impact, for they were simply and frankly written for the workers. Though Carlile and his ilk were violently attacked as "impudent intruders into the sacred privacies of wedded love," John Stuart Mill and

---

[49] Lord David Cecil to the contrary notwithstanding. See Arthur Pollard: "The Novels of Mrs. Gaskell" (*Bulletin of the John Rylands Library*, XLII, 1961, 403–425); Edgar Wright: *Mrs. Gaskell: The Basis for Reassessment* (Oxford, 1965).

[50] The account of this episode in Sidney and Beatrice Webb: *English Poor Law History* (London, 1929), Part II, 163 ff., leaves some doubt whether these eminent authorities actually had read the Marcus essay.

other Radicals endorsed contraception and there appears to have been but little official opposition prior to the 1870's.[51]

Too little is known about the early history of contraception to warrant any firm conclusion as to its importance, but of another nostrum for overpopulation ample data are available. It was a striking feature of the period that colonies were in ill repute—declared by Radical writers to be nothing more nor less than a preserve for the upper classes, who found there opportunities for their younger sons. Yet even Bentham and James Mill were obliged to admit that they might serve the useful purpose of absorbing the homeland's excess population. Charles Buller in 1830 described the chief objective of emigration as the "shovelling out of paupers," and in 1837 Lord Durham, in his famous report on Canada, described colonies as the "ample appanage which God and Nature have set aside in the New World for those whose lot has assigned them but insufficient portions in the Old." The workers in general did not relish the prospect of emigration and did not see why they should be driven from their native land while rich drones stayed at home and enjoyed the good things of life. But it was increasingly clear that emigration was the only effective vent, the only immediate remedy. So the governments in all countries gradually abandoned their opposition and presently reached the point of aiding the departure of the poor. The emigration from England alone rose from about 57,000 in 1830 to 90,000 in 1840 and 280,000 in 1850. From Ireland it has been estimated that over one and a half million had departed prior to the great famine of 1846. As for Germany, large-scale emigration set in only in the 1840's, being heaviest from the most congested areas, such as Hesse, Baden and Württemberg.[52]

[51] Normal E. Himes: *Medical History of Contraception* (Baltimore, 1936; New York, 1963), which may be supplemented with Peter Fryer: *The Birth Controllers* (New York, 1966), Parts I-III. Carlile's booklet contained much information on the *Handbills*, several of which he reprinted. There is also much to be gleaned from Robert Dale Owen's *Moral Physiology* (New York, 1830), which was widely circulated in Britain (10 ed., London, 1833).

[52] See above, Chapter III; in addition, Klaus E. Knorr: *British Colonial Theories, 1570–1850* (Toronto, 1944), chap. ix; William F. Adams: *Ireland and Irish Emigration to the New World* (New Haven, 1932); W. S. Walshaw: *Migration to and from the British Isles* (London, 1941); William S. Shepperson: *British Emigration to North America* (Minneapolis, 1957); Wilhelm Monckmeier: *Die deutsche überseeische Auswanderung* (Jena, 1912); Mack Walker: *Germany and the Emigration, 1816–1885* (Cambridge, 1964).

Great hopes were staked also on philanthropy. Everywhere in Europe charitable organizations proliferated, most of them with ponderous names, specialized programs (often esoteric) and complex procedures. In 1844 there were 450 relief organizations in London alone.[53]

In industry as in agriculture there were good employers, who provided cheap lodgings and wholesome luncheons for their workers. One of them felt that if he could civilize the girls the latter would exercise a good influence on the boys. He therefore established an Order of the Silver Star for those girls who distinguished themselves by their conduct and good morals.[54] But perhaps the greatest effort was devoted to the problem of popular schooling. This was deprecated by some as possibly giving the workers a keener awareness of the exploitation of which they were the victims. But among the liberal middle class the idea had become firmly fixed that through education the laborer could be made to understand the inevitability of inequality, the importance of thrift and sobriety and the futility of revolt or violence. Continental countries such as France and Germany were in advance of Britain in provision for popular education, though in those countries, too, the requirements of the law were one thing and the realities quite another.

In any case, the situation being most pressing in Britain, much is to be learned from the evolution of the problem there. In 1830 primary education was still largely of the monitorial type as developed in the early years of the century by Andrew Bell and Joseph Lancaster and financed by the two rival organizations, The National Society for the Education of the Poor in the Principles of the Established Church, which was intent above all on teaching the children of the poor to read the Bible, and the British and Foreign School Society, which pursued the more secular aim of teaching reading, writing and arithmetic, but also "the ascertained truths of political science," such as the iron law of wages and the necessity for Malthusian moral restraint to limit the

---

[53] John W. Dodds: *The Age of Paradox* (New York, 1952), 86. See further E. C. P. Lascelles: "Charity" (in George M. Young, ed.: *Early Victorian England*, London, 1934, II, chap. xv); David Owen: *English Philanthropy, 1660–1960* (Cambridge, 1964), Part II, chaps. v and vi; David Johnston: *A History of the Present Condition of Public Charity in France* (Edinburgh, 1829); Louis M. Moreau-Christophe: *Du problème de la misère* (Paris, 1851), III, 491.

[54] W. E. H.: *Hints to Employers* (London, 1841), 9 ff., 15 ff.; Ure: *Philosophy of Manufactures*, 32 ff., 45 ff.; Taylor: *Tour of the Manufacturing Districts*, 25 ff., 60 ff.

number of competing workers. In addition there were the Ragged School Union, founded for the purpose of teaching waifs and outcasts the truths of the Bible, and Lord Brougham's Society for the Diffusion of Useful Knowledge (1826), which alone was interested in education for its own sake and devoted itself to the distribution of short, popular treatises on natural science, literature and biography, and economics, such as the pamphlets by Charles Knight which explained to the workers the futility of opposition to the new machine age. Its appeal was necessarily to the literate stratum of the working class, as were the many Mechanics' Institutes which sprang up in all larger cities and became centers of intellectual life, even for the middle class. It must be emphasized, however, that the prime motive of all these efforts was to implement the Malthusian teaching of moral restraint. Even so great a humanitarian as Dr. James Kay could write that in the schools "the evils which imprudent marriages entail on those who contract them, on their unhappy offspring, and on society at large, should be exhibited in the strongest light." He was convinced that "the increase of intelligence and virtue amongst the people will prove our surest safeguard, in the absence of which the possessions of the higher orders might be, to an ignorant and brutal populace, like the fair plains of Italy to the destroying Vandal."[55]

In the gravely overpopulated regions of Central Europe the governments of West and South Germany, including Austria, attempted to check the birth rate by far-reaching restrictions on marriage, as described in Chapter I. These measures were not adopted in laissez-faire England, where William Cobbett and others bitterly attacked all such proposals.[56] But they were seriously considered by the authors of

[55] Quoted by Brian Simon: *Studies in the History of Education, 1780–1870* (London, 1960), 133 ff., 166 ff. Other excellent accounts are those of John W. Adamson: *English Education, 1789–1902* (London, 1930); G. Birchenough: *History of Elementary Education in England and Wales from 1800 to the Present Day* (London, 1938); W. H. G. Armytage: *Four Hundred Years of English Education* (Cambridge, 1964); Hugh M. Pollard: *Pioneers of Popular Education, 1760–1850* (Cambridge, 1957); Carter Jefferson: "Worker Education in England and France, 1800–1914" (*Comparative Studies in Society and History*, VI, 1964, 345–366). On the adult side, see M. Tylecote: *The Mechanics' Institutes of Lancashire and Yorkshire* (London, 1957); J. F. C. Harrison: *Learning and Living, 1790–1960* (Toronto, 1961); R. K. Webb: *The British Working Class Reader* (London, 1955), 66 ff.

[56] William Cobbett: "The Sin of Forbidding Marriage" in his *Twelve Sermons*, new ed., London, 1828, 196–212), and his comedy: *Overpopulation* (1834).

the new poor law of 1834, which, it will be recalled, provided at least for separation of the sexes in the poorhouses, so as to reduce the fertility of the most indigent elements.[57]

At almost the same time the British government showed an increasing readiness to intervene in social affairs by the provisions of the Factory Act of 1833. This act, applicable to textile mills (except lace and silk), forbade the employment of children under the age of nine, limited the workday of those aged nine to thirteen to nine hours a day and those aged thirteen to eighteen to twelve hours. Furthermore, children under thirteen were to attend school for two hours a day, subject to the supervision of government inspectors, who for the first time were appointed to ensure implementation of the law. It has been pointed out by critics that the Factory Act was motivated less by humanitarian considerations than by the thought that child labor was creating adult unemployment and that therefore steps must be taken to reduce its extent.[58] Nonetheless the humanitarian influence should not be underrated. Evangelicals and Radicals in Parliament, warmly supported by the newly enfranchised middle class, inspired a remarkable series of investigating commissions and reports. The revelation that in the mines women and children (aged six or even younger) were being employed for long hours in hauling coal trucks through low and narrow galleries, often in darkness and suffocating heat (see Illustrations 21, 22), aroused so much indignation as to produce the Second Factory Act of 1844. This prohibited the employment of women and of males under the age of ten in underground work, and again provided for government inspection. The workday of children was reduced to six hours and more schooling arranged for. Besides, the act, by regulating the work of adults (women), encouraged renewal of the agitation for a reduction of the general workday to ten hours, which would, of course, have made for the employment of larger numbers of grownups. A bill was introduced in 1846 and was backed by the Central Short Time Committee, a national propaganda organization modeled on the Anti-Corn Law League. First defeated, the bill was passed

57 The information assembled by the poor-law commission was published separately by Nassau W. Senior: *Statement of the Provision for the Poor in America and Europe* (London, 1835).

58 Guy Chapman: *Culture and Survival* (London, 1840), 82; Reinhard Bendix: *Work and Authority in Industry* (New York, 1956), 39.

by a substantial majority in 1847. The preceding abolition of the corn laws and introduction of free trade have tended to obscure this new factory act, but in perspective it must obviously be ranked with the major innovations of the nineteenth century. The ten-hour day and sixty-hour week were important not only in relieving unemployment but also in opening new vistas in the lives of the workers.[59]

Any discussion of early social legislation must of necessity focus on Britain, where the problems were most urgent and the forces favoring reform most active and effectual. France suffered less in readjusting than did Britain, though there too there was a degree of overpopulation and pressure for work. The French made progress in primary education through the law of 1833 and through private enterprise. As in England, it was supposed that education would reduce social unrest. In the primary field the Society for the Improvement of Elementary Education maintained many monitorial schools to supplement the government schools. By the 1840's about 75 per cent of the children aged six to twelve were attending school. Furthermore, the Polytechnic Association (founded in 1830) set up courses for adult workers much like those offered by the British Mechanics' Institutes. Before long the government was subsidizing these efforts, so that by 1847 there were some 115,000 grownups enrolled in almost 7,000 courses. In the matter of factory legislation a law of 1841 forbade the employment of children under eight years of age and restricted the workday of those eight to twelve to eight hours, of those between twelve and sixteen to twelve hours. All factory children were to receive some schooling, but no provision was made for inspection or enforcement.[60]

The English legislation against child labor was the model for similar factory laws in many Continental countries as well as in France. The Swiss canton of Zürich decreed in 1837 that children between the ages of twelve and sixteen should work in factories no longer than fourteen

---

[59] Maurice W. Thomas: *The Early Factory Legislation* (Leigh-on-Sea, 1948), chaps. iv; John Duffy: "Early Factory Legislation" (in Samuel G. McCulloch, ed.: *British Humanitarianism*, Philadelphia, 1950, 63–83); and the detailed account of the political maneuvering in J. T. Ward: *The Factory Movement* (London, 1962). On the educational side see footnote 55 above, and Gertrude Ward: "The Education of Factory Child Workers, 1833–1850" (*Economic History*, III, 1935, 110–124).

[60] Moreau-Christophe: *Du problème de la misère*, III, 493 ff.; Maurice Gontard: *L'enseignement primaire en France* (Paris, 1959); Carter Jefferson: "Worker Education." On the factory law, see Henri Sée: *Histoire économique de la France*, 190 ff.; Félix Ponteil: *Les institutions de la France de 1814 à 1870* (Paris, 1966), 205 ff.

hours in daytime or eight hours at night! The Prussian Law of 1839 forbade the employment of children under nine in factories and limited the hours of those between nine and sixteen to ten per day. Bavaria and Baden followed suit in 1840, Piedmont in 1843 and Russia in 1845. But this legislation was for the most part ineffective, since no provision was made for government inspection or other machinery of enforcement. How important such supervision was is shown by the English experience. There the inspectors, during only a few months in 1836, visited 596 factories, took 504 "informations" and convicted 458 employers, in most cases for employing children for more than nine hours a day without a certificate of school attendance. In that same year seventy-two mill owners petitioned Parliament to undo the work of 1833: "it is absolutely necessary to the carrying on of the cotton trade with advantage, to allow the employment of children eleven years of age for sixty-nine hours a week." A bill to this effect was defeated only by a narrow margin.[61]

Reviewing the social question of the early nineteenth century, it would seem that the tension can be attributed largely to the overpopulation resulting from the rapid population increase and the consequent pressure for work, which in turn brought in its train low wages and widespread unemployment. The resulting problems were mostly new and no one, even the economists, could offer satisfactory solutions. The situation was at its worst in the 1840's, but began to improve after 1850, when large-scale emigration began to drain Europe of large numbers of surplus workers, when industrialization had reached the point of providing more jobs, and when possibly birth control was affecting the rate of population growth, as it certainly was in France, where the teaching of the Catholic Church was frequently ignored and the clergy was instructed not to make an issue of contraception.[62] As for German efforts to restrict marriage, it seems questionable whether they resulted in much more than a marked rise in the rate of illegitimacy and also in the rate of emigration, which was highest in the regions where restrictions were in force.

---

61 John Fielden: *Curse of the Factory System*, 2, 17; Robert H. Greg: *The Factory System* (London, 1837).

62 The case of Bishop Bouvier in 1843, dealt with in some detail in John T. Noonan, Jr.: *Contraception* (Cambridge, 1965), 400 ff. See also Hélène Bergues *et al.*: *La prévention des naissances dans la famille* (Paris, 1960), chap. xii; Alfred Grotjahn: *Geburten-Rückgang und Geburten-Regelung* (Berlin, 1914), 22, 230 ff.; Jean Bourgeois-Pichat: "Evolution de la population française depuis le XVIIIe siècle" (*Population*, VI, 1951, 635–662).

The great hopes placed by liberals on the education of the lower classes would appear to have been generally misplaced, for the workers were not persuaded by the doctrines of the economists. Having learned to read, they tended to read the wrong things. In the long run the education of the workers paved the way for better labor organization and labor action and so undermined the traditional order which it was supposed to fortify. On the other hand, the abandonment of laissez faire in social matters, the emergence of a trained bureaucracy and the gradual adoption of social legislation were definite achievements of the period and departures of greatest significance in the evolution of the modern welfare state. By 1848 the European governments had come to recognize, albeit in varying degrees, their responsibility for the entire population. But of course by that time the situation had degenerated to the point where acute class antagonisms had become firmly rooted. The Manchester mill owners who built high fences or walls around their homes as protection against the menacing proletarians provided a vivid demonstration of the anxiety and dismay which filled the souls of many among the propertied classes.[63]

[63] W. Cooke Taylor: *Notes on a Tour in the Manufacturing Districts of Lancashire* (2 ed., London, 1842), 6, 164 ff.

Chapter Seven

TOWARD A NEW SOCIETY

I. THE FRENCH SOCIALISTS

THE increasing magnitude and acuity of the social question had, even before 1830, produced an impressive body of both destructive and constructive criticism. Robert Owen, Henri de Saint-Simon, Sismonde de Sismondi, Charles Fourier and others had, in the spirit of the Enlightenment, analyzed the social structure and pursued the quest for a more perfect, a juster social order. Humanitarians and men of reason, these writers had faith in progress and were willing to accept the advances of science and industry. What they objected to was the system of economic individualism and free competition which in essence meant the exploitation of the poor by the rich and so produced class antagonism. Free competition they would replace by "co-operation" or "association," of whose advantages they hoped to convince the propertied classes. Owen never tired of the effort to persuade kings and statesmen to throw off the yoke of the "old moral order" and embrace the new system of co-operation. Saint-Simon likewise appealed to the mighty, to rulers, bankers and businessmen, to take the lead in the crusade for a new society, while Fourier waited patiently for some benefactor to provide the funds for his projected new order.[1]

The early social critics were mostly opponents of organized religion, but considered some form of religion essential to human welfare. Owen dreamed of a new rational religion of brotherly love as the indispensable basis for social reform. Saint-Simon considered himself the prophet of a new Christianity, which was to be more than primitive Christianity, directed to the speediest amelioration of the lot of the poorest class. Fourier, in turn, was convinced that the social crisis derived from disregard of God's law. He saw himself as a Messiah, a "social Augustine," sent to inaugurate a new social order.[2]

---

[1] On these early writers, see the preceding volume of this series, Artz: *Reaction and Revolution,* 208 ff.

[2] See D. C. Charlton: *Secular Religions in France, 1815–1870* (New York, 1963), *passim.*

Analytically the early writers started from the paradox that in a period of rapidly mounting productivity, pauperism was becoming more and more general: the rich were becoming richer and the poor, poorer. Society was being split between the "haves" (the capitalists) and the "have-nots" (those who had had nothing but their labor). It was necessary, therefore, to put an end to the exploitation of the masses, whose labor, according to the teaching of Ricardo and others, gave value to goods. Instead of a mere subsistence wage, the worker was entitled to the full product of his labor. Sismondi constantly stressed the antagonism of classes, while Saint-Simon foresaw the eventual struggle between "all the parasites on the one hand and the mass of producers on the other, to decide whether the latter should continue to be the prey of the former."[3]

Another significant contribution of these writers was the provision of a historical setting for the social problem, in keeping with the general historical-mindedness of the period. Fourier thought he could distinguish four great historical periods corresponding to infancy, youth, manhood and old age, each of these divided into lesser ages of advance or decline. But it was Saint-Simon and his followers who gave the greatest impetus to the philosophy of history. They had a clear conception of society as in constant evolution, passing from "critical" (i.e., static) to "organic" (i.e., dynamic) periods. The French Revolution, they held, marked the completion of a critical, essentially destructive phase. The time had now come for a constructive era involving the remaking of society to conform with technological change. This new age would belong not to the traditional upper classes—the nobles, the soldiers and the clergy—but to the producers, who would exploit the wealth of the globe by working in association rather than in competition. The state would control all instruments of production, assigning them to producers according to their capability for using them in the common interest. Such was the inexorable force of historical development, which, however, the intelligent intervention of man might hasten.[4]

---

[3] Pierre Angrand: "Notes critiques sur la formation des idées communistes en France" (*La Pensée*, No. 20, 1948, 57–67); Armand Cuvillier: "Les antagonismes des classes dans la littérature sociale français de Saint-Simon à 1848" (*International Review of Social History*, I, 1956, 433–463).

[4] Walter M. Simon: "History for Utopia: Saint-Simon and the Idea of Progress" (*Journal of the History of Ideas*, XVII, 1956, 311–331). For an excellent brief account, see Frank E. Manuel: *The Prophets of Paris* (Cambridge, 1962), chap. iv.

From the foregoing remarks it will be plain that many of the fundamental ideas of socialism were advanced by these pioneers. The words "socialist" and "socialism" appeared first in England (1827) and then in France (1831). But they were for many years far from attaining the precise definitions to be found in present-day dictionaries. In the 1830's and 1840's socialism meant chiefly criticism of the existing political and social order as unjust and advocacy of a new order consistent with moral values; in other words, a program of fundamental reform of human institutions if not of human nature, with the objective of establishing labor's control over capital and securing for the workman the dominant position in society. In 1840 there then appeared the further terms "communist" and "communism," which, if anything, were even more nebulous. The main thrust was the replacement of private ownership of property by collective ownership. The distinction between socialism and communism prior to 1848 was chiefly one between nonviolent reform (co-operation, association, and reconciliation of social classes) and revolutionary activism (class struggle and eventual domination of the proletariat). Hence communism was rated far more dangerous and was closely associated with the republicanism of the secret societies.[5]

In the *Communist Manifesto* (1848) Karl Marx distinguished various types of socialism and communism as they existed in his day, yet the concepts remain cloudy and the distinctions interesting only as reflecting the great variety of thought on the social question, along with the absence of any agreed program. Society, remarked Saint-Beuve, was like a sick man eager to recover and therefore turning constantly from one remedy to another. The great historian, Michelet, noted that there was "a volcano of books, an eruption of utopias."[6] Though the early socialists were not by any means all utopians, they

---

[5] Arthur E. Bestor: "The Evolution of the Socialist Vocabulary" (*Journal of the History of Ideas*, IX, 1948, 259–303), which may be supplemented by Jacques Gans: "L'origine du mot 'socialiste' et ses emplois les plus anciens" (*Revue d'histoire économique et sociale*, XXXV, 1957, 79–83), and M. Schneider: "Kanttekening het eerste Gebruik van de woorden 'socialisme' en 'communisme'" (*International Spectator*, XI, 1957, 688–689).

[6] Saint-Beuve, quoted in Roger Picard: *Le romantisme social* (New York, 1944), 62; Michelet, quoted in Maxime Leroy: *Histoire des idées sociales en France* (2 ed., Paris, 1950), II, 396.

were romantics and liked to leave their imaginations free rein in the construction of new and better societies.[7]

The historian, confronted with such a diversity of theory and doctrine, must at least make an effort to distinguish the major trends. He may well begin with one of the most influential, though one of the haziest, writers of the period, the Abbé Félicité Lamennais, who, prior to 1830, had been one of the foremost proponents of Catholicism and the Papacy. A man of great magnetism and eloquence, and a superb writer of the romantic type, Lamennais tried, in the years 1830–1832, to reconcile the church to liberalism and, having failed (see Chapter XV), began to preach the doctrine of social equality and political democracy. His best-known booklet, *The Words of a Believer* (*Paroles d'un croyant,* 1834), ran through many editions, was quickly translated into most European languages and proved to be one of the most influential writings of the period. It was followed in 1837 by *The Book of the People,* which sold 10,000 copies in a few days and brought would-be readers in droves to the cafés and reading rooms. The author's essay on *Modern Slavery* (1839) was no less avidly consumed.

It is difficult, more than a century later, to understand Lamennais' extraordinary appeal to his contemporaries. The pope condemned the *Words of a Believer* as false, impious, scandalous and inflammatory (encyclical *Singulari vos,* 1834), yet it was not a revolutionary work. Indeed, it preached respect for private property and for the rights of others. But it did denounce tyrants and oppressors of the people and in rhapsodic, almost Biblical, language bemoaned the sufferings of the poor and preached the need for mutual love and association. Lamennais conjured up a new religion of social democracy, under which men would love each other as brothers and there would no longer be "great" people and "little" people. The greatest curse of mankind, he asserted, was sordid self-interest, "the passion to acquire and possess." In the *Book of the People* he was to argue that "the people" constitute the majority of mankind. Without them there could be no prosperity, no development, no life, for without work there is no life and work is the unique contribution of the people. Yet in fact only a few men make the laws and exploit the masses. There can be no improvement in society until this situation is changed. Men should recognize their duties

<hr>

[7] See Frank E. Manuel, ed.: *Utopias and Utopian Thought* (Boston, 1966), especially 69 ff.

toward their fellowmen; they should co-operate to the end that privilege be abolished and the instruments of production made available to all.[8]

Lamennais can hardly be called a socialist, even in a general sense, but his emotional humanitarianism aroused widespread interest in the plight of the lower classes and enhanced the workers' feeling of being the victims of injustice. Many of the leading writers of the period, such as Saint-Beuve, Victor Hugo, George Sand, Lamartine and Michelet, were impressed by the Abbé's teaching. Even the conservative realist, Balzac, was deeply moved and became convinced that the lower classes were worse off than the slaves of antiquity. The historian Michelet's rhapsody on the workers and their family life, written in 1846, is in much the same strain as Lamennais' *Book of the People*.[9]

The class consciousness of the workers was stimulated also by the radical secret societies which, under the influence of Buonarrotti, revived the program of social revolution associated with the conspiracy for equality during the French Revolution. What was at issue here was less a coherent doctrine than a social democratic movement. Auguste Blanqui, the most prominent leader of the republicans, at his trial in 1832, equated "the people" with the proletariat, "the profession of thirty million Frenchmen who live from their labor and are deprived of their public rights." Convinced that social reform was inseparable from political revolution, Blanqui proclaimed the war of the poor against the rich and undertook to organize among the skilled and literate workers a revolutionary elite or shock troop to overthrow the government, set up a dictatorship of the proletariat and introduce a system of social democracy. Blanqui had a clear conception of the class struggle and was perhaps the first to advance the notion of a dictatorship to act in behalf of the ignorant proletariat.[10]

---

[8] Claude Carcopino: *Les doctrines sociales de Lamennais* (Paris, 1942); Yves Le Hir: *Les "Paroles d'un croyant" de Lamennais* (Paris, 1949); René Rémond: *Lamennais et la démocratie* (Paris, 1948), 10 ff.; Alec R. Vidler: *Prophecy and Papacy* (London, 1954), 242 ff.; Jean-Baptiste Duroselle: "Quelques vues nouvelles sur Lamennais" (*Rassegna storica del Risorgimento*, XLIII, 1956, 322–328); Peter N. Stearns: *Priest and Revolutionary* (New York, 1967), 138 ff.

[9] There is a new edition of Michelet's *Le peuple* by Lucien Lefort (Paris, 1946). On Balzac see Bernard Guyon: *La pensée politique et sociale de Balzac* (Paris, 1947); Herbert J. Hunt: *Balzac's "Comédie humaine"* (London, 1959), especially p. 354.

[10] On the revolutionary mystique, see Jean Skerlitch: *L'opinion publique en France d'après la poésie politique et sociale de 1830 à 1848* (Lausanne, 1901), 74 ff.; V.

Turning now from propagandists and agitators for social reform to the more systematic writers and exponents of specific programs for a new society, it was the French who excelled in the elaboration of utopian schemes. Fourier, of whom it has been said that he widened the dimensions of Utopia beyond anything that had been dreamed of before, worked out his plan in lavish mathematical detail. Hating the immoral practices of urban business, he envisioned a return to the simple life, with kitchen gardens, flower beds and lovely orchards. His dream was to get rid of the wage system, to establish a regime of association and to unite all social classes in a new Kingdom of God on earth. His basic communities were to consist of 1,620 persons living on 5,000 acres of land and working according to impulses and preferences. These "phalansteries" would produce all that was needed and would consume the product without employing middlemen or making profit.

Fourier, in his demand for complete emancipation of human instincts and passions, was one of the first to call for the emancipation of women, for the abolition of marriage, and for complete sexual freedom. This feminist program was soon taken over by the Saint-Simonians and by other socialist groups. Prosper Enfantin, the leader of the newly founded Saint-Simonian religion, had a marked weakness for vivacious young women. He argued that inconstant human nature should not be bound to constancy in marriage. Only through complete sexual freedom (the "rehabilitation of the flesh") could adultery and prostitution be overcome. It was teachings such as these that led to suppression of the Saint-Simonian communities in 1832, but the feminist doctrine was further propagated by that remarkable woman writer, George Sand, whose first novel, *Indiana* (1832), declaimed against established morality and had an important impact on the intellectual life of Europe.[11]

Volguine: "Idées socialistes et communistes dans les sociétés secrètes, 1835–1840" (*Questions d'histoire*, II, 1954, 9–38); Georges Sencier: *Le Babouvisme après Babeuf* (Paris, 1912); Elizabeth Eisenstein: *The First Professional Revolutionary: Filippo Buonarroti* (Cambridge, 1959), chaps. v and vi. On Blanqui, Edward S. Mason: "Blanqui and Communism" (*Political Science Quarterly*, XLIV, 1929, 498–527); Alan B. Spitzer: *The Revolutionary Theories of Louis Auguste Blanqui* (New York, 1957), 97 ff., 162 ff.; Maurice Dommanget: *Les idées politiques et sociales d'Auguste Blanqui* (Paris, 1958). See also Leo A. Loubère: "The Intellectual Origins of French Jacobin Socialism" (*International Review of Social History*, IV, 1959, 415–431).

[11] Léon Abensour: *Le féminisme pendant le règne de Louis-Philippe* (2 ed., Paris, 1913); Marguérite Thibert: *Le féminisme dans le socialisme français de 1830 à 1850*

Fourier's doctrine of associative living, though elaborated prior to 1830, became influential only after that date and largely through the efforts of his gifted disciple Victor Considérant, who founded a propaganda journal, Le Phalanstère (1832; later La démocratie pacifique, 1843), and published a well-written exposition of Fourierism in three volumes, La destinée sociale (1834–1844). In the new societies, he promised, "the phalansteries which arise in the plains and the valleys, in the foothills of the mountains and at the confluence of the rivers will make elegant and noble homes for populations that are leisured, educated, industrious and happy." In another statement, of which thousands of copies were sold, Considérant insisted that the crux of the social problem was to make work attractive. The aim of Fourier's teaching, he maintained, was no other than the realization of Christianity in society.[12]

The vision of Fourier was so alluring that various efforts were made to translate it into reality. In France several agricultural associations were set up, while in the less complicated society of the United States many experimental communities were organized, of which the Brook Farm Phalanx of Agriculture, Domestic Industry and Mechanic Arts (West Roxbury, Massachusetts) was made famous by the interest of Hawthorne and Emerson. These hopeful beginnings ended, however, in failure, partly for purely mundane reasons but chiefly because Fourier's theories of human nature proved too idealistic. Nonetheless, it would be difficult to exaggerate the impact of his teaching on even some of the greatest intellects of the midcentury, on both sides of the Atlantic and as far eastward as Russia.[13]

Of a more popular character and indeed more widely read was

Paris, 1926); Célestin Bouglé: "Le féminisme saint-simonien" (in his Chez les prophètes socialistes, Paris, 1918); Edouard Dolléans: Féminisme et mouvement ouvrier: George Sand (Paris, 1951).

12 Considérant: Exposition abrégée du système phalanstérien de Fourier (Paris, 1845); La destinée sociale (4 ed., Paris, 1851), II, 93 ff., 101. See also Charles Gide: Fourier, précurseur de la coöpération (Paris, 1913); F. Armand and R. Maublanc: Fourier (Paris, 1937); Maurice Dommanget: Victor Considérant (Paris, 1929).

13 On the Fourierist communities in America, M. Holloway: Heavens on Earth: Utopian Communities in America, 1660–1880 (London, 1951); Everett Webber: Escape to Utopia: the Communal Movement in America (New York, 1959); Edith R. Curtis: A Season in Utopia: the Story of Brook Farm (New York, 1961); Maren Lockwood: "The Experimental Utopia in America" (in Frank E. Manuel, ed.: Utopias and Utopian Thought, Boston, 1966), 183–200.

Etienne Cabet's 600-page novelistic fable *Travels in Icaria (Voyage en Icarie,* 1840). The author, a well-known democrat and republican and the first to employ the term "communist," imagined a country far, far away over the western seas, where a great nation, Icaria, was organized on a communistic basis. After describing all aspects of its life Cabet analyzed the ways by which European states might be transformed along similar lines, not immediately nor by revolution, but gradually and with popular support (see Illustration 34). Icaria was indeed a new terrestrial paradise, governed by a popularly elected dictatorship, which functioned through an elaborate system of committees and subcommittees. All production and distribution of goods, indeed all activities, were carefully regulated and so efficiently managed that the necessities of life could be supplied by a workday of only seven hours in summer and six in winter. Everyone shared in the work, which was made "short, easy and attractive," and carried on in shops that were "healthy, clean, comfortable and indeed splendid." For instance, there was the millinery factory, where 2,500 young women (most of them beautiful, all of them happy) took delight in arranging flowers on hats, while sweetly singing. But hats, like all feminine fashions, were scrupulously regulated: "a certain number of predetermined hats, toques, turbans and bonnets, each model decided on by a commission of modistes and painters." Icaria, in short, was a community well designed to appeal to poverty-stricken workers. It was "a reverie, charming as a fairy tale." Its popularity, then, is not difficult to understand. By 1850 various efforts had been made to establish Icarian settlements, both in France and in Texas.[14]

As aforesaid, not all Utopian socialists were Utopians. Several of even the more prominent were practical men, groping for some solution to a baffling problem of horrendous magnitude. Pierre Leroux, for example, was a revered figure, a religious mystic and a democrat devoted to social reform. Yet in a number of essays (1843, collected as *De la ploutocratie,* 1848), he set out to demonstrate that economic as well as political power was in France concentrated in 196,000 individuals out of a population of some 34 million.[15]

---

[14] Jules Prudhommeaux: *Icarie et son fondateur Etienne Cabet* (Paris, 1907); Pierre Angrand: *Etienne Cabet et la république de 1848* (Paris, 1948). Sylvester A. Piotrowski: *Etienne Cabet and the "Voyage en Icarie"* (Washington, 1935) is of little value.

[15] Henri Mougin: *Pierre Leroux* (Paris, 1938); Evans: *Social Romanticism in France,* 41 ff.; Charlton: *Secular Religions in France,* 82 ff.

Editor of a forty-volume collection of the records of the French Revolution was another religiously oriented democrat, Philippe Buchez. He recognized more clearly even than Saint-Simon that possession of the instruments of production enabled one class to exploit another. In order to secure for the workers the largest possible share of the product, he tried to organize co-operative societies of producers, in the first instance among intelligent, literate craftsmen. He also supported the foundation, by a group of artisans, of the first newspaper (*L'atelier,* 1840), owned and managed entirely by workers and for workers. Its device was "He who will not work, shall not eat," and its program called for gradual reform through mutual-aid societies, workers' organizations, universal suffrage, and so on. In a short time the newspaper had established for itself a European reputation.[16]

Of considerable interest, too, was Constantine Pecqueur, a gentle humanitarian whose ideal was a society based on morality, as set forth in his *Of God's Republic* (1844). Pecqueur was noteworthy for pointing out (in his *New Theory of Social and Political Economy,* 1842) the marked tendency of modern industry toward ever greater concentration and the possible role this might play in furthering co-operation.[17]

But for concrete, hardheaded proposals for social reform no other writer had the appeal of Louis Blanc, whose *Organization of Labor* was published serially in 1839 and in book form in 1840. An intelligent journalist, alert to the social forces of his time, Blanc consolidated many of the ideas prevalent in socialist literature. The remedy for the ills of competition, he argued, lay in association, which could be achieved only within the framework of the existing society and by nonviolent means. The workers should agitate first for universal suffrage, through which they could hope to attain control of the state. Thereafter, "the full power of the state must be brought into play; what the proletarians lack in order to attain their emancipation are the instruments of production. It is the function of the state to provide them." The state, in other words, should act as "banker of the poor," buying up enterprises of all kinds and, through state credit, turning them over to workers' associations of production (*ateliers sociaux*), much like those envisaged by Buchez. These workshops would be

16 Armand Cuvillier: *P. J. B. Buchez et les origines du socialisme chrétien* (Paris, 1948), and *Un journal d'ouvriers: l'atelier* (new ed., Paris, 1954).
17 Max Beer: *Allgemeine Geschichte des Sozialismus* (Berlin, 1924), 412; Labrousse: *Le mouvement ouvrier,* 155 ff.

operated by workers and for workers. They would sound the death knell of the system of exploitation. In fact, they would soon show themselves so superior to private enterprise that they would be able presently to supplant it. In this way society would be gradually transformed and the state as a regulatory power would fade away.[18]

While Blanc's program lacked profundity, it had a practical, modern ring, and its author showed himself in 1848 a man devoted to the workers' cause and imaginative in dealing with the crisis. A man of greater intellectual power was Pierre Joseph Proudhon, a largely self-educated typesetter and one of the few socialist theorists who could be termed a worker. Proudhon defies classification, for he railed at socialists and communists alike and refused to put his faith in any ingenious remedy for the social problem. His approach was essentially analytical and scientific. Hating all authority (especially the religious), he was a doughty champion of liberty and justice, by which he meant essentially equality.

Proudhon's reputation derived from three essays of the early forties: *What Is Property?* (1840); *Letter to Blanqui* (1841); and a larger work, *The System of Economic Contradictions, or the Philosophy of Want* (1846), which attempted a dialectical analysis of the capitalist system. The first of these writings is the best known and contains the kernel of his thought. In it he answers his own question by arguing that property is theft. But this proposition, by no means new, was not as incendiary as Proudhon made it sound, for he distinguished between "property" and "possession." He had no objection to possession, but denounced property in the sense of profit taken by the employer at the expense of the producing worker. His concern, incidentally, was less with the urban laborer than with the agrarian worker. In any case, he considered labor alone as productive, and so protested against rent, interest and profit as unearned increments. He wanted a "juster" balance of economic forces, which he hoped might be achieved through a system of mutual exchange of goods, somewhat along the lines of Owen's labor exchanges.[19]

[18] Edouard Renard: *La vie et l'oeuvre de Louis Blanc* (Toulouse, 1922); Paul Keller: *Louis Blanc und die Revolution von 1848* (Zürich, 1926); Hermann Pechan: *Louis Blanc als Wegweiser des modernen Sozialismus* (Jena, 1929); Jean Vidalenc: *Louis Blanc* (Paris, 1948); Leo R. Loubère: *Louis Blanc* (Evanston, 1960).

[19] Proudhon exercised a lasting influence on the French labor movement and has provoked a large number of studies. Among the more recent are Dennis Brogan: *Proudhon* (London, 1934); Armand Cuvillier: *Proudhon* (Paris, 1937); J. Bourgeat:

The French socialist writers naturally reacted one upon the other. The so-called Utopian literature reveals certain common ideas (evils of competition, the right of the worker to the product of his labor, etc.) in various combinations and with differing emphasis. But the basic ideas had an impact on at least the upper crust of the working population. They could be derived not only from the original works but from the debates in the secret societies and from the journals and newspapers, which could be had in the reading rooms for a small monthly fee.[20] It was only natural, then, that efforts should be made to organize labor and so pass from theory to practice. Noteworthy among such efforts were those of a remarkable woman, Flora Tristan, who for several years had been in domestic service in England. Having made something of a reputation as a novelist, she returned to England, became involved with the Chartists and reported brilliantly on English conditions (*Promenades dans Londres,* 1840). Influenced by Owen, Saint-Simon and Fourier, she became an ardent champion of women's rights as well as a labor propagandist. It was futile, she argued, to wait for generous philanthropists to save the situation, or to rely on state action. In her programmatic work *The Union of Labor* (1843), she advised the workers to depend exclusively on their own efforts. They must educate themselves, strive toward a union of workers of all sexes and nationalities, and oblige the propertied classes to recognize the "right to work." "You have on your side numbers, and numbers mean a great deal," she pleaded. Traveling far and wide through France, she aroused considerable interest and even enthusiasm, but the police made life difficult for her and she died (1844) before being able to accomplish much.[21]

Proudhon, père du socialisme français (Paris, 1943); Edouard Dolléans: *Proudhon* (Paris, 1948); Henri de Lubac: *The Un-Marxian Socialist: a Study of Proudhon* (London, 1948); George Woodcock: *Pierre-Joseph Proudhon* (New York, 1956).

[20] Jules Bertaut: *L'époque romantique* (Paris, 1947), chap, xiv; Claude Pichois: "Les cabinets de lecture à Paris durant la première moitié du XIXe siècle" (*Annales*, XIV, 1959, 521–534); Jean Morienval: *Les créateurs de la grande presse en France* (Paris, 1934); Maurice Reclus: *Emile de Girardin, le créateur de la presse moderne* (Paris, 1934).

[21] Jules L. Puech: *La vie et l'oeuvre de Flora Tristan* (Paris, 1925); Margaret Goldsmith: *Seven Women against the World* (London, 1935), chap. iii; Emile Coornaert: "La pensée ouvrière et la conscience de classe en France de 1830 à 1848" (in *Studi in onore di Gino Luzzatto*, Milan, 1950, III, 12–33).

2. SOCIALISM ABROAD

The ideas of French theorists had an almost immediate impact on the intellectuals of other countries. The teachings of the Saint-Simonians and the Fourierists both made a great appeal. Indeed, in 1832 the Saint-Simonians sent a mission to London, which carried on active and generally successful propaganda. Notable figures such as Carlyle and John Stuart Mill were favorably impressed and definitely influenced in their own thinking. Somewhat later, in 1840, Hugh Doherty published a biography of Fourier and founded a newspaper, the *London Phalanx,* in which Fourierist literature was regularly reviewed. Many pamphlets were published and projects drawn for a College of Attractive Industry.[22] But in England the interest centered on Chartism, that is, on action rather than speculation. About the only social doctrine of significance after Owen's was the Young England movement of the 1840's, which was inspired by the bitter critique of Carlyle. It was basically an aristocratic, traditionalist doctrine, and of a very loose kind. Several young men (George Smythe, Lord John Manners, Benjamin Disraeli) inveighed against utilitarianism, denounced the exploitation of man by man, called for a revival of the aristocratic spirit, envisaged a social harmony based on renewed paternal feudalism, and advocated a union of the upper and lower classes against the exploiting business class. Though it had but little impact on public opinion, this elitist group provided spectacular opposition in Parliament to Sir Robert Peel and his conservative following.[23]

In Prussia a similar school of conservative socialism developed at about the same time. Joseph Maria von Radowitz, the eminent diplomat and statesman, was typical of certain nobles who resented industrialism and charged the system of free competition with ruining the lower classes. He dreamed of an alliance between the monarchy and the proletariat against the moneyed business elements, but on a traditional, patrimonial basis. In his influential book *Contemporary Talks on State and Church* (1846), Radowitz revealed his knowledge of

[22] Richard K. P. Pankhurst: *The Saint-Simonians: Mill and Carlyle* (London, n.d.), and "Fourierism in Britain" (*International Review of Social History,* I, 1956, 398–432).

[23] Charles Whibley: *Lord John Manners and His Friends* (London, 1925); William F. Monypenny: *The Life of Benjamin Disraeli* (New York, 1912), I, chap. vi.

French and British socialism, confessed to general sympathy with socialist aims, and more or less endorsed Blanc's program of state aid in
financing workshops which might eventually eclipse the system of free
competition.[24]
This "feudal socialism," as Marx was to call it in the *Communist
Manifesto,* was to have no future and its impact was in any case not to
be compared with that of French ideas in Belgium, Switzerland and
even Germany, where the essential literature was smuggled in by
agents of the German workers' societies in Paris or simply by journeymen returning from their foreign tour. In Belgium, Edouard Ducpétiaux, the leading writer on the social problem, was deeply influenced
by Saint-Simonism, while Adolphe Bartels published an *Essay on the
Organization of Labor,* which followed closely Blanc's program for
state socialism under a democratic republic. Bartels' newspaper, *Le
débat social,* kept in close touch with developments in Paris and
chronicled labor activities throughout Europe. Under the editorship of
Félix Delhasse (1846) it was given a definitely Fourierist slant.[25]
Switzerland was one of the great refuges for political exiles, many of
whom, like Mazzini, were influenced by the Saint-Simonian teaching
and the writings of Lamennais. Mazzini, though attracted by the
notions of evolutionary progress and association, was, however, averse
to the basic tenets of socialism.[26] On the other hand, the numerous
German exiles and workers in Switzerland had their own social and
political societies and even a press which published translations of
French socialist writings.[27] Presently connections were established
between the Swiss societies and the more radical organizations of the
German workers in Paris, such as the League of the Just (*Bund der*

---

[24] Hildegard Goetting: *Die sozialpolitische Idee in den konservativen Kreisen der
vormärzlichen Zeit* (Berlin, 1920); Walter Früh: *Radowitz als Sozialpolitiker* (Berlin,
1937); Wolfgang Scheel: *Das Berliner Politische Wochenblatt und die politische und
soziale Revolution in Frankreich und England* (Göttingen, 1964).

[25] Louis Bertrand: *Histoire de la démocratie et du socialisme en Belgique depuis 1830*
(Paris, 1906), 138 ff., 174 ff., 200 f.; Harry Isay: *Liberalismus und Arbeiterfrage in
Belgien, 1830–1852* (Berlin, 1913), 39 ff.; Rudolf Rezsohazy: *Origines et formation du
catholicisme social en Belgique, 1842–1909* (Louvain, 1958), 5 ff.

[26] Michele Mazzitelli: *Il socialismo di Mazzini* (Florence, 1953); Renato Treves:
L'idea sansimoniana e il Risorgimento (Turin, 1931); Delio Cantimori: *Utopisti i
riformatori italiani* (Florence, 1943), 177 ff.

[27] Otto Brugger: *Geschichte der deutschen Handwerkervereine in der Schweiz, 1836–
1843* (Berne, 1932); Hans G. Keller: *Die politischen Verlagsanstalten und Druckereien
in der Schweiz* (Zürich, 1935), chaps. vii and viii.

Gerechten), founded in 1836 by Karl Schapper and Theodor Schuster, who were members of the French secret societies and tinged with socialist notions. Intellectually the League of the Just soon fell under the influence of Wilhelm Weitling, a tailor by trade who, by his earnestness, ardor and eloquence made a deep impression on his fellow workers. In 1838 the League financed the publication of Weitling's first book, *Humanity as It Is and as It Should Be*. This was an emotional, deeply religious tract, clearly influenced by Lamennais, whose *Book of the People* Weitling had translated into German. Weitling's book was noteworthy, however, for its appeal to the workers to find their own salvation, that is, to struggle for a return to simple Christianity, without private property or inheritance, but with complete equality in the rewards of labor.[28]

Weitling went to Switzerland in 1841 and soon converted several of the workers' societies to his views. They in turn provided the funds for his second book, *Guarantees of Harmony and Freedom* (1842), which is the best exposition of his teaching, written in simple, intimate language. This work was much appreciated by men of the stature of Heine, Feuerbach and Marx, and was soon translated into French, English, Norwegian and Hungarian. It was a passionate denunciation of the social system, followed by an outline for a communal society. Like Proudhon, Weitling declared property to be theft; like Saint-Simon, he envisaged the leadership of the best qualified; like Fourier, he envisaged simple communal units. But to all these items he added a religious element. Though strenuously opposed to the organized churches, which he charged with having corrupted primitive Christianity and early communism, he regarded a simple faith as indispensable. In an essay, *The Gospel of a Poor Sinner* (1844), he cited the Bible to demonstrate that Jesus, as a member of the communist Essene sect, was an advocate of the abolition of private property, inheritance and money: "So Jesus, too, was a communist, teaching the principle of community and the need for this principle, while leaving the realiza-

---

[28] Karl Mielcke: *Deutscher Frühsozialismus* (Stuttgart, 1931), 182 ff.; Thilo Ramm: *Die grossen Sozialisten als Rechts- und Sozialphilosophen* (Stuttgart, 1955), 475 ff.; Carl Wittke: *The Utopian Socialist: a Biography of Wilhelm Weitling* (Baton Rouge, 1950), 24 ff. On the League of the Just and Weitling's Paris period, see the recent works of Werner Kowalski: *Vorgeschichte und Entstehung des Bundes der Gerechten* (Berlin, 1962), a Communist study; Wolfgang Schieder: *Anfänge der deutschen Arbeiterbewegung* (Stuttgart, 1963), 45 ff., and, on Weitling, 245 ff.

tion and form of the system to the future." Thus Weitling appeared as a second and possibly greater Messiah heralding the advent of a new social order.[29]

Weitling's sincere, emotional books, written by a worker for workers, made a deep impression on such societies, mostly secret, as already existed among the workers of the Rhineland. But it was French socialism that attracted the German intellectuals. The writers of the Young German School, like their patrons, Heine and Börne, were much taken with Saint-Simonian doctrine.[30] Similarly, economists such as Carl Rodbertus and Victor Aimé Huber engaged in criticism of the existing social order and called for drastic action if an upheaval was to be avoided. Rodbertus was one of the first to call for state ownership of the means of production so as to assure the workers a fair share of the product of their labor. Huber, who was widely traveled in France and England, suggested as a solution of the social problem the establishment of Owenite communities which were to be essentially rural factory settlements with communal facilities, the entire system to be supported by employers, the church and the state.[31]

Educated Germans were fully instructed in French socialist doctrine through a remarkable book, *Socialism and Communism in Contemporary France,* published in 1842 by a young German scholar, Lorenz von Stein. Inspired by the ideas of Saint-Simon on social evolution and the conflict of social classes, Stein analyzed in detail and with great impartiality the rise of the proletariat and the emergence of the various brands of socialism and communism.[32] As a result of Stein's work

---

[29] Wittke: *Utopian Socialist,* chaps. iii and iv. On Weitling's activities in Switzerland, see also Brugger: *Geschichte,* Part II, and Bernhard Kaufhold's excellent introduction to the new edition of *Guarantees* (Berlin, 1955), and Eduard Fuchs' introduction to the *Gospel* (Munich, 1896).

[30] Eliza M. Butler: *The Saint-Simonian Religion in Germany* (Cambridge, 1926); Werner Suhge: *Saint-Simonismus und Junges Deutschland* (Berlin, 1935); William Rose: *Heinrich Heine: Two Studies of His Thought and Feeling* (Oxford, 1956), 35 ff., 58 ff.; Gerhard Schmitz: *Ueber die ökonomischen Anschauungen in Heine's Werken* (Weimar, 1960), 111 ff.

[31] Hanns E. Jansen: *Das Proletariat im Vormärz in den Anschauungen deutscher Denker* (Kiel, 1928), 48 ff., 67 ff.; William O. Shanahan: *German Protestants Face the Social Question* (Notre Dame, 1954), chaps. ii and iii; Joseph Hoffner: *Die deutschen Katholiken und die soziale Frage* (Paderborn, 1956), 12 ff.

[32] The third edition (1850) of the Stein book bore the title *The History of the Social Movement in France, 1789–1850.* There is an English translation of this edition, with a useful introduction by Kaethe Mengelberg (Totowa, 1964).

there was much reference to socialist doctrine in the vast German literature on the social question which marked the 1840's. But the only coherent doctrine that emerged, apart from Marxism, was "true socialism," as expounded by Moses Hess, Otto Lüning, Karl Grün and others who were active in the industrial Rhineland. Hess had visited Paris in 1832 and had brought back ideas of social democracy. But he frowned on the idea of class conflict and looked to reason to convince mankind of the advantages of co-operation and fraternity. He and his associates published a number of socialist journals and carried on extensive propaganda. But their appeal was less to the worker than to the enlightened business class which, they argued, stood only to gain by a juster and more humane order of society.[33]

How fascinating socialist ideas were to many European intellectuals is perhaps best shown by the impact of socialist writing on the early Russian revolutionaries, whose activities have been described in Chapter V. Herzen read both Saint-Simon and Fourier early in his career and later, under the influence of the Young Hegelians, began to speculate that a general upheaval would not only destroy all obstacles to human freedom but might pave the way to an entirely new social order. His notes reveal the fact that he read Considérant, Blanc, Proudhon, and George Sand, and that he was much impressed by Proudhon's readiness to contemplate the total destruction of the existing social order. After his arrival in France in 1847, Herzen became completely committed to the idea of total revolution, which, like Bakunin, he regarded as terrible yet majestic.[34]

Belinski, too, read widely in the works of Fourier, Blanc, Cabet and especially Proudhon. By the time of his death in 1848 he had become a confirmed revolutionary, looking to a social cataclysm to clear the air

[33] Auguste Cornu: "German Utopianism: 'True' Socialism" (*Science and Society*, XII, 1948, 97–112); Isaiah Berlin: *The Life and Opinions of Moses Hess* (Cambridge, 1959); Edmund Silberner: *Moses Hess: Geschichte seines Lebens* (Leiden, 1966); Jacques Droz and Pierre Aycoberry: "Structures sociales et courants idéologiques dans l'Allemagne prérévolutionnaires, 1835–1847" (*Annali*, VI, 164–236); Karl Obermann: "Die soziale Frage in den Anfängen der sozialistischen und kommunistischen Bewegung in Deutschland, 1843–1845" (*ibid.*, 237–286); Kurt Kozsyk: "Die Bedeutung des Jahres 1845 für den Sozialismus in Deutschland" (*ibid.*, 510–520).

[34] See especially Herzen's own essay: *Du développement des idées révolutionnaires en Russie* (Paris, 1851), 135 ff.; E. Lampert: *Studies in Rebellion* (New York, 1957), 201 ff.; Martin E. Malia: *Alexander Herzen and the Birth of Russian Socialism* (Cambridge, 1961).

and open the way to a new era of equality and fraternity.[35] Michael Bakunin, too, moved from Young Hegelianism to revolutionary socialism. In Switzerland he met Weitling, and in Paris Lamennais, Blanc, Cabet, Proudhon and Marx, as well as George Sand, whom he adored. From Proudhon he derived the ideas underlying his eventual anarchism.[36]

That the impact of socialist doctrine was not confined to a few outstanding figures was clearly shown by the story of the Petrashevski circle, as narrated in Chapter V. Petrashevski, while himself a confirmed Fourierist, built up a library containing all important items of western socialist thought and his home became the meeting place for a considerable group of St. Petersburg officials and intellectuals. Nothing more need be said to demonstrate how widely and deeply socialist doctrine had penetrated in the 1840's.[37]

3. THE RISE OF MARX AND ENGELS

Among the innumerable critics of the existing social order and would-be improvers of mankind and society were also Karl Marx and his associate, Friedrich Engels, who undertook to put socialism on a "scientific" basis and so transcend the bourgeois humanitarianism and idyllic dreamings of the "Utopian" socialists. Both Marx and Engels were bourgeois by origin—sons of well-to-do families of converted Jews in the Rhineland—and both had enjoyed an excellent education. Marx studied philosophy at the University of Berlin and fully intended to become a teacher of that subject. His great intellectual endowment was early recognized by his teachers as well as his fellow students and a brilliant career could confidently be predicted for him. But because of his keen critical sense it was perhaps inevitable that he should identify himself with the radical wing of the dominant philo-

[35] Lampert, *Studies in Rebellion,* chap. ii; Richard Hare: *Pioneers of Russian Social Thought* (New York, 1951), 35 ff.; Peter Scheibert: *Von Bakunin zu Lenin* (Leiden, 1956), chap. x; and especially Herbert E. Bowman: *Vissarion Belinski* (Cambridge, 1954).

[36] Edward H. Carr: *Michael Bakunin* (London, 1937) and the works mentioned in the foregoing notes.

[37] Georges Sourine: *Le Fourierisme en Russie* (Paris, 1936), chaps. ii–vi; Nicholas V. Riasanovsky: "Fourierism in Russia" (*American Slavic and East European Review,* XIII, 1953, 289–302); Frederick I. Kaplan: "Russian Fourierism of the 1840's" (*ibid.,* VII, 1958, 161–172); Iogenson Zilberfarb: *Sotsialnaia filosofiia Sharlia Fure i ee mesto v istoriia sotsialisticheskoi mysli* (Moscow, 1964).

sophical school, the Young Hegelians, whose attacks on the established religion and on the institutions of the old regime soon brought them into ill repute with the authorities. Marx, like others of the group, had to recognize that his chances of academic preferment were decidedly slim.[38]

Marx appears to have been from the beginning of his career more interested in the realities of political and social life than in philosophical abstractions. As editor of the *Rhineland Gazette (Rheinische Zeitung)* in 1842–1843 he had attempted to unite all progressive elements of that advanced region in the struggle against feudal absolutism and had begun to study social conditions, problems and theories.[39] But his editorial policy was far more radical than his sponsors had ever intended and it was not long before the authorities suppressed the journal, leaving Marx without much prospect of further employment. He therefore welcomed the chance to co-operate with Arnold Ruge, a prominent Young Hegelian publicist, in floating a German-French review in Paris. In the autumn of 1843 the Marx family arrived in the French capital, where it was to stay for the next fourteen months.

Unlike most German exiles, Marx did not join any of the secret societies, though he soon made the acquaintance of prominent fellow countrymen, notably Heine, and met about all of the active French socialists. What was perhaps more important, he had an opportunity to study French conditions and to read widely and thoughtfully in French and English political and social literature. He evidently had a great urge to understand human society past and present and, if possible, to grasp the dynamism of its development.[40] His intellectual voracity is attested by the twenty-four large notebooks in the possession of the Marx-Engels-Lenin Institute in Moscow, which cover the years 1843–1847. He read the bourgeois historians (Mignet, Thierry, Guizot), all of whom had much to say of social classes and their struggles. He

[38] Among the countless biographies of Marx the following titles, in English, are of particular interest or value: Franz Mehring: *Karl Marx* (New York, 1936, 1962); Boris Nicolaievsky and Otto Maenchen-Helfen: *Karl Marx* (New York, 1936); Edward H. Carr: *Karl Marx: A Study in Fanaticism* (London, 1934); Isaiah Berlin: *Karl Marx: His Life and Environment* (3 ed., London, 1963). The magistral biography of Auguste Cornu: *Karl Marx et Friedrich Engels: leur vie et leur oeuvre* has thus far appeared in only the first two volumes (Paris, 1955, 1958).

[39] Georg Lukacs: *Der junge Marx* (Pfüllingen, 1965), 15.

[40] Paul Kaegi: *Genesis des historischen Materialismus* (Vienna, 1965), 29.

studied the records of the French Revolution and seriously planned to write a history of the Convention of 1793. And he devoured the entire economic and socialist literature of England and France. There was probably no man of his time who was better informed and certainly none with more of a scholar's passion to get to the root of a problem or with greater analytical power. His training in the Hegelian philosophy gave him in addition the power of broad interpretation. Bertrand Russell has called him the last of the great system builders.[41]

In February, 1845, Marx was expelled from France at the request of the Prussian government, in revenge for his articles attacking the Prussian monarchy. Thenceforth he lived in Brussels until 1848, continuing his researches and publishing essays criticizing his former associates, the Young Hegelians, whom he charged with idle speculation and controversy divorced from the realities of their time, and attacking also various socialist writers for their sentimental humanitarianism and loose imagination. Ricardo and other English economists he accused of basing their doctrine on considerations of profit rather than on thought for the welfare of the workers. Marx soon established himself as a formidable, merciless and often disagreeable opponent. His prodigious knowledge and exceptional analytical power made him impatient and disdainful of his contemporaries. Deeply convinced of the soundness of his own position, he would brook no contradiction. One can sympathize with those who called him "Jupiter Marx."

It was in Paris in 1844 that Marx renewed his acquaintance with Engels, who thenceforth remained his close friend and selfless collaborator. Engels' career was not that of the scholar or writer, but of the businessman. He lived much of the time in Manchester, where his family had a cotton mill. There he observed the condition of the industrial workers and saw the social problem at first hand, as can be seen from his classic account of *The Condition of the Working Class in England in 1844*. He was therefore able to teach Marx much about

[41] Bertrand Russel: *A History of Western Philosophy* (London, 1946), 810 ff. On Marx' notebooks and early writings, see V. Adoratsky: *The History of the Communist Manifesto of Marx and Engels* (New York, 1938), 7; Heinrich Popitz: *Der Entfremdete Mensch: Zeitkritik und Geschichtsphilosophie des jungen Marx* (Basel, 1953); Giuliano Pischel: *Marx giovane* (Milan, 1948); Karl H. Breuer: *Der junge Marx: sein Weg zum Kommunismus* (Köln, 1954); Jean-Yves Calvez: *La pensée de Karl Marx* (Paris, 1956); Auguste Cornu: *The Origins of Marxian Thought* (Springfield, 1957); Lukacs: *Der junge Marx*. Maximilien Rubel: *Karl Marx: essai de biographie intellectuelle* (Paris, 1957) attempts to trace Marx's thought on a strictly chronological basis.

the British economy and the British labor movement. It has been well said of him that he filled in the blank face and figure of Marx's proletarian and placed him in a real house and a real factory.[42] Without a doubt Engels deserves much credit for his contribution to Marxian doctrine.[43]

By 1847 Marx's communist doctrine was just about complete.[44] The point has often been made that it was an amalgam and synthesis of much contemporary thought on economics and the social question.[45] But the same could be said of most great seminal writings. The fact remains that Marx, taking over most of his ideas from the British economists, the "Utopian" socialists, the revolutionaries of the secret societies, and the sociological writers such as Sismondi, Buret and Lorenz von Stein, welded them into a new, comprehensive system and provided that system with a grandiose philosophy of history. Where Hegel had seen ideas in constant conflict, leading to an ever higher synthesis and thereby creating the new forces for further opposition, Marx introduced the conflict of social forces which, in like dialectical fashion, marked progress in the organization of society. The institutions of society are, he argued, at any time a reflection of the system of production and distribution, subject to change and therefore requiring constant readjustment. This means that there is nothing eternal or sacred about the capitalist system, which is simply a transient phase reflecting the victory of the middle class over the forces of feudalism. Its achievements have, admittedly, been impressive, notably in the vast increase of production. But the system of free competition involves not only the exploitation of the lowest class but also the gradual elimination of the lesser units of production, unable to compete on equal terms with the large enterprises, which in turn end in huge monopolies.

[42] Edmund Wilson: *To the Finland Station* (New York, 1940, 1953), 146. Marx learned a great deal about actual conditions also from Eugène Buret: *De la misère des classes laborieuses en France et en Angleterre* (1841). See Kaegi: *Genesis,* 227 ff.

[43] The standard biography and at the same time one of the best accounts of German socialist thought is Gustav Mayer: *Friedrich Engels* (2 ed., The Hague, 1934; abbreviated English version, London, 1936). There is a recent Communist biography by Yelena Stepanova: *Frederik Engels* (Moscow, 1956).

[44] In the *Communist Manifesto* Marx explained his preference for the term "communist" as a fighting term, in contrast to the well-intentioned vaporings of "Utopian" socialism. But he was firmly opposed to "raw communism," that is, to the radicalism that would destroy cities, communize property and women, and ruin the arts. See Kaegi: *Genesis,* 238 ff.

[45] See, e.g., Élie Halévy: *L'ère des tyrannies* (Paris, 1938), 30.

However, the concentration of economic power will eventually facilitate the overthrow of the capitalist system by the proletarians, who, according to the dialectic, will constitute the new opposition and prepare the way for a higher synthesis. Since proletarians comprise about nine-tenths of the population, their emancipation will lead to the emancipation of all humanity, will mark the advent of a classless society and, presumably, the end of a long historical process, the end of the dialectic.

This all-too-brief survey hardly does justice to the richness of Marx's thought and argumentation, but it should at least point up the dialectical materialism, that is, the materialist interpretation of history, which Marx himself regarded as his great contribution, since it was the real dynamic of social evolution. No longer was the future to be dependent on the well-intentioned projects of wiseacres who dreamed up idyllic communities and hoped to persuade others to support their programs. Communism was seen by Marx as part of the inexorable march of history. The proletariat was to be the driving force and ultimate victory was as certain as that day follows night. "Our task," wrote Marx, "is not that of trying to bring some kind of utopian system into being, but of consciously participating in an historical process by which society is being transformed before our very eyes."[46]

Circumstances decreed that Marx should formulate his doctrine in the famous *Communist Manifesto* just as the revolutions of 1848 were about to break over Europe. In the years following 1845 he had undertaken to organize a communist party to serve as an elite, leader group for the international labor movement. The Paris League of the Just had a branch in Brussels and another in London, where there were some 10,000 German artisans. These German workers had, in 1840, founded a Workers' Educational Society as a screen for the League, which was under Weitling's influence and Karl Schapper's leadership. There were probably not more than a few hundred members in the group and they spent much time in doctrinal dispute, since they gradually became estranged by Weitling's messianism and lacked any other platform. It was in the course of one of their disputes that Marx

---

[46] Quoted in Nicolaievsky and Maenchen-Helfen: *Karl Marx*, 122. On his philosophy of history, see Herbert Marcuse: *Reason and Revolution* (2 ed., New York, 1955), Part II; Mandell M. Bober: *Karl Marx' Interpretation of History* (Cambridge, 1950); Gustav A. Wetter: *Dialectical Materialism* (New York, 1959); Kaegi: *Genesis*.

and Weitling met head on in March, 1846. The former called on Weitling to specify what strategy he thought should be followed, and then attacked him for raising false hopes among the workers. Weitling, who was no match for his adversary either in education or debate, allowed himself a caustic reference to "library criticism and analysis deployed apart from the suffering world and the people's torments." Marx thereupon banged his fist on the table and roared "ignorance never did anyone any good." Weitling's day was soon done and he emigrated to America.[47]

Marx gradually converted the members of the League, and presently accepted regular membership in it. In June, 1847, after long harangues, the League was supplanted by a new Communist League, the draft statutes of which were strictly Marxian: "The aim of the League is the downfall of the bourgeoisie and the ascendancy of the proletariat, the abolition of the old society based on class conflicts and the foundation of a new society without classes and without private property." At Engels' suggestion the slogan "All Men Are Brothers" was replaced by a new one, "Proletarians of All Countries, Unite."[48]

It was at the request of the new League that Marx in the winter of 1847-1848 drafted the *Communist Manifesto,* after various leaders such as Hess, Schapper and Engels had made preparatory contributions. This epoch-making document, a mere pamphlet of thirty-five pages, was written in six weeks by an inspired Marx and was published in late February, 1848 (see Illustration 35). In the course of the next century it was to have five hundred or more editions in some thirty languages and to become one of the most influential writings of all time. Of the millions of Marxists throughout the world in 1950, it is probably safe to say that most rested their convictions on this slight essay.[49]

[47] Wittke: *Utopian Socialist,* 101 ff.; Hans Mühlstein: "Marx and the Utopian Wilhelm Weitling" (*Science and Society,* XII, 1948, 113-129).

[48] The basic account is still Franz Mehring: *Geschichte der deutschen Sozialdemokratie* (latest ed. in his *Gesammelte Schriften,* Berlin, 1960, I); but see also Werner Brettschneider: *Entwicklung und Bedeutung des deutschen Frühsozialismus in London* (Königsberg, 1936); Boris Nicolaievsky: "Toward a History of the Communist League" (*International Review of Social History,* I, 1956, 234-252); Herwig Foeder: *Marx und Engels am Vorabend der Revolution* (Berlin, 1960); Wolfgang Schieder: *Anfänge der deutschen Arbeiterbewegung* (Stuttgart, 1963), 61 ff., 101.

[49] Among the numerous histories and commentaries may be mentioned D. Riazanoff's introduction to the translation by Eden and Cedar Paul (London, 1930); the introduc-

The *Manifesto* is divided into four parts, of which the first, entitled "Bourgeois and Proletarians," takes almost half the text and is by far the most important. Here, in what can only be called a masterpiece of compression, Marx outlined the class struggle, the victory of the bourgeoisie over the nobility and clergy, the achievement of the middle class in creating "more massive and more colossal productive forces than all preceding generations together," the development of opposing forces in the form of the proletariat, and the future role of the new class as "gravediggers" of the bourgeoisie. The second part ("Proletarians and Communists") argues that the Communists have no interests apart from those of the proletariat as a whole and are therefore not in opposition to other workers' parties. They are simply "the most advanced and most resolute section of the working-class parties of every country, the section that pushes the others forward." As such, they, will be maligned and attacked, but charges of their wanting to destroy the very foundations of society are malicious: "Communism deprives no man of the power to appropriate the products of society; all it does is to deprive him of the power to subject the labor of others by such appropriation."

The third part of the *Manifesto* provides a systematic criticism of other schools of socialist thought, the great shortcoming of which was the effort to contrive beautiful schemes, "pocket editions of the New Jerusalem," without reference to the compelling forces of historical development. The concluding part is then devoted to discussion of Communist strategy, stressing the point that for the time being the Communists must support all revolutionary movements so as to advance the time for the historically inevitable proletarian revolution. Marx, whose attention was at all times riveted on his native Germany, was persuaded that the social revolution must be fought out there. He was far too well informed to think that Germany was as yet sufficiently developed economically to make a proletarian overturn possible. But it was plain that the country was on the verge of a liberal (bourgeois) revolution and he was convinced that the proper strategy for the Communists would be to support the middle class in destroying the feudal, absolutist system as the prelude to the further class conflict. At this time he still thought

tion by Harold J. Laski to the centennial edition (London, 1948); the introduction by A. J. P. Taylor to the Penguin edition (London, 1967); and Bert Andreas: *Le manifeste communiste* (Milan, 1963).

of the transformation of society through revolution as a short-term proposition.[50]

In 1848 the truly revolutionary elements, in the secret societies and labor organizations, were still few in number, divided in viewpoint and uncertain as to programs of action. In London a segment of the Chartists, the Fraternal Democrats, and in Brussels the Association Démocratique were only just beginning the effort to draw the workers of all countries together. There was an acute social problem and there was a plethora of critical and programmatic writing. A "muffled restlessness" pervaded society, as Lamartine remarked, and "the phantom of revolution" was at every feast, to borrow the expression of Louis Blanc. Heine, who knew Marx well, had the poet's intuitive sense of the troubles to come. He dreaded "the great logicians" such as Marx, who were "cohorts of destruction, undermining and threatening the whole social structure, infinitely superior to the levelers and revolutionaries of other countries because of the terrible logic of their doctrine."[51] But the time was not yet. The discontent of the workers, at least on the Continent, had not yet crystallized and the real proletarians were too ignorant and miserable to play a useful role. Marx, it has been said, gave the proletariat a soul; he assigned to it a grand and glorious part in the struggle for a new social order. But the *Communist Manifesto,* which was so much a product of conditions and a reflection of socialist thought, was well in advance of its time, less a program for immediate action than a portent of the future.

[50] See George Lichtheim: *Marxism: a Historical and Critical Study* (New York, 1961), 51 ff.

[51] Quoted by William Rose: *Heine: Two Studies on His Thought and Feeling* (Oxford, 1956), 83. See also Antonina Vallentin: "Henri Heine et la révolution en marche" (*Europe,* XXVI, 1948, 51–64); Laura Hofrichter: *Heinrich Heine* (Oxford, 1963), 66 ff.

Chapter Eight

PEOPLES AND NATIONS

I. INTRODUCTION

THE PERIOD preceding the revolutions of 1848 is often spoken of as the "springtime of nations" (from the German *Völkerfrühling*), referring specifically to the growing sense of national consciousness, especially among many peoples of central and eastern Europe that had long been submerged under Hapsburg or Ottoman rule. The origins of nationalism lay far back in history, but national sentiment was given great impetus by the teaching of Johann Gottfried Herder, the German philosopher who, at the end of the eighteenth century, advanced the doctrine of a national soul (*Volksgeist*) which, in each people, finds expression in language, literature, law and other institutions.[1]

The cultural or humanitarian nationalism of Herder, which envisaged a world where each nation would contribute according to its peculiar genius to the ultimate good of humanity, was reinforced and expanded by the ideas of the French Revolution, with their emphasis on popular rights, on political duty and on the right of every people to self-determination. Thereby the principle of nationalism was given a distinctly political turn. It tended to become identified with democracy and radicalism and for that reason was largely ignored in the international settlements of 1814–1815, despite the fact that in 1813 many governments had encouraged nationalism as an inspiration to their peoples in the struggle against French domination.

During the first half of the nineteenth century, cultural nationalism continued to flourish, celebrating some of its greatest triumphs in the Romantic movement with its love of the past, of the colorful and of the distinctive. But political nationalism also persisted and in fact gained many converts. From being a radical, revolutionary concept, it became

[1] See the preceding volume of this series, Artz: *Reaction and Revolution,* 103 ff., and more specifically Robert H. Ergang: *Herder and the Foundations of German Nationalism* (New York, 1931); Robert T. Clark, Jr.: *Herder: His Life and Thought* (Berkeley, 1955), 336 ff.

more and more respectable until by 1848 it had merged not only with
cultural nationalism but with the constitutional liberalism of the
middle classes. The economic changes that were transforming European society seemed to call for the union of related states (as in Germany or Italy), and much interest was shown in economic union (as
in the German *Zollverein*) as a first step toward political unification.
To the eastward, it is true, the upsurge of national feeling threatened
the disruption of the Hapsburg and Ottoman empires, or at least their
fundamental reorganization along federal lines. In any event, nationalism, for all its cultural achievements, had by 1848 become an additional
factor of instability and tension.[2]

2. IRELAND: O'CONNELL AND THE REPEAL MOVEMENT

In the 1830's and 1840's the national movements that attracted most
attention and caused governments the greatest anxiety were the Irish
and the Polish. Yet neither of these movements fitted very well the
pattern of reawakening national consciousness as outlined above. In
Ireland, for example, cultural nationalism dated only from 1842, when
a group of brilliant young writers founded a newspaper, the *Nation*,
and floated the Young Ireland movement. They based their nationalism squarely on Irish history—not Celtic or Saxon, not Catholic or
Protestant, but simply Irish. They venerated and tried to revive as a
literary language the Gaelic which, though neglected and even scorned
by the educated class, was still the spoken language of at least a third of
the peasantry. Thomas Davis, one of the leaders of Young Ireland, did
much to stir interest in Irish history, literature and music, while the
Nation published many volumes of the *Library of Ireland,* one a
month at one shilling apiece. Most numbers dealt with historical
episodes, traditions, ballads, songs and other matters of strictly Irish
concern.[3]

[2] The problems involved in the concept of nationalism and nationality are analyzed in
books such as Alfred Cobban: *National Self-Determination* (Oxford, 1945); Karl W.
Deutsch: *Nationalism and Social Communication* (New York, 1953); Boyd C. Shafer:
Nationalism: Myth and Reality (New York, 1955). For the historical development, see
Carlton J. H. Hayes: *The Historical Evolution of Nationalism* (New York, 1931); Hans
Kohn: *The Idea of Nationalism* (New York, 1944); Eugen Lemberg: *Geschichte des
Nationalismus in Europa* (Stuttgart, 1950).

[3] The classic account is still that of the leader Charles Gavin Duffy: *Young Ireland*
(London, 1880). See also E. Strauss: *Irish Nationalism and British Democracy* (London,
1951), 105 ff.; Daniel Corkery: "Thomas Davis and the National Language" (in M. J.

The Young Ireland movement was initially a part of the great and spectacular movement for repeal of the union with England, organized and led by Daniel O'Connell, the brilliant Irish lawyer and politician. He had risen to fame and earned the name "The Liberator" by organizing, in 1823, the Catholic Association, the first of the great pressure groups in modern history, which by 1828 boasted some 15,000 dues-paying members and some three million "associates," who paid a trifling monthly "rent." This mobilization of the entire male population of Ireland was "the most powerful political machine British history had ever witnessed" and played a decisive role in the success of the bill emancipating the Catholics from their political disabilities.[4]

O'Connell's ultimate objective, however, was to force repeal of the Act of Union of 1800, which abolished the Irish Parliament and gave the British Parliament, with only 100 Irish members, control of Irish affairs. O'Connell, who was one of the few Irish Catholic landlords, was convinced that all the woes of Ireland, which were many, derived from the union, which had been more or less imposed upon the Irish Parliament in the interest of British security. He showed little concern with the burning social problem. In fact, as a landlord he was no better and no worse than the Anglo-Irish landlords who owned most of the land and exploited the peasantry. O'Connell was a strictly political figure, a shrewd lawyer, an ambitious politician and a charismatic leader. He rallied the Irish business classes of the towns and the more prosperous tenants and hoped, through his agitation for repeal, to dragoon the British Parliament (of which he had become a member) into adopting reforms for Ireland to the advantage of the Catholic elements. In other words, to reduce the position and power of the Anglo-Irish "Protestant Ascendancy" and strengthen the position of the native Catholic majority.

Since the British Parliament and people were unalterably opposed to

---

MacManus, ed.: *Thomas Davis and Young Ireland*, Dublin, 1945, 14–23); Thomas N. Brown: "Nationalism and the Irish Peasant" (*Review of Politics*, XV, 1953, 403–445). On the *Nation* and the *Library*, see Brian Inglis: "The Press" (in R. B. McDowell, ed.: *Social Life in Ireland, 1800–1845*, Dublin, 1957, chap. vii); P. S. O'Hegarty: "The Library of Young Ireland" (in MacManus: *Thomas Davis*, 107–113).

[4] The quotation is from Angus Macintyre: *The Liberator* (London, 1965), 10. See also R. B. McDowell: *Public Opinion and Government Policy in Ireland, 1801–1846* (London, 1952), 120 ff.; and especially James A. Reynolds: *The Catholic Emancipation Crisis in Ireland* (New Haven, 1954).

repeal of the union (it was voted down 523–38 in the House of Commons in 1834), it may well be asked whether O'Connell ever believed it could be achieved. Probably not. Indeed, he carefully avoided saying just what was involved in repeal and seems to have calculated that tremendous pressure, if it did not bring complete victory, would at least produce a harvest of concessions. Throughout his career he was uncompromisingly opposed to violence or revolution. His was a program of organized agitation and in this field he was not only a pioneer but a past master.[5]

O'Connell was able to enlist some thirty-five or forty members of Parliament (less than one-half of the Irish representation) for an Irish Party, which, in the 1830's, held the balance of power between the Tories and the Whigs, and often enjoyed the support of the Radicals, with whom O'Connell had many affinities. Through adroit tactics and effective debate he made the Irish question the central theme of British politics.

It has been well said of the English that no nation was less fitted to rule Ireland, for the gulf opened by racial, historical, religious and social factors was so great as to be all but unbridgeable.[6] But in the 1830's the Whig government, under pressure from the Irish Party and the Radicals, undertook various measures of reform along the lines of those introduced in Britain itself. To combat illiteracy, nonsectarian schools were built and considerable advances made in popular education.[7] Steps were taken also to limit the wealth of the Protestant Church hierarchy and reduce the tithe paid by the Catholic peasantry to support the Established Church. In 1838 a poor law, modeled on the British, was enacted and a start at least made toward combating indigence.[8]

[5] J. H. Whyte: "Daniel O'Connell and the Repeal Party" (*Irish Historical Studies*, XI, 1959, 297–316); Macintyre: *The Liberator*, 13; Kevin B. Nowlan: *The Politics of Repeal, 1841–1850* (London, 1965), 8.

[6] Nicholas Mansergh: *The Irish Question, 1840–1921* (new ed., Toronto, 1965), 294 ff.

[7] Johann G. Kohl: *Ireland* (New York, 1844), 58; Count Camillo Cavour: *Thoughts on Ireland* (1844; Eng. ed., London, 1868); Thomas W. Freeman: *Pre-Famine Ireland* (Manchester, 1957), 17.

[8] Kohl: *Ireland*, 72 ff., describes the new workhouses. See also George O'Brien: *The Economic History of Ireland from the Union to the Famine* (London, 1921), 162 ff., 177. The reforms of the 1830's are analyzed in some detail in Macintyre: *The Liberator*, chaps. v–vii.

The situation changed drastically after the election of 1841 and the advent of the Tory government of Sir Robert Peel. O'Connell and Peel were constitutionally antagonistic to each other and there was no possibility of an Irish deal with the Tories like the one with the Whigs. O'Connell therefore resumed the agitation of the Loyal National Repeal Association. Stimulated by the new Young Ireland group and its deeper conception of Irish nationalism, the movement gained tremendous momentum in the winter of 1842–1843. Weekly meetings were held in the larger towns, while "repeal wardens" campaigned throughout the country and repeal reading rooms were opened to supply propaganda literature. By 1843 (the "Repeal Year") the income of the association had risen to £48,000, a very large sum indeed for pressure purposes at that time.[9]

Although O'Connell continued to stress his opposition to violence or insurrection and his faith in "moral means, reasonable peaceful combination, and the electricity of public opinion," the authorities in both Dublin and London became increasingly troubled. The Liberator, through his passionate eloquence, his diatribes against the English and his shameless flattery of the Irish ("The bravest, most virtuous, most religious race the sun of God ever shone upon"), was whipping up tremendous popular enthusiasm. "With repeal you will be happy and rich and obtain all you wish and strive for," he told the people. In one of the "monster meetings" in August, 1843, he assumed the role of prophet and called upon the throng to

rejoice, for your fatherland is fated to become a nation again. Rejoice, for the day-star of Irish liberty is already on the horizon, and the full moon of freedom shall beam around your native land. The hour is approaching, the day is near, the period is fast coming when your country shall be a nation once more.[10]

Though he still did not say just what repeal would involve, O'Connell now talked of summoning a Council of Three Hundred to

[9] Sir James O'Connor: *History of Ireland, 1798–1924* (New York, 1925), I, 253; Michael Tierney: *Daniel O'Connell: Nine Centenary Essays* (Dublin, 1949), 155; Sean O'Faolain: *King of the Beggars* (New York, 1938), 328; Macintyre: *The Liberator*, 265 ff.; Nowlan: *Politics of Repeal*, 38 ff.; and the detailed account in Lawrence J. McCaffrey: *Daniel O'Connell and the Repeal Year* (Lexington, 1966).

[10] Quoted in Duffy: *Young Ireland*, 349. Further, O'Connor: *History of Ireland*, I, 201, 203, 254; Tierney: *Daniel O'Connell*, chap. ix. For an eyewitness account, see Kohl: *Ireland*, 67 ff.

Dublin, which would constitute a national assembly and *de facto* government. "Monster meetings" were staged at various historical sites and drew the populace from large surrounding areas. Led by their priests, as many as 300,000 persons would assemble, according to even the conservative estimates.[11] It stands to reason that such spectacles aroused wild enthusiasm and led to excessive language. When, in May, 1843, Peel declared in Parliament that the government was determined to preserve the union even at the cost of civil war, O'Connell ridiculed him as "the merest man of words that the world ever produced." In a monster meeting at Mullinghmast (October 1, 1843) he practically challenged the authorities to act. He boasted of having an army such as Wellington had never had, and his lieutenants talked of the formation of a repeal cavalry and other paramilitary preparations.[12]

Wellington and other Tory leaders were increasing their pressure on Peel to stop the agitation, but the prime minister could not see how the Repeal Association could be outlawed without treating the related Anti-Corn Law League in the same fashion, an action which seemed as dangerous as it was futile. However, substantial military forces were concentrated in Ireland and every effort was made to assemble incriminating evidence which would serve to convict O'Connell, who was said to have a pathological fear of imprisonment. The test of strength came on October 8, when the government, with almost no advance notice, prohibited the last great meeting of the season, at Clontarf, near Dublin. O'Connell, of whom Cavour once remarked that he was "audacious only in proportion to the patience of his adversaries," saw that he had overdrawn the bow and hastily canceled the meeting, but was nevertheless arrested, with eight others, for conspiracy to alter the government and constitution of the country "by intimidation and the demonstration of great physical force." He and his associates were tried by an all-Protestant jury. O'Connell was sentenced to twelve months in prison, from which he was presently freed when the House of Lords reversed the verdict on technical grounds. Given an enthusiastic reception on his

[11] See the account by the historian William E. H. Lecky: *Leaders of Public Opinion in Ireland* (new ed., New York, 1903), II, 235 ff.; also Duffy: *Young Ireland,* chaps. xi and xii.
[12] Dennis Gwynn: *Daniel O'Connell* (rev. ed., Oxford, 1947), 231; Nowlan: *Politics of Repeal,* 45 ff.; McCaffrey, *O'Connell and the Repeal Year,* 138 ff., 175 ff.

release, he still affirmed his faith in "the peaceful majesty and tranquil might of the people." But his abject surrender when the showdown came had seriously discredited his movement and he himself, suffering from a brain disease, lacked the energy to revive it. He died in Italy in 1847, when Ireland was sunk in the misery of the great potato famine. His passing was no longer a matter of much importance.[13]

One of the remarkable features of O'Connell's career was his ability to evoke so enthusiastic a response among the Irish peasants despite the fact that he did not advocate any drastic social reforms and was not prepared to make an issue even of repeal. Among his followers the Young Ireland group criticized him for misleading the people into thinking he would resist. They claimed that popular enthusiasm was such that the crowd would have been more than a match for armed force. John Mitchel, whose hatred of the English knew no bounds, was quite prepared to resort to violent means to liberate his country. His propaganda led to a complete break between his followers and the old and ailing O'Connell.[14]

The activists saw their chance when news arrived of the revolution of February, 1848, in Paris. Hoping for French sympathy and support, Mitchel launched a new journal, *The United Irishman,* in which he preached insurrection, complete separation from England, and the proclamation of a republic. Arrested in May, 1848, he was tried for treason and deported. His "martyrdom" had the effect, however, of increasing popular antagonism to England. His successor, James Finton Lalor, was if anything even more radical. He put aside repeal as "a petty parish question" and demanded drastic land reform. In July he staged an insurrection in Tipperary, but only to meet with speedy discomfiture. The insurgents were few in number, poorly armed, untrained and without clear plan. On July 25 they barricaded themselves in Widow McCormack's farmhouse in Ballingary, where they held the widow and her five children as hostages while police forces surrounded the house. The leader, O'Brien, could not bring himself to blow up the

[13] For an authoritative account of the Clontarf affair, see McCaffery: *Daniel O'Connell,* 191 ff. The pros and cons of O'Connell's decision are set forth in Lecky: *Leaders,* II, 240 ff.; O'Connor: *History of Ireland,* I, 205; Patrick S. O'Hegarty: *A History of Ireland under the Union* (London, 1952), 159 ff.

[14] Randall Clarke: "The Relations between O'Connell and the Young Irelanders" (*Irish Historical Studies,* III, 1942, 18–30); and the detailed studies of Denis Gwynn: *Young Ireland and 1848* (Cork, 1949); Nowlan, *Politics of Repeal,* chap. x.

property and its inmates and so the affair ended in fiasco. The insurgents were captured, convicted and deported to the penal colonies. The "insurrection in the cabbage patch" proved a damp squib.[15]

The Irish repeal movement, though a failure, nonetheless brought moderate but essential reforms in Ireland and, in addition, had important repercussions throughout Europe. In all countries, even in remote Finland, the course of the agitation was watched with lively interest. Liberals everywhere took the doctrine of "organized intimidation" to heart and hoped eventually to succeed in their programs through legal, peaceful organization and pressure. They laid O'Connell's failure to the ruthlessness of his opponents rather than to any weakness in his strategy. After all, they could point to the resounding success of the Anti-Corn Law League, which was the counterpart of the Repeal Association and modeled upon it.[16]

3. POLAND, THE MARTYRED NATION

The Polish Revolution and war against Russia in 1830–1831 were only the most recent of various attempts by the Polish gentry and intellectuals to throw off the Russian yoke and eventually re-establish the Polish state, which meant not the territory clearly inhabited by Poles but the frontiers of 1772, including millions of Lithuanians, White Russians and Ruthenians living submerged under Polish landlords. One could hardly, under the circumstances, speak of Polish "nationalism." Even in the Revolution of 1830 none of the leaders showed much concern for the lot of the peasantry. The peasantry, in turn, took no interest in the struggle of the landlords to recover their independence from Russia. The notion of Polish nationalism was to be developed only after 1831 among the *émigrés* who sought refuge in the West.

The emigration, it will be recalled, consisted of 9,000 to 10,000 men, mostly officers of the Polish army and intellectuals, the majority of whom were settled in France. Like *émigrés* of other times and places,

---

[15] Manus O'Neill" "John Mitchel" (in MacManus: *Thomas Davis*, 43–45); Cathol O'Shannon: "James Finton Lalor" (*ibid.*, 68–70); Donagh MacDonagh: "Ballingary" (*ibid.*, 57–60); and especially Gwynn: *Young Ireland*, chap. xv *et seq*.

[16] Cavour: *Thoughts on Ireland*, 1 ff.; John Hennig: "Continental Opinion" (in Tierney: *Daniel O'Connell*, chap. viii); Karl Holl: *Die irische Frage in der Ära O'Connells und ihre Beurteilung in der politischen Publizistik des deutschen Vormärz* (Mainz, 1958); John H. Wuorinen: *Nationalism in Modern Finland* (New York, 1931), 82.

the Polish exiles spent much time in factional dispute, in endless recrimination and competitive planning. In the main there were two rival organizations: the more conservative, monarchical League of National Unity under the leadership of Prince Adam Czartoryski, who, after vain attempts to enlist the support of the British government, moved to Paris in 1833 and established his headquarters at the Hôtel Lambert. Czartoryski was by profession a diplomat. He staked his hopes on governments hostile to Russia, set up his own extensive intelligence network, and attempted to organize a Balkan coalition that might support Poland in a renewed conflict with Russia, a conflict which he expected and hoped would soon spring from the antagonism of West and East.[17]

A much more numerous faction was the Polish Democratic Party, founded in 1832 and led by the eminent historian-politician Joachim Lelewel, who had been the chief spokesman of the democratic, republican elements in the Revolution. Lelewel put his faith not in governments but in peoples. He and his followers were in close touch with the French secret societies and identified the Polish cause with that of the European Revolution. Though obliged in 1833 to leave Paris for Brussels, Lelewel continued his agitation for revolution and democracy, while in 1835 an extreme group broke away from the Polish Democratic Society to found the Polish People, a faction which adopted the doctrines of socialism and envisaged a revolution that would be social as well as political.[18]

One of the subjects most ardently debated among the émigrés was

---

[17] On the Polish factions, see the contemporary account of Charles F. Henningsen: *Eastern Europe and the Emperor Nicholas* (London, 1846), I, chap. vi; further, W. Feldman: *Geschichte der politischen Ideen in Polen* (Munich, 1917), chap. iv; Gunther Weber: *Die polnische Emigration im 19 Jahrhundert* (Essen, 1937); A. P. Coleman: "The Great Emigration" (in *Cambridge History of Poland*, Cambridge, 1941, II, chap. xivA); R. F. Leslie: *Polish Politics and the Revolution of November, 1830* (London, 1956), chap. viii; M. Kukiel: *Czartoryski and European Unity* (Princeton, 1955), 218 ff.

[18] Ignacy Chrzanowski: "Joachim Lelewel" (in Stephen P. Mizwa: *Great Men and Women of Poland*, New York, 1942, 184–189); Marcel Handelsman: *Les idées françaises et la mentalité politique en Pologne au XIXe siècle* (Paris, 1927), chap. v; Michel Sokolnicki: "Les Polonais et la révolution projetée de 1833" (*Revue des sciences politiques*, XVIII, 1912, 333–343); M. K. Dziewanowski: "The Early Beginnings of Socialism in Poland" (*Slavonic and East European Review*, June, 1951); Peter Brock: "The Socialists of the Polish Great Emigration" (in Asa Briggs and John Saville, eds.: *Essays in Labour History*, London, 1960, 140–173).

the failure of the revolutionary leadership in 1830–1831 to enlist the support of the peasantry, that is, to give the insurrection a broad, popular base. Even conservative elements were ready to admit that this had been a serious shortcoming and that something would in future have to be done to satisfy the vast working majority of the population and give it a stake in the national cause. Czartoryski was willing to have the peasants given the land which they cultivated for their own purposes, but only with compensation to the landlords and with no fringe benefits. Lelewel, on the other hand, wanted to endow the peasants with enough land to ensure more than a bare subsistence. In fact he came close to agrarian communism in his belief that the land should belong to those who work it, and that in the Polish peasant commune (*gmina*) might be found the nucleus for a new social order.

Though Lelewel, like all good Poles, insisted on Poland's right to the frontiers of 1772, which would have meant the return of large non-Polish populations to Polish rule, he was in a sense the founder of genuine Polish nationalism, that is, of the cult of the Polish nation in contrast to mere devotion to the Polish state. He was himself the son of a Polonized German and was deeply influenced by German Romanticism. In his lectures at the University of Vilna he had, even before 1830, preached the doctrine of Poland's peculiar genius and the uniqueness of Polish civilization. It was from him that the great Polish poet, Adam Mickiewicz, derived the inspiration that was to lead him to the exaltation of nationalism far beyond anything previously known. Mickiewicz, too, owed much to German Romanticism.[19] Though he took no part in the Revolution of 1830, he soon became the intellectual leader of the emigration. At heart a mystic, he believed in the divine mission of great men such as Napoleon and rather fancied himself in the role of a spiritual leader of his people, a sort of moral Napoleon.[20]

[19] Josef Nadler: "Adam Mickiewicz, deutsche Klassik, deutsche Romantik" (in Albert Brackmann: *Deutschland und Polen*, Berlin, 1933, 51–62); Iza Saunove: "Der deutsche Einfluss auf die Entwicklung der literarischen und aesthetischen Theorien Mickiewicz" (*Germanoslavica*, III, 1935, 64–94).

[20] On his extravagant admiration for Napoleon, see his lectures in 1844, published as *Les Slaves*, especially 316, 354. Further, Wiktor Weintraub: "Adam Mickiewicz, the Mystic-Politician" (*Harvard Slavic Studies*, I, 1953, 137–178), and *Literature as Prophecy* (The Hague, 1959), 12 ff.; Edouard Krakowski: *Adam Mickiewicz, philosophe mystique* (Paris, 1935), chap. viii; Manfred Kridl: *Adam Mickiewicz, Poet of Poland* (New York, 1951), 11 ff., 264 ff.; Waclaw Lednicki: "The Secret of Mickiewicz's Greatness" (in B. R. Bugelski, ed.: *Mickiewicz and the West*, Buffalo, 1956, 11–18).

In the part entitled "Improvisation" of his lyric drama *Forefather's Eve* (1832), Mickiewicz wrestled with the problem of how a just and loving Deity could have permitted a free, independent, pious people to be crucified by three iniquitous neighbors. This led him to the doctrine of Polish messianism: the Poles were a chosen people, crucified, as Christ had been, in the cause of human freedom. Their suffering is but the prelude to a great exaltation, for even as Christ rose from the dead, so would Poland rise and, transfigured by suffering, assume the leadership of the Slavic and indeed of all Christian nations, ushering in a new and higher epoch of humanity, when all nations would be united in justice, liberty and brotherly love.[21]

Of even greater and wider influence was the poet's next work, the prose poem entitled *The Books of the Polish Nation and of the Polish Pilgrims* (1832), which, in hardly fifty pages, gave a highly idealized survey of Polish history. The Polish exiles appear transformed into pilgrims and made to assume a supranational mission. The Poles are characterized as a people of higher morality, deserted by the selfish nations of the West, sacrificed to expiate the sins of other nations, but called on to lead in the destruction of the existing impious order and open the way to a new federation of free nations. Mickiewicz exhorted them to be worthy of their high calling, to forget the errors of the past, to eschew recrimination, to become self-dependent. "Your endeavors are for all men, not only for yourselves. You will achieve a new Christian civilization." The Polish pilgrims, in short, were the forces of light struggling against darkness. The *Books* end in a litany beseeching God "for a universal war for the freedom of peoples," and "for a happy death on the battlefield."

The Books of the Polish Nation ran through six editions in little more than a year, and were quickly translated into French, German and English. Their impact was tremendous. They soon became the bible of the religion of humanity. Lamennais called them "beautiful as the Gospel" and adopted their Biblical style for his own equally influential *Words of a Believer* (1833), as did Mazzini for his *Faith and the Future* (1834). The great Italian nationalist's admiration for Mickie-

---

21 Excellent analyses in Monica M. Gardner: *Adam Mickiewicz* (London, n.d.), 6 ff. and chap. iv; George R. Noyes in the introduction to *Poems of Adam Mickiewicz* (New York, 1944); Wiktor Weintraub: *The Poetry of Adam Mickiewicz* (The Hague, 1954), chap. xi.

wicz and the Poles knew no bounds. He declared the former the greatest poet of his time and the prophet of a new era, while the latter were for him the people of faith and hope who would set the spark for the great revolution.[22]

Mickiewicz failed to overcome the factional strife among his fellow countrymen, but his writings were undoubtedly a great solace to the common man, whether in exile or at home. Many copies were smuggled into Poland, where they made an impression far beyond anything the revolutionary agents could achieve. The poet's third great work, the epic *Pan Tadeusz* (1834), was a radiant reaffirmation of Polish cultural values and has been justly described as "the immortalization of 'Polishness,' " the best-loved poem in the Polish language.

With these exaltations of the Polish cause and of nationalism in general, Mickiewicz' poetic inspiration ran dry. Yet he continued to exercise a widespread influence, for in 1840 he was appointed the first professor of Slavic literature at the Collège de France, where he was one of the brilliant trio of lecturers of whom Jules Michelet and Edgar Quinet were the other two. His lectures were more or less improvised rhapsody and prophecy, conveying the notion that God spoke most clearly through the Poles.[23] Nonetheless, they were received enthusiastically not only by the Paris exiles of many nations but by the French literary elite, which came to adore the Slavs and more particularly the Poles, to say nothing of Mickiewicz himself, "the august image of crucified Poland."[24]

Mickiewicz presently fell under the spell of Andrej Towianski, a Lithuanian mystic of eloquence and personal magnetism. Like the poet, Towianski was convinced that he was called by God to be Napoleon's successor in establishing social justice and the brotherhood of

[22] On Mazzini, the unpublished part on Poland of his 1847 essay on the Slavic national movements (now in *Scritti editi ed inediti*, XXXVI, 180–218); Giovanni Mayer: "Mazzini e Mickiewicz" (*Richerche slavistiche*, IV, 1955–1957, 7–30); further, Eric P. Kelly: "Guidance for a Conquered People" (in Bugelski: *Mickiewicz and the West*, 19–30); Weintraub: *Poetry of Adam Mickiewicz*, chap. xiii; Manfred Kridl: *A Survey of Polish Literature and Culture* (New York, 1956), 255 ff.

[23] Weintraub: *Literature as Prophecy* is essentially an analysis of Mickiewicz' lectures.

[24] For a contemporary account, see Hippolyte Desprez: "Les Polonais dans la révolution européenne" (*Revue des deux mondes*, August 15, 1849, 537–558); further, Waclaw Lednicki: "Mickiewicz at the Collège de France" (*Slavonic Review*, XX, 1941, 149–172); Z. L. Zaleski: "Michelet, Mickiewicz et la Pologne" (*Revue de littérature comparée*, VIII, 1928, 433–487).

nations. To the Poles he preached acceptance of God's will, arguing that not world revolution but only humility, love and sacrifice could bring on the new day.[25]

The French government in 1844 suspended Mickiewicz' lectures, which had become more and more a rhapsody on Napoleon and were producing hysterical reactions, especially among his female auditors.[26] But Polish messianism lost none of its appeal. Juliusz Slowacki, another eminent Romantic poet and also a disciple of Towianski, envisaged (in his poem *King-Spirit*, 1846) the redemption of Poland through sacrifice of a sinless youth.[27] At the same time Zygmunt Krasinski, in his long poem *Dawn* (1846), argued that since humanity is divine, nations are also divine. The destruction of Poland was a crime against humanity, and therefore a crime against God. But God gave the world his daughter, Poland, as formerly he had given his son, Christ. Poland's death, like Christ's, will be followed by resurrection and the dawn of a new and better age.[28]

The extravagant messianism of the Polish poets did not go unchallenged even in their own time. The eminent philosopher I. M. Hoene-Wronski, who first used the term *messianisme*, insisted on the supremacy of reason over intuition or inspiration, while Count Adam Gurowski reminded the Poles of their traditional factionalism and recommended acceptance of Russian rule.[29] Later Polish historians have, on the whole, been even more severe in their rejection of the Romantic vision. Oscar Halecki denounced messianism as "an aberration of national idolatry." Roman Dyboski declared it "obviously unhistorical, fantastically absurd, and blasphemously and immorally proud," while Manfred Kridl deplored the exorbitant notions that it implanted in Polish minds. Yet even these writers recognize that

[25] For analyses of his teaching, see Gardner: *Adam Mickiewicz*, 206 ff.; Krakowski: *Adam Mickiewicz*, 192 ff.; and, in greater detail, N. O. Lossky: *Three Chapters from the History of Polish Messianism* (Prague, 1936), 11–22; Henri Desmettre: *Towianski et le messianisme polonais* (2 vols., Lille, 1947).

[26] See the police reports in the appendix of Krakowski: *Adam Mickiewicz*.

[27] Stefan Treugott: *Juliusz Slowacki, Romantic Poet* (Warsaw, 1959); Julian Krzyzanowski: *Polish Romantic Literature* (New York, 1931); Kridl: *Survey*, 268 ff.; Lossky: *Three Chapters*, 23–31.

[28] Monica M. Gardner: *The Anonymous Poet of Poland: Zygmunt Krasinski* (Cambridge, 1919); A. E. Tennant: *Studies in Polish Life and History* (London, 1924), 243; Krzyzanowski: *Polish Romantic Literature*, chaps. x and xi.

[29] Lossky: *Three Chapters*, 1–10; Hans Kohn: *Panslavism* (Notre Dame, 1953), 32 ff.

messianism in the midcentury was more than a conceit: in providing the Polish people with an explanation of their suffering, it became a source of moral and national strength, "a mighty antidote against despair."[30]

4. ITALY AND ITS PRIMACY

The most persistent and systematic exponent of nationalism in the Europe of the midcentury was the Italian revolutionary, Giuseppe Mazzini, whose political doctrines and activities have already been recounted in Chapter III. Although nationalism was an integral part of Mazzini's program, it deserves special consideration in the larger context of the awakening of peoples.

Like other peoples, the Italians disliked foreign rule, whether Spanish, French or Austrian. After centuries of subjection, their hopes of independence and unity had been kindled by the Napoleonic regime, and their disappointment was correspondingly great when, in 1815, the individual states were restored, mostly under princes of foreign stock. The repressive policies of the Restoration fanned popular hostility to Austria, which was made responsible for everything. In 1832 the Italian dramatist Silvio Pellico published a little book entitled *My Prisons* which, in emotional, Romantic language recounted his ten years of imprisonment at the hands of the Austrians. The book was soon translated into most European languages and made a deep impression on countless readers. Not that it was a summons to revolution. Far from it, for Pellico was moved by humility and resignation. His memoir, which is hardly readable today, was important solely for its exposure of Austrian brutality and its encouragement of dreams of independence from arbitrary, foreign rule.[31]

The role of Mazzini was to crystallize anti-foreign sentiment and provide a rationale for what had thitherto been nebulous aspiration. As a young man he had read Herder's *Ideas* (in French translation) and had absorbed the notions of the national soul and the role of individual peoples in the unfolding of the cosmic drama. He was influenced also

[30] Weintraub: *Poetry of Mickiewicz*, 151; Roman Dyboski: "Literature and National Life in Modern Poland" (*Slavonic Review*, III, 1924–1925, 117–130); and the eloquent conclusion of Feldman: *Geschichte der politischen Ideen*, 118.

[31] E. M. Gray: *Silvio Pellico* (Milan, 1936); G. Vitali: *Silvio Pellico* (Milan, 1941); Giovanni Spadolini: "La vita religiosa in Italia nei secoli XIX e XX" (in Ettore Rota, ed.: *Questioni di storia del Risorgimento*, Milan, 1951, 822–865).

by Saint-Simonian teaching, with its stress on association as the key to a new social order. Finally, he was completely captivated by Mickie-wicz' *Books of the Polish Nation* with their theme of redemption of the nation through suffering.[32]

Italy, too, Mazzini was convinced, had an important, indeed a divine mission to fulfill. He was quite ready to recognize the primacy of the Poles among the Slavic peoples, but he was much provoked by the claims of the French to leadership in the future as in the past of Europe. Guizot, in his famous and influential lectures on modern history (1828–1830), saw France as the very hearth of European civilization and Michelet, in his *Introduction to Universal History* (1831), declared France "the pilot of humanity," destined to be the harbinger of a new age of the peoples and of a new social order. Particularly offensive to Mazzini was the fact that Buonarroti, the prominent revolutionary leader, was, despite his Italian origin, insistent on the necessity of French initiative in the approaching upheaval. For him, as for Michelet, Italy was to be merely one of the daughters of the free French Republic.[33]

Mazzini, despite his concern for humanity and international brotherhood, could not accept the idea of having Italy play second fiddle in the future concert of nations. He therefore convinced himself that God himself had ordained Italian primacy: the first (republican) Rome and the second (papal) Rome were to be succeeded by a third Rome which would lead the peoples of Europe to a new world order based on association: "The destiny of Italy is that of the world. . . . Rome, by design of Providence . . . is the eternal city, to which is entrusted the mission of disseminating the Word that will unite the world."[34]

---

[32] Gwilyn O. Griffith: *Mazzini: Prophet of Modern Europe* (New York, 1932), 41 ff.; Gaetano Salvemini: *Mazzini* (Stanford, 1957), 25 ff.; Renato Treves: *L'idea sansimoniana e il Risorgimento* (Turin, 1931); Otto Vossler: *Mazzinis politisches Denken und Wollen* (Berlin, 1927), 32 ff.; Hans Holldack: "Probleme des Risorgimento" (*Historische Zeitschrift*, CLXXIII, 1952, 505–527).

[33] H. F. Stewart and Paul Desjardins: *French Patriotism in the 19th Century* (Cambridge, 1923), 272 ff., 311; Hans Kohn: *Prophets and Peoples* (New York, 1946), chap. ii; Lewis Namier: "Nationality and History" (reprinted in his *Avenues of History*, London, 1952); Adolfo Omodeo: "Primato francese e initiativa italiana" (reprinted in his *Figure e passioni del Risorgimento Italiano*, Palermo, 1932, 27–57); Elizabeth L. Eisenstein: *The First Professional Revolutionist: Filippo Buonarroti* (Cambridge, 1959), 87 ff.

[34] The argument is best developed in his essays "On the Revolutionary Initiative" (1834) and "Faith and the Future" (1834). See further Salvemini: *Mazzini*, 77 ff.;

The main purpose of Mazzini's Young Italy was to prepare an insurrection that would first engulf Italy, then set the stage for a national crusade against Austria, and eventually spread to all Europe, after which the Continent could be reorganized along the lines of nationality. His efforts were generally abortive and his Young Europe movement ("The Holy Alliance of the Peoples") led to more discord between national leaders than to positive progress toward the ideal of a new Europe. Nonetheless, Mazzini's teaching fired the imagination of many young Italians. Giovanni Berchet, in his ode on the insurrections of 1831, called on his countrymen to rise against the foreign oppressor and strive to the end for national unity. The satirist Giuseppe Giusti in turn reviled the foreigner and his princely lackeys, while the dramatist Giovan Niccolini and the novelists Francesco Guerrazzi and Massimo d'Azeglio drew on medieval themes to illustrate former Italian resistance to foreign domination. Fanatical patriotism was reflected particularly in the stirring songs of the youthful Goffredo Mameli, whose verses "God and the People" and "Brothers of Italy" enjoyed an immense popularity.[35]

The more moderate elements of Italian society were never willing to adopt Mazzini's political principles and, as far as nationalism was concerned, regarded real unity as hardly more than a dream. However, the pressure of economic developments did suggest the need for a closer relationship between the various Italian states and there grew up gradually a school of thought directed toward a confederation of the Italian states (including the Austrian provinces), this end to be attained not through revolution but through propaganda and other peaceful pressures along the lines of the British Anti-Corn Law League. Gioberti's *Moral and Civil Primacy of the Italians* (1843), already discussed in Chapter III, outdid Mazzini in denigration of French civilization and in elaborate demonstration that Italy had been chosen by God to be the depository of his work. In the past, Italians had proved their superiority in thought, art and religion. By divine decree

---

Luigi Salvatorelli: *Il pensiero politico italiano dal 1700 al 1870* (5 ed., Turin, 1949), chap. vii; Hermann Raschhofer: *Der politische Volksbegriff im modernen Italien* (Berlin, 1936), 72 ff.; Maurice Vaussard: *De Pétraque à Mussolini: évolution du sentiment nationaliste italien* (Paris, 1961), 44 ff.

[35] Ernest H. Wilkins: *A History of Italian Literature* (Cambridge, 1954), 389 ff.; August Bock: *Grundzüge der italienischen Geistesgeschichte* (Urach, 1947), 95 ff.; Klara Steger: *Der politische Charakter der italienischen Romantik* (Bonn, 1952).

the Papacy had been established in Italy and the national revival must therefore be bound up with the Papacy, which, in turn, must be reformed and modernized. In concrete terms Gioberti envisaged a federal union under the titular presidency of the pope and the military leadership of the king of Piedmont. His more distant ideal was a reunited Christendom, a brotherhood of Christian nations under the aegis of the pope, with Italy pointing the way toward a spiritual conquest of the globe by the reformed church.[36]

Despite Gioberti's gross exaggerations and distortions of history, his book contributed greatly to the restoration of Italian self-esteem. His program of federation under papal leadership, on the other hand, held but little appeal for other intellectuals, most of whom had little faith in the possibility of papal reform. Cesare Balbo, the eminent historian, shared to the full the Romantic nationalism of Gioberti, but in his *Hopes of Italy* (1844) rejected the idea of Italian primacy and the program of federalism under presidency of the pope. "Before attaining primacy, we must first arrive at parity, and the first requirement for parity among independent nations is independence." Believing that the future of the Hapsburg Monarchy lay in Southeastern Europe, he thought a deal could be made by which Lombardy and Venetia could be acquired by Piedmont. Thus Italy would be freed of foreign rule and influence and could then consider reorganization, preferably under Piedmont as the strongest state. The novelist Massimo d'Azeglio took a similar line, trusting that European complications might provide the opportunity for a national crusade against Austria, under Piedmontese leadership. Luigi Torelli, too, approached the problem in realistic terms and suggested, in his *Thoughts on Italy* (1846), that after the expulsion of the foreigner, Lombardy, Venetia and Parma might be annexed to Piedmont; Modena and the northern part of the Papal States to Tuscany; and the remainder of the Papal States to Naples. The pope

---

[36] Carmelo Sgroi: *Introduzione alla studio del Gioberti* (Undine, 1935). The standard biography of Antonio Anzilotti: *Gioberti* (Florence, 1922) should be supplemented by Giovanni Saitta: *Il pensiero di Gioberti* (2 ed., Florence, 1927); Adolfo Omodeo: *Vincenzo Gioberti e la sua evoluzione politica* (Turin, 1941); Tullio Vecchietti: *Il pensiero politico di Vincenzo Gioberti* (Milan, 1941). See also Antonio Monti: *Il Risorgimento* (3 ed., Milan, 1948), chap. iv; Vaussard: *De Petraque à Mussolini,* 50 ff.; F. Catalano, R. Moscati and F. Valsecchi: *L'Italia nel Risorgimento* (Milan, 1964), 411 ff.

would then retain only Rome, as a free city, while all the Italian states would join in a confederation.[37]

The election of Pius IX (the "liberal pope") restored confidence in the future of the Papacy and the Catholic Church and revived interest in the notion of papal leadership in the national cause. Pius disliked foreign rule as much as did other Italians, but he must have realized that, in view of the international character of the church, it would be impossible for him to take a stand against a major Catholic power. He was at times troubled by the frenzied enthusiasm of the crowds that cheered him, but at other times allowed himself to be carried away by popular emotion. On one occasion he publicly invoked the blessing of the Almighty on Italy, after which it became impossible for him to disabuse the patriots.[38]

National feeling in Italy reached fever pitch in July, 1847, when the Austrians, who, by treaty, maintained a garrison in the citadel of Ferrara, sent reinforcements to that city. Disorders broke out and presently the troops occupied the city itself. Pius protested and appealed to Charles Albert of Piedmont for support. The king, with public sentiment egging him on, put up a bold front and thereby further fanned the flames of patriotism. Negotiations were initiated between Piedmont, Tuscany and the Papacy for the formation of a customs union, which was meant as the first step in the direction of some type of federation. So tense was the situation that the French and Austrian governments began to discuss joint intervention in case the pope found it impossible to further resist popular pressures. By January, 1848, open conflict seemed unavoidable. In Milan the so-called "tobacco riots" led to serious clashes between the troops and the populace, and on January 12 an insurrection took place in Palermo, which was to prove the spark that set off the revolutions of 1848. By that time nationalism in Italy had become completely identified with both liberalism and radicalism.

[37] Aldo Ferrari: *L'Italia durante la Restaurazione* (Milan, 1935), 229 ff.; George F. H. Berkeley: *Italy in the Making* (Cambridge, 1936), 154 ff., 186 ff.; Rosario Romeo: *Dal Piemonte sabaudo all'Italia liberale* (Turin, 1963), 61 ff.; Francesco Landogna's introduction to the new edition of Balbo's *Hopes of Italy* (Milan, 1930); Paolo E. Santangelo: *Massimo d'Azeglio, politico e moralista* (Turin, 1937).

[38] Robert M. Johnston: *The Roman Theocracy and the Republic, 1846–1849* (New York, 1901). See also Berkeley: *Italy in the Making*, II, chaps. iv and v; Luigi Salvatorelli: *Prima e dopo il Quarantotto* (Turin, 1948), 108 ff.; Antonio Monti: *Pio IX nel Risorgimento italiano* (Bari, 1928).

Mazzini, Gioberti and others had stamped their ideas on the minds of at least the articulate sector of the population. In the revolutions of 1848 the nationalist theme in fact tended at times to dominate even constitutional aspirations.[39]

5. GERMANY: DREAMS AND REALITIES

The unification of the German states was to prove the overriding problem of the Central European revolutions of 1848 and, as finally achieved by Bismarck, was to be one of the major events of nineteenth-century history. Yet the problem defies straightforward treatment. It is nebulous and elusive. To begin with, the Germans needed no cultural revival. They had for centuries performed a great cultural mission not only in Central but in Eastern Europe. They were pre-eminent in literature, art and learning, and were distinguished for their enlightenment, humanitarianism and cosmopolitanism. Indeed, the whole doctrine of cultural nationalism was a product of German philosophy. It stands to reason that these great intellectual achievements should have contributed to a sense of national pride and a desire for greater political identity and unity, but the cosmopolitan outlook was to persist for a long time. The German philosopher Fichte was to argue that it was the peculiar mission of the Germans to represent not one nation but the whole of humanity.[40]

The struggle against French domination in 1813–1815 was borne on a wave of patriotic enthusiasm and led to much discussion of a new German Empire to replace the defunct Holy Roman Empire of the past. The hopes of the nationalists were disappointed in 1815, but the agitation was continued in the universities until the Carlsbad Decrees of 1819 put an end to it, at least temporarily.

[39] For the crisis of 1847–1848, see the valuable contemporary analysis of an Austrian diplomat in Angelo Filipuzzi: *Pio IX e la politica austriaca in Italia* (Florence, 1958); also Friedrich Engel-Janosi: *Oesterreich und der Vatikan, 1846–1918* (Graz, 1958); A. J. P. Taylor: *The Italian Problem in European Diplomacy, 1847–1849* (Manchester, 1934), 24 ff.; Ruggero Moscati: *La diplomazia europea e il problema italiano nel 1848* (Florence, 1947), chap. i.

[40] Friedrich Meinecke: *Weltbürgertum und Nationalstaat* (new ed. in his *Werke*, Munich, 1963) is the classic study of the transition from cosmopolitan to nationalist thinking, but see also Hermann Oncken: "Deutsche geistige Einflüsse in der europäischen Nationalitätenbewegung des 19 Jahrhunderts" (reprinted in his *Nation und Staat*, Berlin, 1935); Eugen Schmahl: *Der Aufstieg der nationalen Idee* (3 ed., Stuttgart, 1933), 11 ff.

The early nationalists, who constituted a small minority even in the universities, were ardent Romanticists who rhapsodized about Germanism without being able to advance any concrete program. In all conscience, the problem bristled with difficulties. It was impossible, for instance, to say just what territories should be included in a new German state. The Confederation established in 1815 embraced territories of non-German states such as The Netherlands and Denmark, yet did not take in the entire territory of the Prussian Monarchy. Furthermore, it comprised about half of the Hapsburg Empire, despite the fact that in that half the German element was definitely a minority. An additional problem arose from the fact that the German world contained two major powers, Prussia and Austria, which were traditional rivals and competitors for leadership. Each of these powers had, in a sense, developed a nationalism of its own. They were not inclined to merge their states in a larger unity. To a degree this was true also of the thirty-odd lesser states of the Confederation, many of them of recent date, whose rulers were suspicious of the designs of their more powerful fellow members. The religious split, too, presented serious obstacles to the realization of unity.[41]

The issue of nationalism emerged again in the commotion following the July Revolution of 1830, when it was definitely associated with political radicalism. At the Hambach Festival (1832), for example, there was much denunciation of the existing Confederation along with demands for an all-German federal republic, which was to form part of a European federation of national states. At the same time Paul Pfizer, in a remarkably prescient book *The Correspondence of Two Germans* (1831), pointed to Prussia as a youthful, progressive and truly German state which alone was fitted to assume leadership of a national state, provided it would espouse constitutional government. Pfizer was, however, troubled by Prussia's disproportionate size and power. He therefore speculated about the dissolution of the Prussian Monarchy and the possible establishment of relative equality of size and power among the members of the prospective federal state. The nature of his meditations reflects the tremendous inherent difficulties in the way of unification.

---

[41] Heinrich von Treitschke: *Deutsche Geschichte im 19 Jahrhundert* (1879–1894), IV, 407. Basic studies of the problem of German unity are Erich Brandenburg: *Die Reichsgründung* (Leipzig, 1916); Erich Marcks: *Der Aufstieg des Reiches* (Stuttgart, 1936); Heinrich Ritter von Srbik: *Deutsche Einheit* (3 ed., Munich, 1940).

They were to plague the liberals in 1848 and, so far as the partition of Prussia is concerned, found a solution only in the mid-twentieth century.[42]

Prussian leaders were by no means converted by doctrines such as Pfizer's. Following Fichte, they argued that the peculiar nature of Germanism called for variety and multiplicity. Even Leopold von Ranke, the great historian, preferred the maintenance of the many German states, each of which could make a peculiar contribution to the broader *Kulturnation*. According to the influential *Berlin Political Weekly*, of which Ranke was the editor, "Germany's unity consists in the fact that each part, even the smallest part of the German fatherland, has its own pulse beat and that all these pulse beats together provide nourishment to the heart." It was such thinking that led men such as Joseph Maria von Radowitz to dream of something like the restoration of a medieval patrimonial state and a medieval German Empire.[43]

In Germany as in other countries nationalism became dynamic during the 1840's. The famous *Zollverein,* organized in 1834 under Prussian leadership, united most of non-Hapsburg Germany in a customs union and thereby created a strong sense of common interest. At the same time the steamboat and the railway were facilitating intercourse between the different states. Professional men began to meet periodically to discuss common problems. Of particular importance were the congresses of Germanists, that is, university teachers of German language, literature, history and law. These led to the establishment in 1847 of a new, pronouncedly nationalist newspaper, *The German Gazette,* which appealed to all liberal, nationalist elements. The struggle for constitutional government thus became merged with the striving for national union.[44]

In a meeting of liberal leaders from many states at Heppenheim

[42] Meinecke: *Weltbürgertum und Nationalstaat,* Part II, chap. i; Ignaz Jastrow: *Geschichte des deutschen Einheitstraumes und seiner Erfüllung* (2 ed., Berlin, 1885), 119 ff.

[43] Meinecke: *Weltbürgertum und Nationalstaat,* 217; Paul Hassel: *Joseph Maria von Radowitz* (Berlin, 1905); Friedrich Meinecke: *Radowitz und die deutsche Revolution* (Berlin, 1913), especially the introductory chapter; E. Ritter: *Radowitz, ein katholischer Staatsmann Preussens* (Köln, 1948).

[44] R. Hinton Thomas: *Liberalism, Nationalism, and the German Intellectuals, 1822–1847* (Cambridge, 1951).

(Hesse) in October, 1847, the problem of unity was discussed at length. There was strong sentiment for transforming the *Zollverein* into a political organization with a representative Parliament. The German parts of the Hapsburg Monarchy (which were not included in the *Zollverein*) might be invited to join. Some even went so far as to envisage the inclusion of the entire Hapsburg Monarchy and possibly even the Balkan region. Thus the rapidly growing industry of Germany might find needed markets and Germany's surplus population might be settled in these underdeveloped areas. These were the projects for a Middle Europe (*Mitteleuropa*) as formulated by the influential economist Friedrich List and, in a less strictly economic sense, by Paul Pfizer and eventually Radowitz. These men were all convinced that any future organization of the German world would have to be on a federal basis and that, in view of the largely non-German character of the Hapsburg Monarchy, to say nothing of its ultraconservative orientation, the leadership of Prussia was imperative. On the other hand, none could bring himself to advocate the abandonment of the German element in Austria, so the idea emerged that the German states should be united under Prussia, but that there should be a firm alliance with the entire Hapsburg Empire, so as to ensure a common foreign policy, a common military establishment, and a common trade policy.[45]

Schemes for German unification and for a greater Middle Europe reflected the growing concern of thoughtful Germans for the security of their country. The Near Eastern crisis of 1840 (see Chapter IX) threatened a general European conflict. War fever in France led to talk of a campaign on the Rhine and reconquest of the Rhineland. In response the Germans, indignant and apprehensive, united in opposition to French pretensions. Nicholas Becker's song "They shall not have the free, the German Rhine" was on all lips.[46] Unity had clearly become urgent and discussion of the ways and means of attaining it became chronic. The final straw came in 1846 with the efforts of the Danish

---

[45] On the Heppenheim meeting, see Brandenburg: *Die Reichsgründung*, I, 170 ff.; Ernst R. Huber: *Deutsche Verfassungsgeschichte* (Stuttgart, 1960), II, 450 ff. On the Middle Europe schemes, see Otto Wagner: *Mitteleuropäische Gedanken und Bestrebungen in den vierziger Jahren* (Marburg, 1935), 65 ff., 95 ff.

[46] Max Schneckenberger's familiar song "The Watch on the Rhine," though written at this time, became popular only after appropriate music had been written for it. Hoffmann von Fallersleben's "Germany Above All" was written in 1841, but also in the context of the French threat.

government to integrate the province of Schleswig with the rest of the Danish Monarchy. Schleswig's population was largely German and its fate was regarded by all German nationalists as a German responsibility. Yet the Germans seemed helpless in the face of the efforts of a small country to coerce the province. Questions of national power and prestige became overriding in the minds of German patriots. "One reason for dissatisfaction is universal in Germany, and every thinking German feels it deeply and painfully," wrote Prince Hohenlohe in his diary: "it is the nullity of Germany vis-à-vis other states." As yet the struggle against absolutism was of highest priority, but before long the issue of unification was to overshadow all else.

6. THE NORTHERN NATIONS

The history of the Scandinavian countries, too often slighted by historians, provides a classic example of cultural nationalism and the gradual emergence of a strong political trend. Northern scholars were much influenced by German philosophers and by writers of the Romantic school and began to collect folklore and folk songs which were still current in the North and which, by definition, were regarded as the true expression of the national spirit.[47] Nicholas Grundtvig, the Danish religious leader, had done pioneer work in this direction and made great efforts to encourage Danish national consciousness. His *Northern Mythology* (1832) propounded a philosophy of history based on the notion of the national soul. "He was so bewitched by the Danish spirit," says one of his biographers, "that whenever he met Danishness, whether in nature or history or speech, he saw mighty visions which so overwhelmed him that his eyes brimmed with tears and his tongue was moved to sing, to praise and to extol," as shown by the hundreds of patriotic poems, songs and hymns which came from his industrious pen.[48]

Grundtvig made an important contribution to Danish cultural development through the establishment of folk high schools, of which a number were opened between 1844 and 1852. These schools were of more than local importance, for they were based on the principle that

---

[47] For a concise review, see John H. Wuorinen: "Scandinavia and the Rise of Modern National Consciousness" (in Edward M. Earle, ed.: *Nationalism and Internationalism*, New York, 1950, 455–480).

[48] Hal Koch: *Grundtvig* (Yellow Springs, 1952), 132–133.

character building was more important than mere factual knowledge. However, they were also schools of Danish nationalism, for every session opened and closed with the singing cf patriotic songs and a great deal of attention was paid to the study of the Danish language, literature and history.[49]

Norway had, prior to 1815, been united with Denmark and its "national Romanticism" was in a sense the counterpart of the Danish national revival. The Association for the History of the Norwegian People and Language was founded in 1832 by the historians Jacob R. Keyser and Peder A. Munch, of whom the latter spent many years in foreign libraries and archives collecting materials for his great history, which began to appear in 1851. Keyser and Munch did their utmost to assign the medieval Eddas to Norway and claimed a national individuality for the Norwegians on the theory that in the hazy past they had entered the Scandinavian peninsula from the north, while the Danes and Swedes had supposedly come in from the south. The Norwegians, therefore, were more purely Nordic and early Norse literature was not loosely Scandinavian but strictly Norwegian-Icelandic.[50]

Along with the historical efforts of Keyser and Munch went the work of the collectors of fairy tales and songs. Many of these were published in 1842–1843 by Peder C. Asbjörnsen and Jörgen Moe, while some time later Magnus Landstad and Olea Cröger brought out an edition of Norwegian ballads. Ivar Aasen, after extensive researches, in 1848 published a grammar of the Norwegian language and a dictionary. On the strength of these a new literary language, distinct from Danish, was then constructed.[51]

---

[49] Axel Garde: *Bauernvolk* (Berlin, 1939), chaps. xv and xvi; John C. and Katherine Watson: *Education in Democracy: the Folk Schools of Denmark* (London, 1944); Elisabeth Sontag: *N. F. S. Grundtvig: Erzieher seines Volkes* (Berne, 1946), chap. iii; and the magistral study of Erica Simon: *Réveil national et culture populaire en Scandinavie: la génèse de la hojskole nordique, 1844–1878* (Paris, 1960), Part I, chaps. ii and iii.

[50] Oscar J. Falnes: *National Romanticism in Norway* (New York, 1933), chaps. iv to ix; Andreas Elviken: *Die Entwicklung des norwegischen Nationalismus* (Berlin, 1930), 117 ff.; Theodore Jorgenson: *History of Norwegian Literature* (New York, 1933), chap. xiii; Simon: *Réveil national*, 248 ff.

[51] Falnes: *National Romanticism in Norway,* chaps. xii–xvi; G. M. Gathorne-Hardy: *Norway* (London, 1925), chap. viii; Harald Beyer: *A History of Norwegian Literature* (New York, 1956), 141 ff.

By the midcentury the Norwegians were completely enamored of their rugged country and their rugged people. "Even their bleak and dreary mountains are dear to their hearts," according to an American visitor; "everything that relates to Gamle Norge (Old Norway) has a perfect charm for them."[52] The mountains that seemed bleak to foreigners were painted in Romantic glow by the fine Norwegian artist Johan C. Dahl, while the great violinist, Ole Bull, took immense pride in introducing Norse music to a larger European public. Among the poets, Johan S. Welhaven still tried for beauty of form and elegance of style, and yearned for the cultivated world of Copenhagen. But his rival Henrik Wergeland championed the homely virtues of his native land, defended the cause of the common man, preached Norwegian nationalism and rejected utterly all Danish connections.[53]

The Swedes, for their part, had no need to rediscover their past greatness. Culturally their ties to Germany were strong and the influence of German Romanticism was immediate. By 1830 the current of nationalism was already in full flow, as shown by Esais Tegner's *Frithjof's Saga,* which idealized all that was Nordic and extolled all that was anti-Russian. Erik G. Geijer at the same time wrote heroic poetry and published a standard *History of the Swedish People* (1832–1836). More popular writers, such as Per H. Ling and Anders Fryxell, contributed patriotic epics, dramas and stories for home consumption.[54]

The national revival in Finland was, in many ways, more instructive than the others, for Finland, prior to its annexation by Russia in 1809, had been ruled for centuries by Sweden. The upper classes were either Swedish or, when Finnish, had become Swedish in language and manners. There had been some reaction to this even before the nineteenth century, for a beginning had been made by Henrik Porthan and Zachris Topelius toward collecting Finnish poetry and sagas, while Adolf Arwidsson had raised objections to the neglect of Finnish

---

[52] Robert Baird: *Visit to Northern Europe* (New York, 1842), II, 67.

[53] Gathorne-Hardy's introduction to his edition of Wergeland's poems (London, 1929); Illit Gröndahl and Ola Raknes: *Chapters in Norwegian Literature* (Oslo, 1923), chaps. iv and v; Simon: *Réveil national,* 138 ff.

[54] B. J. Hovde: *The Scandinavian Countries, 1720–1865* (Boston, 1943), II, 456 ff.; Helmut de Boor: *Schwedische Literatur* (Breslau, 1924), chap. iv; Andrew A. Stromberg: *A History of Sweden* (New York, 1931), 622 ff.; Ragnhild Hatton: "Some Notes on Swedish Historiography" (*History,* XXXVIII, 1952, 96–113); Simon: *Réveil national,* 285 ff.

culture and advanced a doctrine of nationalism.[55] The first lectureship in the Finnish language was established at the University of Helsinki in 1828 and the Finnish Literature Society was founded in 1831 to propagate "more accurate notions about the fatherland and its history, to cultivate the Finnish language and establish in this language a literature both for the educated classes and for the people." However, progress was slow, for Swedish culture was firmly entrenched. Eminent champions of Finnish nationalism continued to write in Swedish and even the Literature Society, while providing textbooks for the study of Finnish, continued to conduct its proceedings in Swedish until 1850.[56]

Finland's great poet, Johan L. Runeberg, a devotee of German and Swedish Romanticism, idealized the Finnish peasant in his epic *The Elk-Hunters* (1832) and, in his cycle of narrative poems *The Tales of Ensign Stahl* (1848), glorified Finnish resistance to the Russian conquest.[57] But best-known of all the Finnish intellectuals was Elias Lönnrot, the secretary of the Literature Society. On a dozen journeys by foot through eastern Finland, Karelia and Lapland he collected folk songs (runes), stories, proverbs and incantations. He noticed that the rune singers, who were still active in Karelia, never sang a song twice in exactly the same way. There were endless variants and combinations of runes. Lönnrot became convinced that, like the Homeric poems, the runes were really parts of one great epic, which he undertook to reconstruct. Acting as a rune singer, he selected themes from thousands of songs and combined them as he saw fit to form a consistent saga. In 1835 he published the first part of his *Kalevala,* consisting of some 12,000 lines. This was followed in 1840 by his *Kanteletar* (a collection of folk lyrics), in 1844 by a volume of riddles, and in 1849 by a much-enlarged edition of the *Kalevala,* consisting now of almost 23,000 lines. This edition was soon translated into the principal European lan-

[55] Magnus G. Schybergson: *Politische Geschichte Finnlands, 1809–1919* (Gotha, 1925), 84 ff., 133 ff.; John H. Wuorinen: *Nationalism in Modern Finland* (New York, 1931), 15 ff., 47 ff.; Jalmari Jaakkola: *Die Geschichte des finnischen Volkes* (Berlin, 1942), 133 ff.

[56] Ernest G. Palmen: *L'oeuvre demi-séculaire de la Société de Littérature Finnoise* (New York, 1916), chap. ii; Arthur Reade: *Finland and the Finns* (New York, 1916), chap. ii; Wuorinen: *Nationalism in Modern Finland.*

[57] Edmund Gosse: *Northern Studies* (London, 1890); Edvard R. Gummerus: *Storia delle letterature della Finlandia* (Milan, 1957), 87 ff.

guages. Lönnrot was warmly praised by Jakob Grimm, the great philologist, while Longfellow was so impressed by the German version of the *Kalevala* that he adopted its style and meter for his own epic *Hiawatha*.[58]

Another of Lönnrot's achievements was the melding of the western and eastern Finnish dialects to form a modern literary language. Thereby he prepared the way for Johan W. Snellman, who gave Finnish nationalism its political twist. Snellman, after extensive travel and study abroad, in 1842 published *The Theory of the State,* a treatise in the Hegelian style. The state, he argued, is nothing but the expression of nationality, and nationality can prosper only if firmly rooted in a common language and based on common feeling. Finnish must, therefore, replace Swedish as the national language. A born controversialist, Snellman did what he could to arouse his countrymen, bridge the gulf between the upper and lower classes, and further the process of Finnization. It was largely due to his efforts that the language issue became so burning a one in the ensuing decades.[59]

Like the Norwegians, the Finns were concerned to legitimize their position historically. The philologist Mathias A. Castrén demonstrated that they were not a small, isolated people, but were related to at least a seventh of the population of the earth. After difficult researches among the primitive tribes of Russia and Siberia, Castrén in 1849 advanced the theory of the basic relationship of the Ural-Altaic peoples as demonstrated by the Finno-Ugrian languages. This doctrine held a mighty appeal for the new generation. The Academic Reading Club (founded in 1846) began to subscribe to foreign books and journals and to interest itself in foreign politics. Thus even remote Finland attempted to fit itself into the larger European scene.[60]

It was only natural that Scandinavian nationalists, concerned with questions of national prestige and power, should have conjured up the vision of a united Scandinavia, for which there was ample historical precedent. This was Grundtvig's dream and Wergeland's plea. Pres-

[58] Domenico Comparetti: *The Traditional Poetry of the Finns* (New York, 1898), 4 ff.; Martin Buber: introduction to the new edition of Schiefner's German translation of the *Kalevala* (Munich, 1922); Francis P. Magoun's introduction to his new prose translation into English (Cambridge, 1963). See also Emil Setälä: "Die finnische Literatur" (in *Die Kultur der Gegenwart*, Berlin, 1908, I, 9, 309–332).

[59] Wuorinen: *Nationalism in Modern Finland*, 84 ff.; Gummerus: *Storia delle letterature*, 107 ff.; Reade: *Finland and the Finns*, chap. iii.

[60] Wuorinen: *Nationalism in Modern Finland*, 98 ff.

ently there emerged the movement known as Scandinavism, with the aim of eventually recovering Finland from Russia, possibly with British support. The various governments, to be sure, would have nothing to do with such a program, the more so as there were serious differences between them. The movement, therefore, remained almost entirely academic. In the severe winter of 1838–1839 Swedish and Danish students crossed the frozen Sound for mutual visits. Scandinavian student congresses were arranged and in 1845 all Scandinavian universities joined in observance of the Feast of the Forefathers, in honor of the Nordic past. At the student congress in Copenhagen in 1845 Orla Lehmann, the Danish liberal leader, forecast a Scandinavian union based not, as in the past, on force, but on freedom and mutual affection. Amid great enthusiasm those present took an oath to work in every way for Nordic unity.[61]

In the years preceding 1848 the Scandinavian movement became entwined not only with the liberal agitation in Denmark but also with the Schleswig-Holstein question, which provided a perfect example of the impact of nationalist feeling on old and well-established relationships of a feudal or dynastic character. The question of these two duchies was so heavily overlaid with claims of traditional rights and the requirements of age-old agreements that it defies adequate brief statement. The population of Schleswig and Holstein constituted about two-fifths of the total population of the Danish Monarchy, but was German, except for a strip in northern Schleswig. The duchies had long been connected with Denmark through the ruler and were supposedly inseparable, though in fact only Holstein had belonged to the Holy Roman Empire and was included in the Germanic Confederation of 1815. Trouble began in the early nineteenth century, when the Germans in the duchies became nationally conscious and clamored for what would have amounted to autonomous institutions, while the nationalists in Germany agitated for their inclusion in a unified German empire.[62]

[61] Christian Degn: *Orla Lehmann und der nationale Gedanke* (Neumünster, 1936), 71 ff.; 93 ff.; Theodore Jorgenson: *Norway's Relation to Scandinavian Unionism, 1815–1871* (Northfield, 1935), 76 ff.; Torvald Höjer: "Die Genesis der swedischen Neutralität" (*Historische Zeitschrift*, CLXXXI, 1958, 65–79); John Sanness: *Patrioter Intelligens og Skandinaver* (Oslo, 1959); Raymond E. Lindgren: *Norway-Sweden: Disunion and Scandinavian Integration* (Princeton, 1959).

[62] Otto Brandt: *Geschichte Schleswig-Holsteins* (5 ed., Kiel, 1957); Johannes Brock: *Zur Vorgeschichte der schleswig-holsteinischen Erhebung von 1848* (2 ed., Göttingen, 1925); Harald Thurau: *Die Anfänge eines deutschen national-politischen Bewusstseins*

The question of the duchies entered the critical phase when, in 1830, Uwe Lornsen, a Danish government official of German nationality, published a pamphlet calling for a modern constitution for the combined duchies, along with complete administrative independence. An ardent German nationalist, Lornsen did not advocate the disruption of the Danish state, but called for its division into two parts, connected only through the person of the ruler.

Lornsen was at once arrested and imprisoned for a year, after which he emigrated to the New World. Though his political career had been little more than episodic, he had launched the new Schleswig-Holsteinism and had precipitated the constitutional issue. The initial reaction of the Danish government was to establish separate provincial diets for each of the duchies (1834). But this move did little to relieve the situation. The liberals in the duchies clamored for a really modern representational system for the combined provinces, while the Danish liberals began to espouse the demands of the Danish minority leaders in the duchies for the optional use of Danish in the administration of North Schleswig. In 1838 they helped to establish the first Danish newspaper, *Dannevirke*, in Schleswig.

The clash of German and Danish nationalism had now become unavoidable. In Copenhagen the liberal leader, Orla Lehmann, took an uncompromising stand. Historical rights and claims weighed little, he argued, as against the requirements of the modern national state. He was prepared to accept the separation of Holstein from the Danish Monarchy, but insisted that Schleswig be fully incorporated with the other territories of the Danish crown.

To further complicate the situation there arose a dispute about the eventual succession to the Danish throne. Christian VIII, who succeeded Frederick VI in 1839, had an only son, who was childless. The throne would therefore pass eventually to the related house of Sonderburg, but to which branch of that family was a question. In Denmark proper, where succession through females was permissible, the heir presumptive was Duke Christian of Sonderburg-Glücksburg. But in Schleswig, where the Salic Law applied, the nearest male claimant was Christian August, Duke of Sonderburg-Augustenburg. The question

---

in *Schleswig-Holstein* (Flensburg, 1939); and the admirable study of W. Carr: *Schleswig-Holstein, 1815–1848* (Manchester, 1963), chaps. iii and iv.

of the succession was not immediate, but it raised the specter of eventual disruption of the monarchy through different successions. Lehmann and the Danish liberals urged the new king to forestall such a crisis by granting a liberal constitution to Denmark proper and Schleswig, leaving Holstein to its own devices. In a major speech in 1842 Lehmann declared that Denmark would fight if necessary to retain Schleswig for the monarchy.

The lines were now clearly drawn: on the one hand, the Schleswig-Holsteiners, led by the young historians Johann G. Droysen and Georg Waitz and ardently supported by all German nationalists; on the other, the Eider-Danes (so-called from the river Eider, which forms the boundary between Schleswig and Holstein), who enjoyed the support of the Scandinavian movement. Both sides carried on an active propaganda in Schleswig and so contributed to the growing tension. The Danish king, unable to resist the pressure of the Eider-Danes, on July 8, 1846 issued an "open letter" dealing with the question of the succession. This, he declared, should be the same in Schleswig as in Denmark. Indeed, he promised to do his utmost to ensure it in Holstein also. Furthermore, he indicated his intention of promulgating a constitution which would bind Schleswig more firmly to the remainder of the monarchy.[63]

This "open letter" naturally raised a storm of protest in the duchies. Most of the deputies left the provincial diets, while the Duke of Augustenburg objected loudly to the prospective violation of his claims. In Germany, too, indignation mounted. Nationalist elements united in support of their threatened fellow Germans in the duchies. And presently, in the midst of the excitement, Christian VIII died (January 20, 1848) and was succeeded by his son Frederick VII, the last ruler of the Oldenburg dynasty. The new king, shaky in his position and frightened by the Eider-Danes, hastily promised a constitution that should apply equally to all parts of the monarchy. While the Germans in the duchies threatened to resist, news arrived of the revolution in Paris and the flight of Louis Philippe. The Eider-Danes insisted on the immediate incorporation of Schleswig, in reply to which the Schleswig-Holstein diets sent a delegation to Copenhagen demanding a new, joint constitution for the two duchies and, what was more, the inclusion of

---

[63] A wealth of interesting detail, which must be omitted here, can be found in the books by Brandt, Degn and Carr, cited above.

Schleswig in the Germanic Confederation. The Eider-Danes were quick to accept the challenge. Under threat of revolution they obliged the king to appoint a popular ministry (the "Casino Cabinet"), which promptly rejected the demands of the diets. Thereupon the Schleswig-Holsteiners set up a provisional government at Kiel (March 24) and began to resist the Danish troops attempting to occupy Schleswig. But they were too unprepared. On April 9 they were defeated near Flensburg, after which the Danish forces took over all of Schleswig.

The further evolution of the problem is part of the German Revolution of 1848, for the question of the duchies became merged with the larger question of German unity and as such became a major issue of European politics.

7. RUSSIA: THE SLAVOPHILES

In Chapter V the Russian nationalists or Slavophiles, as they came to be known, were discussed as constituting an important segment of the growing opposition to the czarism of Nicholas I. The Slavophile movement, like nationalist movements elsewhere, was inspired in its cultural phase by the German writers such as Herder and Schiller, and led initially to the collection of old chronicles, charters and other records, and to the effort to establish a literary language. It was given great impetus by the resistance to Napoleon's invasion, and thereafter by the publication of the various volumes of Nicholas M. Karamzin's great *History of the Russian State* (1816–1829), which carried the narrative to the seventeenth century. In glowing, romantic language, Karamzin provided the Russians with an impressive image of their past and thereby contributed mightily to national pride.[64]

In 1829 Ivan Kireevski, one of the leaders of the budding Slavophile movement, published an article in which he contended that the West, however admirable its past, had completed its mission and that Russia in future would assume the leadership of the European world.[65] The same line was presently taken by the historians S. P. Shervyrev and Michael P. Pogodin. The latter, who in 1835 became the first regular professor of Russian history at the University of Moscow, argued in

[64] Anatole G. Mazour: *Modern Russian Historiography* (2 ed., New York, 1958), 50 ff., 62 ff.; Nicholas V. Riasanowsky: *Russia and the West in the Teaching of the Slavophiles* (Cambridge, 1952), 7.

[65] See the admirable study by Eberhard Müller: *Russischer Intellekt in europäischer Krise: Ivan V. Kireevskij* (Köln, 1966), especially 95 ff.

1838 that while the West was torn by war, social conflicts and revolutions, Russia was the very picture of peace and harmony. The Russian claim to primacy and mission was, it is clear, much like the pretensions of other nations in the first flush of national pride.[66]

The publication of Chaadaev's *Philosophical Letter* in 1836 opened the great debate between the Westerners and the Slavophiles as to the Russian past and the relative merits of Russian culture. This topic, discussed in an earlier context, need not be rehearsed here. The Slavophiles (Alexis B. Khomiakov, Ivan and Peter Kireevski, Constantine and Ivan Aksakov, George Samarin) were men well acquainted with the West but convinced of the superiority of Russian institutions and Greek Orthodoxy. They were highly critical of Peter the Great for having broken the continuity of Russian development, and hated the autocracy and bureaucracy which derived from his efforts to imitate the West. They dreamed of a return to a patriarchal society and a patrimonial system, when the organic relationship between the nobility and the people would be restored and the Greek Orthodox Church, the only true faith, would serve to hold Russian society together. Western civilization, they held, had been undermined by rationalism and materialism; it was corrupt and doomed to rot away. "The entire West is wrapped in the shroud of death," wrote Khomiakov. Russia, as a young, fresh, organic state, had the mission to redeem the West and lead it back to the true faith.[67]

Slavophilism is sometimes confused with Pan-Slavism, a movement which, after the midcentury, became influential in Russia. As the name suggests, Pan-Slavism aimed at some form of union of all Slavic peoples under Russian aegis, so as to form a dominant power. To this end the Russian government, according to Pan-Slav doctrine, should defend the rights of the Slavic peoples of the Hapsburg Monarchy against the pressures exerted by the Germans, and should give support, even to the

<hr/>

[66] Alexandre Koyré: *La philosophie et le problème national en Russie* (Paris, 1929), chap. v; Karl Stählin: "Die Entstehung des Panslawismus" (*Germanoslavica*, IV, 1936, 1–25); Waclaw Lednicki: "Panslavism" (in Feliks Gross, ed.; *European Ideologies*, New York, 1948, 805–912); Hans Kohn: *Panslavism* (Notre Dame, 1953), 113 ff.; Nicholas V. Riasanowsky: *Nicholas I and Official Nationality in Russia* (Berkeley, 1959), 52 ff.

[67] A. Gratieux: *A. S. Khomiakov et le mouvement slavophile* (Paris, 1929); Peter K. Christoff: *An Introduction to Nineteenth Century Slavophilism: A. S. Xomjakov* (The Hague, 1961); Edward C. Thaden: *Conservative Nationalism in Nineteenth Century Russia* (Seattle, 1964), Part I; Wolfgango Giusti: *Il Panslavismo* (Milan, 1941), chaps. iii–v; and the literature cited in preceding footnotes.

extent of military aid, to the Slavic peoples of the Balkans struggling to throw off the Turkish yoke. In the period prior to 1848 this doctrine was expounded chiefly by Czech and Slovak intellectuals, such as Šafařik and Kollár, and to lesser extent by Yugoslav leaders such as Gaj. They found some sympathy and support among Russian nationalists and managed to create, throughout the West, the specter of Pan-Slavism, which was equated with Russian thirst for conquest. But actually it played as yet but an insignificant role and was much less influential than Slavophilism, which was a strictly cultural movement.

8. THE HAPSBURG EMPIRE: A MULTINATIONAL STATE

In the rich Danube basin more different nationalities lived together under Hapsburg rule than could be found anywhere else in Europe. The Germans, though comprising hardly more than a quarter of the population, were the dominant element. In terms of nationalism they had always been loyal to the dynasty, but by the midcentury were being torn between traditional attachment to the polyglot empire and the desire to participate in a new German national state. Next in importance to the Germans were the Magyars, who, though a minority even in the Kingdom of Hungary, were nevertheless the ruling element in the eastern half of the empire. In addition there were various segments of the great Slav family—Poles, Ruthenians, Czechs, Slovaks, Slovenes, Croats, Serbs—as well as the Italians of Lombardy and Venetia and the Rumanians of Transylvania. It is perhaps not too daring a generalization to say that most of these peoples had long been nationally conscious, since for centuries their upper classes (nobility and gentry) had been resisting the efforts of the imperial government to weld the diverse lands into a centralized state. Defense of traditional local rights and institutions was one of the roots of modern nationalism, the other important one being the cultural revival which was inspired by German thought and greatly reinforced by the Romantic movement. The final impetus was then given by the tribulations of French rule and the popular risings which encompassed the downfall of Napoleon.[68]

[68] A standard account is that of Robert A. Kann: *The Multinational Empire* (2 vols., New York, 1950), but see also Hugo Hantsch: *Die Nationalitätenfrage im alten Oesterreich* (Vienna, 1953); Emil Franzel: *Der Donauraum im Zeitalter des Nationalitätenprinzips* (Berne, 1958); and the two articles by Peter F. Sugar: "The Nature of the Non-Germanic Societies under Habsburg Rule" (*Slavic Review*, XXII, 1963, 1–30) and "The Rise of Nationalism" (*Austrian History Yearbook*, III, Part I, 1967, 91–120).

In Hungary the struggle of the Magyar upper classes against encroachment by Vienna on the hoary rights of the Kingdom of St. Stephen had been going on ever since the reconquest of the country from the Turks. But the cultural revival hardly dated further back than the early nineteenth century, when the German-speaking upper classes absorbed the German doctrines of nationalism and undertook the purification of the Magyar language, which hitherto had been scorned as a "gypsy jargon." By 1825, when Count Stephen Széchenyi embarked upon his program of reform and modernization, the nationalist movement in literature was already well under way. Francis Kazinczy had systematized the language and the great Romantic poet Michael Vörösmarty was about to publish his great national epic, *Zalan's Flight*. During the ensuing decades a veritable galaxy of poets and novelists produced epics, historical dramas and ballads, all in the spirit of Romantic nationalism.[69]

Széchenyi, whose interest was in domestic reform, was anxious to avoid conflict with the Vienna government and was opposed to efforts being made to force the Magyar language on the other nationalities living under the Hungarian crown. Like Herder, he believed that each nationality had a contribution to make and argued that the dominant Magyar nationality should set a moral example to the others. But this was not the view of Louis Kossuth and the more uncompromising nationalists who began to overshadow Széchenyi and his friends in the 1840's. This gentry faction was much troubled by the threat of Russian power and was haunted by Herder's prediction that the Magyars might eventually disappear, overwhelmed and absorbed by the non-Magyar nationalities among whom they lived. In an address to the Hungarian Academy in 1842, Széchenyi complained bitterly that his fellow countrymen were stricken with blindness and had lost all sense of reason and justice when questions of the Magyar language and nationality were raised. But nothing he could do would stem the tide. The more rabid the Magyar nationalists became, the more determined were they to impose their language on other nationalities such as the Slovaks and

[69] Julius Farkas: *Die Entwicklung der ungarischen Literatur* (Berlin, 1934), 137 ff., and *Die ungarische Romantik* (Berlin, 1931); I. Kont: *Geschichte der ungarischen Literatur* (Leipzig, 1906), still valuable. Among recent studies, see G. F. Cushing: "The Birth of National Literature in Hungary" (*Slavonic and East European Review*, XXXVIII, 1960, 459–475); D. Mervyn Jones: *Five Hungarian Writers* (Oxford, 1966), 103 ff.

the Croats. Language, it was thought, was the essential bond holding the various peoples of the kingdom together. In 1844 Magyar was made the official language of the kingdom. But the revolutions of 1848 were to show that the intolerance of the Magyars ruling class, far from strengthening its position, only exposed it to the most disastrous internal conflicts.[70]

Magyar nationalists were understandably troubled by the realization that their people were in a minority in the country and that in the north and the south there were solid blocks of Slavs, the Slovaks and the Slovenes, Croats and Serbs, among whom a national renascence, along cultural lines, was already far advanced by 1830.[71] The Czechs of Bohemia were pathfinders in this respect. Living more or less intermingled with a large German minority and economically far more developed than other peoples of the Austrian Empire, the Czechs had for long been in the main stream of western thought. A substantial middle class, consisting of intellectuals and professional people, provided a broad base for nationalism, which therefore far transcended the traditional efforts of the aristocracy to protect its privileges from the encroachments of the Vienna government. Most Czech nationalist leaders were educated at German universities and continued to write in German, drawing heavily on German thinking. Herder had been full of praise for the virtues of the Slavs, whom he hailed as the representatives of a future higher humanity. He pictured them as essentially one nation, peaceful and democratic by nature but brutally subjugated by the warlike Germans. Thereby he provided his Czech disciples with some of their principal arguments.[72]

---

[70] Francis S. Wagner: "Széchenyi and the Nationality Problem in the Hapsburg Empire" (*Journal of Central European Affairs*, XX, 1960, 287–313); George Bárányi: "The Awakening of Magyar Nationalism before 1848" (*Austrian History Yearbook*, II, 1966, 19–54). For an excellent contemporary analysis and criticism, see the letter of the British agent, J. A. Blackwell, to Lord Palmerston, August 21, 1846, printed in "Reports on the Hungarian Parliament of 1843–1844" (*South Eastern Affairs*, I–IV, 1931–1934, Vol. I, 220 ff.); also Hippolyte Desprez: "La Hongrie et le mouvement magyare" (*Revue des deux mondes*, 1847, 1068–1089).

[71] On the earlier phase of this renascence, see the preceding volume in this series, Artz: *Reaction and Revolution*, 241 ff.

[72] Konrad Bittner: *Herders Geschichtsphilosophie und die Slawen* (Reichenberg, 1929), 97 ff.; Hermann Oncken: "Deutsche geistige Einflüsse in der europäischen Nationalitätenbewegung des 19 Jahrhunderts" (in his *Nation und Geschichte*, Berlin, 1935, 305–326); Ernst Birke: "Einflüsse der deutschen Geistesbewegung von Herder bis Hegel auf den Osten" (*Deutsche Ostforschung*, II, 1943, 289–334).

The great period of the Czech cultural renascence fell between the years 1825 and 1848, when scholars such as Josef Jungmann, Paul Šafařik, and Francis Palacký published a great German-Czech dictionary, a history of the Slavic language and literature, and various studies of Slavic antiquities and ethnology. All these writers stressed the common origin and common characteristics of the Slavic peoples and dilated on the past glories and present strength of the Slavs taken as a whole. Particularly influential was the poet-preacher Jan Kollár, the second edition of whose sonnet cycle *Slava's Daughter* appeared in 1832. In 622 sonnets the author rhapsodized about the Slavs and pleaded with them to put aside their quarrels and work together toward mutual understanding: only through unity could they fulfill their high historical mission of leadership in Europe in the cause of peace. For Kollár foresaw for them a wonderful future. A century hence "flood-like, Slavic life will inundate all, expanding its influence everywhere."

Kollár's poetic imagination knew no bounds. Though he recognized that there were really four Slavic nations—the Russians, the Poles, the Czechs and the Southern Slavs—he could not get away from the thought of what they would amount to if only they pulled together. In his famous treatise on the reciprocity of the Slavic languages (1836), he derived the name *Slav* from the word *Slovo,* meaning "word," and persuaded himself that the Slavs were specially chosen to interpret the Word of God, to achieve a more perfect form of Christianity and to establish true humanity among nations. There were, he calculated, seventy to eighty millions of Slavs in Europe, far more than Germans or Latin peoples. Furthermore, in the time of Moses they had occupied most of Europe, and their language was clearly the most ancient of European tongues. Kollár had no idea of aggression. On the contrary, his nationalism was strictly literary and cultural. But to escape from smallness he found it necessary to inflate the Slavic idea to the utmost.[73]

[73] Albert Prazák: "The Slovak Sources of Kollár's Pan-Slavism" (*Slavonic Review,* VI, 1928, 579–592), and the anonymous article "Jan Kollár and Literary Pan-Slavism" (*ibid.,* VI, 1927, 336–343). See further, Alfred Fischel: *Der Panslawismus bis zum Weltkrieg* (Berlin, 1919), 72 ff.; Hans Kohn: *Panslavism* (Notre Dame, 1953), 14 ff.; and on the Czech national revival, Joseph Chada: *The Czech National Revival* (Chicago, 1934); Hans Raupach: *Der tschechische Frühnationalismus* (Halle, 1939); Otakar Odložilik: "The Czechs on the Eve of the 1848 Revolution" (*Harvard Slavic Studies,* I, 1953, 179–218); Karel Trejci: "La lutte pour la libération nationale des Tchèques et des

Czech nationalism was given a political turn by Francis Palacký, the sober, scholarly secretary of the National Academy. In his great *History of the Czech People,* of which the first three volumes appeared between 1836 and 1848, Palacký, while still writing in German, turned the teachings of his German masters against themselves. The Czech people appear as a small, valiant nation fighting heroically in the cause of freedom and justice. The Hussite Wars are pictured as a great clash between the ideas of the past and those of a new age, between the principle of authority and the claims of individual understanding. Thus Czech nationalism was given a firm historical substructure and a sense of mission. Palacký, it has been said, "restored to the nation its buried past and sounded a veritable clarion call for the future."[74]

Palacký provided the Bohemian aristocracy with strong arguments for the defense of the historic rights of the Bohemian-Moravian crown, and at the same time induced the intellectual elite to give up the romantic ideas of Pan-Slavism in favor of a more realistic if narrower Czech nationalism. It was he, too, who launched on his journalistic career the youthful Charles Havlícek, who became editor of the *Prague Gazette* in 1846. In a series of programmatic articles Havlícek undertook to dispel the nebulous idealism of the poets and substitute an entirely realistic policy. Pan-Slavism, he contended, was simply unworkable, the more so as the various Slavic nations differed widely in their histories and institutions. The practical thing was to work for complete equality with the Germans within the Hapsburg Monarchy and to strive for the reorganization of the empire on a federal basis, in which the various national groups should have complete autonomy. A great admirer of Daniel O'Connell, Havlícek was instrumental in founding (1847) the Czech Repeal Club, devoted, like O'Connell's movement, to constitutional reform by peaceful, legal pressure tactics. Havlícek's lively writing proved a great stimulus to political nationalism. Countless pamphlets, plays and stories poured from the presses,

---

Slovaques" (*Journal of World History,* V, 1960, 700–733); S. H. Thomson: "The Czechs as Integrating and Disintegrating Factors in the Habsburg Empire" (*Austrian History Yearbook,* III, Part II, 1967, 203–222).

[74] R. W. Seton-Watson: *A History of the Czechs and Slovaks* (London, 1943), 171 ff.; Hans Kohn: "The Historical Roots of Czech Democracy" (in Robert J. Kerner, ed.: *Czechoslovakia,* Berkeley, 1945, 91–105); Richard G. Plaschka: *Von Palacký bis Pékar* (Graz, 1955), chap. i.

and projects for a national theater were made the excuse for national balls and civic clubs throughout the country. But 1848 Bohemia was in ferment, much like Hungary under the influence of Kossuth.[75]

By the 1840's the Czech national movement had become clouded by the growing insistence of the related Slovaks on a nationalism of their own. The Slovaks were a peasant people under Hungarian rule whose upper classes had become completely Magyarized. The small intellectual class, mostly clerics and teachers, recognized their kinship with the Czechs and indeed generally used the Czech language for literary purposes when they did not employ German. It so happened that a number of the leaders of the Czech renascence, notably Kollár and Šafařik, were Slovaks by birth. From them the Slovaks received the ideas of cultural Pan-Slavism and national mission. They soon convinced themselves that the Slovakian Mountains (the Tatra) were the cradle of the Slavic peoples and that therefore the Slovaks were the primal, the purest Slavs, entitled to leadership in the age to come.[76]

It was the Pan-Slavic aspect of Czech and Slovak nationalism that aroused the suspicions of the Hungarian as of the Austrian government, which watched Kollár's activities and writings carefully.[77] Hence the efforts of the Hungarians to impose the Magyar language on the Slav minorities, which in turn met with the resistance of the Slovaks. Leadership was provided by Louis Stúr, a man of dynamic personality and vibrant enthusiasm, perhaps not an original thinker,

---

[75] Ernest Denis: La Bohême depuis la Montagne Blanche (2 ed., Paris, 1930), 197 ff.; Berthold Bretholz: Geschichte Böhmens und Mährens (Reichenberg, 1924), IV, 47 ff.; Hanns Schlitter: Aus Oesterreichs Vormärz, II: Böhmen (Vienna, 1920), 72 ff.; Kann: Multinational Empire, I, 165 ff.; Stanley B. Kimball: Czech Nationalism: a Study of the National Theater Movement (Urbana, 1964), chap. i; S. E. Mann: "Karel Havlícek: A Slav Pragmatist" (Slavonic and East European Review, XXXIX, 1961, 413–422).

[76] Ernest Denis: Les Slovaques (Paris, 1917), 156 ff.; Theodor J. G. Locher: Die nationale Differenzierung und Integrierung der Slovaken und Tschechen in ihrem geschichtlichen Verlauf bis 1848 (Haarlem, 1931), 112 ff.; 146 ff.; Jan Hanak: "Slovaks and Czechs in the Early Nineteenth Century" (Slavonic Review, X, 1929, 588–601); C. Krofta: "Tchèques et Slovaques jusqa'à leur union politique" (Le monde slave, n.s., X., 1933, 1–38); Heinz Brauner: "Die geschichtlichen Kräfte beim Aufbau der Slowakei" (Jahrbuch des Osteuropa-Instituts, 1940, 45–65); Julius Mésáros: "Magyaren und Slowaken: zur Frage des Panslawismus in der Vormärzzeit" (Jahrbücher für Geschichte Osteuropas, n.s., XV, 1967, 393–414).

[77] J. F. N. Bradley: "Czech Pan-Slavism before the First World War" (Slavonic and East European Review, XL, 1961, 184–205).

but a brilliant speaker and writer. Fully persuaded of the mission of the Slovaks to unite the Slavs and perform a great civilizing role, he undertook to supplant Czech as the literary language and substitute a Slovakian dialect as the best means of uniting all Slovaks in opposition to the introduction of the Magyar language. Though forced out of his teaching position by the Hungarian government, Stúr was granted permission by the Vienna authorities to found a *Slovakian National Gazette,* with a literary supplement, the *Tatra Eagle.* He and his associates, the Lutheran pastors Michael Hodža and Josef Húrban, used these vehicles to introduce the new literary language, for which Stúr provided the orthography and grammar.[78]

Stúr and his friends outraged the Czech leaders, who argued that the Czech literary language had always been recognized in Slovakia and that that province clearly belonged, with Bohemia, Moravia and Silesia, to the so-called West Slav people. Havlícek denounced the Slovak nationalists as hack writers posing as national leaders. But in the stress of the revolutionary year 1848 a reconciliation was effected and the ranks of Czechs and Slovaks were closed. As a matter of fact, Stúr was to emerge, in the last years of his short life, as one of the chief theorists of political Pan-Slavism under Russian aegis.[79]

Concurrent with the national revival of the Czechs and the Slovaks was that of the South Slavs or Yugoslavs, who formed a belt across the southern part of the Hapsburg Empire and extended eastward as far as Bulgaria and the Black Sea. But these South Slavs differed so greatly in their history, in their religion and in their cultural orientation that a unified national movement was all but impossible of realization. Farthest to the west the Slovenes, while inhabiting several Hapsburg lands, were in a minority everywhere but in Carniola and Gorizia. These lands had always been included in the Germanic Empire and had always been oriented toward the West. In religion they were Roman Catholic. The upper classes were almost entirely German and made use of Latin and German for cultural purposes. For a few years

---

[78] Hélène Tourtzer: *Louis Stúr et l'idée de l'indépendance slovaque* (Paris, 1913), 144, 233 ff.; Mésáros: "Magyaren und Slowaken"; Vaclav L. Benés: "The Slovaks in the Habsburg Empire" (*Austrian History Yearbook,* III, Part 2, 1967, 335–364).

[79] Michael B. Petrovich: "Ludevít Stúr and Russian Panslavism" (*Journal of Central European Affairs,* XII, 1952, 1–19); Vladimir Matula: "Ludovít Stur und Russland" (*Jahrbücher für Geschichte Osteuropas,* n.s., XV, 1967, 29–58).

(1809–1813) Napoleon had united most of the Slovene territories with other Slav lands to form the Illyrian Provinces, with their capital at Ljubljana in Carinthia. The French administration had encouraged use of the Slovene language in the lower schools and had thereby stimulated notions of national renascence. At the same time Germanized Slovene scholars such as Jernez Kopitar, the great philologist, had supported efforts to establish a single alphabet and orthography for all the South Slavs. But the road was long and hard. By 1848 the editor Janez Bleiweiss and the poet Francis Prešeren had worked out a Slovene literary language based on the Carniolan dialect and the way was clear for formulation of a political program for union of all Slovenian territories in an autonomous Slovenia, within the framework of a federal Austrian Empire. But of all the South Slavs, the Slovenes had been least touched by nationalist aspirations.[80]

The Serbs, on the other wing, had established a self-governing principality, but this included far less than half the Serb population. There were fully as many Serbs living in southern Hungary and almost as many in the still Turkish provinces of Bosnia and Herzegovina, as well as in Montenegro. The Serbs had always been connected culturally with the Byzantine world. They were Greek Orthodox in religion and used the Kyrillic rather than the Latin alphabet. Religion if nothing else had kept alive a profound suspicion between the Serbs and their near relatives, the Croats, who inhabited the regions to the west. By 1830 the Serbs had not only established their own state but had arrived at a literary language, the work largely of the philologist Vuk Karadžíc, who had been educated in Germany and had been encouraged and helped by Jakob Grimm. Karadžíc purged the Serbian language, which had degenerated into a barbarous mixture of Old Church Slavic, Russian and various Serbian dialects. Through his grammar and phonetic system he raised the dialect of southern Herzegovina, which Mickiewicz once described as the "most harmonious

[80] Fran Zwitter: "L'Illyrisme et sentiment yougoslave" (*Le monde slave*, n.s., X, 1933, 38–71, 161–185, 358–375), and "The Slovenes and the Habsburg Monarchy" (*Austrian History Yearbook*, III, Part II, 1968, 159–202); Robert Auty: "The Formation of the Slovene Literary Language against the Background of the Slavonic National Revival" (*Slavonic and East European Review*, XLI, 1963, 391–402); Anton Slodnjak: *Geschichte der slowenischen Literatur* (Berlin, 1958).

and most musical of all the Slavic dialects," to the status of a literary language. By 1848 his reforms had been generally accepted.[81]

Furthermore, in these years Serbian national pride was much stimulated by Sima Milutinovich's history of the insurrection of 1813–1815 and his patriotic drama *The Tragedy of Kossovo* (1837). It was in this period, too, that Peter II, the prince-bishop of Montenegro, began to publish his romantic poems on the struggles of his people against the Turks, to be followed in 1847 by his masterpiece *The Wreath of the Mountain,* which, in more than three thousand verses, recounted episodes of Montenegrin life and heroism.[82] Politically the Serbs began to listen to the alluring proposals of Polish agents who were intent on organizing Balkan opposition to Russia. Czartoryski encouraged the Serbs to expand their rule so as to include all South Slavs and to ally themselves with the Hungarians and Poles to form a bulwark. Ilija Garashanin, the leading Serb statesman of the period, worked out a secret program in 1844 envisaging just such a Greater Serbia.[83]

Neither the Serbian nor the Slovenian national revival could be compared with that of the Czechs and the Slovaks. But among the Croats there developed a more sophisticated and effective movement, the Illyrian. In 1830 Louis Gaj, educated at German universities and inspired by the teachings of Kollár and other Czech and Polish nationalists, proposed language reforms along the lines marked out by Karadžíc. A man of great personal magnetism as well as literary and oratorical talent, Gaj quickly aroused enthusiasm among younger members of the gentry, whose elders had become completely Magyarized. In 1834 he founded an *Illyrian Gazette* with a literary supplement, *Danica,* in which he gradually introduced his language

[81] V. Corović: "Vuk Karadjíc" (*Slavonic Review,* XVI, 1938, 667–677); George R. Noyes: "The Serbo-Croatian Language" (in Robert J. Kerner, ed.: *Yugoslavia,* Berkeley, 1949, 279–301); Ivan Popović: *Geschichte der serbokroatischen Sprache* (Wiesbaden, 1960); Wayne S. Vucinich: "The Serbs in Austria-Hungary" (*Austrian History Yearbook,* III, Part II, 1968, 3–47); Dimitrije Djordjević: "The Serbs as Integrating and Disintegrating Factor" (*ibid.,* 48–82).

[82] Louis Leger: *Serbes, Croates et Bulgares* (Paris, 1913), 122 ff.; Milos Savković: *La littérature yougoslave moderne* (Belgrade, 1936), 45 ff.; Noyes: "Serbo-Croatian Language."

[83] Marcel Handelsman: *Czartoryski, Nikolas I et la question du Proche-Orient* (Paris, 1934), 32 ff.; Paul N. Hehn: "Prince Adam Czartoryski and the South Slavs" (*Polish Review,* VIII, 1963, 76–86); G. Y. Devas: "Les origines de l'unité yougoslave" (*Le monde slave,* II, 1918, 532–549); Albert Mousset: *Le Serbie et son église* (Paris, 1938), 190 ff.; L. S. Stavrianos: *Balkan Federation* (Northampton, 1942), 51 ff., 63 ff.

reforms, rejecting the local dialect of the capital, Zagreb, and adopting that most widely used by the Croats and Serbs. Basically it was the same dialect already chosen by Karadžíc, though Gaj retained the Roman alphabet. Thus was born the Serbo-Croatian literary language, which is much the same whether written in the Roman or Kyrillic script.[84]

Politically the Illyrian movement envisaged the ultimate union of all South Slavs ("from Villach to Varna"), but it held little appeal either for the Slovenes or the Serbs. It remained throughout essentially a Croat movement which rallied a number of patriotic poets and writers and enabled the Croats to resist the efforts of the Hungarian government to impose the Magyar language on the Croat provinces.[85] According to the Magyars, Croatia and Slavonia were annexed territories (*partes adnexae*) of the crown of St. Stephen, while the Croats on their side claimed to be freely allied on the basis of well-defined historical agreements (*pacta conventa*). The Croatian Diet (*sabor*) offered no resistance to Hungarian policy until Gaj and his friends began to advance the Illyrian program. In 1832 one of the younger nobles, Count Janko Draskovíc, drew up instructions to the Croat delegates departing for the meeting of the Hungarian Diet at Pressburg. This was one of the first writings in the new language and perhaps the earliest political pamphlet. Draskovíc urged the delegates to use their own language in the debates and to work for the eventual union of Croatia, Slavonia and Dalmatia in a Greater Illyria. It was his hope that the Hapsburg emperor would aid in establishing an independent South Slav state, with close ties to Hungary. Gaj went even further. In 1840 he paid a visit to Russia and secured financial aid from sympathetic groups, though the czar refused to have anything to do with "revolutionary" activities.[86]

[84] Franco Fančev: "Les origines autochtones du mouvement illyrien-croate" (*Le monde slave*, n.s., XII, 1935, 384–393); Stjepan Tropsch: "Les influences allemandes sur les Illyriens et leurs précurseurs" (*ibid.*, 439–452); A. Wenzelides: "Ludevít Gaj, réformateur de la littérature croate" (*Les Balkans*, VII, 1935, 328–338); Popović: *Geschichte der serbokroatischen Sprache.*

[85] On the literary side, see Gerhard Gesemann: *Die serbo-croatische Literatur* (Potsdam, 1930), 33 ff.; Antun Barać: "Les études critiques sur la littérature de l'Illyrisme" (*Le monde slave*, n.s., XII, 1935, 353–373).

[86] Philip E. Mosely: "A Pan-Slavist Memorandum of Liudevít Gaj" (*American Historical Review*, XL, 1935, 704–715); Bogdan Krizman: "The Croatians in the Habsburg

The Vienna government at first encouraged the Illyrian movement, if only to vex the Hungarians. In fact the emperor in 1841 sent Gaj a diamond ring by way of recognition. But the pressure exercised by the pro-Magyar aristocracy led the Vienna authorities in 1843 to prohibit the use of the term "Illyrian." In 1844 the Hungarian government decreed that after six years Magyar should be the official language of Croatia. Thenceforth there was open war between the factions. In 1845 the nationalists secured control of the diet and in 1847 they proclaimed Serbo-Croatian the official language of the Croat administration. By 1848 the conflict of Magyars and Croats had reached the stage of a thinly veiled civil war, which was soon to erupt in open hostility.

To the east of Hungary, in the historic land of Transylvania, lived yet another emerging nationality, the Rumanian. They were equal in number to the South Slavs of the empire (about three million), but were mostly illiterate peasants without privilege or recognition, dominated by a landowning aristocracy that was chiefly Magyar or German. Transylvania was loosely connected with the Hungarian crown and, like Hungary, underwent a reform period influenced by the work of Széchenyi, but this had nothing to do with the development of Rumanian national sentiment, which affected both the Rumanians of Transylvania and the Rumanians of the two Danubian Principalities. During the preceding generation Rumanian scholars had discovered, to their own satisfaction, that their people were the direct descendants of the Roman legionaries and that their language was closely related to Latin. On this basis rested the cult of Latinity stressing the kinship of the seven or eight million Rumanians, wherever their home.[87]

The cultural revival of the Rumanians centered, as was natural, in the Principalities, which were largely self-governing. John Eliade-Radulescu in Wallachia and George Asachi in Moldavia promoted the use of the Latin script and reformed the orthography. They wrote textbooks, made translations and supported national theaters. Michael

Monarchy" (*Austrian History Yearbook*, III, Part II, 1968, 116–158). See also Emile Haumant: *La formation de la Yougoslavie* (Paris, 1930), 321 ff.; Fischel: *Der Panslawismus*, 146 ff.

[87] R. W. Seton-Watson: *A History of the Roumanians* (Cambridge, 1934); Zoltan Toth: "Die siebenburger Rumänen im 19 Jahrhundert" (in L. Galdi and L. Makkai: *Geschichte der Rumänen*, Budapest, 1942, 316–355); Ladislas Makkai: *Histoire de Transylvanie* (Paris, 1946), 303 ff.; Stephen Fischer-Galati: "The Rumanians and the Habsburg Monarchy" (*Austrian History Yearbook*, III, Part II, 1967, 430–459).

Kogalniceanu began the collection of historical sources while various poets, novelists and dramatists produced works on patriotic subjects.[88]

Among the Rumanians, as among other awakening nationalities, the national theme was bound up closely with agitation for liberal reform and constitutional government. In Transylvania the main drive was for recognition of the Rumanians as a "community" on a par with Magyars, Germans and Szeklers. In the Principalities the political opposition was directed against Russian tutelage and the absolutist policies of the princes. But among the enlightened, progressive younger members of the nobility, the sentiment of Latinity was strong. The nationalists made no secret of their desire to see the two Principalities united and independent of Russian "protection." Beyond that they dreamed also of the union of all Rumanians in one national state. In 1839 one of the liberal leaders, John Campineanu, strongly influenced by the British consul and by Czartoryski's emissaries, paid a visit to Paris and London in the hope of enlisting diplomatic aid for the national program. But his mission ended in disappointment. It could not have been worse timed, for the great Near Eastern crisis of 1839–1841 was just beginning. In Paris Thiers and in London Palmerston received him cordially, but left him no hope that the western powers would take a stand against Russian treaty rights in the Principalities. On his return home Campineanu was imprisoned for his pains.[89]

In the years just prior to 1848 the nationalist movement centered in the Society of Rumanian Students in Paris, to which reference has been made in Chapter V. This group, which included most of the young opposition leaders, was able to enlist the patronage of the poet Lamartine and the sympathetic interest of Mickiewicz and Michelet, from whose book *The People* (1846) they translated and distributed the chapter dealing with nationality. They were in close touch with Prince Czartoryski and with the publicist Henri Desprez, who had traveled through the Rumanian lands in 1845–1846 and presently became a

---

[88] Nicolas Iorga: "La société roumaine du XIXe siècle dans le théatre roumain" (*Revue historique du sud-est européen,* III, 1926, 98–112, 189–231); Petre V. Hanes: *Histoire de la littérature roumaine* (Paris, 1934), 78 ff.

[89] Radu R. N. Florescu: *The Struggle Against Russia in the Rumanian Principalities, 1821–1854 (Acta Historica,* II, 1962), chap. vii, and "R. G. Colquhoun, Ion Campineau and the pro-Western Opposition in Wallachia, 1834–1840" (*Slavonic and East European Review,* XLI, 1963, 403–419); Nicolas Iorga: *Histoire des relations entre la France et les Roumains* (Paris, 1918), chap. ix.

leading proponent of the notions of Rumanian unity and of a Slav-Hungarian-Rumanian bloc to support the Poles against Russia in the great conflict which was thought imminent. By 1848 the Rumanian democrats and nationalists were in ferment and eager for action, though the form and extent of such action were still uncertain.[90]

90 Mathieu Fotino: *L'influence française sur les grands orateurs politiques roumains* (Bucharest, 1928), 49 ff.; John C. Campbell: "The Influence of Western Political Thought in the Rumanian Principalities, 1821-1848" (*Journal of Central European Affairs*, IV, 1944, 262-273); Hélène Vacaresco: "La mystique nationale roumaine aux environs de 1848" (*Revue d'histoire diplomatique*, XLII, 1929, 8-19); and especially Vasile Maçiu: "Un centre révolutionnaire roumain dans les années 1845-1848: la Société des Étudiants Roumains à Paris" (*Nouvelles études d'histoire*, 1965, 243-270); Cornelia Bodea: "Le problème de l'unité roumaine, 1845-1848" (*Revue roumaine d'histoire*, IV, 1965, 497-521).

Chapter Nine

HOLY ALLIANCE AND ENTENTE CORDIALE

I. THE BELGIAN SETTLEMENT

By 1832 the acute danger of war, which dated from the July Revolution in France and the insurrection of the Belgians, had fairly subsided. The eastern powers, diverted by the Polish Revolution and by serious upheavals in Germany and Italy, had reluctantly followed the example of the British in recognizing the new regime of Louis Philippe and accepting the establishment of Belgium as an independent state, despite the revolutionary character of these settlements. But what had emerged was a new alignment of the great powers along ideological lines. On the one hand were Britain and France, with Belgium dependent, and on the other Austria, Prussia and Russia, the three eastern powers commonly designated the Holy Alliance. "It is vain," wrote the *Edinburgh Review* in April, 1832, "to deny that two great antagonist principles now divide Europe: freedom and despotism. They are to be found contending from Lisbon to St. Petersburgh, and we meet them in every political question."[1]

It was the Belgian question that had most sorely tried the patience of the powers in the critical years 1830–1832. In as much as the breakaway of the Belgian provinces from the Netherlands was a breach of the 1815 settlement, the powers were technically obligated to come to the assistance of the king of the Netherlands when he appealed to them. But such intervention would almost certainly have entailed war with France, where public opinion was rabid on the "natural" frontiers and hopeful of the early reunion of the Belgian provinces with France. There was nothing for it but to accept what Metternich called the "mournful reality," and strive for the least objectionable settlement.[2]

---

[1] Quoted in Élie Halévy: *Histoire du peuple anglais au XIXe siècle* (Paris, 1923), III, 67 n.

[2] On the general crisis of 1830–1832, see Eugène, Vicomte de Guichen: *La révolution de 1830 et l'Europe* (Paris, 1916), 153 ff.; Gustav Huber: *Kriegsgefahr über Europa, 1830–1832* (Berlin, 1936), 34. On French aspirations, Philippe Sagnac: "La crise de l'Occident et la question du Rhin, 1832–1840" (*Revue des études napoléoniennes*, XVI,

In these circumstances great credit accrued to Lord Palmerston, the newly appointed British foreign secretary, who, through the clarity of his policy and the adroitness of his diplomacy, guided the London Conference of ambassadors through the many shoals of the Belgian problem. The British had played a leading role in 1815 in uniting the Dutch and Belgian provinces so as to establish a strong bulwark against further French aggression. But by 1830 they had convinced themselves that this arrangement was not workable. They were therefore prepared to recognize Belgium's independence. They were as determined, however, as they had ever been to prevent any part of The Netherlands falling under French control. Since Louis Philippe realized that any attempt in that direction would unite all Europe against him, he undertook to run counter to French sentiment and aspiration and accept the British policy. There remained for Palmerston the truly Herculean task of mediating not only between the king of The Netherlands and his former subjects, but also between the Belgians and the eastern powers, all of which were sympathetic to the Dutch king and most reluctant to make any concessions to Belgian or French claims.

There would be no point in rehearsing here the many complications of the Belgian issue, the problem of selecting a king, the question of the new state's frontiers, and so on.[3] Eventually Prince Leopold of Saxe-Coburg, the widowed husband of Princess Charlotte of Britain and the uncle of the future Queen Victoria, was chosen for the throne. The Dutch forces which had reinvaded the country were driven out by combined French and British action. The powers then agreed to the Twenty-Four Articles (October 14, 1831), by which King William was awarded a favorable territorial settlement: he was to have the larger, eastern part of the province of Limburg, with the fortress of Maastricht, and also the eastern, German-speaking part of the Duchy of Luxembourg, which was included in the Germanic Confederation. To

---

1919, 284–300). On pro-French sentiment in Belgium, the excellent analysis of Jean Stengers: "Sentiment national, sentiment orangist et sentiment français à l'aube de notre indépendance" (*Revue belge de philologie et d'histoire*, XXVIII, 1950, 993–1029; XXIX, 1951, 61–92).

[3] See the previous volume in this series, Frederick B. Artz: *Reaction and Revolution*, 270 ff., and on Palmerston's role Herbert C. F. Bell: *Lord Palmerston* (New York, 1936), I, chap. vi; Charles K. Webster: *The Foreign Policy of Palmerston, 1830–1841* (London, 1951), I, chap. ii; Donald Southgate: *"The Most British Minister . . ."*: *The Policies and Politics of Palmerston* (New York, 1966), 30 ff.

everyone's surprise the obstinate king rejected these terms, which the Belgians had accepted only with heavy hearts. The Dutch still held the citadel of Antwerp and so were able to close the Scheldt River to Belgian traffic, thus crippling the economic life of the country. To break the deadlock the British blockaded the Dutch coast and within a month intercepted merchandise valued at a million pounds sterling. At the same time a French army crossed Belgium and forced the capitulation of Antwerp after heavy bombardment. Though in order to lift the disastrous blockade King William promised in May, 1833, not again to attack Belgium, he still refused to sign the Twenty-Four Articles. The Belgians therefore remained in possession of the disputed territories. For years the entire issue hung fire until finally, in March, 1838, King William, under pressure from his Parliament, announced his readiness to accept the terms agreed to by the powers. But by this time the Belgians were so opposed to the cession of any territory that it was only under heavy pressure that the Brussels Parliament was induced to yield. On April 19, 1839, the powers were at last able to sign the Treaty of London, which recognized not only the independence of the Belgian state but its perpetual neutrality under guarantee of the signatory powers. However, to the eastern powers the settlement was still extremely distasteful. They had accepted the Twenty-Four Articles only because the alternative seemed to be war. In the last analysis the Belgian question, born of revolution, had fallen almost completely into the hands of the British and French, and so had contributed substantially to the division of Europe into the western and eastern blocs.[4]

2. THE FIRST EGYPTIAN CRISIS

Near Eastern crises were a chronic affliction of European diplomacy throughout the nineteenth century. They stemmed from the growing debility of the Ottoman Empire and the interest of most of the great powers in either hastening or delaying its dissolution. Sultan Mahmud II (1808–1839) made valiant but unsystematic efforts to reform and

---

[4] The standard study of the international aspects of the Belgian problem is still F. de Lannoy's *Histoire diplomatique de l'indépendance belge* (Brussels, 1930), of which the same author's shorter account (Brussels, 1948) is a useful summary. Valuable monographic studies are Wolfgang von Franqué: *Luxemburg, die belgische Revolution und die Mächte* (Bonn, 1933); Stanley T. Bindoff: *The Scheldt Question to 1839* (London, 1945); C. Smit: *De Conferentie van London: het Vredesverdrag van 19 April, 1839* (Leiden, 1949).

modernize his empire, but was interrupted by the Greek insurrection of the 1820's, which, if only for geographical reasons, was difficult to suppress. He had therefore resorted to the aid of his powerful vassal, Mehemet Ali of Egypt, who, with the support of European officers and advisers, had been successful in building up an efficient army and navy. However, the intervention of the Egyptian forces, while it promised an early end of the revolution, provoked the interference of the European powers and this in turn led to in the Russian-Turkish War of 1828–1829. By the Treaty of Adrianople, which ended the conflict, the sultan was obliged to recognize the independence of Greece and accept a Russian protectorate over the now self-governing Danubian Principalities and Serbia.[5]

Hardly less serious than these losses were the pretensions of Mehemet Ali,[6] who by 1831 had reconstructed his army and navy and now began to press for cession of the territories promised him in return for his aid. These were the island of Candia (Crete) as well as the governorship of the Morea (Peloponnesus). Since the powers had obliged the Egyptians as well as the Turks to evacuate the Morea, Mehemet Ali now insisted that he be awarded Syria instead. The exchange would hardly have been an equable one, for Syria was a territory of great strategic and economic importance. For the Egyptians it would have meant control of the road leading to Mesopotamia as well as command of the passes to and from Anatolia. Syria (which included modern Palestine and Lebanon) was valuable also for its resources—timber, wood and charcoal, as well as olive oil, raw silk and cotton—and for its manpower, for the Syrian highlanders were rated as far better soldiers than the Egyptian peasants or even the Sudanese tribesmen.[7]

[5] On the problem of reform, see Bernard Lewis: *The Emergence of Modern Turkey* (London, 1961), 76 ff.; Roderic H. Davison: *Reform in the Ottoman Empire, 1856–1876* (Princeton, 1963), chap. i.

[6] Mehemet Ali is the French spelling of the pasha or viceroy's name. It is so well established in the literature that to now insist on a better English transliteration, such as Muhammad Ali, would seem to invite unnecessary confusion.

[7] Henry Dodwell: *The Founder of Modern Egypt: a Study of Muhammad Ali* (Cambridge, 1931), chap. iv; Mohammed Sabry: *L'empire égyptien sous Mohammed Ali et la question d'Orient, 1811–1849* (Paris, 1930); and for greater detail, Asad J. Rustum: *The Royal Archives of Egypt and the Origins of the Egyptian Expedition to Syria, 1831–1841* (Beirut, 1936); Mehmet Sinas: *Studien zur Geschichte der syrischen Politik Mehmed Alis von Aegypten* (Göttingen, 1936); William R. Polk: *The Opening of South Lebanon, 1788–1840* (Cambridge, 1963), 81 ff.

The dispute between sultan and vassal came to a head when the pasha of Acre refused Mehemet Ali's demand for the surrender of six thousand Egyptian peasants who had fled their homes to escape conscription. The viceroy suspected the sultan of encouraging this resistance and decided to wait no longer. He dispatched an army to invade Palestine and sent his son Ibrahim with a fleet to join in the operations against Acre. Ibrahim quickly overran Palestine and finally took Acre (May 27, 1832) after a long siege.

By this time the sultan had outlawed both Mehemet and Ibrahim, and had sent his best forces to relieve Acre. But these troops proved no match for the Egyptians. Ibrahim defeated them in a series of engagements and on July 29, 1832, captured the Beylan Pass, which commands the road to Antioch and Cilicia, which he then invaded. After some months spent in resting and refitting, he resumed his advance through the passes of the Taurus Mountains and eventually reached the ancient capital, Konya. There, on December 21, 1832, he met a Turkish army greatly superior to his own, commanded by Reshid Pasha, the most outstanding of the Turkish generals. Again Ibrahim won a resounding victory, not only because of his excellent generalship and the superiority of his troops in training and equipment, but also because of the fact that, in a heavy fog, Reshid lost his way and was captured.[8]

In the sultan's council an influential group had been pressing for some time for an arrangement with Mehemet Ali even at the expense of major concessions. But Mahmud, obstinate by nature, was determined to crush his presumptuous vassal. He sent missions to London begging for naval aid with which to threaten Egyptian communications through Syria. But Palmerston returned only a polite refusal, both before and after the disaster at Konya. Strange though it may seem in the light of later developments, the British government and the foreign secretary in particular were slow in arriving at the conclusion that British interests demanded the maintenance of the Ottoman Empire. There is no evidence to suggest that Palmerston at any time showed partiality for Mehemet Ali, but it was apparently only at the very end of January, 1833, that he came to realize that the viceroy, if he had posses-

---

[8] For the operations, see Dodwell: *Founder of Modern Egypt,* chap. iv; Pierre Crabitès: *Ibrahim of Egypt* (London, 1935), chap. xi; Georges Douin: *La première guerre de Syrie* (Paris, 1931), Vol. I; Vice-Admiral Durand-Viel: *Les campagnes navales de Mohammed Aly et d'Ibrahim* (Paris, 1930), II, 55 ff.

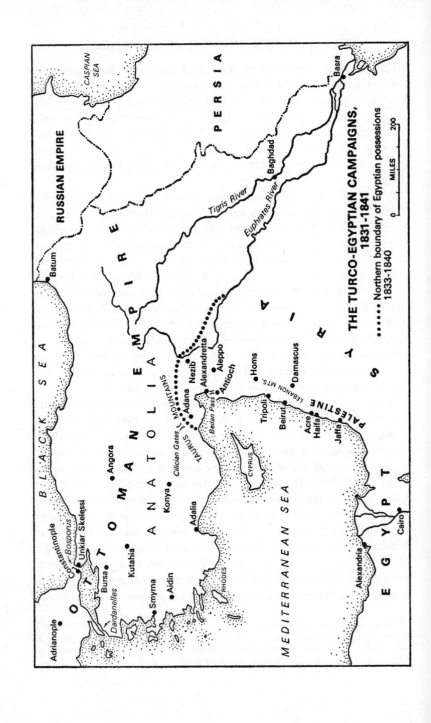

THE TURCO-EGYPTIAN CAMPAIGNS,
1831-1841

•••••• Northern boundary of Egyptian possessions
1833-1840

0   MILES   200

sion of Syria, was bound to secure control of Mesopotamia. This, in turn, would so weaken the Ottoman Empire as to make it an easy prey to Russian influence. By that time Palmerston was ready to use strong language at Alexandria to force Mehemet to halt the Egyptian advance. But the British government was not willing to go even that far. The British navy was fully occupied in blockading the Dutch coast and in supporting Dom Pedro's operations against Portugal. There were simply not enough ships available for a third major undertaking. So nothing much was done, a "tremendous blunder," as Palmerston was to admit later on.[9]

Meanwhile Czar Nicholas had been taking an active interest, unexpectedly in behalf of the sultan. The czar, in his fear of revolution and disorder, had sent General Nicholas Muraviev to Constantinople even before the Egyptian victory at Konya. "This whole affair," he had told his emissary, "is nothing but the result of the spirit of revolt which has taken hold of all Europe and especially France. If Constantinople is conquered, we shall have as neighbors a nest of all the stateless people who now surround the Pasha of Egypt." Muraviev, who reached the Turkish capital on the morrow of the Konya battle, assured the sultan of Russia's "unalterable friendship" and offered aid by land and sea to drive back the Egyptians. Pending Mahmud's decision, he sent a delegate to Ibrahim warning him against further advance, while he himself proceeded to Alexandria to urge upon the viceroy the dangers inherent in the situation.[10]

The policy of protecting rather than dismembering the Ottoman Empire was a new departure in Russian diplomacy and one which, understandably, was rarely credited at the time. It is now known, however, that following the Treaty of Adrianople the czar allowed himself to be convinced by his advisers that the Ottoman Empire, as a weak neighbor, would be quite unobjectionable to Russia, while any effort to disrupt that empire would inevitably lead to intervention by

---

[9] Webster: *Foreign Policy of Palmerston,* I, 278 ff.; Southgate: *"The Most English Minister,"* 63 ff.; M. Vereté: "Palmerston and the Levant Crisis, 1832" (*Journal of Modern History,* XXIV, 1952, 142–151); Christopher J. Bartlett: *Great Britain and Sea Power, 1815–1853* (Oxford, 1963), 88 ff.; M. S. Anderson: *The Eastern Question, 1774–1923* (New York, 1966), 77 ff.

[10] Theodor Schiemann: *Geschichte Russlands unter Kaiser Nikolaus I* (Berlin, 1913), III, 208 ff.; Vladimir P. Potemkin: *Histoire de la diplomatie* (Paris, 1946), I, 411 ff.; Constantin de Grunwald: *Tsar Nicholas I* (New York, 1955), 184 ff.

other powers and possibly to the establishment of a strong state on Russia's frontiers.[11]

Before accepting suspect Russian aid, Mahmud was finally induced by his counselors to make Mehemet Ali an offer: namely, the southern half of Syria (Palestine), which the viceroy rejected as inadequate. Mehemet now had his victorious son to deal with. Ibrahim's plan seems to have been to press the advance on Constantinople, force the deposition of Mahmud and then extort from his young son and successor the concessions which he regarded as indispensable: not only all of Syria but also the rich province of Cilicia (Adana) and possibly the island of Cyprus. Mehemet may have seen the dangers and may have wanted to call a halt. But Ibrahim, ignoring instructions, resumed his advance and on February 1 reached Kutayia, only a few weeks' march from the Turkish capital.[12]

Mahmud, unable to stem the progress of the Egyptians and in danger of being deposed by the pro-Egyptian faction in the palace, on February 2 appealed to the Russians for military and naval aid. An army was prepared in the Principalities for advance on Constantinople, while in less than three weeks a Russian squadron of nine warships appeared in the Bosporus and began to disembark troops for use against the Egyptians (see Illustration 54). To the protesting French chargé d'affaires the Turkish vizier replied that "a drowning man will clutch at a serpent."

The international crisis now quickly overshadowed the initial dispute between sultan and viceroy. New French and British ambassadors (Admiral Roussin and Lord Ponsonby) arrived on the scene and exerted themselves to the utmost to reverse the course of events by engineering an agreement between the contestants and then securing the withdrawal of the Russians. It would be tedious to follow in detail the involved negotiations with Ibrahim at Kutayia and Mehemet at Alexandria, the more so as the multiplicity of effort resulted more in confusion than in progress. Meanwhile (April 8) more Russian ships arrived and additional troops encamped on the hill at Unkiar Skelessi,

---

11 Robert J. Kerner: "Russia's New Policy in the Near East after the Peace of Adrianople" (*Cambridge Historical Journal*, V, 1937, 280–290); G. H. Bolsover: "Nicholas I and the Partition of Turkey" (*Slavonic Review*, XXVI, 1948, 115–145).

12 Crabitès: *Ibrahim of Egypt*, chap. xi; Douin: *Première guerre de Syrie*, II, introduction.

just opposite the British and French residencies at Therapia. As they arrived the Russian ships made a graceful sweep before the embassies: "A corvette, with her decks crowded and a band playing, was particularly conspicuous in paying this compliment; one of the most unwelcome serenades to which Lord Ponsonby had probably ever been treated." These were great days for the Russians, which they celebrated with endless saluting and cannon firing. One day the sultan, accompanied by the diplomatic corps, visited the Russian camp: "Men and officers were decked in their best attire, the soldiers having their mustachoes stiffened with grease and their chests thickly padded."[13]

The upshot of the many *pourparlers* was that Mahmud had to yield. By the Convention of Kutayia (May 4, 1833) he assigned Syria to Mehemet Ali for the duration of the latter's life and appointed Ibrahim "collector of the taxes" for the pashalik of Adana. Ibrahim thereupon began the evacuation of Anatolia. The sultan no longer required Russian protection and the British and French, who had used pressure to effect the Kutayia agreement, now prepared to concentrate naval forces at the entrance to the Dardanelles so as to demonstrate to the Russians their determination to resist any effort to exploit the unprecedented situation in which the latter found themselves.

Actually Czar Nicholas had no intention of keeping his forces in the Bosporus, once the Egyptians had begun to withdraw. Already on May 5 Count Orlov had arrived in Constantinople to arrange their evacuation. Little is known of his discussions with the Turks, except that they bore fruit in the Treaty of Unkiar Skelessi (July 8, 1833), after the signature of which the Russian troops embarked and departed (July 10). This famous treaty was in effect a defensive alliance for a period of eight years. Each party was to come to the aid of the other in the event of attack by another power. However, a secret clause relieved the sultan of this obligation in return for his promise to close the Dardanelles to foreign warships in the event of war. Actually this obligation rested on

---

[13] Miss Pardoe: *The Beauties of the Bosporus* (London, 1838), 156 ff., reporting the account of a British diplomat. On the development of the crisis, F. S. Rodkey: *The Turco-Egyptian Question in the Relations of England, France and Russia, 1832–1841* (Urbana, 1921) is still useful, but should be supplemented by Sabry: *L'empire égyptien*, and Harold Temperley: *The Crimea* (London, 1936); Webster: *Foreign Policy of Palmerston*. Both C. Giglio: "La questione egiziana dal 1798 al 1841" (*Oriente moderno*, XXIII, 1943, 455–500) and Anderson: *Eastern Question* are admirable, up-to-date summaries.

the sultan under the terms of earlier international agreements and so, on the face of it, was altogether unobjectionable. Nonetheless, it was feared at the time that the sultan, while closing the Dardanelles to the warships of Britain or France, was at least tacitly promising to leave open the Bosporus to Russian warships. There was nothing to support such an interpretation. Indeed, it is now known that the astute Russian foreign minister, Count Nesselrode, had urged the czar not to claim any special rights in the Straits, knowing as he did that other powers would not recognize them. There remained the fact, however, that the treaty amounted to a Russian protectorate over the Ottoman Empire. Nicholas expected the sultan "to come to agreement without reserve on all matters concerning their respective tranquillity and safety," in short, to consult the Russians and take their advice in preference to that of any other power. In Palmerston's words: "The most objectionable part of the treaty is the mutual engagement between the two Powers to consult each other confidentially upon all their respective interests, and by which the Russian Ambassador becomes Chief Cabinet Minister of the Sultan."[14]

Because of the uncertainty respecting the terms of the Russian-Turkish treaty and the suspicions to which the uncertainty gave rise, the effect of this first Egyptian crisis was to heighten the tension between the western and the eastern powers and so to accentuate the division of Europe. This was the more regrettable because the Russian policy, all appearances to the contrary notwithstanding, was quite unobjectionable, for the British and the French too were interested in protecting the Ottoman Empire from further disruption. Russian objectives became clear from the discussions at the meeting of the czar with the Austrian emperor at Münchengrätz in Moravia, on September 18, 1833. The Russian and Austrian governments there came to a far-reaching agreement: Nicholas promised to support the Hapsburg dynasty in Austria, where a change of ruler was imminent. He

---

14 Webster: *Foreign Policy of Palmerston,* I, 304. The secret clause was leaked to the British almost at once, but there were grave suspicions that yet further secret arrangements were involved. The confusion about the treaty was actually enhanced by the volume of Serge Gorianov (a Russian Foreign Ministry official): *Le Bosphore et les Dardanelles* (Paris, 1910), 40 ff., but the full facts have since been brought out by Philip E. Mosely: *Russian Diplomacy and the Opening of the Eastern Question in 1838 and 1839* (Cambridge, 1934), 9 ff.; J. C. Hurewitz: "Russia and the Turkish Straits: a Revaluation of the Origins of the Problem" (*World Politics,* XIV, 1962, 605–632).

promised also to uphold the Ottoman Empire under the existing dynasty. Austria and Russia reaffirmed the principle of intervention against revolution and undertook to co-operate in action against Polish revolutionaries. With respect to the Near East they engaged to work together to prevent Mehemet Ali from acquiring a foothold in European Turkey and, if the breakup of the Ottoman Empire became unavoidable, to act in consultation with each other. In October the Prussian government reluctantly subscribed to the Münchengrätz agreement (much of which was of little concern to the Prussians) and thereby completed the renewal of the Holy Alliance. In the West, where the exact terms of the convention were not known, the very fact of the meeting and agreement was viewed as an unfriendly if not a hostile move. In a matter of months the answer was given to the Holy Alliance of Münchengrätz by the formation of the Entente Cordiale between the western powers.[15]

3. THE OPPOSING CAMPS

To Palmerston the Münchengrätz meeting and agreement, coming hard on the Russian successes in the Near East, appeared as an out-and-out challenge to the western powers, and one which he was not loath to take up. In the Belgian question Britain and France had had their way and there was good reason to suppose that these two powers, now under comparable political regimes, might constitute a liberal bloc in opposition to the league of the absolute powers of the East. The British desired such an alignment, for even though many, like Palmerston, were suspicious of French designs in Belgium, Italy and even Poland, the monarchy of Louis Philippe, obviously intent on avoiding trouble, was much more agreeable to the British than its predecessor. Furthermore, the best way to forestall French adventures was to be associated with France and so be in a position to restrain it by co-operation. On the French side, the readiness for an understanding with Britain was even stronger. To be sure, the French disliked the British, to put it mildly, but the new king and his ministers, exposed as they were to intervention by the eastern powers, felt the support of Britain to be essential.

[15] On Münchengrätz, Ernst Molden: *Die Orientpolitik des Fürsten Metternich, 1829–1833* (Vienna, 1913), 80 ff., with the complete text of the agreements, 119 ff.; also Heinrich von Srbik: *Metternich, der Staatsmann und der Mensch* (Munich, 1925, 1954), I, 684 ff.; III, 151; Erzsebet Andics: *Das Bündnis Habsburg-Romanow* (Budapest, 1963), 14 ff.

For that reason the French had sacrificed their opportunities in Belgium and had turned a deaf ear to the appeals of Poles, Italians and other oppressed peoples. It would hardly be too much to say that by 1833 the Entente Cordiale already existed, though it rested on no specific agreements.[16]

Palmerston, however, wanted more than a close understanding with France. What he aimed at was a league of all liberal, constitutional states, for he was convinced that order and progress could best be ensured through representative government and that British interest would be best served through a liberal world controlled by the middle classes. "I consider the constitutional states to be the natural allies of this country," he had declared in Parliament in August, 1832; "I am persuaded that no English ministry will be performing its duty if it is inattentive to their interests." To him this was more than a matter of paper protests. It meant intervention when necessary, intervention which he regarded as altogether justifiable so long as it fell short of actual armed force.[17]

The Belgian question provided a clear example of Palmerston's views and procedures. Another was to be the joint problem of Portugal and Spain, where again liberalism and constitutionalism were at stake, challenged by the forces of reaction. Here was the ideal opportunity for the foreign secretary to respond to the revived Holy Alliance. Writing to the British ambassador to Madrid in February, 1834, Palmerston explained:

The great object of our policy ought now to be to form a Western confederacy of free states as a counterpoise to the Eastern League of the arbitrary governments. England, France, Spain and Portugal, united as they now must be, will form a political and moral power in Europe which must hold Metternich and Nicholas in check. We shall be on the advance, they on the decline; and all the smaller planets of Europe will have a natural tendency to gravitate towards our system.[18]

[16] On the general problem of Anglo-French relations, see John Hall: *England and the Orleans Monarchy* (London, 1912), chap. vi; Raymond Guyot: *La première Entente Cordiale* (Paris, 1926), chap. iii; Charles Pouthas: "Sur les rapports de la France avec l'Angleterre pendant la Monarchie de Juillet" (*Revue d'histoire moderne*, II, 1927, 455–469); Jean Duhamel: *Louis Philippe et la première Entente Cordiale* (Paris, 1951).

[17] Charles K. Webster: "Palmerston and the Liberal Movement, 1830–1841" (*Politica*, III, 1938, 299–323); Southgate, *"The Most English Minister,"* 52 ff.

[18] Webster: *Foreign Policy of Palmerston,* I, 390.

Such a confederacy was in fact established by the Quadruple Alliance of April 22, 1834, by which the Spanish government was induced to send an army into Portugal to support Dom Pedro and the liberals in their effort to defeat Dom Miguel and the absolutists, while Britain and France committed themselves to provide financial, naval and other aid. The risks involved were minimal, for the eastern powers, while sympathetic to the conservative elements, were unable to intervene effectively, if only for geographical reasons. On the other hand, the British and French, for all their earlier protests against intervention by the eastern powers in Italy and elsewhere, now carried their interference to the limit short of war. The liberals in both Portugal and Spain were given generous financial support, and were permitted to recruit large numbers of volunteers. The British fleet saw to it that the northern coasts should not fall into the hands of the Carlists, and at times actually took part in the operations. The story has been told in some detail in a previous chapter and need not be repeated here.[19] The British had ample opportunity to query the fitness of their clients for liberal government, and the French had increasing reasons for resenting the policies of their British ally. But the outcome was a foregone conclusion: neither the British nor the French would tolerate a victory of the reactionary Carlists, while the latter had neither the strength nor the military competence to win without subsantial foreign aid. The eastern powers provided some financial support and a few hundred volunteers or adventurers, but they realized from the start that they would have to stand by while the western powers imposed their will on the Iberian nations.

What the Entente Cordiale might accomplish in the Near East was, of course, another question. In reaction to the treaty of Unkiar Skelessi, Palmerston had declared in Parliament (July 11, 1833) that "the integrity and independence of the Ottoman Empire are necessary to the maintenance of the tranquillity, the liberty and the balance of power in the rest of Europe." The British and French were at one in their opposition to any attempt of the Russians to dismember the Turkish Empire (which the czar had no intention of doing) and they had the naval power in the Mediterranean to make their weight felt. For that very reason Czar Nicholas busily reinforced his Black Sea fleet and in addition strengthened the Russian Baltic fleet till it was thought a

[19] See Chapter III.

potential threat to British naval supremacy. The Russian Black Sea forces had standing orders to seize control of the Straits the very moment when the British or French made a move in that direction, whether or not they were called upon by the sultan for aid.[20] On the other side the British and French squadrons were under orders to pass the Dardanelles and hasten to the defense of Constantinople "in case of certain and imminent danger," if appealed to by the sultan.[21]

The sultan no doubt rejoiced to see the western powers pitted against the Russians, whose protection he had accepted only under duress. He did in fact make repeated efforts to enlist British support, if not against the Russians, at least against Mehemet Ali. But Palmerston, while willing to provide supplies and even conclude a defensive alliance, would not countenance aggression on the sultan's part.[22]

On the problem of Mehemet Ali and his ambitions, Britain and France tended to drift apart. Frenchmen held key positions in the Egyptian administration and contributed heavily to the modernization of the country. A number of Saint-Simonians were particularly active in the effort to improve education, regulate the Nile waters, and develop agriculture. More and more the French looked upon Mehemet Ali as a useful client. They were ready to defend him against efforts to deprive him of the gains of 1833, and they seem to have encouraged him in his designs on the remaining Arab territories of the sultan.[23]

The very fact that Mehemet Ali favored the French was probably enough to induce the British to distrust him, but they were bound to actually oppose him, first, because they were developing a growing interest in the Ottoman Empire and, second, because he obstructed projects which they regarded as vital to their own purposes. In 1833 David Urquhart, an emotional young romantic, had reported most favorably on the trade prospects of the Near East after traveling through the Balkans and Circassia, where native tribesmen were resisting Russian efforts to take over the territory acquired from the

---

20 Vernon J. Puryear: *England, Russia and the Straits Question, 1844–1856* (Berkeley, 1931), 30; Mosely: *Russian Diplomacy,* chap. iii.

21 G. H. Bolsover: "Lord Ponsonby and the Eastern Question, 1833–1839" (*Slavonic Review,* XIII, 1934, 98–118); Webster: *Foreign Policy of Palmerston,* II, 603.

22 Mosely: *Russian Diplomacy,* 120 ff.; Temperley: *Crimea,* 98.

23 Sébastien Charléty: *Histoire du Saint-Simonisme* (Paris, 1931), Book III, chaps. i and ii; Jacques Lajard de Puyjalon: *L'influence des Saint-Simoniens sur la réalisation de l'isthme de Suez et des chemins de fer* (Paris, 1926).

Turks in 1829. Urquhart, whose hatred of the Russians was positively pathological, urged his government to support the Circassians. Eventually he induced a British merchant to send a ship, the *Vixen,* with munitions and supplies. The ship was intercepted by the Russians, who thereby provoked a tense though momentary crisis in their relations with Britain.

Urquhart played a major role in stimulating anti-Russian feeling in Britain. In his paper, *The Portfolio,* he published documents compromising to the Russians that had been supplied him by the Polish exiles. Palmerston had him discharged from the diplomatic service, whereupon he turned his very considerable propaganda talents against the foreign secretary. Nonetheless, he retained considerable influence among business circles, for whom he pictured "the infinite riches" of the "inexhaustible" Ottoman Empire. The empire, he argued, could supply Britain not only with grain but with most of the raw materials needed for manufactures. However, the empire must be reformed and modernized, and this should be the task of the British. Largely through his efforts the sultan in 1838 assented to the Convention of Balta Liman, a trade treaty which for the first time opened the empire wide to foreign trade as other powers concluded similar agreements. By 1840 the British exports to Turkey (cotton cloth, refined sugar, iron and steel, woolens and hardware) had already trebled as compared with those of 1825. Presently Turkey ranked third or fourth among Britain's export markets.[24]

Although Smyrna (Izmir) was the chief Turkish emporium, Beirut on the Levant coast was developing rapidly. The export of Syrian raw silk and cotton doubled in a few years, while British manufactured yarns and cotton cloths came in such quantities as to upset the traditional economy of the region. Syria being under Egyptian rule, the administration made every effort to maintain monopolies and controls, which in turn were much resented by the British.[25]

Of equal if not greater concern to the British was the question of communications with India and the East, a question which in large

---

[24] John H. Gleason: *The Genesis of Russophobia in Great Britain* (Cambridge, 1950); Frank E. Bailey: *British Policy and the Turkish Reform Movement* (Cambridge, 1942), chaps. ii and iii; G. H. Bolsover: "David Urquhart and the Eastern Question, 1833–1837" (*Journal of Modern History,* VIII, 1936, 444–467); Charles K. Webster: "Urquhart, Ponsonby and Palmerston" (*English Historical Review,* LXII, 1947, 327–351); Peter Brock: "The Fall of Circassia" (*ibid.,* LXXI, 1956, 401–427).

[25] William H. Polk: *The Opening of South Lebanon* (Cambridge, 1963), chap. x.

part depended on Mehemet Ali for a favorable solution. The steamship and the railroad had opened the prospect of supplanting the long and tedious passage around the Cape by new and much shorter routes through the Red Sea or the Persian Gulf. In 1830 the first of several voyages from Bombay to Suez by steamship had been satisfactorily completed. In the same year Captain Francis Chesney had surveyed the Isthmus of Suez and disproved the well-established notion that there was a significant difference in level between the Red Sea and the Mediterranean. Thus it appeared for the first time that a Suez Canal would be feasible.[26] For the time being, however, the British government was more interested in a possible route from the Syrian coast through Mesopotamia to the Persian Gulf, a route which would have greater strategic value and would avoid exposure to the southwest monsoon. Chesney reported favorably on this route in 1832 and was sent out in 1835 with steam-powered flatboats to navigate the Euphrates. Once again Egyptian officials did everything possible to delay and obstruct the expedition, which was not completed until June, 1836. It was to be another two years before Captain John Hawkins first succeeded in ascending the Euphrates by steamboat.

Meanwhile French and British steam packets had in 1835 and 1836 opened service through the Mediterranean to Alexandria, and postal service to India by way of Egypt had been inaugurated. But the Red Sea route to India was almost entirely under the control of Mehemet Ali. There were reports, in fact, that he was preparing to take Aden, Hadramaut, Oman and Muscat. In 1838 Egyptian troops overran Nejd and threatened Bahrein, on the Persian Gulf. There was every indication that the viceroy was indeed planning to make himself master of the entire Arab world. In response to his designs the British therefore occupied the important coaling and supply station of Aden in January, 1839, at the same time warning Mehemet Ali that the occupation of Bahrein by Egyptian forces "could not be viewed with indifference by the British government." Preparations were made at once to defend Bahrein by force if necessary.[27]

<hr />

26 It should be noted, however, that Chesney's conclusions were not generally accepted until 1847.

27 Thomas E. Marston: *Britain's Imperial Role in the Red Sea Area, 1800–1878* (Hamden, 1961), 51 ff.; Halford L. Hoskins: *British Routes to India* (New York, 1928), chap. viii and p. 221; Dodwell: *Founder of Modern Egypt,* 137 ff.

In effect, then, a real clash of interest had developed between Britain and the Egyptian viceroy. The latter would do nothing to further the construction of either a railroad or a canal to connect the Mediterranean with the Red Sea. At the same time he threatened to block the route through Mesopotamia and the Persian Gulf, which, at the time, seemed to the British the more preferable one. By 1839 Palmerston could no longer see anything good in the "Napoleon of the East."

"For my part I hate Mehemet Ali," he wrote to the ambassador at Paris, "whom I consider as nothing but an ignorant barbarian, who by cunning and boldness and mother-wit has been successful in rebellion. . . . I look upon his boasted civilisation of Egypt as the arrantest humbug, and I believe that he is as great a tyrant and oppressor as ever made a people wretched."[28]

No doubt the sultan counted heavily on British hostility to Mehemet Ali to aid him in taking revenge on that presumptuous vassal. Between the two Egyptian crises Mahmud did his utmost to press on with the modernization and strengthening of his empire. The administration was reformed, missions were sent to the western capitals and European dress was introduced. Above all, the effort was made to raise the effectiveness of the armed forces. Polish and German officers (notably General Chrzanowki and Captain, later Field-Marshal, Helmuth von Moltke) were called in. Regular conscription was introduced, soldiers were put into serviceable uniforms, given modern equipment and carefully disciplined: beards were to be no longer than the width of two fingers and mustaches were limited to the length of eyebrows. Many of these reforms of course remained superficial. They met with much criticism from the conservative upper classes, whose contempt for western institutions was exceeded only by their ignorance. Nonetheless the sultan persisted. He had only one all-consuming desire and that was to put Mehemet Ali in his place, and his great hope was that when the showdown came the British would give him effective support.[29]

4. THE SECOND EGYPTIAN CRISIS

After Mehemet Ali's avowal of his intention to proclaim his independence (1838), no admonitions by the European ambassadors could

---

[28] Quoted by Temperley: *Crimea*, 89.
[29] For studies of the Turkish reforms, see the references in footnote 5 above.

longer deter the sultan from the attempt to discipline his fractious vassal. In April, 1839, Turkish forces crossed the upper Euphrates and began offensive operations against Ibrahim and the Egyptian forces. Despite Moltke's urgent advice to stand on the defensive until further Turkish troops could arrive from Konya and Angora, the Turkish commander insisted on attacking. Ibrahim, ably supported by Soliman Pasha (the Frenchman Colonel Sève), avoided a frontal attack and began an enveloping movement which caused the Turkish troops to flee to escape capture. The battle of Nezib (June 24) lasted hardly two hours, yet opened the way once again to an invasion of Anatolia by Ibrahim's army. Mercifully, Mahmud died of a lingering disease (July 1) before he learned of this disaster and of the equally calamitous, unexpected surrender of the Turkish fleet, which, on July 14, sailed into the harbor of Alexandria and gave itself up without fighting. This amazing event was due chiefly to the fear of the commanding officer, Ahmed Pasha, lest the new grand vizier, Chosrev Pasha, throw himself and the empire on the mercy of the czar. Before taking his fateful step, Ahmed had consulted Admiral Lalande, commander of the French Mediterranean squadron, who evidently gave it his blessing. Mehemet Ali, suddenly presented with so valuable a prize, at once announced that he would return the fleet to the sultan only when and if the latter dismissed Chosrev and recognized the viceroy's hereditary possession of Egypt, Syria and Candia.[30]

The new sultan, Abdul Mejid, was a boy of sixteen, quite unprepared for the crisis which now confronted him. Chosrev, it seems, was so panic-stricken that he would have quickly made a deal with the viceroy. But this time Palmerston was not to be caught napping. Even before news of the Turkish disasters had reached him, he had had instructions sent to the British fleet to cut the sea communications between Egypt and Syria. Peace in the Levant, he declared, could not be assured until the desert were interposed between Egypt and the rest of the empire: Mehemet Ali might be given hereditary possession of Egypt, but he simply must give up Syria. Furthermore, Palmerston welcomed Metternich's proposal for collective action by the powers. On July 27 the British, French, Austrian and Russian ambassadors at Constantinople presented a note requesting the Turkish government to

---

[30] For a full account of this episode, see Vice-Admiral Durand-Viel: *Les campagnes navales de Mohammed Ali et d'Ibrahim* (Paris, 1937), 183 ff.

take no action pending the efforts of the powers to arrange a settlement. The collective note, which the Turks naturally accepted with alacrity, meant in effect that Russia, as one of the signatories, was abandoning its claim to a special protectorate. The explanation for this shift lies in the czar's realization that neither Britain nor France would ever permit the Treaty of Unkiar Skelessi to be put in operation. Palmerston, who had come to the conclusion that "Russia is a great humbug," and that Britain could throw Russia back half a century in one campaign, had warned the czar's government as recently as 1838 that, as regards the Near Eastern problem, "Europe never would endure that the matter should be settled by the single, independent and self-regulated interference of any one power." Unable and unwilling to face the opposition of the western powers, Nicholas was therefore intent on forestalling separate action by those powers. This could best be done through collective action.[31]

Mehemet Ali's cause would now have become hopeless, had it not been for the fact that the French government, having joined in the collective note in the expectation that it would be opposed by Russia, now began to regret its action and attempt to undo it by furthering an understanding between Constantinople and Alexandria, which would have made any effort by the powers superfluous.[32] However, in defending the viceroy's claim to Syria the French inevitably met head on the British determination to expel the Egyptians from that province and force Mehemet Ali to return the Turkish fleet. Palmerston's position was reinforced by the special missions which Czar Nicholas sent to London in September and December, 1839. No doubt the czar's larger aim was to undermine the Entente Cordiale between Britain and France and so isolate the latter, but he was also and more directly intent on securing for Russia what the Treaty of Unkiar Skelessi had failed to afford. His emissary, Baron Brunnow, was therefore instructed to say that the objectionable treaty would not be renewed on its expiration in 1841, provided an international agreement could be arrived at closing the Straits to all foreign powers while the Ottoman Empire remained at peace. Russia, he declared, would support the

---

[31] R. W. Seton-Watson: *Britain in Europe* (New York, 1937), 184 ff.; Webster: *Foreign Policy of Palmerston,* II, 594.

[32] Emile Bourgeois: *Manuel historique de politique étrangère* (8 ed., Paris, 1927), III, 148 ff.; Paul Henry: *La France devant le monde de 1789 à 1939* (Paris, 1945), 125 ff.

British stand with respect to Syria even without French co-operation.[33]

Despite the fact that many of his colleagues were opposed to abandonment of the French alliance in favor of a new and questionable agreement with Russia, Palmerston was ready to accept support wherever he could find it. An agreement for joint action was arrived at in January, 1840, and necessarily exacerbated the relations between Britain and France, the more so after Thiers succeeded to the premiership on March 1. Thiers, who was generally regarded as the embodiment of French patriotism and the chief proponent of an active foreign policy, had publicly criticized the position of his predecessor and committed himself to support of the Egyptian claim to Syria. He clearly had an exaggerated notion of Egypt's ability to defend Syria, and of the reluctance of the powers to apply force in the face of French opposition. He therefore attempted to wear down the other governments by continuing obstruction, while at the same time forestalling their action by promoting a deal between the sultan and the viceroy. By June, 1840, these efforts seemed to be bearing fruit.[34]

That Thiers miscalculated on almost every count was quickly demonstrated by events. Palmerston was at last able to induce a reluctant cabinet to consent to the conclusion of the Treaty of London (July 15, 1840), by which the four powers (Britain, Russia, Austria and Prussia) accepted the principle of closure of the Turkish Straits to all powers while Turkey was at peace and, with respect to Mehemet Ali, agreed to offer him hereditary possession of Egypt and South Syria (Palestine) for the duration of his life (he was already seventy-one years old). He was to evacuate Candia, Adana, northern Syria and the Holy Places of Arabia (Mecca and Medina), and he was to return the Turkish fleet to its rightful owner. Failure to accept these terms within ten days of their receipt was to entail withdrawal of the offer of South

---

[33] Perhaps still the best account of Russian policy is that of Theodor Schiemann: *Geschichte Russlands unter Kaiser Nikolaus I* (Berlin, 1913), III, 387 ff., but see also Constantin de Grunwald: *Tros siècles de diplomatie russe* (Paris, 1945), 189; Barbara Jelavich: *A Century of Russian Foreign Policy, 1814–1914* (Philadelphia, 1964), 87 ff.; Ettore Anchieri: *Costantinopoli e gli stretti* (Milan, 1948), chap. ii.

[34] De Guichen: *La crise d'Orient,* chap. viii; John M. S. Allison: *Thiers and the French Monarchy* (London, 1926), 271 ff.; Henry: *La France devant le monde,* 125 ff.; François Charles-Roux: *Thiers et Mehemet Ali* (Paris, 1951), 46 ff.; and especially Charles H. Pouthas: "La politique de Thiers pendant la crise orientale de 1840" (*Revue historique,* CLXXXII, 1938, 76–96).

Syria. After the lapse of another ten days, the sultan was to be free to make other arrangements, even with regard to Egypt.[35]

Despite the united front presented by the powers, the viceroy rejected these terms and indeed threatened to have the sherif of Mecca proclaim a Holy War against the Europeans. In his obstinacy he was relying on French support. France at that time had naval squadrons in the Mediterranean superior even to those of the British.[36] It seemed most unlikely that Britain and its associates would act without France or against it. In this he was as mistaken as, on the French side, was Thiers. Palmerston was convinced that the French, for all their bluster, would not dare precipitate a war against all Europe, and that if they did, the British by themselves could take care of the situation. Thiers, like all French patriots, was dumfounded and enraged by the Treaty of London. He at once called up reserves, strengthened the fleet, embarked upon the fortification of Paris and in general threatened to repay his opponents by fomenting revolutions in Italy and Germany. French opinion, says one French historian, was seized by a kind of collective folly and accepted the idea of war without due regard to the menacing coalition.[37]

Thiers counted heavily on the ability of the Egyptians to defend their position in Syria and so prepare the way for a compromise settlement. But in this he was again overoptimistic. Palmerston warned the French that if they started a war they would soon lose their ships, their colonies and their commerce, and that Mehemet Ali would "just be chucked into the Nile."[38] British, Austrian and Russian squadrons, loaded with Turkish troops, now arrived off the Levant coast, while the Druse mountaineers rose in revolt against the Egyptians, stoutly supported if not instigated by the British. On September 10 Sir Charles Napier, in command of the combined fleets, bombarded Beirut and landed a substantial force of British marines and Turkish troops north of the city. Beirut and other towns were taken by October 10 and Ibrahim, defeated at Ardali Heights, was obliged to fall back. Acre fell

[35] Francis Waddington: "La politique de Lord Palmerston et le traité du 15 juillet, 1840" (*Revue d'histoire diplomatique*, XLIX, 1935, 1–27).

[36] The British had twelve ships of the line, the French seventeen, while the combined Egyptian-Turkish fleets made an additional nineteen ships of the line (Gerald S. Graham: *The Politics of Naval Supremacy*, London, 1965, p. 76).

[37] Henry: *La France devant le monde*, 127.

[38] Herbert C. Bell: *Lord Palmerston* (New York, 1936), I, 303–304.

early in November (see Illustration 57). At the end of the month Napier appeared at Alexandria and at last induced Mehemet Ali to give up the Turkish fleet.[39]

By this time the sultan had, on British advice, deposed Mehemet Ali as viceroy of Egypt and the French, reacting to the complete debacle of their plans and hopes, had become so belligerent that the Egyptian crisis was soon engulfed in a much greater war scare. A French attack on the Rhineland seemed so imminent that King Leopold of Belgium and others made heroic efforts to break the tension. Eventually Louis Philippe, who throughout remained devoted to peace, dismissed Thiers and appointed in his stead Marshal Soult, with the historian Guizot as foreign minister. The latter, as ambassador to London, had been greatly disturbed by Thiers' bellicosity. Not sharing the general enthusiasm for Mehemet Ali and concerned lest war in Europe end in a general revolutionary conflagration, Guizot was prepared to yield. Meanwhile Palmerston, too, was under pressure from his colleagues and from the Austrian and Prussian governments, which were most directly exposed to French aggression. He therefore agreed that the viceroy's deposition should be revoked and that he should be given hereditary possession of Egypt, under Turkish suzerainty. By the sultan's firman of February 13, 1841, Mehemet was recognized as ruler of Egypt, with the provisos that he keep an army of not more than 18,000 men and that he pay 25 per cent of the Egyptian revenue as tribute to the sultan.[40]

The severe and explosive Egyptian crisis was finally brought to a close on July 13, 1841, when France joined the other four powers in signing the Straits Convention, the terms of which had already been laid down in the Treaty of London. It specified that the sultan, so long as the Ottoman Empire remained at peace, should admit no foreign warship to either strait (the Dardanelles or the Bosporus). However, in the event of Turkey's being at war, the sultan was left free to call upon any foreign power for aid, on the understanding that if the warships

[39] Sir Charles Napier: *The War in Syria* (London, 1842); Durand-Viel: *Les campagnes navales*, II, chap. xvii; E. Simion and M. Nani Mocenigo: *La campagna navale di Siria del 1840* (Milan, 1933). On the revolt of the Druses, see François Charles-Roux: "La domination égyptienne en Syrie, 1833–1840" (*Revue d'histoire des colonies françaises*, XXI, 1933, 187–212); Polk: *Opening of South Lebanon*, 205 ff.

[40] Joseph E. Cattaui: *Histoire des rapports de l'Egypte avec la Sublime Porte du XVIIIe siècle à 1841* (Paris, 1919), chaps. x and xi.

of such a power were to pass either strait, other signatories of the convention should have the same right to send their ships through. This convention established the international law of the Straits until 1923. Though it did not include a formal guarantee of the independence or integrity of the Ottoman Empire, it did supersede the unilateral protectorate of the Russians and documented the concern of all the powers in the affairs of the Near East.

A by-product of the Egyptian crisis was the inauguration of the reform era in Turkey known as the *Tanzimat*. It may be dated from the "exalted rescript" of Gülhané (November 3, 1839), which guaranteed the life, liberty and property of all the sultan's subjects, promised regularity in the fixation and collection of taxes, and envisaged reform of the military service. To many Europeans this high-sounding document was mere window dressing, "the offspring of frippery, French philosophy, and ignorant vanity," in the words of the British ambassador. To a certain extent this was true. The Turkish statesman, Reshid Pasha, had persuaded the young sultan that, in order to enlist the sympathy and support of the western powers, he should at least proclaim enlightened principles. But more than that was involved. Reshid, who had served as Turkish ambassador in Paris and London, had convinced himself that if the Ottoman Empire were to survive it would have to embark courageously on the course of modernization. Under his guidance the sale of offices was abolished, the tax system revised, the law codes reformed. In the spring of 1840 he went so far as to convoke an assembly of notables which, though it did little more than listen to an imperial address, nonetheless suggested the possibility of an eventual representative system. It stands to reason that Reshid's efforts should have provoked opposition. He was presently driven from power, after which the conservatives staged a reaction so severe that Reshid appealed to the powers to intervene and assume at least temporary supervision of the Ottoman government. Nothing came of this amazing proposal, but in 1845 Reshid returned to power and, with British support, resumed his reforming program. A western administrative code was introduced, the equality of all religions recognized, mixed tribunals with western procedures established, local government reorganized, secular education promoted, and the military establishment modernized. Naturally these reforms were often incomplete. But they reflected the penetration of liberal ideas in the East, in the Islamic world. Feudalism gradually died out and something like a modern administration emerged, the prelude to the constitutional movement of the 1870's.[41]

5. PERSONALITIES AND POLICIES

Despite the growing importance of national feeling and of economic interests as factors influencing international relations, foreign policies continued in the years preceding 1848 to be determined largely by the personalities of rulers and statesmen. Among the eastern powers, where the word of the prince was still law, this is not greatly to be wondered at, the more so as Czar Nicholas had an absorbing interest in diplomacy and fancied himself the protector of law and authority wherever they were threatened by revolution. Thus in Austria, where the feeble-minded Ferdinand I had succeeded to the throne in 1835 and where the state was increasingly shaken by nationalist forces, the czar not only responded favorably to Metternich's appeal for support of the dynasty but realized at an early date that Hungary was becoming a revolutionary danger spot, against which Russia might eventually have to intervene. Nicholas did everything he could to stiffen the Vienna government in opposition to the forces of disintegration.[42]

The czar was equally concerned about developments in Prussia, where his brother-in-law Frederick William IV ascended the throne in 1840. The king's romanticism, weakness and vacillation, above all his flirtation with liberal ideas, were profoundly disturbing. When in 1847 Frederick William convoked the United Diet, the czar was filled with dismay. Such policies could lead only to the victory of constitutionalism, to the weakening of Prussian power and to the subversion of the Holy Alliance. But admonitions proved futile. Nicholas had to admit to himself that the coalition of conservative powers had lost much of its pristine solidarity.[43]

---

[41] The basic study in a western language is Edouard Engelhardt: *La Turquie et le Tanzimat* (Paris, 1882). See also Nicolas Milev: "Réchid Pacha et la réforme ottomane" (*Zeitschrift für osteuropäische Geschichte*, II, 1912, 382–398); Bailey: *British Policy and the Turkish Reform Movement*, chaps. v and vi; Bernard Lewis: *The Emergence of Modern Turkey* (London, 1961), chap. iv.

[42] Eduard Winter: "Eine bedeutsame Unterredung zwischen Zar Nikolaus I und Metternich am Neujahrstag, 1846" (*Zeitschrift für Geschichtswissenschaft*, IX, 1961, 1861–1870); Andícs: *Das Bündnis Habsburg-Romanow*, 24, 347.

[43] Willy Andreas: "Die russische Diplomatie und die Politik Friedrich Wilhelms IV von Preussen" (*Abhandlungen der preussischen Akademie der Wissenschaften: Philosophisch-Historische Klasse*, 1926, No. 6).

Added to this was the czar's dislike of Louis Philippe, his fear of France as the wellspring of unrest, the hearth of revolution and the possible instigator of war. In 1840 Britain and Russia had worked together against France, but it was clear that Guizot would try to revive the entente between France and England and that there was at least the possibility that in another Near Eastern crisis the two western powers might co-operate to the detriment of Russian interests. Far from being reassured by the agreements of 1840 and 1841, Nicholas kept agonizing over the future of the Ottoman Empire. He did not think it could last long and he knew that Russian pretensions to the inheritance of any substantial part of it would be resisted by force. Under the circumstances it seemed best to him that Austria, over which he expected to exercise increasing influence, should take over the Turkish possessions in the Balkans. He discussed this matter with Austrian statesmen in the autumn and spring of 1843–1844, without eliciting a clear reply. Nonetheless, the czar assumed that in the event of another crisis he would be able to count on Austrian co-operation.

Even more important, from Nicholas' point of view, would be a further development of the agreement with Britain. In June, 1844, the czar quite suddenly appeared in England for a visit and for discussions with Sir Robert Peel and Lord Aberdeen, the successors of Melbourne and Palmerston after the election of 1841. Nicholas expatiated upon the weakness of the Ottoman Empire and freely avowed his fear of French designs in the Levant. Though he was eager to maintain the Ottoman Empire as long as possible, he had grave doubts whether it could last much longer. Would it not, he queried, be advisable to come to an agreement between Britain, Austria and Russia as to the terms of partition, if such were to become unavoidable? His interlocutors were made uneasy by such talk and in any case were unwilling to commit themselves in what was still a hypothetical situation. They expressed gratification over the czar's assurances and agreed that it would be wise to discuss matters if another crisis ensued. Such "agreement" as there may have been was purely personal and certainly did not bind the British to any specific program. The entire episode is important rather as revealing Nicholas' fears and views than as an indication of British intentions or policies.[44] That it left the czar still in fear and trembling

---

[44] An extreme interpretation is that of Vernon J. Puryear: *England, Russia and the Straits Question, 1844–1856* (Berkeley, 1931), 41 ff., 64 ff. See further G. H. Bolsover: "Nicholas I and the Partition of Turkey" (*Slavonic Review*, XXVII, 1948, 115–148);

is indicated by his conversation with Metternich on New Year's Day, 1847. In the event of a collapse of the Ottoman Empire, he remarked, Russia would covet no territory, but would be content to leave the Balkans and Constantinople to Austria. But, he added with a flare-up of suspicion, if the British or the French should make a move to occupy the Turkish capital, Russian forces would get there first and would stay there.[45]

If Nicholas' prime objective was to keep France isolated, it stands to reason that Guizot was equally intent on breaking out of such isolation. His aim was to restore the Entente Cordiale, the coalition of the liberal powers of the West, and for this policy he was bound to evoke a sympathetic response from the British foreign secretary, Lord Aberdeen, a statesman of conciliatory disposition, ever devoted to peace. The prime minister, Sir Robert Peel, and other prominent Britons were also favorably inclined, for, despite their co-operation with Russia in 1840, many remained uncomfortable in the company of the Holy Alliance and distrustful of the ultimate objectives of Russian policy. In 1840 there had been violent protest against Palmerston's treatment of France by those for whom the alliance with that country was the natural and most congenial one.[46]

Logical though the combination of the liberal powers may have been, there was little popular sentiment on either side to support it. To the British the French remained a troublesome people and, according to Thackeray's *Paris Sketchbook* (1840) and other travel literature, a shockingly immoral people, of whom anything could be expected. For the French, the British were as of old the enemies of French aspirations, the mean-spirited shopkeepers, the ruthless realists. Many eminent writers, such as Tocqueville, Lamartine, Michelet, made no secret of their dislike of the British and their policies.[47]

Much like the entente of the 1830's, that of the 1840's was to suffer

---

Temperley: *Crimea*, 251 ff.; and on the Russian side, Potemkin: *Histoire de la diplomatie*, I, 420 ff.

45 Winter: "Eine bedeutsame Unterredung."

46 Douglas Johnson: *Guizot* (London, 1963), 275 ff.; Raymond Guyot: *La première Entente Cordiale* (Paris, 1927), chaps. vii and viii; A. B. Cunningham: "Peel, Aberdeen and the Entente Cordiale" (*Bulletin of the Institute of Historical Research*, XXX, 1957, 189–206).

47 Llewellyn Woodward: "Les caractères généraux des relations franco-anglaises de 1815 à 1870" (*Revue d'histoire moderne*, XIII, 1938, 110–125).

many strains, despite good intentions in high places. Limitations of space preclude anything but the most summary reference to the disputes that occurred in the economic, colonial and even the strictly political fields. For instance, the British in their intense search for foreign markets were constantly pressing for reductions in the high French tariffs that were, as a matter of fact, designed expressly to keep out the cheaper British manufactures.[48] On the other hand, the British were offended by Guizot's schemes for a customs union between France, Belgium and eventually the Netherlands, Switzerland and Piedmont as a counterweight to the German *Zollverein*. This project, foreshadowing the Common Market of the twentieth century, was pursued vigorously in 1842–1843, only to be wrecked by the pressure brought to bear by Britain, Prussia and Austria on King Leopold, as also by the insistent protests of French industrialists.[49]

For years (1842–1845) French opinion was irritated by the question of slave-trade control, charging the British with trying to monopolize that important activity. But it was the clash of influence and interest in the Mediterranean that caused most enmity. French influence remained dominant in Egypt, while in both Spain and Greece the advent of new cabinets meant French gains at the expense of the British.[50] Furthermore, there was the entirely new problem of naval rivalry and the related one of colonial expansion. The advent of the steamship, independent of wind and tide, meant that British sea power, unchallenged since 1805, called for modernization and revised strategy if it were to retain its ascendancy. In 1844 there appeared in Paris an anonymous pamphlet, actually the work of the Duke of Joinville, the sailor son of Louis Philippe. The author argued that through the introduction of steam-powered warships the French navy could be made the equal of the British and indeed that a landing of troops in England might become possible. Though promptly disavowed by the French king, these effusions were at once translated into English. They made a deep and most unpalatable impression in London, where the fear of invasion

[48] Peter Stearns: "British Industry through the Eyes of French Industrialists, 1820–1848" (*Journal of Modern History*, XXXVII, 1965, 50–61).

[49] Alfred de Ridder: *Les projets d'union douanière franco-belge et les puissances européennes, 1836–1843* (Brussels, 1933); Henry-Thierry Deschamps: *La Belgique devant la France de Juillet: l'opinion et l'attitude françaises de 1839 à 1848* (Paris, 1956); Salvo Mastellone: *La politica estera del Guizot* (Florence, 1957), chaps. iv–vi.

[50] See above, Chapters III, V.

became chronic, despite steps taken to strengthen the naval establishment.[51]

Ominous, too, from the British standpoint, was French activity in North Africa. The decision had been taken in 1834 to retain the foothold established in Algeria in 1830, and systematic colonization, along with military conquest, had been initiated. In 1837 the French captured the important town of Constantine. Still, the British regarded Algeria as a part of the Ottoman Empire. While they did not make an issue of French expansion there, they were determined to oppose any moves against Tunisia or Morocco. The situation became tense after 1840, when the French embarked on a major campaign against Abd el-Kader, a young and energetic religious leader who had rallied Moslem opinion against the French and had come to dominate the western half of the country. Operating from various strong points, General Bugeaud sent out columns that devastated the country and decimated the tribesmen. By 1844 he had driven Abd el-Kader over the frontier into Morocco, where his presence aroused such enthusiasm that the sultan felt impelled to join forces with him.[52]

The British, determined to prevent French intervention in Morocco, had warned the sultan against throwing in his lot with Abd el-Kader, and had secured from Guizot a promise that the French troops, in their operations, would not attempt a permanent occupation of Moroccan territory. The situation therefore became tense when, in August, 1844, a French squadron under Joinville bombarded Tangiers and French forces under Bugeaud invaded Morocco and defeated Abd el-Kader in the Battle of Isly. Fortunately, restraint was shown on both sides, the French withdrawing from Morocco in the following month.[53]

At this very time the area of conflict was extended to the Pacific.

[51] Emil Daniels: "Die Engländer und die Gefahr einer französischen Landung zur Zeit Louis Philippes und Napoleons III" (*Festschrift für Hans Delbrück*, Berlin, 1908, 257–291); Bartlett: *Great Britain and Sea Power*, 155 ff.

[52] Georges Hardy: *Histoire de la colonisation française* (5 ed., Paris, 1947), 176 ff.; Christian Schéfer: *La politique coloniale de la Monarchie de Juillet: l'Algérie et l'évolution de la colonisation française* (Paris, 1928); Paul Azan: *Conquête et pacification de l'Algérie* (Paris, 1931), chaps. x and xi. On Abd el-Kader see the excellent study of Paul Azan: *L'émir magnanime: Abdel-Kader le croyant* (Paris, 1959); and Wilfrid Blunt: *Desert Hawk: Abd el-Kader and the French Conquest of Algeria* (London, 1947).

[53] James E. Swain: *The Struggle for the Control of the Mediterranean prior to 1848* (Boston, 1933), 119 ff.; Francis B. Flournoy: *British Policy towards Morocco in the Age of Palmerston* (Baltimore, 1935), 72 ff.

There, on various islands, French missionaries, traders and whalers were competing with the British, often with marked success. On Tahiti, however, they collided with George Pritchard, the British consul and at the same time the leader of the Protestant missionaries. The details of the ensuing duel are too unimportant to warrant extended treatment. In 1842 Admiral Dupetit-Thouars and a French squadron dragooned the Tahitian queen, Pomaré, into guaranteeing the Catholics freedom of religion and, what was more, into accepting a French protectorate. Naturally this highhanded procedure evoked passionate protests from British missionary and trading circles. Pritchard, following an absence in Australia, returned to his post and induced Pomaré to appeal to Queen Victoria for support. Endless confusion resulted, if only because it took four to six months for news to reach Paris or London from the mid-Pacific. In Tahiti the French admiral deposed Pomaré and proclaimed the annexation of the island to France, an action which the French government at once disavowed. Meanwhile Pritchard did what he could to obstruct the French until, in March, 1844, they arrested and, after four days of imprisonment, deported him. He arrived in England on July 30, to be hailed as a martyr. So excited was public opinion that the prime minister felt obliged to denounce the French action as "a gross outrage accompanied with gross indignity."[54]

The British government demanded satisfaction for the treatment meted out to Pritchard. Guizot, under constant attack by the opposition for his "truckling" to the British, delayed action until the Moroccan crisis could be brought under control. He then expressed regret for what had happened in Tahiti and agreed to compensate Pritchard for whatever damages he had sustained. But Pritchard did not return to the Pacific, and the French within a few years (1847) established their protectorate over Tahiti.

While opinion on both sides of the Channel was kept inflamed by this succession of incidents, the governments, both desirous of peace, managed to keep their heads and the rulers maintained more than just cordial relations. In September, 1843, Queen Victoria and Prince Albert

---

[54] Schéfer: *La politique coloniale*, 363 ff.; J. R. Baldwin: "England and the French Seizure of the Society Islands" (*Journal of Modern History*, X, 1938, 212–231); L. Joré: "George Pritchard, l'adversaire de la France à Tahiti" (*Revue d'histoire des colonies françaises*, 1939).

paid a visit to the French royal family at the Château d'Eu, a visit which Louis Philippe and Queen Amélie returned at Windsor in October, 1844 (see Illustration 19). In September, 1845, the British royal couple again visited at the Château d'Eu. On these occasions pending problems were discussed, especially the overriding dynastic question of the day, the prospective marriage of the Spanish girl queen, Isabella. It was no secret that the British court would have liked to see a Coburg prince (Leopold, born 1824, nephew of the reigning duke of Saxe-Coburg and of King Leopold I of Belgium, and younger brother of Ferdinand, who in 1836 had married Queen Maria II of Portugal) chosen for the honor. But the British foreign secretary, Aberdeen, out of deference for French susceptibilities, was prepared to leave the matter to the decision of the Spaniards themselves. At the first Château d'Eu meeting he and Guizot had come to a gentleman's agreement barring the candidacy of any one of Louis Philippe's sons but specifying that only princes of the Bourbon family should be eligible.[55]

The twentieth-century reader, apt to lose patience over the complicated marriage problems of an unattractive, wayward girl of fourteen, should remember that in the mid-nineteenth century dynastic affairs were still of great importance. Thus the British regarded the possibility of an Orléans prince as altogether unacceptable, while the French were constantly on their guard against the growing power and influence of the Coburg "tribe." So a number of attractive young princes were ruled out and the choice narrowed down to several decidedly unimpressive Bourbons. Prominent among these was Carlos Luis, who, as Count of Montemolín, succeeded to the Carlist claims in 1845. He appealed to the conservative clerical circles in Spain and enjoyed the warm support of the governments of the Holy Alliance. But since his candidacy involved recognition of the Carlist claims, Carlos Luis was anathema to the Spanish court and the liberals.

Among Spanish princes were also the dukes of Cadiz and Seville, sons of the younger brother of the late Ferdinand VII and of Maria Cristina's sister, Carlota. The older, Cadiz, was unprepossessing even as

[55] E. Jones Parry: *The Spanish Marriages, 1841–1846* (London, 1936) is the authoritative account, but must be supplemented with the scholarly study, based on the Spanish Royal Archives, by Maria Teresa Puga: *El matrimonio de Isabel II* (Madrid, 1964); see also Mastellone: *La politica estera del Guizot,* chaps. vii–x; Johnson: *Guizot,* 302 ff. On the personal relations, see Jean Duhamel: *Louis Philippe et la première Entente Cordiale* (Paris, 1951).

THE SPANISH MARRIAGES

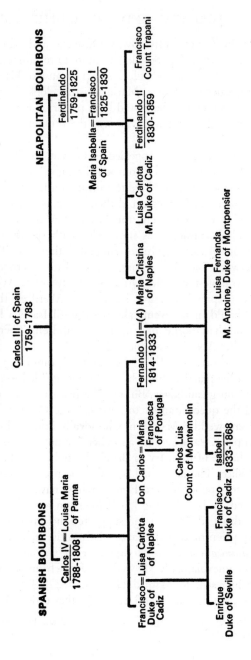

SPANISH BOURBONS

NEAPOLITAN BOURBONS

Carlos III of Spain
1759-1788

Carlos IV = Louisa Maria
1788-1808   of Parma

Francisco = Luisa Carlota
Duke of   of Naples
Cadiz

Don Carlos = Maria
                   Francesca
                   of Portugal

Carlos Luis
Count of Montemolin

Fernando VII = (4) Maria Cristina
1814-1833   of Naples

Francisco = Isabel II
Duke of Cadiz 1833-1868

Enrique
Duke of Seville

Luisa Fernanda
M. Antoine, Duke of Montpensier

Ferdinando I
1759-1825

Maria Isabella = Francisco I
of Spain   1825-1830

Luisa Carlota
M. Duke of Cadiz

Ferdinando II
1830-1859

Francisco
Count Trapani

Bourbon princes went. His downy mustache and falsetto voice made him seem the perfect fop. Seville had more to recommend him, but was regarded in royal circles as a black sheep because of his liberal leanings. The young queen's mother, Maria Cristina, looked upon both these princes with contempt. She would have preferred her own sixteen-year-old brother, Count Trapani, who was the brother also of the king of Naples.

The Trapani candidacy appealed to Guizot, for it would bring the Kingdom of Naples into a "Bourbon Triangle" or Occidental League dominating the western Mediterranean under French leadership: "France, Spain and Naples could then move as one their fifty million inhabitants."[56] Unfortunately, the Neapolitan Bourbons were not interested and the project was unpopular with the Spanish public. To make it more attractive, Guizot suggested the possibility of a second match, between Isabella's younger sister, Luisa Fernanda, and Louis Philippe's youngest son, the Duke of Montpensier. At the second Eu conference (September, 1845) he assured Aberdeen that this second marriage should in no event take place until Isabella had been safely married and had borne one or more children. There was no fast agreement, but Aberdeen acquiesced.

The delays occasioned by the Trapani candidacy and Isabella's eagerness to be married "somehow to someone" led to renewed discussion of a Coburg candidacy. Bulwer, the British ambassador at Madrid, persuaded the queen mother to approach the Coburg family, but was at once disavowed by Aberdeen, who loyally informed Guizot of what had taken place. Paris became apprehensive nonetheless when, in June, 1846, the change of ministry in Britain brought back Palmerston to the Foreign Office. The latter had for years been criticizing Aberdeen for his conciliatory policy toward France, whose naval and colonial policies he distrusted. Guizot, fearing lest Palmerston revive the Coburg candidacy, now dropped Trapani and supported the Duke of Cadiz, suggesting to the queen mother that as a solatium the Infanta Luisa might be married *simultaneously* to Montpensier. It was at this juncture that Palmerston unexplainably showed the French ambassador a dispatch which he had sent to Madrid (July 19, 1846), listing as appropriate candidates Coburg, Cadiz and Seville in that order. Palmerston seems

---

[56] These Mediterranean designs are discussed in detail by Mastellone: *La politica estera del Guizot,* chap. viii.

to have had but little interest in the Coburg aspirations, but was intent of wrecking the Montpensier project. So he now put forward the liberal, pro-British Duke of Seville for Isabella's hand and suggested Coburg as a possible husband for Luisa.

The final solution was to inflict upon Isabella the least desirable of the candidates (one can hardly call them suitors). The queen mother, frightened by the prospect of a *Progresista* regime, requested the French to arrange for the marriage of the queen with Cadiz, and to "associate" with this project the marriage of Luisa to Montpensier. The French king was reluctant to go back on his engagements to the British court, but Guizot finally persuaded him that Palmerston's revival of the Coburg candidacy had nullified all previous commitments. On August 28 Isabella, weeping copiously, was dragooned into accepting her unattractive cousin. On October 10, 1846, the double nuptials took place.

Guizot, it is said, regarded the Spanish marriages as a master stroke on his part, as French revenge for the isolation imposed by Palmerston in 1840. He was evidently surprised by the virulence of Palmerston's reaction, and even more by that of the British court and people, who resented what they took to be his double-dealing. If indeed he was so purblind, events were soon to show him that his schemes and maneuvers had ruined relations with Britain beyond repair. Thenceforth Palmerston not only rejected all efforts to revive co-operation but made a point of obstructing and thwarting French policy everywhere and on all occasions.

The Holy Alliance, now relieved of the Entente Cordiale, took immediate advantage of the new situation to extinguish the little Republic of Cracow, which, in violation of the treaties of 1815, was now annexed to Austria. The background for this coup was provided by the uprising of the Poles in Galicia in February, 1846. The peasantry (mostly Ruthenian), far from supporting the insurgents, turned upon their Polish landlords, set fire to the manor houses and slew some 2,000 members of the landlord class in what was one of the most savage outbreaks of class hatred in modern European history.[57]

[57] Ludwig von Mises: *Die Entwicklung des gutsherrlich-bäuerlichen Verhältnisses in Galizien, 1772–1848* (Vienna, 1902); Hanns Schlitter: *Aus Oesterreichs Vormärz: I, Galizien und Krakau* (Vienna, 1920); Stefan Kieniewicz: "The Social Visage of Poland in 1848" (*Slavonic and East European Review*, XXVII, 1948–1949, 91–105); Jerome Blum: *Noble Landowners and Agriculture in Austria, 1815–1848* (Baltimore, 1948),

The Poles at once charged the Austrian authorities with having encouraged the attacks on the Galician gentry, a charge which liberals and radicals everywhere were only too ready to repeat. It was true that some local officials, badly frightened by the Polish insurrection, had called on the peasants for help, and there were a few cases where the peasants were rewarded for bringing in rebels dead or alive. But the Austrian government as such certainly did nothing to provoke massacre. Metternich, though pleased to learn that the peasants had refused to join in the uprising, was deeply shocked by news of the horrible outrages that followed.[58]

Cracow had long been a center of Polish conspiracy and one of the first acts of the insurgents in February, 1846, was to proclaim a provisional government there. This government was quickly liquidated by Austrian and Prussian troops that marched in and took over. Czar Nicholas now insisted that this hotbed of revolution be suppressed by annexation to Galicia, that is, to Austria. But Metternich, reluctant to break the public law of Europe, embarked on long-winded negotiations to secure the consent of Britain and France. Guizot tried hard to induce Palmerston to join him in opposition, but the latter declined joint action. In the end the western powers filed separate, relatively mild protests.[59]

Since co-operation with Britain had obviously become hopeless, Guizot reverted to a policy dear to Louis Philippe and conservative circles, namely a *rapprochement* with Austria which would strengthen the position of the dynasty. He dispatched secret agents to Vienna to assure Metternich of France's readiness to adopt a truly conservative policy in international affairs. The Austrian chancellor was wary of

---

225 ff.; R. F. Leslie: "Polish Left-Wing Political Tactics, 1831–1846" (*Slavonic Review,* XXXIII, 1954, 120–139).

[58] Heinrich von Srbik: *Metternich, der Staatsmann und der Mensch* (Munich, 1925), II, 151 ff.; and the judicious treatment of the subject in Lewis B. Namier: *1848: the Revolution of the Intellectuals* (London, 1944), 15 ff. That the charge against the Vienna government is not yet dead is shown by J. Feldman: "The Polish Provinces of Austria and Prussia" (in *Cambridge History of Poland,* II, 352 ff.); Oscar Halecki: *A History of Poland* (New York, 1943), 236.

[59] Marcel Szarota: *Die letzten Tage der Republik Krakau* (Breslau, 1910), to be supplemented with the writings of Schlitter and Srbik, and by Stefan Kieniewicz: "The Free State of Cracow, 1815–1846" (*Slavonic and East European Review,* XXVI, 1947–1948, 69–89); Élie Halévy: "Palmerston et Guizot, 1846–1848" (*Revue des sciences politiques,* LIX, 1936, 321–346).

definite commitments, but was understandably pleased by the assurance that, in the Swiss crisis as in the affairs of Italy, France would work with rather than against Austria.[60]

In the Swiss crisis, which has already been dealt with in an earlier chapter,[61] France definitely aligned itself with Austria and the Holy Alliance in support of the Sonderbund, while Britain made no secret of its sympathy with the federal Diet, now controlled by the radicals (i.e., liberals). It is clear that neither France nor Austria dared go so far as to intervene because of the position taken by the British. Palmerston, for his part, did not share the widely held opinion that in the event of armed conflict the Sonderbund would be victorious. Nonetheless, he kept warning the Diet against precipitating war, pointing out the serious danger of international complications. When the war did break out, in October, 1847, Guizot proposed a collective *démarche* calling for the cessation of hostilities and the settlement of political questions (reform of the federal constitution) in conference with the five powers responsible for the arrangements of 1815. Palmerston then proposed a number of changes and several weeks were spent in arriving at agreement. When finally a joint note was ready, the British decided not to submit it to Berne (as the others did), on the plea that the victory of the federal forces over the Sonderbund made it superfluous. It has been supposed by many writers that Palmerston, intent not only on protecting the federal Diet against intervention but also on frustrating Guizot's efforts, purposely complicated and delayed action on the joint note. But there is little serious evidence to support this thesis. The British, siding with the Diet, raised altogether legitimate objections to Guizot's original draft, and communications with Switzerland were still slow in the pre-telegraphic days. On the other hand, the victory of the federal forces was not only unexpected but incredibly swift, leaving inadequate time for the governments to concert action. In the last analysis, however, Guizot and the conservative powers shared in the defeat of the Sonderbund, while Britain and the liberals everywhere exulted in the spectacular triumph of their principles.[62]

[60] Pietro Silva: "La politica francese in Italia nell'epoca delle riforme, 1846–1848 e l'accordo Metternich-Guizot" (*Revue des études italiennes*, I, 1936, 276–295).

[61] See above, Chapter IV.

[62] Edgar Bonjour: *Geschichte der schweizerischen Neutralität* (Basel, 1946), the best general diplomatic history; Arnold Winkler: "Metternich und die Schweiz" (*Zeitschrift für schweizerische Geschichte*, VII, 1927, 60–116, 126–163); Carl Eckinger: *Lord*

In Italy, too, Guizot and Palmerston found themselves on opposite sides, the former supporting Austrian policy and opposing the aspirations of Piedmont and the nationalists, while the latter encouraged the proponents of liberalism and unification. In October, 1847, Palmerston sent Lord Minto, a member of the government, on a special mission to Rome, Florence and Turin. Minto sustained the pope in his efforts at reform and warned him against appeals to Austria or France for support against revolutionary pressures. During his six months' stay he worked also for a customs union which might serve as a base for "national and united sentiment," but the importance of his rather unusual mission has often been exaggerated.[63]

Palmerston und der schweizer Sonderbundskrieg (Berlin, 1938); Margrit Hatze: "Lord Palmerstons Stellung zur Sonderbundskrise" (*Schweizer Rundschau*, XLVII, 1947–1948, 305–314); Ann G. Imlah: *Britain and Switzerland, 1845–1860* (London, 1966), 19 ff.

[63] Letizia Falcone: "La missione di Lord Minto" (*Giornale di politica e di letteratura*, V, 1929, 636–652); A. J. P. Taylor: *The Italian Problem in European Diplomacy, 1847–1849* (Manchester, 1934), 24 ff.; Ottavio Barié: *L'Inghilterra e il problema italiano, 1846–1848* (Milan, 1955).

Chapter Ten

1848: THE SECOND REPUBLIC

I. THE EVE OF UPHEAVAL

It HAS been perhaps too readily assumed that the revolutions which broke over the Continent in 1848 reflected the rising power of the middle class and its determination to force the recalcitrant governments to accept liberal reforms and constitutional government. Tocqueville's great speech in the Chamber of Deputies on January 27, 1848, in which he warned of the danger of social as well as political revolution, has been frequently quoted as prophetic. But a passage in Tocqueville's *Recollections,* frequently overlooked, tends more or less to deflate the importance of his address, for he remarks that in the political melee of the time it was common practice to charge one's opponents with endangering society. For that reason his warnings were met with ironical sneers as well as with applause. Tocqueville admits, furthermore, that he was not actually as alarmed as he claimed to be; that in fact he did not expect so early or so formidable an uprising. While perceiving the general factors making for revolution, he did not, he confesses, foresee the accidents which were to precipitate it.[1]

Since it was the revolution in Paris on February 22, 1848, that set the spark for the European conflagration, it is essential to understand its causes and origins. In the first place, it should be remembered that in France the well-to-do or upper middle class had gathered the fruits of the July Revolution of 1830 and that the July Monarchy represented the type of liberal government established in Britain in 1832 and aspired to by the rising middle classes in other countries. There was from the outset opposition to this regime on the part of intellectuals (writers, artists, lawyers, doctors, educated workers), who regarded it as too restricted and who in any case resented their exclusion from political life for lack of sufficient income. Parenthetically, it might be remarked that

---

[1] J. P. Mayer, ed.: *The Recollections of Alexis de Tocqueville* (New York, 1959), 13–15; see also Edward T. Gargan: *Alexis de Tocqueville: the Critical Years, 1848–1851* (Washington, 1955), 55 ff.

perhaps the most serious error committed by the governments of that time was the refusal to extend the franchise to this able, articulate and influential element of the population. Politically speaking, the opposition in France was nothing more than a parliamentary group, that is, a faction within the ruling class. Basically it objected to Guizot's monopoly of power and hoped to break his control by agitating for electoral reform. But even the more advanced wing of this "dynastic" opposition, the group around the newspaper *La Réforme,* though it advocated universal suffrage and some social legislation, was by no means revolutionary. Socialist writers, such as Louis Blanc, regarded revolution as premature and therefore doomed to failure resulting in a serious setback. All these men, from the parliamentary opponents of the regime, such as Thiers and Odilon Barrot, to the socialists, followed the career of Cobden and his Anti-Corn Law League. They hoped through propaganda and peaceful agitation to wear down the resistance to reform on the part of the government. The whole program of political banquets, also modeled on the British, was intended to open the way to a peaceful victory.[2]

In the Central European countries the professional and business classes were still striving to secure the type of political regime which already existed in France and Britain. The strength of the liberal movement varied from state to state, but the demand for the abolition of privilege and the introduction of constitutional government was common to all. Furthermore, the liberal program was everywhere a peaceful one, and everywhere it was beginning to bear fruit by 1848. In France most of the prominent deputies had joined the ranks of the opposition, and the National Guard, designed as the shield of the regime against revolution, was turning against it. It is hard to believe that the king and his prime minister could much longer have withstood the pressure from their opponents. In Germany the liberals of the Rhineland and Westphalia had become so insistent on reform that even the obstinate Prussian king was beginning to give way. Even in Vienna, the headquarters of reaction, many officials were in the ranks of the liberal opposition and in the court, too, there were advocates of reform. The dismissal of Metternich had by 1848 become a question

[2] Stanislas Mitard: *Les origines du radicalisme démocratique* (Paris, 1952), chap. iii; Alvin R. Calman: *Ledru-Rollin and the Second French Republic* (New York, 1922), 23 ff.; Leo R. Loubère: *Louis Blanc* (Evanston, 1960), 55 ff.; John J. Baughman: "The French Banquet Campaign of 1847–1848" (*Journal of Modern History,* XXXI. 1959, 1–15).

merely of time. As for Italy, the liberals there enjoyed the personal inspiration provided by Cobden's visit and Lord Minto's mission. They fully expected to realize their political program through peaceful agitation. The victory of the constitutional movement in the opening months of 1848 seemed to justify their expectations.[3]

There were, of course, genuinely revolutionary forces in Europe, as described in the foregoing chapters. But they were neither as numerous nor as well organized as the governments believed. The rulers, ever mindful of the French Revolution and the execution of Louis XVI, sat uneasily upon their thrones. They lived in chronic fear of secret societies and conspiracies aimed at themselves and at the whole political-social order. Actually the secret societies, even in Paris, were relatively weak in numbers and more or less paralyzed by dissension. They lacked leadership and clear programs. Their time had not yet come, as those clearheaded revolutionaries, Marx and Engels, were quick to realize. While trying to organize urban workers and unite them, they recognized that hopes of an early proletarian victory were illusory. They argued, therefore, that the correct strategy would be to support the *bourgeoisie* in its campaign to destroy the remnants of the feudal order, and thereafter to make war on it in its turn.

One is left then with the interesting problem of explaining how revolutions could break out in France and other countries and how they could triumph so easily. That the various governments had at their disposal the armed forces needed to suppress insurgency there can be no doubt. In France, for example, serious outbreaks had been beaten down on various occasions during the 1830's. And Czar Nicholas showed how, when confronted with seething discontent, one could escape revolution by using huge numbers of troops to snuff out opposition wherever it appeared and before it could attain dangerous proportions. By the application of ruthless measures he could even play the role of "gendarme of Europe."[4]

[3] Veit Valentin: *Geschichte der deutschen Revolution von 1848–1849* (Berlin, 1930), I, 400 ff., 416–417; Jacques Droz: *Les révolutions allemandes de 1848* (Paris, 1957), 71–83; Rudolf Stadelmann: *Soziale und politische Geschichte der Revolution von 1848* (Munich, 1948), 6 ff.; Heinrich von Srbik: *Metternich, der Staatsmann und der Mensch* (Munich, 1925), II, 259 ff.; Rudolf Kiszling: *Die Revolution im Kaisertum Oesterreich, 1848–1849* (Vienna, 1948–1952), I, 35.

[4] A. S. Nifontov: *Russland im Jahre 1848* (Berlin, 1954); Benjamin Goriely: "La Russie de Nicolas I en 1848" (in François Fetjö, ed.: *Le printemps des peuples*, Paris, 1948, 355–394); and especially John S. Curtis: *The Russian Army under Nicholas I* (Durham, 1965), chap. xi.

Other rulers, however, were more reluctant to have the troops shoot upon the populace and, what was more, they could not be sure that the troops would do so. The common soldiers of the new conscript armies could not be relied upon to fire upon their unarmed fellow citizens, as was shown in 1830 when two regiments of Marshal Marmont's forces defected in the very heart of Paris, and similar incidents took place in some of the disturbances in Germany. What this meant in effect was that the governments, while they had adequate military forces available, hesitated about using them, the more so as the new technique of barricade fighting, made possible by the paving blocks with which the streets were paved and the availability of other material for effective obstruction, greatly complicated the business of urban disorder.[5] One of the striking features of the revolutions of 1848 was the failure of the authorities to use the means of suppression which were at their disposal.

In retrospect it is hard to understand how the governments and the opposition elements could have been so purblind as to underestimate the dangers of truly popular insurrection. Much has already been said of the overcrowding of the cities, the unemployment and general misery of the lower classes. But all this must be underlined in speaking of the years 1846 and 1847, which were probably the worst of the entire century in terms of want and human suffering. For to the chronic hardships of the workers were added the tribulations resulting from crop failures, financial crisis and business depression. In the autumn of 1845 the potatoes, on which in many localities the lower classes depended for their food supply, suddenly turned black, became mushy and to a large extent inedible. It was an unknown disease, later identified as a fungus. In the following year the potato crop was again an almost complete failure. It was somewhat less disastrous in 1847, but again very poor in 1848. And to compound the food crisis, the grain crops, too, were below average in these years, so that the prices of wheat and rye quickly rose till they were double those of the preceding decade.[6]

[5] For greater detail, see the author's article "The Pattern of Urban Revolution in 1848" (in Evelyn M. Acomb and Marvin L. Brown, Jr., eds.: *French Society and Culture since the Old Regime,* New York, 1966, 90–118).

[6] T. P. O'Neill: "The Scientific Investigation of the Failure of the Potato Crop in Ireland, 1845–1846" (*Irish Historical Studies,* V, 1946, 123–138).

In Ireland, as might be expected, the potato famine led to one of the greatest tragedies of the century. Over 21,000 people died of actual starvation, while much larger numbers were taken off by hunger diseases such as typhus, dysentery and cholera, of which the latter occurred in violent epidemic form in 1849. It has been estimated that the "great hunger" claimed a million and a half victims, while another two hundred thousand fled annually on the typhus-stricken "plague ships," only to find a watery grave before reaching their destination. Travelers in Ireland saw corpses lying by the roadside and found the dead unburied in their deserted hovels. Everywhere strangers were besieged by starving, naked, desperate wretches (see Illustration 36). The 1851 Census reported that "the starving people lived upon the carcasses of diseased cattle, upon dogs, and dead horses, but principally upon the herbs of the field, nettle tops, wild mustard, and water-cresses. In some places dead bodies were found with grass in their mouths."[7]

During the famine England continued to import from Ireland large quantities of foodstuffs, even grain, which has led indignant critics to charge the London authorities with deliberately allowing the crisis to run its course in the hope of reducing the Irish population.[8] Although this charge is probably unwarranted, it is a fact that the British government was so deeply committed to the principles of private enterprise that it was most dilatory in taking relief action. At first it imported modest amounts of maize from America and sold them at low prices, and ultimately it set up a fairly extensive program of public works and introduced direct relief in the form of soup kitchens. But all these measures were taken without conviction. The prime minister, Lord John Russell, thought the idea of feeding a whole nation fantastic and was troubled about disturbing industry and trade by special grain

---

[7] Quoted in John E. Pomfret: *The Struggle for Land in Ireland, 1800–1923* (Princeton, 1930), 34. See also Lord Dufferin and G. F. Boyle: *Narrative of a Journey from Oxford to Skibereen* (London, 1847). The classic account of the famine is J. O'Rourke: *The History of the Irish Famine of 1847* (Dublin, 1875). There is a more recent, splendid co-operative study edited by R. D. Edwards and T. D. Williams: *The Great Famine* (Dublin, 1956), and a reliable, vividly written account by Cecil Woodham-Smith: *The Great Hunger* (London, 1962). On the horrors of the plague ships, see Arnold Shrier: *Ireland and the American Emigration* (Minneapolis, 1958), 157; and especially Oliver MacDonagh: *A Pattern of Government Growth, 1800–1860* (London, 1961).

[8] Francis Hackett: *The Story of the Irish Nation* (New York, 1922), 267 ff.; Edwards and Williams, *Great Famine*, viii–ix.

imports and public works. Charles E. Trevelyan, the official most directly responsible, was convinced that the situation must be left to "the operation of natural causes." The record of the government was certainly unedifying, but it was probably due more to "obtuseness, short-sightedness and ignorance" than downright heartlessness.[9]

On the Continent the crisis was only a little less disastrous than in Ireland. In Flanders many people were eating roots, grasses and carrion, and many others died of starvation and disease. By 1847 some 700,000 persons in Belgium were on public relief, while unknown numbers were succored by private charity. Thousands of wretched workers invaded the industral regions of northern France in search of work at almost any wage, only to be soon turned back over the frontier.[10]

In Germany the plight of the populations was such that the governments were obliged to import grain, open soup kitchens and provide employment through public works. Nonetheless serious food riots known as the "potato war" broke out in the spring of 1847 in Berlin and other cities (see Illustration 53). Barricades were thrown up and eventually troops had to be called out to quell the rioting. In Vienna, too, the workers attacked and plundered the foodshops before the government provided relief through the opening of soup kitchens.[11]

Unrest in France, too, produced food riots and attacks on grain transports, which in some localities had to be protected by troops. In Paris the price of bread rose by 50 per cent between 1845 and 1847, while the price of potatoes just about doubled.[12] Presently the situation

---

[9] Woodham-Smith: *Great Hunger*, chap. vii. Charles E. Trevelyan: *The Irish Crisis* (London, 1848) is practically an official defense. See further E. Strauss: *Irish Nationalism and British Democracy* (London, 1951), 85 ff.; Edwards and Williams: *Great Famine*, chap. iv.

[10] G. Jacquemyns: *Histoire de la crise économique des Flandres, 1845–1850* (Brussels, 1929), especially Books II and III; M. Défourny: "Histoire sociale" (in *Histoire de la Belgique contemporaine*, Brussels, 1928–1930, II, 258 ff.); Laurent Dechesne: *Histoire économique et sociale de la Belgique* (Paris, 1932), 418 ff.

[11] Sigmund Fleischmann: *Die Agrarkrise von 1845–1855* (Heidelberg, 1902); Jürgen Kuczynski: *Die Bewegung der deutschen Wirtschaft von 1800 bis 1946* (Berlin, 1947), 59 ff.; Theodore S. Hamerow: *Restoration, Revolution, Reaction* (Princeton, 1958), 77 ff.; and on Austria, Ernst von Zenker: *Die Wiener Revolution in ihren sozialen Voraussetzungen und Beziehungen* (Vienna, 1897), 96 ff.; Julius Marx: "Die Wirtschaftslage im deutschen Oesterreich vor dem Ausbruch der Revolution, 1848" (*Vierteljahrschrift für Sozial- und Wirtschaftsgeschichte*, XXXI, 1938, 242–282).

[12] Jeanne Singer-Kérel: *Le coût de la vie à Paris de 1840 à 1954* (Paris, 1961), 454, 462 ff.

was aggravated by a financial crisis and a business depression, which were much discussed but not fully understood.[13] The inevitable result was a rapid rise in the rate of unemployment. Thousands of workers, already faced with prohibitive food prices, had to rely on charity or public relief to keep body and soul together.[14]

Many writers, including Karl Marx, attributed the outbreak of revolution in 1848 to the misery and desperation of the masses.[15] This is true to a large extent, though the role and responsibility of the middle class should not be lost from view. Their demonstrations were often the occasion for the popular outbreaks. The banquet campaign of the French opposition illustrates the point perfectly. While the dining and speechmaking were the affair of those who could pay ten francs, huge numbers of non-diners gathered to listen to the denunciations of the government and the demands for reform. The opposition unwittingly fanned the discontent of the masses without realizing the implications. Thiers was one of the few who objected to the banquet program, saying that he could see the red flag of the revolution under the banquet tables. But for the most part the government and the opposition were alike oblivious of the tremors already shaking society. As late as January, 1848, Louis Philippe is reported to have said to his Belgian relatives that he was so firmly in the saddle that "neither banquets of cold veal nor Bonaparte could unseat him."[16] And at the very same time the leaders of the dynastic opposition who were planning the monster Paris banquet actually called upon the populace

---

[13] Bertrand Gille: "Les crises vues par la presse économique et financière, 1815–1848" (*Revue d'histoire moderne*, XI, 1964, 5–30); T. J. Markovitch: "La crise de 1847–1848 dans les industries parisiennes" (*Revue d'histoire économique et sociale*, XLIII, 1965, 256–260).

[14] Henri Sée: *Histoire économique de la France* (Paris, 1951), II, 142 ff.; and the valuable studies collected by Ernest Labrousse, *Aspects de la crise et de la dépression de l'économie française, 1846–1851* (Paris, 1956), together with the lengthy review by Charles Pouthas in the *Revue d'histoire moderne et contemporaine*, IV, 1957, 309–316. See also Arthur L. Dunham: "Unrest in France in 1848" (*Journal of Economic History*, Suppl., VIII, 1948, 74–84); and on the situation in the northern industrial areas, the articles assembled in the *Revue du Nord* (XXXVIII, 1956).

[15] See Ernest Labrousse: "1848, 1830, 1789: comment naissent les révolutions" (*Actes du Congrès Historique du Centenaire de la Révolution de 1848*, Paris, 1948, 1–30); François Fejtö: "L'Europe à la veille des révolutions" (in his *Le printemps des peuples*, Paris, 1948, I, 25–126).

[16] Quoted by Brison D. Gooch: *Belgium and the February Revolution* (The Hague, 1963), 18.

to demonstrate, so as to make the function more impressive. Political myopia and stupidity could hardly be carried further.

2. FRANCE: THE FEBRUARY REVOLUTION

The French Revolution of 1848 was, like that of 1830, a matter of "three glorious days" of rioting and barricade fighting. It was the work of the opposition leaders, both inside the outside the Parliament, whose objective was to force Guizot from office and impose upon the king a cabinet that would put through political reforms. The occasion for the demonstrations was a monster banquet, to be held in Paris on February 22, 1848, with reduced rates to attract members of the lower middle class. The government, having first prohibited the project, agreed that it might be held in a well-to-do neighborhood, near the Champs Elysées, but only symbolically: that is, the banqueters were to disband at once on orders of the police and then test the legality of such assemblies in the courts. Many of the opposition leaders became soured on the whole enterprise, fearing it might have unwanted consequences, but a hard core of activists, such as Ledru-Rollin and others of the *Réforme* group, insisted on accepting the government's challenge. They called on the populace to assemble on the morning of February 22 at the Place de la Madeleine and invited the National Guard to join in a grand procession preceding the banquet. Deputies, National Guards in formation (though unarmed), students, and journalists were to march together up the Champs Elysées to the banqueting place. News of these arrangements, when it appeared in the newspapers, struck fears into the hearts of most of the opposition, who in a hastily convoked meeting, voted by a large majority to drop the whole business, parade, banquet and all. Even the most advanced newspapers now counseled the people to avoid trouble, to observe legality, and to deny the government a bloody success. Only a few, the poet Lamartine among them, stuck to the plan. He would march, declared Lamartine, though accompanied only by his shadow.[17]

Doubts as to the wisdom of the enterprise proved fully warranted.

[17] John J. Baughman: "The French Banquet Campaign of 1847–1848" (*Journal of Modern History*, XXXI, 1959, 1–15). On the February events, still the fullest study is that of Albert Crémieux: *La Révolution de février* (Paris, 1912). There are several more succinct and lively accounts, such as Maurice Soulié: *Les journées de février* (Paris, 1929); Jean Bruhat's book of the same title (Paris, 1948); and most recently the stimulating essay by Georges Duveau: *1848: the Making of a Revolution* (New York, 1967).

On the morning of February 22 a substantial crowd collected on the Place de la Madeleine, despite the cold and rainy weather. Presently a group of students appeared from the Left Bank and led a contingent to the Chamber of Deputies, where they were turned back by the police. Soon the crowds became unruly: street lamps were broken, omnibuses overturned, and efforts made to throw up barricades. However, the disturbances were desultory and sporadic. The police, occasionally supported by troops, seemed quite capable of dealing with the rioters and their barricades. In the evening the troops were ordered back to their barracks, which were scattered throughout the city. The king congratulated his ministers on their handling of the situation.[18]

It is little short of amazing that the situation should have been viewed with so much equanimity in court circles, for even though the crowds were as yet shouting only for the dismissal of Guizot and the adoption of reforms, the plight of the populace was certainly common knowledge and it could hardly have been supposed that the fracas would end with the pillage of gunshops and a few futile efforts to construct barricades. Furthermore, the Paris police, consisting chiefly of the Municipal Guard, was never intended to cope with larger disturbances. It numbered only about 3,500 men, mostly former soldiers, organized militarily in sixteen companies of infantry and five squadrons of cavalry. This Municipal Guard was renowned for its toughness and brutality, but its function, according to the prefect of police, was to prevent crime and forestall disturbances rather than to suppress them. Under the French system it was the National Guard, numbering in Paris about 80,000 and organized by legions (one for each of the twelve *arrondissements,* plus an elite cavalry legion), that was responsible primarily for protection of the regime. The National Guard was basically a bourgeois organization, hence meant to be the mainstay of the bourgeois monarchy. It had performed well in the early 1830's, but since 1840 had become more and more disaffected, so that by 1848 most of the legions were on the side of the opposition, not necessarily hostile to the monarchy, but certainly hostile to Guizot. The garrison troops, some 30,000 in number, were intended only for use in extreme situations, if called upon by the National Guard. In a nutshell, then, the

---

[18] Sébastien Charléty: *La Monarchie de Juillet* (Paris, 1921) is still one of the best accounts. The valuable police report for February 22 has now been published by Jean Tulard: *La préfecture de police sous la Monarchie de Juillet* (Paris, 1964), 168 ff.

police force, while excellent and devoted, was too small to handle a large-scale uprising. The troops were meant only for use as a reserve. All then depended on the National Guard, which was known to be discontented and unreliable. It is impossible to understand the optimism prevalent in government circles on the evening of February 22 without assuming that Louis Philippe expected that the Guard, when officially called out, would stand by the regime.[19]

On the morning of February 23, despite the foul weather, the crowds were larger than ever. The center of disturbance moved from the open avenues of the west to the old, congested, narrow streets of the center, where barricades could more easily be built. The mood of the people, too, had become more aggressive. To the shouts of "down with Guizot" and "long live reform" were now added denunciation of the king and the dynasty. The National Guard proved itself utterly ineffectual from the government standpoint. Even the legions from the wealthiest districts joined in the demand for reform. Those from the poorer sections were alarmingly radical. To quote an eminent French historian, the government, faced by a leaderless, amorphous riot, called up the National Guard and thereby created another, armed and official, riot. Naturally frightened by the almost total defection of the *bourgeoisie*, Louis Philippe in the early afternoon precipitately and unceremoniously dismissed Guizot.[20]

Had the king now called opposition leaders such as Thiers or Barrot to form a ministry, the situation might have been saved. But he disliked Thiers and detested the idea of reform. So matters remained in suspense while the disorders became more and more widespread and violent. Eyewitnesses are agreed that the Municipal Guard fought valiantly and well. But 3,500 men could hardly master the situation, the more so as the National Guardsmen openly fraternized with the rioters. As for the troops, they were badly shaken by the unwillingness

[19] On the police, Paul Pichon: *Histoire et organisation des services de police en France* (Issoudun, 1949), 88 ff., and especially Tulard: *La préfecture de police*, 61 ff. On the National Guard, the excellent monograph of Louis Girard: *La garde nationale, 1814–1871* (Paris, 1964); and on the troops, Jean Vidalenc: "L'armée française sous la Monarchie Constitutionelle" (*Information historique*, XI, 1949, 57–62).

[20] Charléty: *La Monarchie de Juillet*, 389. Crémieux: *La Révolution de février*, chap. iv, contains an analysis of the attitude of the various Guard legions. See also Girard: *La garde nationale*, 284 ff.; Adeline Daumard: *La bourgeoisie parisienne de 1815 à 1848* (Paris, 1963), 595 ff.

of the National Guard to play its assigned role. Without clear directives, army officers became discouraged and the troops demoralized.[21]

Events took a turn for the worse when, on the evening of February 23, a surging mob, accompanied by National Guards, collided with a detachment of troops on the Boulevard des Capucines (see Illustration 58). The troops, hard pressed, became panicky and opened fire, with the result that forty or fifty persons were left dead or wounded on the pavement. The populace, furious over this "massacre," paraded the dead through the town and spent the night in preparations to resist the government's alleged plan to slaughter the workers. To the wild sound of the tocsin, well over a million paving stones were torn up and over 4,000 trees felled to build the more than 1,500 barricades that by morning studded the city (see Illustration 59).[22]

When finally the king came to a decision, it was one that involved contradictory action. On the one hand he called on Thiers and Barrot to form a ministry, which was meant as a gesture of conciliation, and on the other he appointed General Bugeaud, the victor of the Algerian campaigns and a soldier itching to put "the rabble" in its place, to command both the troops and the National Guard, an obviously provocative move.[23] Both steps proved utterly futile. Thiers, who had greeted the downfall of Guizot with enthusiasm as ridding him of a hated opponent without jeopardizing the regime, found himself on the morning of February 24 swept along the streets by a menacing crowd and was, by the time he reached the Chamber of Deputies, so unnerved that he refused to take part in the debates and hurried back to his home by a roundabout route. His companion reported him as almost out of his wits, gesticulating, sobbing, uttering incoherent phrases.[24]

The fire-eating Bugeaud fared no better. He tried hard, on the morning of the 24th, to reopen communications between key points of the city, but failed, chiefly because of the almost complete defection of the National Guard and the demoralization of the troops, many of whom abandoned their weapons to the insurgents. By noon he was obliged to give up the attempt and proclaim a cease-fire. Louis Philippe made a last effort to rally at least some of the legions of the National

[21] P. Chalmin: "La crise morale de l'armée française" (in *L'armée et la Séconde République*, Paris, 1955, 27–76).

[22] Henri Guillemin: *La tragédie de quarante-huit* (Paris, 1948).

[23] Pierre de La Gorce: *Louis Philippe* (Paris, 1931), 403.

[24] Alexis de Tocqueville: *Recollections*, 60.

Guard and, having failed, decided to abdicate and flee the country. Only in disguise and secrecy was the royal family able to reach Le Havre and embark for England.

In the last analysis the bourgeois National Guard, organized solely to protect the dynasty and the regime, had become disgusted with both and had proved altogether unwilling to fight for it. Tocqueville quotes one guardsman as saying: "We don't want to get killed for people who have managed their business so badly." Not that the middle classes, either in or out of Parliament, had wanted a revolution. On the contrary, they feared disorders. But they had themselves aroused the populace with banquets and demonstrations, and appear to have thought, even in the February days, that they could manage the people once Guizot had been gotten rid of. The revolution was a remarkably bloodless one. On the government side there were only eighty dead, and on the popular side about 290. As revolutions go, this one proved mild because the resistance was so ineffectual.[25]

The tumult of February, 1848, ended with the insurgent assault on the Tuileries Palace, only minutes after the precipitate departure of the king and his family (see Illustration 43). Meeting with little resistance, the crowd overran the palace, threw the throne into the courtyard and wrecked the furnishings: "The common herd ironically wrapped themselves up in laces and cashmeres. Gold fringes were rolled around the sleeves of blouses. Hats with ostrich feathers adorned blacksmiths' heads, and ribbons of the Legion of Honor supplied waistbands for prostitutes" (Flaubert).

Meanwhile several members of the more moderate opposition (those of the newspaper Le National) had worked out a plan for a regency. Louis Philippe had abdicated in favor of his nine-year-old grandson, the Count of Paris, whose father had been killed in a carriage accident some years before. Since his uncle, the Duke of Nemours, was an archconservative and extremely unpopular, it was the idea of Barrot, the most recently appointed premier, that the boy's mother, Princess Hélène of Mecklenburg, who was attractive and well-liked, should

---

[25] For a vivid account of the final phase, see Les barricades: scènes les plus saisissantes de la Révolution de 1848 (Paris, 1848). Gustave Flaubert: L'éducation sentimentale (1869) conveys a sense of complete confusion. The recently published observations of a Swiss eyewitness are particularly revealing: see "William de La Rive: un témoin génévois de la Révolution de 1848" (Etudes, XV, 1953, 143–163).

serve as regent. But this scheme, adopted with some enthusiasm by the deputies, was wrecked in almost no time. The crowds were shouting for a republic and were hardly in a mood to accept an arrangement so reminiscent of the deal of July, 1830. Furthermore, Lamartine had been won to the idea of a republic, on the theory that any other solution would mean renewed conflict and disastrous divisions. Having disappeared during the days of greatest crisis, the poet now emerged as the man called upon to lead "the people" along the road to a democratic republic, which in turn would unite all Frenchmen and usher in a new age of general welfare. In the critical days of late February, Lamartine of all men showed himself self-assured and courageous. He had helped to precipitate the troubles, and he was now to contribute substantially to the restoration of order.

It was about 1:30 P.M. on February 24 when the Duchess of Orleans arrived at the Chamber of Deputies with the heir to the throne and his younger brother. In the general hubbub she was unable to make herself heard, but Barrot spoke eloquently in favor of her regency until he was shouted down by a crowd of armed men—National Guards and workers—who invaded the hall. Ledru-Rollin, the confirmed republican, then made a windy speech calling for appointment of a provisional government, a demand supported by Lamartine. The latter, after a moving tribute to the courageous princess fighting for the rights of her son, proceeded to argue that what was needed was a government that could stop the flow of blood and forestall a civil war. The ultimate decision must be left to the country, to "that sublime mystery of universal sovereignty," but a provisional government was necessary to tide over. At this point a second and more ferocious invasion took place. Ruffians, coming from the sack of the Tuileries, brandished their guns and insulted the deputies, most of whom, including the president, fled for safety, leaving their seats to the newcomers. The duchess and her party, almost suffocated, barely managed to escape through a side corridor.[26]

Despite the pandemonium, Lamartine finally secured approval of a

---

[26] Crémieux: *La Révolution de février,* 373 ff. analyzes the often contradictory sources for this episode. See also Paul Bastide: *Doctrines et institutions politiques de la Séconde République* (Paris, 1945), I, 36 ff., 104 ff., and recent studies of the revolution such as Felix Ponteil: *1848* (Paris, 1937); Jean Dautry: *1848 et la Deuxième République* (2 ed., Paris, 1957); Emile Tersen: *Quarante-huit* (Paris, 1957); Georges Duveau: *1848* (New York, 1967).

provisional government, the membership of which was a distillation of numerous lists then in circulation. The president was an eighty-year-old revolutionary war horse, Dupont de l'Eure, who would serve as a figurehead. Lamartine, who was presently to become minister of foreign affairs, was to be the real leader. The others (Arago, Marie, Garnier-Pagès, Crémieux) were members of the moderate wing of the opposition, while Ledru-Rollin, a wealthy lawyer and eloquent republican agitator, represented the left wing. Late in the afternoon these harassed men set out on foot for the Hôtel de Ville, traditionally the focal point of Parisian affairs, where they had reason to fear lest the populace had already set up its own revolutionary government.

It was only with great difficulty that Lamartine and his associates could make their way through the throngs and into the building. Once inside, they were so beset with delegations that they had to move from one room to another in search of a spot for quiet deliberation. Presently a group, headed by Louis Blanc, arrived from the offices of *La Réforme,* the journal of the democratic, socialist group. Blanc demanded that members of his party be included in the government, and it was finally decided that Blanc, Flocon (editor of *La Réforme*) and a mechanic named Albert should be appointed secretaries to the provisional government. Though in the sequel they were to play a role equal to that of the regular members, this initial episode is instructive as revealing the reluctance of the moderate element to admit the more radical leaders to full standing.

During the hectic days that followed, the government was obliged, under popular pressure, to make a number of decisions, some of which at least went beyond what was palatable. Freedom of speech, assembly and association were proclaimed and the death penalty abolished in political cases. The troops, humiliated and disgruntled, were ordered withdrawn from the city and the detested Municipal Guard was dissolved. Caussidière, a prominent member of the revolutionary clubs, took over as chief of police and began to form a new Popular Guard (*garde du peuple*) drawn from recently released political prisoners. The government hastened, too, to order the recruitment of 24,000 volunteers between the ages of sixteen and thirty, to be organized as a National Mobile Guard (*garde nationale mobile*), two battalions for each *arrondissement,* the men to be paid 1.50 francs per day. By these measures it was hoped to re-establish an effective police force and at the same time take off the streets some of the restless, unemployed youngsters and ne'er-do-wells.[27]

The overriding issues, however, were those of the form of government and the "organization of labor." The crowds, milling about in front of the Hôtel de Ville, insisted on the proclamation of the republic, so as not again to be wheedled out of the fruits of their revolution. Most members of the provisional government had come to the conviction that any other form of government was for the time being impractical and likely to lead to further conflict. But Lamartine for one was unwilling to proclaim the republic out of hand. The whole country, he thought, was entitled to a voice in the matter. Time and again he harangued the crowd while his colleagues devised a formula saying that while the provisional government desired a republic, the final decision should be left to a nationwide vote, which should be taken as soon as possible. However, in the tumult and confusion Blanc and others gave the people to understand that the republic had in fact been proclaimed. There was little to be done about this, but Lamartine managed at least to talk the crowds out of adopting the red flag of the revolution in place of the tricolor. But here again something had to be done by way of compromise: members of the government agreed to wear a red rosette in their buttonholes and decreed that there should be a similar rosette at the peak of all flagstaffs.[28]

But the crowds wanted a social as well as a political republic. The "organization of labor" and the "right to work" were slogans on every tongue. The new regime must do something to ensure against unemployment, hunger and general misery, which were the chief grievances of the populace in these critical years. "Every trade, every industry was looking to the government to put a complete end to its miseries," says Flaubert. Around noon of February 25 an unknown young worker forced an entrance into the council chambers of the government and,

[27] P. Chalmin: "Une institution militaire de la Séconde République: la garde nationale mobile" (*Etudes d'histoire moderne et contemporaine*, II, 1948, 37–82); Max Jahns: *Das französische Heer* (Leipzig, 1873), 339 ff.

[28] Maurice Dommanget: *La Révolution de 1848 et le drapeau rouge* (Paris, 1948); J. S. Shapiro: "Lamartine: a Study of the Poetic Temperament in Politics" (*Political Science Quarterly*, XXXIV, 1919, 632–643); Ethel Harris: *Lamartine et le peuple* (Paris, 1932), Book III, chap. i; Henri Guillemin: *Lamartine en 1848* (Paris, 1948); André Becheyras: "Lamartine au pouvoir" (in *Esprit de 1848*, Paris, n.d., 41–76); Gordon Wright: "A Poet in Politics: Lamartine in 1848" (*History Today*, VIII, 1958, 616–627).

banging his rifle butt on the floor, exclaimed: "Citizens, the revolution was achieved twenty-four hours ago and the people is still waiting for results." Lamartine's attempt to reply was cut off with the words: "Enough of phrases, enough of poetry." The government was to proclaim the organization of labor within the hour. Lamartine refused, saying that he did not even know what was meant by the term. At this point Blanc saved the day by promising that the government would guarantee the workers employment and would give recognition to their associations. Thereupon the worker withdrew, never again to be heard from.[29]

Since Blanc and the workers were in control of the situation, it was impossible for other members of the government to gainsay his social-istic program. On February 26 it was decreed that national workshops (*ateliers nationaux*) should be opened in various sections of the city and that those admitted should be paid 2.00 francs a day when employed and 1.50 francs (later reduced) when not employed. Had Blanc had his way, these workshops would have been organized by trades and would have been producers' co-operatives such as he had long advocated. As it was, the national workshops had little in common with the social workshops (*ateliers sociaux*) beyond the resemblance in name. They were really nothing but a new version of the familiar *ateliers de charité*, or relief works in which the unem-ployed were put on grading or other unskilled jobs, without reference to trade. As for Blanc, the government, while rejecting his demand for a ministry of progress, appointed him chairman of a commission of labor, which became known as the Luxembourg Commission, from the palace where it held its sessions. Blanc quickly assembled repre-sentatives of different trades and, with their support, obliged the government on March 2 to decree the reduction of the workday in Paris to ten hours, and in the provinces to twelve. Needless to say, this regulation was not very scrupulously observed, since no provision was made for supervision or enforcement.[30]

---

[29] J. A. R. Marriott: *The Right to Work* (Oxford, 1919), lviii ff.; Donald C. McKay: *The National Workshops* (Cambridge, 1933), 10–11; Georges Lefranc: *Histoire du travail et des travailleurs* (Paris, 1957), 325 ff.

[30] Still valuable is the contemporary article by the economist Michel Chevalier: "Question des travailleurs: l'amélioration du sort des ouvriers; l'organisation du travail" (*Revue des deux mondes*, March 15, 1848, 1057–1086). See also Pierre Loustau: *Louis Blanc à la commission du Luxembourg* (Paris, 1908); Paul Keller: *Louis Blanc und die Revolution von 1848* (Zürich, 1926).

3. THE SECOND REPUBLIC

For several months after its proclamation the history of the Second Republic was one of stormy uncertainty. The provisional government, composed largely of men of moderate views, was more or less at the mercy of the populace, which meant the lesser middle class and the skilled artisans as well as the workers and paupers. For the time being Paris was without police protection of any kind. The Municipal Guard, which had done its duty all too well and had thereby incurred the undying hatred of the people, was at once dissolved, to be replaced gradually by the new *garde mobile*. The National Guard, whose part in the revolution had been crucial, was thrown open to all, so that by mid-March almost a hundred thousand were enrolled. It stands to reason that time would be required before these huge numbers could be integrated and the legions reformed and trained. As for the troops, they had been withdrawn from the city, utterly demoralized and disgruntled over their humiliating experience. In these circumstances the government had nowhere to look for support against the excesses of the population.

The situation, bad enough to begin with, was much aggravated by the onset of a severe financial and business crisis. The disorders of late February brought business to a standstill and provoked a panic. There were runs on the banks, bankruptcies and failures, so that the Bourse had to be closed. Government 5 per cent bonds fell from 116 on February 23 to 89 on March 7 and to 50 by April. With the economy paralyzed, it was inevitable that vast numbers of workers should find themselves idle. Where in 1847 about 335,000 had been employed in Paris, in 1848 there were only 147,000. An official investigation revealed that over 50 per cent of the work force was thrown out of work, and that production declined by about 53 per cent.[31] The government, faced by a rapidly mounting deficit, decided that the only alternative to national bankruptcy was the levy of a surtax of 45 centimes on every franc paid in direct taxes, exemptions to be made only at the discretion of the tax collector. By this device the unpropertied urban workers

---

[31] T. J. Markovitch: "La crise de 1847–1848 dans les industries parisiennes" (*Revue d'histoire économique et sociale*, XLIII, 1965, 256–260), which analyzes the voluminous inquiry of the Paris Chamber of Commerce. On the financial crisis, see also Jean Bouchary: "Economie et finances" (in Charles Moulin, ed.: *1848: le livre du centenaire*, Paris, 1948, 257–268).

would not be affected. The burden would fall on the landed classes, who did not for the moment present a threat to the regime or to society.[32]

The general acceptance of the republic not only by the middle class but by the aristocracy and the Catholic Church has often been commented on. There was indeed a closing of ranks to meet the threat of radical political and social revolution. For the new freedom removed all obstacles to the formation of radical clubs and the launching of radical newspapers. Within a few weeks there were 170 new journals and more than 200 clubs, in which popular leaders could expound the most advanced political and socialistic ideas. Thus Auguste Blanqui, the uncompromising revolutionist, founded the Central Republican Committee on the very day (February 28) of his release from prison. It soon had 3,000 members, with meetings every evening except Sunday. There Blanqui, in his prison rags, wearing black gloves, made a frightening appearance—dour, emaciated, fanatical, according to Victor Hugo "a gloomy apparition in which all the hatred born of all the miseries was incarnated."[33] One can understand how members of the middle class, once they had overcome their initial stupefaction, should have been agreeably surprised to find themselves still alive (Flaubert), but one can also understand their growing dread of the radical tide that confronted them.

Radical leaders kept harping on the theme that the people would not again allow the government to betray the principles of the revolution. There was to be not another bourgeois regime, but a political and social democracy. Furthermore, France was to resume its traditional role of champion of the rights of the people everywhere: it was to embark, if need be, on a crusade of liberty. Once freed of the yoke of tyranny, Europe could be reorganized as "the great European republic," a federation of free peoples transcending the narrow limits of

---

[32] See Rémi Gossez: "La resistance à l'impôt: les quarante-cinq centimes" (*Etudes*, I, 1953, 89–131); Ernest Labrousse: *Aspects de la crise et de la dépression de l'économie française, 1846–1851* (Paris, 1956).

[33] Charles Moulin: "Les clubs et la presse" (in *1848: le livre du centenaire*, 139–158); Suzanne Wassermann: *Les clubs de Barbès et de Blanqui* (Paris, 1913); Peter Amann: "The Changing Outlines of 1848" (*American Historical Review*, LXVIII, 1963, 938–952). Flaubert, in his *Education sentimentale*, gives a vivid account of a meeting of the Club of the Intellect, where everyone talked at once about altogether unrelated matters.

nationality: "In that holy, blessed day there will be no more wars of partition, of domination, of nationality, of influence."[34] Of course France, as the recognized leader of the new order, would see that a "just" settlement replaced the treaty of 1815, and a just settlement would mean the "natural" frontiers of the Rhine and the Alps. Thus French patriots, defying all logic, were eager to fight for the liberties of other peoples, but equally prepared to relieve them of part of their territory.[35]

Once again, then, the French Republic appeared as a threat to the peace of Europe. Czar Nicholas at once mobilized a large army to support any victim of French aggression. The Austrians prepared to fight in Italy, and the German states looked to Prussia to meet a possible assault on the Rhine. Most immediately threatened were the Belgians, who promptly appealed to the British for support. But Palmerston did not share the general alarm. He looked with scorn upon the new republic as the rule of forty or fifty thousand of the "scum of the faubourgs of Paris" and firmly believed that, if left to themselves, the French would soon restore the Orleans dynasty.[36] He therefore urged the other governments to avoid interference with France unless the latter actually embarked upon aggression.

Lamartine, Ledru-Rollin and Blanc had all, in the past, denounced Guizot's compliant foreign policy and had voiced hopes of sometime regaining France's "lost" territories. But Lamartine, now that he was responsible for France's security, proved himself a hardheaded realist. He at once made a bid for British friendship, so as to forestall attack by the Holy Alliance, and gave assurances with respect to Belgium and Spain, the areas of greatest British concern. Then on March 4 he published a directive to French diplomats, which was a masterpiece of contradiction. As a sop to French opinion he declared that in the eyes

[34] Garnier-Pagès, quoted by Pierre Quentin-Bauchart: *Lamartine et la politique étrangère de la Révolution de Février* (Paris, 1913), 26.

[35] Emile Tersen: *Le gouvernement provisoire et l'Europe* (Paris, 1948), 21; Quentin-Bauchart: *Lamartine,* 27: "They spoke less of the Rhine frontier and more of the deliverance of their oppressed brothers, but it was always the treaties of 1815 that they wanted to destroy." See also Paul Henry: *La France devant le monde* (Paris, 1945), 144 ff.

[36] Herbert Bell: *Lord Palmerston* (New York, 1936), I, chap. xix; Brison D. Gooch: *Belgium and the February Revolution* (The Hague, 1963), 27 ff.; Eugène de Guichen: *Les grandes questions européennes et la diplomatie des puissances sous la Seconde République* (Paris, 1925), I, 52 ff.

of the French Republic the treaties of 1815 were no longer valid. He then hastily added that as a practical matter the new regime would respect the *status quo*. France would not attack its neighbors, but would, if appealed to, come to the aid of oppressed peoples struggling for their freedom. In substance this long and windy document proclaimed a policy of peace, as Palmerston at once recognized. British opinion, as well as the foreign secretary, paid tribute to Lamartine, who was obviously a man of sense.

On the other hand, French opinion was far from satisfied. The provisional government, it seemed, was reverting to the pusillanimous policy of the past regime. Paris was full of foreigners, political exiles and workers, many of whom were members of the secret societies and now established clubs of their own. In addition, delegations began to arrive from "oppressed" peoples everywhere, soliciting support. There were English Chartists, Irish Nationalists, Belgians, Swiss, Poles, even Hungarians, Rumanians and Portuguese. Various members of the government received these delegations sympathetically, and put them off with promises of support in the event of active repression by their governments. "We love Poland, we love Italy, we love all oppressed peoples," said Lamartine to the Poles; "but we love France above all else and we are responsible for its destinies and perhaps for those of all Europe."[37]

The activists heard only as much as they wanted to hear. During March the Belgians, the Germans and the Savoyards all organized filibustering forces, confident that in a crisis the French government would come to their aid and meanwhile hoping to set the spark of revolution in their homelands. No doubt the French government was glad to be rid of these restless foreigners. Ledru-Rollin, the minister of the interior, gave them moral as well as modest financial support. But the foreign "legions" were poorly organized and ill-equipped. On crossing the frontiers they were quickly defeated. Beyond reviving the fears and suspicions of neighboring countries, they accomplished nothing. On the French side the radicals were profoundly disappointed. In every club and coffeehouse they had been busily rearranging the map of Europe and laying plans for the forthcoming crusade. They dreamed of landing in England, joining the Chartists, overthrowing the government and eventually liberating the Irish. Similar dreams were

[37] Henry: *La France devant le monde,* 150 ff.

indulged in with respect to Continental countries. Yet here was Lamartine and the government putting off foreign revolutionaries with fine words. In retrospect the workers' paper *L'atelier* in 1849 wrote that by refusing to liberate Poland, Italy, Hungary, the provisional government had given the tyrants of Europe a chance to recover their breath and at home had hastened the restoration of the conservative elements. Indeed, a whole century later the eminent socialist leader Léon Blum, though a confirmed pacifist, was to bemoan the failure of the government in 1848 to take the lead in a general revolution of the European peoples.[38]

The members of the provisional government were generally agreed that France could under no circumstances afford to become involved in foreign war, which would inevitably lead to radical dictatorship at home. On equally pressing domestic policies, however, opinion was divided. On March 2 the government had yielded to popular demand and decreed the introduction of universal manhood suffrage, which meant enlarging the electorate from 250,000 to 9,000,000. But even Ledru-Rollin, long the proponent of this system, now began to have doubts about suddenly calling upon the political scene millions of uneducated peasants and workers. In the hope of preparing a favorable outcome of the elections, which were fixed for April 9, he sent out special commissioners to replace the prefects. In late March several commissioners-general were appointed as "veritable proconsuls" for different regions. Despite opposition these commissioners worked hard and generally successfully to see that the right candidates were on the electoral lists and that influence and patronage were applied in the right places.[39]

Ledru-Rollin's misgivings about the possible outcome of early elections were fully shared by the radicals, who feared that the ignorant peasants and workers would be completely under the domination of employers, landlords and clergy, whose enthusiasm for the republic was thought to be superficial at best. Blanqui for one foresaw civil war

[38] Léon Blum: "La Révolution de Février" (*Revue socialiste*, n.s., No. 20, 1948, 321–336). In general see Georges Duveau: "Les relations internationales dans la pensée ouvrière, 1840–1865" (*Actes du Congrès Historique du Centenaire de la Révolution de 1848*, Paris, 1949, 277–283).

[39] P. Haury: "Les commissaires de Ledru-Rollin en 1848" (*La Révolution française*, LVII, 1909, 438–474); Calman: *Ledru-Rollin and the Second French Republic;* Felix Ponteil: *1848* (Paris, 1937), 34 ff.

between Paris and the provinces if the elections turned out to be re-actionary. Since the forces of counterrevolution had been in control for fifty years, it was not unreasonable to ask at least one year for the forces of liberty.[40]

The growing antagonism between the moderates, who were a majority in the provisional government, and the radicals, together with the continuing economic crisis and the general instability, led to a series of episodes comparable to the "days" of the great French Revolution. The first of these, on March 16, had to do with the National Guard, which had been opened to all on March 14, with provision for new elections of the officers. The well-to-do elements, known as the *bonnets à poil* from their fur caps, were outraged by the mass influx of the lower classes and vagabonds. In formation, but unarmed, about 25,000 of them marched to the Hôtel de Ville to protest. The government was shocked, and Lamartine and other members roundly re-buked a delegation of the demonstrators, who thereupon disbanded. The sole effect of the affair was to arouse the radicals, who were planning a demonstration to press for social reforms. On March 17 a huge crowd gathered to congratulate the government for resisting the demands of the "reactionaries." Some 150,000 workers marched peace-fully from the Place de la Concorde to the Hôtel de Ville, where the popular "communist" Etienne Cabet headed a delegation petitioning the government to postpone the elections by at least two months. The authorities, highly gratified by the orderliness of the multitude, prom-ised a decision within a week. Though all went off well, Lamartine and his associates were shaken by the realization that they were at the mercy of the populace. They were, said Lamartine in private, living on a volcano, with no knowing when it might erupt.[41]

On March 26 the government decreed the postponement of the elec-tions from April 9 to April 23, due evidently to the difficulty of organizing so vast a poll in short order. Meanwhile the election of National Guard officers took place on April 5 and turned out most satisfactorily from the conservative or even moderate point of view. The workers of Paris, it appeared, were still under the influence of the

[40] Neil Stewart: *Blanqui* (London, 1939), 102 ff.; Sylvain Molinier: *Blanqui* (Paris, 1948), 38.

[41] Girard: *La garde nationale,* 294 ff.; Henri Guillemin: *La tragédie de quarante-huit* (Paris, 1948), 122 ff.; Duveau: *1848: the Making of a Revolution,* 81 ff.

upper classes. As Blanqui feared, they were not prepared to assume control. In any event, the National Guard, numbering now some 100,000 men, was to become once more a defense force at the command of the government. This was to be clearly shown by the events of April 16, the origins of which remain even more obscure than those of March 17. As background one must remember the increasing virulence of the propaganda war on both sides. The conservatives were floating every kind of charge and rumor about the plans of the "revolutionists," and made little secret of their intention of recalling the troops so as to ensure the preservation of order. The radicals, on their part, plastered the city with threatening placards and made their clubs forums for the most incendiary oratory. The Club of the Mountain, for example, announced that the people would boil the blood of the aristocrats in the cauldron of the revolution and make a stew that would sate the appetite of the famished proletarians.[42]

On April 14, respectable people were alarmed to read in the *Bulletin of the Republic,* a publication of the ministry of the interior, an article which, as it turned out later, was written by no less a person than the well-known novelist George Sand, who had been converted to socialism and was now an ardent advocate of a new society. "Unless the elections bring the victory of social truth," she wrote, "there will be only one road to the safety of the people who built the barricades, and that will be to make its will known again and to postpone the decisions of a false national representation."[43]

There was some justification, then, for the fear that there was a radical plot in the making and that its objective was the removal of Lamartine and the moderates and the substitution of a committee of public safety for the objectionable provisional government. Blanc obligingly warned his colleagues that another great demonstration was planned for April 16, so precautions could be taken, and the radical leaders, including Blanqui, could be confidentially warned. As a result they tended to hold aloof at least in the initial stages. The demonstrators who, 40,000 strong, on April 16 marched from the Champs de Mars to the Hôtel de Ville found their procession hedged in on both sides by National Guards, while the new police, the *garde mobile,*

---

[42] Quoted by Moulin: "Les clubs et la presse."

[43] Albert Fournier: "George Sand en 1848" (*Europe,* XXVI, 1848, 140–150); André Maurois: *Lélia: the Life of George Sand* (New York, 1953), Part VII.

broke the crowd into sections. Shouts of "down with the communists" and "down with Cabet" began to be heard, and the demonstrators, for the most part leaderless, were soon faced with complete fiasco. Conservative newspapers crowed over their victory over the "barbarians" and rhapsodized over the "sublime élan" shown by the reconstituted National Guard.[44]

To celebrate this happy turn of events the government arranged a festival of fraternity for April 20. For hours the members stood in array at the Arc de Triomphe and presented new colors to the legions of the National Guard, as well as to five regiments of the army, which were now restored to their Paris barracks.

No less gratifying to the moderate elements was the outcome of the elections on Sunday, April 23, when fully 84 per cent of the electorate went to the polls. Ledru-Rollin's commissioners, it will be recalled, had done their utmost short of corruption to secure the election of "true" republicans, but on the other hand the conservatives, organized in the Republican Club for Freedom of the Elections, and the church hierarchy with its Committee for Defense of Religious Liberty had thrown their influence on the side of the traditional ruling classes. In many areas the bishops drew up lists of candidates for the priests to recommend to their flocks and in countless villages the priest joined the mayor in leading the procession to the polls. When one considers further that the small landholders and peasants suffered particularly from the imposition of the 45 per cent surtax, one can understand that the vote came out on the conservative side. Most of those elected belonged to the class of local notables. They would have been just as eligible for election under the highly restricted franchise of the July Monarchy. Indeed, 165 of them had sat in the Chamber of the previous regime. Almost half of them were local lawyers, while only about thirty could be classed as workers; actual peasants were completely absent.

Politically just about all the successful candidates described themselves as republicans, partly because for the time being no other regime was in prospect. It has generally been supposed that about half of them were moderate republicans, but recent studies suggest that this figure is exaggerated. There were evidently about 300 monarchists, mostly members of the dynastic opposition of the July Monarchy. On the other wing there were some seventy-five or eighty radicals and social-

[44] Guillemin: *La tragédie de quarante-huit*, 177.

ists. The "true" or confirmed republicans numbered not 500 but somewhat less than 300. In any event, the elections were a resounding victory for the moderate and conservative elements. Even in Paris only one radical leader, Armand Barbès, and twelve socialists were elected. Blanqui, Raspail and other radical leaders failed of election. In other words, even in Paris, the focus of the revolution, the workers and lower classes generally voted for the respectable, well-to-do candidates.[45]

The lines were now more clearly drawn than ever before. On the one side many of the new deputies might have said, with one of Flaubert's characters: "I had as much trouble as five hundred devils in making my fortune. And now people want to tell me that I'm not the master, that my money is not my own; in short, that property is theft. . . . Don't bother me with your Proudhon: I think I'd strangle him if he were here." On the other side were the radicals who, in one of their placards, warned the Assembly: "If you persist in defending the old social order, you will find our sections well organized and in the van on the day of reckoning."[46] No less an authority than Tocqueville, himself one of the deputies, tells us that everywhere the idea of an inevitable and imminent conflict was current.[47]

The members of the provisional government had all secured election to the new Assembly (see Illustration 60). Lamartine, who had so successfully held the fort during three critical months, was elected in ten departments and received 260,000 votes in the Seine. Ledru-Rollin polled 131,000 votes, but the more radical Blanc received only 120,000. Lamartine was generally looked upon as the man who could suppress the "socialists." He might have become provisional president had he so desired. But he had always taken a middle position and had been genuinely concerned with the plight of the common people. He now tried to mediate between the opposing wings and insisted that Ledru-Rollin be included in the new executive commission of five which was

[45] Alfred Cobban: "Administrative Pressure in the Election of the French Constituent Assembly, April, 1848" (*Bulletin of the Institute of Historical Research*, XXV, 1952, 133–159), and "The Influence of the Clergy and the 'Instituteurs primaires' in the Election of the French Constituent Assembly" (*English Historical Review*, LVII, 1942, 334–344); Rémond: *La Droite en France*, 87 ff.; Bastid: *Doctrines et institutions politiques de la Seconde République*, I, 176 ff. The analyses of Duveau: *1848*, 96 ff., and earlier writers should be corrected by the researches of George W. Fasel: "The French Election of April 23, 1848: Suggestions for a Revision" (*French Historical Studies*, V, 1968, 285–298).

[46] Quoted in Jean Dautry: *1848 et la Seconde République* (2 ed., Paris, 1957), 149.

[47] Tocqueville: *Recollections*, 107.

to replace the provisional government. His unwillingness to serve as the instrument of reaction naturally cost him much of his popularity among the deputies. When it came to the election of the new executive, Arago obtained 725 votes, Garnier-Pagès 715, Marie 702, Lamartine only 643 and Ledru-Rollin 458. Actually this body did little beyond appointing the ministers, who reported directly to the Assembly. The Assembly, in turn, operated through fifteen key committees.[48]

Since the majority of the Assembly was set on putting an end to the radicalism and socialism of Paris, it rejected out of hand Blanc's plea for the establishment of a ministry of labor and indeed gave short shrift to his commission of labor, which had been holding its sessions in the Luxembourg Palace and had long since become a thorn in the flesh of his bourgeois colleagues in the provisional government. Blanc, a dynamic idealist fertile in practicable ideas, had assembled several hundred employers and workers in something like an economic parliament. His commission received numerous petitions, aided in settling wage disputes and encouraged the organization of labor unions. Much time, understandably, was given to doctrinal debate on subjects such as the nationalization of the railroads, banks and major industries. From the profits, Blanc hoped, the government could then finance the producers' workshops which he had so much at heart. There was nothing subversive about this. Not even the workers called for a social revolution. What they asked was state action to guarantee work, a minimum age, insurance for old age, and so on. Even in the so-called "socialist" propaganda put out by the well-known writer Eugène Sue, there was talk only of a progressive income tax, nurseries for the children of working women, homes for the aged, free education, government insurance against fire, and the like. Nonetheless, the idea became firmly rooted that Blanc and his associates were intent on making over society along socialist lines.[49]

[48] Bastid: *Doctrines et institutions politiques*, I, 197 ff. On Lamartine's attitude, see his revealing letter to his niece, June 1, 1848, quoted in Edouard Vellay: "L'impopularité de Lamartine peu après l'ouverture de l'Assemblée Constituante" (*1848*, No. 188, 1951, 61–62).

[49] K. Bloch: *Geschichte der Kommission des Luxembourg* (Frankfurt, 1925); Jean Vidalenc: *Louis Blanc* (Paris, 1948); Leo R. Loubère: *Louis Blanc* (Evanston, 1960); Alexandre Zévaes: "La propagande socialiste dans la campagne en 1848" (*La Révolution de 1848*, XXXI, 75–94); Rémi Gossez: "L'organisation ouvrière à Paris sous la Seconde République" (*1848: Revue des révolutions contemporaines*, XLI, 1949, 31–45).

The antagonism between conservatives and radicals broke wide open on May 15, when, despite the efforts of Blanqui and Barbès to prevent a premature clash, huge crowds assembled on the Place de la Bastille and marched thence to the hall of the Assembly, a huge, hastily constructed wooden building within the courtyard of the Palais Bourbon. There the procession, largely unarmed, found a detachment of the National Guard, as well as the police and some regular troops. Since the officers of these forces had no particular directives and were uncertain of themselves, they gave no orders. The crowd easily brushed aside the National Guard, invaded the chamber and dropped from the galleries to the floor. Tocqueville, who was present, has left a vivid picture of the confusion that ensued as the invaders surged about while the deputies sat stone still, like the Roman senators awaiting the invasion of the Gauls. One radical leader, Raspail, read a petition calling for action on behalf of the Poles and for the formation of an army of liberation to be financed by a tax of a billion francs levied on the rich. Finally, after unconscionable delays, large contingents of the National Guard were called out. But by the time of their arrival, the crowd had for the most part disappeared, partly to escape the intolerable heat and partly to march to the Hôtel de Ville and set up a revolutionary government. Lamartine and Ledru-Rollin thereupon mounted horses and led a squadron of dragoons to the same destination. The demonstrators were easily dispersed and the upshot of the affair was that some 400 persons, including most of the radical leaders (Blanqui and Barbès had belatedly joined in the demonstration), were arrested and imprisoned. In March, 1849, the high court at Bourges sentenced them to life imprisonment. Blanc escaped indictment only by a narrow vote of the Assembly. Many of the radical clubs were closed down and more drastic legislation was enacted to forestall further risings. The first round of the conflict had been fought; the first victory of the conservatives had been won.

Once more, to celebrate so auspicious an event, a grand festival of concord was held on the Champs de Mars (May 21). Tocqueville tells us that some 200,000 bayonets flashed in the sun, but that the deputies were nevertheless so apprehensive of the populace that they came secretly armed with pistols, daggers and blackjacks. Nothing untoward happened as hour after hour the various guards and troops marched past the reviewing stand. But the bouquets of the sturdy young women from the industrial *faubourgs,* says Tocqueville, fell on the assembled deputies like hailstones, reminding the authorities that concord was somewhat less than perfect.

4. THE JUNE DAYS

Although the primary purpose of the newly elected Assembly was to draft a constitution for republican France, the deputies felt obliged to deal first of all with the problem of the national workshops, in which by June no less than 100,000 men were enrolled. The reader will recall that these workshops had never been intended as a socialist experiment. They were, in fact, not workshops at all, but merely a traditional system of public relief in time of great unemployment (see Illustration 40). Initially the plans called for decentralized administration dealing with perhaps 10,000 or 12,000 men. But the influx was so great that the project had to be put under central direction. At the suggestion of the director, a brilliant young engineer named Emile Thomas, the workers were organized in paramilitary fashion, by squads, brigades and companies. They were a motley crew which included many skilled workers and even professional men as well as ordinary day laborers. In the acute economic crisis of the spring of 1848, the unemployment, by official count, ran to 65 per cent in the construction trades, 72 per cent in the furnishing trades, 58 per cent in hardware, 51 per cent in textiles and clothing. Even artists were hard hit, as shown by the fact that the eminent sculptor David d'Angers recommended many hungry dramatists, painters and designers for admission to the workshops.[50]

It was utterly impossible, at short order, to find useful work for so many men. Actually, no more than 10,000 were employed at any one time, mostly on grading jobs. Marie, the minister of public works, proposed that a circumferential railway be built around Paris, and Thomas suggested repavement of the roads running into the city. These projects would have taken large numbers of workers out of the center of the city, but they were all so expensive that the government, financially hard pressed, could not seriously contemplate them.[51]

---

[50] Thomas' analysis of mid-May, 1848, is given in the appendix of Charles Schmidt: *Des ateliers nationaux aux barricades de juin* (Paris, 1948). See also T. J. Markovitch: "La crise de 1847–1848 dans les industries parisiennes" (*Revue d'histoire économique et sociale,* XLIII, 1965, 256–260).

[51] Donald C. McKay: *The National Workshops* (Cambridge, 1933), 31; Schmidt: *Des ateliers nationaux,* 22.

The government and the propertied classes were from the beginning beset with fear lest this huge conglomerate of hungry, desperate people be used by radical leaders for a new, social revolution. "These poor people," says Tocqueville, "were told that the wealth of the rich was in some way the produce of a theft practiced upon themselves." Since with only one franc a day they were on the very verge of subsistence, they constituted a real danger. For that reason Thomas had organized and disciplined them. Presently they were permitted also to enroll in the National Guard, where again they were under control. Nonetheless the new government was convinced that an end must be put to the workshop system, which was an intolerable drain on the exchequer as well as a social menace. The deputies, coming mostly from the provinces, shared the feeling prevalent among the peasants that, through the 45 per cent surtax, they were paying for the upkeep of the lazy ruffians of the capital.

Finally, after weeks of debate, it was decided on May 24 to close the workshops to new enrollment as the first step toward dropping from the rolls all those who had been resident in Paris less than six months and sending those aged eighteen to twenty-five into the army. Thomas, when he protested these decisions, was spirited away to distant Bordeaux under police escort.

Before long, thousands on thousands of unemployed workers, barred from the dole, were threatened with starvation, as shown by the numerous delegations begging for bread. The new director of the workshops foresaw France being engulfed in the misery of Ireland and warned the government that soon the flood would break the dykes.[52] One of the radical clubs began to campaign for a great popular banquet of the people in imitation of the earlier bourgeois banquets. At five sous (twenty-five centimes) some 30,000 subscribed and the movement became so formidable that the leaders themselves became alarmed. On June 10 it was decided to postpone the banquet to July 14, Bastille Day. But the project had stirred the lower classes, despite the fact that it had no specific objective or revolutionary intent. After its deferment workmen would gather in large numbers in the evening, knowing not where to turn. Presently these assemblies had to be

[52] See especially the evidence adduced by A. I. Molok: "Problèmes de l'insurrection de juin, 1848" (*Questions d'histoire*, II, 1954, 57–100).

broken up by the mounted police. The scene was then already set for the ensuing conflict.[53]

The majority in the assembly was more than ever convinced that there was on foot a widespread socialist conspiracy to establish a democratic and social republic. In preparation for defense the government therefore appointed as commander of the troops, the National Guard and the police (Mobile Guard) General Eugène Cavaignac, veteran of sixteen years of campaigning in Algeria and only recently named governor-general of that colony. Cavaignac's assignment was hardly an enviable one, for the 30,000 troops he had in and around Paris were still rather demoralized and not entirely reliable. The huge National Guard, too, was a questionable asset, for it was socially such a conglomerate that there was no knowing how much or what part of it could be counted on to fight the workers. His most effective force was the new Mobile Guard, 15,000 strong, well-drilled and tough.[54]

Hostilities began around noon on June 23, following vain protests by the workers against the government's decree dissolving the workshops. Barricades sprang up by the hundreds in the poorer sections of the city, and presently the entire area east of the present-day Boulevard Saint-Michel on the Left Bank and the Boulevards Sebastopol, Strasbourg and Barbès on the Right Bank was in the hands of some 50,000 insurgents. It must be emphasized that among the insurgents there were relatively few members of the workshops, whose dole the government promised to pay during the disturbances. The vast majority of the barricade fighters were destitute, unemployed workers who had been denied admission to the workshops and had no resources beyond charity. Most of them had come to Paris within the preceding year or two and were in a state of utter desperation, as shown by the doggedness of their resistance. Though a few of them may have been class-conscious fighters for a republic of the workers, most of them appear to have been utterly devoid of notions of political or social renovation.

[53] Peter Amann: "Prelude to Insurrection: the Banquet of the People" (*French Historical Studies*, I, 1960, 436–440), and "Du neuf on the 'Banquet of the People' " (*ibid.*, V, 1968, 344–350).
[54] General Doumenc: "L'armée et les journées de juin" (*Actes du Congrès du Centenaire de la Révolution de 1848*, 255–266); P. Chalmin: "Une institution militaire de la Séconde République: la garde nationale mobile" (*Etudes d'histoire moderne et contemporaine*, II, 1948, 37–82); Girard: *La garde nationale*, 309 ff.; Rémi Gossez: "Notes sur la composition et l'attitude de la troupe" (*Etudes*, XVIII, 1955, 77–110).

There is a real danger of reading into the June Days ideas which were to crystallize only much later.[55]

The June insurrection, in which not a single radical leader participated and which was therefore an unplanned, disorganized outbreak, never had much chance of success. It was able to secure control of a large part of the city simply because Cavaignac refused to take action until all his forces were ready and concentrated in three localities: at the National Assembly, at the Panthéon, and at the Place de la Concorde. An ominous development was the failure of the National Guard to respond in strength to the *rappel* of June 23. Many stayed in their own localities to protect their property. Only about 10,000 (10 per cent) reported for active duty. In these circumstances the government sent out an appeal to nearby *départements* to send contingents of their National Guards, and for the first time in French history the steamboat and railroad made the intervention of the provinces possible. On June 24 and 25 thousands of provincials, eager "to defend society against the threat of anarchic doctrines and to put an end to the intolerable dictation of the chronically insurgent Parisian workers" arrived in the capital. For the most part they were too late to share in the fighting, but they were used for guard duty and in general exercised a significant moral influence.[56]

On June 24 Cavaignac opened his offensive. His forces drove a wedge between the insurgents on the left and the right banks of the river and gradually closed in on the main centers of resistance, using artillery to blast the barricades. Much of the fighting was done by the Mobile Guard, the National Guardsmen participating to some extent on both sides, while the troops of the line were committed only where success seemed certain. By June 26 the workers had been driven back into the Faubourg Saint-Antoine, which, attacked from all sides, soon had to surrender (see Illustration 59). In four days of desperate fight-

---

[55] Marx, to be sure, saw the June Days as "a fight for the preservation or annihilation of the bourgeois order" (*The Class Struggles in France*). On the social diversity of the insurgency, see McKay: *The National Workshops*, 145 ff.; Emile Tersen: "Juin, 1848" (*La Pensée*, No. 19, 1948, 16–24); Rémi Gossez: "Diversités des antagonismes sociaux vers le milieu du XIXe siècle" (*Revue économique*, VII, 1956, 439–457); George Rudé: *The Crowd in the French Revolution* (Oxford, 1959), chap. xv.

[56] All told, about 100,000 provincials had arrived by July 1. See the archival study of Jean Vidalenc: "La province et les journées de juin" (*Etudes d'histoire moderne et contemporaine*, II, 1948, 83–144) and the remarks of Tocqueville (*Recollections*, 169, 182 ff.), many of whose friends hurried in from Normandy.

ing the insurgents had lost 400–500 men, while the attacking forces had something like twice that number of dead. In terms of human life, the worst, however, was still to come. The insurgents were hunted through houses and alleys and some 3,000 were cut down in cold blood. Alexander Herzen, watching the slaughter, noted that Russian Cossacks and Austrian Croat troops were meek as lambs compared to the ferocious French guards. In addition to the slain, about 12,000 persons were arrested, some of whom were released after four to six months, while most were summarily deported to Algerian labor camps.[57]

Karl Marx was to describe the June Days as "the most colossal event in the history of European civil wars," and they were indeed to occupy a central place in socialist historical writing. As such, it would be hard to exaggerate their importance. Yet in fact no socialist writer or leader played any role in the insurrection, which was not in any sense a revolt of a class-conscious industrial proletariat, but rather an uprising of skilled as well as unskilled workers made desperate by hunger and want. It is interesting chiefly as marking the culmination of a long-term development. Population pressure and the social dislocations occasioned by industrialization, reinforced by the crop failures of 1846 and 1847 and crowned by the sudden economic crisis provoked by the February Revolution, had created such widespread unemployment that no government, least of all the provisional government, could cope with it over a longer period. The decision of the government to close down the national workshops is understandable, but surely the transition should have been more gradual and some alternative solution should have been sought. The abruptness of the action was, of course, due to the great fear of social revolution. One might almost say that the government, by its drastic action, seized the initiative and broke the opposition of the workers before it could crystallize. The end result, however, was to deepen class antagonisms and strengthen suspicions and fears, making even gradual social reform ever more difficult. The fruits of the June Days took the form not of democracy but of reaction.

---

[57] For Herzen's remark, see Edward H. Carr: *The Romantic Exiles* (London, 1933), 43, and for the repression Roger Ikor: *Insurrection ouvrière de juin, 1848* (Paris, 1936), 58; Schmidt: *Des ateliers nationaux*, 53 ff.

Chapter Eleven

UPHEAVAL IN CENTRAL EUROPE

I. THE REVOLUTION IN VIENNA

THE REVOLUTIONS in Central Europe, which were directly inspired by news of the easy success of the insurrection in Paris, to a large extent followed the pattern of their prototype. A flood of petitions and a series of demonstrations brought the common people upon the scene, with the inevitable result that the liberal middle class, once it had realized its program of constitutional government, was confronted by a radical movement which in certain places took on a distinct socialistic tinge. It stands to reason that in this area, where society was far less industrialized than further west, the forces of both liberalism and radicalism were less formidable than in France, and the chances of lasting success therefore greatly reduced. Besides, in Central Europe nationalism soon made its influence felt, so much so that eventually nationalist aspirations and claims overshadowed the issues of liberal government. In the entire Danube Basin the struggle of nationalities threatened the disintegration of the Hapsburg Monarchy, while in Germany proper the contrary drive toward unification became overriding. These crosscurrents created a situation so complex that the historian, able to speak of only one thing at a time, is at a loss for an acceptable pattern of discourse.

The impetus to revolution in the Hapsburg Empire was given by Louis Kossuth, who, in a passionate speech to the Hungarian Diet on March 3, 1848 declared that even though the peoples of the empire were loyal to the dynasty, the time had come to put an end to absolutism, to centralized bureaucratic government and indeed to all the repressive measures of the "Metternich System." All parts of the empire should be given representative institutions and the special position of the Kingdom of Hungary should be respected. Hungary must insist on complete autonomy under a responsible ministry.

It was this resounding address that raised excitement throughout the empire to fever pitch. The government, however, was too paralyzed to formulate an effective policy. The emperor was feeble-minded and the council of state dominated by his uncle, the Archduke Louis, who, like the chancellor, Prince Metternich, was dead opposed to surrender under popular pressure. Metternich, now old and discouraged, recognized that the old regime was becoming impossible, but insisted that such changes as might be necessary should be made deliberately by the government, not by the people.[1]

Pressure of events, however, soon deprived the court of freedom of decision. On the morning of March 13, a bright spring day, the Estates of Lower Austria, an essentially feudal assembly in which, however, there were a number of liberal-minded aristocrats, were meeting in the Herrengasse to discuss a petition for reform to be presented to the emperor. Presently several thousand or more students from the university, who had suffered particularly under close police supervision and whose own petition had been rejected by the Court, arrived to persuade the Diet to adopt an advanced position. Crowds of bystanders assembled and there was much milling about in the narrow street. Excitement mounted as one student took it upon himself to read the full text of the Kossuth speech. Students began to invade the council chamber and presently the presiding officer of the Diet felt impelled to appeal to the Archduke Albert, commanding the garrison troops, to intervene and restore order.[2]

In Vienna, as in Paris, the preservation of public order devolved upon the paramilitary police (*Militär-Polizeiwache*), numbering about 1,200 men. The fact that the police on March 13 stood idly by during the disturbances was evidently due to the commander's view that large-scale riots were the business of the army. There was also a citizen's guard (*Bürgerwehr*) of 14,000 men recruited from the upper and middle *bourgeoisie* but, unlike the Paris National Guard, unarmed for the most part and used chiefly for parade purposes. In the last analysis, protection against civil disorders devolved upon the garrison troops,

[1] Heinrich Friedjung: *Oesterreich von 1848 bis 1860* (2 ed., Stuttgart, 1908), I, 17–18; Heinrich von Srbik: *Metternich, der Staatsmann und der Mensch* (Munich, 1925), II, 259 ff.; Constantin de Grunwald: *Metternich* (London, 1953), 286 ff.; Rudolf Kiszling: *Die Revolution im Kaisertum Oesterreich* (Vienna, 1948–1952), I, 35.

[2] For the background of the student agitation, see Julius Marx: "Polizei und Studenten" (*Jahrbuch des Vereins für Geschichte der Stadt Wien*, XIX–XX, 1963–1964, 218–250).

numbering about 15,000 men, who were quartered in barracks outside the ancient walls of the Inner City.[3]

The military forces at the disposal of the government were certainly sufficient to quell disturbances before they assumed the proportions of a revolution, but in Vienna as in Paris the authorities failed to issue specific orders. The archduke, left to his own devices, dispatched several squadrons of cavalry into the city, where they found it extremely difficult to operate because of the narrow, crowded streets. Presently missiles were thrown from the roofs and guns went off, no one knew just how or why. There were several dead, with resulting popular hostility. Before long, crowds of workers began to appear from the industrial suburbs. Only in the nick of time were the gates closed against them, whereupon they returned to their homes to engage in an orgy of machine breaking, incendiarism and looting.[4]

By late afternoon the disorder was such that a group of prominent citizens persuaded the lord mayor to call out the Citizen Guard and have the military withdraw from action. The archduke did in fact evacuate the Inner City and for several highly critical days the garrison troops stood idle on their parade ground outside the walls. The Citizen Guard, in turn, duplicated the role of the Paris National Guard: far from defending the regime, it deserted it. A deputation of guard officers proceeded to the palace and firmly demanded that Metternich be dismissed and the students armed, so that they might suppress the disorders among the workers. In the Imperial Council Metternich argued that the police and the troops could and should repress the disturbances. Too hasty dismissal of his chief minister had cost Louis Philippe his throne. The imperial house should not make the same mistake. Concessions to popular demands would lead no one knew where. The chancellor was supported vigorously by Prince Alfred von Windischgrätz, the governor of Bohemia, who on previous occasions

---

[3] Adolf Schmidl: *Wien und seine nächsten Umgebungen* (Vienna, 1847), 162–163; Karl Weiss: *Geschichte der Stadt Wien* (Vienna, 1872), II, 239 ff.; Viktor Bibl: *Die Wiener Polizei* (Vienna, 1927), 313; Hermann Oberhummer: *Die Wiener Polizei* (Vienna, 1937), I, 201 ff.

[4] Ernst Violand: *Die soziale Geschichte der Revolution in Oesterreich* (Leipzig, 1850), 69 ff.; Ernst von Zenker: *Die Wiener Revolution in ihren sozialen Voraussetzungen und Beziehungen* (Vienna, 1897), 112 ff.; Heinrich von Srbik: "Die Wiener Revolution . . . in sozialgeschichtlicher Beleuchtung" (*Schmollers Jahrbuch*, XLIII, 1919, 19–58); R. John Rath: *The Viennese Revolution of 1848* (Austin, 1957).

had suppressed outbreaks of workers in Prague and other cities. Energetic action, argued the prince, would soon end the insurrection. To dismiss Metternich would be nothing short of shameless cowardice. Nonetheless, the court eventually surrendered to popular pressure. In the evening Metternich was obliged to resign and flee in disguise across Germany to England. Meanwhile the students, having received permission to arm, secured several thousand muskets from the arsenal and formed patrols to ensure order.[5]

The success of the insurrection, which was entirely unplanned and unexpected, was due to the ineptitude of the government rather than to the strength of the opposition elements, among which only the students showed much grit and determination. The youths naturally rejoiced at their success, which put the government at their mercy. The court had to consent to the formation of a National Guard, which was to include a separate student corps, the Academic Legion. Though intended to comprise only 10,000 reliable citizens, the Guard soon numbered 30,000 and the Academic Legion another 7,000.[6]

The utmost dreams of the liberals were realized when the helpless government agreed to recognize civil rights, promised a constitution (March 15) and appointed a modern cabinet of well-known officials. Satisfaction with the fruits of the disorders was clearly indicated by the fact that fewer and fewer of the respectable people reported for service in the National Guard. By early April only about 7,200 showed real interest.[7] But the moderate liberal elements were soon to discover that they were now prisoners of more advanced, democratic forces, that is of the students, some 5,000 in number, who in turn were guided by a handful of instructors and junior staff members of the hospitals, such as Dr. Adolf Fischhof and Dr. Josef Goldmark. The students, furthermore, enjoyed the confidence of the workers in the suburbs, from whose midst many of them had come. During the spring of 1848 the popularity of the students was unlimited. Through a student committee they dominated the much larger Central Committee of Citizens, National Guards and Students, which more or less gave the law to the weak and confused government. Through never-ending demonstra-

5 Srbik: *Metternich*, II, 280 ff.; Paul Müller: *Feldmarschall Fürst Windischgrätz* (Vienna, 1934), 66, 88–89.

6 Paul Molisch: "Die Wiener akademische Legion" (*Archiv der oesterreichischen Geschichte*, CX, 1924, 1–207); Hugo Kerchnawe: *Die Ueberwindung der ersten Weltrevolution* (Innsbruck, 1932), 12, 17.

7 Rath: *Viennese Revolution*, 123.

tions and the practice of "serenading" unpopular ministers or officials, the students invariably had their way. With no training in political science and but little acquaintance with western doctrines, they readily took their cue from a few radical leaders. Democratic clubs were opened and extremist newspapers founded that attacked not only the government but the aristocracy and church hierarchy.[8]

Pressures upon the government from the Magyars and the Czechs in addition to the outbreak of insurrection in Milan and the ensuing declaration of war by Piedmont help to explain the weakness of the authorities in dealing with the Viennese situation. Furthermore, developments in the rest of Germany made it imperative that Austria keep pace with the liberalism which was everywhere triumphant. On April 25, after hasty deliberation, the cabinet, under the influence of the liberal-minded Baron Franz von Pillersdorf, proclaimed a constitution generally modeled on the Belgian constitution of 1831, to apply only to those parts of the monarchy which were included in the Germanic Confederation, plus Galicia. There was to be a two-chamber Parliament for the German provinces and Bohemia, Moravia and Galicia. The upper chamber was to consist of imperial princes, landed aristocrats and higher clergy. The lower Chamber of Deputies was to be indirectly elected by qualified taxpayers.

Once again the moderate elements, though they had had no share in the making of the constitution, were quite content with its provisions. But the students and their radical supporters at once protested against limitation of the franchise to taxpayers. The government again yielded, agreeing that all should have the vote except laborers by the day and week, and domestic servants, all of whom were allegedly too dependent on others to exercise their right freely. Once more the students objected. On May 15 there were immense, threatening demonstrations, before which the government, still unwilling to use force, had to capitulate. It now accepted the demand for complete manhood suffrage, and for a single-chamber Parliament. Furthermore, it surrendered its last weapon by promising that in future military forces should not be brought into the city except when requested by the National Guard.[9]

---

[8] Hermann Meyer: *1848: Studien zur Geschichte der deutschen Revolution* (Darmstadt, 1949) as well as Rath: *Viennese Revolution,* chap. v, analyze the forces of radicalism and their leaders.

[9] The electoral issue is admirably analyzed by Peter Burian: *Die Nationalitäten in 'Cisleithanien' und das Wahlrecht der Märzrevolution, 1848–1849* (Graz, 1962), 29 ff.

So complete was now the domination of the radicals that the imperial court arranged for the flight of the emperor and his entourage to Innsbruck (May 17). News of this event caused consternation in moderate circles, where it was feared that the radicals would proclaim a republic. There was a revulsion of feeling against the students, who were blamed for the rampant radicalism. Hoping to capitalize on this turn of opinion, the government on May 25 decreed that the university be closed and the Academic Legion merged with the National Guard. But this heroic decision invited only further disaster. The populace backed the students and thousands of workers arrived from the suburbs to stiffen resistance to the government. For the first time barricades appeared in the streets and preparations were made to fight. Once again Pillersdorf quailed. On May 26 he gave in to all demands: there was to be a Committee of Citizens, National Guards and Students of Vienna for Preservation of the Rights of the People, in short a Committee of Safety. This committee, with a membership of 240, was presided over by Dr. Fischhof, who had been in the forefront of the radical student movement from the outset. It marked the complete triumph of radicalism in the capital, and the first serious effort to combat the prevailing unemployment which, as in Paris, had increased with the political instability. Something akin to the French national workshops was set up, with government pay for the needy. As in Paris, this experiment created new problems, which must be left for discussion in a later context.

2. THE THREAT OF DISRUPTION

The Hapsburg court probably regarded the uprising of the Vienna students and workers as less ominous than the pretensions of the various nationalities and more particularly the terrifying threat of a peasant insurrection as presaged by the Galician troubles of 1846. It will be remembered that by 1848 many Austrian landowners had convinced themselves that serfdom had seen its day and that it would be impossible to maintain it much longer in the face of rising discontent and class hatred. Under the circumstances, they argued, it would be better to take the initiative in its abolition so as to make the most favorable settlement possible. On March 20, therefore, the government decreed that forced labor (*robot*) and other feudal obligations should be abolished as of March 31, 1849, in Bohemia and Moravia. The landowners were to be indemnified by the government and the state in turn was to recoup through additional charges on the peasants. These concessions were extended to Styria, Carinthia, Carniola and Galicia during the following weeks. In Galicia, the most explosive area, the abolition of serfdom was made immediate.[10] By these preventive measures the government certainly exorcized one of the greatest threats to the existing society. The peasants, expecting to receive a much better settlement than was intended, lost interest in revolution and were more and more inclined actually to take sides against the restless townsmen.

In Hungary, where the agrarian problem was equally pressing, the Parliament at Pressburg, frightened by false rumors of a huge insurrection of serfs in the neighborhood of Budapest, voted the immediate abolition of serfdom (March 15).[11] But the great objective of the Magyar nationalists was elimination of the control of the Vienna government and establishment of Hungary as a completely independent state, united with Austria only through the person of the ruler. Kossuth's program of March 3 envisaged not only independence for the "Kingdom of Saint Stephen," but incorporation of Croatia-Slavonia, Transylvania and the so-called Military Frontier in the Kingdom of Hungary. This expanded and reformed Hungarian state was to be national and constitutional, completely self-governing, with a ministry responsible to Parliament. The latter was henceforth to meet not in Pressburg but in Budapest, the center of the Magyar world.

The lower chamber of the Hungarian Diet, the stronghold of the gentry, supported this program wholeheartedly, but the upper house, in which the magnates or great landowners and high clergy dominated, opposed such drastic innovations for fear of a serious clash with the Vienna Court. When news arrived of the insurrection in Vienna, the recalcitrant were soon forced into line. On March 15 a large delegation, including seventy-five parliamentarians as well as leaders such as Széchenyi and Kossuth, set out for Vienna on the Danube steamer *Bela*. The party was given an enthusiastic ovation by the Viennese populace, which idolized Kossuth as the personification of liberalism. At the Court long and heated discussions took place over several days. At issue particularly were the questions of future control over the Hungarian armed forces and disposition of the huge public debt. In the end the

<hr>

[10] Jerome Blum: *Noble Landowners and Agriculture in Austria, 1815–1848* (Baltimore, 1948), 232 ff.

[11] György Spira: "La dernière génération des serfs de Hongrie" (*Annales*, XXIII, 1968, 353–367).

Court, fearful lest Hungary declare its independence and be lost to the dynasty, agreed to defer settlement of these vital matters and accepted the rest of the Hungarian demands.[12]

The Emperor Ferdinand, as king of Hungary, named Count Louis Batthyány, a liberal-minded magnate, to form a new cabinet. When completed, it included most of the leaders of the reform movement. Széchenyi became minister of communications and public works; Déak was given the ministry of justice, and Eötvös the ministry of public instruction. The more moderate reformers would have liked to exclude Kossuth, but fear of the public reaction induced them to give him, not the ministry of the interior, which he hoped for, but the troublesome ministry of finance.[13]

During the next three weeks the Hungarian Parliament approved some thirty "March Laws" which transformed the country from a feudal into a modern state of liberal stamp. These drastic changes were both political and social. Politically the king or the viceroy was to act only through the ministry, which was to be responsible to a Parliament meeting annually. The upper House of Magnates was to remain unchanged, but the lower Chamber of Deputies was henceforth to be elected by all males over the age of twenty, provided they were not in domestic service and possessed urban property worth 300 florins or landed property of at least ten acres. All religions were declared equal; preliminary censorship of the press was abolished; jury trials were instituted for press offenses; and a National Guard was established, to include all those who enjoyed the franchise. On the social side the exemption of the nobility from taxation was terminated; all feudal obligations and manorial jurisdictions were also ended, with provision for indemnification of the landowners by the state; church tithes were abolished without compensation, the state in future to provide the salaries of the clergy.[14]

12 François Eckart: "La révolution de 1848 en Hongrie et la cour de Vienne" (*Actes du Congrès Historique du Centenaire de la Révolution de 1848*, Paris, 1948, 229–242); Julius Miskolczy: *Ungarn in der Habsburger Monarchie* (Vienna, 1959).

13 According to the British agent, Joseph A. Blackwell, Kossuth "was regarded as an unavoidable fatality—a necessary evil by *all* his colleagues" (see the contemporary reports for March 19 and 22 in "England and the Hungarian Revolution," *South Eastern Affairs*, III, 91–132).

14 These laws are well summarized in C. M. Knatchbull-Hugessen: *The Political Evolution of the Hungarian Nation* (London, 1908), II, 25 ff., and in Dominic G. Kosary: *A History of Hungary* (Cleveland, 1941), 221 ff.

The March Laws, in the words of one Hungarian historian, represented the victory of a nation liberating itself not only from a foreign bureaucracy but also from the selfish interests of its own ruling class.[15] But the self-sacrifice of the upper classes was not as wholehearted as might appear. If the nobility rallied to the Kossuth program, it was largely in panic and fear of a major peasant insurrection.[16] Rumor, which proved unfounded, had it that radicals in Budapest were about to rouse the peasantry for a grand assault on the manor houses. There was in fact a radical, republican movement in the capital, which on March 15 had rallied the populace and forced the city council as well as the commander of the troops to accept the Twelve Points, a program similar to that of Kossuth, to whom the radicals looked for leadership.

The leader of this radical movement was the poet Alexander Petöfi, who, at the age of twenty-five, had already won the hearts of the common people by his lyrics and had attracted attention even abroad. Petöfi, who had started life as a poor vagabond actor, had nevertheless educated himself. He had at least a reading knowledge of western languages and was well-acquainted with the poetry of Schiller, Byron, Shelley and contemporary French poets such as Hugo and Béranger. Fascinated by the history of the French Revolution, he idolized the republic and the republican leaders and eventually came to study even socialist writers such as Fourier. He was a man of the people and shared fully in their hatred of the privileged aristocracy. Indeed, he was a most thoroughgoing democrat and republican. In one of his best poems, *The Hungarian Noble* (1845), he had the aristocrat priding himself on his ignorance and idleness:

> Doing no work—that is life.
> I am idle, therefore I am alive.
> Work is for the peasant.
> I am a Hungarian noble.

[15] Heinrich Marczali: *Ungarische Verfassungsgeschichte* (Tübingen, 1910), 145.

[16] Erwin Szábo: "Aus den Parteien und Klassenkämpfen in der ungarischen Revolution von 1848" (*Archiv für die Geschichte des Sozialismus*, VIII, 1919, 258–307); Coloman Benda: "La question paysanne et la révolution hongroise en 1848" (*Etudes d'histoire moderne et contemporaine*, II, 1948, 231–242); Erzsebet Andiċs: "Kossuth en lutte contre les ennemis des réformes et de la révolution" (*Studia historica*, XII, 1954, 1–169), 61 ff.

What do I care about the country?
The hundred troubles of the country?
The troubles will soon pass off.
I am a Hungarian noble.[17]

During the popular demonstration on March 15, Petöfi read his new
National Ode:

Up, Hungarian, your country is calling!
Here is the time, now or never!
Shall we be slaves or free?
This is the question, answer—
By the God of the Hungarians we swear,
We swear to be slaves no more.[18]

The Twelve Points having been agreed upon, a delegation was sent to
the Diet at Pressburg and received by Kossuth on March 17. The latter,
however, displayed great caution, warning against any popular effort to
coerce the Diet. Kossuth was clearly apprehensive lest the democratic-
republican program estrange the nobility from the work of reform.
The Diet was already much upset by the news of the Budapest rising
and the radical program. It was the threat of radicalism that led the
nobility to accept the reform program lock, stock and barrel after only
the most cursory discussion.[19]

The Emperor Ferdinand, beset by countless difficulties, had no
choice but to approve the March Laws (April 11). His entourage,
however, was deeply troubled, not only by the laws, but by the efforts
of the Hungarian government to incorporate Transylvania, Croatia
and the Military Frontier (the eastern part of Croatia, organized as a
military colony for protection of the empire against the Turks, and

---

[17] Quoted from D. Mervyn Jones: *Five Hungarian Writers* (Oxford, 1966), 262. See
also Paul A. Löffler: *La vie d'Alexandre Petöfi* (Rodez, 1953); René Schwachhofen:
Bettelsack und Freiheit: Leben und Werk Alexander Petöfis (Weimar, 1954), which is
excellent.

[18] Jones: *Five Hungarian Writers,* 277.

[19] For the Budapest demonstration, see the excerpts from Petöfi's diary, available in
German translation in Petöfi: *Prosäische Schriften* (Leipzig, 1895), 83 ff. There is a
fairly good translation of the *National Ode* in *Sixty Poems by Alexander Petöfi,*
translated by Eugenie B. Pierce and Emil Delmar. On the fears of the nobility, see
Dominic Kosary: "L'aspect social de la révolution de 1848 en Hongrie" (*Actes du
Congrès Historique du Centenaire,* 133–142), and György Spira: "L'alliance de Lajos
Kossuth avec la gauche radicale et les masses populaires de la révolution hongroise de
1848–1849" (*Acta historica,* II, 1953, 49–150), 49 ff.

under direct jurisdiction of the Vienna government). Another serious problem was the attempt of the Hungarians to apply the taxes, customs and mines of the country to strictly Hungarian needs, and to secure control of the Hungarian regiments, of which only four were serving in Hungary, while six were in Italy and five in Austria and Bohemia.[20]

The dominant figure at the Court was now the Archduchess Sophia, a Bavarian princess married to the Archduke Francis Charles, a prince who was hardly better fitted to rule than his brother Ferdinand. Sophia was intelligent, strong-willed and courageous. Strictly conservative and clerical in her upbringing, she felt humiliated by the emperor's submission to the demands of "a mess of students," as well as by the many concessions that followed. She was determined to have the childless Ferdinand abdicate the throne as soon as possible in favor of her own eighteen-year-old son Francis Joseph. Prince Windischgrätz, Count Charles Stadion, the governor of Galicia, Archbishop Otmar Rauscher and a few other high officials, soon to be called the Camarilla, concurred entirely in this program. But military suppression of the revolution and the dynastic change would have to wait, for all available troops were needed in Italy. Meanwhile the Court would have to maneuver as best it could to stave off disintegration of the empire.[21]

It was the established practice of the Vienna government to combat the centrifugal forces of feudalism and nationalism by playing off one against the other. To counter Magyar pretensions it was decided to support the Croats, Serbs and Rumanians, all of them subject peoples of the Crown of Saint Stephen who were determined to resist the efforts of the Hungarian government to Magyarize them. On March 23, soon after the departure of the Hungarian delegation from Vienna, the emperor appointed as ban (governor) of Croatia Baron Joseph Jellachich (Jellačič), who was colonel of one of the frontier regiments and a friend of Louis Gaj, the leader of the Illyrian movement. A week later Gaj himself appeared in Vienna at the head of a large delegation requesting the union of Croatia, Dalmatia and Slavonia in one king-

---

[20] Gunther E. Rothenberg: "The Habsburg Army" (*Austrian History Yearbook*, III, Part I, 1967, 70–90).

[21] Little is known of the deliberations of the Camarilla, but see Heinrich Friedjung: *Oesterreich von 1848 bis 1860*, I, 13 ff.; Josef Redlich: *Emperor Francis Joseph of Austria* (New York, 1929), 11 ff.; Egon C. Corti: *Kindheit und erste Jugend Kaiser Franz Josephs I* (Vienna, 1950), 263 ff., which draws upon the archduchess' diaries.

dom, free of Hungarian control. The emperor, though he evaded definite commitments, indicated that the Croats could count on his support in their resistance to Hungarian pressures.[22]

The appointment of Jellachich came as a great blow to Kossuth, who had deluded himself into thinking that the new liberal institutions would counteract separatist, nationalist movements.[23] His disillusionment was complete when in early April Jellachich was made commander of all troops in Croatia and the Military Frontier, and when on April 19 he ordered all Croat officials to cease communication with the Hungarian government.

Kossuth's response, strongly supported by both liberal and radical elements, was to refuse the royal request for more Hungarian troops to be sent to the Italian theater of war. This move quickly brought the Vienna authorities to heel. On May 7 the Court reversed itself, called upon Jellachich to obey the orders of the viceroy of Hungary, appointed Marshal John Hrabovski to supersede Jellachich in command of the troops, and put all Croatian and Military Frontier forces under the Hungarian Ministry of War. Ten days later the Court, exposed to radical revolution in the capital, fled to Innsbruck. It was the moment of greatest crisis, so the imperial government yielded readily to the further proposals of a Hungarian delegation which arrived in Innsbruck. In return for the promise to provide more Hungarian troops for Italy, the Court gave assurances that it would discontinue support of the Croats. On June 10 Jellachich was deprived of all his offices and threatened with impeachment if he disobeyed.[24]

The court Camarilla was appalled by the emperor's repeated compliance and the Archduchess Sophia was now convinced that Ferdinand must be replaced as soon as possible. Jellachich was summoned to Innsbruck and probably encouraged to ignore the imperial orders. In any event, June 15 saw the Court's first important success: Windischgrätz' reduction of insurgent Prague through bombardment of the

[22] Kosary: *History of Hungary*, 226 ff.; M. Hartley: *The Man who Saved Austria: the Life and Times of Baron Jellačić* (London, 1912), 132 ff.; Ferdinand Hauptmann: "Banus Jellačić und Feldmarschall Fürst Windisch-Grätz" (*Süd-Ost Forschungen*, XV, 1956, 373–402).

[23] Zoltan I. Toth: "The Nationality Problem in Hungary in 1848–1849" (*Acta historica*, IV, 1955, 235–277).

[24] For a succinct review of these complicated happenings, see Gunther E. Rothenberg: "Jelačić, the Croatian Military Border and the Intervention against Hungary in 1848" (*Austrian History Yearbook*, I, 1965, 45–67).

city. This was the signal for an open reversal of Imperial policy. On June 19 Jellachich's deposition was revoked and no further secret made of the fact that the Court would again support the resistance of Croatians, Serbs and Rumanians to Hungarian rule. On May 13 a Serbian national congress had met at Karlowitz and declared the Serbs of the empire "politically free and autonomous under the House of Austria and the Crown of Hungary," at the same time voting closest co-operation with Croats, Slavonians and Dalmatians. Shortly after that the Rumanians of Transylvania had protested the action of the Magyar-dominated Diet in voting the union of Transylvania with Hungary. A national council had been set up under Abraham Jancu and the loyalty of the Transylvanian Rumanians to the Hapsburg dynasty reaffirmed.[25]

The duplicity of the Austrian court becomes somewhat more understandable when set in the framework of the war against Piedmont. Kossuth and other members of the Hungarian government made no secret of their sympathies for Italian aspirations and talked constantly of the need for recalling the Hungarian regiments serving outside the country. Beset by the revolt of the subject peoples, all Hungarian troops were needed at home. On July 11 Kossuth in a major speech called upon Parliament to declare the country in danger and authorize an army of 200,000 men for defense. While the Budapest government, therefore, displayed its hostility to the imperial Court, Jellachich proclaimed his loyalty to the dynasty and served as guarantor that the 40,000 Croatian and Frontier regiments in Italy would remain faithful.

An important turn in events came with Field Marshal Radetzky's resounding victory over the Italians at the Battle of Custoza (July 24), which led presently to the conclusion of an armistice in the Italian war. Croatian troops could now be released for reassignment to Jellachich. The Camarilla made up its mind that the time had come to put an end to the Hungarian threat to disrupt the empire. The Court returned to Vienna on August 12 and brushed aside last-minute efforts by Batthyány and Déak to arrive at an accommodation. On August 31 the

[25] G. Y. Develle: *La nouvelle Serbie* (Paris, 1918), 155 ff.; Hermann Wendel: *Der Kampf der Südslawen um Freiheit und Einheit* (Frankfurt, 1925), 229 ff.; L. S. Stavrianos: *Balkan Federation* (Northampton, 1942), 57 ff.; Dragoslav Stranjaković: "La collaboration des Croates et des Serbes en 1848–1849" (*Le monde slave*, n.s., XII, 1935, 394–404); Ladislas Makkai: *Histoire de Transylvanie* (Paris, 1946), 310 ff.; Mihail Roller: *Histoire de la Roumanie* (Bucharest, 1947).

March Laws, on which the new Hungarian regime rested, were declared incompatible with the Pragmatic Sanction of 1723 and destructive of the unity of the empire. A few days later Jellachich, who meanwhile had raised and organized a force of 50,000 men, began the invasion of Hungary. He crossed the Drave (September 11), hoping for the support of the Serbs for a rapid advance on Budapest. On the same day Batthyány, representative of the moderate element in Hungarian politics, resigned as premier and left Kossuth the undisputed leader in the conflict confronting the country.

3. THE AUSTRO-SLAVS

The counterpart of the Hungarian drive for independence was the effort of the Slavs of the empire to unite and attain equal status with the Germans and the Magyars in a federally organized state. The Czechs, as the most advanced of the Slavic peoples of the empire, naturally assumed the lead, making Prague the focal point of the movement. There, even before the outbreak of the revolution in Vienna, a spontaneous popular assembly had called for civil rights, the equality of the Czech and German languages, and even the "organization of labor." A committee, which was to draft an appropriate petition to the emperor, appealed to intellectual leaders such as Palacký and Havlícek, who produced the petition of March 22. Couched in submissive, moderate terms, it asked for the administrative union of Bohemia, Moravia and Austrian Silesia to form an autonomous state, roughly like the Hungarian state of the March Laws. On April 8 the hard-pressed Imperial Court granted most of these demands, though the question of the union of the three provinces was left for decision to the general Austrian Parliament which was to meet in early summer.

Thus far the Germans and Czechs of Bohemia had co-operated. The upper middle class (largely German intellectuals and businessmen) and the lesser middle class (mostly Czech shopkeepers and artisans) were united in the campaign for a liberal regime. The Germans, though dominant, appear to have been quite prepared to accept the Czech language as equal to the German and to have raised no objection to the projected union of the three historic lands. All were agreed that the feudal system must be ended. The rural population, half of which was landless and in great distress, was becoming menacingly restless. That feudal obligations and jurisdiction must be abolished was obvious even to the landowners. Palacký urged immediate action, so that the landowners might at least obtain compensation for the loss of their "property." There was real danger, he maintained, that the urban radicals might mobilize the peasants for a social revolution, which was the last thing the propertied classes wanted to see.[26]

The rift between the two nationalities was first revealed by an important episode in early April. At Frankfurt a commission (the *Vorparlament*) was preparing for the meeting of a German national assembly which was to work out the unification of the German states. Since Bohemia, Moravia and Silesia were included in the Germanic Confederation of 1815 and were always regarded by Germans as German territory, the Frankfurt commissioners invited Palacký to join them as a representative of the three provinces. To this invitation Palacký replied (April 11) in what was hardly less than a historical-political essay. He must decline the invitation, he said, because he was not a German, but a Czech devoted to his Czech nationality. The past connection of Bohemia with the Germanic Confederation, he continued, was "a mere dynastic tie" to which the Czech nation, that is, the Czech states, paid no attention. German nationalists, he charged, were undermining the Hapsburg Empire, but that empire was one "whose preservation, integrity, and consolidation is, and must be, a great and important matter not only for my own nation, but also for the whole of Europe, indeed for humanity and civilization itself." Only through that empire could the peoples of Eastern Europe be protected against Russian expansion and domination, "an infinite and inexpressible evil, a misfortune without measure or bound." None of the nationalities of the Danube Basin being strong enough to stand by itself, their union in one state was essential: "Assuredly, if the Austrian state had not existed for ages, it would have been a behest for us in the interests of Europe and indeed of humanity to endeavor to create it as soon as possible," he wrote in an oft-misquoted passage. He recommended that the Germans proceed to the unification of the German states and leave the peoples of the Hapsburg Monarchy to reorganize

---

[26] Arnost Klima: "Ein Beitrag zur Agrarfrage in der Revolution von 1848 in Böhmen" (*Studia historica*, No. 51, 1961, 15–26). The landowners, industrialists, merchants and intellectuals had been organized since 1833 in the Society for the Encouragement of the Industrial Spirit in Bohemia, which became more or less a political debating society. See Hans Raupach: *Der tschechische Frühnationalismus* (Halle, 1929), 57 ff., 109 ff. On Czech radicalism, see Berthold Bretholz: *Geschichte Böhmens und Mährens* (Reichenberg, 1924), IV, 75 ff.; and the suggestive Marxian study by I. I. Udalzow: *Aufzeichnungen über die Geschichte des nationalen und politischen Kampfes in Böhmen im Jahre 1848* (Berlin, 1953), 43 ff.

their empire on a federal basis, with full equality for all nationalities. Ultimately the German and Austrian Empires might enter upon a firm alliance, reinforced by a customs union.[27]

Palacký's famous letter amounted to a formulation of the doctrine known as Austro-Slavism, which hinged on the maintenance of the Hapsburg Empire in the interests at least of the Austrian Slavs, who, as nations, were too weak to hold their own in the modern world. It involved rejection of German efforts to incorporate any part of the empire (not only the Czech provinces but also the essentially German ones) in a new German Empire, and at the same time insistence on reorganization of the empire along federal lines, so that each nationality might be autonomous.[28]

An important step in the realization of this program would be the union of the Slavic peoples of the monarchy and an effort to put them on a par with the Germans and the Magyars. The idea was given impetus when in May the Vienna government ruled that the issue of elections to a German Parliament should be left to the provincial authorities. Thereupon the Bohemian Germans seceded from the National Committee which, since mid-April, had been the *de facto* government of Bohemia. The Czechs, on their side, did all they could to block the elections to the Frankfurt Parliament, so that in the end only the eighteen strictly German electoral districts (out of a total of sixty-eight) chose delegates.

After this first bout, the Czech leaders decided to convoke a Congress of the Slavs to counterbalance the Frankfurt Parliament and also the Magyar Parliament at Budapest. The rift between the Czechs and Slovaks was quickly bridged when, after the Hungarian government had rejected Slovak demands for self-government, the Slovak leaders fled to Prague and threw in their lot with the Czechs. It was Stúr in fact who drafted the invitation to the congress.[29]

27 A full English translation may be found in the *Slavonic Review*, XXVI, 1948, 303–308.

28 The doctrine is well analyzed in Otakar Odložilik: "A Czech Plan for a Danubian Confederation, 1848" (*Journal of Central European Affairs*, 1941, 253–274); Rudolf Wierer: "Palacký's staatspolitisches Programm" (*Zeitschrift für Ostforschung*, VI, 1957, 246–258).

29 Albert Prazák: "Czechs and Slovaks in the Revolution of 1848" (*Slavonic Review*, V, 1927, 565–579), and "The Slavonic Congress of 1848 and the Slovaks" (*ibid.*, VII, 1928, 141–159); Daniel Rapant: "Slovak Politics in 1848–1849" (*ibid.*, XXVII, 1948–1949, 67–90, 381–403).

Palacký's intention was to invite only Slavs of the Austrian Empire, but some of the Galician Poles demanded that all Slav nations be invited, hoping no doubt that the entire Polish problem could then be put on the docket. In the end it was decided that non-Austrian Slavs might attend the congress, but only as guests, without vote. Actually only a few Prussian Poles and a few non-Austrian Serbs appeared, along with two Russians (one of them the great revolutionist Michael Bakunin). They were too few to act as a group. As individuals they were finally permitted to vote along with the Austrians, though Palacký made it clear that the sole issue before the congress was the future of the Austrian Slavs and the integrity of the Austrian empire.[30]

The Congress of the Slavs (or Slavic or Slavonic Congress, for short) opened its sessions in Prague on June 2. It was a typical midcentury assembly of middle-class intellectuals. There were only 35 aristocrats and 16 clerics among the 340 members. Most of the Austrian Slav leaders were present and gave the congress a distinctly moderate cast. Czechs and Slovaks were in the vast majority (237), while Poles and Ruthenians from Galicia numbered 61 and the South Slavs only 42. Each of the three sections, based on the foregoing classification, was to prepare a manifesto to the nations of Europe, establishing the claims of the Austrian Slavs; a petition to the emperor; and a plan for reorganization of the empire. There was evidently a good deal of heated debate, for by no means all the members were enamored of the Palacký program. The Poles disliked the Czechs and distrusted the Vienna government. They would have liked the co-operation of the Austrian Slavs in the struggle for Polish independence and in the effort to unite all Slavs on a democratic basis. Bakunin, who played an important part in the Polish-Ruthenian section, was utterly committed to the destruction of "the monstrous Austrian Empire" and considered Austro-Slavism pure utopia. The Slovaks, again, were reluctant to sever all connection with Hungary and were irked by Czech pretensions to leadership. The Poles, in contrast to the Slovaks and Croats, were well-disposed to the Magyars. And in addition to these divergent views there was the fundamental question whether the empire should be federalized on the

[30] Alfred Fischel: *Der Panslawismus bis zum Weltkrieg* (Stuttgart, 1919), 262 ff.; Lewis B. Namier: *1848: the Revolution of the Intellectuals* (London, 1944), 105; Henryk Batowski: "The Poles and their Fellow-Slavs in 1848" (*Slavonic and East European Review*, XXVII, 1949, 404–413).

basis of the historic lands (which was the Czech desire), or on the basis of ethnographic divisions.[31]

Failure to agree on so many points meant that in the end the congress produced little more than a vague, emotional manifesto to the nations of Europe, almost entirely the work of Palacký. The great historian reverted to his favorite thesis: the peace-loving Slavs who had been conquered and exploited by the warlike Germans were no longer willing to be victimized. They asked only liberty and equality for all nations as for all individuals. His manifesto called for justice to Poland, demanded that the Magyars cease their oppression of the Slavs, and expressed the hope that the Slavs still under Turkish rule might soon be given a chance to develop. After insisting on the federal reorganization of the Hapsburg Monarchy, it closed with a universal appeal:

We, the youngest but by no means the weakest people, in entering once more the political arena of Europe, propose that a general European Congress of Nations be summoned for the discussion of all international questions; being thoroughly convinced that free nations will more easily come to agreement than paid diplomats.[32]

When on June 12 the manifesto was approved by the congress, the sessions came to an end. Bakunin, writing some months later, described the meeting as "the resurrection of the Slavs," and declared that for them "it was the first day of a new life." Later commentators have described the congress as "the peak of the Slavonic renascence."[33] No doubt its effect was to enhance the national self-consciousness of Slavs everywhere and, despite all differences of interest and aim, make for mutual understanding and tolerance. In the last analysis the congress must be viewed as a product of the 1848 upheaval. The learned and high-minded intellectuals gathered there were genuinely moved by the

---

31 Fischel: *Der Panslawismus*, 268 ff.; Hans Kohn: *Pan-Slavism* (Notre Dame, 1953), 72 ff.; and the excellent essay by Otakar Odložilik: "The Slavic Congress of 1848" (*Polish Review*, IV, 1959, 3–15). Some of the basic differences are discussed by Benoît P. Hepner: *Bakounine et le panslavisme révolutionnaire* (Paris, 1950), 253; see also Peter F. Sugar: "The Nature of the non-Germanic Societies under Habsburg Rule" (*Slavic Review*, XXII, 1963, 1–30).

32 Full text in *Slavonic Review*, XXVI, 1948, 309–313; see also Namier: *1848*, 114; Josef Mačurek: "The Achievement of the Slavonic Congress" (*Slavonic Review*, XXVI, 1948, 329–340).

33 Bakunin's remark is taken from the draft of his own appeal (see Josef Pfitzner: *Bakuninstudien*, Prague, 1932, 84). For the second question, see Mačurek: "Achievement of the Slavonic Congress."

ideals of liberty, equality and fraternity. They made a point of proclaiming their love and respect for all peoples. At the same time they approached their immediate political problem in realistic fashion. Austro-Slavism, as expounded by Palacký, was an excellent solution for the problem of the Czechs, but it held less appeal for some of the other Slavs. Before long the idealism of June was to give way to the conflict of divergent aims and policies.

June 12, the day of the official end of the congress, was also the first day of the insurrection in Prague which many historians regard as an unfortunate episode and a severe blow to the notion of Slavic unity. But the rising should be studied in its own right and not only in the context of the congress. It was, in a sense, the counterpart of the Vienna revolt of late May, an uprising of the unemployed and destitute, for which students provided a rudimentary leadership. It had no specific plan nor program, and seems to have had no reference whatever to the nationalist issues which were being debated at the congress. German and Czech students and workers acted in concert and were opposed by the German and Czech upper classes without regard to nationality.

In Prague as in Vienna there had been a proliferation of radical literature during the spring of 1848, followed presently by strikes and gatherings of workers. The peasants, too, were beginning to demonstrate opposition: they were refusing to wait a full year for abolition of feudalism, were defaulting on their duties and threatening an agrarian terror. Meanwhile Prince Windischgrätz, the governor, had returned to his post on May 17. He had, in 1844, put down workers' revolts and was all for applying military force to restore order in Vienna and other centers of disturbance. In collaboration with the court Camarilla he worked out a plan for combating urban insurrection: the strong points of the city were to be occupied; the bayonet rather than the musket was to be used in dispersing crowds; troops were to avoid involvement in the narrow streets of the old cities; every effort was to be made to keep open the main lines of communication; if necessary, artillery was to be used to batter down barricades prior to their storming in bayonet charges.[34]

By early June, Windischgrätz had concentrated all available forces in the vicinity of Prague and had mounted artillery on the heights

[34] Hermann Kriebel: *Feldmarschall Fürst Windisch-Grätz* (Innsbruck, 1929), 13–14.

surrounding the city. The students, to whom his very name was anathema, demanded his recall and the cessation of military preparations. They even went so far as to ask for 2,000 muskets, so that they could preserve order. Naturally these demands were ignored by the governor. As a result, the closing of the congress was made the occasion for a great popular demonstration. Guns went off around the palace and Princess Windischgrätz, standing indiscreetly at a window, was shot dead. In almost no time hundreds of barricades went up all over the town. Several days of street fighting ensued, during which the insurgents made great efforts to instigate a peasant rising. Palacký and other leaders tried in vain to mediate. Windischgrätz, it seems, allowed the revolt to develop for some days so as to make the repression more complete. Eventually he withdrew his troops from the city and on June 16 began a systematic bombardment, despite the fact that the popular leaders had already indicated their readiness to capitulate.

Once the rising was suppressed, the local government or National Committee and the National Guard were dissolved and martial law established. There were numerous arrests and the foreign members of the congress were expelled. The revolutionary movement in Prague, basically a moderate movement, was thus snuffed out along with the radicalism of the students and workers. A flood of recriminations followed. The *bourgeoisie,* frightened by the specter of social upheaval, charged German and Magyar agents with having stirred up the populace. At the same time the Germans rejoiced at the suppression of the "anti-German" movement of the Czech nationalists and even debated the desirability of calling in Bavarian or Saxon troops to save the Bohemian Germans from a further "blood bath." Social as well as national lines were now sharply drawn.

Viewed in the framework of general Hapsburg history, the bombardment and reduction of Prague was an epoch-making event. It was the first "victory" of the conservatives over the revolutionaries, of the governments over the peoples. Windischgrätz had demonstrated that as long as the troops remained loyal, urban insurrections could be mastered. The popular movements had only ideas and ideals to support them. They could not hope to hold out against organized military power. That power none of the governments had been willing to apply in February and March. But by June they had recovered from their initial surprise and fright, or at least had begun to yield to the pressure of the military men, who, many of them, made no secret of their eagerness to give short shrift to the revolutionary "canaille." In doing just that, Windischgrätz had opened a new chapter in the story of the midcentury revolutions.[35]

4. ITALY: REVOLUTION AND WAR

The overriding concern of the Viennese government in the spring of 1848 was with Italy, where revolution had broken out in Milan, followed by Piedmontese intervention and war against Austria. The tension in Milan was already acute when news of the Vienna revolution arrived on March 17. The substantial liberal group, consisting of progressive nobles, merchants and bankers, was committed to the struggle for a constitution and dreamed of the expulsion of the Austrians and the organization of Italy as a national state along federal lines. But it hoped to attain its ends by propaganda and agitation, not by revolution.[36] It was rather the more radical, republican element that forced the pace and planned for a monster demonstration with a petition calling for freedom of the press, liquidation of the police force, formation of a civic guard, and convocation of a National Assembly.

On the morning of March 18 Count Gabrio Casati, the podestà or mayor, informed Count O'Donnell, the vice-governor, of the coming demonstration and, arguing that any show of military power would only enhance the unrest, persuaded him to request the commander of the garrison, General Radetzky, not to intervene unless expressly called upon to do so.[37] By noon on the same day about 10,000 people, some

---

[35] For a detailed history of the Prague insurrection, see the Marxist study of I. I. Udalzow: *Aufzeichnungen über die Geschichte des nationalen und politischen Kampfes in Böhmen im Jahre 1848* (Berlin, 1953), especially 122 ff.; but see also the "bourgeois" accounts of Bretholz: *Geschichte Böhmens*, IV, 100 ff.; and Namier: *1848*, 116 ff. On the military aspects, see Paul Müller: *Feldmarschall Fürst Windischgrätz* (Vienna, 1934), 112 ff.

[36] Gaetano Salvemini: *I partiti politici Milanese nel secolo XIX* (reprinted in his *Scritti sul Risorgimento*, Milan, 1961, 27–123); Walter Maturi: "Partiti politici e correnti di pensiero nel Risorgimento" (in *Nuove questioni di storia del Risorgimento e del unità d'Italia*, Milan, 1961, 39–130, especially 99 ff.).

[37] Joseph A. von Helfert: *Mailand und der lombardische Aufstand, März, 1848* (Frankfurt, 1856), 5 ff.; Cesare Spellanzon: *Storia del Risorgimento e dell'unità d'Italia* (Milan, 1936), III, 711; G. F. H. Berkeley and J. Berkeley: *Italy in the Making* (Cambridge, 1940), III, 81 ff.; and the critical analysis of Casati's activity in Alessandro Luzio: "L'apologia di O'Donnell" (in his *Studi critici*, Milan, 1937, 108 ff.).

armed with pistols, daggers or clubs, surged about the Broletto or city hall and all but forced Casati to lead a parade to the government palace to secure acceptance of the petition. When Casati arrived at the palace, two of the imperial guards had already been slain and the mob had begun to invade the building. O'Donnell, badly frightened, agreed to all the demands made upon him and followed the mob back to the Broletto as a hostage.[38]

Presently the narrow, winding streets of the old city bristled with barricades. The troops, who now belatedly intervened, were met with bottles, pans and other missiles thrown from the roofs. The crowd plundered the famous Uboldi collection of medieval armor and raided La Scala opera house for halberds, pikes and other weapons. During the night a central committee was formed to direct insurgent operations. Carlo Cattaneo, the eminent philosopher-economist and republican theorist, who at first had urged the folly of fighting while unarmed against the Austrian troops, became the guiding spirit of the committee. With only about 600 muskets the populace put up a ferocious fight, much more bloody than the Paris insurrection of the month before.

Radetzky, an octogenarian hero of the Napoleonic Wars and probably the ablest military man of his time, had long since foreseen trouble and had called for reinforcements, only to have his fears discounted in Vienna. As a result he had at his disposal only 13,000 men to preserve order in a city of 170,000, the rest of his forces being dispersed as garrisons in other towns.[39] Nonetheless he took up the fight, calling in 6,000 or 7,000 additional troops from neighboring towns. By the evening of March 18 he had retaken several key points, including the Broletto and the government palace. Violent fighting continued during the following days, until a heavy rain set in on the 20th. It then became increasingly difficult to hold and supply numerous scattered posts, so the troops were called back to the Castello, which many of them reached only through torrents of rain and showers of rocks, tiles and

38 Antonio Monti: *Il 1848 e le cinque giornate di Milano* (Milan, 1948); Berkeley and Berkeley: *Italy in the Making,* III, 81 ff.; Spellanzon: *Storia del Risorgimento,* III, 711 ff.; Giorgio Candeloro: *Storia d'Italia moderna* (Milan, 1960), III, 165 ff.

39 Feldmarschall Graf Radetzky: "Die Märztage des Jahres 1848 in Mailand" (*Oesterreichische Rundschau,* XIV, 1908, 339–348); Oskar von Arno: *Der Feldherr Radetzky* (Vienna, 1934), 54 ff.; Hugo Kerchnawe: *Radetzky* (Vienna, 1944), 62 ff.; Oscar Regele: *Feldmarschall Radetzky* (Vienna, 1957), 236 ff.

hot water poured from the rooftops. However, the Austrian forces still held the walls and gates of the old city and so prevented intercourse between the insurgents and the surrounding territory.

On March 22 Radetzky with heavy heart decided to evacuate the city. His troops, few in number, were weary and hungry, the country round about was seething with insurrection, and the threat of Piedmontese intervention might soon make withdrawal impossible. On March 23 the troops succeeded in making an orderly exit, "one of those sorry masterpieces of the art of war," to borrow Radetzky's own words. The "Five Days" of Milan were indeed among the most remarkable cases in history of successful street fighting.[40]

The Austrian troops, many of them barefoot and but scantily clad, reached Verona on April 1, having lost their munitions and other equipment on the way. They took refuge in the forts of the Quadrilateral: Peschiera and Mantua on the Mincio River and Verona and Legnago on the Adige, commanding the narrow passage between Lake Como and the Po River, and forming the boundary between Lombardy and Venetia. Both provinces were now in open revolt, for in Venice a popular rising had forced the Austrian troops to evacuate, after which the leaders, Daniele Manin, a prominent lawyer, and Niccolò Tommaseo, a well-known man of letters, had proclaimed the Republic of San Marco.[41]

Radetzky had lost upward of 11,000 men through the defection of Italian units in his army and isolation of a further 7,000 who were cut off in various places. All told he had hardly more than 35,000 men and with these he had now to face the prospect of attack by Piedmont and other Italian states supporting the Milanese revolution. The moderates in the Lombard capital had at once appealed to Charles Albert of Piedmont for support, not only against the Austrians, but against the

[40] Berkeley and Berkeley: *Italy in the Making*, III, 78. The literature on the Five Days is almost endless. On the Italian side, see Monti: *il 1848 e le cinque giornate*, Pietro Pieri: *Storia militare del Risorgimento* (Turin, 1962), 187 ff.; and the contemporary account of a Swiss officer, A. Le Masson, translated as *Military Events in Italy, 1848–1849* (London, 1851). On the Austrian side, General Karl von Schönhals' *Erinnerungen eines oesterreichischen Veteranen aus dem italinischen Kriege, 1848–1849* (Stuttgart, 1852) is something of a classic.

[41] Vincenzo Marchesi: *Storia documentata della rivoluzione e della difesa di Venezia negli anni 1848–1849* (Venice, 1913) is fundamental, but far less readable than George M. Trevelyan: *Manin and the Venetian Republic of 1848* (New York, 1923); Alessandro Levi: *La politica di Daniele Manin* (Milan, 1933), 9 ff.

violent, revolutionary elements in their own city. Perhaps if he had crossed the frontier at once, the king might have hampered the Austrian retreat or possibly have destroyed Radetzky's whole army, for he had a standing army of 45,000 men which could be raised to a strength of 60,000 in a short time. But Charles Albert, irresolute by nature, was kept from reaching a prompt decision by many and varied considerations.

In the first place, the king was deeply religious and conservative, much under the influence of the Jesuits. He still felt bound by the alliance concluded with Austria in 1831 to meet the threat of war with France. Although he had now turned against Austria and had more or less accepted the role assigned to him by Italian nationalists, his fears of revolution and of aggression by France had been reawakened by the February Revolution. Much as he would have liked to acquire Lombardy and if possible Venetia, he was most reluctant to aid and abet revolution in Milan, the more so as intervention might lead to renewed French claims to Savoy and Nice, or even to war. Furthermore, the British, Prussian and Russian ministers were all warning him against aggression as likely to result in a larger conflict. On the other hand, the pressure from liberals and nationalists was hardly to be resisted. On March 23 Count Cavour had published an unequivocal warning: "One way only lies open to the nation, to the government, to the king: war, war immediately and without delays."[42]

Later that day the decision for intervention was made, at a time when the insurrection in Milan was already successful and a provisional government had already been set up by Casati and his friends.[43] By March 26 the first Piedmontese troops reached Milan, while news of the expulsion of the Austrians evoked a storm of enthusiasm throughout the peninsula. Charles Albert, in the hope of discouraging French intervention, had announced that the Italians alone would liberate Italy: *Italia farà da se*. In the same spirit volunteers enrolled everywhere and popular pressure forced the various governments to contribute contingents of troops to the national war. The Tuscan

42 William R. Thayer: *The Life and Times of Cavour* (Boston, 1911), I, 87; Amadeo Tosti: "L'età contemporanea" (in *Storia d'Italia*, Rome, 1958), 114.

43 Salvemini: *I partiti politici Milanese*, 61 ff.; Adolfo Omodeo: *La leggenda di Carlo Alberto nella recente storiografia* (Turin, 1940), 93 ff.; and the standard biography of the king by Niccolò Rodolico: *Carlo Alberto negli anni 1843–1849* (Florence, 1943), 289 ff.

government dispatched 7,000 men (March 29), and the Duke of Parma a comparable number (April 9). Even the papal government fell in line: 7,000 regulars were sent to defend the Po frontier against any attempt by the Austrians to advance south. In addition 9,000 militia and volunteers were allowed to start for the north. Ferdinand of Naples, too, was obliged to participate by sending 14,000 men to the north by land and sea. Under the circumstances success seemed certain at an early date. Patriotic fervor ran high and everywhere the youth hoped to be in on the final triumph.[44]

At first all went well, for Radetzky remained inactive and thereby made it easy for Charles Albert to overrun Lombardy and reach the Mincio River (April 6). After winning the Battle of Goito (a minor engagement) the Italians crossed the river and invested Peschiera. But little more was done to exploit their temporary advantage. Military critics argue that if the Piedmontese had crossed to the south side of the Po and invaded Venetia, they might have cut the Austrian communications and deprived Radetzky of all hopes of reinforcement. Strong terms have been used in condemnation of the king for allowing himself to be torn this way and that by the conflicting counsels of his generals, none of whom had any real plans of campaign. In any event, several weeks were lost in argument.[45]

Political as well as military considerations help to explain Charles Albert's procrastination. He was hoping to acquire Lombardy and Venetia so as to establish a strong and prosperous North Italian kingdom. He was therefore troubled by the possibility that the Milan provisional government might set up an independent Lombard state and turn to the French Republic for support. He therefore regarded as urgent the "fusion" of Lombardy with Piedmont. This solution was entirely agreeable to most members of the Lombard provisional government, who as nobles and landowners felt uneasy about their revolutionary role and lived in fear lest radical elements in town and country

---

[44] General Mario Caracciolo di Ferolete: "Il contributo militare degli Stati Italiani" and General Cesare Cesari: "I voluntari," both in the General Staff official history *Il primo passo verso l'unità d'Italia, 1848–1849* (Rome, 1948).

[45] Rodolico: *Carlo Alberto*, 311 ff., defends the king. Among the critics, see Guido Porzio: *La guerra regia in Italia nel 1848–1849* (Rome, 1955), 24 ff., 47 ff., 64 ff.; Pieri: *Storia militare del Risorgimento*, chaps. vii and viii, and the same author's more extended treatment in "La guerra regia nella pianura padana" (in Ettore Rota, ed.: *Il 1848 nella storia italiana ed europea*, Milan, n.d., I, 169–479).

set off a social uprising. Dubious of their ability to maintain an independent Lombard state, they were in favor of union with Piedmont, which was conservative and monarchical. On the other hand the republican minority, led by Cattaneo, detested Charles Albert and despised the "backward" Piedmontese. Their ideal was in fact an independent Lombard republic, united with other Italian states on a federal basis like that of the Swiss Confederation or the American Union. "Italy," they maintained, "is physically and historically federalist."[46] As for defense against possible attack by Austria, the French Republic would undoubtedly lend assistance. Indeed, Cattaneo was in favor of calling in the French at once so as to clinch the victory over the Austrians.

Unfortunately for the republican minority, it was to meet with opposition even from that great republican theorist Joseph Mazzini, who on April 8 arrived in Milan and met with an enthusiastic popular reception. Mazzini regarded liberation from foreign rule as the matter of highest priority and had recently founded a National Italian Society in the effort to bring all factions together, "reserving till the day of victory measures that would enable the people to decide upon the form of government." Agreeing that Italy must do the job itself, he was bitterly opposed to French interference. He would support Charles Albert as long as the Piedmontese remained in the field.

In a famous meeting on April 30 Cattaneo made a supreme effort to convert Mazzini to his views. He argued that during the Five Days no one had come to the aid of the city, but that in the hour of victory Charles Albert, the man who in 1821 had betrayed the liberals and in 1834 had fired on the democrats, put in a prompt appearance: "I will be accused of irreverence," Cattaneo added, "but I swear that I would prefer to see the return of the Austrians rather than see a traitor as chief of Lombardy." Yet Mazzini remained unmoved. He would have nothing to do with plans to overturn the provisional government and call in the French. The meeting broke up in a huff and the republicans, politically speaking a distinct minority, could not recover from the blow dealt them by Mazzini's intransigence.[47]

---

[46] Bruno Brunello: *Il pensiero di Carlo Cattaneo* (Turin, 1925), 168 ff.

[47] The only full account of this meeting, written in 1852 at Cattaneo's request, was discovered and published by Antonio Monti: *Un dramma fra gli esuli* (Milan, 1921). For a good discussion of the problem of fusion, see Leopoldo Marchetti: "I moti di Milano e il problema della fusione col Piemonte" (in Roto: *Il 1848 nella storia italiana,*

The provisional government decided on May 12 to submit the question of fusion to a popular vote, which was taken on May 29. The fact that the voting was open may help to explain the outcome: 561,000 in favor of fusion and only 681 in opposition. Fusion with Piedmont was proclaimed on June 13 and was followed by similar action on the part of Parma (June 16), Modena (June 21) and the Republic of Venice (July 4). Manin and his associates were by no means enamored of the idea of fusion, but Venice was being blockaded by the Austrian fleet and was therefore obliged to look to Piedmont for aid.

Meanwhile the military situation worsened. The vision of a united effort by all Italian states faded away. In sending contingents to the north the various governments had acted under popular pressure. At bottom they disliked and feared Piedmont and had no desire whatever to assist Charles Albert to expand his kingdom. They made efforts, therefore, to induce the pope to take the lead in organizing an Italian League which would afford the individual states protection against the designs of others.

Pope Pius, for his part, was confronted with a painful dilemma. The papal cabinet, created under the new constitution to deal with temporal affairs, was headed by Count Recchi and consisted almost entirely of patriotic liberals, in close touch with Piedmontese nationalists. Supported by popular sentiment, the ministers urged His Holiness to declare war on Austria and participate actively in the campaign. Pius, who from the outset saw the conflict between his Italian patriotism and his responsibilities as head of an international church, saw no way of intervening in the national war except under cover of a League of Princes. He did what he could to bring such a league into being (see Illustration 56). But by mid-April it had become clear that Charles Albert, confident of victory, would not bind himself to share the spoils with others. [48]

II, 653–723); see also Franco Valsecchi: "L'intervention française et la solidarité révolutionnaire internationale dans la pensée des démocrates lombards en 1848" (*Actes du Congrès Historique du Centenaire*, 165–176); Brunello: *Il pensiero di Carlo Cattaneo*, 160 ff., 202; Mario Borsa: *Carlo Cattaneo* (Milan, 1945), 164 ff.; Gwilyn O. Griffith: *Mazzini* (New York, 1932), 185 ff.

[48] Pietro Pieri: "La missione di Mons. Corboli-Bussi in Lombardia e la crisi della politica italiana di Pio IX" (*Rivista di storia della Chiesa in Italia*, I, 1947, 38–84); Roger Aubert: *Le pontificat de Pie IX* (Paris, 1952), 27 ff.; Candeloro: *Storia d'Italia moderna*, III, 206 ff.

To complicate matters still further, the commander of the papal forces, General Giovanni Durando, was a Piedmontese officer who had as his adviser the ardent nationalist, Massimo d'Azeglio. Durando evidently had no intention of halting his advance at the Po, but was determined to invade Venetia and fight the enemy. On April 5 he issued an order of the day, written by D'Azeglio, which implied that the pope approved and indeed blessed the campaign "to exterminate the enemies of God and of Italy . . . . Such a war is not merely national, but highly Christian."[49] Pius, furious at Durando for presuming to proclaim a crusade against a Catholic power, at once rebuked him, but this did not prevent the general from crossing the Po (April 22). In Rome the ministers redoubled their efforts to secure a declaration of war, while the cardinals were equally energetic in opposing it. To terminate the argument the pope published an allocution to the College of Cardinals which was meant as an address to the entire Catholic world. He rejected the charge that by his reforms he had precipitated the revolutionary movements of 1848 and repudiated all thought of working for an Italian republic under his own presidency. As representative of God on earth he could not, he declared, make war, for, "according to the order of Our supreme Apostolate, We seek after and embrace all races, peoples and nations, with equal devotion of paternal love."

This famous allocution completed the disillusionment of the patriots, who had tried to make the pope the champion of Italian nationalism. He was now charged with betrayal of the national cause. His ministers resigned and disorder spread. Popular clubs and radical groups proliferated in Rome and agitation against priests, cardinals and even the Papacy became the order of the day. Then, to crown the pope's misfortune, the Austrian government on May 4 severed relations with the papal government.[50]

Ferdinand of Naples at once took heart from the pope's refusal to declare war. During April his situation had been extremely precarious,

[49] Berkeley and Berkeley, *Italy in the Making*, III, 164; Edward E. Y. Hales: *Pio Nono* (New York, 1954), 73.

[50] Friedrich Engel-Janosi: *Oesterreich und der Vatikan, 1846–1918* (Graz, 1958), 37 ff.; R. M. Johnston: *The Roman Theocracy and the Republic, 1846–1849* (New York, 1901), 357 ff.; Antonio Monti: *Pio IX nel Risorgimento italiano* (Bari, 1928), 97 ff.; Domenico Demarco: *Pio IX e la rivoluzione romana del 1848* (Modena, 1947), 71 ff.; Hales: *Pio Nono*, 76 ff.; D. Massé: *Pio IX e il gran tradimento del 1848* (Alba, 1948).

for Sicily, except for the citadel of Messina, had been lost to the insurgents and they had rejected all offers of autonomy. On April 13 they had declared the Sicilian throne vacant. On the mainland the government was wrestling with a financial crisis, with unemployment and general disorder. A radical minority, inspired by events in the north, demanded active intervention in the war against Austria and called for revision of the constitution which had been so recently granted. By mid-May the tension between the king and the radicals in the Parliament had reached the breaking point over the questions of the oath to the constitution and the right of the chamber to undertake revisions of the charter. Presently barricades appeared in the streets around the palace and fighting broke out between the royal troops and Swiss guards on the one hand and the radicals, supported by the National Guard and the people, on the other (see Illustration 63). After considerable loss of life, the insurrection was mastered on the evening of May 15.[51]

Ferdinand thus scored the first success of the governments against the forces of revolution. Yet he did not abolish the constitution. On the contrary, after driving the insurgent leaders from the city and dissolving the National Guard, he set a date for new elections and allowed a new Parliament to meet on July 1. It seems that the king in his policy had the support of the upper classes—the landowners and the businessmen—as well as of the landed middle class which was so characteristic of southern Italy. These propertied classes were much disturbed by the unrest, especially in the countryside. In certain places there were peasant outbreaks so serious that the landlords had to barricade themselves in their manor houses or seek refuge in the cities. At Cosenza the radicals in May set up a provisional government which was suppressed only through use of organized military forces.[52]

Relief from radical pressure enabled Ferdinand to recall the Neapolitan troops from the north, on the plea that they were needed for the reconquest of Sicily. General Guglielmo Pepe, veteran revolutionist and

---

[51] Domenico Demarco: *Il crollo del Regno delle Due Sicilie* (Naples, 1960), I, 152 ff.; Harold Acton: *The Last Bourbons of Naples* (New York, 1961), 228 ff. On the Sicilian revolution, see Federico Curato: *La rivoluzione siciliana del 1848–1849* (Milan, 1940).

[52] A. Williams Salomone: "The Liberal Experiment and the Italian Revolution of 1848" (*Journal of Central European Affairs*, IX, 1949, 267–288). On the agrarian unrest in the south, see Demarco: *Il crollo del Regno*, 157 ff.; Acton: *Last Bourbons of Naples*, 251 ff.; Pasquale Villani: *Mezzogiorno tra riforme e rivoluzione* (Bari, 1962), 75.

ardent patriot, followed Durando's example and disobeyed. About 1,000 men followed him in joining forces with the papal contingent, but the great majority returned to Naples, thus depriving Charles Albert of a substantial auxiliary force.[53]

Meanwhile Radetzky had received reinforcements of some 30,000 men who had managed to evade Durando's troops and pick their way through the foothills of the Alps to reach Verona. Charles Albert still failed to undertake major operations. He now deluded himself into thinking that he might acquire Lombardy and Venetia through diplomacy rather than war. The Austrian government, desperately beset by events in Vienna, in Bohemia and in Hungary, was approaching the verge of hopelessness, the more so as even the pope, through a special envoy, was begging the emperor to accept the inevitable and leave the Italian provinces to the Italians.[54] The French and British governments, too, were bringing pressure to bear in the same direction. Lamartine was genuinely sympathetic to Italian national aspirations, the more so as they promised to put an end to Austrian control and influence in the peninsula. Starting with the resolution not to countenance Austrian aggression against any Italian state, he soon reached the point of being ready to aid Piedmont to expel the Austrians, provided Lombardy and Venetia should then constitute one or two independent states. Their "fusion" with Piedmont would not be in France's interest, for it would result in the formation of a strong north Italian kingdom on France's frontier. Such a solution could be made palatable only through the cession to France of the Piedmontese provinces of Savoy and Nice, which would give France the "natural" frontier of the Alps in the southeast. Assuming that Charles Albert would not be able to defeat the Austrians without French aid, the French provisional government began to concentrate on the frontier a corps of observation (the "Army of the Alps"), which soon reached a strength of 60,000 men. At the same time the sale of large stocks of ammunition to the

---

[53] Giuseppe Paladino: "Il governo napoletano e la guerra de 1848" (*Nuova rivista storica*, III, 1919, 565–600; IV, 1920, 61–80, 341–372; V, 1921, 220–245); Rota: "L'antagonismo politico fra Torino e Napoli durante la guerra del 1848" (in his *Il 1848 nella storia italiana e europea*, I, 123–169).

[54] Monti: *Pio IX nel Risorgimento italiano*, 97 ff.; Engel-Janosi: *Oesterreich und der Vatikan*, 39, and *Die politische Korrespondenz der Päpste mit den oesterreichischen Kaisern, 1804–1918* (Vienna, 1964), 230 ff.

provisional government of Milan was authorized, and a special envoy sent to Turin to arrange for French intervention.[55] Charles Albert was still convinced that the Italians could win on their own. He flatly refused to appeal to the French for aid, thinking the price exorbitant and fearing above all lest the presence of the French stimulate republicanism in Lombardy and elsewhere. He was reinforced in his attitude by Palmerston, who was greatly troubled by the threat of French action, the repercussions of which were hard to foresee. Convinced by Foreign Office representatives in Italy that the Italians were bound to succeed, he concluded that the sooner the Austrians were gotten out of Italy, the better it would be for all concerned. It made no difference to him whether Lombardy became an independent state or was united with Piedmont. The important thing was to forestall French intervention or a possible alliance of France with a Lombard republic. Not only in northern Italy but in Sicily also the British were exerting themselves to block the republican movement. Thus in Sicily they supported the candidacy of the duke of Genoa, younger son of Charles Albert, for the Sicilian throne, and actually succeeded in having him elected by the Palermo Assembly on July 10.[56]

As the threat of French intervention grew, the Austrian government sent to London Baron Karl Hummelauer to canvass the terms on which British diplomatic support might be obtained. In conversations with Palmerston (May 23–25), Hummelauer stressed the danger of French intervention and the impossibility for Austria to fight against France as well as Piedmont. In order to reach a settlement the Austrian government might be willing to agree to the establishment of a

[55] Paul Henry: "La France et les nationalités en 1848" (*Revue historique*, CLXXXVI, 1939, 48–77; CLXXXVIII, 1940, 234–258); César Vidal: "La France et la question italienne en 1848" (*Etudes d'histoire moderne et contemporaine*, II, 1948, 162–183); and the following studies by Ferdinand Boyer: "Lamartine et le Piémont" (*Revue d'histoire diplomatique*, LXIV, 1950, 37–57); "Les fournitures d'armes par le gouvernement français aux patriotes italiens en 1848 et 1849" (*Rassegna storica del Risorgimento*, XXXVII, 1950, 95–106); "Charles Albert et la Seconde République" (*ibid.*, L, 1963, 463–512); "L'armée des Alpes en 1848" (*Revue historique*, CCXXIV, 1965).

[56] Ruggero Moscati: *La diplomazia europea e il problema italiano nel 1848* (Florence, 1947), chap. ii; and the same author's more recent essay: "L'Europa e il problema italiano nel 1848–1849" (in F. Catalano, R. Moscati, and F. Valsecchi: *L'Italia nel Risorgimento*, Verona, 1964, 431–478); further, Gaetano Falzone: *Il problema della Sicilia nel 1848 attraverso nuove fonti inediti* (Palermo, 1951), which stresses French policy in Sicily.

self-governing Lombardo-Venetian kingdom under an Austrian arch-duke as viceroy. Parma and Modena might be added to this kingdom so as to form a new north Italian state. Palmerston, however, argued that the return of Lombardy to Austrian rule in any form would be impossible. He proposed that Lombardy be ceded to Piedmont so as to make a strong state on the French frontier, while Venetia might be given autonomy within the Hapsburg Empire. Hummelauer, con-vinced that Austria must secure British mediation at any price, took Palmerston's proposals *ad referendum,* only to learn a few days later that the British cabinet, under the passionately Italophile Lord John Russell, would agree to mediate only if Venetia as well as Lombardy were abandoned by Austria.

On these same days the Lombard and Venetian leaders induced Charles Albert to promise not to make peace as long as a single Austrian soldier remained on Italian soil, and the French National Assembly, recently elected, voted unanimously a resolution in favor of the liberation of Italy (May 24). The French government, enraged by Lombardy's vote for fusion with Piedmont, began to bring pressure on Vienna to give up the Italian provinces on the understanding that they should not be annexed to Piedmont. But the Vienna court could not bring itself to accept the loss of more than Lombardy and that only providing the problem of the public debt could be satisfactorily solved. Venetia was to be given complete autonomy. A special envoy was sent to Milan to negotiate with the Lombard authorities, while Radetzky was instructed to take steps toward securing an armistice.[57]

Radetzky was furious at Vienna's defeatism and sent one of his officers, Prince Felix zu Schwarzenberg, to argue the increasingly favorable prospects of military success and plead for continuance of the war. After much confabulation the Court abandoned the idea of making cessions and arranged to send Radetzky yet another 20,000 men. Military operations now entered the concluding phase.[58] At first the Piedmontese and Tuscans were able to block Radetzky's attempted advance beyond the Mincio and scored a last success in the

[57] A. J. P. Taylor: *The Italian Problem in European Diplomacy, 1847–1849* (Man-chester, 1934), 120 ff.; Moscati, "L'Europa e il problema italiano," 458 ff.; Ferdinand Boyer: "Le problème de l'Italie du Nord entre la France et l'Autriche de fevrier à juillet, 1848" (*Rassegna storica del Risorgimento,* XLII, 1955, 206–217); and, on the Austrian policy, Vittorio Barbieri: "I tentativi di mediazione anglo-francesi durante la guerra del 1848" (*ibid.,* XXVI, 1939, 683–726).

[58] Rudolf Kiszling: *Fürst Felix zu Schwarzenberg* (Graz, 1952), 34 ff.

reduction of Peschiera. But once again the Piedmontese king failed to follow up his successes, evidently hoping still that French threats and British pressure would induce the Austrians to abandon their Italian provinces. By early July, however, he was sufficiently disillusioned to be willing to settle for Lombardy, Parma and Modena, leaving Venetia to the emperor. But the Turin government, thinking less dynastically than the king, flatly refused to abjure its commitments and abandon Venetia, which had voted fusion with Piedmont, to its fate.

The Austrian government, staking everything on Radetzky's assurances, now resisted all efforts of the French and British to divest it of its Italian possessions. By the end of July Radetzky, provided now with superior forces and fire power, was ready for the decisive blow. On July 23 he attacked the long-strung Italian lines stretching from Rivoli in the north to Mantua in the south. Several days of fighting culminated in the Battle of Custoza (July 23–27), after which the defeated Italian forces were obliged to fall back to the Mincio. Presently they were in full retreat on Milan, in the outskirts of which city they suffered another defeat on August 4. Mazzini and other Lombard leaders were eager to defend the city, but the king and his high command were by this time demoralized, convinced as they were that further resistance was hopeless. Booed by the populace and denounced as a traitor by the Milanese leaders, Charles Albert was smuggled through the streets by night while his forces abandoned the city. They were followed by some 100,000 Lombards, who now sought refuge in Piedmont or Switzerland (see Illustration 37). Between the Lombards and the Piedmontese there was now nothing but bitterness. According to the former the Piedmontese had served only their own selfish ends, while according to the latter the Milanese had failed to make an appropriate contribution in men and supplies. There was more than a grain of truth in both charges.[59]

Consternation overcame the Italian governments on news of the disaster at Custoza. From both Turin and Milan envoys were dispatched to Paris to explore the possibilities of military aid. Charles Albert, still unwilling to pay the price for such aid, finally left the decision to his ministers. But the moment for action had passed. General Cavaignac, provisional head of the French government, and the new minister for foreign affairs, Jules Bastide, had learned from

[59] On the Milan crisis, see Pietro Silva: *Il 1848* (Rome, 1948), 138 ff.; Porzio: *La guerra regia*, 202 ff.; Pieri: *Storia militare*, 258 ff.

their agents in Italy that the Austrian armies were in great strength, numbering some 130,000 men. Since in any event it would take the French forces three weeks to cross the Alps, there was a real possibility that the Austrians might reach and occupy the passes before the French could get there. The French authorities were determined to intervene if the Austrians undertook an invasion of Piedmontese territory, but for the rest they fell back on the plans for joint mediation with Britain. On August 8 they proposed to London that mediation be offered on the basis of the Hummelauer memorandum of May 24, which envisaged the cession of Lombardy to Piedmont, autonomy for Venetia, and self-determination for Parma and Modena. But before anything could come of this project, Charles Albert had had his chief of staff, General Canera di Salasco, conclude an armistice for a six-week period. He seems to have hoped that within that period French and British pressure on Vienna would bring him Lombardy without his having to sacrifice Savoy. But the Austrian government temporized and evaded until on August 22 the Austrian foreign minister notified the French and British that Vienna would negotiate with Piedmont directly and that in any event Austria, having reconquered Lombardy, could no longer accept the Hummelauer memorandum as a basis for discussion.[60]

The Austrian reply was only the prelude to long and tedious negotiations which dragged on through the autumn of 1848 while the Austrian government was still too unsure of itself to speak categorically. But these discussions belong properly to the later phase of the Italian question. For the time being, the Battle of Custoza was decisive for Italian affairs and indeed for the entire development of the revolutionary situation in Europe. For Custoza had demonstrated even more conclusively than the reduction of Prague that so long as the governments could rely on their armies they could sooner or later master the forces of upheaval. They could in fact hope that in the work of repression they would enjoy the at least tacit support of the liberal middle class, which was not revolutionary to begin with and had quickly taken fright at the radicalism of the lower strata of the population, in the countryside as well as the towns.

Italian historians have long concerned themselves with the social structure of the 1848 revolution and more particularly with the ques-

[60] Taylor: *Italian Problem*, 137 ff., and the articles by Barbieri and Boyer cited in previous footnotes.

tion whether and to what extent the lower classes played a significant role. For the first phase of the revolution the answer is fairly clear.[61] The strongest element in the opposition was the liberal group, consisting of progressive nobles, the landed middle class and the banking and business class of the towns, together with professors at the universities, writers and other professional men. These people were most of them well-to-do. They were intent on reform while avoiding revolution. It was the much smaller, lower-middle-class element in the towns, many of whom were democrats and republicans, who in Milan provided the impetus for the huge popular demonstrations which introduced the revolution. The fighting on the barricades was done largely though not exclusively by workers—not factory workers, for the factory system was in its infancy, but artisans and journeymen suffering from unemployment, high food prices and generally low wages. Once the Austrians had been expelled, however, it was relatively easy for the respectable liberal classes to take over the provisional government and throw in their lot with Piedmont, if only as one way to avoid the growth of radicalism. As for the vast majority of the population, the peasantry, it was certainly moved by profound but ill-defined discontent. It is clear that the propertied classes, even radicals such as Cattaneo, were apprehensive of rural insurrection and were at times deterred in their activities by fear of stirring up forces which would or at least might end in social upheaval. In the early days of the Milan revolt, large numbers of peasants hurried to the city to enroll in the civic guard and aid in driving out the foreigner. But the provisional government, badly frightened by the prospect, refused them admittance to the guard and ordered them to return home. They were not even allowed to enter the gates.[62]

Actually, because of the predominant position of the liberals, the

---

[61] See, e.g., A. M. Ghisalberti: "Ancora sulla participazione populare al Risorgimento" (*Rassegna storica del Risorgimento*, XXXI–XXXIII, 1944–1946, 5–13); Niccolò Rodolico: "Atteggiamenti di gruppi sociali nel Risorgimento italiano" (*Accademia nazionale dei Lincei: Atti di convegni*, X ,1949, 351–363); Antonio Monti: "Guerra regia e guerra di populo nel Risorgimento" (in Ettore Rota, ed.: *Questioni di storia del Risorgimento*, Milan, 1951, 183–216); Palmiro Togliatti: "Le classi populari nel Risorgimento" (*Studi critici*, III, 1964); and most recently the excellent analysis by Franco Valsecchi: "Le classi populari e il Risorgimento" (*Cultura e scuola*, No. 15, 1965, 82–93).

[62] Valsecchi: "Le classi populari e il Risorgimento"; Denis Mack Smith: "The Italian Peasants and the Risorgimento" (in *Italia e Inghilterra nel Risorgimento*, London, 1954, 15–30); Albert Soboul: "Risorgimento et révolution bourgeoise" (*La pensée*, No. 95, 1961, 63–73).

revolutions of the spring of 1848 followed a normal course. The provisional governments were not seriously challenged or threatened. The really important feature was the war against Austria. This, it must be admitted, ended in complete fiasco, not only because the Piedmontese and their supporters had the bad luck to have a real military genius as their opponent, but because of the suspicions and rivalries between the Italian governments and above all because of the irresolution and military ineptitude of Charles Albert, to say nothing of the narrow selfishness of his aims. Having undertaken to expel the Austrians, he was afraid to act for fear of French intervention. He then turned to the British and French to mediate, a policy in which he was bound to fail if only because of the differences between those two powers as to what should be done with Lombardy once it had been abandoned by the Austrians. Radetzky solved this problem by squelching the defeatism of Vienna and then dealing the Piedmontese so decisive a blow that they were obliged to abandon the prize which they thought already in the bag. As for Mazzini's dream of the united Italians, who would be more than a match for an Austrian empire rent by conflicting forces, it turned out to be merely a pipe dream. In every Italian state there were patriots anxious to back Piedmont to the limit, but they were too few to impose their policy of intervention on the governments. Among the governments, one may safely conjecture, there were at least some that secretly rejoiced at Charles Albert's discomfiture.

Chapter Twelve

GERMANY: THE HEYDAY OF LIBERALISM

I. THE MARCH REVOLUTIONS

MARX and Engels, reflecting on the German situation in January, 1848, asked themselves whether the *bourgeoisie* of any country had ever been in a more splendid position to carry on its struggle against the existing government.[1] They were referring, of course, to the widespread distress and unrest and to the apparent failure of the liberals to take advantage of their opportunity. But these liberals—progressive officials, the upper stratum of the intellectuals and professional men, and especially the new business class—were as reluctant in Germany as they were elsewhere to provoke a revolution. Remembering the excesses of the 1793 Terror in France, they dreaded a major upheaval almost as much as did the princes and the aristocrats. Their hope was to attain their objective of constitutional government through peaceful organization and agitation along the lines of Cobden's Anti-Corn Law League. They might value popular unrest and demonstration as providential additional pressure on the governments, but they never intended anything remotely resembling the political or social overturn of the existing order.

Many of the German states experienced unwanted revolutions in the spring of 1848, the circumstances often varying widely from one locality to another. Perhaps most typical was the course of events in Baden, one of the most overpopulated parts of Germany, where distress among the people was chronic. There, too, parliamentary life was fairly well-developed and the forces of liberalism and even radicalism reasonably well-organized. On receipt of the news of the February Revolution, huge popular meetings took place at once in Mannheim and other cities. The demands of the people were for freedom of the press,

[1] Quoted by Karl Obermann: "Die Rolle der Volksmassen in Deutschland zu Beginn der Revolution von 1848" (*Geschichte in der Schule*, XI, 1958, 142–157), and "Die Volksbewegung in Deutschland von 1844 bis 1846" (*Zeitschrift für Geschichtswissenschaft*, V, 1957, 503–525).

establishment of a citizen guard and other familiar liberal items. So formidable were the demonstrations that the government yielded at once. On March 2 a new cabinet, headed by the well-known liberal leaders Welcker and Bassermann, was installed. But before the liberal regime could get its footing, peasant outbreaks occurred, marked by attacks on Jewish moneylenders and especially on manor houses. Led by their elders the populations of whole villages hacked down the doors of their landlords, threw out the feudal records, forced the lords to sign away their traditional privileges, and plundered the forests. Troops had to be called out to restore a semblance of order.[2]

The pattern of development was much the same in other German states, for example, in Würtemberg, Hesse-Darmstadt, Saxony, Hanover, and the Hanseatic cities. Everywhere there were the same crowds, the same deputations, petitions and demonstrations, often accompanied by destruction of machines and in the countryside by sporadic outbreaks which in Würtemberg came to be a veritable peasant insurrection. In all these states the princes and governments were so terrified that they offered no resistance to popular demands. By mid-March, that is, even before the revolution in Vienna, most of the smaller German states had introduced responsible government and accorded civil liberties. The action of the masses in town and country had forced the procrastinating rulers to accept a solution which the changes of the foregoing decades had made all but inevitable.

In Bavaria the pressure for reform was curiously enmeshed with an old-fashioned court scandal. The aging king, Louis I, was infatuated with a young "Spanish" dancer, Lola Montez, who was actually the daughter of a British officer and a Creole mother. She was born, not in Andalusia, but in Ireland. All are agreed that she was an exceptionally beautiful creature, a young woman whose dark eyes, jet-black hair, and marvelous figure (invariably clothed in tight-fitting black velvet) left few men unmoved. But there was more to Lola than that. She had an alert mind and genuine wit, in fact, enough of a personality to have

---

2 Friedrich Lautenschläger: *Die Agrarunruhen in den badischen Standes- und Grundherrschaften im Jahre 1848* (Heidelberg, 1915), chap. iii; Gunter Franz: "Die agrarische Bewegung im Jahre 1848" (*Zeitschrift für Agrargeschichte und Agrarsoziologie*, VII, 1959, 176–192); Franz Schnabel: "Das Land Baden in der Revolution von 1848–1849" (in Wilhelm Keil, ed.: *Deutschland, 1848–1948*, Stuttgart, 1948, 56–70); and the excellent account in Theodore S. Hamerow: *Restoration, Revolution, Reaction* (Princeton, 1958), chap. ix.

attracted Franz Liszt and Alexander Dumas, both of whom had been her lovers. Liszt had introduced her to the circle of George Sand, which was one of the most sophisticated and advanced in European society. There Lola absorbed, from Lamennais and others, the principles of republicanism and socialism with which she attempted to indoctrinate the Bavarian king.

Louis, so it seems, was captivated as much by her mind as by her beauty. Soon after her arrival in Munich (October, 1846) he began to turn to her for political advice. She soon became arrogant and dictatorial. She publicly insulted ministers and insisted on the appointment of officials of her own choice. Nonetheless, the king adored her, wrote her numberless romantic poems and eventually created her countess of Landsberg. All the warnings of his ministers, of the high clergy, even of the pope, fell on deaf ears. Presently the whole country was outraged. In January and February of 1848, students staged demonstrations against her and even launched an attack on her residence. The king ordered the university closed, but this move only provoked more disturbances and led to clashes between the troops and the populace. Finally the king, under heavy pressure from his ministers, asked Lola to leave. It was at this point that news arrived of the revolution in Paris. Larger and larger crowds appeared on the streets, singing the "Marseillaise" and calling for a republic. Soon barricades appeared and the crowd attacked the arsenal. Louis was obliged to yield to demands for freedom of the press and other concessions (March 6). When, ten days later, it became known that Lola had visited the city in disguise, the popular indignation was such that the king had to banish his favorite from the country. For him this was the final straw. An absolutist at heart, he could not envisage governing under the new system. Besides, the loss of Lola was more than he could bear. So on March 20 he abdicated the throne in favor of his son, Maximilian II.[3]

[3] Erich Pottendorf: *Lola Montez* (Vienna, 1955) is devoted almost entirely to her stirring eighteen months in Munich; Helen Holdredge: *The Woman in Black* (New York, 1955), on the contrary, is particularly full on Lola's further career in America. These rather colorful books should be supplemented by the sober professional accounts of Michael Doberl: *Entwicklungsgeschichte Bayerns* (Munich, 1931), III, 135 ff.; Karl Bosl and H. Schreibmüller: *Geschichte Bayerns* (Munich, 1955), II, 92 ff.; and especially Egon C. Corti: *Ludwig I of Bavaria* (London, 1938), chaps. x, *et seq.*, which contributes many new letters.

The Lola Montez affair had the effect of uniting all influential elements in Bavarian society in opposition to the king. The popular agitation against his favorite took on the character of political pressure and obliged the king to accept the principle of responsible government and indeed the entire liberal program. But the disorder and lawlessness was such in South Germany that the radicals were bound to take advantage of it. Led by Friedrich Hecker and Gustav Struve, they staged a meeting at Offenburg at which there was much talk of setting up clubs on the Jacobin model, organizing a committee of public safety and eventually proclaiming a German republic. Hecker did proclaim a republic at Konstanz (April 12), hoping for support of the peasantry and the defection of the troops, and trusting that a filibustering force of Germans, under the poet George Herwegh, would stage an invasion from Alsace. But the venture, which was poorly planned, led to much dissension among the leaders and ended in fiasco. On appeal from the grand duke of Baden, the federal Diet at Frankfurt sent Hessian and other troops which defeated Hecker's forces at Kandern (April 20). Hecker fled to Switzerland and the radical insurrection proved to be a mere flash in the pan. It was, nevertheless, indicative of the activist element in the revolution.[4]

But what mattered most was what happened in Prussia, the largest, most populous, and both economically and militarily the strongest of the non-Hapsburg states. The Rhineland, though still preponderantly agricultural, had already become an industrial center. It was a region where the transition to the factory system was causing much technological unemployment and where the economic crisis of 1846–1847 was making itself severely felt. In Cologne, for example, a third of the population was receiving relief at the beginning of 1848. Government officials were profoundly disturbed by the growing number of popular meetings and the appearance of radical newspapers.[5]

Of particular interest was the monster demonstration of March 3 in Cologne, engineered by Andreas Gottschalk and August von Willich, which spawned a petition going far beyond the usual radical program

---

[4] These events are treated in all the basic histories of the revolution, such as Veit Valentin: *Geschichte der deutschen Revolution* (Berlin, 1930), I, 240 ff.; Jacques Droz: *Les révolutions allemandes de 1848* (Paris, 1957), 158 ff.; Ernst R. Huber: *Deutsche Verfassungsgeschichte* (Stuttgart, 1957), II, 509 ff.

[5] Konrad Repgen: *Märzbewegung und Maiwahlen des Revolutionsjahr 1848 im Rheinland* (Bonn, 1955), chap. iv; Gerhard Becker: *Karl Marx und Friedrich Engels in Köln, 1848–1849* (Berlin, 1963), 12 ff.

and including such drastic demands as government by revolutionary committees, the protection of labor, and the satisfaction of human needs for all members of the population. Though the leaders were both members of the Communist League, there is no evidence that they were directly inspired by Marxist doctrine. It was only within the past few months that the Communist League had adopted the Marxian teaching and only a matter of weeks since the publication of the *Communist Manifesto*. Gottschalk and Willich were socialists on their own, whose radicalism was enough to frighten liberals as well as conservatives. Troops were called in, the meeting dispersed and the leaders arrested.[6] But both officials and businessmen promptly renewed their pressure on the king to concede the demands of the liberals. Frederick William stuck obstinately to his notions of paternalistic government until the demonstrations in Berlin itself became so formidable that, reluctantly and with some mental reservations, he decided to accept the principle of constitutional government and a responsible ministry.[7]

A group of radical intellectuals had existed in the capital at least since 1846, when Julius Berends and Friedrich Schmidt had appeared in the Artisans' Society. They gathered about the newspaper *Zeitungshalle,* which took its name from a reading room not far from the royal palace. These same men seem to have been instrumental in arranging the popular meetings in an entertainment park known as Unter den Zelten. On March 11, after the Berlin city council had rejected a popular petition, the crowds became aggressive, so that the council had to request the government to permit the formation of constabulary forces or security commissions to help preserve order without calling in the military.[8]

By this time it was almost too late to forestall an explosion. On

[6] Karl Obermann: *Die deutschen Arbeiter in der Revolution von 1848* (Berlin, 1950), 73 ff., is a standard Marxist account. On the non-Marxist side, see Rudolf Stadelmann: *Soziale und politische Geschichte der Revolution von 1848* (Munich, 1956), 70 ff.; and the excellent study by P. H. Noyes: *Organization and Revolution: Working-Class Associations in the German Revolutions of 1848–1849* (Princeton, 1966), 62 ff.

[7] Wilhelm Busch: *Die Berliner Märztage von 1848* (Munich, 1899), 4, 10; Ernst Kaeber: *Berlin 1848* (Berlin, 1948), chap. ii; Alfred Hermann: *Berliner Demokraten* (Berlin, 1948), 114 ff.

[8] Karl Haenchen: "Zur revolutionären Unterwühlung Berlins vor den Märztagen des Jahres 1848" (*Forschungen zur brandenburgischen und preussischen Geschichte,* LV, 1943, 83–114); Hermann Meyer: *1848: Studien zur Geschichte der deutschen Revolution* (Darmstadt, 1949), 61 ff.

March 13 cavalry forces charged the crowds and as usual showed themselves brutal. The populace, which hated the troops for this very reason, began to shout insults and hurl stones. Two days later huge throngs surged about the royal palace and attacked the guards with rocks and bottles. The crowds became more and more insistent that the troops be withdrawn from the city. Only at this juncture did the government authorize the formation of the security commissions. Modeled on the British special constabulary, these commissions were to consist of respectable citizens, such as guild masters, to be armed only with truncheons and to wear white armbands for identification. At this late hour these prosperous citizens were met by the populace only with ridicule. Defeated in their efforts to restore order, they were presently obliged to appeal to the military for protection.[9]

News of the victory of the revolution in Vienna naturally put the situation in Berlin out of control completely. The king now began to make concessions: he announced on March 18 that the press censorship would be abolished, the Diet would be convoked on April 2, a constitution would be granted, and Prussia would assume the leadership in the effort to achieve German unity. The crowds responded enthusiastically until they spotted the troops massed in the courtyard of the palace, when they renewed their demands that the troops be withdrawn. So great was the commotion that the king eventually ordered General von Prittwitz to clear the palace square (see Illustration 64). The general and his cavalry escort were soon surrounded by the crowd and had to be rescued by an infantry detachment. In the process two musket shots rang out. No one was hurt, but the crowd began to panic. Barricades began to appear as though by magic. By evening severe fighting had broken out in many sections of the city.

The question has been much debated whether the Berlin uprising was the work of foreign instigators. The king and his generals were firmly convinced that French and Polish revolutionaries had come in and stirred up the population. Though this charge can hardly be substantiated from the available evidence, it is worth recalling that Berlin like other big cities was experiencing a large and constant influx.

[9] Anon.: *Die Berliner Märztage, vom militärischen Standpunkte geschildert* (Berlin, 1850), 12 ff., is an official account. See further C. Nobiling: *Die Berliner Bürgerwehr, 1848* (Berlin, 1852), 55 ff.; Kaeber: *Berlin 1848*, 40 ff.; and Karl Haenchen: "Aus dem Nachlass des Generals von Prittwitz" (*Forschungen zur brandenburgischen und preussischen Geschichte*, XLV, 1933, 99–125).

Ten thousand workers are reported to have come to Berlin in 1847 and many of these were desperate people in search of work. They may in fact have contributed significantly to the insurrection. Furthermore, the radicals of the *Zeitungshalle,* some of whom had contacts with foreign revolutionary organizations, may well have provided leadership. Berends and Bisky, for example, are known to have taken part in the fighting.[10]

General Prittwitz commanded the garrison of about 15,000 troops and a number of light guns. The rebels, on the other hand, lacked weapons and munitions. They hurled paving stones from the roofs and poured boiling water from the windows. Though the insurgents fought ferociously, the military blew up the barricades by artillery fire, after which the troops, as ruthless as their opponents, broke into the houses, chased the insurgents up to the garrets and massacred those whom it was inconvenient to drag off as captives. By midnight Prittwitz had secured control over the center of the city, but he had become convinced, from the violence of the conflict, that to suppress the uprising everywhere would be a long and costly undertaking. He therefore advised the king to leave for Potsdam and withdraw the troops from the city, which could then be blockaded and eventually bombarded into submission. But the king, fully convinced that his people had not spontaneously revolted against him, refused to abandon the capital. Instead, he composed during the night a pathetic appeal *To my dear Berliners* in which he offered to discuss the situation with representatives of the people and evacuate the troops as soon as the barricades were taken down. This document, which was tantamount to surrender, has been called by one German historian "the swan song of political romanticism and the patriarchal concept of government."[11]

What followed was utter confusion. The king, in a state of near collapse, was beset on all sides by generals and city councilors, all with their own ideas. Eager to close out the painful matter one way or

---

[10] Haenchen: "Zur revolutionären Unterwühlung Berlins"; Hermann: *Berliner Demokraten,* 64.

[11] Erich Brandenburg: *Die Reichsgründung* (Leipzig, 1916), I, 195. Although on the morning of March 19 the outcome of the fighting was at best a draw, most writers consider that the eventual victory of the military was inevitable. On Prittwitz and his plans, see Felix Rachfahl: *Deutschland, König Friedrich Wilhelm IV, und die Berliner Märzrevolution* (Halle, 1901), 163, 172; Hermann: *Berliner Demokraten,* 125; Gordon A. Craig: *The Politics of the Prussian Army* (Oxford, 1955), 93, 99.

another, Frederick William readily gave credence to unconfirmed rumors that the barricades were being dismantled. Brushing aside the protests of his brother William and the military men, he thereupon ordered the withdrawal of the troops to their barracks. Whether or not he then planned to leave for Potsdam is unimportant, for in the early afternoon a huge throng appeared before the palace accompanied by seven or eight wagons filled with the dead, wounds fully exposed. The king was obliged to appear on the balcony and salute the victims of the insurrection. Nothing, certainly, could have demonstrated more clearly the capitulation of the Prussian monarchy. It was indeed the deepest humiliation ever suffered by the Hohenzollern dynasty (see Illustration 65).

Frederick William completed his surrender by finally agreeing to the establishment of a Civic Guard (*Bürgerwehr*). Each district of the city was to supply a hundred men, drawn from among those who enjoyed full citizen rights. By evening this new force of 6,000 men was able to take over guard duties at the palace.[12] Thus the king placed himself entirely under the protection of his subjects. He was as defenseless, wrote the American minister on March 21, "as the poorest malefactor of the prisons." On March 22 Prince William, the leader of those who counseled suppression of the rebellion, fled to England to escape the public wrath.[13]

Careful analysis of the records of those who gave their lives in the Berlin barricade fighting leaves no shadow of doubt that it was an insurrection of the workers, by which must be understood artisans and journeymen in the traditional trades, since the number of factory workers was still insignificant. There were only about fifteen representatives of the educated class in a total of some 300 dead, and only thirty master craftsmen. The vast majority consisted of journeymen, among whom the cabinetmakers, tailors and shoemakers were most prominent.[14] Motivated chiefly by want and without a specific program of reform, the effect of their valor was to oblige the king to grant the

[12] C. Nobiling: *Die Berliner Bürgerwehr,* 1 ff.; O. Rimpler: *Die Berliner Bürgerwehr im Jahre 1848* (Brandenburg, 1883), 3 ff.

[13] Karl Haenchen: "Flucht und Rückkehr des Prinzen von Preussen im Jahre 1848" (*Historische Zeitschrift,* CLIV, 1936, 32–95).

[14] Ruth Hoppe and Jürgen Kuczynski: "Eine Berufs-bzw. auch Klassen und Schichtenanalyse der Märzgefallenen 1848 in Berlin" (*Jahrbuch für Wirtschaftsgeschichte,* 1964, Part IV, 200–276); Noyes: *Organization and Revolution,* 68 ff.

demands of the liberals. He adopted the national black-red-gold flag, promised to convoke an assembly to collaborate in the drafting of a constitution, announced that henceforth Prussia should be merged or fused with the new German national state, and, lastly, named a liberal cabinet under Ludolf Camphausen, in which David Hansemann was to serve as minister of finance. These eminent Rhineland businessmen were certainly ideal representatives of moderate liberalism.

The liberal press was at first lavish in its praise of the workers, who had served so well. Workers were taken into the clubs and programs were drafted for relief of the needy. On March 25 the city council set up a Deputation for Consideration of the Well-Being of the Working Classes and two days later the king promised to establish a ministry for trade, industry and public works which was to concern itself chiefly with the labor situation.[15] But propertied people were nonetheless uneasy about the demonstration of proletarian discontent. The American minister noted violent newspaper articles suggesting that the workers, having won the victory, were being excluded from the Civic Guard and so deprived of a rightful share in the new regime. Talk of this kind, he reported, had so frightened the propertied classes that many were leaving the city "from fear that a practical organization on the part of the communists has been effected." Even the ambassadors of foreign powers, he observed, were feeling uneasy whenever they appeared on the streets attended by liveried servants. On March 26 there was a monster assembly of workers which put forth demands for universal suffrage, a ministry of labor, a minimum wage and a ten-hour day.[16]

It was in this context that one of the king's friends, Josef Maria von Radowitz, urged him to court the support of the workers by an extensive program of social insurance and so obtain a counterweight to the forces of liberalism. These proposals were too much for the ultra-conservative court Camarilla, which was much more sympathetic to Otto von Bismarck's plans for a counterrevolution. Bismarck, a young Pomeranian Junker who was eventually to become Germany's Iron

[15] Noyes: *Organization and Revolution*, 71 ff.

[16] For the reports of Mr. A. J. Donelson, see *American Historical Review*, XXIII, 1918, 355–373. Further, Wilhelm Friedensburg: *Stefan Born und die Organisationsbestrebungen der Berliner Arbeiterschaft bis zum Berliner Arbeiterkongress* (Leipzig, 1923), 50 ff.; Obermann: *Die deutschen Arbeiter*, 89 ff., 100; Noyes: *Organization and Revolution*, 101 ff.

Chancellor, made his debut at this time with an attempt to organize the agrarian interests in support of the king's authority. He laid his plans before Princess Augusta, the wife of the refugee Prince William, but was refused her support (March 23). Neither the princess nor the king would envisage further civil strife, but the king at least was much inclined to look to conservative circles for counsel and support.[17]

Camphausen and the moderates aimed at a constitutional regime like that of the July Monarchy, but they were not in a position to resist the popular pressure for universal suffrage. They attempted, however, to minimize its effect by requiring a one-year residence for the franchise (thus excluding traveling journeymen and migrant workers) and by barring those who were on relief or served as domestics. The Diet (*Landtag*), which met on April 2, realized that these restrictions would not be tolerated and so reduced the residence requirement to six months and excluded only those on relief or convicted of crime. Even the Diet, however, rejected the idea of direct elections: voters were to choose members of electoral colleges who in turn would elect the deputies to Parliament. The efforts of the new, liberal regime to curtail the influence of the lower classes were unmistakable.[18]

Reflecting on the German revolution of 1848, Lenin bemoaned the fact that after March 18 the workers had not set up a revolutionary dictatorship. As it was, he remarked, they were left with nothing but "freedom to remain the party of extreme revolutionary opposition."[19] It seems clear, however, that the workers, having won the victory on the barricades, were by no means prepared to assume control of the government. They were probably more generally literate than the French or even the British workers, but they were quite unorganized and had nothing like united leadership. Friedrich Held and Gustav Schlöffel were popular, radical journalists, of whom the second has

---

[17] Erich Marcks: *Bismarck und die deutsche Revolution* (Stuttgart, 1939), and the extended critical review by Fritz Hartung: "Bismarck und die deutsche Revolution, 1848–1851" (*Die Welt als Geschichte*, VI, 1940, 167–178), as well as the same author's essay "Verantwortliche Regierung, Kabinette und Nebenregierung im konstitutionellen Preussen" (*Forschungen zur brandenburgischen und preussischen Geschichte*, XLIV, 1932, 1–45); G. Adolf Rein: "Bismarck's gegenrevolutionäre Aktion in den Märztagen 1848" (*Die Welt als Geschichte*, XIII, 1953, 246–262).

[18] Gerhard Schilfert: *Sieg und Niederlage des demokratischen Wahlrechts in der deutschen Revolution, 1848–1849* (Berlin, 1952), 49 ff.

[19] V. I. Lenin: "Two Tactics of Social Democracy in the Democratic Revolution" (1905), reprinted in his *Collected Works* (Moscow, 1962), IX, 17–140.

been described as "perhaps the only open advocate of violent class warfare and continuation of the revolution."[20] But their influence was limited. The workers were less interested in revolutionary theory than in securing better wages and shorter hours. There were numerous strikes in separate trades, most of which led to surrender by the timorous employers. These isolated efforts served to point up the need for better organization, and that was the chief aim of Stefan Born, who was to play the most prominent role in the German labor movement. Born, a journeyman typesetter only twenty-four years of age, had worked abroad and had become converted to Marxian Communism. He had arrived in Berlin on March 20 and had at once joined the radical *Zeitungshalle* group. He was instrumental in setting up a Central Committee of Workers (April 19), of which he became president, and in launching a genuine labor newspaper, *The People* (May 25). Born's basic objective was to organize the workers so that they might co-operate effectively in establishing a truly democratic regime and preparing the way for an eventual socialist state. He believed that disorder and revolution were more harmful than beneficial. Only through organization and peaceful political action could the workers attain their ends. So he never tired of warning the workers against the lure of fire-eating demagogues and against seduction by utopian schemers.

Born has at times been accused of betraying his Marxist origins, but he seems always to have adhered to the Marxist interpretation of history and indeed to the basic ideas of the *Communist Manifesto*. The point is that Born recognized the unpreparedness of the workers to assimilate highfalutin doctrine and in any case realized that their efforts would be futile unless organized. It has been well said of him that he put organization above program and that he emphasized the organization of laborers rather than the organization of labor.[21]

During the spring of 1848, workers' societies or clubs sprang up in many German cities, the one in Cologne being of particular interest because of the industrially advanced character of the city and because

---

[20] Noyes: *Organization and Revolution*, 108.

[21] The basic account of Eduard Bernstein: *Geschichte der Berliner Arbeiterbewegung* (Berlin, 1907) must be supplemented by intensive later studies such as Max Quarck: *Die erste deutsche Arbeiterbewegung* (Leipzig, 1924); Friedensburg: *Stefan Born*, 56 ff.; Obermann: *Die deutschen Arbeiter*, 107 ff., 118 ff.; Noyes: *Organization and Revolution*, 124 ff.

of the activity of Marx and Engels. Marx spent several weeks in Paris during March and there arranged to have the headquarters of the Communist League moved from London to the French capital. The notion that he took an active part in the debates of the Society for the Rights of Man appears to rest on a case of mistaken identity.[22] Marx devoted himself especially to the drafting of a program, *The Seventeen Demands of the Communist Party of Germany,* which was as much or more political than socialist. Its very first item called for a unified, indivisible German republic, while others included the arming of the people, the abolition of feudal dues without compensation to the owners, separation of church and state, free and equal education, and so on. This program was taken by the Paris Communists to various cities of Germany, where they attempted to found Communist cells. Those who, like Born in Berlin, devoted themselves to the organization of the workers for practical ends, came to play a significant role in the labor movement, while those who stuck more closely to the doctrines of Communism appear to have had but little success. Only a few labor leaders, such as Andreas Gottschalk in Cologne, were indifferent to political radicalism and indeed to socialist doctrine. Gottschalk was a benevolent doctor who knew the misery of the workers from personal experience. His objective was direct action by the workers to attain a workers' republic. His prestige in Cologne was unrivaled and the Workers' Society or union which he founded on April 13 had some 6,000 members in June. With its directorate of fifty, representing all the chief trades and industries of the city, it was a formidable organization which in general resisted merger with other groups.[23]

Marx arrived in Cologne on April 11, on the eve of the founding of Gottschalk's Workers' Society. Convinced as he was that a rising of the unorganized lower classes would be premature and that the soundest strategy for the workers was to support the radical elements of the *bourgeoisie* in winning control of the governments, Marx was intent

---

[22] S. Bernstein: "Marx in Paris, 1848" (*Science and Society,* III, 1939, 323–355; IV, 1940, 211–217); and especially Peter Amann: "Karl Marx: 'Quarante-huitard francais' " (*International Review of Social History,* VI (2), 1961, 249–255).

[23] Hans Stein: *Der Kölner Arbeiterverein, 1848–1849* (Cologne, 1921); Gerhard Becker: *Karl Marx und Friedrich Engels in Köln* (Berlin, 1963); Frolinde Balser: *Sozial-Demokratie, 1848/49—1863* (Stuttgart, 1962); Noyes: *Organization and Revolution,* 111 ff.; Werner Conze and Dieter Groh: *Die Arbeiterbewegung in der nationalen Bewegung* (Stuttgart, 1966), 33 ff.

above all on reviving the *Rhenish Gazette* and making it the organ for expression of his views. The problem was to find the needed funds and this proved difficult because even the radicals were suspicious of Communist designs. "They shy away from any discussion of social problems as from the pest," wrote Engels to Marx from Elberfeld; "the root of the matter is this, that even the radical bourgeois see in us their chief enemies of the future and therefore refuse to put any weapons into our hands that we would turn against them." In short, the radicals saw through Marx's game. In the end the Communist leaders had to put up their own money for the *New Rhenish Gazette,* which began to appear on June 1 and soon reached a circulation of 5,000 copies. By this time Marx had dissolved the Communist League (May), arguing that a secret organization was out of place under prevailing circumstances, but perhaps more in order to avoid conflict with Gottschalk. During the ensuing months Marx and his paper preached democracy more than socialism or communism. Indeed, he founded the Democratic Society (April 25) for co-operation with the radicals in the forthcoming elections. In July, when Gottschalk was arrested, Karl Schapper, a close collaborator of Marx, assumed the presidency of the Workers' Society and after Schapper's arrest (October) Marx himself took over.[24]

The later importance of Marx and Engels and their Communist doctrine has led, naturally, to much study of their activity in 1848 and certainly on the part of Marxist historians to some exaggeration of their contribution. German workers felt themselves close to the democratic elements of the lesser *bourgeoisie* and shared their hopes for a democratic republic. Some of their emerging leaders were members of the Communist League and even more of them were acquainted with the socialist doctrines of Weitling, Hess and the French theorists. But the

---

[24] Auguste Cornu: "Karl Marx et la révolution de 1848 en Allemagne" (*Europe,* XXVI, 1948, 238–252); Jean Meerfeld: "Der achtundvierziger Karl Marx" (in Wilhelm Keil, ed.: *Deutschland, 1848–1948,* Stuttgart, 1948, 89–99); Walter Schmidt: "Der Bund der Kommunisten und die Versuche einer Zentralisierung der deutschen Arbeitervereine im April und Mai, 1848" (*Zeitschrift für Geschichtswissenschaft,* IX, 1961, 577–614); Karl Obermann: "Ueber die Bedeutung der Tätigkeit von Friedrich Engels in Frühjahr und Sommer, 1848" (*ibid.,* IX, 1961, 28–47); August W. Fehling: *Karl Schapper und die Anfänge der Arbeiterbewegung* (Rostock, 1926), appendix; M. A. Kotschetkowa: "Die Tätigkeit von Marx und Engels in der Kölner Demokratischen Gesellschaft, April bis Oktober, 1848" (*Sowjetwissenschaft: Gesellschaftswissenschaftliche Beiträge,* 1960, Heft 11, 1155–1167).

strictly Marxist doctrine was of only recent date and evidently had but little impact. The contribution of the workers to the revolution must be sought, then, not in doctrine or organized action, but in the readiness of desperate men to mount the barricades and fight even against hopeless odds.[25]

This does not mean that the propertied classes were not deeply disturbed by the upsurge of artisan radicalism. After all, there had been for years endless discussion of the social question and the need for social reform. The liberals had not been unsympathetic to the plight of the workers, but they had expected to obtain reforms by peaceful methods. Never having envisaged the use of violence, they were appalled by the excesses to which the agitation for reform had led. More and more they recoiled from the implications of revolution until ultimately many of them found themselves in the conservative camp. To charge them with "betrayal of the revolution" is going too far, for they never intended revolution and can therefore hardly be blamed for shrinking from events which presaged a social as well as a political upheaval.

2. THE CHALLENGE OF POLAND

Europe in the spring of 1848 resounded not only with the tumult of revolution but also with threats of war. It seemed at first that Nicholas of Russia would draft the Prussians and Austrians for a crusade against the French Republic. The insurrections in Germany ruined any plans the czar may have had for such intervention, for his own armies could not be ready in less than several months and he could hardly expect support from the revolutionary governments of Germany. On the contrary, liberals and especially radicals were everywhere consumed with "flaming hatred of Russia," to quote a contemporary newspaper. They regarded liberty and tyranny as altogether incompatible and dreamed of setting up their own democratic republics. After destroying despotism they would eventually join all countries in a grand European republic which would once and for all dispose of the disputes

---

[25] This admittedly bourgeois evaluation is essentially the same as that of Karl Griewank: "Vulgärer Radikalismus und demokratische Bewegung in Berlin, 1842–1848" (*Forschungen zur brandenburgischen und preussischen Geschichte*, XXXVI, 1924, 14–38); Stadelmann: *Soziale und politische Geschichte*, chap. xi; Noyes: *Organization and Revolution*, 122; Conze and Groh: *Die Arbeiterbewegung*, 39 ff.

from which professional diplomats made their living. By many, war was regarded as inevitable, indeed, as highly desirable as a means of rallying all popular forces for the revolutionary task.[26]

Poland, of course, called for special consideration. What task could be more urgent than to undo the "crime" of 1772 and restore the "martyred" nation to independence and integrity? The pressure brought by Paris radicals on Lamartine was almost more than he could bear. Not that he lacked sympathy for the Poles, but he realized, in early March, that any effort to resurrect Poland would meet with the combined resistance of the three partitioning powers. He dared not even raise the issue of Russian Poland for fear of provoking war. There was, however, the possibility of working with the new liberal government of Prussia which emerged from the Berlin revolution.[27]

Prussia held the Grand Duchy of Posen (Poznan), which had been assigned to it in 1815 on the understanding that it should be given a large measure of autonomy. Though it was Polish territory and not included in the Germanic Confederation, Posen had a large German minority of some 700,000 souls. King Frederick William was well-disposed toward his Polish subjects and had, on his accession, introduced the use of the Polish language in the courts and schools. The minister for foreign affairs in the Camphausen cabinet, Baron von Arnim-Suckow, was prepared to go much further. On taking office he had at once used his influence to have the Polish insurgent leaders of 1846, Louis Mieroslawski and others, released from prison and presented to the king. Furthermore, he persuaded his colleagues to receive a deputation of Poles from Posen who asked for what amounted to autonomy. On March 24 the king reluctantly promised the Poles the "national reorganization" of the grand duchy under a commissioner aided by a board consisting of both Germans and Poles. Indeed, the Prussian government went so far as to permit droves of Polish refu-

[26] Eberhard Meyer: *Die aussenpolitischen Ideen der Achtundvierziger* (Berlin, 1938), 20 ff.; Lewis B. Namier: *1848: the Revolution of the Intellectuals* (London, 1944), 43 ff. On the rabid bellicosity of Marx and Engels, see Bertram D. Wolfe: "Nationalism and Internationalism in Marx and Engels" (*American Slavic and East European Review,* XVII, 403–417).

[27] Pierre Quentin-Bauchart: *Lamartine et la politique étrangère de la Révolution de février* (Paris, 1907); Eugène de Guichen: *Les grandes questions européennes et la diplomatie des puissances sous la Seconde République française* (Paris, 1925); Theodor Schiemann: *Geschichte Russlands unter Kaiser Nikolaus I* (Berlin, 1919), IV, 151 ff.; A. S. Nifontow: *Russland im Jahre 1848* (Berlin, 1954), 228 ff.

gees from France and Belgium to cross Germany to Posen, where Mieroslawski was organizing an incursion of Russian Poland.[28]
Arnim and other liberals were ready to give up Posen for the sake of restoring Poland. They realized that such a policy would mean war with Russia, but they actually desired such a conflict as a setting for establishing Prussian leadership in the unification of Germany and, more importantly, as forging an alliance with the western powers that would put an end, once and for all, to the pretensions of the Russian autocracy. On March 31 Arnim proposed to the French the conclusion of an alliance for the purpose of restoring Poland. This was going beyond suggestions which Lamartine had made, but he nevertheless promised Prussia armed support in the event of a Russian attack. The British, for their part, replied to unofficial soundings that they sympathized with Polish aspirations but felt that provocation of Russia should be avoided. Neither Britain nor France wanted to become involved in a major European war for the sake of Poland, the more so as Czar Nicholas was concentrating large forces on the Prussian and Austrian frontiers.[29]

While the French continued their efforts to induce the Prussians to give up Posen, events in the grand duchy itself soon made the question academic. The Poles soon took control of the local administration, whereupon the Germans began to organize resistance. Through pressure on the Berlin government they had the "reorganization" restricted to the purely Polish areas, which meant that a line of demarcation had

---

28 Namier: *1848*, 57 ff., takes account of the Polish literature. On the German side, see Wolfgang Hallgarten: *Studien über die deutsche Polenfreundschaft in der Periode der Märzrevolution* (Munich, 1928); Wolfgang Kohte: "Deutsche Bewegung und preussische Politik im Posener Lande, 1846–1848" (*Deutsche wissenschaftliche Zeitschrift für Polen*, XXI, 1931, 1-216); Friedrich Schinkel: *Polen, Preussen und Deutschland* (Berlin, 1932); R. Hepke: *Die polnische Erhebung und die deutsche Gegenbewegung in Posen im Jahre 1848* (Posen, 1948). See also Stefan Kieniewicz: "The Social Visage of Poland in 1848" (*Slavonic and East European Review*, XXVII, 1948–1949, 91-105); Cyril E. Black: "Poznań and Europe in 1848" (*Journal of Central European Affairs*, VIII, 1948, 191-206).

29 Erich Marcks: "Die europäischen Mächte und die 48-er Revolution" (*Historische Zeitschrift*, CXLII, 1930, 73-87); Friedrich Ley: "Frankreich und die deutsche Revolution, 1848-1849" (*Preussische Jahrbücher*, CCXIII, 1928, 199-216); Wislawa Knapowska: "La France, la Prusse et la question polonaise en 1848" (in *La Pologne au VIe Congrès Internationale des Sciences Historiques*, Warsaw, 1928, 147-166); Paul Henry: "Le gouvernement provisoire et la question polonaise en 1847" (*Revue historique*, CLXXVIII, 1936, 198-240), and *La France devant le monde* (Paris, 1945), 153 ff.

to be established. Meanwhile the Prussian commander, secretly encouraged by the king and court, began to suppress the Polish movement. Rather desperate fighting ensued, during which many of the Polish landlords sided with the Germans, blaming Mieroslawski and the revolutionaries for all the trouble. After Mieroslawski's defeat (May 9) the demarcation line was fixed so as to assign about two-thirds of the duchy (the mixed as well as the strictly German areas) to the German sphere. This part was then to be admitted to the Germanic Confederation and to send twelve deputies to the national Parliament at Frankfurt.

The French, encouraged by the Polonophilism of the Frankfurt radicals, protested against this "fourth partition" of Poland, but the debates in the Frankfurt Parliament (July 24-27) put the quietus on Polish hopes. While the radicals Robert Blum and Arnold Ruge pleaded the Polish cause, Wilhelm Jordan, from East Prussia, sounded a note of crass realism. The time had come, he argued, to renounce sentiment and concentrate on German rights: "It is time to wake up to a policy of healthy national egotism." It would be ridiculous to abandon Germany's mission in the East for the sake of "a few families who revel in court splendor and for a few charming mazurka dancers." At the end of the debate the vote was 342 to 31 in favor of recognizing the demarcation line and receiving the "German" part of the duchy into the new German Empire. The vote has been rightly taken as marking the triumph of political nationalism over the cosmopolitanism to which theretofore the liberals had been devoted.[30]

In Posen itself talk of reorganization became fainter and fainter until in 1851, when the tumult and shouting had died, the *status quo* was restored: the grand duchy remained a part of the Prussian Monarchy, and none of it was included in the revived Germanic Confederation. With the onset of reaction all thought of autonomy was abandoned. German officials resumed control and Polish nationalism was in eclipse.

In retrospect the pro-Polish policy of Count Arnim and Lamartine seems "risky and almost fantastic."[31] Yet it remains instructive evidence not only of the rabid popular hatred of Russian tyranny but also

---

[30] Roy Pascal: "The Frankfurt Parliament and the 'Drang nach Osten' " (*Journal of Modern History*, XVIII, 1946, 108-122).
[31] Erich Marcks: *Der Aufstieg des Reiches* (Stuttgart, 1936), I, 260 ff.

of the idealism of the period. Call it sentiment or romanticism if you will, yet one must pay tribute to the sense of justice which led the revolutionaries of 1848 to regard the righting of the wrong done the Poles as a matter of high priority, to be settled even at the expense of territorial sacrifices. It is important, too, as setting the stage for the period of realism that was to follow. The "reorganization" of Posen precipitated the conflict between German and Polish nationalism and provided the Prussian court and military a welcome opening for repression. Karl Marx, furious over the outcome of the debate in the Frankfurt Parliament, recognized at once that the "betrayal" of Poland was to be the first move in the offensive of the counterrevolution.

3. SCHLESWIG-HOLSTEIN: GERMAN AGAINST DANE

Even more ominous than the Polish question was the problem of Schleswig and Holstein, the German-speaking provinces of the Danish crown whose earlier, much involved history has been recounted in a previous chapter.[32] The local patriots, having challenged Copenhagen and been defeated, called upon the Germanic Confederation for help and thereby presented German nationalism with a supreme test. The problem was to be further aggravated by the fact that two major powers, Britain and Russia, had compelling interests in the maintenance of Denmark's integrity, since that state was the guardian of the Sound, the entrance and exit of the Baltic Sea. From the outset the future of Schleswig and Holstein was a European as well as a German-Danish problem.

German public opinion was all but unanimous in its demand that something be done to protect Germanism in the North and to demonstrate that German national interests were not to be trifled with, least of all by a minor power such as Denmark. King Frederick William of Prussia, though reluctant to countenance a revolutionary movement, felt obliged to champion the national cause, if only to recover the prestige he had lost during the Berlin insurrection. When, on April 12, 1848, the federal Diet at Frankfurt recognized the provisional government of the duchies at Kiel, voted to admit Schleswig to membership in the Germanic Confederation, and called upon the German governments to provide troops for action against the Danish king, Frederick William, like the rulers of Hanover and Brunswick, sent a contingent

[32] See above, Chapter VIII.

under General Friedrich von Wrangel which on April 23 crossed the boundary between the two duchies and began the invasion of Schleswig. Wrangel easily expelled the Danish forces and presently (May 2) carried the operations into Jutland, that is, the mainland part of the Danish Monarchy. In response the Danes blockaded the German coast and captured a number of German merchantmen. The Swedes, too, caught up in the revolutionary excitement, forced their king to appoint a liberal cabinet, which at once responded to Danish appeals by promising 15,000 men, provided either Britain or Russia should come to Denmark's support. In June some 4,500 Swedish-Norwegian troops did in fact land in Denmark.[33]

The impending defeat of Denmark and the consequent loss of the duchies at once brought Britain and Russia to the scene. Czar Nicholas, indignant over the Prussian king's support of a revolutionary movement, brought great pressure to bear in Berlin to have the German forces withdrawn from Danish territory. He even threatened to send Russian troops to force the evacuation of the Germans, if necessary. In Britain there was criticism of the Eider-Danes, the extreme Danish nationalists, but even more vigorous censure of German pretensions. The idea that any and all lands inhabited by Germans should belong to the projected German Empire raised suspicions of German designs on the Baltic provinces of Russia and revived fears of German claims to Alsace. Political nationalism threatened to undermine the entire public law of Europe. Benjamin Disraeli, in a famous speech of April 19, ridiculed German nationalism as "dreamy and dangerous nonsense" and warned that the German objective in the Schleswig-Holstein business was to acquire seaports and more particularly a suitable naval base. He called upon the British government to defend Denmark's possession of the duchies. Palmerston, for his part, had done his utmost to prevent the outbreak of war and was now intent on bringing hostilities to an end, if only to forestall intervention by Russia. He therefore at once offered to mediate.[34]

---

[33] Halvdan Koht: "Die Stellung Norwegens und Schwedens im deutsch-dänischen Konflikt" (*Videnskabs-Selskabets Skrifter, Hist.-Fil. Klasse,* Christiania, 1907), chap. i; A. Buscher: *Schweden-Norwegen und die schleswig-holsteinische Frage in den Jahren 1848–1863* (Greifswald, 1927).

[34] Alexander Scharff: *Die europäischen Grossmächte und die deutsche Revolution* (Leipzig, 1942), chap. iii, and "Europäische und gesamtdeutsche Zusammenhänge der schleswig-holsteinischen Erhebung" (in K. von Raumer and Theodor Schieder, eds.:

The Berlin government, under Russian pressure, ordered Wrangel to withdraw from Jutland (May 22) and accepted the British offer of mediation on the basis of a compromise: northern (that is, Danish-speaking) Schleswig to be incorporated with Denmark proper and the remainder to be united with Holstein in a new German state which, though a member of the Germanic Confederation, should remain connected with Denmark through a common sovereign. Unfortunately this proposal, which foreshadowed the settlement of 1919, was rejected both by the Danish king and by the provisional government of the duchies. Weeks of argumentation and bickering followed until eventually the Prussian government accepted Swedish mediation and signed an armistice at Malmö (August 26), to be valid for seven months. The agreement was clearly in Denmark's favor, for it would take the country through the winter, when blockade operations would be all but impossible. Furthermore, it provided for the evacuation of the duchies by the German forces and for the annulment of all acts of the Kiel government. The provisional government of the duchies was to be replaced by a joint Danish-German commission, the chairman of which was known to be pro-Danish.

Among German liberals the Malmö armistice was seen as a major defeat for national interests, and the Berlin government was therefore accused of treason to the national cause. The issue precipitated a severe crisis in the Frankfurt Parliament, as will appear presently. Yet the Prussian government could hardly have acted otherwise. It had the choice between signing the armistice or facing military intervention by Russia and Sweden, and perhaps even by Britain and France. Technically speaking, it should not have concluded the armistice without the concurrence of the Frankfurt authorities, for in the duchies Prussia and the other German states were acting only as agents of the Germanic Confederation. But the national Parliament was known to be rock-ribbed in its opposition to any compromise and would only have complicated matters through its obstruction. Yet the fact remained that Berlin had capitulated in behalf of all Germany and had thereby aroused the indignation and resentment of all nationalists, whether

Stufen und Wandlungen der deutschen Einheit, Stuttgart, 1943, 197–233); W. E. Mosse: *The European Powers and the German Question, 1848–1871* (Cambridge, 1958), 18 ff.; and the painfully detailed study of Holger Hjelholt: *British Mediation in the Danish-German Conflict 1848–1850 (Historisk-Filosofiske Medellelser,* XLI, No. 1, Copenhagen, 1965).

liberal or radical. They refused to see and in the sequel were slow to learn that German problems were not exclusively the affair of the Germans. The organization of Germany rested on the international treaties of 1815, and it was to be expected that the signatories of those treaties would insist on having their say where their interests were concerned. In 1848 three major powers—Britain, Russia and France—were at one in rejecting the German claim to the duchies merely on the basis of language and race. More specifically, they denied the right of the Germanic Confederation to declare Schleswig a member without even consulting the king of Denmark, who, under the public law of Europe, was the undisputed possessor. Against the opposition of the united powers neither Berlin nor Frankfurt could hope to stand.

4. GERMAN UNITY: PROGRAMS AND PROBLEMS

By 1848 the question of German unity had been examined from every conceivable angle: political, economic, sentimental—and all means of attaining it had been critically scrutinized. So urgent had the matter become that several moves were made by official circles even before the insurrections in Vienna and Berlin had taken the problem out of the hands of the governments. Two Hessian aristocrats, the liberally minded brothers Heinrich and Max von Gagern, were particularly active. They had concluded that the Hapsburg Monarchy could hardly introduce representative government without running the risk of disintegration and that therefore Germany, if it was to be unified at all, must look to Prussia for leadership. But such leadership would be acceptable only on two conditions: one, that Prussia become a liberal, constitutional state; and two, that Prussia agree to its own dissolution. Each of its eight constituent provinces should become a separate state in the new Germany, so that no single power should be dominant. On February 28 Heinrich called for the election of a popular parliament to work out the new system. A week later the duke of Nassau sent Max on a tour of the German courts to propose the convocation of a national Parliament elected by the state legislatures, this national Parliament to serve as a lower house in conjunction with the existing federal Diet.

In the turmoil of early March the German princes hardly dared oppose the Gagern project, no doubt hoping that the king of Prussia would raise objection to sacrificing his state on the altar of German unity. As a matter of fact, however, Gagern arrived in Berlin just as the revolution triumphed and just as Frederick William in a public address promised to put himself at the head of the national movement and announced (with mental reservations, it seems) that henceforth Prussia should be merged with Germany. In conversation with the king, Gagern was to discover that Frederick William was indeed reluctant to envisage the partition of the monarchy, and furthermore that in the spirit of romantic loyalty he objected to the exclusion of Austria from the projected German national state. "Germany without the German provinces of Austria would be worse than a face without a nose," he declared.[35]

The king's friend, Radowitz, had already persuaded him to take the initiative in reforming the Germanic Confederation through agreement between the member governments. Radowitz had gone to Vienna and had induced Metternich to concur in a meeting of ministers at Dresden on March 25, where the problem could be explored. But this project was wrecked by the outbreak of revolutions. There remained only the possibility that the federal Diet at Frankfurt might itself do the job. It had already (on March 10) invited the German governments to send special emissaries (*Vertrauensmänner*) to Frankfurt for this purpose. Seventeen delegates, all prominent liberals, presently put in an appearance and, under the chairmanship of Heinrich von Gagern, threw themselves into the task. For a time there seemed at least a fair chance that the new liberal governments emerging from the revolutions might in this way forge the new German national state.

But nonofficial groups were soon to steal the show. As early as March 5, fifty-one notables, mostly liberal deputies from the South German parliaments, had met at Heidelberg to discuss the problem of unification. The Baden radicals, Friedrich Hecker and Gustav von Struve, had proposed that a democratic republic be proclaimed at once, but this was too much for the majority of those present and was at once defeated. Instead it was decided to convoke a preliminary Parliament (*Vorparlament*) at Frankfurt on March 31 to plan elections for a national Parliament.[36]

The members of the pre-Parliament were for the most part deputies

[35] Quoted by Heinrich von Srbik: *Deutsche Einheit* (Munich, 1935–1942), I, 326. See also Friedrich Meinecke: *Weltbürgertum und Nationalalstaat* (Munich, 1908); 301 ff.; George Kuntzel: *Heinrich von Gagern und der grossdeutsche Gedanke* (in *Gesammt-deutsche Vergangenheit: Festgabe für Heinrich Ritter von Srbik*, Munich, 1938, 266–275).

[36] For a succinct account, see Richard K. Ullmann and Sir Stephen King-Hall: *German Parliaments* (New York, 1954), 46 ff.

or former deputies of the South and West German states. The 141 Prussian representatives came chiefly from the liberal Rhineland and carried much weight, since only two Austrians took part. Though it had neither governmental nor popular mandate, the pre-Parliament brushed aside the program of the group of seventeen and also rejected Struve's proposal that it assume supreme power and proclaim a federal republic. It decided that the projected national Parliament should be elected by universal suffrage, the details to be left to the various state governments. East and West Prussia and the "German" part of Posen, as well as Schleswig, were also to be included though not members of the Germanic Confederation. Those parts of the Hapsburg Monarchy that were in the Confederation (that is, Bohemia, Moravia, Silesia, Slovenia, as well as the German-speaking provinces) were also to be included. Pending the meeting of the national Parliament, set for May 1, the pre-Parliament appointed a committee of fifty to deal with matters of federal concern in conjunction with the federal Diet.

In setting the regulations for the elections most of the governments not only ignored the pre-Parliament's recommendation of direct election of deputies but also restricted the concept of universal suffrage. For example, they required a six months' residence, thus shutting out from the vote the numerous itinerant workers. Furthermore, those on relief were almost everywhere denied the vote. In many states domestics, day laborers and apprentices were excluded from the franchise, as being not really independent. In the elections it seems that many abstained who were entitled to vote. In certain places abstentions ran to 30 per cent, due evidently to lack of interest in politics in areas where economic distress was great or else to desire to protest against the electoral restrictions.[37]

In the larger cities Democratic Societies had been hastily organized, mostly by radical groups, to formulate programs and nominate suitable candidates. But the time was short and the voters for the most part were left to their own devices, unless they followed the counsel of their priest or pastor. The lower classes, in so far as they voted at all, tended to choose electors who were often more radical than the deputies whom they in turn elected. In the industrial city of Düsseldorf, for instance, the electoral college consisted of artisans (one-third), inn-

---

[37] Gerhard Schilfert: *Sieg und Niederlage des demokratischen Wahlrechts in der deutschen Revolution* (Berlin, 1952), 122 ff.; Theodore S. Hamerow: "The Elections to the Frankfurt Parliament" (*Journal of Modern History*, XXXIII, 1961, 15–33).

keepers (one-fifth), merchants and factory owners (one-eighth) and lawyers (one-tenth).[38] The members of the so-called Frankfurt Parliament were for the most part men of influence and repute, either on the national or the local level. Out of over five hundred members there were only four journeymen and no common laborer. However, the upper classes were also poorly represented. There were only thirty-eight landlords, of whom only twenty-five were nobles. The number of merchants and industrialists was even smaller.

The phrase "Professors' Parliament," coined at the time, has stuck to the assembly ever since, much as the revolution in Germany has been stamped "the revolution of the intellectuals." Actually there were in the Parliament about fifty professors and sixty secondary-school teachers, but they were definitely outnumbered by the government officials, lawyers, clergymen and writers. It was not really a Professors' Parliament, though it is true that the vast majority of the members were well-educated and belonged to the liberal upper middle class. Certainly no popularly elected assembly has ever been intellectually more distinguished.[39]

The Frankfurt Parliament opened its sessions on May 18 in the Church of St. Paul, a circular structure well adapted to the purpose.[40] Heinrich von Gagern was chosen president, and before long political groupings (hardly organized parties) began to form and meet in various hostelries, from which they presently took their names. The majority of the deputies belonged to the center, being men of bourgeois origin devoted to the principles of political and economic liberalism and eager to achieve national unification, but in no sense revolutionary. Many of them were, in fact, much disturbed by the threat of political and social upheaval. For this reason, if for no other, they wanted to avoid conflict with the governments, with which they hoped to co-operate in remaking Germany. They have often been accused, espe-

---

[38] Konrad Repgen: *Märzbewegung und Maiwahlen des Revolutionsjahres 1848 im Rheinland* (Bonn, 1955), 227, 305 ff.

[39] Efforts to classify the members by social standing have produced only divergent estimates. See Karl Demeter: "Die soziale Schichtung des deutschen Parlaments seit 1848" (*Vierteljahrschrift für Sozial- und Wirtschaftsgeschichte*, XXXIX, n.d., 1–29); Paul Albrecht: *Die volkswirtschaftlichen und sozialen Fragen in der Frankfurter Nationalversammlung* (Halle, 1914), 5 ff.; Droz: *Les révolutions allemandes*, 270; Huber: *Deutsche Verfassungsgeschichte*, 610 ff.; Schilfert: *Sieg und Niederlage*, 402 ff.

[40] This historic church was largely destroyed during the Second World War, but was rebuilt in expectation that it would become the seat of the post-war German Parliament. The present interior arrangement is quite different from what it was in 1848.

cially by Marxist writers, of having "betrayed" the revolution and having turned to support the reaction. It should be remembered, however, that the revolution was not of their making, nor even desired by them. Of the Parliament it has been well said that it was a revolutionary assembly of which the membership was preponderantly nonrevolutionary.[41]

To the left of center were a number of radicals, mostly lawyers and writers, poorly paid and without much prestige, who were described at the time as the *ecclesia militans* of the fourth estate.[42] These men were radicals in the political sense, men out of patience with the existing institutions and desirous of really popular government, with a German national state on a centralized, democratic, republican base. Although closely related to the artisans and skilled workers, the radicals concentrated on political reform and left the workers more or less to find their own salvation.

Not only Marxist but also liberal historians have criticized the Frankfurt Parliament for its indecision, not to say its pusillanimity. Marx maintained that it should at once have declared its full sovereignty and acted dictatorially. Veit Valentin, author of the standard history of the 1848 revolution, attributed the failure of the Parliament to its unwillingness to employ revolutionary methods and its inability to recognize the requirements of the new democracy. An even more recent writer, Wilhelm Mommsen, has charged the leaders of the Parliament with wanting to close out the revolution before it had really gotten under way, and was convinced that thereby the liberal cause was already lost when the Parliament assembled.[43]

Marx, who had counted on supporting the bourgeois revolution as

[41] Gustav Radbruch: "Die frankfurter Grundrechte" (in Wilhelm Keil, ed.: *Deutschland, 1848–1948*, Stuttgart, 1948, 80–88); see also Reinhart Kosseleck, in Werner Conze, ed.: *Staat und Gesellschaft im deutschen Vormärz* (Stuttgart, 1962), 77 ff.; Veit Valentin: "La date de 1848 dans l'histoire de l'Allemagne" (*Société d'histoire moderne*, séance de March 1, 1936); Friedrich Meinecke: *1848: eine Säkulärbetrachtung* (Bonn, 1948), 12 ff., 22; Karl Griewank: "Ursachen und Folgen des Scheiterns der deutschen Revolution von 1848" (*Historische Zeitschrift*, CLXX, 1950, 495–523).

[42] Lenore O'Boyle: "The Democratic Left in Germany, 1848" (*Journal of Modern History*, XXXIII, 1961, 374–383); Wilhelm Abel: "Der Pauperismus in Deutschland" (in *Wirtschaft, Geschichte und Wirtschaftsgeschichte, Festschrift für Friedrich Lütge*, Stuttgart, 1966, 284–298).

[43] Auguste Cornu: "Karl Marx et la révolution de 1848 en Allemagne" (*Europe*, XXVI, 1948, 238–252); Lenin: "Two Tactics of Social Democracy in the Democratic Revolution" (in *Collected Works*, IX); Valentin: *Die deutsche Revolution;* Mommsen: *Grösse und Versagen des deutschen Bürgertums* (Stuttgart, 1949), 217–218.

the prelude to the rising of the proletariat against the capitalist system, was naturally disappointed when he discovered that the *bourgeoisie* had no intention of fighting the governments to the death. But the criticism of the liberal historians is harder to understand, for the Parliament did in fact at once assume the sole right to draft a federal constitution and presently decreed that this constitution should be binding on all German states. Furthermore, it applied itself at once to the establishment of a provisional federal executive. Due to the fact that the Czechs of Bohemia and Moravia had refused to take part in the elections, the Hapsburg Monarchy, which was entitled to 190 seats, actually had only 120 deputies, while Prussia had 198. For this reason the sentiment of the moderates favored Prussian leadership or at least an executive directory of three, yet the Parliament eventually yielded to the radical demand for a single head and on June 28 chose Archduke John as vicar-general (*Reichsverweser*). John, though an uncle of the Austrian emperor, was a man well known for his progressive views. Having accepted the Frankfurt appointment, he at once named Prince Leiningen, a half-brother of Queen Victoria of Great Britain and a confirmed liberal, to head the federal cabinet.

These were undeniably important strides in the direction of federal control, taken while the governments were still paralyzed and prevented by radical pressures from offering active resistance. But the efforts of the Frankfurt Parliament were soon to meet ominous setbacks abroad as well as at home. The attempt to secure full control of foreign affairs failed when both Britain and France declined to receive fully accredited ambassadors and protested formally against the Parliament's action in the Schleswig affair. The attitude of these powers, initially well-disposed toward the aspirations of German nationalism, underwent drastic changes as the territorial implications of German unification began to emerge. Only the United States continued to be wholly sympathetic, offering to exchange ministers. Other powers preferred to wait and see.[44]

On the domestic front the issue was control over the armed forces. Liberals and radicals were at one in their hatred of standing armies,

<hr />

[44] See footnote 34 above, and in addition Hans Precht: *Englands Stellung zur deutschen Einheit, 1848–1850* (Berlin, 1925); Günther Gillesen: *Lord Palmerston und die Einigung Deutschlands* (Hamburg, 1961), 32 ff.; Paul Henry: *La France devant le monde* (Paris, 1945), 153 ff.

regarded by them as instruments of repression. Their ideal was a militia on the Swiss model, but as a first step the Frankfurt government on July 16 called on the armies of all states to adopt the national colors and take an oath of allegiance to the Archduke John as commander-in-chief. Many of the lesser states complied, but both Prussia and Austria refused. In Prussia the king was already involved in dispute with his own Parliament over control of the forces. Since his army was the one really powerful German force, he fancied himself as the ultimate commander-in-chief. In any event, the Frankfurt government had no way of enforcing its decree and had to accept defeat. It was the first serious contest between nationalism and state particularism and its outcome was soon to becloud other efforts at popular control.[45]

The Frankfurt Parliament spent the early weeks of its existence in receiving countless deputations and petitions, and in working out its organization. Committees (twenty-four in all) were set up to draft a statement of fundamental rights, to study constitutional problems, to handle foreign affairs, and so on. One of the most important committees was the Economic Committee, which, in addition to questions of trade and industry, had responsibility also for the problems of labor. For some time the debates of the Parliament centered on basic rights (*Grundrechte*). Indeed, the Parliament has been charged with spending so much valuable time on learned discussion of principles that by the time it arrived at the problem of federal organization the governments had already recovered sufficiently to obstruct the popular will. It should be remembered, however, that prevention of a return to the Metternich system was a matter of great and immediate importance and also that it was necessary to arrive at uniform principles in order to counteract the forces of particularism. Allowing for the expansive rhetoric of the period, the debates reveal not only eloquence and learning but the kind of hardheaded reasoning with which professors are rarely credited.[46]

Considering its nature and membership, it was only to be expected

---

[45] Gerhard Ritter: *Staatskunst und Kriegshandwerk* (Munich, 1954), I, 148 ff.; Gordon A. Craig: *The Politics of the Prussian Army* (Oxford, 1955), 111 ff.; Huber: *Deutsche Verfassungsgeschichte*, II, 647 ff.

[46] Radbruch: "Die Frankfurter Grundrechte," and the analytical study of Herbert A. Strauss: *Staat, Bürger, Mensch: die Debatten der deutschen Nationalversammlung über die Grundrechte* (Aarau, 1947).

that the Parliament should hold to the principles of liberalism. Its treatment of the agrarian problem is a   good example. During the spring of 1848 several governments, confronted with peasant disturbances, had decreed the abolition of all feudal dues, usually with provision for compensation to the owners of servitudes resting on the land. The Parliament took much the same line. It declared all patrimonial rights at an end, abolished without compensation feudal obligations of the peasantry (including the hated hunting and forest rights), but decreed that dues connected with the land should be commuted into money payments. The details were left largely to the state governments.[47]

Equally important, in the light of later developments, was the question of industrial labor, more particularly the plight of craftsmen and artisans working at the traditional trades and suffering greatly from technological unemployment and the growing competition of machine production. These were the people who, in their desperation, had fought on the barricades and who now staked their hopes on the radical democratic program. They were not, in general, Communists or even socialists. It is true that Karl Marx, through his *New Rhenish Gazette,* was exercising increasing influence, but his policy and that of his paper was at the time directed more toward political democracy than toward communism. Furthermore, the sophisticated reasoning, what Heine once called "the terrible logic," of the Communists was definitely beyond the comprehension of the ordinary worker. Even in Cologne the Communists were almost exclusively middle-class intellectuals.

The average artisan, whether a master craftsman or a journeyman, tended to look not forward but backward. His greatest dread was that of losing respectability and sinking to the status of the true proletarian. His difficulties, as he saw them, derived from the machine and from the system of economic liberalism, that is, from free competition. Little interested in politics, the workers made concerted efforts to organize, nationally as well as locally, in a general labor union as well as in separate trade unions. Their great aim was to revive the guild system

---

[47] Paul Albrecht: *Die volkswirtschaftlichen und sozialen Fragen in der Frankfurter Nationalversammlung* (Halle, 1914), 29 ff.; Walter Schneider: *Wirtschafts- und Sozialpolitik im Frankfurther Parlament* (Frankfurt, 1923), 62 ff.; Hamerow: *Restoration, Revolution, Reaction,* chap. ix.

with all its protective features, and beyond that to enlist the aid of the state to guarantee work, to protect industry through tariffs, and to regulate if not actually check the spread of the factory system and of railway and steamship transportation.[48]

During the summer of 1848 various efforts were made to organize the artisans. An important congress, representative chiefly of the master craftsmen of southern Germany, met at Frankfurt from July 15 to August 18 and undertook to play an economic role co-ordinate with the political role of the Frankfurt Parliament, indeed, to draft a new labor code to supplement the new political constitution. The congress, which refused admittance to ordinary journeymen, called for return to the guild system and for free, compulsory elementary education, a progressive income tax, a protective tariff and state provision of employment when necessary.

From the very beginning the German labor movement was weakened by the rift between the masters and their employees, most of whom lived in the home of the master and were therefore subject to his authority.[49] On their exclusion from the masters' congress, the journeymen organized their own congress at Frankfurt. They were less enamored of the guild system than their employers and aimed at organization of the workers more or less in opposition to the guilds. Much of their attention was given to practical matters such as a minimum wage and a shorter workday, and to the demand for extensive state aid, foreshadowing the modern welfare state.

Even more important from the organizational standpoint was the Berlin Labor Congress (August 23–September 2), representing about ninety-five workers' clubs, mostly in North Germany. Its president was Stefan Born, the chief advocate of organization and self-help. It was an essentially moderate group which formulated the usual program with-

---

[48] Hans Meusch: *Die Handwerker-Bewegung, 1848–1849* (Alfeld, 1949); Theodore S. Hamerow: "The German Artisan Movement, 1848–1849" (*Journal of Central European Affairs,* XXI, 1961, 135–152); Obermann: *Die deutschen Arbeiter,* 180 ff.; Werner Conze: *Die Arbeiterbewegung in der nationalen Bewegung* (Stuttgart, 1966), 32 ff.; Noyes: *Organization and Revolution,* 122 ff. A useful collection of articles from the *New Rhenish Gazette* has been published under the title: *Karl Marx und Friedrich Engels: Die Revolution von 1848* (Berlin, 1953).

[49] In Frankfurt there were 2,696 shops with 3,965 employees, of whom 3,214 lived with the master. See Paul Kampffmeyer: *Geschichte der modernen Gesellschaftsklassen in Deutschland* (3 ed., Berlin, 1921), 234.

out attacking the capitalist system or private property. Rejecting the guild system even more positively than the journeymen's congress, the Berlin group petitioned the Frankfurt Parliament to recognize and consider the needs of the workers, but at bottom its objective was effective organization to secure its demands. It set up a Labor Brotherhood (*Verbrüderung*) with twenty-six district committees to send delegates to an annual assembly which, in turn, should elect a central committee to transact business on a permanent basis. This organization, which managed to survive the revolution of 1848, went much further than anything attempted by the French workers and marked an important advance in the German labor movement.[50]

The Economic Committee of the Frankfurt Parliament was by no means unsympathetic to the cause of the workers and made an honest effort to balance the demands of the workers' congresses as well as of the numberless petitions that flowed in from local groups and individuals. The main task was to find a middle way between the guild system, called for by the master craftsmen, and economic freedom, which was a chief tenet of liberalism. However, a new industrial ordinance to regulate the conditions of labor was ultimately arrived at and submitted to the full Parliament. The members were all well aware of the social problem and many had read in the extensive literature that had poured out over the preceding years. They recognized that they had a mission to find "the solid ground of improved material and social conditions," and they engaged in long and earnest debates on various aspects of the labor problem. But they were liberals and could not get away from Malthusian thought. Pauperism, they argued, is due largely to the shortcomings of the workers, and in any case is bound to be transitional. Interference by the state would only make matters worse and, as for a return to the guild system, that would be a negation of all that liberalism stood for. The program of the workers, according to one liberal paper, reflected contempt for the demands of science and a shameless passion for monopoly. In the end the projected labor

[50] Ernst Schraepler: *Quellen zur Geschichte der sozialen Frage in Deutschland, I, 1800–1870* (Göttingen, 1955), 104 ff.; Max Quarck: *Die erste deutsche Arbeiterbewegung: Geschichte der Arbeiterverbrüderung, 1848–1849* (Leipzig, 1924); Wilhelm Friedensburg: *Stefan Born und die Organisationsbestrebungen der Berliner Arbeiterschaft* (Leipzig, 1923), 92 ff.; Rudolf Stadelmann: *Soziale und politische Geschichte der Revolution von 1848* (Munich, 1948), 166 ff.; Meusch: *Die Handwerker-Bewegung,* 43 ff.; Noyes: *Organization and Revolution,* 212 ff.

ordinance was quietly shelved. The workers had made a significant start, but they still had a long way to go.[51]

5. THE END OF ILLUSION

The Malmö armistice (August 28) marked the end of the Frankfurt Parliament's golden age. It had started out with illusions of grandeur, arrogating to itself the exclusive right to lay down the terms for the unification of Germany, setting up a federal government, and attempting to assume command of the armed forces. The refusal of the two great powers, Prussia and Austria, to abandon control over their armies was the first serious setback in domestic affairs, highlighting as it did the fact that the Parliament had no means for enforcing its decisions. In the foreign field the Malmö armistice, concluded without consultation of the Parliament, demonstrated, first, that any German state could and would, if its interests demanded it, act without reference to the elected assembly; second, that the question of German unity was not one for the Germans alone to decide. Prussia had acted under pressure from Britain and Russia, powers which left no doubt that they were entitled to be heard and proposed to insist on it. There were those, the historian Dahlmann for example, who counseled resistance at any cost and induced the Parliament at first to reject the armistice (September 5). One deputy talked of replying to the foreign powers with a *levée en masse* of a million and a half men. Count Schmerling, who was about to take over the premiership from Prince Leiningen, observed that war might not be a bad thing, as it would quickly unite all Germans in the national cause. Lord Cowley, the British representative, was horrified by the bellicose talk he heard in political circles. He thought the Parliament "a parcel of children who want whipping and caressing alternately."[52]

One can explain the attitude of the Parliament by the lack of experience of most of its members, but it was above all else a reflection of the ardent passion for national self-assertion which moved not only liberals and radicals but also workers and even Communists such as Marx.

[51] Wilhelm Mommsen: *Grösse und Versagen des deutschen Bürgertums*, 162 ff.; Eugen Barthelmess: "Sozialpolitisches im Revolutionsjahr" (in Wilhelm Keil, ed.: *Deutschland, 1848–1948*, 114–123); Noyes: *Organization and Revolution*, 221 ff.

[52] Günther Gillesen: *Lord Palmerston und die Einigung Deutschlands* (Hamburg, 1961), 40 ff.; Donald Southgate: "The Most English Minister" (New York, 1966), 226.

Ever since the crisis of 1840 they had been painfully aware of the helplessness of the Confederation. They were determined not only on the establishment of constitutional government but also on the attainment of a position commensurate with their numbers, their size, and their cultural achievements. Their economic development called for the extension of the *Zollverein* to the entire German area and the creation of a strong state that could hold its own in international affairs. In 1848 every German state, even the little county of Knyphausen, had its own commercial flag and its own (mostly honorary) consuls abroad. The foreign representatives of powers such as Prussia and Austria, or the great commercial city of Hamburg, were of course treated with respect, but those of the lesser states were often ignored.

The war with Denmark in 1848 emphasized to all the utter helplessness of the Germans at sea. Despite their long coastline and huge merchant marine, they had no fleet, not even a decent coastal defense force. The Danes blockaded the German harbors and captured German ships with impunity. Popular indignation was understandable. Countless pamphlets poured from the presses and everywhere navy societies were founded to agitate for a German fleet. After a navy congress at Hamburg (May 31), the Frankfurt Parliament on June 14 voted almost unanimously that a navy should be built for coast defense and commerce protection. But the Germans lacked the necessary naval shipyards, the experienced officers and the trained men. They converted some merchantmen and bought some warships in England and the United States. Meanwhile the Prussian government decided to build six frigates and six steam corvettes on its own account. But to construct a navy would take time. Prior to the autumn of 1848, very little had been accomplished.[53]

The naval program, whatever its merits, served among other things to arouse the suspicions of the British, who already ascribed German policy in the Schleswig question to the desire to get control of the duchies with the excellent potential naval base at Kiel. But what estranged the foreign powers more than anything else was the apparent claim that all territory inhabited by Germans should be included in the new national empire. This appeared from the affair of the duchies and from the effort to include nonfederal lands in the east, such as East and

[53] Archibald Hurd and Henry Castle: *German Sea-Power* (London, 1913), 72 ff.; Karl Haenchen: *Die deutsche Flotte von 1848* (Bremen, 1925), 12 ff.

West Prussia and the larger part of Posen, to say nothing of the voices that clamored for a Greater Germany in which parts of Switzerland, Belgium, the Netherlands and possibly Denmark might be included.[54] What was particularly disconcerting to outsiders was the readiness of the Germans to incorporate in their national state many non-German territories, the populations of which had nationalist aspirations of their own. This meant the Czechs of Bohemia and Moravia, the Slovenes of Carniola and Carinthia, the Italians of the South Tyrol, the Danes of northern Schleswig and the Poles of Prussia's eastern provinces. The Germans were indignant over the refusal of the Czechs to participate in the elections to the Frankfurt Parliament and many were well pleased when Windischgrätz dealt Czech nationalism a blow by the reduction of Prague. They also subscribed to Prussia's suppression of the Polish movement in Posen, and refused to consider the petition of the South Tyrolese for permission to join the nascent Italian national state.

Meanwhile little progress was made toward the reorganization of the Germanic Confederation. The general sentiment at Frankfurt was in favor of unification under Prussian leadership, but Frederick William made no move to implement his promise that Prussia should be merged or fused with Germany, or to assume the leadership which he romantically believed belonged to the Hapsburgs. Actually the Austrian Empire, which in the spring had seemed done for, had by the summer shown greater vitality than most liberals had dreamed of. Radetzky's victory at Custoza revealed the Austrians as champions of German rights and claims and made the new liberal Austria seem more attractive than the old. One might say that the election of the Archduke John as vicar-general was a tribute to the Hapsburgs and a landmark in the revival of Austrian prestige.[55]

The vital question of precedence and leadership therefore remained open, while the tide was turning against the Parliament, as noted

[54] Richard Haufe: *Die Anschauungen über Gebiet, Staatsform und Oberhaupt des deutschen Nationalstaates in den Flugschriften, 1848–1849* (Leipzig, 1915), 8 ff., 25 ff.; Josef Pfitzner: "Die grenz- und auslandsdeutsche Bewegung des Jahres 1848" (*Historische Zeitschrift*, CLX, 1939, 308–322); Peter Rassow: *Deutschland und Europa im Jahre 1848* (Krefeld, 1954), *passim*.

[55] Adolf Rapp: *Grossdeutsch-Kleindeutsch* (Munich, 1922), xxiii; Hans G. Telle: *Das oesterreichische Problem im Frankfurter Parlament* (Marburg, 1933), 20, 33 ff.; Heinrich von Srbik: *Deutsche Einheit* (Munich, 1935), I, 332 ff.

above. With respect to the Malmö armistice, counsels of moderation finally prevailed. On September 17 the Parliament with heavy heart reversed its earlier decision and approved the armistice by a vote of 258 to 237. Among the opponents were the radicals, who were unwilling to surrender to the will of the hated German governments or the pressure of the foreigners. Marx, who denounced the signers of the armistice as a collection of impotent dreamers and a college of fools, mobilized the Democratic Society and the Workers' Society in Cologne for a huge demonstration (September 13), as a result of which a Committee of Public Safety, with Marx, Engels and other Communists as members, was set up. The Cologne radicals were evidently ready to start a civil war, but this was forestalled by the Prussian government, which proclaimed martial law, suspended the publication of the *New Rhenish Gazette,* and forced many of the Communist leaders to flee the city.[56]

The insurrection that broke out in Frankfurt itself on September 17 faced no such opposition, for the Parliament had no armed forces at its disposal. Radicals and workers threw up barricades and fought bitterly, ostensibly in protest against the approval of the humiliating Malmö armistice, but in reality probably in protest against the failure of the Parliament to make progress in the direction of democracy and relief for the poorer classes. The town garrison being altogether unequal to such an outbreak, the provisional government had to call in federal troops (Austrian, Prussian, Hessian) from the nearby federal garrison at Mainz. The insurrection was suppressed by the evening of September 18 and a week later an attempted republican rising in Baden was also defeated. But the upsurge of discontent and radicalism made a deep impression on the liberal members of Parliament, who had never envisaged barricade fighting at the very doors of the popularly elected assembly. Unable to protect itself, the Parliament would in the days to come have to depend on the collaboration of the governments for any progress toward reform and unification.

[56] Hermann Meyer: "Karl Marx und die deutsche Revolution von 1848" (*Historische Zeitschrift,* CLXXII, 1951, 517–537); Kotschetkowa: "Die Tätigkeit von Marx und Engels in der Kölner demokratischen Gesellschaft"; Becker: *Karl Marx und Friedrich Engels in Köln,* 117 ff.

Chapter Thirteen

CLOSING THE CIRCLE

I. THE REPUBLIC WITHOUT REPUBLICANS

In France General Cavaignac, who had been given dictatorial powers to suppress the insurrection of the June Days, insisted on resigning his extraordinary powers, but was named by the National Assembly to be chief of the executive power. As such he replaced the executive commission set up in May and, as president of the Council of Ministers, named the members of his cabinet. Cavaignac was an incorruptible republican, a man of moderate views who served as the faithful servant of the Party of Order, which in turn commanded a majority in the chamber. He dissolved the dissident elements of the National Guard and brought radical clubs and newspapers to heel. Though the radicals branded him the "butcher" of the June Days, he suited the Assembly very well and worked effectively with it.[1]

During the summer and autumn of 1848 the Assembly devoted itself to the task for which it had been chosen, namely, the drafting of a new constitution. This was urgently necessary, for the charter of 1830 was a thing of the past, the monarchy had been swept away, the Orleanist Parliament had been dissolved, the cabinet of Louis Philippe had given way to a provisional government, then to an executive commission and most recently to a chief of the executive power. These were all makeshift arrangements, operating at a time when stability and permanency seemed so necessary.

The Constitutional Committee of the Assembly numbered eighteen members, among them some of the leading political figures of the time. Tocqueville, an outstanding theorist of that or any period, was among them, but held his colleagues in low esteem as lacking depth and deliberation: "I never witnessed a more wretched display in any committee on which I ever sat," he noted in his Recollections. His disparagement, however, may have been due in part to the unwilling-

---

[1] General Ibos: *Le général Cavaignac* (Paris, 1930), 190 ff.; Paul Bastid: *Doctrines et institutions politiques de la Seconde République* (Paris, 1945), II, 5 ff.

ness of his colleagues to adopt his favorite recipe for a decentralized administrative system and a two-chamber Parliament. The committeemen knew little and perhaps cared less about the experience of the United States or Britain. They thought in terms of French history and French requirements.

The republican form, under the circumstances, had to be taken for granted. As for universal suffrage, radical though it might appear, it had proved itself in the elections of April, when the population at large had demonstrated its sanity in opposition to political and social extremism. Other provisions of a first draft were examined critically by delegates chosen by other committees of the Asssembly, after which another month was devoted to revision. From September 4 to October 23 the full Assembly debated the draft, article by article, and eventually on November 4 adopted the new constitution by a vast majority.

Nothing was done to change the highly centralized administrative system which Tocqueville blamed for so many of France's woes, but which Frenchmen of all stripes seemed to find both efficient and congenial. The constitution recognized the familiar civil rights, but boggled at recognition of the "right to work," which had been recognized by the provisional government and had underlain the establishment of the national workshops. Five full sessions were devoted to this topic. Most members were certainly in favor of rejecting it, but were fearful of further disturbances in Paris and other cities. Thiers, who had been elected to the Assembly in a by-election in June, argued that recognition of the right to work would run counter to the principles of economic liberalism and that, furthermore, it would be tantamount to paying workers a wage for doing nothing. By way of compromise the Assembly voted to recognize only the workers' right to relief: the state would provide for foundlings, for the infirm and for the aged. As for work, it would not recognize the laborers' right but would undertake to provide work as far as possible by favoring public projects suitable for unskilled labor.[2]

The principal debates, however, had to do with the nature of the legislature and the method of electing the executive. There was little sentiment for a two-chamber Parliament, on the theory that in Britain the upper chamber was designed for the aristocracy while in the United States the Senate was necessary because of the federal system.

---

[2] Bastid: *Doctrines et institutions politiques*, II, 82 ff.; Jean Dautry: *1848 et la Seconde République* (Paris, 1957), 214.

France, with a centralized administration, required only a single Assembly with concentrated power, competent to deal with any revolutionary emergency. Hence the constitution provided for a single chamber of 750 members, elected triennially by universal suffrage and by cantonal lists. The Assembly was to appoint a council of state, but this was to have the sole function of preparing legislation.

As for the executive, there was general agreement that its powers, too, should be concentrated: there should be a president with substantially the powers of the American president.[3] The key question, however, was whether the president should be elected by the Assembly, acting as the mandatory of the nation, or by direct vote of the people. Jules Grévy, a radical who was eventually to become president of the Third French Republic, warned that the populace, left to itself, might even elect a pretender to the throne. The Assembly would have sounder political judgment than the people at large. But Lamartine, in one of his most eloquent oratorical efforts, argued that election of the president by the Assembly would surely lead to corruption, which would not be possible in a popular vote: "One poisons a glass of water, but not a whole river." Dangers there were, of course, but if things should turn out badly, he was prepared to accept what fate had in store: "Even though the people should choose him whom perhaps my badly enlightened foresight dreads to see, no matter, the die is cast." The Assembly thereupon voted (October 9) that the president should be elected by universal suffrage for a four-year term, but be ineligible for re-election. In the event of none of the candidates receiving two million or more votes, the election was to revert to the Assembly. This is probably what most of the deputies expected to happen.[4]

The debate on the presidency was carried on very much with Prince Louis Napoleon, the Bonapartist claimant, in mind. The prince had hurried to Paris after the February Revolution and had evidently hoped to be included in the provisional government. But Lamartine had convinced him that his presence was not desired and he had returned to London to await developments. Some of his friends, however, had remained in France and had initiated a propaganda campaign on his behalf, with the result that he was elected to the

[3] The influence of the American constitution made itself felt only in this connection. See Eugene N. Curtis: *The French Assembly of 1848 and American Constitutional Doctrines* (New York, 1918), 186 ff.

[4] Bastid: *Doctrines et institutions politiques*, II, 107 ff.; André-Jean Tudesq: *L'élection présidentielle de Louis-Napoléon Bonaparte* (Paris, 1965), 51 ff.

chamber in a by-election in June. His supporters urged him to return, but in vain. Instead he declined his mandate (June 16) and decided to bide his time.

Members of the Assembly were distinctly troubled by the emergence of the Bonaparte pretender on the political scene and by the crowds that eagerly awaited his appearance at the Chamber. Lamartine proposed enforcement of the law which excluded the Bonaparte family from France, and others talked of nullifying the prince's election, which became unnecessary when he voluntarily resigned his seat. But there was, of course, no knowing what the future would bring. Louis Napoleon's friend and promoter, Victor Fialin de Persigny, soon badgered him into standing for election in the by-election of September 17, on which occasion he was again elected in Paris (Seine *département*) and in four other *départements*. In Paris he polled over 110,000 votes, as against 78,000 for his nearest competitor. This was enough to decide him. On September 24 he arrived in Paris, and two days later took his seat in the Assembly.[5]

Members of the Assembly were not so naïve as to think that a pretender with the charismatic name of Bonaparte would be content with the simple role of deputy. They realized that he might enter the race for the presidency and even attempt to restore the empire. But the prince did not seem a very formidable threat, for he was small, short-legged, and expressionless of countenance. When, on two occasions, he spoke briefly to avow his devotion to the Republic, his embarrassed stammer and his Swiss-German accent moved many of his colleagues to either scorn or ridicule. Experienced politicians put him down as a harmless halfwit (Thiers) or an insignificant numskull (Tocqueville).

The future was soon to tell, for Louis Napoleon announced his candidacy for the presidential elections fixed for December 10, thus entering into competition with Cavaignac, Lamartine, Ledru-Rollin and Raspail. Had the choice been up to the Assembly, it would almost certainly have elected Cavaignac, who, with support of the bureaucracy

---

[5] The basic account is still André Lebey: *Louis-Napoléon et la révolution de 1848* (2 vols., Paris, 1907–1908). Among more recent studies, F. A. Simpson: *The Rise of Louis Napoleon* (London, 1909), chap. xi, is excellent, and the following are important: Bernard de Vaulx: *L'échéance de 1852, ou la liquidation de 1848* (Paris, 1948); Maurice de La Fuye and Emile A. Babeau: *Louis-Napoléon avant l'Empire* (Amsterdam, 1951), chaps. xiv–xvi; Adrien Dansette: *Louis-Napoléon à la conquête du pouvoir* (Paris, 1961), chap. x; Heinrich Euler: *Napoleon III in seiner Zeit* (Würzburg, 1961), 446 ff. On the Napoleonic propaganda, see also Paul Chrétien: *Le duc de Persigny* (Toulouse, 1943), 27 ff.

as well as the army, seems in any event to have been so certain of success that, austere republican that he was, he refused to exercise administrative pressure and instead conducted an unaggressive campaign. He certainly had little to fear from his opponents on the left, for the democratic forces were weakened by the repression following the June Days and sadly divided as between republican democrats and social democrats. Ledru-Rollin represented the former and Raspail the latter. Neither had the remotest chance of obtaining even one million votes. Lamartine, on the other hand, thought he had reason for optimism, considering all he had done in the spring to hold the forces of radicalism in check. As for Louis Napoleon, he soon undeceived those who saw in him only a harmless imbecile. He conducted his campaign with great astuteness. His door was always open to those who had something to say and he showed himself ever ready to listen patiently to suggestions. With prominent politicians he posed as a man above class or party, intent on stabilizing the situation and conciliating conflicting factions. When necessary he would even go so far as to make definite commitments.

By the beginning of December the prince had enlisted the more or less sincere support of leading Orleanists (Guizot, Thiers, Barrot, Molé), of prominent Catholics (Berryer, Montalembert, Veuillot), of literary notables (Victor Hugo, Alexandre Dumas) and of influential editors (Girardin). What he lacked was financial support, for his personal fortune and the contributions of his devoted mistress, Miss Howard, were not sufficient. He managed to float a few modest loans with Paris bankers, but he was chronically short of funds and his backers mostly contributed their services without immediate reward. They launched newspapers, posted pamphlets and broadsides, formed election committees and dispatched agents to the provinces. They made effective use of the Napoleonic legend, which had long since established the great emperor as the champion of progress, the defender of religion and society, and the hero who had exalted France above all nations. The nephew, it was now argued, represented the very same principles. He could be depended upon to put an end to revolutionary agitation, to maintain order, restore property and revive French glory.[6]

The elections of December 10 were to show that Louis Napoleon

---

[6] Jean Lucas-Dubreton: *Le culte de Napoléon, 1815-1848* (Paris, 1960), chap. xviii; André-Jean Tudesq: "La légende napoléonienne en France en 1848" (*Revue historique*, CCXLIII, 1957, 64-85).

enjoyed the widest conceivable support not only throughout the rural areas of France but in the cities as well. Even in Paris the radical candidates, Ledru-Rollin and Raspail, received only 12.5 per cent of the votes. The capital and four other major cities gave the prince an absolute majority.[7] The results no doubt reflected the workers' hatred of Cavaignac and their distrust of Ledru-Rollin for his abandonment of the socialist program, but they certainly expressed also the appeal of Louis Napoleon, who had had nothing whatever to do with the struggles that culminated in the June Days and who, besides, had a well-known interest in the problems of the machine age and the plight of the urban workers. During his exile in England he had visited the industrial centers and made copious notes of his observations.[8] While in captivity in the fortress of Ham he had received the visits of Louis Blanc and had tried his own hand at social theorizing. In his pamphlet *The Extinction of Pauperism* (1844) he had argued that the days of social castes were over. In the future it would be possible to govern only with the support of the masses. The answer to unemployment and the constant fluctuation in the demand for labor was for the state to finance agricultural colonies to which unemployed urban workers could return, to work at a guaranteed soldier's wage until again required for work in the factories. The idea was by no means new. In fact, it was a favorite nostrum of the period. But it was new that a prince should demonstrate such awareness of the social problem and such interest in the welfare of the worker.[9]

Among the peasants, at the same time, the Napoleonic legend apparently had its most devoted adherents. The fact that the empire had meant heavy taxation, conscription and almost continuous war seemed no longer of much account. Bonapartists, said Victor Hugo, were like children: they liked what was flashy. The countryside, furthermore, had no use for revolution. It resented the 45-centime surtax, which was regarded as a case of rank discrimination in favor of worthless city loafers. Even after the June Days the peasants could not rid themselves of the fear of "communism." George Sand, herself accused of being a Communist, remarked that in the provinces one was

[7] Tudesq: *L'élection présidentielle*, 210–211.

[8] Ivor Guest: *Napoleon III in England* (London, 1952), 35.

[9] Ernest Labrousse: *Le mouvement ouvrier et les idées sociales en France de 1815 à la fin du XIXe siècle* (Paris, 1948), 135; Albert Guerard: *Napoleon III* (Cambridge, 1943), 55.

regarded as a Communist if one was a republican, and if one was a socialist republican one was suspected of drinking human blood, of killing babies, of beating one's wife, of being a bankrupt, a drunk and a robber, and one ran the real risk of being assassinated by some peasant who believed you mad because his bourgeois and his priest had told him so.[10]

It was fairly clear from the outset that the peasantry would vote for Louis Napoleon, many no doubt in the hope that he would put an end to the republic. It was thought that he would soon bring back prosperity. According to rumor he was planning to reduce the surtax from 45 centimes to 25 and to draw on his own "immense" fortune to relieve the rural poor. It took only the prince's election manifesto of early December to clinch the election. Though he had discussed it with Thiers, the manifesto was the prince's own work. A masterful political document, it promised in general all things to all men and once again pictured Louis Napoleon as the man above class or party, as the great conciliator.[11]

The victory of Louis Napoleon was, then, hardly the surprise of which many writers speak. The startling thing was not his election but the magnitude of his success, for of the 7,426,252 votes cast, he received 5,534,520, while Cavaignac had only 1,442,302, Ledru-Rollin 371,431, Raspail 36,920 and Lamartine a paltry 17,910. In most *départements* the prince obtained upward of 80 per cent of the votes, especially in the north and center. If the election did not exactly reveal what France wanted, it at least showed what the country did not want, namely, the existing republic. The influential groups, deputies, prefects, notables, editors, had all been swamped by the tidal wave of popular sentiment. Universal suffrage had brought the repudiation of the February Revolution and its fruits. In the words of Karl Marx, it was "the day of the peasant insurrection," marking "their entry into the revolutionary movement." But they entered it not to further it; rather, to ruin it.[12]

[10] Quoted in Pierre Labracherie: "Le paysan de 1848" (in *Esprit de 1848*, Paris, n.d., 215–246).

[11] Albert Soboul: "La question paysanne en 1848" (*La pensée*, No. 20, 1948, 48–56). On the manifesto see Vaulx: *L'échéance de 1852*, 107 ff.

[12] Karl Marx: *The Class Struggles in France*, 71. See also the discriminating evaluation of the election results in Tudesq: *L'élection présidentielle*, 211 ff.

2. ITALY: THE RADICAL PHASE

Many Frenchmen, when they voted for Louis Napoleon, expected him to restore France to its historic position as arbiter of Europe and it was, in fact, only a few months before the new president had involved his country in the traditional struggle for influence in the Italian peninsula. There the trend of events in the autumn of 1848 ran counter to that of most countries, for while elsewhere the forces of conservatism or reaction were in the ascendant, in Italy the liberal elements were being superseded by radical, democratic forces. To a large extent this was a reflection of the shock of the defeat at Custoza. For a time there was still hope that the mediation of Britain and France would bring Piedmont possession of Lombardy, but this mediation soon proved as ineffectual as the military operations. Palmerston preached to the Austrian government the virtues of abnegation and kept warning it of the imminent danger of French intervention, but in vain. In Vienna it was realized that the French were actually opposed to the aggrandizement of Piedmont and that the Cavaignac government, though it might put up a brave front, was intent on avoiding embroilment in foreign adventure. The Anglo-French partnership rested at bottom on distrust rather than confidence, for while the British objective was a strong North Italian state that would be an effective buffer between Austria and France, the French were concerned to keep North Italy divided and thus open to French influence. Neither government was moved by interest in Italian national aspirations. Their thought was of the balance of power and their objectives therefore diametrically opposed.

The Salasco armistice was a strictly military truce, which was periodically renewed while the effort at mediation continued. For months the Vienna government managed to temporize until, by November, the revolution in the Austrian capital had been finally mastered and Prince Felix zu Schwarzenberg had taken over as chief of the cabinet. Schwarzenberg at once struck a more positive note. He charged the British with desiring the annexation of Lombardy to Piedmont merely so as to obstruct French influence. No doubt this was an accurate expression of French opinion, too, for Cavaignac now began to warn the Piedmontese government not to expect French aid if it attempted to renew the war against Austria. Palmerston continued for a time to exert pressure on Vienna until Schwarzenberg, in an amazing dispatch to Austrian representatives abroad, called him to order:

Lord Palmerston regards himself too much as the arbiter of Europe. We for our part are not disposed to accord him the role of Providence. We never impose our advice on him in Irish matters: let him spare himself the trouble of advising us on the subject of Lombardy. . . . We are tired of his eternal insinuations, his protective and pedagogical tone, both offensive and unwelcome. We are resolved to tolerate it no longer. Lord Palmerston said one day to Koller (the Austrian chargé d'affaires in London), that if we wanted war, we could have it. I say, if he wants war, he *shall* have it.[13]

As the outlook for mediation grew dimmer, the Piedmontese government found itself in a quandary. Some political leaders favored an appeal for French intervention, but of this the king would hear nothing and, besides, Cavaignac soon blasted all hopes that French troops might serve as "mercenaries." Meanwhile the Turin government was faced by a deteriorating economic situation, widespread unemployment and threat of social upheaval. Genoa, a center of radicalism like other seaports, seemed on the verge of revolution, while in Turin itself the democratic forces were becoming more assertive. Radical leaders, organizations and newspapers blamed the king and his aristocratic entourage for the defeat of the army. They clamored for constitutional reform and a renewal of the patriotic war, arguing that once the sword were drawn, the French Republic would be bound to aid. Count Cavour, who was rising to prominence, counseled patience, insisted on the need for more preparation and warned that France could no more be counted on to support the Piedmontese than to aid the Poles. The Italians, he thought, should wait at least until the Austrians had become more deeply involved in the war against Hungary. On the other hand, Gioberti was heart and soul with the war party, which was steadily growing in influence. On October 17 a motion for war by the

---

[13] A. J. P. Taylor: *The Italian Problem in European Diplomacy, 1847–1849* (Manchester, 1934), 177 ff.; Vittorio Barbieri: "I tentativi di mediazione anglo-francesi durante la guerra di 1848" (*Rassegna storica del Risorgimento*, XXVI/2, 1939, 683–726); Ruggero Moscati: *La diplomazia europea e il problema italiano nel 1848* (Florence, 1947), and "L'Europa e il problema italiano nel 1848–1849" (in F. Catalano, R. Moscati and F. Valsecchi: *L'Italia nel Risorgimento*, Verona, 1964, Part III, chap. iii); Donald Southgate: *"The Most English Minister"* (New York, 1966), 230 ff.

democratic leader Angelo Brofferio was defeated by a vote of only 77 to 58.[14]

In December, when the chances of successful mediation had become hopeless, Charles Albert felt obliged to yield to popular pressure. He appointed a democratic cabinet with Gioberti at its head. The new administration promptly dissolved Parliament and in January, 1849, held elections which for the first time produced a democratic majority. Pressure for renewal of the war continued to mount, but Gioberti, now that he was in power, began to recognize many obstacles to a policy of unrestrained patriotism. The army, for instance, was still inadequately prepared and the new French president held out no hope of support. Furthermore, the pope, who had been obliged by the radicals to leave Rome, was appealing to the Catholic powers for intervention in his behalf and Gioberti, the champion of an Italian federation under papal leadership, now devoted his efforts to forging a coalition of Italian states for joint action in behalf of the pope which would make foreign intervention superfluous. Presently Gioberti, who showed no aptitude for constitutional procedures, fell out with his colleagues and resigned (February 21). He was succeeded by Urbano Rattazzi, who had long agitated for renewal of the war. On March 12 the Piedmontese government denounced the Salasco armistice and reopened hostilities.

A few words may be said about the projected Italian league or confederation which had become so popular after publication of the Gioberti book in 1843 and then cropped up continually in one form or another during the revolutionary years 1848-1849. After the defeat at Custoza, Gioberti had persuaded Charles Albert to send the eminent philosopher Antonio Rosmini to Rome, where the latter, in collaboration with a papal and a Tuscan representative, had worked out a plan for a confederation under papal leadership resting on an assembly sitting at Rome and having control over foreign policy, the armed forces and the trade policies of the entire peninsula (see Illustration 56). The plan is interesting chiefly as a reflection of Gioberti's thought

14 G. F. H. and J. Berkeley: *Italy in the Making* (Cambridge, 1940), III, 384 ff.; Giorgio Candeloro: *Storia dell'Italia moderna* (Milan, 1960), III, 363 ff.; A. J. Whyte: *The Political Life and Letters of Cavour, 1848-1861* (London, 1930), 14 ff.; Adolfo Omodeo: *Vincenzo Gioberti e la sua evoluzione politica* (Turin, 1941), 78 ff.; Rosario Romeo: *Dal Piemonte sabaudo all'Italia liberale* (Turin, 1963), 108 ff. For the evolution of democratic doctrine in Italy, see Franco della Peruta: *I democratici e la rivoluzione italiana* (Milan, 1958).

and that of the patriotic nationalists. The Piedmontese government, now as ever, was opposed to any scheme that involved sacrifice of sovereignty. Its counterproposal (October) envisaged merely an alliance of independent states for the protection of their territorial integrity and for common military action in defense. In this plan the other governments rightly saw nothing but an effort to enlist support for Piedmontese designs and pretensions to hegemony. The effect of the Piedmontese proposal was to arouse distrust and fan hostility to the Turin government.[15]

Closely related to the problem of Italian confederation were developments in Tuscany and the Papal States. Social conditions in Tuscany, where most of the peasants were illiterate sharecroppers, were so desperate that an insurrection seemed imminent. In the towns, too, there was much unemployment and misery. In August there was an uprising in Livorno, a busy seaport, which forced officials and troops to flee the city. As it was, however, the lower classes were so illiterate, unorganized and leaderless as to be unable to assume power. Their demands were rudimentary: a larger share of the land and reduced obligations to the landlords; in the cities higher wages and public works to provide employment, along with restrictions on the introduction of machinery. There was occasionally a demand for recognition of the right to work and for the organization of labor, but these were only faint echoes of French socialist doctrine, the sole effect of which was to frighten the propertied classes and turn many of them toward reaction.[16]

The uprising in Livorno was finally suppressed by Francesco Guerrazzi, the well-known novelist, who rallied the *bourgeoisie* and organized a Civic Guard to restore and maintain order. Because of the limited franchise the moderate liberals were able to retain a majority in the Tuscan Parliament, but they were so beset by fears of all kinds that they left the government to Guerrazzi and to another celebrated writer,

[15] Antonio Monti: *L'idea federalistica nel Risorgimento italiano* (Bari, 1921); Berkeley and Berkeley: *Italy in the Making*, III, 384 ff.; Candeloro: *Storia dell'Italia moderna*, III, 293 ff.

[16] Gino Luzzatto: "Aspects sociaux de la révolution de 1848 en Italie" (*Revue socialiste*, n.s., Nos. 17–18, 1948, 80–86); Guido Quazza: *La lotta sociale nel Risorgimento* (Turin, 1951), 206 ff.; Franco Catalano: "Socialismo e communismo in Italia del 1846 al 1849" (*Rassegna storica del Risorgimento*, XXXVIII, 1951, 306–316); Salvatore F. Romano: "Le classi sociali in Italia, 1815–1918" (in *Nuove questioni di storia del Risorgimento*, Milan, 1961, 511–572).

Giuseppe Montanelli, who had just returned from volunteer service in the north. Guerrazzi, once in power, tended like Gioberti in Piedmont to adopt a moderate course. He turned his face against republicanism and denounced "the disgraceful greed of men without name, without country, without God, who have designs on the lands and houses of others."[17]

Montanelli for his part busied himself with schemes for an Italian confederation on a popular basis, such as Mazzini had long since advocated. Without union, he was convinced, the foreigner could never be expelled, and this, according to the program he submitted to the governments on November 7, was the real purpose of the confederation. What he proposed was the election of a constituent assembly by universal suffrage, this assembly then to decide what degree of integration was necessary. The Piedmontese government replied promptly that a popular assembly could hardly direct a war and then reverted to its own plan for military collaboration. The Montanelli proposal proved abortive, but remains interesting as a reflection of democratic aspirations. It was, in fact, to have a real influence on the course of events in Rome during the succeeding months.[18]

The situation as it emerged in the Papal States was both complicated and crucial. There, as elsewhere, the economic crisis provided the background for political developments. The government, struggling with a chronic deficit, could not hope to make ends meet without antagonizing influential strata of society. The cabinet of Count Terenzio Mamiani (May to August, 1848) enrolled some 3,000 Roman workers in what amounted to national workshops, only to discover that it had only about a third of the money required. The unrest was such that radical clubs sprang up everywhere and demonstrations became the order of the day. The most popular and powerful club was the Circolo Populare, led by Angelo Brunetti (*Ciceruacchio*), a brawny baker who was constantly proclaiming the right to work and demanding the abolition of want, chiefly through merciless taxation of the rich. The situation in Bologna was no better. An attempt by the Austrians

17 Quoted by Romano: "Le classi sociali in Italia." See also W. K. Hancock: *Ricasoli and the Risorgimento in Tuscany* (London, 1926), 130 ff.

18 R. Cessi: "Il problema della Costituente nel 1848" (*Rassegna storica del Risorgimento*, XLI, 1954, 304–311); A. M. Ghisalberti: *Giuseppe Montanelli e la Costituente* (Florence, 1947); and the heavily documented analysis of the various projects for federation in Renato Mori: "Il progretto di lega neo-guelfa di Pellegrino Rossi" (*Rivista di studi politici internazionali*, XXIV, 1957, 602–628).

in August to occupy the city led to such a ferocious popular outbreak that the troops had to retreat. For several weeks the city was at the mercy of unemployed workers and hoodlums who pillaged, murdered and tyrannized over the population without any specific program or objective. Eventually a government emissary backed by Swiss mercenaries succeeded in restoring order.[19]

The Mamiani cabinet, typical of the moderate liberal governments of 1848, was distrusted by the pope, not only because it was constantly pressing for participation in the war against Austria, but because it attempted to separate the administration of the Papal States from the administration of the Catholic Church. Mamiani had but little chance of success, for not even the Parliament, elected in May, afforded him much support. So great was the political immaturity of the country that of the restricted electorate only about a third had voted and of the successful candidates only about half had accepted their mandate. Though the well-to-do classes commanded a majority in the lower house, they showed themselves strangely apathetic, if not frightened. By way of contrast, the radical wing, led by the Mazzinian Pietro Sterbini and the renegade Carlo Bonaparte (prince of Canino), a nephew of the great French emperor, was aggressive and domineering. Crowds in the galleries and on the streets constantly cheered it on.[20]

The main issue was still that of war or peace. Pius and the cardinals, concerned about their ecumenical obligations, were unalterably opposed to participating in the war, the more so as they considered it primarily a campaign for the aggrandizement of Piedmont. But the majority in Parliament, the right as well as the left, was enthusiastically committed to war. The arrival of volunteers returning from the north, and of liberal and radical refugees from the Kingdom of Naples, added fuel to the fires of patriotism. The pope, in despair, finally appointed a cabinet under Cardinal Soglia, in which the sole member of note was Pellegrino Rossi, one of the truly significant personalities of the period. Rossi, an Italian by birth, had spent his mature years in France, where he enjoyed an enviable reputation as an economist of the liberal school.

---

[19] On the economic crisis in the Papal States, see Domenico Demarco: *Pio IX e la rivoluzione romana de 1848* (Modena, 1947), 92 ff., 105 ff., 122 ff.; also Quazza: *La lotta soziale*, 214 ff.

[20] Demarco: *Pio IX*, 77 ff. R. M. Johnston: *The Roman Theocracy and the Republic, 1846–1849* (New York, 1901), chap. x. See further, Guillaume Mollat: *La question romaine de Pie IX à Pie XI* (Paris, 1932), 225 ff.; Berkeley and Berkeley: *Italy in the Making*, III, 337 ff.; Candeloro: *Storia dell'Italia moderna*, III, 311 ff.

His friend Guizot sent him to Rome as French minister in 1846 and there he had quickly become one of the pope's chief advisers in matters of reform. Though disillusioned about constitutional government, Pius in the summer of 1848 seems to have still hoped that Rossi could make the system work and so save the country from chaos.

Rossi was convinced that war against Austria without foreign support would be sheer folly. For the pope to take part in it would mean working for the king of Piedmont when the Papal States required above all the restoration of order and reform of the administration. Like other liberals, Rossi held that good government was more important than popular government. He devoted himself, therefore, to realistic improvements: restoration of discipline in the army, modernization of the judicial system, increase of government income through taxation of church property, exploitation of the salt deposits, encouragement of trade through abolition of restrictions, and improvement of communications through railroads and telegraphs. Naturally he incurred the enmity of those who suffered from reforms. Unfortunately he made matters worse by the shortcomings of his own personality. A man of complete self-assurance and courage, he was cold and humorless in his dealings with others, contemptuous of opposition and disdainful of public opinion. His arrogance, sarcasm and offensive manners went a long way toward nullifying his great abilities.[21]

Rossi's cold and calculating attitude with regard to the war against the foreigner naturally made him anathema to all good patriots, whether moderate or radical. It was hardly surprising that a group of returned volunteers should plan to assassinate him, which they did on November 15 by stabbing him in the neck as he was ascending the staircase of the Parliament. This tragic event marked the end of the pope's effort to keep a middle course between the reactionary, clerical elements and the radical, nationalist forces. Of course, Pius had long since ceased to be the great hope of the patriots, since he had publicly refused to sacrifice the interests of the church to the cause of Italian unity. He was now in acute danger of being stripped of his worldly power as sovereign of the Papal States.

On the very day following Rossi's assassination, huge crowds

21 Fundamental is Carlo A. Biggini: *Il pensiero politico di Pellegrino Rossi* (Rome, 1937), which deals almost exclusively with the years 1846–1848, but see also Laszlo Ledermann: *Pellegrino Rossi, l'homme et l'économiste* (Paris, 1929), and Tarquinio Armani: "Pellegrino Rossi, ministro federalista e costitutionalista" (*Nuova antologia*, CCCIV, July 1, 1939, 79–95).

gathered about the Quirinal Palace demanding the appointment of a democratic cabinet and a declaration of war against Austria. When the Civic Guard and even units of the armed forces began to fraternize with the populace, His Holiness recognized the hopelessness of his situation. As the mob began to invade the palace and threaten the Swiss palace guards with annihilation, Pius, under protest and in the presence of foreign diplomats, agreed to appoint a cabinet including the radical leaders Sterbini and Galletti. The new government was committed to declare war and call a popularly elected constituent assembly. Since Rome was now in the hands of the revolutionary elements, the pope on November 24 left the city in disguise. With the help of foreign diplomats he was able to reach Neapolitan territory and take refuge in the castle at Gaeta.[22]

Pius now appealed to the European governments to restore his temporal power. At the same time he embarked upon an acrid debate with the government in Rome. Arguing that it had been forced upon him, he now refused to recognize it and appointed a commission of three, under Cardinal Castracane, to take over the administration. The cabinet, while rejecting this attempt to supersede it, sent a deputation to Gaeta begging the pope to return to the capital. Pius, now completely under the influence of Cardinal Antonelli, declined even to receive this delegation, whereupon the cabinet took a further step in setting up a Council of State, an act which Pius again declared illegal and void. The situation was thus completely deadlocked.

Nonetheless, the Rome cabinet proceeded to convoke a constituent assembly for the Papal States, which was to be elected on January 21, 1849, by universal suffrage. Once more Pius tried to intervene. He denounced the projected election as "a monstrous act of unconcealed treason and open rebellion," and excommunicated those responsible for it. Nevertheless, the election took place and returned a democratic majority, chiefly because of the fact that the conservative and moderate elements abstained from voting. Even in Rome itself it is said that only 23,000 out of a possible 60,000 exercised the franchise.[23]

This stirring chapter of Roman history came to a close with the meeting of the constituent assembly on February 5. After a few days of

[22] Berkeley and Berkeley: *Italy in the Making*, III, 411 ff., quotes the accounts of several ambassadors who were eyewitnesses of the events of November 16 and the flight of the pope.

[23] E. E. Y. Hales: *Pio Nono* (London, 1954), 97; Charles Pouthas: *Le pontificat de Pie IX* (Paris, 1962), 47 ff.

debate it declared the temporal power of the popes at an end and proclaimed the Papal States to be thenceforth the Roman Republic (February 9). The vote on this crucial matter was 120 to 10 (with 12 abstentions), but this should not be taken to indicate an overwhelmingly strong republican movement. There was, for the time being, no acceptable alternative. The flight of the pope, like the defection of the princes, had transformed the democratic movement in central Italy into a republican movement and had so paved the way for the victory of Mazzinian principles.

3. ROME: THE ORDEAL OF A REPUBLIC

The European powers, even the Protestant ones, believed that the pope must be restored to his temporal power if he was to have the independence necessary for discharge of his spiritual functions. The problem was simply how the restoration could be accomplished. In France, "the eldest daughter of the Church," the question had from the beginning marked political overtones. Cavaignac, evidently in the hope of securing the support of the Catholic party in the elections of December 10, had (November 26) ordered 3,500 troops to be concentrated at Marseilles preparatory to embarkation for Civitavecchia, the seaport of Rome. At the same time he had dispatched Count François de Corcelle to Gaeta to offer the pope asylum in France. The arrival of His Holiness on French soil would no doubt have been a feather in Cavaignac's cap. Perhaps for that very reason Pius declined the offer, whereupon the French expedition to Civitavecchia was suspended.[24]

On December 4 the pope, despairing of bringing his rebellious subjects to submit, appealed to the powers for armed intervention to restore him to his states. The Spanish government proposed (December 21) a congress of the Catholic powers, but the Piedmontese government, ever fearful of foreign interference in Italian affairs, countered by insisting that the matter be left to the Italians. Gioberti made every effort to effect a reconciliation between the pope and the Roman authorities and was prepared to send troops south into Tuscany and the Papal States to "restore order." But the papal court, as ever suspicious of Piedmontese designs, declined the advances of Turin.

---

24 Ross W. Collins: *Catholicism and the Second French Republic* (New York, 1923), 153 ff.; Guillaume Mollat: *La question romaine de Pie IX à Pie XI* (Paris, 1932), 243 ff.; Guido Quazza: *La questione romana nel 1848–1849* (Modena, 1947), 43 ff.

On February 18, 1849, Pius appealed officially to the Catholic powers (omitting Piedmont) and Gioberti was obliged to resign as Piedmontese prime minister, in favor of Rattazzi.[25]

The Austrian government was at this time still seriously hampered by the threat of renewal of the war by Piedmont and, what was perhaps even more grave, by the major operations against Hungary. France, then, was free to make its decision. Communications being still very poor, several weeks were lost in the mission of various agents and the dispatch of countless messages. During this span of time the Roman Republic had a chance to organize. Mazzini, who arrived on March 5, has generally been credited with having made the short-lived Roman Republic a unique example of a democracy devoted to "God and the People," high-minded and moral to an unprecedented degree. It should be noted, however, that prior to his arrival the government had already introduced many drastic reforms: the nationalization of church properties, the abolition of clerical control over the university, the suppression of the Inquisition, and the abolition of the censorship. It had also made concrete efforts to relieve the sufferings of the poor: church buildings were turned into cheap housing, church lands were being divided and assigned to peasant ownership, the salt and tobacco monopolies were being reformed. Considering the brevity of its existence, this was a not insignificant achievement.[26]

Mazzini approved of all these measures wholeheartedly, but his own contribution was rather on the intellectual and moral plane. On the day after his arrival he expounded to the Roman assembly his doctrine of a Third Rome, the symbol of a new and higher humanity.[27] In concrete terms, he aimed at the union of Tuscany with Rome and the convocation of an Italian constituent assembly to establish an Italian Republic and prepare for resumption of the crusade to drive out the foreigner. He had spent some weeks in Florence prior to coming to

---

[25] Luis Garcia Rives: *La Repubblica Romana de 1849* (Madrid, 1932); Quazza: *La lotta soziale,* chap. vi and 139 ff.; Candeloro: *Storia dell'Italia moderna,* III, 387 ff.

[26] Still worth reading is R. M. Johnston's *The Roman Theocracy and the Republic* (New York, 1901), 240 ff. The best recent study is Luigi Rodelli: *La Repubblica Romana del 1849* (Pisa, 1955), 161 ff. Important also are Domenico Demarco: *Una rivoluzione sociale: la Repubblica Romana del 1849* (Naples, 1944); Georges Bourgin: "L'oeuvre sociale de la République Romaine de 1849" (*Actes du Congrès du Centenaire de la Révolution de 1848,* Paris, 1948, 149–156); Fausto Fonzi: "La Repubblica" (in *La mostra storica della Repubblica Romana,* Rome, 1949, 31–34).

[27] See above, Chapter VIII.

Rome and had tried to persuade Guerrazzi to adopt his program. But the latter had evaded a definite commitment, partly no doubt from fear of provoking intervention by either Piedmont or Austria, but perhaps also from reluctance to merge Tuscany with the radical Roman Republic. Particularism was as strong a force in Italy as in Germany.[28]

The prospect of a united central Italy and a republican war against Austria decided the Piedmontese government to take the plunge which it had been contemplating for several months. It denounced the Salasco armistice (March 12) and prepared for hostilities. The French minister at Turin, who, like his British colleague, had done his utmost to dissuade the Piedmontese from resumption of the war, regarded the decision as "heroic folly." The Piedmontese army was still not completely ready and could not put into the field a force larger than that of a year before. The king had been induced to name as chief of staff and *de facto* commander the Polish general, Joseph Chrzanowski, who, though a competent soldier, had arrived in Italy only six months earlier and had only an imperfect command of the language. Chrzanowski, pessimistic by nature, was hardly edified to note that neither the king, nor the politicians, nor the generals had much hope of success. They were embarking on the war for reasons of prestige and to anticipate action by the republicans of central Italy. By taking the initiative they trusted that other states would come to their support.[29]

Chrzanowski favored a cautious strategy, avoiding a major engagement for the time being. But the king and his advisers, thinking the Austrians far weaker than they were, insisted that a vigorous offensive would oblige Radetzky to fall back and make possible the Piedmontese reoccupation of Milan. Radetzky, for his part, had long anticipated denunciation of the armistice and had done everything possible to encourage the mistaken notions of his opponents. "Give me the opportunity," he wrote to Schwarzenberg on March 7, "and you shall soon see me lay the whole of Italy up to the frontier of the noble king of Naples at the feet of His Majesty the Emperor."[30] In an order of the

---

[28] Gwilyn O. Griffith: *Mazzini* (New York, 1932), 205 ff.; Fausto Fonzi: "Mazzini" (in *La mostra storica*, 55–59); Giorgio Falco: *Giuseppe Mazzini e la Costituente* (Florence, 1946); Ivanoe Bonomi: *Mazzini, triumviro della Repubblica Romana* (3 ed., Milan, 1946), chap. iii; Candeloro: *Storia dell'Italia moderna*, III, 382 ff., 429 ff.

[29] César Vidal: "La Deuxième République et le royaume de Sardaigne en 1848" (*Rassegna storica del Risorgimento*, XXXVII, 1950, 505–530); Piero Pieri: *Storia militare del Risorgimento* (Turin, 1962), chap. ix.

[30] A. J. P. Taylor: *The Italian Problem in European Diplomacy* (Manchester, 1934), 213 ff.

day following the resumption of hostilities, he cheered his troops on to the advance on Turin. They responded with enthusiastic demonstrations and ovations.[31]

The Piedmontese advance across the Ticino was given short shrift. Radetzky had deployed his forces from Milan to Pavia. On March 20 the Austrian forces, like the Piedmontese, crossed the boundary river, but Radetzky's army turned northward to take the enemy on the right flank. The Piedmontese hastily recrossed the river and fell back on Novara, to which Radetzky, expecting to meet the enemy at Mortara, had dispatched only one army corps, under General D'Aspre. The latter, discovering on March 23 that he had the entire Piedmontese army before him, called for support, which was promptly dispatched to him. For several hours D'Aspre was badly outnumbered, but Chrzanowski failed to take advantage of his opportunity. By four in the afternoon the whole Austrian army was on the scene and by early evening the Battle of Novara was over. The Piedmontese were completely defeated. Charles Albert, still nominally in command, abdicated his throne on the field of battle, and his successor, Victor Emmanuel II, promptly sent an emissary to Radetzky with the request for an armistice.

Radetzky was well impressed with the new ruler when he met him in conference on March 26. Victor Emmanuel was known to have disapproved of the war and now declared that he was determined to reestablish royal authority by curbing the pretensions of his democratic Parliament. Radetzky therefore decided to give him a chance. He eschewed an advance on Turin, in part certainly to avoid provoking French intervention. Furthermore, he asked for no cession of Piedmontese territory, but only for occupation of the frontier fortress of Alessandria pending the payment of a formidable indemnity. After some months of quibbling over details, the terms of the armistice were enshrined in the peace treaty of Milan (August 6).[32]

[31] Oskar Freiherr von Wolf-Schneider: *Der Feldherr Radetzky* (Vienna, 1934), 86 ff.; Viktor Bibl: *Radetzky, Soldat und Feldherr* (Vienna, 1955), 304 ff.; Oskar Regele: *Feldmarschall Radetzky* (Vienna, 1957), 287 ff.

[32] The patriotic legend that Radetzky offered Victor Emmanuel easy terms on condition that he agree to "modify" the Piedmontese constitution and that the young king nobly rejected the offer was exploded by Howard M. Smyth: "The Armistice of Novara: a Legend of a Liberal King" (*Journal of Modern History*, VII, 1935, 141–152). Smyth's conclusions have been accepted by authoritative Italian historians such as Angelo Filipuzzi: *La pace di Milano* (Rome, 1955), ii ff.; Candeloro: *Storia dell'Italia moderna*, III, 405 ff.

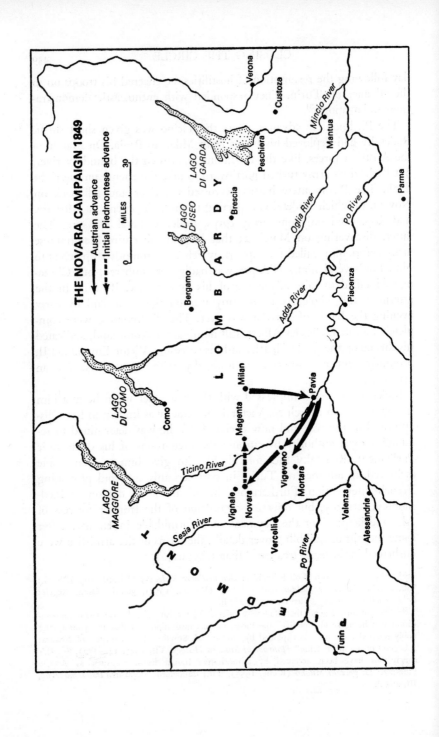

THE NOVARA CAMPAIGN 1849

→ Austrian advance
⇢ Initial Piedmontese advance

MILES
0   30

Verona

Custoza

Mincio River

LAGO
DI GARDA

Peschiera

Mantua

LAGO
D'ISEO

Brescia

Oglia River

Po River

Parma

LAGO
DI COMO

Bergamo

Adda River

Piacenza

L O M B A R D Y

Milan   Pavia

Como

Magenta

Vigevano

Ticino River

Mortara

LAGO
MAGGIORE

Vignale

Novara

Valenza

Alessandria

Sesia River

Vercelli

Po River

P I E D M O N T

Turin

Novara was not, in military terms, a major engagement. It lasted only a few hours and the casualties were extremely modest. But it was decisive in the sense that it brought to an abrupt end Piedmontese aspirations to expel the Austrians from Italy and annex Lombardy and Venetia to form a North Italian kingdom. It left the Austrians free to occupy all central Italy and restore the fugitive princes. Schwarzenberg bemoaned the fact that Radetzky had not gone on to Turin and there imposed on the Piedmontese an indemnity so heavy that the kingdom could barely survive. But the genius of the aged field marshal was political as well as military. He argued that a Carthaginian peace would have generated ever greater animosity, that a huge indemnity would in any case prove uncollectible, that it would only discredit the Piedmontese monarchy and that it might well entail conflict with France. If Piedmont could be kept quiet by easy terms, the Austrians could not only carry through their intervention in central Italy but could redeploy their forces to the Hungarian front.[33]

For France, too, Novara was decisive, in the sense that the government must now intervene in Italy or abandon the affairs of the peninsula to the Austrians. Louis Napoleon, who valued the support of the church in his campaign to restore order in France, was under heavy pressure from the influential minister of public instruction, Count Frédéric de Falloux, and other Catholic notables who clamored for military action on behalf of the pope. The president yielded to the extent of being ready to send an army across the Alps to save the Piedmontese from the wages of their "heroic folly," but was dissuaded by Thiers, who urged negotiations instead. In any case, the leniency of Radetzky's terms obviated the need for French action to save the Piedmontese from occupation.[34]

There remained the threat of Austrian action in central Italy and especially in the Papal States. It was well known in Paris that Naples and Spain as well as Austria were about to intervene against the Roman Republic, which was regarded throughout Europe, even by some liberals, as a den of thieves and ruffians, imposed on the inhabitants by a group of dangerous radicals. The French thought it impera-

---

[33] Bibl: *Radetzky*, 313; Filipuzzi: *La pace di Milano*, 11 ff.

[34] F. A. Simpson: *Louis Napoleon and the Recovery of France* (3 ed., London, 1951), 61 ff.; César Vidal: "La Deuxième République et le Royaume de Sardaigne en 1849" (*Rassegna storica del Risorgimento*, XXXVII, 1950, 505–530).

tive to forestall Austrian domination of central Italy and ensure that the pope, when restored to his capital, would not revert to the old regime, but would maintain and develop the lay institutions introduced in the spring of 1848. It was believed in Paris that the Romans would greatly prefer French to Austrian intervention. The radicals in Parliament, to be sure, protested against coercion of a sister republic and raised the awkward question what was to be done in the event of resistance. But theirs were voices crying in the wilderness.[35]

On April 16 the French assembly, by a huge majority, voted credits for an expedition to Rome and on April 24 a force of 10,000 men landed at Civitavecchia, thirty-five miles from the city. Since there was no resistance, the commander, General Nicolas Oudinot, set out for Rome "full of vain anticipation of a glorious reception and a gratuitous banquet," to quote the report of a British agent.[36] He had at least some justification for his confidence, for the Roman army, while it had secured some munitions abroad, was still far from ready for combat. Conditions in the city were bad and morale low.[37] Only the extremists had faith in the survival of the republic, reported a German consul. Most people, he continued, wished they were a thousand miles away and even some of the leaders were talking of the need for compromise. But Mazzini, who on March 29 had become a member of the directing triumvirate, opposed all accommodation and rallied the non-Roman Italians (exiles and volunteers, who flocked to Rome in great numbers) to organize resistance. He probably realized that the city could not long hold out, but he had an insuperable aversion to French pretensions and in any case felt that the Romans must act as "men working for eternity." The Third Rome, if it had to go under, should meet its doom in a blaze of heroism.[38]

[35] Collins: *Catholicism and the Second French Republic*, 217 ff.; Emile Bourgeois and Emile Clermont: *Rome et Napoléon III* (Paris, 1907), 13; Ruggero Moscati: *La diplomazia europea e il problema italiano nel 1848* (Florence, 1947), 80 ff.; Franco Valsecchi: "Luigi Bonaparte e gli intenti della sua politica d'intervento a Roma nel 1849" (*Rassegna storica del Risorgimento*, XXXVII, 1950, 500–504). George M. Trevelyan: *Garibaldi's Defence of the Roman Republic* (new ed., London, 1908), 101, 109, comments on British hostility to the Roman Republic.

[36] Collins: *Catholicism and the Second French Republic*, 228 ff.

[37] For details, see the excellent analysis in Luigi Mondini: "L'aspetto militare della difesa di Roma nel 1849" (in *Giuseppe Mazzini e la Repubblica Romana*, Rome, 1949, 37–62).

[38] The reports of the Württemberg consul, Kolb, are of great interest. They were published by Moscati: *La diplomazia europea*, 138 ff. For Mazzini's position, see also Alberto M. Ghisalberti: *Roma da Mazzini a Pio IX* (Milan, 1958), chap. ii.

Mazzini's position was reinforced by the arrival, on April 27, of 1,200 Garibaldian legionnaires and 600 Lombard volunteers under Colonel Luciano Manara. Garibaldi had been in Rome since February, but had left his followers at Rieti. Like the Lombards, they were hard-bitten fighters. On Oudinot's approaching the San Pancrazio Gate on April 30, he was suddenly attacked on the flank by the Garibaldians and forced to retreat. Garibaldi was all for pursuing him, but Mazzini vetoed such action on the theory that it would be a mistake to

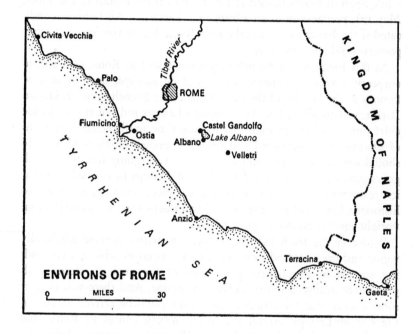

antagonize the French government before seeking a peaceful solution.[39]

The effect of Oudinot's unexpected reverse was to harden French policy. The president wrote at once to the commander: "Our soldiers

[39] The classic account of the military operations is Trevelyan's book, already cited, but this should now be supplemented with Vittorio E. Giuntella: "La difesa della Repubblica" (in *La mostra storica della Repubblica Romana,* 73–77); Pieri: *Storia militare del Risorgimento,* chap. xii; and recent biographies of Mazzini such as Arturo Codignola: *Mazzini* (Turin, 1946), chap. vi, and Garibaldi, such as Denis Mack Smith: *Garibaldi* (New York, 1956), and Christopher Hibbert: *Garibaldi and His Enemies* (Boston, 1966).

have been received as enemies; our military honor is involved. I shall not suffer it to be stained. You will not lack reinforcements." Additional men and munitions were rushed to Oudinot. There was indeed no time to lose, for Austrians, Neapolitans and Spaniards were all poised for action. Early in May the Austrians invaded Tuscany and occupied Pisa and Lucca (May 6), then Livorno (May 11) and, after fierce resistance, Bologna (May 16) and Florence (May 25). Concurrently Neapolitan forces advanced to Albano and Velletri (May 8), while Spanish troops landed at Fiumicino (at the mouth of the Tiber, May 17), preparatory to an advance on Terracina. All haste was indicated if the French were to take over Rome before the forces of other powers could reach the city.

At this juncture the French government sent to Rome as a special emissary a young diplomat, Ferdinand de Lesseps, later to become famous as the builder of the Suez Canal. The French premier, Odilon Barrot, was to admit later that, though Lesseps did not realize it, the chief purpose of his mission was to gain time until the reinforcement of Oudinot was completed and until the French elections of May 19 should have cleared the political atmosphere. Arguing that the French government neither expected nor desired Lesseps to succeed and that its treatment of the Roman Republic was sheer duplicity, authoritative historians have said that the unwitting Lesseps was "no more than an upright agent of a crooked government."[40]

Whatever the truth may be, Lesseps' instructions were admittedly vague and even contradictory. He clearly hoped to achieve a resounding success in negotiating the return of the pope to Rome with guarantees against a return to the old regime. And there was at least some chance that some such arrangement could be arrived at, for on the eve of Lesseps' arrival the Württemberg consul in Rome had visited Oudinot's headquarters at the Roman government's behest, to inquire what the terms of the French might be.[41] However, there is no doubt that Lesseps was overeager and precipitate. He exceeded his in-

---

[40] The standard and by no means friendly account is that of Bourgeois and Clermont, noted above, and the preface by Gabriel Monod. See further Trevelyan: *Garibaldi's Defence of the Roman Empire*, 145 ff.; Griffith: *Mazzini*, 224; and, most recently, G. Edgar-Bonnet: *Ferdinand de Lesseps, le diplomate, le créateur de Suez* (Paris, 1951), 80 ff.

[41] Moscati: *La diplomazia europea*, 154; Mollat: *La question romaine*, 260 ff.; Simpson: *Louis Napoleon*, 70 ff.

structions and outraged the French military men by arranging a suspension of hostilities so as to give Garibaldi time to drive back the Neapolitans from Albano (May 18) and threaten the invasion of the kingdom. Then Lesseps proposed to the Roman government that it request French protection and admit French troops to aid in defense of the city against possible attack by Austria. The city was to be left free, however, to decide its own form of government. Mazzini rejected this offer, evidently in the fantastic hope that the French election would prove a victory for the radicals and that presently the French would come to the help of a sister republic. Only in response to an ultimatum did the Roman government agree (May 31) that the French might occupy cantonments outside the city walls, in return for a promise of aid in repelling an eventual attacker. Oudinot flatly refused to sign this agreement and the French government, on learning of it, not only refused to sign it but recalled Lesseps, who, so rumor had it, had gone plumb mad.

Oudinot was now ordered to attack the city. He had by now some 30,000 men and ample artillery, including thirty siege guns. The defenders, sadly deficient in equipment, could muster hardly half the number of Oudinot's troops. Their army was a miscellaneous force, consisting of former papal troops, Roman Civic Guards, volunteers, students, conscripts, and, of course, many patriots from the north.[42] They were commanded by a competent professional soldier, General Pietro Roselli, for whom, understandably, Garibaldi was a veritable thorn in the flesh. But the latter certainly gave moral courage and dash to the defense. Incapable of commanding large units and often reckless in handling even small ones, he did have a quick sense for tactical situations and the nerve to make decisions. Thus, when Oudinot on June 3 unexpectedly attacked and occupied the villas commanding the approaches to the San Pancrazio Gate, Garibaldi speedily organized resistance and staged one counterattack after another to defeat the French assault.

For the better part of a month the French bombarded the city while constructing approach trenches preparatory to an attack on the walls. The outlook for the defenders became ever more desperate and there

---

[42] Alberto M. Ghisalberti: "Popolo e politica nell' 49 romano" (in *Giuseppe Mazzini e la Repubblica Romana*, 79–102) disputes the charge that the Romans themselves were apathetic and made but a minor contribution.

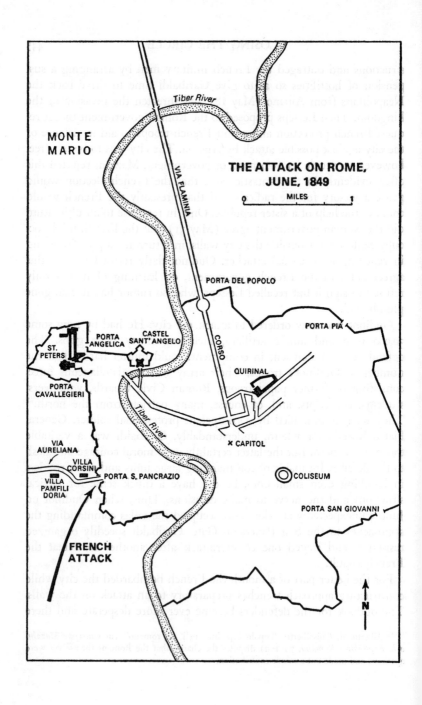

MONTE
MARIO

Tiber River

VIA FLAMINIA

**THE ATTACK ON ROME,
JUNE, 1849**

0 MILES 1

PORTA DEL POPOLO

PORTA PIA

ST.
PETERS

PORTA
ANGELICA

CASTEL
SANT' ANGELO

CORSO

PORTA
CAVALLEGIERI

QUIRINAL

VIA
AURELIANA

Tiber River

✕ CAPITOL

VILLA
CORSINI

PORTA S. PANCRAZIO

◎ COLISEUM

VILLA
PAMFILI
DORIA

PORTA SAN GIOVANNI

**FRENCH
ATTACK**

N

was much popular pressure for surrender. Garibaldi recommended that the army abandon the city and conduct a war of harassment in the open country. But Mazzini, of whom it has been well said that he was less interested in getting the best peace terms than in putting up the best possible battle, was for fighting to the last ditch and then going down in a never-to-be-forgotten blaze of glory. When the assembly voted against such romantic heroism (June 30), Mazzini and his colleagues resigned. Garibaldi, with several thousand men, then left the city (July 2) and tried to make his way north to join in the defense of Venice. Harassed by Austrian forces, many of his party were captured and executed. Others simply disappeared and Garibaldi himself barely succeeded, after a dramatic flight, in reaching the Tuscan coast and escaping by sea. Mazzini remained undisturbed in Rome for some days before he, too, took refuge on a ship at Civitavecchia.

The French troops occupied the city on July 3, after which the Roman assembly was dissolved, the clubs closed down, the population disarmed and the press subjected to censorship. Presently a commission of three cardinals arrived from Gaeta to prepare for the restoration. Oudinot, an innocent in politics, turned over the administration to them, with the result that before long the institutions of the past were re-established. The French were shocked by the prospect of a return to the benighted rule of the priesthood. They made desperate attempts to salvage the liberal institutions, but in vain, for the pope had the support of Austria and other Catholic powers, and even of Russia and Prussia. When French pressure became too irksome, Cardinal Antonelli, the soul of reaction, would threaten the removal of the papal Curia to Austrian-occupied territory. Meanwhile the pope deferred his return from Gaeta until the restoration was substantially completed (April 12, 1850). Thus the French, by their intervention, prepared the ground for the reaction which, in the premises, it had been their objective to forestall.[43]

"In the few hundred meters between the bastions of the Porta San Pancrazio and the Villa Corsini," says an Italian historian, "the Revolution of 1848 was really brought to its close."[44] The Austrians

---

[43] Bourgeois and Clermont: *Rome et Napoléon III*, 192 ff.; Mollat: *La question romaine*, 269 ff.; Roger Aubert: *Le pontificat de Pie IX* (Paris, 1952), 36 ff.; Hales: *Pio Nono*, 149 ff.; and the interesting article by Charles H. Pouthas: "Un observateur de Tocqueville pendant les premiers mois de l'occupation française" (*Rassegna storica del Risorgimento*, XXXVII, 1950, 417–430).

[44] Giunstella: "La difesa della Repubblica."

had all but completed the work of restoration by the time of Rome's capitulation. On July 28 the Grand Duke Leopold had resumed his Tuscan throne. Long before that the Sicilian revolution had met its doom. The British and French had exerted themselves to arrive at a compromise settlement which would have given the island complete autonomy, with a connection with Naples only through a common ruler. Ferdinand, however, had balked at the notion of an independent Sicilian army and eventually ordered his troops to attack (March 29, 1849). Catania fell to the Neapolitans on April 6, after which operations were extended to the west coast. Palermo was obliged to capitulate after the arrival of the Neapolitan fleet (April 27). The populace then rose in revolt, but this could be little more than a gesture of despair. After some severe barricade fighting, the insurrection was suppressed (mid-May) and the island, which a year before had attained *de facto* independence, was once again under Bourbon domination.[45]

There remained only the Venetian Republic, for the other Adriatic seaport, Ancona, had fallen to the Austrians on June 19 after a month of siege and blockade. The Republic of St. Mark, cut off from the mainland and blockaded by the Austrian fleet, had played only a peripheral role in the developments of the period following Custoza. Daniele Manin, the very soul of caution and moderation, had been given dictatorial powers, under which he repudiated the act of fusion with Piedmont, on the plea that the omission of Venice from the provisions of the Salasco armistice had annulled all previous agreements. He appealed to the British and French for support, but received from them little more than the good advice to make the best terms he could with the Austrians. It was obvious to all that Venice's doom would be sealed as soon as the Austrians had disposed of the Piedmontese and the radicals of central Italy.

The day of reckoning approached on the morrow of the Battle of Novara. Yet the Venetian assembly, when called upon by the Austrians to submit, voted to resist. On May 4 the Austrians began to bombard the Venetian fortifications. By July the city, now tightly blockaded, was running out of food and suffering severely from epidemics of cholera and typhus. Finally, on August 22, almost two months after the fall of

---

[45] For an excellent, succinct account, see Federico Curato: *La rivoluzione siciliana del 1848–1849* (Milan, 1940), 207 ff. For the military operations, see Pieri: *Storia militare del Risorgimento,* chap. xiii.

Rome and ten days after the capitulation of the Hungarians at Világos, the city was obliged to surrender. Manin and other leaders were permitted to leave.[46]

The radical phase of the Italian revolution proved just as abortive as the moderate, liberal phase which preceded it. Born of the disillusionment and discouragement following the Custoza disaster, the radical movement was an affair of the lower classes, tradesmen, artisans, journeymen, of the cities, the very people who in March had mounted the barricades but had then left the conduct of the revolution and the war of independence to the upper, educated classes. But the lower classes were no better educated, no better organized in the summer and autumn than they had been in the spring. The radical leaders who now emerged, the men such as Guerrazzi, Montanelli and Galletti, were democrats and republicans, but chiefly in theory. They were themselves disturbed by the prospect of mob rule, and in any case had no thought of serious social revolution. Not even Mazzini, for all his concern for the common man, would have anything to do with socialism or attacks on private property. These men, once they were in power, were almost as intent as their predecessors on the restoration and maintenance of order.

This being so, the debate provoked by Marxist politicians and historians seems rather bootless. They argue that the radicals had only themselves to blame for their failure, because they should have faced up to the need to liquidate the feudal regime and should have roused the peasantry to share in the struggle. To this one can only reply that the radical like the moderate leaders positively dreaded a social upheaval and had not the slightest intention of encouraging the ignorant peasantry to revolt; that, furthermore, many of them, like Mazzini, knew, very little about the peasantry and its problems and sufferings, for they were city-bred intellectuals; and lastly, that the peasantry was so backward and unorganized that it could hardly have been an effective partner.[47]

[46] For a vivid account, see George M. Trevelyan: *Manin and the Venetian Republic of 1848* (New York, 1923); and for a more sober treatment, Pieri: *Storia militare del Risorgimento,* chap. xi.

[47] This debate was given impetus by the Communist leader A. Gramsci: *Il Risorgimento* (3 ed., Turin, 1950) and continued by Palmiro Togliatti: "Le classi popolari nel Risorgimento" (*Studi storici,* III, 1964). On the "bourgeois" side, see Antonio Monti: "Guerra regia e guerra di popolo nel Risorgimento" (in Ettore Rota, ed.: *Questioni di*

In the last analysis it was not so much the shortcomings of the revolutionary regimes as the brutal fact of military power that proved decisive. Radetzky had both the military and political insight to bide his time and take every advantage of the complicated Italian situation. He pressed the Italians as fast and as far as he dared without provoking the intervention of the French and, whether wittingly or not, left it to the French Republic to liquidate the Roman Republic and pave the way for the restoration of clerical rule in the Papal States.

4. FRANCE: THE CONSTITUTIONAL DEADLOCK

Louis Napoleon as president of the French Republic was the choice of the nation, not of the Assembly elected in the previous April. The Assembly had good reason to question the sincerity of the new president's devotion to the Republic, but could do nothing about it, for the recently enacted constitution, that "newfangled bundle of bad laws," made it as impossible for the Assembly to remove the president as for the president to dissolve or even prorogue the Assembly. Not only that: it was all but impossible, too, to revise the constitution. For the first two of the three years of its term the Assembly was forbidden even to entertain motions for revision, and after the two years a motion required for its adoption a two-thirds vote in three consecutive sessions, each a month apart. It would have been literally unthinkable to trammel political action more completely.[48]

At first Louis Napoleon did not appear as a formidable opponent. He allowed Thiers to all but name the members of the new cabinet under the Orleanist Odilon Barrot, and the cabinet in turn worked closely with the conservative elements in the Assembly without much reference to the views or desires of the chief executive.[49] The details of French political life must be omitted in a summary account like the present. The first important landmark of the period was the election of May 13, 1849, held after the Assembly, which had completed its task of

---

storia del Risorgimento, Milan, 1951, 183–216); and Rosario Romeo: Risorgimento e capitalismo (Bari, 1959). For recent critical reviews, see John W. Cammett: "Two Recent Polemics on the Character of the Italian Risorgimento" (Science and Society, XXVII, 1963, 433–457); Franco Valsecchi: "Le classi popolari e il Risorgimento" (Cultura e scuola, No. 15, 1965, 82–93).

48 F. A. Simpson: Louis Napoleon and the Recovery of France (3 ed., London, 1951) is still one of the best treatments of this period.

49 Paul Bastid: Doctrines et institutions politiques de la Seconde République (Paris, 1945), II, 162.

providing a constitution, had reluctantly agreed to dissolve. The monarchical groups—Legitimists, Orleanists, Bonapartists—managed to pull together in a "coalition of fear" directed against radicalism and socialism. On the other hand, the radical or democratic elements had also come together in a "new Mountain," with a program of mildly socialist reforms. The moderate republicans, on the other hand, failed to take advantage of their position. Léon Faucher, the minister of the interior, took his liberalism so seriously that he refused to bring administrative pressure to bear on behalf of his associates.[50] The result was that the monarchists won almost 500 seats out of 750 in the new Assembly, and the leftists some 200. The moderate republicans, who had dominated the previous Assembly, came off with only 80 seats in the new one. The shift toward conservatism was generally expected, but the radical victory was both surprising and alarming. It rested, of course, on the urban populations, where the radicals were fairly well organized. Paris gave them 106,100 votes as against 106,300 for the Party of Order and only 42,300 for the moderate republicans. Ledru-Rollin, who in the presidential election had polled only 370,000 votes, was now elected in no less than five *départements,* with a total vote of 2,000,000. Taking the country at large, the monarchists polled 3,310,000 votes, the "new Mountain" 1,955,000, and the moderate republicans 834,000.[51]

The radicals were so elated by their gains that they presently overreached themselves. In the Assembly the question of French intervention on behalf of the pope was being hotly debated when on June 11 Ledru-Rollin moved the impeachment of the president and the members of the cabinet for violation of Article V of the constitution, which forbade the use of French armed forces against the liberty of any other people. He and his party, declared Ledru-Rollin, would defend the constitution "if necessary by arms." On defeat of his motion, he and the deputies of the Mountain left the assembly and on June 13 attempted to stage an insurrection. They seized the Conservatoire des Arts et Métiers, in the crowded workers' section of Paris, and called on the people to throw up barricades.

The rising proved, however, to be a fiasco. Karl Marx was to ridicule

[50] Theodore Zeldin: "Government Policy in the French General Election of 1849" (*English Historical Review,* LXXIV, 1959, 240–248).

[51] Simpson: *Louis Napoleon,* 37 ff.; Bastid: *Doctrines et institutions politiques,* II, 204 ff. On the recovery of radicalism, see Georges Duveau: *La vie ouvrière en France sous le Second Empire* (Paris, 1946), 57 ff.; and the Communist analysis of N. Zastenker: "La 'Montagne' en 1849" (*Questions d'histoire,* No. 2, 1954, 101–138).

the exaggerated hopes of the Mountain and to compare its noisy claims to the Biblical trumpets of Jericho: "Whenever they stand before the ramparts of despotism, they seek to imitate the miracle."[52] In his opinion recollections of the June Days and distrust of the radical leadership explained the failure of the Paris populace to rise in support of the men they had just elected to the chamber. A further factor no doubt was the severe cholera epidemic which was claiming 600–700 victims daily. People had other things than revolution to think about. Besides, they had been disarmed and were under martial law, that is, state of siege, which was at once proclaimed by the government. General Changarnier easily dispersed the demonstrators, while Ledru-Rollin and his colleagues escaped from the Conservatoire by a back door or, as some would have it, through a skylight. The point has been well made that whereas in June, 1848, the insurrection had plenty of men but no leaders, in June, 1849, it had more than enough leaders but no men.[53]

There was a more serious uprising in Lyons, which cost some 200 lives but was also quickly suppressed. The upshot of these revolts was to provide the government with ample excuses for repression. Some thirty radical deputies were deprived of their seats, martial law was continued in both Paris and Lyons, units of the National Guard from the workers' sections were disbanded, clubs were suppressed and newspapers, though not abolished, were put under strict surveillance.

Louis Napoleon, meanwhile, set out on a tour of the provinces, including some that were known to be unfriendly. His reception was generally satisfactory, sufficiently so to warrant his dismissal of the Barrot cabinet and his appointment of one which, though undistinguished, could be counted on for loyalty. This assertion of control over the executive came as a disagreeable surprise to the majority in the Assembly, but the president carefully abstained from further challenges. It was not that he lacked an organized following, for he had nothing but contempt for party rule and aimed to stand above parties and to set up an efficient administration by nonpolitical experts who could overcome class antagonisms by building a modern, well-

---

[52] Karl Marx: *The Eighteenth Brumaire of Louis Bonaparte* (1852).

[53] Raoul de Félice: "La journée du 13 juin, 1849 à Paris" (*La Révolution de 1848,* VI, 1909–1910, 135–157, 242–252, 314–325); Alvin R. Calman: *Ledru-Rollin and the Second French Republic* (New York, 1922), chaps. xxiii and xxiv; Duveau: *La vie ouvrière en France,* 57 ff.

integrated, productive society.[54] He probably shared the concern of most people over the continued unrest and spread of radicalism and may well have been content to have the Assembly assume the onus of reactionary measures which he regarded as necessary and to which at the very least he assented. For another period of many months he continued to co-operate with the parliamentary majority.

The campaign against radicalism produced, in the spring of 1850, two important acts of Parliament: a new education law and a revised electoral law. In the field of education the Guizot Law of 1833 had marked an important advance, but the situation still left much to be desired. Fully 40 per cent of the French communes had by 1848 failed to open a primary school. Many of those that had opened schools used a barn or granary for the purpose. More than half of the primary-school teachers earned less than 300 francs a year and were obliged to supplement their salary by serving as bell ringer in the church or even as gravedigger.[55] The situation, in brief, was such that liberal, radical and socialist writers all clamored for a system of free, obligatory primary education, in socially integrated schools where the children could be given instruction in both natural and social sciences, to meet the requirements of the modern world.[56]

Following the February Revolution, the provisional government had therefore commissioned Hippolyte Carnot, the minister of instruction and a follower of Saint-Simon, to draft an appropriate bill. When completed, it provided for compulsory education to the age of fourteen, with instruction in civics, history, hygiene, music and other cultural subjects. Private organizations (even the Jesuits) were to have the right to conduct their own schools, but in the public schools religious instruction was to be imparted outside the school building. The salaries of teachers were to be raised to the 600–1,200-franc level. All told, the Carnot project was enlightened and forward-looking. But it was promptly stamped "socialistic" by his opponents and after the June Days Carnot was dismissed.

---

[54] Duveau: *La vie ouvrière en France,* 46, and various biographies that stress the modernity of Napoleon's views and objectives, such as Albert Guerard: *Napoleon III* (Cambridge, 1943); T. A. B. Corley: *Democratic Despot: a Life of Napoleon III* (London, 1961).

[55] George Bourgin: "La question scolaire en 1848 et la loi Falloux" (*Accademia dei Lincei: Atti dei Convegni,* X, 1949, 329–347).

[56] Georges Cogniot: *La question scolaire en 1848 et la loi Falloux* (Paris, 1948).

In the Barrot cabinet, appointed after the presidential election, Count Frédéric Falloux became minister of public instruction. He was an outstanding Legitimist, had been one of the chief advocates of suppression of the national workshops, and was to be an ardent proponent of intervention on behalf of the pope. As a devout Catholic, he was convinced that the most effective way to combat radicalism was to strengthen clerical influence in education, in line with the campaign for "liberty of instruction" long since being waged by Count Charles de Montalembert and other Catholic leaders, who wanted the right to establish church schools at the secondary as well as the primary level, and aimed to end all state regulation or supervision. Montalembert and his friends, who at first had welcomed the February Revolution, now joined the so-called Party of Order. So did many former anticlericals, such as Thiers, who, thoroughly frightened by the threat of social revolution, declared: "Today I regard religion and its ministers as the auxilliaries, the saviors, perhaps, of the social order."[57]

Falloux shelved the Carnot draft and appointed an extraparliamentary commission to re-examine the school problem. Thiers, who served as chairman, came out frankly against free, compulsory education and made no secret of his belief that radical teachers were at the root of much of France's troubles. "To read, to write, to count, that is what needs to be taught; all the rest is superfluous," he declared. Had he had his way, the entire primary-school system would have been turned over to the clergy. This was more than even Montalembert or Falloux desired. The new bill therefore provided for some measure of state control. It was laid before the Assembly in June, 1849, debated at length in various committees and finally adopted on March 15, 1850.

The "Falloux Law" has been called one of the major events in French political history in the nineteenth century, and has also been described, by a Marxist writer, as a law of fear and hate.[58] Its effect was to enhance greatly the influence of the church, for it authorized private organizations to maintain both primary and secondary schools. At the primary level the communes were authorized to entrust the school to the priest, and even to dispense with a public school if the

---

[57] Quoted by Ross W. Collins: *Catholicism and the Second French Republic* (New York, 1923), 271–272. See also Jean Leflon: *L'Eglise de France et la révolution de 1848* (Paris, 1948); R. Aubert: *Le pontificat de Pie IX* (Paris, 1952), 42 ff.

[58] René Rémond: *La droite en France* (2 ed., Paris, 1963); Cogniot: *La question scolaire,* chap. v.

church already provided one. Schooling was not made free or compulsory; religious instruction was made obligatory; state supervision was hardly more than administrative, for the entire educational system was to be under a Superior Council of Public Instruction, with lower departmental councils. On these councils the clergy (Protestant and Jewish as well as Catholic) was to be represented. The Assembly, in its struggle against radicalism, had now enlisted the support of the church. "Fear of the Jacobins outweighed fear of the Jesuits," says Pierre de La Gorce. The extreme wing of the Catholic party, it is true, denounced the law as a betrayal of the church's interests, inasmuch as it did not abolish state "interference," but even the extremists came to see what important gains the church had made.[59]

A few days before passage of the Falloux Law an election took place to fill the seats of the thirty radical deputies excluded in June, 1849. To the disagreeable surprise of political circles, twenty-one radicals were returned. Yet more ominous was the result of a Paris by-election on April 28, when the writer Eugène Sue carried the day against a prosperous merchant who had fought against the workers in the June Days. Sue, who had made millions from his writings, notably his *Mysteries of Paris,* was a confirmed socialist whose victory was hailed with jubilation by radicals of every stripe. Fear of possible revolution led the Assembly to appoint a commission, with well-known members such as Thiers, Molé and Montalembert, to draft additional provisions for the electoral law, which were enacted into law on May 31 by a vote of 433 to 241.

The new law was designed to reduce the electorate by excluding the workers and other undesirables, whom Thiers described publicly as "the vile multitude." Henceforth three-year residence in the canton, to be demonstrated by tax receipts or employers' affidavit, was required for the franchise. In effect this provision raised the voting age from twenty-one to twenty-four, since men were not enrolled on the tax lists until the age of twenty-one and could only vote if they had been on these lists for three years. The reduction in the electorate was drastic: about 30 per cent (from nine and a half million to six). The degree of disfranchisement varied from one region to another. In the *département* of the Rhone it was 40 per cent, in the Nord 51 per cent, in the

---

[59] Collins: *Catholicism and the Second French Republic,* 298 ff.; John K. Huckaby: "Roman Catholic Reaction to the Falloux Law" (*French Historical Studies,* IV, 1965, 320–321).

Seine 63 per cent. In Paris, where the indigent were numbered at 120,000, fully 144,000 out of the previous 220,000 were deprived of the vote.[60]

Another aspect of the new electoral law had an important bearing on the election of the president. The two million votes required for popular election had thus far constituted about one-fifth of the total vote. Under the new law it would amount to about one-third. In other words, the chances of election by popular vote were markedly diminished, and those of election by the Assembly correspondingly enhanced.[61] If Louis Napoleon nevertheless signed the new law, it may well have been that he too was concerned by the rising tide of radicalism, or that he was not yet ready to defy the conservative elements in the assembly. It has been suggested that perhaps he was glad to have the Assembly compromise itself and to leave the reckoning to the future. In any case, it is impossible to believe that he ever positively approved of so drastic a curtailment of universal suffrage, to which he owed so much.

The royalist majority in the Assembly had no more burning desire than to arrange for the restoration of the monarchy. In the summer of 1850 leaders of both the Legitimist (Bourbon) and Orleanist factions conferred with the Bourbon claimant ("Henry V") in Germany, and with the Orleanist family in England. Louis Philippe having died (August 26), it was ardently hoped that his son would agree to "fusion," that is, to a deal by which the Bourbon Henry, who was childless, should ascend the throne, to be succeeded on his death by the Orleanist claimant. In short, there would within a foreseeable time be a return to the July Monarchy. But the project was doomed by the recalcitrancy of the Bourbons. They hated their Orleanist relatives and saw no point in preparing the way for their restoration. Furthermore, Henry was so firmly convinced of his divine right to the throne that he flatly refused to recognize the right of the people to determine the form of government, as they had done in 1830.[62]

During the years 1849–1851 the economic situation continued to be bad, in the countryside as in the cities. The workers appear to have

---

[60] Bastid: *Doctrines et institutions politiques*, II, 256 ff.; Duveau: *La vie ouvrière en France*, 59 ff.

[61] Heinrich Euler: *Napoleon III in seiner Zeit* (Würzberg, 1961), 669.

[62] Simpson: *Louis Napoleon*, 98; Rémond: *La droit en France*, 101; Bernard de Vaulx: *L'échéance de 1852* (Paris, 1948), 168 ff.

accepted the new electoral law without much protest and refused to react to the constant prodding of radical leaders in exile to organize resistance. At most they talked about the regular elections due to take place in May, 1852, when they would take their revenge. It seems clear that there was a steady increase of radicalism, especially in the provinces, where the petite *bourgeoisie* of the rural towns and even the peasants were more democratic, republican and even socialist than they had ever been before.[63]

While the members of the Assembly were working to restore the monarchy, Louis Napoleon was scheming to retain his office beyond May, 1852, the date of the next presidential as well as parliamentary election, in which under the constitution he would not be eligible for re-election. He therefore toured the country once again, appealing for popular support for a revision of the constitution in his favor. Departmental councils were encouraged to petition the Assembly in this sense, and the president took every opportunity to replace prefects, judges and other officials who were unfriendly, while he cultivated the commanders of the local *gendarmerie,* who, in the last resort, controlled the situation in their area. By military reviews and other attentions he flattered the army and secured enough support to enable him, in January, 1851, to insist on the replacement of General Changarnier, who was commander of the Paris garrison and National Guard and at the same time a deputy. The general, regarding Louis Napoleon as an obstacle to an Orleanist restoration, had done what he could to discredit him. He was heard to call him a melancholic parrot and to express his readiness to lock him up in Vincennes whenever the Assembly might so order. Naturally, his dismissal provoked a storm in the Assembly, which ended by censure of the cabinet. The president thereupon replaced the cabinet with one of much the same stripe.[64]

---

[63] Ernst Labrousse: "La propagande napoléonienne avant le coup d'état" (*Accademia dei Lincei: Atti degli convegni,* X, 1949, 313–324); Duveau: *La vie ouvrière en France,* 60; and the interesting analysis of three southern *départements* by Leo A. Loubère: "The Emergence of the Extreme Left in Lower Languedoc, 1848–1851" (*American Historical Review,* LXXIII, 1968, 1019–1051). Of great interest is also the official report of December 1, 1851, which reviews the situation in many parts of France and discusses the ramifications of the radical movement. This was published by Juda Tchernoff: *Associations et sociétés secrètes sous la Deuxième République* (Paris, 1905), chap. ix. Other unpublished reports are cited in Euler: *Napoleon III,* 660 ff.

[64] Bastid: *Doctrines et institutions politiques,* II, 278 ff.; Vaulx: *L'échéance de 1852,* 175 ff.; Howard C. Payne: "Preparation of a Coup d'Etat" (in *Studies in Modern European History in Honor of Franklin Charles Palm,* New York, 1956, 175–202).

By the summer of 1851 matters were approaching a crisis. By that time more than fifty departmental councils, no doubt inspired by the prefects, had petitioned for revision of the constitution so as to allow Louis Napoleon to stand for re-election in May, 1852. The favorite argument was that only thus could a government overturn of which the radicals would take advantage be avoided. The Assembly in fact voted a bill for revision on July 14, but the vote fell far short of the two-thirds required by the constitution. It had now become clear, however, that there was next to no hope that the deadlock resulting from the rigidity of the constitution could be broken by parliamentary action. There was more and more talk of the need for a *coup d'état*, that is, a subversion of the constitutional order by force. Business circles in particular were becoming convinced that stability and confidence depended on the president's taking matters in hand and putting an end to what Palmerston was presently to call "the day-before-yesterday tomfoolery which the scatter-brained heads of Marrast and Tocqueville invented for the torment and perplexity of the French nation." "There is a pronounced feeling in England," wrote *The Times* on November 19, "that financial conditions would be much better if the French political squabble were settled by a successful coup d'état." This was the sentiment everywhere in Europe. The revolutions had been suppressed and only in France did the republic hang on, with radicalism threatening a revival of disorder, with unpredictable ramifications.[65]

5. THE COUP D'ÉTAT OF LOUIS NAPOLEON

The assembly was not deterred by the smoldering crisis from taking its annual vacation from August to November, which gave the president ample time for completing his plans. A number of reliable prefects were appointed and some hard-bitten soldiers brought home from Algeria. General Leroy Saint-Arnaud, famous for his toughness, was made minister of war. Another highly important recruit was the president's half-brother, Count (later Duke) Auguste de Morny, an able, cool-headed and utterly ruthless man of the world, who had made a fortune in industry and banking and had for some years been a deputy under the July Monarchy.[66]

[65] Palmerston's comment quoted by Simpson: *Louis Napoleon,* 167; *The Times* quoted in Franklin C. Palm: *England and Napoleon III* (Durham, 1948), 66.

[66] Morny was the illegitimate son of Queen Hortense and Count Charles de Flahault, who in turn was an illegitimate son of Talleyrand. In the absence of a really adequate

Morny insisted that the coup must wait until the assembly was once more in session, so as to forestall efforts by the members to organize resistance in their constituencies. Planning was made difficult by lack of funds, for the Assembly had kept the president on somewhat less than short rations. Some money was scrounged from bankers and friends, but the major contribution came from Miss Howard, the president's mistress, who mortgaged her London house, pawned her jewels and sold her horses. Her cash contribution is said to have amounted to some 200,000 francs.[67]

When the chamber reassembled early in November, the president at once requested the abrogation of the electoral law and the restoration of universal suffrage, on the plea that the law as it stood was being exploited by radicals for subversive purposes. No doubt Louis Napoleon fully expected the conservatives to reject his proposal, which they did by a vote of 355–348, thus enhancing his own popularity. The majority tried to counter by submitting a bill that would enable the questeurs of the Assembly to requisition troops for its protection and to appoint the commanding officer of such troops. In effect, the assembly proposed to arrange for its own protection in the form of a little private army under the command of Changarnier. In response Saint-Arnaud offered to provide all the protection that might be desired, but insisted that only he, as minister of war, could appoint the commander. After much acrimonious debate the bill was defeated on November 17, the elements of the left all uniting against it.

By this time rumors and dire forebodings were everywhere afloat. There was talk of the return of Ledru-Rollin from his exile in England, and of plans for a grand insurrection in May, 1852. The Orleanists, too, were said to be girding for action. They allegedly were planning to nominate the Prince de Joinville for the presidency and may even have had some thought of provoking insurgency in the provinces. The evidence on these matters is scanty and inconclusive. In

---

biography, see Marcel Boulenger: *Le duc de Morny* (Paris, 1925). Popular biographies are those of Maristan Chapman: *Imperial Brother: the Life of the Duke de Morny* (New York, 1931), and A. Augustin-Thierry: *Son Elégance, le duc le Morny* (Paris, 1951).

[67] Simone André-Maurois: *Miss Howard, la femme qui fit un empéreur* (Paris, 1956), 80–81, 96. On the financial problem in general, see Adrien Dansette: *Louis-Napoléon à la conquête du pouvoir* (Paris, 1961), 291 ff.

any event the plans of others had no bearing on those of Louis Napoleon and his entourage.[68]

The date chosen for the coup was December 2, the anniversary of the great Napoleon's victory at Austerlitz. The detailed plans were executed with exemplary promptitude and efficiency, due largely to the management and direction of Morny. Early in the morning Paris was placarded with three announcements, printed under heavy guard during the night. The first declared the Assembly dissolved, universal suffrage restored, a popular referendum to be held later in the month, and the establishment of martial law in the Paris area. The second charged the Assembly with having become the center for conspiracies against the president, the choice of the people: "When men who have already lost two monarchies wish to tie my hands so that they may destroy the Republic also, it becomes my duty to save the Republic and the country by appealing to the solemn judgment of the people, the sole sovereign I recognize in France." The people were to vote on a new constitution, admittedly based on Napoleon's constitution of the Year VIII (1799), which established a representative but authoritarian regime. The third announcement called upon the army, "the elite of the nation," to make its voice heard.

Early on the same morning the police arrested at their homes sixteen deputies, of whom six were generals, seven radical leaders and three Orleanists. The police took into custody sixty-two other undesirables, most of them men of the left. As news of these happenings spread, a number of deputies hurried to the Chamber, only to find it closed and under military guard. A few managed to get in by back doors, but were quickly ejected by the troops. They then gathered at the homes of various chiefs to denounce the president's action and plan resistance. Most of these groups were soon dispersed by the police, but at 11 A.M. about 250 deputies, mostly royalists, assembled at the town hall of the tenth *arrondissement*. The meeting declared itself a regular session of the Assembly, deposed Louis Napoleon and assumed supreme power. After some hours of debate the military appeared and marched the protesters off to the barracks. By way of resistance the deputies refused

[68] Most of the evidence comes from the correspondence of Count de Flahault, Morny's father, who was privy to Napoleon's plans. See Earl of Kerry and Philip Guedalla, eds.: *The Secret of the Coup d'Etat* (New York, 1924), 36 ff., 159; and the discussion of the problem in Simpson: *Louis Napoleon*, 125 ff., and appendix B; Dansette: Louis-Napoléon, 340–341; Euler: *Napoleon III*, 763 ff.

the liberation pressed upon them by the government, but their resistance met with little sympathy or response. Louis Napoleon and his generals, when they rode through the city on horseback, found perhaps not popular enthusiasm but at least calm acceptance of what had been done.

The Paris workers, many of them still unemployed, had no reason to regret the Assembly which had deprived them of the vote. They were probably more pleased by its discomfiture than by Louis Napoleon's success. In any case they were unarmed and confronted with military forces of some 50,000 men. Under the circumstances an insurrection would indeed have been pure folly.[69] The nearest thing to it was the effort of a few radical leaders, among them the poet Victor Hugo, to initiate a barricade war. Hugo, originally a member of the Party of Order, had deserted the majority in protest against the repressive measures following the abortive uprising of June, 1849, and had become a confirmed radical and republican. He and his friends exhausted themselves in street-corner agitation, but the workers, so Proudhon reported, instead of heeding the call to arms, continued their game of billiards. The revolutionaries rallied only about a thousand supporters, who, in the night of December 3–4, threw up barricades in the congested sections of the city, between the boulevards and the Right Bank of the river.[70]

General Magnan, commander of the Paris garrison, followed the now well-established strategy of allowing the insurrection to mature before attacking the disaffected area from all sides. The barricades were soon taken and the defenders captured or killed. However, a tragic episode occurred in the course of the operation. Large numbers of the curious had collected on sidewalks and balconies to watch the show. The soldiers, excited by taunts hurled at them and fearful of the crowds that hedged them in, suddenly opened fire. In the ensuing panic artillery was turned on the elegant shops while the troops stormed the buildings and cut down everyone they could reach, without discrimination. Many persons, men and women, who had not the slightest intention of resisting fell victims to this fury. Some have

[69] Duveau: *La vie ouvrière en France,* 70 ff. Karl Marx: *The Eighteenth Brumaire of Louis Bonaparte,* 93 ff., rightly stressed the importance of the economic stagnation.

[70] Hugo's own account is in his *Histoire d'un crime.* For his role, see Matthew Josephson: *Victor Hugo* (New York, 1942), chaps. xii and xiii.

charged Louis Napoleon and Morny with having wanted the massacre in order to cow the populace into submission, but this is perhaps going too far. All one can say is that Morny throughout urged firmness. All told, over 500 people, civil and military, were killed or wounded in the aftermath of the *coup d'état,* the big black mark on the record of Louis Napoleon.[71]

The resistance in the provinces was more formidable than in Paris, especially in the poorer *départements* of the center and south (notably Drôme, Ardèche, Gard, Hérault, Aude, Var and Basses-Alpes), where the local lawyer or teacher led the protests of villagers and peasants. There was relatively little violence or plunder, but the resistance was sufficiently widespread and determined to frighten the propertied classes and conjure up the "red specter." Officials, too, were so firmly convinced of the existence of a huge conspiracy that they took this resistance to be the prelude to the grand insurrection planned for May, 1852. Consequently stories were rife of a dreadful *Jacquerie,* of murder, pillage and rape. Even so well-informed a person as the Count de Flahault could write in private letters that only a tenth of the atrocities were being reported in the press. There were, he asserted, whole schools of young girls violated and women killed after horrid tortures. In short, the insurgents were cannibals corrupted by civilization.[72]

The disturbances, such as they were, gave the authors of the *coup d'état* ample excuse for systematic repression. Martial law (state of siege) was proclaimed in thirty-two *départements* and some 27,000 persons were arrested. They were tried by special commissions which had been instructed by Morny to treat as bandits and criminals all members (even past members) of secret societies and opponents of the regime. Verdicts were arrived at on the basis of evidence provided by local officials, many of whom had already prepared lists of undesirables. In the short space of a month (February, 1852) the commissions

---

71 Simpson: *Louis Napoleon,* 172 ff.; Dansette: *Louis-Napoléon,* 355 ff.; Henri Guillemin: *Le coup d'état du 2 décembre* (Paris, 1951), 390 ff.; Howard C. Payne: *The Police State of Louis Napoleon Bonaparte, 1851–1860* (Seattle, 1966), chap. ii.

72 Kerry and Guedalla: *Secret of the Coup d'Etat,* 190, 193, 200; Duveau: *La vie ouvrière en France,* 77 ff.; Dansette: *Louis-Napoléon,* 358 ff.; Guillemin: *Le coup d'état de 2 décembre,* chap. vii; Albert Soboul: "La question paysanne en 1848" (*La pensée,* Nos. 18–20, 1948); and the important studies of Marcel Dessal: "Le complot de Lyon et la résistance au coup d'état dans les départements du Sud-Est" (*1848: Revue des révolutions contemporaines,* No. 189, 1951, 83–96); Loubère: "Emergence of the Extreme Left."

disposed of the thousands of cases before them. Over 11,000 prisoners were released and another 8,000 interned under police surveillance; 9,581 were deported to labor camps in Algeria and 239 to the prison colony in Guiana.[73]

Since Louis Napoleon, on taking office, had promised "to remain faithful to the democratic republic," and "to regard as enemies of the nation all those who may attempt by illegal means to change the form of the established government," it is clear that by the *coup d'état* he violated his oath. However, the moral aspects of his action concerned only those good democrats who bemoaned the shipwreck of their dreams. Heinrich Heine, who idolized the great Napoleon and had nothing to say in favor of the "blockheads" of the Assembly, felt his heart bleed:

The noble ideals of political morality, legality, civic virtue, liberty and equality, the rosy morning dreams of the eighteenth century, for which our fathers went so heroically to their deaths, and which we dreamed after them in the same spirit of martyrdom—there they now lie at our feet, shattered, dashed to pieces, like fragments of chinaware.[74]

But these outbursts were exceptional. Most people, in France and abroad, approved of what Louis Napoleon had done. The Legitimists are said to have secretly rejoiced at the assault on radicalism and socialism, and especially at the suppression of the dreaded *Jacquerie*. The Orleanists, while outraged, were soon reconciled and joined the victorious faction. Like business circles in general, they welcomed the end of uncertainty and the return of confidence. The business recovery was truly phenomenal. In two weeks the quotation of government bonds rose from 91.60 to 100.90.

In London joy was as unconfined as in Paris: "The great French difficulty which has so long loomed like a dim and gigantic terror through the mist, has met with its solution," wrote *The Economist* (December 13). "The French," added the *Illustrated London News*

---

[73] Pierre Dominique: *Louis Napoléon et le coup d'état du 2 décembre* (Paris, 1951) prints in the appendix the verdicts in the *département* of Basses-Alpes. See also Dansette: *Louis-Napoléon*, 370 ff.; Payne: *Police State of Louis Napoleon, op. cit.*, 40 ff., 64 ff.

[74] Heine, letter of February, 1852, quoted in William Rose: *Heinrich Heine, Two Studies of His Thought and Feeling* (Oxford, 1956), 81. The same plaint is in the letters of the Countess d'Agoult to the German poet Georg Herwegh: "There is no longer any law or right: Rome is in the hands of the pretorians, who are gorging themselves on blood and gold" (Marcel Herwegh: *Au printemps des dieux*, Paris, 1929, 157).

(December 27), "begin to love their business much better than they love theories of government." The workers, too, were reported gratified by the economic recovery: "Six weeks ago society was living from hand to mouth," reported Walter Bagehot: "now she feels sure of her next meal. And this, in a dozen words, is the real case—the political excuse for Prince Louis Napoleon."[75]

Foreign governments were relieved that now, at long last, the revolution had been everywhere suppressed. Lord Palmerston was so hasty in his expression of approval that the outraged queen insisted on his resignation, though many of his cabinet colleagues shared his sentiments. The Austrian ambassador in Paris could see in the president only "the chosen instrument of Providence to deal the mortal blow to parliamentarism on the Continent." Even Nicholas of Russia shared in the general satisfaction. At just about all levels of society moral issues were ignored and the gratification of practical interests was supreme.[76]

Under the circumstances, the outcome of the plebiscite of December should cause no surprise. In reply to the question whether or not they desired the maintenance of the president's authority and whether they delegated him to draft a new constitution, 7,439,216 voted in the affirmative and only 640,737 in the negative. Eighty-two per cent of the electorate voted and of these 91.65 per cent expressed approval. These figures seemed for long so implausible that the government was suspected of having doctored them, but recent study of the records has dispelled all such doubts. Incidentally, latter-day dictators have demonstrated that such landslide votes are by no means unobtainable.[77] Nonetheless, the figures of Louis Napoleon's plebiscite do tend to conceal the degree of opposition to his *coup d'état*. The disturbances in several *départements* are instructive in this regard, and so are the abstentions. After all, it may be taken for granted that the almost 20 per cent of the voters who, despite official pressure, refused to cast a ballot were almost all of them opponents of the regime. In some *dé-*

---

[75] Norman St. John-Stevas: *Walter Bagehot* (Bloomington, 1959), 418 ff.; Palm: *England and Napoleon III,* 68 ff.; Guillemin: *Le coup d'état de 2 décembre,* chap. ix.

[76] Herbert C. Bell: *Lord Palmerston* (New York, 1936), chap. xxi; Richard Salomon, "Die Anerkennung Napoleons III" (*Zeitschrift für osteuropäische Geschichte,* II, 1911–1912, 321–366).

[77] Gisela Geywitz: *Das Plebiszit von 1851 in Frankreich* (Tübingen, 1965) provides a definitive analysis.

partements the abstentions ran to more than 50 per cent. In the large cities both the percentages of abstentions and of negative votes were remarkably high: in Lyons, 27 per cent and 35.3 per cent respectively; in Bordeaux, 31 per cent and 33.6 per cent; in Strasbourg, 41 per cent and 36 per cent. Paris, as might be expected, was definitely hostile. There the abstentions were 25.5 per cent and the negative votes 26.2 per cent even in the well-to-do sections, while in the workers' sections the negative votes were as high as 42.9 per cent. Considering the administrative pressure brought to bear by prefects and subprefects and the systematic propaganda picturing Louis Napoleon as the savior of the country from the atrocities of the radicals, the opposition to his coup was by no means negligible. But the fact remains that his action met with overwhelming approval. By and large the rural areas were more favorable than the urban, the poorer rural areas more favorable than the prosperous, the latter more favorable than the provincial towns, and the larger cities least favorable. The conclusion is inescapable that the country, which had become a republic by default, was never really reconciled to the Second Republic and therefore welcomed the rule of a man whose name signified something to all men and who promised the restoration of order, the return of confidence and the recovery of business.

Chapter Fourteen

CENTRAL EUROPE: THE MARCH OF REACTION

I. BALKAN INTERLUDE: THE WALLACHIAN REVOLUTION

THE June Days in France and Radetzky's victory at Custoza marked the turn of the revolutionary tide in Europe. The governments were recovering from their paralyzing fright and were ready to use their armed forces against the insurgents when necessary. Czar Nicholas, too, had completed the deployment of his armies on his western front and reiterated his readiness to come to the aid of his fellow princes if they so desired. No doubt they preferred to settle their problems in their own way and with their own means, but it was comforting to know that the Russian armies stood ready to intervene in case of emergency.

The first instance of Russian armed intervention was in the Danubian Principalities, where, the reader may recall, the czar exercised a certain protectorate by treaty. There was much opposition, even on the part of the upper classes, to Russian domination; and when news arrived of the revolutions in Western and Central Europe, a number of patriotic boyars in April provoked huge demonstrations against the prince of Moldavia. The latter, however, refused to be intimidated. Sure of Russian support, he had the ringleaders arrested and deported. Only a few managed to escape to Transylvania.[1]

Much more serious and important was the revolution which broke out in Wallachia in June. This was largely the work of the young boyars who had been educated in Paris and had there imbibed the ideas of nationalism, democracy and socialism.[2] Despite the repeated warnings of the Russian consul, the government did nothing to supervise or control the activities of these ardent young men on their return home.

---

[1] R. W. Seton-Watson: *A History of the Roumanians* (Oxford, 1934), chap. ix; John C. Campbell: "1848 in the Roumanian Principalities" (*Journal of Central European Affairs,* VIII, 1948, 181–190); Michael Roller: "Les Roumains en 1848" (in François Fejtö, ed.: *Le printemps des peuples.* Paris, 1948, II, 239–266).

[2] See above, Chapter VIII.

466

In a secret meeting at Islaz on the Danube they drew up a program calling for abolition of the Organic Statute, recognition of the equality of rights, election of a Parliament representing all classes, universal education, emancipation of Gypsies and Jews (both numerous in the Principalities), and emancipation of the peasantry, redistribution of the land, and indemnification of the landowners by the state. When the prince rejected these demands, a revolution broke out in Bucharest. The prince was obliged to appoint a revolutionary cabinet before fleeing the country (June 23).

The revolutionary forces now quickly broke ranks. The majority, led by Eliade-Radulescu, was intent on liberating the country from foreign domination and effecting a union of the Rumanian lands. But a radical minority of intellectuals, of whom Nicholas Balcescu was the leader, was determined on fundamental social changes, especially abolition of forced labor by the peasants and distribution of the land among them. The moderates were able for some time to defer elections to a constituent assembly and to exclude the radicals from important offices. But the unrest in the country was such that the provisional government was obliged to set up a commission (composed equally of landlords and peasants) to study the agrarian problem. At the meetings of this commission (August 22-31), the peasants were unexpectedly aggressive: they objected to being bound to the soil and forced to labor on the estates. They demanded land, even if the state had to compensate the landlords. Such shocking talk had never before been heard and to the propertied classes was utterly intolerable. On August 31 the government closed out the work of the commission.[3]

The Wallachian Revolution was doomed from the start because the ideas of the leaders, particularly of the radicals, were imported from the West and far too advanced for Rumanian society at that time. Only a few of the boyar families had any part in it. Most of them were

---

[3] The radical side is presented in the anonymously published account of Balcescu: *La question économique des Principautés Danubiennes* (Paris, 1850), and in the defense of Balcescu by A. G. Golesco: *De l'abolition du servage dans les Principautés Danubiennes* (Paris, 1856). On the more conservative side, Ion Eliade-Radulescu: *Mémoires sur l'histoire de la régéneration roumaine* (Paris, 1851). Among modern treatments, see Marcel Emérit: *Les paysans roumains depuis le traité d'Andrinople* (Paris, 1937), 297 ff.; Helmut Haufe: *Die Wandlung der Volksordnung im rumänischen Altreich* (Stuttgart, 1939); Andre Oțețea: "La révolution de 1848 et les paysans roumains" (*Revue d'histoire comparée*, VII, 1948, 19-34); Vasile Maciu: "De la conception sociale et politique de Nicolae Balcescu" (*Nouvelles études d'histoire*, 1955, 373-390).

outraged by the program of the radicals, which went far beyond anything the upper classes had in view. When the agrarian problem was raised they became completely soured on the revolution and probably regarded the intervention of the powers as a godsend.

The insurgent leaders had tried hard to conciliate their Turkish overlords and enlist the support of the French and British. Lamartine was and always had been sympathetic to Rumanian aspirations, but by June he had already been eclipsed by more realistic politicians. His successor at the Foreign Office, Bastide, was frightened by the whole business, which he thought premature and likely to provoke Russian intervention. Palmerston, too, rejected Rumanian advances, holding that if the Principalities, in the name of nationality, were to be allowed to break away from the Ottoman Empire, the Bulgarians and other Balkan peoples would soon register similar claims and thereby undermine the empire which it was British interest to uphold.[4]

Lord Stratford de Redcliffe, the British ambassador at Constantinople, considered the Bucharest revolution nothing but the work of "a number of young boyars educated abroad, gypsies and students who demanded universal suffrage and the election of every Wallachian to the office of hospodar (prince)." He urged the Turks to intervene and restore order, but the Turks, already under pressure from Czar Nicholas to join in military occupation of the Principalities, were reluctant to collaborate with their traditional enemy. The result was that at the end of July the Russians alone invaded Moldavia, thus almost forcing the Turks to send troops across the Danube into Wallachia (early September). Some weeks later the Turks occupied Bucharest, where they were soon joined by the Russians (October 11). The revolutionary leaders were driven into flight and the revolution was at an end. In May, 1849, the Russians and Turks signed a new convention at Balta Liman. This provided that in the future the two powers should jointly choose the princes, whose term of office should be seven years. The former elected assemblies were to be replaced by appointed councils (*divans*) composed of members of the great nobility and high clergy. Russia and

---

[4] Paul Henry: *La France devant le monde* (Paris, 1945), 165 ff.; Harold Temperley: *England and the Near East: the Crimea* (London, 1936), 258 ff.; Radu R. Florescu: "Stratford Canning, Palmerston and the Wallachian Revolution of 1848" (*Journal of Modern History*, XXXV, 1963, 227–244); Dan Berindei: "La politique extérieure de la Valachie pendant la révolution bourgeois-démocratique" (*Nouvelles études d'histoire*, 1965, 285–297).

Turkey were to name commissioners to "advise" the princes, and were to maintain forces of occupation until a new statute had been worked out. Actually they evacuated only in 1851.[5]

2. THE REDUCTION OF VIENNA

In the Hapsburg dominions the fate of the revolution hinged largely upon the war in Hungary, which broke out in September, 1848 and then precipitated the October Revolution in Vienna. In order to avoid undue fragmentation of the narrative, attention will be directed first to the affairs of the capital. There the radical elements—students, artisans, workers—were firmly in control, for in the absence of the Court at Innsbruck the official government and the city council were helpless, at least where local matters were concerned. The Committee of Safety, really a revolutionary assembly, was directed by Dr. Fischhof and other academic leaders who looked to the Student Committee (the *Aula*) as a link to the general public and especially the workers.

The Committee of Safety, like the Paris provisional government, was confronted by a severe economic crisis and its concomitant unemployment. It appointed a Committee of Labor under an eloquent and enthusiastic student named Willner, who promptly proclaimed the "right to work" and set up "workshops" much like the French national workshops, where large numbers of the indigent were employed on grading and other jobs at relatively attractive pay. Presently 20,000 workers were enrolled and the financial burden was becoming formidable. The propertied classes grumbled about the experiments of this new Louis Blanc and became increasingly impatient with the revolutionary regime. They induced the emperor and Court to return (August 12) and applauded the appointment of Ernst von Schwarzer as minister of public works. He in turn reduced the wage rate in the workshops and thereby precipitated the serious disorders of August 21–23. Students and suburban National Guards backed the protests of the workers, while the National Guards of the Inner City defended the government. Fighting broke out and there were a number of dead. While not comparable in magnitude to the Paris June Days, this clash of conservative and radical forces and the defeat of the workers was a

[5] Seton-Watson: *History of the Roumanians,* chap. ix; Theodor Schiemann: *Geschichte Russlands unter Kaiser Nikolaus I* (Berlin, 1919), IV, 173 ff.; A. S. Nifontow: *Russland im Jahre 1848* (Berlin, 1954), 292 ff.; Berindei: "La politique extérieure de la Valachie."

similar class conflict. The Committee of Safety was obliged to disband and the government took over command of the National Guard. But the student committee and the Democratic Society remained in existence, while the workers boiled with resentment and desire for revenge.[6]

Meanwhile elections for the Austrian Parliament had been held in mid-June and the National Assembly (*Reichstag*) had opened its sessions in Vienna on July 22. The voting had been by universal but indirect suffrage, but there had been many irregularities and many abstentions. In terms of social class the deputies were for the most part members of the lower middle class and peasants, of whom many were illiterate. In terms of nationality it should be noted that no elections were held in Hungary or in the Italian provinces. In the Parliament the Germans were in a minority, as they were in the general population. Of some 400 deputies there were 160 Germans and 190 Slavs. Proceedings of the Parliament were much hampered by the language problem. Fully 25 per cent of the membership were ignorant of German, the only possible language for debate, so that the meaning of the discussion had to be explained to them by interpreters.[7]

Like other revolutionary assemblies, the Austrian devoted itself first to the drafting of a constitution and especially to the formulation of a bill of civil rights. Difficulties between Germans and Czechs soon developed, for while the Germans took the unity of the Hapsburg Monarchy (exclusive of the Kingdom of Hungary) as almost axiomatic, the Czechs now formed a conservative wing determined to work for the federalization of the empire, through which alone they could hope to attain self-government and, as a strong unit, exercise an important if not dominant influence.[8]

The Parliament did, however, act harmoniously in resolving one major problem, that of the peasantry. Emancipation within a year had

[6] Ernst W. Zenker: *Die Wiener Revolution 1848 in ihren socialen Voraussetzungen und Beziehungen* (Vienna, 1897), 200 ff.; Heinrich von Srbik: "Die Wiener Revolution des Jahres 1848 in sozialgeschichtlicher Beleuchtung" (*Schmollers Jahrbuch*, XLIII (3), 1919, 19–58); Rudolf Kiszling: *Die Revolution im Kaisertum Oesterreich* (Vienna, 1948), I, 206 ff.; R. John Rath: *The Viennese Revolution of 1848* (Austin, 1957), 219 ff., 289 ff.

[7] Peter Burian: *Die Nationalitäten in 'Cisleithanien' und das Wahlrecht der Märzrevolution* (Graz, 1962), 36 ff.

[8] Josef Redlich: *Das oesterreichische Staats- und Reichsproblem* (Leipzig, 1920), I, 119, 140; Kiszling: *Die Revolution in Kaisertum Oesterreich*, I, 201 ff.

already been decreed for Bohemia, Moravia and Silesia, as well as immediately for Galicia, but there was much pressure for prompt and more drastic action. On July 26 Hans Kudlich, the son of a Silesian peasant who at the age of twenty-five had already distinguished himself as a student leader, proposed the abolition of all feudal dues and obligations. Adoption of the bill in one form or another was a foregone conclusion because the landlords everywhere, haunted by the fear of peasant insurrection, realized that they must abandon their traditional privileges. But since Kudlich demanded emancipation as a human right, rather than as an economic measure, there was much debate as to whether the holders of these rights should be indemnified and, if so, to what extent and by whom. After forty sessions, during which over a hundred amendments were proposed, it was agreed that there should be no compensation for loss of patrimonial jurisdiction but that, under a law passed on September 7 by a modest majority (174–134), there should be indemnification for loss of rights attached to the land, the amount to be determined by a special commission. The act, whatever its shortcomings, was of major importance and of direct interest to far more people than the political issue then under debate. The Parliament and the government, by satisfying the demands of the peasantry, drained off one of the most dangerous sources of revolutionary unrest. Thenceforth the peasantry as a class showed but little interest in efforts at reform.[9]

Despite the setback suffered in August, the radical press and the clubs became more and more aggressive in September. Many well-to-do people began to leave the city, while the National Guards of the better quarters became discouraged. Class lines were now clearly drawn: on the one hand the Constitutional Club, founded to oppose radicalism, and on the other the Democratic Club, which labored to co-ordinate all radical activities.

Such was the situation when the Croatian forces began to approach Vienna. In mid-September Jellachich had advanced on Budapest until the Hungarians on September 29 made a stand at the towns of Pakozd and Velencze, some forty miles southwest of the capital.

[9] Zenker: *Die Wiener Revolution 1848*, 185 ff.; Jerome Blum: *Noble Landowners and Agriculture in Austria, 1815–1848* (Baltimore, 1948), 232 ff.; Josef Buchinger: *Der Bauer in der Kultur- und Wirtschaftsgeschichte Oesterreichs* (Vienna, 1952), 168 ff.; and on Kudlich, the scholarly biography of Friedrich Prinz: *Hans Kudlich* (Munich, 1962), especially chap. viii.

Though the fighting was indecisive, Jellachich halted his advance and turned northwestward towards Vienna. He had evidently reckoned on the defection of many Hungarian regiments and was now fearful of meeting yet greater forces if he persisted in his effort to take the Magyar capital. It seems that his new plan was to put himself in position to co-operate with the imperial armies advancing from the west.[10]

In Hungary the Croat invasion produced important political changes. Batthyány and most members of the cabinet began to doubt the ability of the Hungarians to maintain their independence and tried repeatedly to arrive at some accommodation with the Court. The high aristocracy or magnates were even more dubious and were disgruntled with the Batthyány government, which they blamed for the impasse in which the country found itself. They counseled the king to break with the ministry and persuaded him to appoint Count Franz Lamberg, who had large estates in Hungary, to be commander-in-chief of all forces in Hungary. These conservative elements had gone along with the revolution in March because, in view of popular pressure, there seemed to be no alternative. Now, eager to break the power of radicalism, they were above all intent on avoiding a conflict with Vienna, the more so as Hungary was already beset with revolt on all its borders.[11]

The liberal gentry, on the other hand, were outraged by what they regarded as the treachery of the Court. They rallied to Kossuth, who already enjoyed the support of all popular elements. He now became the dominant figure of the Committee of National Defense set up by Parliament on September 25. The Lamberg appointment was promptly denounced as illegal and army officers were ordered to refuse him obedience. So great was the excitement and hostility in Budapest that when Lamberg was seen crossing the Danube bridge he was set upon by a mob and brutally murdered (September 28). Unwilling to defend this attack on the royal authority, Batthyány resigned. Kossuth, on the

10 Ferdinand Hauptmann: "Banus Jellačič und Feldmarshal Fürst Windischgrätz" (*Südostforschungen*, XV, 1956, 373–402); Gunther E. Rothenberg: "Jelačič, the Croatian Military Border and the Intervention against Hungary" (*Austrian History Yearbook*, I, 1965, 45–67).

11 Heinrich Friedjung: *Oesterreich von 1848 bis 1860* (2 ed., Stuttgart, 1908), I, 77; Julius Miskolczy: *Ungarn in der Habsburger Monarchie* (Vienna, 1959), 112 ff.; Erzsebet Andićs: "Kossuth en lutte contre les ennemis des réformes et de la révolution" (*Studia historica*, XII, 1954, 1–169).

other hand, set out on a tour of the provinces to secure recruits for the army. The peasants, who regarded him as the author of their emancipation, gave him an enthusiastic reception. Soon thousands of young peasants were flocking to the colors.[12]

Kossuth, far from the capital, did not learn of the fighting at Pakozd until several days later. It strengthened his conviction that the country, if properly inspired, could defend its independence successfully and he therefore urged pursuit and destruction of Jellachich's army. But the commander of the Hungarian forces, Field Marshal Franz Moga, had grave doubts about the legality of the war and little confidence in the fighting qualities of his militia (*Honved*) regiments. In his opinion the first requirement was to ensure the defense of Budapest. Count Denes Pazmandy, presiding officer of the lower chamber of Parliament and temporarily chairman of the Committee of National Defense, shared Moga's opinion.

On Kossuth's return to the capital (October 7) he learned that a royal decree of October 3 had ordered the Hungarian Parliament dissolved, had declared its decisions null and void, and had named Jellachich high commissioner and commander-in-chief of all troops in Hungary. All troops were absolved from their oath of allegiance to the Hungarian constitution. Thus at last the Vienna court had abandoned all pretense and thrown down the gauntlet to the revolutionary regime. Kossuth at once denounced the decree in the most scathing terms and declared that the country would in three weeks provide 300,000 men to defend its honor and independence. Parliament thereupon declared the royal decree illegal and charged Jellachich and all his supporters with treason.

Kossuth, who now became chairman of the Committee of National Defense, pressed for vigorous action by the army. When news arrived of a great insurrection in Vienna on October 6, he urged that Hungary make common cause with the Viennese, even to the extent of invading Austrian territory. Moga was ordered to pursue Jellachich and destroy his forces before they could be reinforced. But Moga still hesitated,

---

12 François Eckart: "La révolution de 1848 en Hongrie et la cour de Vienne" (*Actes du Congrès Historique du Centenaire de la Révolution de 1848*, Paris, 1948, 229–242); Gyözö Ember: "Louis Kossuth à la tête du Comité de la Défense Nationale" (*Studia historica*, VI, 1953); György Spira: "L'alliance de Lajos Kossuth avec la gauche radicale et les masses populaires de la révolution hongroise de 1848–1849" (*Acta historica*, II, 1953, 49–150).

hoping against hope that an accommodation might still be arrived at. Two precious weeks were lost, since Kossuth was reluctant to provoke dissension in the ranks of government.[13]

Before pursuing this theme further, attention must be given to the developments in Vienna, on which so much depended. In the Austrian Parliament many of the German deputies, who were radicals, supported the Hungarian cause enthusiastically, while the Czechs and other Slavs, who were mostly conservatives, stood firmly by the Court. A crisis ensued when, on September 30, it became known that the minister of war, Count Theodor von Latour, had been supplying Jellachich with money and munitions. The decree making Jellachich commander of all the troops in Hungary followed almost at once. Thereupon the radical press began to vilify Latour and demand that he and other ministers be hanged. To all intents and purposes the populace was invited to give Latour the treatment already meted out to Lamberg by the Budapest mob.[14]

The crisis broke on October 6, when a German regiment was being dispatched to reinforce Jellachich. The populace offered resistance, tore up the railroad tracks and blocked the bridge over the Danube. Fighting broke out in the city, so serious that Count Auersperg, the commander of the garrison troops, felt obliged to evacuate his forces to the suburbs. The crowds then besieged the Ministry of War, where the cabinet was in session. Most of the members of the government managed to escape, but Latour was hunted through the building and murdered, after which his body was stripped naked, mutilated and strung up on a lamppost. The final act of this ferocious outbreak was an assault on the arsenal, which was forced to surrender 30,000 rifles to the crowd.[15]

The radicals and the mob were now in undisputed command of the capital. On October 7 the Court fled to Olmütz (in Moravia) and a general exodus of the upper classes followed. Even the Parliament,

[13] For much interesting detail, based on the documents, see the article by Ember: "Louis Kossuth" and Friedrich Walter: "Die Ursachen des Scheiterns der madjarischen Waffenhilfe für die Wiener Oktober-Revolutionäre, 1848" (*Südostforschungen*, XXII, 1963, 377–400).

[14] Hermann Meyer: *1848: Studien zur Geschichte der deutschen Revolution* (Darmstadt, 1949), 43 ff., has revealed the contacts and relations between Hungarian agents and Vienna radicals.

[15] Kiszling: *Die Revolution in Kaisertum Oesterreich*, I, 237 ff.; Rath: *Viennese Revolution of 1848*, chap. xiv.

from which thirty-two Czech deputies had departed, was so shocked by the brutality of the mob that it hesitated to take any initiative. The real power now rested with the Central Committee of the Democratic Societies, which in turn dominated the National Guard. The Guard, from which all but the radical elements had defected, now numbered only 18,000 and was commanded by the radical journalist Wenzel Messenhauser, who, though a former army officer, was better fitted to conduct a propaganda campaign than to wage war. Messenhauser was assisted by General Joseph Bem, hero of the Polish war against Russia in 1831. They felt that, if necessary, they could muster some 50,000 men, with seventy pieces of artillery.

The Viennese radicals were in constant touch with Hungarian head-quarters and repeatedly called for assistance. But in the Hungarian camp all was confusion and indecision. Kossuth and his adviser, General Francis Pulszky, favored energetic action, arguing that if the Vienna revolution were snuffed out, all Austrian forces would be turned against Hungary. But Moga, uncomfortable in the role of op-ponent of the king, hesitated to cross the frontier (the Leitha River) unless formally invited to do so by the Austrian Parliament, which in turn evaded incrimination. Moga must also have had doubts about his own forces. He had only 5,000 regular troops, plus 1,400 cavalry. In ad-dition there were some 15,000 fairly well-armed but untrained troops and 5,000 National Guards armed only with scythes or pitchforks. There was grave reason to fear that many of the men, who had enlisted only for defense of the fatherland, would desert if ordered to cross the frontier.[16]

Jellachich crossed the Leitha on October 10 and joined forces with Auersperg and the Vienna garrison. Had he had his way, he would have attacked the city at once, before the Hungarians could ar-rive. But he was ordered to await the arrival of Windischgrätz, who had been appointed a field marshal and given command of all troops, including Jellachich's. The attacking forces totaled about 70,000 men, with 200 guns. By October 20 the army advancing from the north began to reach the city, which by October 23 was fairly well encircled. Hostilities soon became general. On October 28 Jellachich delivered an assault on the city and an armistice was agreed to, which, however, was almost at once broken under popular pressure.

[16] For details see the articles by Ember and Walter, cited above.

The Viennese were heartened by news that the Hungarians, who had already once sent some men across the frontier river, only to recall them, had now at last cast the die and were on the march toward the city. But on October 30 Jellachich defeated them at Schwechat and forced them to fall back. Kossuth blamed the Viennese for this reverse, remarking that they watched the battle from the cathedral tower without sending forces to the rescue. But Kossuth had throughout overestimated the military strength of the Viennese. He had calculated on assistance by a force of 25,000 or more men, which was utterly out of the question. In any case, the cause of the revolutionaries was now hopeless. On October 31 the city was attacked in the vicinity of the imperial palace. There was vigorous resistance, but the trained and well-equipped troops were soon able to overrun and occupy the entire Inner City. The losses on the government side were about 1,200 men, while the defenders had some 3,000 casualties. Martial law was at once proclaimed, the National Guard and the Academic Legion dissolved, the political clubs suppressed and the newspapers put under rigid censorship. The active insurgents were mostly taken prisoner. Of some 2,400 about half were released after some months, while 400 were given long prison terms and twenty-five were executed. Many of the radical leaders managed to escape and others were protected by their status as deputies. But Messenhauser faced the firing squad and so did Robert Blum, the well-known Saxon radical and member of the Frankfurt Parliament. Blum had come to Vienna not as the official representative of the Parliament but merely as the representative of his radical colleagues, who wished to encourage the Viennese insurgents. He had taken an active part in the operations and was therefore subject to court-martial. His conviction and execution, while technically justifiable, were openly defiant of liberal as well as radical opinion throughout Germany. It was, in a sense, notice given that the Vienna government was not to be trifled with and that, when it came to a showdown, it would ignore the pretensions of the popularly elected Parliament.

3. THE SUBMISSION OF BERLIN

The course of events in the Prussian capital followed closely the developments in Vienna, and the Prussian government's moves were clearly influenced by those of the Hapsburg Court. The Prussian Parliament had been elected early in May and turned out to be much more radical than the Frankfurt Parliament, elected at the same time. Not only the larger cities but also the agricultural regions of Silesia and East Prussia returned confirmed democrats. None of the 1,500 great landholders of Silesia was elected, for example. The majority of the members were lower judges, local officials, schoolteachers and clergy of both faiths. Though there were no organized parties, there was a group of about forty on the right; a center of moderate liberals, much influenced by the economist Karl Rodbertus; and a democratic, republican left led by Franz Waldeck, a prominent judge of known integrity. Since the left wing of the center tended to vote with the left, the more advanced elements could usually command a majority.[17]

The Parliament had been called by the king to "collaborate" with the government in drafting a constitution, and was therefore suprised to find a constitution modeled on the Belgian waiting for its approval. It promptly voted down the government draft as inadequate, and appointed its own Constitutional Committee, under Waldeck, making clear its intention to assume full constituent powers. The king allowed matters to run their course, much to the exasperation of the court Camarilla, which was becoming ever more insistent on the assertion of royal authority. The populace, meanwhile, was becoming more and more assertive. There were endless demonstrations and petitions, while the newspapers bombarded the citizenry with programs worked out by the radical clubs. Of the latter the most influential was the Democratic Club, with a membership of some 1,200 journalists, students and artisans. The workers had in addition the Workers' Club, organized and led by Stefan Born, which aimed at self-help in the attainment of labor's demands. To alleviate the widespread unemployment the government in Berlin as in Vienna assigned some 3,000 workers to road and grading jobs, and at the same time instituted an inquiry into the conditions of the agrarian laborers.[18]

The task of maintaining order under these circumstances devolved

[17] Gerhard Schilfert: *Sieg und Niederlage des demokratischen Wahlrechts in der deutschen Revolution, 1848–1849* (Berlin, 1952); Ernst R. Huber: *Deutsche Verfassungsgeschichte* (Stuttgart, 1960), II, 584 ff. On the attitude of the rural areas, see Gunter Franz: "Die agrarische Bewegung im Jahre 1848" (*Hessisches Jahrbuch für Landesgeschichte,* IX, 1959, 150–178); Hans Hübner: "Die ostpreussichen Landarbeiter im Kampf gegen junkerliche Ausbeutung und Willkür, 1848–1849" (*Zeitschrift für Geschichtswissenschaft,* XI, 1963, 552–569).

[18] Ernst Kaeber: *Berlin, 1848* (Berlin, 1948), 101 ff., 137 ff.; Hermann Meyer: *1848: Studien zur Geschichte der deutschen Revolution* (Darmstadt, 1949), 67 ff.

upon the Civic Guard (*Bürgerwehr*), which consisted of some 22,000 men organized in battalions and companies. Associated with it were several "flying corps," one composed of students, another of young workers, another of artists, all of them highly activist. However, neither the Civic Guard nor the flying corps had a clear mandate or charter defining their duties. The Civic Guard, like its Vienna counterpart, tended to be fluid, the well-to-do elements shirking their obligations except on crucial occasions. On June 14 there was a serious clash between the Guard and the populace when the latter attempted to storm the arsenal and seize weapons. Another grave episode occurred on October 12 when the Guard fired on unruly canal workers, with some loss of life. By that time the Guard, long since ridiculed by the regular troops, was scorned even by the radicals.[19]

By the autumn the conservative elements were regaining confidence and beginning to organize for resistance to radicalism. Prince William returned from exile to take the seat in Parliament to which he had been elected. Presently Fatherland Societies and Prussian Societies sprang up and a new and influential newspaper, the *Gazette of the Cross* (*Kreuzzeitung*), began to assert the rights and virtues of the old order. On August 18–19 a group of landlords met in a so-called Junker Parliament to protest against proposed laws to end tax exemptions of the nobility and labor obligations of the peasants. They founded an Association for the Protection of Property which soon courted the support of the workers by agitating against the Civic Guard and the cabinet, while at the same time denouncing the system of free competition and advocating a return to the guild system.[20]

The aggressiveness of the Junkers, among whom were many army officers, provoked the ire of the liberals and radicals, who detested the army as an instrument of repression and aimed at replacing it by a popular militia. On August 9 a resolution was introduced in Parliament directing army officers to refrain from reactionary agitation or else resign. So flagrant was this attack on the royal prerogative that Frederick William at long last decided to take action. He worked out a plan for dissolving Parliament and introducing a government-made

---

[19] O. Rimpler: *Die Berliner Bürgerwehr im Jahre 1848* (Brandenburg, 1883). Rimpler was the last commander of the Guard.

[20] Kaeber: *Berlin, 1848*, 182 ff.; Theodore S. Hamerow: *Restoration, Revolution, Reaction* (Princeton, 1958), 177 ff.; Sigmund Neumann: *Die Stufen des preussischen Konservatismus* (Berlin, 1930).

constitution. But before plans were complete a crisis developed which led to the resignation of the Auerswald-Hansemann cabinet and its replacement by a cabinet of bureaucrats under General Ernst von Pfuel. The latter was an enlightened soldier of the earlier reform period, who was interested in the success of the constitutional experiment. To the utter disgust of the Court and the army, he accepted the resolution of the Parliament, which, in turn, became more and more arrogant in its dealings with the government.[21]

The situation came to a head in October, in Berlin as in Vienna. The Prussian Parliament, coming at last to discussion of the constitution, voted on October 13 to make the Civic Guard permanent, and to abolish the hunting rights of the nobility. Far more defiant was the vote (217–134) to strike the words "by the Grace of God" from the king's title, to forbid the use of all titles of nobility and eventually to abolish the nobility itself. This was too much for Pfuel, who resigned. Co-operation between the government and the elected Parliament had clearly become impossible, the more so as the radicals were becoming intransigent. On October 26–29, just as the Vienna insurrection was coming to a head, a great Democratic Congress, with delegations from 140 cities, was held in Berlin. While much given to theoretical debate, the congress called upon the Prussian Parliament to aid the Viennese revolutionaries. On October 31 there were great demonstrations in front of the theater which was the seat of the Parliament. But in the end the Parliament rejected a motion for military intervention at Vienna and belatedly referred the whole question to the Frankfurt Parliament for decision.[22]

News of Windischgrätz' victory at Vienna emboldened the king to take the offensive against his own revolutionaries. On November 1 he appointed General Friedrich Wilhelm von Brandenburg, a natural son of Frederick William III, to be minister-president. The Parliament promptly protested, demanding a cabinet which could enjoy its support. This time the protest was ignored and Brandenburg was instructed to liquidate the entire revolutionary movement. On November 9 he announced the adjournment of the Parliament to November 27

[21] Gordon A. Craig: *The Politics of the Prussian Army* (Oxford, 1955), 115; Huber: *Deutsche Verfassungsgeschichte*, II, 736 ff.

[22] Karl Obermann: *Die deutschen Arbeiter in der Revolution von 1848* (Berlin, 1953), 234 ff.; Huber: *Deutsche Verfassungsgeschichte,* II, 706 ff.

and its transfer to the provincial town of Brandenburg. But this attempt to imitate Windischgrätz' procedure met with more resistance than had been expected. The Parliament voted by a huge majority (252–30) to declare the decree illegal and refuse compliance. The Civic Guard ignored orders to keep the Parliament from meeting and the Workers' Club offered to support the assembly against the reactionary government. But there was no popular upheaval. The populace was evidently weary of turmoil and disorder and above all appears to have been deeply discouraged by the news from Vienna.[23]

General Wrangel, who occupied the capital with 13,000 troops on November 10, met with no significant opposition from the Civic Guard or the populace. There was no bloodshed as in Vienna. Troops closed the Parliament building, whereupon a substantial number of deputies attempted, during the following days, to meet in other places. As a parting shot they called upon the country to refuse taxes. But these moves proved ineffectual. The Parliament remained closed and only the diehard radicals, such as Karl Marx, attempted to carry through the denial of taxes.[24]

In Berlin as in Vienna martial law was proclaimed, the Civic Guard dissolved, the clubs closed and the newspapers subjected to censorship. On November 26 about 260 of the original 400 members of the Parliament, mostly the conservative and moderate elements, assembled dutifully at Brandenburg. Had the court Camarilla had its way, the Parliament would have been abolished entirely and the objectionable members arrested. The king, while unwilling to go back on his promise of March, wanted to couch the future constitution in traditional terms. But the cabinet, unwilling to provoke further crises, proposed that Parliament be dissolved while the government at the same time promulgated a reasonably liberal constitution based on the Parliament's earlier draft. There was to be a two-chamber Parliament, of which the lower chamber was to be elected by universal suffrage. Parliament was to have the right to initiate legislation and the cabinet was to be responsible to it. The king reluctantly agreed, but only after adding a provision giving him an absolute veto on legislation and the

---

[23] Rimpler: *Die Berliner Bürgerwehr*, 86 ff.; Obermann: *Die deutschen Arbeiter*, 243 ff.; Hamerow: *Restoration, Revolution, Reaction*, 185 ff.

[24] Hermann Meyer: "Karl Marx und die deutsche Revolution von 1848" (*Historische Zeitschrift*, CLXXII, 1951, 517–537).

power to rule by decree in an emergency. On December 5 the Parliament was dissolved and the new constitution proclaimed.[25]

The evidence suggests that Count Brandenburg and the Court intended the constitution to be provisional, designed to pacify the country and tide matters over until revisions in a conservative direction became feasible. But the elections to the new Parliament on January 22 again produced a lower chamber strongly oriented toward the left: as against 184 conservatives and moderates, there were 160 radicals. In response to this situation the government submitted and Parliament approved a new labor code which to some extent undid the work of 1845 and restored some of the controls of the guild system, for which the workers had been clamoring. At the same time a bid was made for support of the peasantry by out-and-out abolition of patrimonial jurisdiction.[26]

The strength of the radicals made it difficult if not impossible for the government to carry through its plan for conservative revision of the constitution. So when the Parliament, on April 27, 1849, called upon the government to approve the liberal constitution worked out for all Germany by the Frankfurt Parliament, the decision was taken to dissolve it and then promulgate a new electoral law that would produce a more satisfactory chamber. The new law introduced the three-class system of voting, which remained in effect until 1918. While every adult and "independent" male retained the franchise, the electorate was divided into three classes according to taxpaying ability. The first class, paying in the aggregate one-third of the direct taxes, comprised only 5 per cent of the population but elected one-third of the deputies. Its voting power was four times as great as that of the second class and about twenty-five times as great as that of the third class. In Berlin, for instance, the first class in 1849 numbered 2,000, the second 7,000 and the third 70,000 persons. Obviously, the effect of the law was to exclude from the franchise the miners, factory workers and domestics who could be classified as not independent. Political control

[25] Friedrich Meinecke: *Weltbürgertum und Nationalstaat* (1962 ed.), 349 ff.; Friedrich Frahm: "Entstehung und Entwicklungsgeschichte der preussischen Verfassung" (*Forschungen zur brandenburgischen und preussischen Geschichte*, XLI, 1928, 248–301); Huber: *Deutsche Verfassungsgeschichte*, II, 763 ff.

[26] Rudolf Stadelmann: *Soziale und politische Geschichte der Revolution von 1848* (Munich, 1948), 171; Hamerow: *Restoration, Revolution, Reaction*, 188 ff.; P. H. Noyes: *Organization and Revolution* (Princeton, 1966), 318.

was in the hands of the propertied classes, the large landholders and the upper middle class. These people had never favored universal suffrage and asked nothing better than a franchise based on property, as in France, Belgium and Britain. In the elections of June, 1849, the results were entirely satisfactory to the government. The lower classes were accorded so little power that many of them ignored the election. In the industrial Rhineland and Westphalia abstentions were as high as 80 or even 90 per cent. Even in rural Brandenburg they reached 60 per cent.[27]

The new Parliament worked harmoniously with the government in revising the constitution, which was promulgated on January 31, 1850. The upper chamber now became a house of peers, the cabinet became responsible to the king alone, and in general the royal authority was fully restored. The revolution was over. What is surprising is that in Prussia it should have had so radical a complexion. It is readily understandable that in the industrialized areas, where unemployment was prevalent, the democratic forces should have enlisted support among the workers. Evidently the situation of the rural workers under feudal conditions was just as bad and produced just as much radicalism. The situation in Prussia, which was ostensibly favorable was actually parlous. But the forces of radicalism were too unorganized and the leadership too inexperienced to establish effective control. Furthermore, the government still had the loyalty of the armed forces and so was able, when the time seemed ripe, to defeat the revolution. Nonetheless, much had been gained. The old system of government through the patrimonial estates had been replaced by a form of parliamentary government; absolutism had given way to constitutionalism. The common people, it is true, had suffered defeat and were not to play a much larger role under the new system than under the old. But the upper middle class, which had led the opposition in the years before 1848, had established its position on the political stage. Popular insurrection, for all the fear and danger it involved, had forced the governments to accept a large installment of liberal demands. To master insurgency the governments had been obliged to purchase the support of the moderates by adopting reforms which, though partial, breached the walls of the old order and opened the way to modernization.

[27] Schilfert: *Sieg und Niederlage,* 267 ff.; Jacques Droz: *Les révolutions allemandes de 1848* (Paris, 1957), 476 ff.; Huber: *Deutsche Verfassungsgeschichte,* III, 49 ff.

4. SCHWARZENBERG AND THE HUNGARIAN WAR

The suppression of the revolution in Vienna enabled the court Camarilla to prepare openly for the counterrevolution. On the recommendation of Windischgrätz a new cabinet was appointed under Prince Felix zu Schwarzenberg, who, however, insisted that first of all the dynastic change, so long planned by the Archduchess Sophia and her entourage, should be carried through. On December 2, then, the Emperor Ferdinand abdicated in favor of his nephew Francis Joseph, who had just turned eighteen and was therefore legally of age.[28] For the next three years, however, the government was in the firm and energetic hands of Schwarzenberg, who is generally regarded as the prototype of the realistic statesmen who were to dominate both domestic and international politics during the ensuing period. The new chancellor was a man of high intelligence but quite unhampered by moral considerations. Though a member of one of the greatest landholding families, he was by no means the rock-ribbed feudalist that Windischgrätz was. Determined to put an end to revolution, he nevertheless recognized the need for some progressive change. His own class, the high aristocracy, was too hidebound for the modern world. It was necessary and desirable, he thought, to bring at least the upper middle class into political life. He had associated with him in the cabinet Count Franz Stadion, the liberal-minded governor of Galicia; Alexander Bach, an outstanding lawyer and former leader of the liberal *bourgeoisie;* and Karl Ludwig Bruck, a Rhinelander by birth who had made himself a great merchant and shipowner. These men, whatever their differing views on details, were united in the effort to counteract revolutionary agitation by overhauling and modernizing the old system of feudal privilege. Schwarzenberg, in presenting his cabinet to the Austrian Parliament, which had been transferred to Kremsier, near Olmütz, announced the intention of the government to work with the representatives of the people in establishing a constitutional state: "We honestly and unreservedly desire the constitutional monarchy."[29]

The sequel was to demonstrate that Schwarzenberg was insincere in this affirmation, made no doubt to rally popular support until the

---

[28] Josef Redlich: *Emperor Francis Joseph of Austria* (New York, 1929), 27 ff.

[29] Rudolf Kiszling: *Die Revolution im Kaisertum Oesterreich* (Vienna, 1948), I, 303 ff.; Adolf Schwarzenberg: *Prince Felix zu Schwarzenberg* (New York, 1946), 27 ff.; Rudolf Kiszling: *Fürst Felix zu Schwarzenberg* (Graz, 1952), 45 ff.

revolutionary unrest had been ended. Nonetheless, the work of the next few years must not be ignored. For example, the government made no effort to return to the feudal system, nor to undo the emancipation of the peasantry. Much was done to put the administration, the tax system and the tariff on a uniform basis. The administration of justice was taken from the bureaucracy and trial by jury was introduced. The civil service was thoroughly reformed and a substantial measure of local self-government instituted. All in all, the upheaval of 1848 brought not inconsiderable changes in the direction of modernization.

Schwarzenberg's immediate objectives were to restore the authority of the government throughout the empire, and to re-establish the position of Austria as a great power in German and European affairs. Most pressing was the need for liquidating the Hungarian problem, which meant the military defeat of the "rebel" kingdom and the destruction of the historic rights and claims of the Crown of St. Stephen. The Hungarian government refused to recognize the accession of Francis Joseph as king of Hungary on the plea that the dynastic change had been engineered without consultation with the Budapest Parliament. The Hungarians were further provoked and outraged by Schwarzenberg's contention that the new ruler was not bound by the concessions which had been extracted from his predecessor under duress. By the new year the break between the two governments was complete. Francis Joseph declared Kossuth and his supporters rebels and traitors and ordered Windischgrätz to proceed militarily against them.[30]

The commander of the forces was slow in getting operations under way, partly because he doubted the ability of the Austrians to subdue the Hungarians without Russian help and therefore hoped to induce the Hungarian aristocrats to assert themselves against Kossuth and the extreme nationalists, and then offer their submission to the emperor-king. These hopes were by no means groundless, for many of the Hungarian magnates felt that Kossuth had driven matters too far and that the revolutionary reform movement might well end in the destruction of the entire social structure. Had Windischgrätz been willing to

<hr />

[30] C. M. Knatchbull-Hugessen: *The Political Evolution of the Hungarian Nation* (London, 1908), II, 108 ff.; Heinrich Marczali: *Ungarische Verfassungsgeschichte* (Tübingen, 1910), 151.

agree to terms short of unconditional surrender, a compromise might indeed have been arrived at.[31]

Initially the prospects of the Hungarians seemed dim indeed. General Arthur Görgei, a thirty-year-old engineer officer, who had been appointed to command of the army, had a hard time in recruiting, training and equipping a force of even 30,000 men. When Kossuth tried to induce him to attack the Austrians, he flatly refused, with the result that serious dissension quickly developed between the politician Kossuth and the soldier Görgei, who resented civilian interference with operations. Görgei, like many others, had doubts about Kossuth's extreme nationalism and was not ill-disposed toward negotiations which might lead to a return to the *status quo*.[32]

When finally Windischgrätz began his advance (December 15), Görgei refused battle and fell back so as to keep his forces intact. Since he did not believe defense of the capital militarily advisable, Kossuth and the government were obliged to move to Debreczen, to the east of the Tisza (Theiss) River. On January 5, 1849, Austrian troops occupied Budapest, to the immense rejoicing of those who, like Windischgrätz, considered the war all but concluded, especially after a victory over the Hungarian field forces at Kapolna on February 26.

This easy success probably decided Schwarzenberg to cut short the constitutional labors of the Austrian Parliament, which had reached completion. The Parliament had eschewed consideration of Austria's place in the projected German Empire, partly because the Czech deputies were so firmly opposed to the program of German unity and partly because that problem was within the province of the Frankfurt Parliament, in which Austria had representation. Hungary, too, had been omitted from its deliberations on the grounds that that kingdom had been granted virtual independence in March, 1848. The long and arduous debates had therefore focused on the knotty problem of organizing a state in which there were many nationalities living inter-

---

[31] Friedrich Walter: *Die Nationalitätenfrage im alten Ungarn* (Munich, 1959), 8k ff.; Erzsebet Andics: *Das Bündnis Habsburg-Romanow* (Budapest, 1963), 139 ff.

[32] Fritz Valjevec: "Ungarn und die Frage des oesterreichischen Gesamtstaates zu Beginn des Jahres 1849" (*Historische Zeitschrift*, CLXV, 1941, 81–98); Gyözö Ember: "Louis Kossuth à la tête du Comité de la Défense Nationale" (*Studia historica*, VI, 1953, 40 ff.); Erzsebet Andics: "Kossuth en lutte contre les ennemis des réformes et de la révolution" (*ibid.*, XII, 1954, 82 ff.); Julius Miskolczy: *Ungarn in der Habsburger-Monarchie* (Vienna, 1959), 114.

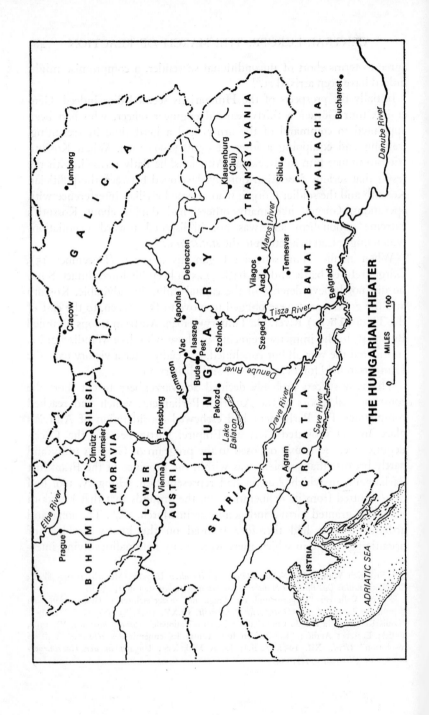

THE HUNGARIAN THEATER

spersed in many areas and having various historic rights and claims. The Czechs took the conservative view and opposed all efforts at centralization, which they believed certain to end in domination by the German element. The Parliament's draft, the so-called Kremsier Constitution, was unanimously approved by the assembly on March 1, 1849. It is historically of great interest, for it proposed a compromise solution for the multinational empire. In the first place it provided for popular sovereignty and so marked the end of absolutism and the patrimonial state. The emperor was to appoint the ministers, but they were to be responsible also to the Parliament. The emperor's veto on legislation enacted by Parliament was to be only suspensive, and his power to dissolve Parliament was limited by the proviso that a new Parliament should meet within three months. Parliament was to consist of an upper house (*Länderkammer*) composed of delegations from the historic local diets or *Landtage*. The lower house (*Volkskammer*) was to be popularly elected by direct vote. The constitution declared all peoples of the monarchy to have equal rights in matters of language and administration. The provincial Diets were to have broad autonomy in cultural matters, and the districts (*Kreise*), into which the historic lands (*Länder*) were to be divided, were to be based on nationality and to have popularly elected councils. In sum, the Kremsier draft constitution envisaged a liberal representative system and at the same time a federal organization based on the historic lands with a large measure of local self-government and full scope for national self-expression. This was probably as close to a satisfactory solution of the nationalities problem as one could hope to come.[33]

Schwarzenberg, who had been watching the work of the Parliament with ill-concealed hostility, had long since made up his mind to dissolve it as soon as possible. If he had not done so prior to March 1, it was chiefly out of consideration for public opinion in Germany, where Austria's position would be further weakened by an attack upon the popularly elected Parliament. Now, when the assembly voted

[33] The basic study is Josef Redlich: *Das oesterreichische Staats- und Reichsproblem* (Leipzig, 1920), I, Part III. See also Paula Geist-Lanyi: *Das Nationalitätenproblem auf dem Reichstag zu Kremsier* (Munich, 1920); Fritz von Reinöhl: "Die Frage der deutschen Einheit und der Wien-Kremsier Reichstag" (in *Festschrift für Ritter von Srbik*, Munich, 1938, 276–286); Robert A. Kann: *The Multinational Empire* (New York, 1950), II, 21 ff.

approval of the draft constitution, further delay was impossible. On March 4 the Parliament was prorogued and the government promulgated its own constitution, largely the work of Count Stadion. In many respects this "provisional constitution" was hardly less liberal than that of the Parliament, though the franchise was restricted to taxpayers and the powers of the emperor were more extensive. The important difference was in the projected organization of the empire. The government constitution was to apply to all Hapsburg possessions, described as "the free, indivisible, indissoluble, constitutional hereditary monarchy." This meant the inclusion of Hungary, of which the constitution was to remain valid only in so far as it did not conflict with the imperial constitution. Hungary was reduced to the status of any other crown land, and was to be deprived of all its historically associated territories (*partes adnexae*). Thus Croatia, Slavonia, Voivodina and Transylvania were all given the status of individual crown lands, each with its own Diet.[34]

An eminent authority has described the government constitution of March 4 a "supreme piece of political jugglery," designed by its ostensible liberalism to mislead German public opinion and by its all-inclusiveness to challenge Hungarian nationalism.[35] This it certainly did, despite the fact that in April the tide of victory had begun to turn in favor of the Hungarians. Windischgrätz, by his procrastination, had given Görgei time to complete his preparations. In a brilliant campaign the Hungarian army evaded the Austrians and, marching north, joined forces with the new levies concentrated east of the Tisza River. On March 5 Görgei had won a first victory at Szolnok, to be followed by a second at Isaszeg (April 6). Meanwhile another Hungarian force, commanded by the Polish general Bem, who had escaped from Vienna, drove the Austrians out of Transylvania and threatened to invade Galicia. Under these favorable auspices Kossuth was able to override the compunctions of the more moderate elements. In response to Schwarzenberg's constitution he proclaimed the Hapsburg dynasty deposed and Hungary completely independent, with the inclusion of

---

[34] Redlich: *Das oesterreichische Staats und Reichsproblem*, I, Part IV, chap. i; Kann: *Multinational Empire*, II, 59 ff. The important documents are printed in the fundamental study of Hanns Schlitter: *Versäumte Gelegenheiten: die okroyierte Verfassung vom 4 März, 1849* (Vienna, 1920); see also Walter: *Die Nationalitätenfrage im alten Ungarn*, 88 ff.

[35] Redlich: *Emperor Francis Joseph*, 77.

Transylvania and other associated territories (April 14). The Committee of National Defense was dissolved and Kossuth became governor-president. Though not officially a republic, the new regime was in every respect *de facto* republican. For a month or six weeks the miracle of Hungarian victory was several times repeated. Görgei advanced to Budapest, which he besieged and finally captured (May 21). By this time the Vienna government was panic-stricken, fearing a Hungarian advance on Vienna and a recrudescence of insurgency in the capital. Windischgrätz was replaced by General Welden, who, after inspecting the situation, gave up all hope. There was now no alternative to calling on Czar Nicholas for aid.

The czar felt bound by the agreements of Münchengrätz (1834) and by his promise to the Emperor Francis in 1835 to stand by his successors. Fearful lest the revolutionary upheaval in Central Europe spread to Russia, he had concentrated large armies on the frontiers so as to be ready to intervene when necessary. He watched developments in Germany with as much interest as the affairs of his own country and as for Austria was convinced that its maintenance as a great power was of supreme interest to Russia, not only as a bulwark against revolutionary ideas coming from the West, but also as a counterweight to a possible united Germany under Prussian leadership. "No one needs a strong and powerful Austria more than I do," he had written the Archduchess Sophia when she begged his support for her son in December, 1848. Nicholas kept urging the Hapsburg government to take a strong line against the revolutionaries and had applauded every success of Windischgrätz, Jellachich and Radetzky. Time and again he reiterated his readiness to help, but only on condition that he be appealed to by the emperor himself and that he be allowed to conduct the intervention on his own terms.[36]

On the Austrian side Schwarzenberg as well as Windischgrätz had envisaged the probable need for Russian aid against Hungary, but the chancellor was naturally reluctant to suffer the humiliation of an

---

[36] Fundamental are the studies of Revekka Averbuch: *Tsarkaiia interventsiia v borbe s vengerskoi revolutsiei* (Moscow, 1935); Eugene Horvath: "Russia and the Hungarian Revolution" (*Slavonic Review*, XII, 1934, 628–659); Dionys von Janossy: "Die russische Intervention in Ungarn im Jahre 1849" (*Jahrbuch des Wiener Ungarischen Historischen Instituts*, I, 1931, 314–335); A. S. Nifontow: *Russland im Jahre 1848* (Berlin, 1954); Andics: *Das Bündnis Habsburg-Romanow*, 68 ff.

appeal. He tried to induce the Russians to intervene spontaneously and secretly encouraged the Austrian commander in Transylvania to call upon General Lüders and the Russian forces occupying the Danubian Principalities for support when Bem threatened to take over the entire area. When, on March 11, Bem defeated both the Austrians and the Russians near Sibiu, Schwarzenberg felt obliged to ask for 30,000 Russian troops to intervene in Transylvania.[37]

Finally, on April 20, when the Austrian commander ordered the evacuation of Budapest and there was reason to fear that the Hungarians might presently stage an advance on Vienna, Schwarzenberg formally requested Russian intervention in Galicia, despite the fact that the cabinet was still reluctant to take the plunge. Nicholas, dreading the possibility of an invasion of Galicia by Bem and an eventual Polish insurrection, ordered General Paskievich to act. The intervention was publicly announced on May 8 as urgently necessary to forestall the spread of revolution. The presence of Polish officers and refugees in the Hungarian army, possibly 5,000 in number, was greatly exaggerated by the Austrian authorities, who reported 20,000 Poles, organized in separate regiments and corps, so as to impress the Russians. In any case, the czar felt that he must crush the revolution or be incessantly menaced by it.[38]

On June 6 the main Russian army of 100,000 men poured over the Carpathians and into Galicia and Hungary, while another force of 30,000 invaded Transylvania from Wallachia. But the opening of the campaign was delayed not only by the indecision and circumspection of the commander-in-chief, Field-Marshal Paskievich, but by lack of provisions and supplies and by the outbreak of a severe cholera epidemic which, during July and August, took a heavy toll. However, more and more troops were dispatched to clinch the victory, until ultimately the Russians had sent about 360,000 men into the country. The Hungarians, who had enjoyed a superiority in numbers over the

[37] Hugo Kerchnawe: *Feldmarshall Fürst Windischgrätz und die russische Hilfe, 1848* (Innsbruck, 1930); Andićs: *Das Bündnis Habsburg-Romanow,* 106 ff., 116 ff., 126 ff., 136.

[38] His remarks to the French representative, cited by Constantin de Grunwald: *Tsar Nicholas I* (New York, 1955), 249 ff. See also Nifontow: *Russland im Jahre 1848,* chap. viii; Walter: *Die Nationalitätemfrage im alten Ungarn* 107 ff.; Andićs: *Die Bündnis Habsburg-Romanow,* 137, 144 ff.

Austrians, now saw the scales swing violently against them. There was, in fact, little or no hope of holding out for long.[39] In this extremity Kossuth tried to arrive at a separate agreement with the czar, suggesting the possibility of electing a Russian grand duke to the Hungarian throne, but Nicholas would not parley with a revolutionary. Kossuth also approached the Frankfurt Parliament, stressing the common interest of Germans and Hungarians in forestalling the domination of Central Europe by the Slavs. But his appeal impressed only the German radicals, and came to nothing. Britain and France, on whom Kossuth for a time placed high hopes, proved equally disillusioning. Both powers were interested chiefly in preserving the Hapsburg Monarchy as a bulwark against Russia. Though radicals such as Cobden and Urquhart might sympathize, Palmerston refused to be moved, even by suggestions of a favorable trade treaty. On July 21 he summed up the British interest as he saw it, in a speech to Parliament:

The political independence and liberties of Europe are bound up . . . with the maintenance and integrity of Austria as a great European power; and therefore anything which tends by direct or even remote contingency to weaken and to cripple Austria, but still more to reduce her from the position of a first-rate Power to that of a secondary State, must be a great calamity to Europe, and one which every Englishman ought to deprecate and to try to prevent.[40]

With conservative circles in all countries, even Britain, on the Austrian and Russian side, the Hungarians had only the military genius of Görgei, the determination of Kossuth, and the valor of the troops to fall back upon. Fortunately for them Paskievich, who had been ordered by the czar to "strike like a thunderbolt," did nothing of

[39] One of the best studies of the campaign is the contemporary account of Max Schlesinger: *The War in Hungary* (London, 1850). Of modern treatments, see Kiszling: *Die Revolution im Kaisertum Oesterreich*, II, and John S. Curtiss: *The Russian Army under Nicholas I* (Durham, 1965), chap. xv.

[40] Quoted by Charles Sproxton: *Palmerston and the Hungarian Revolution* (Cambridge, 1919), 21. For other aspects of the international situation, see Wilhelm Alter: *Die auswärtige Politik der ungarischen Revolution* (Berlin, 1912), 25 ff.; Eugene Horvath: "Kossuth and Palmerston, 1848–1849" (*Slavonic Review*, IX, 1931, 612–631); N. J. Szenczi: "Great Britain and the War of Hungarian Independence" (*ibid.*, XVII, 1939, 556–570); Denes A. Janossy: "Great Britain and Kossuth" (*Archivum Europae Centro-Orientalis*, III, 1937, 53–190); Andić: *Die Bündnis Habsburg-Romanow*, 165 ff.

the kind. Though the Hungarians were obliged to abandon Budapest and move the government to Szeged (July 2), Görgei succeeded in evading the Russian armies and retreating to the northeast, whence he then marched southward beyond the Tisza River toward Szeged. At the same time, however, the Austrian general, Count Julius von Haynau, advanced from the west, crossed the Tisza and defeated a Hungarian force under General Dembinski near Temesvar. Since the Russians had managed also to drive the Hungarians in Transylvania across the border into Turkey, the Hungarians were being gradually surrounded. Görgei, who had been at odds with Kossuth for some time, insisted on his resignation (August 11) and two days later surrendered with his 25,000 men at Világos, not to Haynau and the Austrians, but to the Russians. Kossuth and other leaders fled to Turkish territory, where their presence soon created an international crisis. The Austrians and Russians demanded their extradition, while the British and French supported the sultan in refusing it. Under threat of a British-French naval demonstration, Austria and Russia finally gave way.[41]

Görgei was given his freedom by the Russians, who found it easy to get along with the Hungarians, whose plucky resistance they admired. But Russian efforts to intercede in their behalf with the Vienna government proved utterly futile. The Austrians were furious with the Hungarians for having forced upon them the humiliation of appealing for foreign help. They had even considered asking the czar for a tract of territory in northern Asia to which they could exile the revolutionaries. Haynau, an able general but a heartless brute, was beside himself when the Hungarians surrendered to the Russians. He secured from the emperor a free hand to try and execute thirteen Hungarian generals, as well as the former premier, Count Batthyány.[42] Thousands of other Hungarians were sentenced to long prison terms. Pleas for moderation by the British and other governments were ignored or

41 Eduard von Wertheimer: "Die Kossuth-Emigration in der Türkei" (*Ungarische Jahrbücher*, VIII, 1928, 377 ff.); Harold Temperley: *The Crimea* (London, 1936), 292 ff.; Vernon J. Puryear: *England, Russia and the Straits Question, 1844–1856* (Berkeley, 1931), 153 ff.

42 For a discussion of responsibilities, see Walter: *Die Nationalitäten Frage im alten Ungarn*, 123 ff.; Andics: *Die Bündnis Habsburg-Romanow*, 158, 195.

rejected. In a letter to the British ambassador in Vienna, Palmerston felt impelled to describe the Austrians as "the greatest brutes that ever called themselves by the undeserved name of civilised men."[43]

For some years Hungary remained under martial law, divided into five military districts and ruled by German officials sent from Vienna. Croatia, Slavonia and other lands, which had espoused the imperial cause against the Hungarians, were treated no better. All nationalities, it was said, were given equal rights to Germanization. Soon it became clear that the March 4 constitution had been meant solely as window dressing. It was never put into effect. Once the Hungarian problem was solved, the government felt free to ignore it and eventually (December 31, 1851) it was replaced by an imperial decree or "patent" which restored absolute rule. There was to be an appointed council (*Reichsrat*) with consultative powers only, but the government was in reality left to a ministry appointed by the emperor and a bureaucracy recruited from the German population. German was made the official language. This was the so-called "Bach System," from the name of the man who had started as a liberal and had in 1849 succeeded Count Stadion as minister of the interior. Actually it was inspired by Baron von Kübeck, a close adviser of the emperor and an unrepentant conservative.[44]

The surrender of the Hungarians capped the victory of the counter-revolutionary forces in the Hapsburg Empire. Looking back on the great revolutionary upheaval, it is rather surprising that it ever developed as far as it did, for the truly revolutionary forces were weak and unorganized. The liberal elements, who never contemplated a resort to violence, were carried away by the students and workers of Vienna and were soon so frightened that they either retired from the scene or actively supported the government. The threat of peasant insurrection, which was real and formidable, was eliminated by the prompt abolition of remaining feudal obligations and dues.

There remained the problem of nationalities, which gave the court an opportunity to play off one group against another, the more so as

[43] Sproxton: *Palmerston and the Hungarian Revolution*, 109–111.
[44] Redlich: *Das oesterreichische Staats und Reichsproblem*, I, Part IV, chap. iii; Kann: *Multinational Empire*, II, 115 ff.; Schwarzenberg: *Prince Felix zu Schwarzenberg*, 98 ff.; Kiszling: *Fürst Felix zu Schwarzenberg*, 166 ff.

the Hungarians, under Kossuth's influence, overshot the mark in demanding a degree of independence that might have destroyed the monarchy as a great power and in any case antagonized the other nationalities. The majority of the Hungarian aristocracy and even many of the gentry disapproved of Kossuth's policies, but he was able to rally the support of the workers and peasants and eventually over-reached himself. Even so, the resistance of the Hungarians was truly impressive. It is most unlikely that the government would have been able to suppress the Hungarian revolution without the massive aid of the Russians.

The story of the Hapsburg insurrections is filled with subterfuges, deceits and brutalities of many kinds. Yet the fact remains that despite the repression some progress was made. The government leaders, Radetzky, Schwarzenberg, Stadion, Bach, whatever their transgressions, were not dyed-in-the-wool feudalists like Windischgrätz. True, they were determined to forestall popular sovereignty and representative government and to frustrate the reorganization of the empire along federal lines, but they would not go back to the patrimonial system of hoary privilege and feudal rights. The revolution, it must be said, had at least the effect of opening the way to modernization in Central Europe.

5. GERMANY: THE DILEMMA OF NATIONALISM

It was indeed a tragedy that the Parliament at Frankfurt should have arrived at debate on the composition and organization of the new national state at a time when the revolutionary movements in the two principal capitals were being suppressed and the governments again securing control of their affairs. The Parliament has sometimes been blamed for spending months on discussions in the Constitutional Committee and so allowing the golden moment when the governments were relatively helpless to pass. But a few months devoted to so difficult and complicated a problem would hardly seem excessive. In France the Constitutional Committee took almost as long to debate a far less thorny problem. The Frankfurt committee included many of Germany's most outstanding scholars. It is not true that they lost themselves in rhetoric and theory. The records of their proceedings reveal much hardheaded thinking in addition to an impressive knowledge of the British, French and American constitutional systems and their operation.[45]

There was basic agreement among the men of the Frankfurt Parliament that the new German state must be a federal state (*Bundesstaat*), that is, something more than a mere confederation of states (*Staatenbund*), such as the Germanic Confederation of 1815. The federal government would have extensive executive power, including control over foreign policy, the armed forces, justice, trade, and so on. The more conservative men of the right wished to preserve as much as possible of the authority of the individual states; they were "particularists." Those on the left, by contrast, wanted the powers of the princes and their governments pared to the bone and almost complete authority vested in the federal government. In between were the center groups whose members, far from being contemptuous of local traditions and interests, were enamored of the variety of German life. While desirous of preserving the individuality of the member states, they were nevertheless determined to have a federal system endowed with effective power. Differences of opinion in these matters were susceptible of compromise and what finally emerged was an intermediate solution.

Far more baffling was the question what territories should be included in the new German Empire. In the early months of the revolution it was generally believed that the Hapsburg Monarchy was doomed to disintegration and that, if it survived at all, it would be little more than a loose aggregation of national units. The Germans of Austria were, in these circumstances, eager to be included in the new Germany, and the non-Austrian Germans were just as keenly desirous of having them. In the summer of 1848 it still looked as though the emerging German state would comprise all major German populations, that is, would be a truly national state.

Yet after Radetzky's victory at Custoza it seemed increasingly likely that the Hapsburg government would regain its footing. By October the chances of the counterrevolution were even brighter. At Frankfurt some of the radicals began to argue that if the Hapsburg Empire was to be disrupted, it was high time to act. They pleaded for aid to the

[45] Anton Scholl: *Der Einfluss der nordamerikanischen Unionsverfassung auf die Verfassung des Deutschen Reiches vom 28 März, 1849* (Leipzig, 1913); Eckart G. Franz: *Das Amerikabild der deutschen Revolution von 1848–1849* (Heidelberg, 1958); Halvdan Koht: *The American Spirit in Europe* (Philadelphia, 1949), chap. iv, who stresses the profound influence of Tocqueville's *Democracy in America*.

Viennese insurgents and support for the Hungarians. But the majority would not hear of such a provocative policy. Most members were convinced that it would be a fatal mistake to antagonize the governments, with which co-operation was necessary if the German problem was to be solved without major ructions. So the Parliament remained inactive while the counterrevolution triumphed, while Windischgrätz defiantly executed Robert Blum, one of the most prominent leaders of the left.[46]

Just as the revolution in Vienna was about to go under, the Frankfurt assembly on October 27 voted (316–90) approval of paragraphs II and III of the constitutional draft, which specified that no part of the new German Empire should be connected with non-German territories save through purely personal union. This posed the "great query" which the Austrian government would have to answer: whether to allow its German provinces to join the new Germany and reorganize the Hapsburg Monarchy as a loose conglomeration of lands held together only through the dynastic tie, or whether to accept its exclusion from the projected German national state.

Austrian historians have complained that the historian Gustav Droysen, who drafted these fateful paragraphs, was a North German who lacked understanding or appreciation of Austria's position and mission; that he looked upon the monarchy simply as "an irrational complex of states." Perhaps so, but the fact remains that of the 115 Austrian deputies in the Frankfurt Parliament, 74 voted in favor of Droysen's draft. Like their colleagues, most of the Austrian deputies had set their hopes on the nascent German state and were prepared to bid the Hapsburg Monarchy farewell.[47] The great majority of the members had convinced themselves that the Hapsburg government would never accept the solution offered it and that therefore the inclusion of the German lands of Austria was impossible. With heavy hearts they had decided that it was better to abandon the Austrian Germans than to jeopardize the future of all Germany. It seems that the Austrian Germans (in contrast to the Austrian deputies in the Parliament) were in fact opposed to any plan that involved the breakup of

---

[46] Hans G. Telle: *Das oesterreichische Problem im Frankfurter Parlament im Sommer und Herbst, 1848* (Marburg, 1933), 78 ff.

[47] Heinrich von Srbik: *Deutsche Einheit* (3 ed., Munich, 1940), I, 366 ff.; Rudolf Kiszling: *Die Revolution im Kaisertum Oesterreich* (Vienna, 1948), I, 337 ff.

the historic Hapsburg Empire. They had a deep conviction of mission to rule the congeries of nationalities in the Danube Basin. Yet, unwilling to sacrifice the monarchy, they were indignant at the attempt to exclude them from German affairs.[48]

Following the subjugation of Vienna, the Austrian government made it increasingly clear that the empire would be maintained as a single state (*Gesamtstaat*) and that, as soon as it had put its own house in order, it would discuss its relations with the rest of Germany. In other words, while the Italian and Hungarian problems were still unsettled, the Vienna government did not propose to challenge the Frankfurt Parliament.

Schwarzenberg's negative stand led to the resignation (December 15) of the Frankfurt cabinet of Anton von Schmerling, a prominent Austrian liberal. Heinrich von Gagern headed the new cabinet, while Eduard von Simson succeeded him as presiding officer of the Parliament. Gagern, it will be recalled,[49] had from the outset held that the only feasible solution of the German problem lay in establishment of a federal state under Prussian leadership, with the exclusion of the German provinces of Austria. The German and the Austrian Empires could then be united through a constitutional alliance. It was an integral part of his plan, however, that the king of Prussia should exchange his royal crown for the imperial one, which was to carry real power and authority. Meanwhile, in order to avoid the domination of the new federal state by one powerful member, and to establish something like equality between the member states, Prussia was to be dissolved and each of its eight provinces was to become a separate member state of the empire, while many of the smallest German states were to be merged with the larger states. The end result would be the emergence of eight German states to match the eight former provinces of Prussia. Lest the reader suppose that such a fundamental recasting was fantastic, he should be reminded that Napoleon in 1803 had carried through just such a restructuring of the German world and that, since most of the German states had existed in their present form only since 1815, they could all be regarded as still in a formative stage. This was particularly true of Prussia, which many looked upon as a mere

[48] Adolf Rapp: *Grossdeutsch-Kleindeutsch* (Munich, 1922), xxiv; Jacques Droz: *L'Europe centrale: évolution historique de l'idée de 'Mitteleuropa'* (Paris, 1960), 79 ff.
[49] See above, Chapter XII.

"bundle of provinces." Bismarck was partially to remake the German world in 1866, while later, in 1919, many liberals were to advocate the dissolution of the Prussian state. It was something of a tragedy that this was accomplished not in 1848 but only after two world wars.[50]

That Frederick William of Prussia had a genuine interest in the larger problem of German unity is not in dispute. Indeed, in the days of his tribulation he had talked of his readiness to "merge" or "fuse" Prussia with Germany. But these were merely beautiful words, designed to still the popular clamor. Neither the king nor the court had any intention of breaking up the glorious monarchy of Frederick the Great. They were particularists, almost to a man. Even the liberal leaders of the industrialized Rhineland, where separatist feeling was stronger than elsewhere, were opposed to disruption of the monarchy. Gagern and other members of minor South German states might cook up alluring schemes, but neither one of the two great powers was willing to be carved up or merge its identity in a still-nebulous national state. The Frankfurt leaders had soon to deal with the further fact that the so-called "middle states," that is, those of intermediate size, were one and all opposed to the surrender of substantial authority to the projected federal government. All told, the Gagern program, however intelligent and carefully planned, from the outset ran serious danger of shipwreck.

The suppression of the Berlin revolution in November led many to fear that Prussia would adopt an out-and-out reactionary policy and so make itself impossible as the leader of liberal Germany. Gagern himself hurried to Berlin, which, incidentally, he had never before visited. He tried to persuade the king to replace the cabinet of Count Brandenburg by one enjoying the confidence of the Prussian Parliament and did what he could to forestall the promulgation by the government of a constitution that might conflict with that being worked out at Frankfurt. By holding before Frederick William the prospect of the imperial crown, he hoped to prevent a reorganization of the Prussian state that would nullify plans for its dissolution. His efforts, however, proved vain and his sole consolation was the realization that the Prussian

[50] For full treatment of this subject, see the classic study of Friedrich Meinecke: *Weltbürgertum und Nationalstaat* (7 ed., now in his *Werke*, Munich, 1962).

constitution of December 5 was more liberal than might have been expected.[51]

Despite the independent procedure of the Berlin government, the Frankfurt Parliament proceeded on what was now the only remaining course of action. On January 3, 1849, it adopted the Gagern plan for an "inner" federal state and an "outer" federation to include the Austrian Empire. Two days later it defeated a radical proposal for a federal republic under a popularly elected president and adopted a motion for a federal empire under a hereditary emperor. The Parliament had by this time split into a greater German (*grossdeutsch*) and a lesser German (*kleindeutsch*) faction. The former, commanding some 125 votes, favored inclusion of either the German provinces of Austria or the entire Hapsburg Monarchy in the new federal state, and looked with disdain on the lesser German faction, which commanded more votes (about 225), as compromisers who would exclude Austria and so betray the German national cause.[52]

The final decision was forced on the Frankfurt Parliament when Schwarzenberg on March 4 promulgated the constitution which treated the Hapsburg Monarchy as a single unit and then followed up (March 11) with the demand that the entire empire be included in the new German state. This state, he proposed, should be governed by a directory of seven, assisted by a chamber of states (*Staatenhaus*) appointed by the state governments, and in this Austria, on the basis of population, should have thirty-eight seats, as against thirty-two for all the other German states combined.

This was too much for the *Kleindeutschen*. Gagern and his associates now made a deal with the radicals: they agreed that provision for an upper house of Parliament should be dropped and that election for the lower house should be by universal, equal and direct suffrage. In return, the radicals undertook to vote the rest of the constitution and not to obstruct the election of the king of Prussia as emperor. The constitution was then voted on March 27 and the final step, the election

---

[51] Meinecke: *Weltbürgertum und Nationalstaat*, 340 ff.; Huber: *Deutsche Verfassungsgeschichte*, II, 756 ff.

[52] The two terms appeared first in December, 1848. See Heidrun von Möller: *Grossdeutsch und Kleindeutsch; die Entstehung der Worte in den Jahren 1848–1849* (Berlin, 1937).

of Frederick William as emperor, was taken on March 28, by a vote of 290 in favor and 248 abstaining.

On April 2 the presiding officer, Eduard von Simson, led a delegation of thirty prominent members of the Parliament to offer Frederick William the imperial crown. The king was gracious but enigmatic. He spoke of the desirability of strengthening the powers of the executive and referred to his obligations toward his fellow princes, without whose approval he could not consider acceptance. The majority of the delegation took the royal remarks as a veiled refusal and they were right. As the king's letters to his friends (published much later) were to reveal, he was most contemptuous of the Frankfurt Parliament and its pretensions to organize the future of Germany. He would have nothing to do, so he wrote, with a crown offered him by bakers and butchers, and reeking with the stench of the revolution. He would not allow the revolutionaries to fasten about his neck a dog collar by which to chain him forever to the principle of popular sovereignty and so make him the slave of the revolution. In short, he would accept the crown only if it were offered to him by his fellow princes. As for the German national state, he could envisage that only in medieval terms, with the Hapsburgs at the head and with government by divinely appointed princes, assisted by their feudal estates.

The temptation is strong to ridicule the king and his antiquated romanticism. It was a real misfortune that at this crucial moment the Prussian crown should have been worn by a man so little fitted to the requirements of the modern world. The men of Frankfurt were as saddened as they were helpless in the face of this situation, for their wisdom would not compensate for their lack of material power. They could neither force the Hapsburgs to accept their exclusion from the new Germany nor induce the Prussian king to change his nature.

At first there was a period of confusion, during which the definitive reply of the king was awaited. There was still some hope that, at the price of certain concessions, he might be persuaded to accept the crown. The Prussian Parliament and even the ministry urged Frederick William to seize the God-given opportunity to assume the leadership of Germany, and in other German states, too, the parliaments and public opinion staunchly backed the Frankfurt program. On April 14 many of the German states (though not the four kingdoms) approved the Frankfurt constitution and recognized the election of Frederick

William as emperor. But all to no avail. The Austrian government advertised its uncompromising opposition and recalled the Austrian deputies from Frankfurt. Frederick William, in turn, was further deterred by the attitude of the Vienna government and may have feared war with Austria and possibly Russia in the event of his accepting the crown. However, these considerations were only ancillary to his deeply felt aversion to the revolution and its objectives. On April 27 the Prussian government informed Frankfurt of the king's rejection of both the constitution and the crown. The Archduke John promptly resigned the post of vicar-general (May 8) and two days later Gagern, too, laid down his office. The final move came when, on May 14, the Berlin government recalled the Prussian deputies and the governments of Saxony, Hanover and other states followed suit.

The Parliament now had no alternative to proclaiming a federal republic and electing a president. This had been the radical program right along, but even now the moderates still hoped that federal reform could somehow be worked out in collaboration with the governments. To this end the Parliament called for new elections and the meeting of the new assembly in August. However, many of the members, now quite disillusioned, left for home. Those who remained voted (May 30) to move to Stuttgart, to be further removed from the federal troops stationed at Mainz. Before they could reassemble, all South Germany was in the turmoil of a new revolution. Only a meager rump gathered at Stuttgart and this was easily dispersed by local troops on June 18. Thus ingloriously ended the Parliament which had brought together so much ability and good will and had embarked a year before with so much confidence and enthusiasm upon the task of national unification.

6. GERMANY: THE RADICAL REVOLUTIONS

Germany, like France, Italy and Hungary, was to experience an outburst of radicalism in the spring and early summer of 1849, the last desperate protest of the revolutionary forces before being overwhelmed by the tide of reaction. The radicals, drawing their strength chiefly from the lesser *bourgeoisie* of southwest Germany and from the artisans, journeymen and factory workers of the industrialized Rhineland, Westphalia and Saxony, were a distinct minority in the Frankfurt Parliament, but were well represented by intellectuals such as teachers and writers. They had been critical of the Frankfurt constitution, which they regarded as not sufficiently democratic and as far too considerate of governments and vested rights. But now that the revolution was threatened with shipwreck, they rallied in support of the constitution, which was approved by many of the state governments under pressure from democratic societies and workers' clubs. The popular movement was, on the whole, political rather than social. In fact, many of the radical leaders were troubled by the extremism of the socialists and communists, whose objectives were suspect. Thus, when Engels attempted to exploit the insurrection in the Rhineland, the revolutionary committee of Elberfeld requested him to leave, lest he create an erroneous impression of the nature of the movement. In the Palatinate and Baden, too, the *élan* seems to have gone out of the revolution as socialists and communists came flocking from all over Europe and started to give the insurrection an unwanted turn.[53]

In the Rhineland the disorders began early in May when the militia regiments refused to obey orders and proclaimed their readiness to defend the Frankfurt constitution. For some days Elberfeld was in the hands of a revolutionary government, of which the Communists tried to secure control. The propertied classes, even the shopkeepers and craftsmen, actively opposed the extremists and the Civic Guard intervened to restore order until regular troops were brought in. The revolution was suppressed. Marx, Engels and other Communists were expelled, and the last number of the Communist organ, the *New Rhenish Gazette,* appeared on May 19.[54]

Dresden was one of the chief centers of insurgency. There the king had defied the popular will by dissolving his Parliament for urging acceptance of the Frankfurt constitution. Great meetings of protest thereupon led to the formation of a Committee of Public Safety (May 3). The king fled the city and appealed to the Prussian government for military aid. When the troops marched in, the barricades went up and some 10,000 insurgents fought desperately for four days and nights.

[53] Rudolf Stadelmann: *Soziale und politische Geschichte der Revolution von 1848* (Munich, 1948), 180 ff.; Karl Obermann: *Die deutschen Arbeiter in der ersten bürgerlichen Revolution* (Berlin, 1950), 256 ff.

[54] Marx and Engels have left their own account in their *Germany: Revolution and Counterrevolution* (1852), chap. xvii, conveniently reprinted with an introduction by Leonard Krieger as Engels: *The German Revolution* (Chicago, 1967). See also Auguste Cornu: "Karl Marx et la révolution de 1848 en Allemagne" (*Europe,* XXVI, 1948, 238–252); Hermann Meyer: "Karl Marx und die deutsche Revolution von 1848" (*Historische Zeitschrift,* CLXXII, 1951, 517–537).

The Dresden rising was noteworthy not only for the ferocity of the struggle but for the participation of several figures of world repute. Bakunin's role is still somewhat obscure, as he seems to have been more interested in stimulating a revolt in Bohemia than in defending the Frankfurt constitution. Without much confidence in the success of the rising, he enjoyed the fighting for its own sake. Another name to become famous throughout the world was Richard Wagner, at that time music director of the Dresden Opera. He had been consorting with Bakunin and other radicals for some time and had become a republican. His radicalism, however, was more cultural than political, and his objective a new and better world for art and artists than for the downtrodden and disfranchised. When finally the Prussian troops had beaten down the rebellion, Wagner managed to escape to Switzerland, but Bakunin was captured, convicted and eventually turned over to the Russian government, which sent him to exile in Siberia.[55]

In southwest Germany, the traditional center of radicalism, where there had already been two serious upheavals, the revolution was first successful in the Bavarian Palatinate, where again some of the troops rallied to the support of a provisional government. For a brief spell the Palatinate was an independent democratic republic. The Bavarian government, faced by the threat of insurgence elsewhere, lacked the forces needed to suppress the revolution and hesitated, as a matter of pride, to call upon the Prussians for aid. But presently Prussian forces, coming from the Rhineland, intervened in the Palatinate without being asked. By mid-June they had snuffed out the insurrection and driven the provisional government into flight.

In Baden the revolution, though last to materialize, proved to be the most formidable. In mid-May the troops of the Rastatt garrison revolted and a huge popular assembly at Offenburg led to the formation of a provisional government, followed by the flight of the grand duke. Radicals of every stripe and every nationality quickly flocked to Baden from every part of Germany and indeed from all over Europe. The

---

[55] Josef Pfitzner: *Bakuninstudien* (Prague, 1932); Edward H. Carr: *Michael Bakunin* (New York, 1937, 1961), 196; Frederick Barghoorn: "Russian Radicals and the West European Revolutions of 1848" (*Review of Politics*, III, 1949, 338–354). On Wagner, see Ernest Newman: *The Life of Richard Wagner* (New York, 1933–1945), II, chaps. iv and v; K. R. Ganzer: *Richard Wagner, der Revolutionär gegen das 19 Jahrhundert* (Munich, 1934); Maurice Boucher: *The Political Concepts of Richard Wagner* (New York, 1950).

Poles and Hungarians formed separate legions and the well-known Polish revolutionary, Mieroslawski, was given command of the insurgent forces. The Communists, too, appeared on the scene. Marx, for example, badgered the provisional government to march on Frankfurt to defend the Parliament. But once again the Prussian regulars were to give the radical revolt short shrift. At the grand duke's request they invaded Baden as soon as they had suppressed the revolution in the Palatinate. Mieroslawski, with 40,000 men, mostly untrained and poorly equipped, fought valiantly but was soon defeated at Waghäusel (June 20). The insurgents were obliged to abandon Karlsruhe and the provisional government took flight as the Prussian forces occupied the entire duchy. But only on July 23 did the beleaguered Rastatt garrison finally surrender. Prussian courts-martial then went into action, showing themselves no less ruthless than their Austrian counterparts in Hungary. About a thousand persons were convicted, of whom twenty-seven died before firing squads. Most of the insurgents, however, managed to escape. Over 10,000 of them reached Switzerland, among them Carl Schurz, who at the age of twenty had taken a prominent part in the fight and was presently to emigrate to the United States, there to make for himself a distinguished career as soldier, diplomat and statesman.[56]

The insurrections of May–June, 1849, sometimes called the Second German Revolution, revealed widespread popular support for the work of the Frankfurt Parliament, but they were the expressions only of forlorn hopes, partly because of their internal weaknesses and partly because of the forces now marshaled against them. There was, in the first place, no unity to the radical movement. The radical leaders could rarely see eye to eye and the provisional governments were usually so taken up with internal conflicts that they could not concentrate on the task of defense. At the same time the liberals had become so disheartened and so averse to further disorder and violence that they either stood aloof or else supported the governments in the work of repression. In any event, the hastily organized insurrections had no chance of survival now that the Prussian government had re-estab-

56 *The Reminiscences of Carl Schurz* (New York, 1906–1908), I. Of the many books on Schurz, the following are particularly full on his early, German period: Otto Dannehl: *Carl Schurz, ein deutscher Kämpfer* (Berlin, 1929); Hanns Höwing: *Carl Schurz, Rebell, Kämpfer, Staatsman* (Wiesbaden, 1948).

lished its position at home and was willing if not eager to act as gendarme for all Germany. The fighters of 1849 were, for all their heroism, champions of a lost cause.

7. POSTLUDE: THE AUSTRO-PRUSSIAN CONFLICT

Frederick William of Prussia rejected the imperial crown offered him by the Frankfurt Parliament not because he was opposed to German unification but because he wanted to carry it through according to his own ideas, that is, along traditional lines of agreement between the German princes. The details of his program had been worked out by his friend Radowitz, whose knowledge of the German problem was derived from years of experience as Prussian military representative at the federal Diet, followed by service as deputy in the Frankfurt Parliament. Radowitz was convinced that German unity was the best antidote to revolution and that the Frankfurt constitution, revamped in a conservative direction and approved by the German princes, might well serve the purpose. According to the plan which he worked out for the king, membership in the projected empire was to be entirely voluntary. The king of Prussia was to be the head, and was to have an absolute veto on legislation enacted by the Parliament. The emperor was to be assisted by a college of six princes, as well as by a two-chamber Parliament: an upper chamber representing the member states, and a lower chamber elected on the three-class system of government just being introduced in Prussia. This German Empire was, however, to be a component part of a larger federation to include the entire Hapsburg Monarchy, under Austrian leadership. The larger federation would be governed by a directory of four, two members of which would be Austrian. It would have control of foreign affairs and trade for the entire federation, comprising all of Central Europe.[57]

This program, submitted to the German governments on May 9, 1849, was politely rejected by Schwarzenberg on May 25, for even though it met his demand of March 7 that the entire Austrian empire

[57] Friedrich Meinecke: *Radowitz und die deutsche Revolution* (Berlin, 1913) provides the basic account, but see also Erich Brandenburg: *Die Reichsgründung* (Leipzig, 1916), I; Erick Marcks: *Der Aufstieg des Reiches* (Stuttgart, 1936), I, 334 ff.; and the excellent, succinct treatment by Egmont Zechlin: *Die deutsche Einheitsbewegung* (Frankfurt, 1967), 157 ff. On the Austrian side, see Heinrich von Srbik: *Deutsche Einheit* (3 ed., Munich, 1940), II; Kiszling: *Fürst Felix zu Schwarzenberg*, 107 ff.

be included in the new Germany, its provision for a well-integrated inner German empire under Prussian leadership was highly objectionable. For the time being, however, the position of Austria, obliged to call on Russia for aid against the Hungarians, was exceedingly weak, while that of Prussia, called upon to suppress the revolutionary movements in South Germany, was strong. The Austrian chancellor was unable, for the moment, to do much more than encourage Bavaria and other important states to resist the Prussian proposals, baiting them with hopes of eventually being allowed to absorb the smaller states and so form a third unit on a par with Austria and Prussia.

Prussia, meanwhile, seemed to make real strides forward. On May 26 Hanover and Saxony agreed to an alliance with Prussia, on condition that Bavaria and Württemberg do likewise. These two states, under Austrian influence, declined, but in all, twenty-eight German states accepted, under varying degrees of dependence on Prussian support and with varying degrees of enthusiasm. In June, 148 members of the Frankfurt Parliament (most of them liberals) convened at Gotha and voted to support the Prussian program, on the theory that the objectives of the Frankfurt Parliament were more important than the exact means by which they were to be attained.

Within a few months, however, storm clouds began to gather. Once the Hungarians had surrendered, Schwarzenberg went over to the offensive. On August 27 he protested that the constitution envisaged by the Prussian program would be incompatible with the treaties of 1815, by which all German states were still bound. The Prussian government, never very much enamored of the schemes of the "outsider" Radowitz, drew back to the extent of accepting the establishment of a provisional federal executive, on which both Austria and Prussia were to have two members, this to continue until May 1, 1850. The agreement on this point meant that Prussia recognized the continued validity of the old Confederation and by implication expressed readiness to abandon what had become known as the "Prussian Union." Nonetheless, the Berlin government went on with its plans for elections to a Parliament that was to meet on March 20, 1850. Schwarzenberg, in turn, threatened in veiled terms that war might result if the Prussian government persisted on this course. The chancellor had by this time adopted the plan worked out by his minister of commerce, Karl Ludwig Bruck, for a vast Middle European customs union which would comprise a population of seventy million and give German industry access to the Mediterranean and the entire lower Danube Basin. This was reminiscent of the program advanced some years earlier by the famous economist, Friedrich List.[58]

For the Austrian chancellor this progressive economic concept provided a useful instrument of power politics, for he proposed that the projected customs union be given extensive jurisdiction under the federal authority at Frankfurt. He also induced Hanover and Saxony to abandon their alliance with Prussia and join with Austria in a new alliance envisaging the absorption of the smaller German states and the reorganization of Central Europe on the triune basis.[59] Much of this was undoubtedly tactical maneuvering and need not be traced in detail. The point is that the Prussian Union was under increasingly frequent and heavy attack. Yet neither Frederick William nor Radowitz would yield. They felt in honor bound to stand by their program, to which twenty-six governments still subscribed, and to protect the smaller states from the victimization that threatened them. They therefore opened the Union Parliament on March 20, 1850. Since the radicals had boycotted the elections, the membership was safely conservative or moderately liberal. It soon accepted the modifications in the draft constitution proposed by the Prussian government, subject to eventual approval also by the member governments. It then adjourned (April 29).

But on the very eve of the Erfurt meeting the federal Diet, inspired by Schwarzenberg, had invited the German states to send delegates to Frankfurt to discuss the resurrection of the old Germanic Confederation. The Prussian government insisted on prior recognition of the Union, but the Middle States stood by Austria. When the delegates assembled at Frankfurt on May 10, only ten out of the thirty-five German states were represented, but they were all the important ones, save Prussia. The two great powers were now deadlocked. Each of them appealed to Czar Nicholas for support. Since the Russian interest was to keep Central Europe only loosely federated and therefore weak,

[58] Franz J. Schoeningh: "Bruck und der grossdeutsche Zollverein" (*Hochland*, XXXI (1), 1933–1934, 325–332), and "Karl Ludwig Bruck und die Idee Mitteleuropas" (*Historisches Jahrbuch*, LVI, 1936); Henry C. Meyer: *Mitteleuropa in German Thought and Action* (The Hague, 1955), 11 ff.; Jacques Droz: *L'Europe centrale: évolution de l'idée de "Mitteleuropa"* (Paris, 1960), chap. ii.

[59] Michael Doberl: *Bayern und das preussische Unionsprojekt* (Munich, 1926).

the czar had no sympathy for the Prussian Union and hardly more for the vast Mitteleuropa scheme. He had been greatly relieved when Frederick William declined the "revolutionary" crown offered him by the Frankfurt Parliament, and was irritated when Radowitz, whom the Russian ambassador in Berlin described as "a charlatan and phrase-maker," advanced a new scheme which borrowed substantially from the Frankfurt constitution. As between the Prussian and the Austrian schemes, the latter was far less advanced and less likely to materialize. Nicholas was therefore disposed to support Vienna and bring pressure on Berlin to abandon the Union.[60]

This was the more so as the Prussian policy in the troublesome Schleswig-Holstein affair continued to estrange not only the Russian but also the British and French governments. Efforts to reconcile German and Danish views during the Malmö armistice having failed, the Danish government had in March, 1849, denounced the armistice. In the ensuing hostilities Prussian and federal troops advanced to the point of invading Jutland (July) when the powers again intervened. Russia, supported by Britain and France, obliged the Prussian government to agree to another armistice, under which matters continued to simmer for another year, until the Berlin government, fearful of losing Russian support in the German question, agreed to the Treaty of Berlin and withdrew its troops entirely from Schleswig (July 2, 1850). The Schleswigers, who refused to join in this abject surrender, kept on fighting, only to be defeated by the Danes at Idstedt (July 25). As for Holstein, which was part of the Germanic Confederation, the Danish king appealed to the revived federal Diet for aid in restoring his control. Thus the fate of the duchies, which so influenced the attitude of the European powers toward Prussia, became a key issue also in the duel between Prussia and Austria.[61]

Matters came to a head in September, 1850, when the electoral prince of

[60] Eduard Heller: *Mitteleuropas Vorkämpfer: Fürst Felix zu Schwarzenberg* (Vienna, 1933), 102 ff.

[61] W. E. Mosse: *The European Powers and the German Question, 1848–1871* (Cambridge, 1958), 28 ff.; W. Carr: *Schleswig-Holstein, 1815–1848* (Manchester, 1963), 294 ff.; Willy Andreas: "Die russische Diplomatie und die Politik Friedrich Wilhelms IV" (*Abhandlungen der Preussischen Akademie der Wissenschaften: Phil.-Hist.* Klasse, 1926, 1–64); Ernst G. Lange: *Frankreichs Preussenpolitik in den Jahren 1849 und 1850* (Berlin, 1930); Günther Gillesen: *Lord Palmerston und die Einigung Deutschlands* (Lübeck, 1961), 77 ff.; Holger Hjelholt: *British Mediation in the Danish-German Conflict, 1848–1850* (Copenhagen, 1965–1966), II, chaps. viii, ix, xiv.

Hesse turned to the federal Diet for aid against his Parliament, which, supported by the people and the army was in revolt against his violation of the constitution. The Prussian government protested against federal action either in Holstein or in Hesse. It denied the competence of the rump federal Diet and furthermore insisted that since Hesse was still a member of the Union its case should be referred to the court of arbitration of that body. The situation was further complicated by the fact that Hesse lay between the two parts of the Prussian Monarchy and that the Prussian government had rights of military transit on two of the main roads. In Berlin the decision was made to occupy Hesse if federal troops were sent in. Schwarzenberg, relying on Russian support against the "revolution" in Hesse, resolved on his part to accept the challenge. On October 12 Austria concluded military agreements with Bavaria and Württemberg by which those states agreed to employ military force in Hesse if the federal Diet so ordered.

At this juncture the Prussian minister-president, Count Brandenburg, hurried off to Warsaw to plead with the czar, only to be followed by Schwarzenberg on the same errand. After long discussions the Prussian minister, long since soured on the Union scheme, agreed to recognize the resurrection of the old Confederation and its enlargement by inclusion of the entire Hapsburg Empire. This was tantamount to abandonment of the Union. In return Schwarzenberg would agree only that the reorganization of Germany should be decided upon by a conference of state ministers. Neither on the Holstein nor the Hesse problem was any progress made.

Meanwhile the federal Diet voted to send a commissioner to Holstein to take charge of affairs and report on the need for intervention. On October 16 it voted to send Bavarian and Hanoverian troops into Hesse. When on November 1 Bavarian forces crossed the frontier, Prussian troops at once occupied the military routes and the territory between them. Radowitz, who had been appointed Prussian minister of foreign affairs, felt that the challenge must be accepted and the federal troops be resisted even at the cost of war. He seems to have hoped that, in a showdown, if Russia supported Austria, Britain and France would stand by Prussia.[62] But the king was unwilling to contemplate a German civil war and the majority of the cabinet was also opposed to a trial of strength which they feared might have a disastrous outcome.

[62] Lange: *Frankreichs Preussenpolitik*.

Radowitz was obliged to resign (November 2) and the Prussian Union was doomed.

As for Holstein and Hesse, Schwarzenberg would not even discuss these issues until the Prussians had evacuated Hesse. This the Berlin government felt would be too great a blow at its prestige. Full mobilization was ordered (November 5). On the following day Count Brandenburg died quite unexpectedly. His successor, Count Otto von Manteuffel, had even less use for the Union and was ready to make whatever settlement was possible. How dangerous the situation had become was revealed by a minor clash between Prussian and federal (Bavarian) troops in Hesse on November 8. So close did war appear that some of the Middle States were already looking forward to an Austrian victory that would end the threat of Prussian domination.[63] Schwarzenberg might quite possibly have welcomed a military decision, but was naturally anxious to avoid further dependence on Russian good will. Furthermore, he had to reckon with the hostility of France and Britain. The French had begun to concentrate large forces on the Rhine and were clearly determined to participate in any readjustment of the balance of power. The British, while they were much irritated by the Prussian policy in the duchies and regarded the Union as a half-baked project which was endangering the peace, were nonetheless unwilling to see Prussia defeated. And finally, in all this welter of conflicting interests, Czar Nicholas was constantly urging a peaceful solution, the reflection of his conviction that war between the two German powers could result only in renewed revolution.[64]

The crisis came to a head when, on November 24, Schwarzenberg sent an ultimatum to Berlin demanding the evacuation of the Hessian fortress of Cassel within forty-eight hours. The Prussian government, hopeless of success and unwilling to invoke French aid, made no resistance. Manteuffel journeyed all the way to Olmütz to confer with the Austrian chancellor, who, after first taking a hard line, showed himself fairly conciliatory, evidently so as to strengthen the conservative elements in the Berlin government. The result of long discussion was the Convention (*Punktation*) of Olmütz (November 29), by which the

[63] Heller: *Mitteleuropas Vorkämpfer,* 125 ff.

[64] Andreas: "Die russische Diplomatie," 42 ff.; Lange: *Frankreichs Preussenpolitik;* Hans Precht: *Englands Stellung zur deutschen Einheit* (Berlin, 1925), 158 ff.; Gillesen: *Lord Palmerston,* 95 ff.

two powers agreed to send commissioners to Holstein as agents of the Germanic Confederation. As for the Hessian issue, Prussia agreed to permit federal forces to cross the military roads and to admit Austrian forces to share in the garrisoning of Cassel. Austria dropped the demand for complete evacuation of Hesse by the Prussians. As for the reorganization of Germany, Prussia was to abandon the Union plan, while Austria agreed that the foreign ministers of all German states should meet immediately at Dresden to study the problem. In a secret protocol Manteuffel agreed that Prussia should demobilize completely before the Dresden meeting, though Austria was obliged to demobilize only partially and the Middle States not at all.[65]

In German histories the Punctation of Olmütz is usually referred to as the "humiliation" of Olmütz. It certainly was humiliating for Prussia to sacrifice the Union and yield on both the Holstein and Hesssian issues. In the Prussian Parliament the vote of approval (January 8, 1851) was exceedingly close (146–142), despite the brilliant, realistic defense of the government's policy by Otto von Bismarck, who was now rising to prominence. The widespread feeling of frustration and defeat was further enhanced by the outcome of the Dresden conferences, which lasted from December 3, 1850, to May 15, 1851. Schwarzenberg again pressed for the inclusion of the entire Hapsburg Monarchy in the revamped Germanic Confederation, while the Prussian delegates insisted on complete equality with Austria in the leadership of the new Germany. Once more agreement proved impossible and there remained no alternative but to return to the arrangements of 1815, that is, to the reconstitution of the Germanic Confederation, with all its faults and weaknesses. "A threadbare, shabby coat is still better than none at all," the Austrian chancellor is reputed to have said.[66]

Thus liberal hopes for the unification of the German states on the basis of popular, constitutional government went up in smoke. As a result of the Dresden conferences Schwarzenberg's program for a great Middle Europe went the way of the Prussian Union. In short, all

---

[65] For an excellent analysis of the convention, see Huber: *Deutsche Verfassungsgeschichte*, II, 919 ff. Joachim Hoffmann: "Russland und die Olmützer Punktation" (*Forschungen zur osteuropäischen Geschichte*, VII, 1959, 59–71) has disposed of the story that it was the intervention of the Russian ambassador to Vienna that induced Schwarzenberg to relent.

[66] Friedrich Engel-Janosi: "Ein Kampf um Oesterreich in Berlin und Frankfurt, 1849–1855" (in his *Geschichte auf dem Ballhausplatz*, Graz, 1963, 65–102).

projects for an integrated national state were wrecked in one way or another. At the root of the failure lay the strong particularism of the German states. Prussia refused to be dissolved in a new Germany, and the Austrians were equally unwilling to have the historic Hapsburg Empire disrupted. The small German states, in turn, were in terror of being devoured by the Middle States. For that reason they were willing to join the Prussian Union, which was exactly what the Middle States refused to contemplate. And to these fundamental obstacles must be added the fact that neither Frederick William of Prussia nor Francis Joseph of Austria would have any truck with revolution or the revolutionary Frankfurt Parliament. Yet the Frankfurt constitution was probably the most practicable and forward-looking of all the projects advanced at that time and the liberal forces that created the Frankfurt Parliament were the forces of the future. If the princes and their governments were obtuse in their refusal to adopt much-needed reforms before 1848, they were even more benighted in their determination to overrule the forces making for a progressive program of national unification. It was fear and hate of popular forces that led the ruling classes to defend the old regime by armed power, which to them still seemed more important than the dictates of reason.

Chapter Fifteen

PHILOSOPHY, RELIGION AND SCIENCE

I. PHILOSOPHY

HEGEL, the last of the great philosophers of the idealist school, died, a victim of the cholera, in November, 1831, just when the period of the present study begins. So comprehensive, closely reasoned and impressive was his philosophical system that it left its mark on almost every field of modern learning and to some extent has continued to influence the world even to the present day. For a couple of decades following the master's death, the Hegelian philosophy dominated the teaching of the German universities and through those great institutions radiated far and wide, especially in the Slavic world. Devoted followers, the "Old Hegelians," expounded and elaborated the doctrine and thereby built up a vast and imposing literature. Almost from the start, however, Hegel's pretensions to finality provoked criticism. In his later years especially, the master seemed to justify the existing social and political as well as the religious order, and to suggest that centuries if not millennia had labored to bring forth the regime of the Restoration period. It was natural to ask why Hegel's fundamental thesis that reality is forever in process of organic development should not apply to the present as well as the past; why existing institutions, like former ones, should not call forth opposing forces that, through evolutionary change, would eventually produce new and better forms. By the mid-1930's there had emerged in Germany the so-called Young (or Neo) Hegelian school, a group of scholars who applied the Hegelian dialectic first to religious and then to political and social problems, making major contributions not so much to the field of pure philosophy as to the broader field of general ideas. The Young Hegelians all prided themselves on bringing philosophy down from the chilly heights of abstraction to the level of concrete reality. It therefore makes sense to discuss them in the context of religious and social thought, where, as in science, the greatest advances were made in this period.

The British at this time were absorbed in the utilitarian teaching of

Bentham and James Mill, which was altogether congenial to a society dominated by material problems. The French, on the other hand, outshone other nations in the volume and variety of their social thought. But in the field of pure philosophy the French Eclectic School, which was almost officially accepted during the July Monarchy, was at best second-rate. Its recognized head was Victor Cousin, who had studied in Germany and was fully conversant with the idealist philosophy. He was a great scholar, as shown by his editions of Descartes' works and his translation of Plato, as well as an eloquent lecturer and influential educator. But as a philosopher he leaned heavily on others: his aim was to lift from any and all systems what was "true," and to fit the assembled "truths" into a system based on reason and observation. Like Hegel and many other thinkers of the period, he devised a philosophy of history, based on the notion of constant progress by which humanity advanced through various stages before reaching its culmination in European Christianity. However, Cousin's orientation was at least as much political as philosophical. He groped for a doctrine that would be non-Catholic but not atheistic, liberal but not radical. He was, in short, the man of the middle way, perfectly fitted to be the intellectual dictator of the July Monarchy.[1]

The Positivist School of Auguste Comte was equally characteristic of the period, but of more lasting importance. Comte, educated at the École Polytechnique, began his career as secretary and collaborator of Saint-Simon. He was no doubt influenced by that extraordinary thinker, but at the same time seems to have contributed to the Saint-Simonian doctrine many ideas that were original with him. Striking out on his own even before Saint-Simon's death, he attempted to construct a vast philosophical system comparable to the Hegelian. Philosophy, he believed, should focus on the moral and political improvement of mankind. For abstract, metaphysical speculation he had no use whatever. Convinced that the laws of society could be determined by direct observation, by experiment and by the study of history, he attempted a strictly "scientific" approach. His *Course of Positive*

---

[1] His chief philosophical works were *Fragmens philosophiques* (1826), and *Du vrai, du beau et du bien* (1836). See Jules Simon: *Victor Cousin* (5 ed., Paris, 1921); George Boas: *French Philosophies of the Romantic Period* (Baltimore, 1925), 197 ff.; D. G. Charlton: *Secular Religions in France, 1815–1870* (London, 1963), 96 ff. and chap. vii.

Philosophy (six volumes, published between 1830 and 1848) was a detailed and complex synthesis of many diverse ideas and doctrines, based on a philosophy of history. Comte envisaged the development of human knowledge through three stages—the theological, the metaphysical, and the scientific. All discipline, he held, passed through the same stages, though not concurrently. The result was a hierarchy of sciences (mathematics, astronomy, physics, chemistry, biology) culminating in sociology (a word he himself coined), which was just entering its final, scientific phase under Comte's direction. Positivism was to be the philosophy of the sciences. Through it society was to be reorganized and humanity regenerated.[2]

Comte was as unstable emotionally as he was brilliant intellectually. Following a violent love affair in the mid-forties, he became deeply religious and, like other Saint-Simonians, felt impelled to found a new religion of humanity, complete with a leader (himself), a priesthood, sacraments and prayers, as expounded in his four-volume *System of Positivist Politics, or Treatise of Sociology Introducing the Religion of Humanity* (1851–1854). John Stuart Mill, an early admirer of Comte, spoke of this second phase of positivism as the "melancholy decadence of a great intellect." It belongs to the history of the later nineteenth century when, in fact, Comte's earlier doctrines, too, had their greatest impact. He and his followers were only on the fringe of the July Monarchy. They advocated a new society but were opposed to revolution. Comte was hostile to the workers in 1848 and was an early supporter of Louis Napoleon. It follows then that socialists and communists have been hard on him and his teaching. According to Lenin, positivism is "a deplorable mess." Communist historians see in it only "the scientific philosophy of the dominant bourgeoisie."[3]

The Germans, who had already produced such intellectual giants as

---

[2] Henri Gouhier: *La vie d'Auguste Comte* (Paris, 1931); F. S. Marvin: *Comte, the Founder of Sociology* (London, 1936). On the origins of his ideas, see Boas: *French Philosophies,* 254 ff.; Henri Gouhier: *La jeunesse d'Auguste Comte et la formation du positivisme* (Paris, 1933–1941); Frank E. Manuel: *The Prophets of Paris* (Cambridge, 1962), 251 ff. For analyses of his doctrine, see H. B. Acton: "Comte's Positivism and the Science of Society" (*Philosophy,* XXVI, 1951, 291–310); Henri Gouhier: "La philosophie d'histoire d'Auguste Comte" (*Journal of World History,* II, 1955, 503–519); W. M. Simon: *European Positivism in the Nineteenth Century* (Ithaca, 1963), 4 ff.

[3] M. A. Dynnik and others: *Geschichte der Philosophie* (Berlin, 1961), II, 182 ff. The later history of positivism is dealt with in detail by Charlton: *Secular Religions in France,* 87 ff., and especially by Simon: *European Positivism, passim.*

Kant, Herder, Fichte and Hegel, continued to be pre-eminent in the field of philosophy and, in the person of Arthur Schopenhauer, went beyond the wrangle over Hegelian doctrine. Schopenhauer's basic work, *The World as Will and Idea,* was written in his late twenties and first published in 1818. But at that time the scholarly world was so engrossed in Hegelianism that it had no use for the thoughts of a young writer who, at the University of Berlin, was so presumptuous as to schedule his lectures at the same hour as the master's. Little attention was paid to Schopenhauer's book, despite the brilliance of its style, and in 1835 the publisher sold the remainder of the 800 copies as waste paper. When, in 1844, the author had completed a second volume, the publisher reluctantly agreed to a new edition, again of only 800 copies, and again he had to report a few years later that the book had done poorly. In 1850 he and several other publishers refused Schopenhauer's essays (*Parerga and Paralipomena*), which were at long last to make his reputation. Small wonder that the author withdrew from academic life at an early age and spent more than thirty years in embittered isolation. Life to him appeared completely pointless and man's constant reproduction of his kind an absurd comedy.

Schopenhauer's pet aversion was Hegel and the Hegelian philosophy, a "senseless and extravagant maze of words" and "the most barefaced general mystification that has ever taken place." His great objective was to bring philosophy down to the facts of real life and to demonstrate that the will, not the intellect, governs the actions of men. The will, as he saw it, is an imperious, vital driving force, sometimes conscious, often unconscious, aiming always at the satisfaction of recognized or unrecognized desires. Since the realization of one desire leads invariably to another, the end result of all this striving is suffering, for happiness is only occasional relief from pain. Basically life is strife and conflict, "a business which does not cover expenses."

Schopenhauer's ideas were brilliantly expounded in his principal work and in his essays. They were to make a great impression on Wagner, Nietzsche and other opponents of rationalism, and they clearly foreshadowed the theories of Freud. Schopenhauer was above all "modern" in his preoccupation with human psychology and the hidden drives of human nature. In the late nineteenth century, after many of the hopes of the earlier period had been blasted, he was to come into his own. His work was substantially complete by the midcentury; its impact was to come only later.[4]

Philosophy has been traditionally concerned with fundamental problems of religion, and it is therefore difficult to decide to which discipline certain eminent thinkers should be assigned. Ludwig Feuerbach, whose book, *The Essence of Christianity* (1841), was to make him the most widely read philosopher in the immediate post-Hegelian period, started as a critic of accepted religious ideas and proved in the long term to be highly influential in the formation of Marxist thought as well as of twentieth-century existentialism. In reaction to flights of philosophical idealism, he dealt with reality and made man the measure of all things. "We will not find happiness on earth," he asserted, "until we put man in the place of God, and reason in the place of faith." Christianity as he saw it was merely an *idée fixe,* "in flagrant contradiction with our fire and life insurance companies, our railroads and steam engines, our picture and sculpture galleries, our military and industrial schools, our theaters and scientific museums." Religion he would study only "in terms of the known manifestations of human nature." Such study revealed to him that religion is really nothing but the objectification of man's basic, essential needs. God is the reflection of human thoughts and aspirations. Once it is understood that God is a name for man's own idealized essence projected into a transcendent sphere, man will overcome the self-alienation involved in religion, will recover faith in himself and in his future. Thus Feuerbach's materialist philosophy led to renewed stress on the need for freeing mankind from the trammels man had imposed upon himself and to restore to him dignity and confidence. This teaching obviously fitted well with socialist doctrine. It had a profound influence on the development of Marxist thought and on the emergence of realism in literature and art. In the period just prior to 1848, Feuerbach was indeed the intellectual hero of the hour.[5]

[4] Arthur Hübscher: *Arthur Schopenhauer* (Leipzig, 1938), 95; Hans W. Wolff: *Arthur Schopenhauer, Hundert Jahre später* (Bonn, 1960), 99; and the eloquent appreciation by Thomas Mann: *Schopenhauer* (Stockholm, 1938).

[5] Feuerbach himself wrote an interesting statement of his position in the introduction to the second edition of his book. See further, Johann Fischl: *Geschichte der Philosophie* (Vienna, 1953), IV, 18 ff.; Frederick Copleston: *A History of Philosophy* (Westminster, 1963), VII, 293 ff.; Dynnik: *Geschichte der Philosophie,* II; Karl Barth: *Protestant Thought from Rousseau to Ritschl* (New York, 1959), chap. ix; and especially Karl Löwith: *From Hegel to Nietzsche* (New York, 1964), 343 ff.

While Feuerbach preferred reality to abstractions and stressed the human as against the divine, Max Stirner went to the very limits of individualism. In his book *The Individual and His Individuality* (1845), he rejected Feuerbach's generalized man and concentrated on the unique personality of the individual. In the urge to assert his identity the individual must not allow himself to be checked by any higher power, such as God or the state, or by abstractions, such as humanity and natural law. Stirner's thought was really too logical, too extreme, to have wide or profound influence.

On the other hand the numerous writings of the Danish thinker, Søren Kierkegaard, most of which belong to the 1840's, were eventually to have a significant, worldwide impact. Kierkegaard was a neurotic, perplexing personality, a man deeply read in the German philosophy who, like the Young Hegelians, became an enemy of philosophical systems and of institutionalized religion. To him the clergy was little more than "a guild which had gotten control of the firm of Jesus Christ and had done a big business." Basically a moralist, he became, like Feuerbach and Marx, a relentless critic of modern society and its threat to the individual. He dreaded the leveling effect of egalitarian doctrines such as majority rule, and never tired of preaching the need for the individual to cultivate personal integrity, to commit himself, to assume responsibility for decisions freely made, and so eventually to attain a personal religious faith expressing itself in action.

Kierkegaard made but a slight impression on his own time and his own people, who thought of him chiefly as another antagonist of the Established Church. Outside Denmark he was all but unknown until in the 1870's the Danish critic George Brandes called attention to his work. Even so, it was only after the First World War that many of his works were translated into other languages and began to contribute to the formulation of existentialist teaching.[6]

---

[6] Since 1920 the literature in English alone has reached vast proportions. There is a useful anthology with annotations by Robert Bretall: *A Kierkegaard Anthology* (Princeton, 1946), and good biographies by Walter Lowrie (London, 1938) and Johannes Hohlenberg (London, 1954). Of recent analytical studies may be mentioned H. V. Martin: *Kierkegaard, the Melancholy Dane* (London, 1950); James D. Collins; *The Mind of Kierkegaard* (Chicago, 1953); Edward J. Carnell: *The Burden of Søren Kierkegaard* (London, 1965). Among German works the essay by Walter Nigg, in his *Prophetische Denker* (Zürich, 1957), and the account in Arthur Hübscher: *Von Hegel zu Heidegger* (Stuttgart, 1961) are valuable.

2. RELIGION

Karl Marx was by no means the first or only critic to describe religion as the opiate of the people. In the midcentury the churches everywhere in Europe were under state control and religion was thought of as an important factor in upholding the political and social structure, that is, in fortifying the resistance to innovation or reform. The Roman Catholic Church during the pontificate of Gregory XVI (1831–1846) may be taken as the perfect example of unyielding opposition to new ideas or demands. The pope was a man of aristocratic background, more interested in theology than in politics, but in all things given to strong convictions and even firmer resolve. Having ascended the papal chair at a time when the States of the Church were in open revolt, he determined to suppress liberalism at all costs and so took his stand by the Holy Alliance. Even the Catholic powers urged upon him the need for some measure of lay government, but Gregory interested himself only in reform of the papal (clerical) government, the regulation of old and the foundation of new religious orders, and particularly the furtherance of foreign missions. For him liberalism was synonymous with freemasonry and secret societies, and these with revolution. Not even the struggle of the Catholic Poles against the heretical Russian government would induce him to compromise with his principles. Following the suppression of the Polish insurrection, he urged upon the Polish hierarchy submission to the powers ordained by God.[7]

The pope's conservatism did not necessarily gain him recognition of papal authority or claims. The Russian government continued, despite his pleas, to persecute the Catholic Church in Lithuania and Poland, and even the Austrian government refused to surrender control over the clergy and Church. Many of the German states, which had acquired former ecclesiastical territories in the Napoleonic period, were jealous of outside influence and at times made things quite uncomfort-

---

[7] Josef Schmidlin: *Papstgeschichte der neuesten Zeit* (2 ed., Munich, 1933), I, Book III; Charles H. Pouthas: *L'église catholique de l'avènement de Pie VII à l'avènement de Pie IX* (Paris, 1945), 273 ff.; Jean Leflon: *Histoire de l'Eglise: la crise révolutionnaire, 1789–1846* (Paris, 1951), 431 ff.; Kenneth S. Latourette: *Christianity in a Revolutionary Age* (New York, 1958), I, chaps. vii and viii; E. E. Y. Hales: *Revolution and Papacy, 1769–1846* (London, 1960), chap. xviii; Henri Daniel-Rops: *The Church in an Age of Revolution, 1789–1870* (New York, 1965), 186 ff.

able for the Catholic hierarchy. In Prussia serious tension developed over the issue of mixed marriages or, more accurately, over the question whether the Catholic clergy should follow the instructions of the Vatican and require the parties to a mixed marriage to commit themselves to the education of their future children in the Catholic faith. The Prussian government had in 1825 decreed that in the newly acquired Catholic Rhineland the children of mixed marriages should be brought up in the faith of the father, and had obliged the archbishop of Cologne to comply. But in 1837 the new archbishop, Klemens von Droste-Vischering, insisted on adherence to the papal directive. The government arrested and imprisoned him, despite great popular excitement and vigorous protests by the pope and even some foreign governments. Only after the accession of the more conciliatory Frederick William IV in 1840 was the archbishop released and the papal instruction accepted by the government.[8]

The victory of the Papacy in the duel with the Prussian government contributed substantially to the growth of ultramontanism, which had been revived by the writings of Joseph de Maistre and Abbé Lamennais and was strongly supported by the Jesuit Order. Another factor working for papal authority was the attitude of the July Monarchy in France, which, far from upholding the traditions of Gallicanism, displayed indifference in religious matters and so almost forced the Catholic clergy to look to Rome for guidance. In any event the prestige and authority of the Vatican had reached new heights by 1846, which in part explains the storm of enthusiasm that greeted the supposed liberalism of Pius IX.[9]

The Protestant churches were nowhere in a position to challenge the control of the governments. On the contrary there were many German theorists who preached the divine right of the ruler and defended the alliance between throne and altar. In Prussia E. W. Hengstenberg and his *Evangelical Church News* denounced the French Revolution as the work of Satan and vigorously opposed all forms of liberalism. In the

8 Franz Schnabel: *Deutsche Geschichte im 19 Jahrhundert* (Freiburg, 1937), IV, 106 ff.; Jacques Droz: *Le libéralisme rhénan* (Paris, 1940), 80 ff.; Wilhelm Neuss: *Die Kirche der Neuzeit* (Bonn, 1954), 450 ff.; Hajo Holborn: *A History of Modern Germany* (New York, 1964), II, 505 ff.

9 John M. S. Allison: *Church and State in the Reign of Louis Philippe* (Princeton, 1916); Charles S. Phillips: *The Church in France, 1789-1848* (London, 1929); Adrien Dansette: *Religious History of Modern France* (New York, 1962), I.

1840's the eminent theorist Friedrich J. Stahl advanced a comprehensive doctrine of the Christian state. With such support the Prussian king could impose upon his Protestant subjects a union of the Lutheran and Reformed (Calvinist) churches and press for the eventual union of all Protestant sects in one United Evangelical Church. Here was a classic example of the undisputed control of the government in religious affairs.[10]

The case of the Established (Anglican) Church in England is particularly instructive because the great political and social changes of the period were reflected in significant modifications of the relations between church and state. The English church was a state church, without corporate organization of its own, and wholly under the control of Parliament, even in matters of liturgy. In social terms it was, in 1832, still closely knit with the system of aristocratic privilege. The higher clergy, and even some of the country parsons, were often younger sons of the nobility, appointed according to political considerations: "Soundness of Tory views was a better passport to general acceptability than pastoral zeal or theological orthodoxy."[11] The upper, landed classes that controlled the government controlled the church also. The atmosphere was one of passive conservatism, of "complacent worldliness."[12]

In 1833 there was published, anonymously, an *Extraordinary Black Book* which revealed the huge wealth of many bishoprics and cathedral chapters that had at their disposal numerous livings and benefices. Corporations and private individuals possessed other livings, which they assigned without reference to professional qualification. In almost half the livings the vicar was a nonresident, his duties being discharged by a curate with an annual income of one hundred pounds or less, which might well leave him and his family on the very verge of destitution, like the Reverend Josiah Crawley in Trollope's novel.[13]

[10] Georges Goyau: *L'Allemagne religieuse: le Protestantisme* (Paris, 1911); André L. Drummond: *German Protestantism since Luther* (London, 1951).

[11] C. K. Francis Brown: *A History of the English Clergy, 1800–1900* (London, 1953), 125 ff.

[12] Spencer C. Carpenter: *Church and People, 1789–1889* (London, 1933), 50.

[13] Anthony Trollope: *Last Chronicle of Barset*. See also William L. Mathieson: *English Church Reform, 1815–1840* (London, 1923), 22 ff.; John R. Moorman: *A History of the Church in England* (London, 1953), 332 ff.; Owen Chadwick: *The Victorian Church* (New York, 1966), I, 34 ff.; Brown: *History of the English Clergy*, 15 ff.

The *Black Book* appeared at the very time when English bishops were in the forefront of opposition to the Reform Bill. Its "tale of cynical rapacity" quickly sold 50,000 copies and contributed to the outbreak of violent anticlericalism which impelled the government to attack the problems of church administration. The changing membership of Parliament, since 1829 no longer restricted to communicants of the Established Church, meant a greater readiness to attack the abuses of privilege. Following the report of a royal commission, Parliament in the years 1836–1840 enacted a series of laws equalizing the income of bishoprics, creating new sees (e.g., Manchester), forbidding the holding by one person of more than two livings at the same time, abolishing nonresident prebends and sinecure rectories, and commuting the tithes. A permanent Ecclesiastical Commission was set up to supervise the affairs of the church.[14]

Criticism of the Established Church came largely from Evangelicals and Dissenters—Methodists, Congregationalists, Unitarians, and so on—many of whom were influenced by the pietism of the eighteenth century and sought a more vital, more personal religion. While many intellectuals had turned agnostic or even atheist under the influence of rationalism and utilitarianism (e.g., Bentham, J. S. Mill, Grote, George Eliot), religious devotion led to the foundation of Bible societies and missions, which were busy extending their activities from the homeland to even remote parts of the world. Some of the best minds, indeed, were entering the ministry (e.g., Keble, Milman, Thomas Arnold, Newman, Maurice) and re-examining the entire problem of the place of religion in the modern world. All hoped to breathe new life into religion and revitalize the church. Thus several bishops (Blomfield of London, Stanley of Norwich, Wilberforce of Oxford and Winchester) were active members of the Ecclesiastical Commission and convinced advocates of church reform.[15]

The efforts of the government to reform and modernize the Estab-

[14] Mathieson: *English Church Reform*, 43 ff.; Olive J. Brose: *Church and Parliament: the Reshaping of the Church of England, 1828–1860* (Stanford, 1959), especially chap. v; Chadwick: *Victorian Church*, I, chap. ii.

[15] Alfred W. Benn: *The History of English Rationalism in the Nineteenth Century* (New York, 1906), I, 295; Ernest E. Kellett: *Religion and Life in the Early Victorian Age* (London, 1938), 22 ff.; George Kitson Clark: *The English Inheritance* (London, 1950), chaps. v–viii; Kathleen Heasman: *Evangelicals in Action* (London, 1962), 17 ff.; Anthony O. J. Cockshut: *The Unbelievers: English Agnostic Thought, 1840–1890* (London, 1964), 10.

lished Church called forth in England the interesting movement known as the Oxford or Tractarian movement, of which John Keble, Edward Pusey and John Henry Newman were the outstanding figures. The leaders were young Oxford dons, ordained Anglican clergymen, inspired by Romanticism and Evangelicalism. The reform measures of the 1830's roused them to oppose the interference of Parliament in the affairs of the church. Thus it was the decision of the government in 1833 to reduce the number of Irish bishops from eighteen to ten and assign part of the immense wealth of the Irish Church to other purposes that led to the publication of the first of the *Tracts for the Times*. In less than a decade, ninety of these tracts, varying greatly in subject matter and length, were published, most of them from the pen of Newman. They reflected an ardent emotional reaction not only against secular influence in church affairs but against the rationalism of the eighteenth century and the utilitarianism of the nineteenth. The Tractarians were at war against the materialism of their time, and strove to recover the piety and spirituality of primitive, apostolic Christianity. They rejected liberalism, industrialism and science and were quite indifferent to the so-called social problem deriving from the Industrial Revolution.[16]

The *Tracts* explored many aspects of dogma and liturgy, but their main thrust was directed against the notion of the church as a human institution. The church, they argued, is a spiritual entity of divine origin, independent of the state, and with an episcopal authority of its own transmitted from the earliest times through apostolic succession. The true church is the ancient Catholic Church purged of corruption and liberated from the usurped power of the bishop of Rome. The church alone has the right to define its beliefs and establish its jurisdiction. Continued study and reflection led Newman further and further in the direction of the Roman Catholic Church until in the last (ninetieth) *Tract* (1841) he argued that the thirty-nine articles of the

---

[16] The classic account is R. W. Church's *The Oxford Movement* (3 ed., London, 1891), which may be supplemented by the excellent brief treatment by Sidney L. Ollard: *A Short History of the Oxford Movement* (3 ed., London, 1963). One of the best analyses is Yngve Bilioth: *The Anglican Revival* (London, 1925), especially chap. v. See also Hoxie N. Fairchild: "Romanticism and the Religious Revival in England" (*Journal of the History of Ideas*, II, 1941, 330–338); Charles F. Harrold: "The Oxford Movement: a Reconsideration" (in Joseph E. Baker, ed.: *The Reinterpretation of Victorian Literature*, Princeton, 1950, 33–56).

Anglican Church were not incompatible with Roman dogma. Charged with heresy, he went into retirement and in 1845 became converted to Roman Catholicism, eventually to be elevated to the cardinalate.[17]

The Oxford movement had only a limited influence in its day, yet has continued to fascinate the Christian world. It has been severely criticized as being completely out of tune with the early railroad age, as being the expression of a few young men in perplexity who had too much time on their hands, too few problems of real life and too much proselytizing zeal. No doubt there is something to be said for the view that the movement would have evoked little interest except for the sincerity and eloquence of Newman, reflected in a remarkably clear and brilliant style. It has been well said of him that he and his movement continue to interest others because he was so deeply interested in himself and so honestly recounted his struggle to attain true Christian piety.[18]

The Oxford movement had some impact in Germany and Scandinavia, but on the Continent the revival of religious interest among Protestants took the form chiefly of renewed pietism, spreading even to high society. Thus in Pomerania Adolf von Thadden organized a pietist group among the Junkers which was made memorable by Bismarck's association with it. Frederick William IV of Prussia and his immediate friends were also interested in it. The king, in fact, was impressed by the Oxford movement and dreamed of reorganizing the Prussian Church along episcopal lines, of eventually uniting the Prussian and Anglican churches, and even of ultimate reunion with the Roman Catholic Church. But these vague notions of ecumenism touched only a few people. They are worth mentioning only as illustrating the radiation of ideas from country to country.[19]

[17] Among recent biographical studies may be mentioned Charles F. Harrold: *John Henry Newman* (New York, 1945); R. D. Middleton: *Newman at Oxford* (New York, 1950); Meriol Trevor: *Newman: the Pillar and the Cloud* (London, 1962). Convenient selections from the *Tracts* may be found in Owen Chadwick, ed.: *The Mind of the Oxford Movement* (London, 1960); Eugene R. Fairweather, ed.: *The Oxford Movement* (New York, 1964).

[18] See the severe criticism of Bishop Edmund A. Knox: *The Tractarian Movement, 1833–1845* (London, 1933); Sir Llewellyn Woodward: *The Age of Reform, 1815–1870* (2 ed., Oxford, 1962), 512 ff.; Ronald Pearsall: "The Oxford Movement in Retrospect" (*Quarterly Review,* January, 1966, 75–83).

[19] Schnabel: *Deutsche Geschichte,* IV, 383 ff., 529 ff.; Latourette: *Christianity in a Revolutionary Age,* II, chap. v; Erich Marcks: *Bismarcks Jugend* (Stuttgart, 1909), 244 ff.; Otto Pflanze: *Bismarck and the Development of Germany* (Princeton, 1963), I, 54 ff.

In the Catholic countries the reaction to state control of the church and the stagnation of religious life took the form of Liberal Catholicism, which was initially closely related to the July Revolution in France. It was in October, 1830, that the Abbé Lamennais and some of his friends founded the newspaper *The Future* (*L'avenir*) which, during the thirteen months of its existence, became the mouthpiece for advanced ideas in the entire realm of modern culture. Lamennais, whose reputation had been made as an exponent of papal power and ultramontanism, had convinced himself that the future of nations rested with the peoples and not with the princes; that democracy and nationalism were the keynotes of the new age. To ensure the sound development of the new democratic society, he regarded the leadership of the Catholic Church as essential. But to be effective the church must be freed of dependence on princes and governments. His program therefore called for separation of church and state and the alliance of the church with the forces of liberalism and democracy. Following the example of Daniel O'Connell in the campaign for emancipation of the Catholics in Britain, Lamennais and his followers attempted to organize Catholics not only throughout France but throughout Europe. In France he secured the support of men such as Lamartine, Hugo and Saint-Beuve, while in Belgium and even in Bavaria the ideas of Liberal Catholicism evoked much interest.[20]

The opposition of the French hierarchy to Lamennais' religious and political radicalism was to be anticipated. Neither could the liberals of the July Monarchy be expected to subscribe to the doctrine that God was fashioning a new society, "the final era of humanity," through revolution and popular sovereignty. Even foreign governments were disturbed and brought pressure on the pope to condemn such subversive teaching. Lamennais, for his part, was convinced that the so-called *Avenir* movement was entirely orthodox and unobjectionable on religious grounds, while its political platform was beyond the authority of the pope. In the spring of 1831 he and his friends, Count Charles de Montalembert and Abbé Henri Lacordaire, set out for Rome as "pilgrims of God and Liberty." It was the time of the insurrections against papal rule in the Romagna and the new pope, Gregory XVI, was in

---

[20] André Latreille *et al.: Histoire du catholicisme en France* (Paris, 1962), III, 282 ff.; Louis Le Guillon: *L'évolution de la pensée religieuse de Félicité Lamennais* (Paris, 1966); Peter N. Stearns: *Priest and Revolutionary: Lamennais and the Dilemma of French Catholicism* (New York, 1967), chaps. iv and v.

no mood to be instructed in revolutionary doctrine. Bombarded by warnings from Metternich, he temporized and when finally he did receive Lamennais it was only for a short courtesy visit. The pilgrims were obliged to leave Rome without having had a chance to expound their views. Presently their failure was underlined by a papal encyclical, *Mirari vos* (1832), which, without naming Lamennais specifically, denounced everything for which he stood: separation of church and state, freedom of conscience, liberty of the press, in fact all truck with "liberal revolutionaries" and all rebellion against "our dearest sons in Jesus Christ, the princes." Lamennais at first submitted, but by the publication of his famous *Words of a Believer* (1834) he provoked the pope to condemn his teachings as heretical, execrable, absurd and perverse (encyclical *Singulari vos,* 1834). Lamennais left the priesthood, but continued his agitation for democracy and a new social order. This later phase of his career belongs to the history of social thought and has been treated in Chapter VII, above.[21]

Despite the pope's denunciation Liberal Catholicism, reflecting the new forces in society, continued to grow and spread. In France its principles inspired the preaching of Lacordaire and the agitation of Montalembert for freedom of instruction, that is, for the freedom of Catholic schools from state interference. They were reflected also in the teachings of Christian socialists such as Buchez and Leroux. In Italy they informed the efforts of Abbé Rosmini, Abbé Ventura and Abbé Gioberti to modernize the church and redefine its place in society. In Germany two different movements, though not directly influenced by French developments, were of the same type: the Protestant Friends (*Lichtfreunde*), an association founded in 1841 in reaction to government control of the church and for the purpose of advocating democratization of religion so as to accord with the demands of the modern world; and the German Catholic movement (1844), which rejected papal dictation and adopted freedom of conscience even to the extent of entertaining radical, socialist ideas.[22]

[21] On Lamennais and the papacy, see Schmidlin: *Papstgeschichte,* I, 556 ff.; R. Vidler: *Prophecy and Papacy* (London, 1954); Hales: *Revolution and Papacy,* 290 ff.; Stearns: *Priest and Revolutionary,* chap. vi.

[22] Michael Fogarty: *Christian Democracy in Western Europe, 1820–1953* (South Bend, 1958); Maurice Vaussard: *Histoire de la démocratie chrétienne* (Paris, 1956), I, 26 ff., 133 ff., 201 ff.; II, 15 ff.; Walter Nigg: *Geschichte des religiösen Liberalismus* (Zürich, 1937), 176 ff., 188 ff.; D. C. Charlton: *Secular Religions in France* (New York,

Interesting though they be as efforts toward modernizing religion and the churches, these movements touched only very few people. The upper classes and particularly the intellectuals were for the most part agnostics or atheists. In France the church was looked upon as the staunch ally of the old regime and the July Revolution brought on a wave of violent anticlericalism. The sacking of the Abbey of Saint-Germain l'Auxerrois in February, 1831, was followed by lesser outrages in various parts of France as the triumphant liberals harried the priests and pillaged church property. Louis Philippe was himself a freemason who made no effort to conceal his disdain for religion. In the *lycées* and colleges the professors proclaimed their contempt for the church as intolerant, corrupt and reactionary. They positively went out of their way to shake the faith of their pupils. It is said that at the highest school, the Ecole Polytechnique, there were not more than a dozen practicing Catholics among the two hundred students. The great historian, Michelet, lecturing at the Collège de France, declared publicly that Christianity was the religion of slaves and that it had, through the ages, served the purposes only of the masters. Proudhon proclaimed that God is tyranny and misery, God is evil. Small wonder that an English cleric, visiting France in 1845, should have noted with dismay that "infidelity not only stalks openly through the land, but bears open sway in it."[23]

The religious disillusionment of the educated classes was due in part to the critical writing which at this time poured from the numerous German universities, where eighteenth-century rationalism and the romantic, noninstitutional Christianity of Friedrich Schleiermacher had already done much to undermine the traditional faith. In the mid-nineteenth century the theological and philosophical faculties were producing literally hundreds of scholarly studies of the Bible and the history of Christianity. For the most part these writings were not

---

1963), 82 ff.; Henri Haag: *Les origines du catholicisme libéral en Belgique, 1789–1839* (Louvain, 1950).

[23] Thomas W. Allies: *Journal in France in 1845 and 1848* (London, 1849), 5 ff., 239. The testimony of Lacordaire and Montalembert as to their schooldays is in Waldemar Gurian: *Die politischen Ideen des französischen Katholizismus, 1789–1914* (München-Gladbach, 1929), 84. See also Mgr. J. Lestocquoy: *La vie religieuse en France du VIIe au XXe siècle* (Paris, 1964), 282, 292, 299; Christiane Marcilhacy: "L'anticléricalisme dans l'Orléanais pendant le première moitié du XIXe siècle" (*Archives de sociologie des religions, No. 6, 1958, 91–103*); Louis Trenard "Aux origines de la déchristianisation: la diocèse de Cambrai de 1830 à 1848" (*Revue du Nord*, XLVII, 1965, 399–459).

polemical, but the impact or implications of some of them were devastating.

Liberal theology is generally dated from the appearance in 1835 of David Friedrich Strauss's two-volume *Life of Jesus,* a book which Albert Schweitzer once described as "one of the most perfect works of scholarly literature." Strauss, at that time a young instructor at the University of Tübingen, applied his great erudition and keen critical sense to an objective and dispassionate examination of the Gospels as a body of historical evidence. After meticulous analysis he came to the conclusion that the Gospel narratives will not qualify as a historical record; that they were in fact merely imaginative stories reflecting the myths of the Jews in the time of Augustus. The life of Jesus, then, was simply the expression of the age-old messianic myth, and Christianity less the creation of Jesus than a product of the popular spirit of that period.[24]

Strauss' masterpiece, of which four editions appeared in five years, was followed in 1840 by his *The Christian Religion,* in which he analyzed the principal Christian dogmas and drained many of them of authority. His writings naturally evoked a storm of criticism and denunciation, and presently led to his academic ostracism. On all sides it was recognized that his books were a blow at the very foundations of European culture, threatening to destroy the faith from which mankind had over the centuries derived its consolation. On the other hand, Strauss' work stimulated further investigations. Ferdinand C. Baur, Strauss' teacher and a theologian of the first rank, published studies of *The Apostle Paul* (1845) and the *Canonical Gospels* (1847) in which again he demonstrated that Christianity was the product of various forces and drew sharp distinctions between early Christianity and the later Catholic Church. Meanwhile Bruno Bauer, one of the keenest minds among the Young Hegelians, between 1840 and 1850 published a series of studies of the authorship of the various Gospels which led him to deny the divinity as well as the historicity of Jesus. Having turned

---

[24] Albert Schweitzer: *The Quest of the Historical Jesus* (London, 1954), chap. vii ff.; Karl Barth: *Protestant Thought from Rousseau to Ritschl* (New York, 1959), chap. x; Heinrich Hermelink: *Das Christentum in der Menschengeschichte* (Stuttgart, 1953), II, 3 ff.; Emanuel Hirsch: *Geschichte der neueren evangelischen Theologie* (Gütersloh, 1954), V, chap. liv; Nigg: *Geschichte des religiösen Liberalismus,* 157 ff.; Adolf Rapp: "David Friedrich Strauss: seine Lebensleitung und sein Schicksal" (*Die Welt als Geschichte,* XVII, 1957, 213–220).

atheist, Bauer denounced Christianity as a religion of slaves and a misfortune for the human race.[25]

Feuerbach's highly influential book *The Essence of Christianity* (1841) belongs in this context, though more a philosophical inquiry as to the nature of religion than a critical analysis of texts. Its effect was bound to be the destruction of all religious faith, what the papal nuncio described as "the entire prostration of religious sentiment," so that "atheism was openly avowed and Christianity ridiculed as the invention of priestcraft."[26]

Though Strauss' books had but little impact in France, they aroused violent protest in England, where Henry H. Milman's *History of the Jews* (1829) had already begun the deflation of the Old Testament narratives. The *Life of Jesus* was translated by George Eliot in 1846 and produced a severe shock which is well reflected in the writings of Francis Newman, the brother of John Henry. He expressed himself as irked by Jesus' "enigmatic and pretentious style of teaching," and refused to accept his claims to religious authority. In a scholarly *History of the Hebrew Monarchy* Newman stripped the Old Testament narratives of their supernatural elements and interpreted the story of the Jews strictly in terms of historical evidence. In much the same temper the historian Anthony Froude, wholly under the influence of Strauss, published a novel, *The Nemesis of Faith* (1849), whose hero was tortured by doubts as to the truth of the Bible story and weighed down by feelings of guilt.[27]

The lower, less educated classes were, of course, not touched by the researches of the intellectuals. They remained benighted and neglected so far as religion was concerned. No doubt there were among the lower middle class, the small landowners and especially the shopkeepers and artisans, many who were God-fearing and devout, as may be inferred from the novelists of the period and from the increase of membership in the nonconformist sects. But among the peasants and city workers

---

[25] Schweitzer: *Quest of the Historical Jesus,* chap. xi; Nigg: *Geschichte des religiösen Liberalismus,* 166 ff.; Karl Löwith: *From Hegel to Nietzsche* (New York, 1964), 343 ff.

[26] Schmidlin: *Papstgeschichte,* I, 256–257; C. H. Cotterill: *Religious Movements of Germany* (London, 1849), quoted in J. M. Robertson: *A History of Free Thought in the Nineteenth Century* (New York, 1930), 44; Schnabel: *Deutsche Geschichte,* IV, 570 ff.

[27] Benn: *History of English Rationalism,* I, 318 ff., 381 ff.; II, 18 ff., 37 ff.; Chadwick: *Victorian Church,* I, 527 ff., 558 ff.

religion was of little if any importance. The French peasantry went through the motions of religious observance and would probably have been shocked by failure of the traditional ritual, but they lived more in accord with hoary superstitions than with the doctrines of Christianity.[28] The plight of the city workers was no better, as noted in Chapter VI, above. Deprived of church service, they regarded religion as a luxury of the upper classes and resented the indifference of the churches to the sufferings of the poor.[29]

Among the upper classes, who were themselves religiously indifferent, there was growing concern about the irreligion of the lower classes, who, it was thought, must be taught to accept their fate as an expression of God's will. In England the government subsidized the building of more churches, of which 1,864 were opened in the twenty years following 1831.[30] Through the Ecclesiastical Commission it also diverted part of the wealth of certain bishoprics to the foundation of new dioceses in industrial areas. It even went so far as to subsidize the two school societies which were teaching a million or more children the need for obedience and submission.[31] Private interests, too, redoubled their efforts. Countless societies for charitable purposes, for the salvation of souls and for moral uplift were springing up everywhere. But these organizations were directed more toward the conversion of unbelievers than to the larger problem of religious faith. They had little if any grasp of the over-all social problem, nor had they any general program of social reform. Neither the Established Church nor the nonconformist sects in England had much interest in the social problem prior to 1848. The Tractarians, for their part, looked the other

[28] Monique Vincienne and Hélène Courtois: "Notes sur la situation religieuse en France en 1848" (*Archives de sociologie des religions*, No. 6, 1858, 104–118); Yver-Marie Hilaire: "La pratique religieuse en France de 1815 à 1878" (*Information historique*, XXV, 1963, 57–69); Louis Trenard: "Aux origines de la déchristianisation: le diocèse de Cambrai de 1830 à 1848" (*Revue du Nord*, XLVII, 1965, 399–459).

[29] George Kitson Clark: *The Making of Victorian England* (London, 1962), chap. vi; Donald O. Wagner: *The Church of England and Social Reform* (New York, 1930), chap. i; Kenneth S. Inglis: *Churches and the Working Classes in Victorian England* (London, 1963), 1 ff.; Chadwick: *Victorian Church*, I, 332 ff., 363 ff.; M. H. Vicaire: "Les ouvriers parisiens en face du catholicisme de 1830 à 1870" (*Schweizerische Zeitschrift für Geschichte*, I, 1951, 226–244); François A. Isambert: *Christianisme et classe ouvrière* (Tournai, 1961), 180 ff.

[30] Brown: *History of the English Clergy*, 237; Kitson Clark: *Making of Victorian England*, 169.

[31] Carpenter: *Church and People*, chap. iv.

way and for all their ardor and devotion allowed the "spiritual starvation of the millions" (E. B. Pusey) to go its way.[32]

Only after 1848 was a new start made through the Christian Socialist movement, the leaders of which were the eminent theologian Frederick D. Maurice and the London barrister John M. Ludlow. Maurice had for some years concerned himself with the spiritual needs of the workers. He had become a determined opponent of economic liberalism, which he hoped to see replaced by the principle of co-operation within a classless Christian community. Ludlow had received his education in Paris and was well acquainted with the writings of the French socialists, from whom he took over the idea of association, "one of the greatest discoveries of our age." He had joined the French Society of Friends of the Poor and in 1847 had undertaken social work in the slums of London. He had hailed the Revolution of 1848, but with insistence that the new order should have religious foundations. He and Maurice joined forces and were presently reinforced by Charles Kingsley, Tom Hughes and other young reformers. They founded a newspaper for discussion of workers' problems and attracted the support of some of the Chartist leaders. Holding that philanthropy could at best be but a patchy business, they challenged the entire industrial system and aimed at replacing free competition by co-operation. In the years 1848–1852 they established a number of producers' associations among tailors, shoemakers, printers and bakers. The movement was making real progress when, in 1854, personal disagreements among the leaders led to its disintegration. Christian Socialism, though hardly more than a flash in the pan, at least established the obligation of the churches to deal with the social problem, in addition to furthering the development of coöperatives.[33]

[32] David Owen: *English Philanthropy, 1660–1960* (Cambridge, 1964), Part II, chaps. v–vi; Brian Harrison: "Philanthropy and the Victorians" (*Victorian Studies*, IX, 1966, 353–374); Wagner: *Church of England and Social Reform*, chap. i; Kellett: *Religion and Life in the Early Victorian Age*, 25–27; Heasman: *Evangelicals in Action*, 48 ff., 71 ff.; Inglis: *Churches and the Working Classes*, 5–18; E. P. Thompson: *The Making of the English Working Class* (London, 1963), chap. xi.

[33] Kitson Clark: *English Inheritance*, 155 ff. The classic account is Charles E. Raven's *Christian Socialism, 1848–1854* (London, 1920), but this should now be supplemented by Torben Christensen: *Origin and History of Christian Socialism* (Aarhus, 1962); Neville C. Masterman: *John Malcolm Ludlow, the Builder of Christian Socialism* (London, 1963); and Alec R. Vidler: *Frederick D. Maurice and Company* (London, 1966).

In France the government of the July Monarchy did less than its English counterpart by way of relief.[34] But the Catholic hierarchy, at least in the industrial areas, was becoming seriously troubled by the ruthless exploitation of the workers, who were not even given their Sundays for rest and devotion.[35] Among the radicals, too, there developed a Catholic Socialism akin to Lamennais' doctrine. Philippe Buchez was outstanding among the early socialists in finding in Christianity the equality and brotherhood which he regarded as fundamental principles of the new social order. He converted a group of skilled workers and encouraged them to found the newspaper *The Workshop* (*L'atelier*). He also drafted the program of workers' co-operatives which was later taken over by Ludlow and the English Christian Socialists.[36]

Active efforts at relief along Christian lines were initiated by laymen such as Frédéric Ozanam and Count Armand de Melun. To enlist the support of the church and convince the workers of the value of religion, Ozanam in 1835 founded the Society of St. Vincent de Paul, which by 1848 had 282 branches in France and 106 abroad. Groups of thirty or forty members would meet weekly for discussion and each would undertake to visit, instruct and provide for a couple of destitute families. Another organization, the Society of St. Francis Xavier (1840) undertook similar religious and relief activities in the workers' sections of the larger cities.[37]

These efforts undoubtedly help to explain the "idyllic interlude" of 1848, when, after the outbreak of the revolution, the Catholic hierarchy hailed the brotherhood of man and the advent of a new society, while Buchez taught the people to identify God and liberty. Catholic leaders founded a newspaper, *The New Era,* of which Lacordaire was editor and Ozanam one of the prime movers. For a few months this journal advocated social reform as well as democratic institutions, but after the

---

[34] A. de Watteville: *Essai statistique sur les établissements de bienfaisance* (Paris, 1846), 7–10.

[35] Paul Droulers: "L'épiscopat devant la question ouvrière en France sous la Monarchie de Juillet" (*Revue historique,* CCXXIX, 1963, 335–362).

[36] Armand Cuvillier: *P. J. B. Buchez et les origines du socialisme chrétien* (Paris, 1948). The basic over-all study is Jean-Baptiste Duroselle: *Les débuts du catholicisme social en France, 1822–1870* (Paris, 1951), but see also the shorter treatment in Alec R. Vidler: *A Century of Social Catholicism* (London, 1964), chap. i.

[37] Allies: *Journal in France,* 62; Latourette: *Christianity in a Revolutionary Age,* I, 336 ff.; Daniel-Rops: *Church in an Age of Revolution,* 326 ff.; Georges Bourgin: "Les catholiques sociaux sous la Monarchie de Juillet" (*Revue d'histoire économique et sociale,* XI, 1923, 498–515).

horrors of the June Days prominent Catholics, like the upper classes in general, became frightened by the specter of socialism and communism, and abandoned their previous efforts. Most of them supported Louis Napoleon and were rewarded, during the Second Empire, by the support and encouragement of the government.[38]

In Germany as in France churchmen as well as laymen began in these years to denounce the system of free competition. At the Prussian court Radowitz, the king's friend, urged the need for social reform and hoped for a new order along Christian-patrimonial lines.[39] At Hamburg the eminent preacher, Johann von Wichern, undertook an extensive and highly successful program of training laymen for relief work among the destitute.[40] Noteworthy, too, was the establishment in 1846 of the Journeymen's Union (*Gesellenverein*) by the Rhineland priest Adolf Kölping. This was an organization for mutual aid which spread rapidly over Germany and Austria and in the late nineteenth century came to be a most effective instrument of Catholic action.[41]

The position of the German churches with respect to the social problem crystallized in 1848, when a conference of Catholic bishops called for complete freedom of the church from government control and for "solution of the social problem." In 1848 Wilhelm von Ketteler, the later bishop of Mainz, preached a series of sermons which were then published under the title *The Great Social Questions of Our Age*. In these he castigated social injustice and attacked the social problem vigorously in terms of Christian doctrine.[42]

Despite these interesting beginnings, the efforts of the churches to

---

[38] Ross W. Collins: *Catholicism and the Second French Republic* (New York, 1923); Jean Leflon: *L'église de France et la révolution de 1848;* Jean-Baptiste Duroselle: "L'attitude politique et sociale des catholiques français en 1848" (*Revue d'histoire de l'église en France*, XXXIV, 1948, 44–62); Vidler: *Century of Social Catholicism,* chap. ii.

[39] Josef Maria von Radowitz: *Gespräche aus der Gegenwart über Staat und Kirche* (1846); Walter Früh: *Radowitz als Sozialpolitiker* (Berlin, 1937).

[40] His book, *Die innere Mission der deutschen evangelischen Kirche* (1849), contains a vivid description of proletarian conditions in the German cities. There is a recent edition of this by Martin Gerhardt (1948).

[41] Schnabel: *Deutsche Geschichte,* IV, 202 ff., 429 ff.; William O. Shanahan: *German Protestants Face the Social Question* (Notre Dame, 1954), I, 185 ff.; Latourette: *Christianity in a Revolutionary Age,* II, chap. viii; Holborn: *History of Modern Germany,* II, 495 ff.; Joseph Hoffner: *Die deutschen Katholiken und die soziale Frage in 19 Jahrhundert* (Paderborn, 1956), 12 ff.

[42] Mainz, 1849. There is a new edition of these sermons by Ernst Deuerlein (Mainz, 1948). M. Neuefeind: *Bischof Ketteler und die soziale Frage seiner Zeit* (Cologne, 1926); Wilhelm Neuss: *Die Kirche der Neuzeit* (Bonn, 1954), 456 ff.; Daniel-Rops: *Church in an Age of Revolution,* 341 ff.

bring religion to the lower classes and to alleviate the lot of the workers were very slight indeed in the period prior to 1850. Indifference and unbelief remained widespread and deeply rooted throughout the lower classes and anticlericalism was rampant among the middle classes, especially in France. The churches had barely made a start in facing the problems raised by the forces of democracy and socialism when they were called upon to combat the destructive criticism of historical theology and the equally threatening impact of scientific discoveries.

3. SCIENCE

The midcentury was noteworthy in the history of science not only for a considerable number of important discoveries but also for the foundation of modern science in terms of organization and professionalization. By 1850 science had ceased being primarily the pursuit of leisured amateurs working in private laboratories for the satisfaction of their own curiosity. In both France and Germany, as in Scotland, it had become identified with learned academies and universities, which provided systematic instruction and well-equipped facilities. The English, on the other hand, tended to stick by tradition. They produced a number of really great scientists and contributed most of the fundamental concepts upon which future developments depended, but there was little systematic training prior to 1840. An increasing number of would-be scientists went to Edinburgh or to the German universities, and the new University of London (1827) as well as the British Association for the Advancement of Science (1831), both modeled on German prototypes, began to provide professional training, but only in the 1840's did Oxford and Cambridge reluctantly fall in line. As late as 1853 the eminent philosopher, Sir William Hamilton, expressed the opinion that the physical sciences could be fully taught "to all, at once" by one competent demonstrator.[43]

The English had the reputation of being constitutionally averse to pure speculation and preferring direct observation of facts. On the Continent, too, there was in this period a growing distaste among scientists for elaborate abstract systems. Schelling's philosophy of

[43] George Haines: *German Influence upon English Education and Science, 1800–1866* (New London, 1957), 3, 13 ff. The British attitude and neglect were castigated by Charles Babbage in his *Reflexions on the Decline of Science in England* (1830). See Charles F. Mullett: "Charles Babbage, a Scientific Gadfly" (*Scientific Monthly*, LXVII, 1948, 361–371).

nature, the great Romantic effort to establish the essential unity of all natural phenomena, was rejected as the construction of a dilettante. Alexander von Humboldt, the dean of European scientists, like some of his French friends, called for concentration of effort on observation of facts, while somewhat later Justus von Liebig, the great chemist, was to describe philosophical speculation as the pestilence of the century. It was Liebig who, after receiving his training in Paris, founded the chemistry laboratory at the University of Giessen in 1825, not only for research, but for systematic instruction. His inspired teaching revolutionized scientific training. Students flocked to Giessen from all over the world, while other universities established laboratories in various fields and governments began to finance the construction of institutes and observatories.[44]

This was the age, too, of progressive specialization in scientific work. A few great generalists there still were, such as the greatest of mathematicians, Johann K. F. Gauss, who has been called "the Titan of science" because of his contributions to many fields: astronomy, geodesy, physics, electromagnetism, and so on, to say nothing of his profound interest in linguistics, literature and even world politics.[45] More widely known and admired was Humboldt's farewell effort at popular education in science, the publication (1845) of the first two volumes of his *Kosmos,* which undertook to describe the entire universe—everything from celestial nebulae to the geography of mosses, to use his own words, and to put scientific knowledge into its historical and social setting. The venerable scientist succeeded brilliantly in presenting his age with a well-organized and interestingly written guide to the understanding of man's place in the universe. Translated at once into all principal European languages, *Kosmos* was sold in the hundreds of thousands of copies and is said to have been more widely read than any book except the Bible.[46]

---

[44] Theodor Heuss: *Justus von Liebig* (Hamburg, 1949), 42; Florian Cajori: *A History of Physics* (rev. ed., London, 1929), 286 ff.; Aaron J. Ihde: *The Development of Modern Chemistry* (New York, 1964), chap. x; D. S. L. Cardwell: "The Development of Scientific Research in Modern Universities" (in A. C. Crombie, ed.: *Scientific Change,* New York, 1963, 661–677).

[45] Eric T. Bell: *Men of Mathematics* (New York, 1937), chap. xiv; G. Waldo Dunnington: *Carl Friedrich Gauss: Titan of Science* (New York, 1955).

[46] Herbert Scurla: *Alexander von Humboldt* (Berlin, 1955), 375 ff.; Ewald Banse: *Alexander von Humboldt* (Stuttgart, 1953), 102 ff.

Men of this type became more and more exceptional. The rapidly growing volume and complexity of scientific knowledge made greater specialization inevitable. Even in 1826 Faraday was complaining that, if he was to devote time to experiment, he could not keep up with the literature of science, which, in that age of innocence, he described as "immense." By the 1840's societies and journals were being founded everywhere to meet the requirements of particular fields.[47]

Notable advances were also made in these years in the construction of key instruments. In the 1820's Josef von Fraunhofer and Pierre Guinand had refined the manufacture of glass and produced achromatic lenses which, when applied to telescopes, were to revolutionize astronomical observation. Equally important was the achromatic lens system devised for the microscope by Giovanni Amici in 1827, for this made possible the intensive study of cells and microorganisms essential to the biological sciences.[48]

Another important feature of the period was the popularization of science and the increasingly close relationship between science and industry. Humboldt's lectures in Berlin were attended by more than a thousand people, and so were Faraday's in London. Innumerable mechanics' institutes and local societies provided ample and varied scientific fare and the British Association for the Advancement of Science, founded in 1831 when reform of the old Royal Society proved impossible, did much to stimulate interest. The public became fascinated by the discoveries which came at an ever faster tempo. Science changed from "an elegant ornament of society, practiced by virtuosi, to an essential factor in the everyday production of goods and services."[49]

The impact of science upon industry was surprisingly slow and gradual. It is well known that the great inventions on which modern industry depended were made by ingenious craftsmen working by trial and error. The great engineers, too, were generally innocent of scientific theory and attacked their problems empirically. But by 1850 important changes were already taking place. Liebig's experiments led to the development of chemical fertilizers, while Faraday's studies of electromagnetism underlay the invention of the electric telegraph and indeed the entire electric industry of the next hundred years. Photog-

[47] James G. Crowther: *British Scientists of the Nineteenth Century* (London, 1935), 96.

[48] Erik Nordenskiöld: *The History of Biology* (New York, 1949), 389 ff.; Charles Singer: *A History of Biology* (rev. ed., New York, 1950), 506.

[49] John D. Bernal: *Science and Industry in the Nineteenth Century* (London, 1953).

raphy and later the development of the chemical and dye industries derived from researches in chemistry. By 1850 science was becoming an integral part of human thought and a crucial factor in human society. If the "age of science" had not yet arrived, it was at any rate definitely on the way.[50]

Limitations of knowledge and understanding on the part of the author preclude anything more than a cursory review of the scientific achievements of the midcentury. Mathematics was dominated by the figure of Gauss, "the last complete mathematician," who solved many of the most difficult mathematical problems before he was twenty-five and continued active until his death in 1855. Gauss, mercilessly rigorous in his standards, published only the results of researches for which he felt he had ironclad proof. His diaries, published much later, reveal that some of his major contributions were withheld from his contemporaries. Such was the elaboration of a non-Euclidean geometry well before Nicholas Lobachevski in 1829 and Janos Bolyai in 1831 published their systems. In the years after 1830 Gauss devoted himself chiefly to mathematical physics, more particularly to the measurement of magnetic phenomena. In 1833 he, in collaboration with his Göttingen colleague Wilhelm Weber, devised an electric telegraph connecting the astronomical observatory with the physics laboratory. This line, which remained in operation until 1845, transmitted whole sentences and was full of promise, but Gauss did nothing to promote it. He was at all times indifferent to worldly rewards.[51]

In the light of later developments in data processing, Charles Babbage, that petulant genius, deserves a tribute. He spent many years at work on a calculating machine which he never completed, though he made basic discoveries in the use of punch cards, memory storage and record printing. Of great importance in the sequel was also the contribution of George Boole, who in 1847 brought out the first small book on the algebra of logic, a treatise which paved the way for modern symbolic or mathematical logic. In a related field Adolphe Quetelet, an astronomer turned mathematician, founded the modern

[50] A. R. Hall: "The Scientific Movement and its Influence on Thought and Material Development" (*New Cambridge Modern History*, X, 1960, chap. iii); Albert E. Musson and E. H. Robinson: *Science and Technology in the Industrial Revolution* (London, 1967).

[51] Dunnington: *Carl Friedrich Gauss*, 147 ff.; H. W. Turnbull: *The Great Mathematicians* (London, 1939), chap. x; George Hubbard: *Cooke and Wheatstone and the Invention of the Electric Telegraph* (London, 1965).

science of statistics. His book *On Man* (1835) established the method of human measurements and introduced the use of vital statistics.

Major advances were made in astronomy, thanks to improved telescopes and modern observatories. Friedrich Bessel in 1838 first determined the parallax of a star and reckoned the distance of 61 Cygni from the earth. He was also the first to employ the concept of light-years for measuring astronomical distances. In 1843 Heinrich Schwabe determined the sunspot cycle, while two years later the Earl of Rosse, with a giant reflector telescope, succeeded in studying star clusters and discerning the spiral nebulae. But the greatest astronomical achievement was the discovery in 1846 of the new planet Neptune, described as the most sensational (astronomical) discovery of the nineteenth century.[52] The existence of an unknown planet had been suspected for years, since only so could the irregularities of the orbit of Uranus be explained. In 1845–1846 the Frenchman Urbain Le Verrier and the Englishman John C. Adams undertook quite independently what was "probably the most daring mathematical enterprise of the century." In a mere matter of months they determined the location of the presumed planet, which was soon verified by the Berlin Observatory's discovery of an unknown star of the eighth magnitude moving with relation to other stars, and therefore a planet.[53]

Chemistry and physics were not as yet distinct, specialized fields. Many scientists worked and achieved notable progress in both. Much research was inspired by the atomic theory advanced by John Dalton early in the century. Thus the eminent Swedish chemist Jöns Jakob Berzelius, accepting the proposition that chemical compounds are combinations of different atoms in fixed proportions, was able to draw up the first fairly accurate table of atomic weights (1828). He was also the author of the system of symbols for chemical elements, and one of the first to study the effects of electrical charges upon chemical compounds.[54] Meanwhile Friedrich Wöhler, who in 1828 had first synthesized an organic compound (urea), and Justus von Liebig gave a new impetus to researches in organic chemistry. Liebig's studies of

[52] Giorgio Abetti: *The History of Astronomy* (New York, 1952), 214; Maurice Daumas, ed.: *Histoire de la science* (Paris, 1957), 763 ff.

[53] Reginald L. Waterfield: *A Hundred Years of Astronomy* (London, 1938), 30 ff.

[54] Frank S. Taylor: *A History of Industrial Chemistry* (London, 1957), 175; J. Jacques: "Esquisse pour une histoire de la chimie au XIXe siècle" (*Journal of World History*, IV, 1958, 723–752); Ihde: *Development of Modern Chemistry*, chap. x; Alexander Findlay: *A Hundred Years of Chemistry* (3 ed., London, 1965), 13 ff.

plant physiology and soil analysis made clear the role of chemicals in restoring fertility. His book *Organic Chemistry Applied to Agriculture and Physiology* (1840), which appeared simultaneously in German, English and French, was revolutionary in its impact, while his periodical *Letters on Chemistry* (1844—) popularized the use of artificial fertilizers, thereby increasing the production of food immeasurably. The first chemical fertilizer was manufactured in 1843.[55]

The discoveries in physics were no less fundamental than those in chemistry. The period started with Michael Faraday's demonstration (1831) that magnetism could be converted into electricity, which led him to formulate the theory of electromagnetic induction, one of the greatest scientific achievements of all time. Faraday was credited with having an almost instinctive sense of scientific truth, as well as single-minded devotion and "ferocious" perseverance in research. Between 1830 and 1862 he performed no less than 16,000 experiments, never allowing himself to become discouraged or distracted from the search for what his intuition told him must exist. During the 1830's he established the laws of electrolysis, studied electric currents and lines of force, and devised the basic terminology of electricity (electrodes, anodes, cathodes, etc.). His generators and dynamos laid the basis for all later electrical engineering. Few men indeed have done so much to alter the conditions of human existence.[56]

Comparable in long-term importance were the discoveries in thermodynamics, namely, the establishment of the mechanical equivalent of heat and the formulation of the theory of conservation of energy. Three different scientists, working concurrently but independently, deserve credit for these achievements. In 1842 Julius Mayer, a physician turned physicist, submitted a figure for the mechanical equivalent of heat, expressed the idea of the conservation of energy, and even advanced the notion that the sun was the source of all energy, whatever its form, existing on earth. At the same time James Joule, a gentleman scientist, reflecting on the conversion of coal into power in the steam engine, carried out numerous experiments and demonstrated

[55] Richard Blunck: *Justus von Liebig* (Berlin, 1938); Theodor Heuss: *Justus von Liebig* (Hamburg, 1949), 47 ff.; Archibald and Nan L. Clow: *The Chemical Revolution* (London, 1952), 467 ff., 487 ff.

[56] Henry Crew: *The Rise of Modern Physics* (Baltimore, 1928), chap. xi; James C. Crowther: *British Scientists of the Nineteenth Century* (London, 1935), chap. ii; Sir William H. Bragg: *Michael Faraday* (London, 1931); James Kendall: *Michael Faraday* (London, 1955).

that heat is not a substance but a form of energy. Use of an extremely sensitive thermometer enabled him to measure the relationship between heat and work and in 1847 to publish the principle of the conservation of energy. In the very same year the German physiologist Hermann Helmholtz, studying the heat produced by combustion of food in animals, published his essay on *The Conservation of Energy* in which the principle was analyzed in detail. Mayer's work, as that of a nonprofessional speculator, attracted no attention, and that of Joule and Helmholtz was at first viewed with much skepticism, but before long the principles of thermodynamics were recognized as among the most important generalizations of science.[57]

Among the principal advances in physics in the midcentury was also the measurement of the speed of light by Armand Fizeau in 1849. Using a revolving cogwheel, he arrived at results not greatly at variance from those obtained later with more sophisticated instruments.

The biological sciences were dominated at this time by the figure of Johannes Müller, professor at Berlin, a highly productive scholar and a most influential teacher. Müller brought the findings of chemistry and physics to bear on biological problems and stressed the need for microscopic experimentation. His own work centered on the study of the structure of animal tissue and the nervous system. Further work on nerves was carried out in the 1840's by Emil Du Bois-Reymond and Johannes Purkinye, but the greatest advances were made in the study of cells, for which the improved microscope was invaluable. In 1831 the botanist Robert Brown described the nucleus of the cell, to be followed in 1838 by Matthias Schleiden, who advanced a complete theory of the cell structure of plants. A year later Theodor Schwann discovered the cell structure of animals and advanced the general theory of the cell as the unit of life in all living organisms. He had already (in 1837) demonstrated that the process of fermentation, long a mystery of science, was not spontaneous or vital, but the action of vegetable (yeast) cells upon the fermenting material.[58]

[57] Crew: *Rise of Modern Physics,* chap. viii; Crowther: *British Scientists,* chap. iii; Robert H. Murray: *Science and Scientists in the Nineteenth Century* (London, 1935), chap. iv; A. E. E. McKenzie: *The Major Achievements of Science* (Cambridge, 1960), chap. xiii; Charles Gillispie: *The Edge of Objectivity* (Princeton, 1960), 370 ff.; John D. Bernal: *Science in History* (3 ed., London, 1965), 396 ff.

[58] Murray: *Science and Scientists,* chap. iv; Nordenskiöld: *The History of Biology,* 394 ff.; Charles Singer and E. Ashworth Underwood: *A Short History of Medicine* (2 ed., Oxford, 1962), 320 ff.

Marked progress was made in these years in the identification of individual diseases. Laënnec's stethoscope (1819) made possible the analysis of indicators in the chest, for example. In the vast General Hospital in Vienna, Carl Rokitansky and his associates carried out thousands of autopsies and described various diseases. A general theory of disease, however, was still lacking and progress in therapy therefore continued to lag. Many medical men still held all disease to be manifestations of over- or understimulation, taking the form of inflammation, of which fever was a symptom. To relieve this condition bloodletting was still the accepted method. In 1833 no less than 41 million leeches were imported into France alone.[59]

The theory of cells promised an answer to the problem of disease. In 1835 Agostino Bassi, studying the disease of the silkworm, found that a vegetable microorganism or fungus could cause infection. Soon afterward Johannes Müller published a treatise on morbid tumors (1838) in which he demonstrated the cellular character of these growths. Presently (1840) Jakob Henle advanced the theory that all infectious disease is caused by minute, invisible forms of life. This interesting thesis had little impact until Pasteur and Koch reinforced it by their experiments.[60]

Karl von Baer, who in 1827 had discovered the mammalian ovum, in 1837 completed his great work on the evolution of animals. He noted the resemblance of the embryos in lower and higher forms, a resemblance the closer the younger the embryo. Then, in the closing years of the period, three of the greatest scientists of the century produced their early works. Claude Bernard in 1843 began his studies of the chemistry of digestion, especially the action of glycogen on the liver and the function of the pancreatic juice. Hermann Helmholtz, equally great in physiology, pathology, chemistry and physics, made significant contributions to the physiology of the eye and ear, and in 1852 succeeded in measuring the speed of nerve impulses. Rudolf Virchow, in turn, began by describing leukemia (1845), then made important studies of thrombosis and embolism, and in 1847 founded the leading journal of pathology, *Virchows Archiv*. He was presently to advance the notion

---

[59] Singer and Underwood: *Short History of Medicine;* Richard H. Shryock: *The Development of Modern Medicine* (New York, 1947), 153 ff., 185 ff.; Esmond R. Long: *A History of Pathology* (rev. ed., New York, 1965), 95 ff.

[60] Singer: *History of Biology,* 442 ff.; Paul Diepgen: *Geschichte der Medizin* (2 ed., Berlin, 1959), II, 104 ff.; Long: *History of Pathology,* 114 ff.

of the human body as an organized aggregation of cells in which each microscopic unit performed a specific function.[61]

The advances in pathology, though significant, were not of such a character as to alter the impact of disease on society. Too little was yet known of the nature of disease, hence little progress could be made toward prevention or cure. Despite vaccination, smallpox still carried away large numbers of children. Among the youth the ravages of tuberculosis were positively terrifying. To these afflictions must be added the horrible and highly lethal Asiatic cholera, which first appeared in 1830–1833 and then recurred in even more virulent form in 1848–1850. Of those afflicted about half died within three days. The causes of these sudden visitations were not known, but there was no escaping the fact that the lower classes were more affected than the higher, a fact which stimulated medical research. Some studies of blood changes in cholera victims were made as early as 1831, but it was only in 1849 that John Snow, examining the stomach and intestines of victims, concluded that the disease was caused by a poison (or fungus) carried by water and reproducing itself in the body. The cholera epidemics then gave the impetus to improvements in water supply and sanitation, first in England and then on the Continent.[62]

An important stage in the history of surgery was reached in the 1840's with the introduction of ether and chloroform as anesthetics. Ether was first used in dental work and in 1846 in a major operation in Boston, Massachusetts by Dr. W. G. T. Morton. A year later the Edinburgh gynecologist Sir James Simpson, after many experiments, suc-

---

[61] Shryock: *Development of Modern Medicine*, 202 ff.; Singer and Underwood: *Short History of Medicine*, 294 ff.; Long: *History of Pathology*, 117 ff.

[62] Charles Creighton: *A History of Epidemics in Britain* (Cambridge, 1891–1894) and Georg Sticker: *Abhandlungen aus der Seuchengeschichte* (Giessen, 1912) both contain a wealth of data. On smallpox, see W. Scott Jebb: *A Century of Vaccination* (2 ed., London, 1899); on tuberculosis, Arturo Castiglioni: *History of Tuberculosis* (New York, 1933); S. L. Cummins: *Tuberculosis in History* (London, 1949); René and Jean Dubos: *The White Plague* (Boston, 1952); E. R. Long: "Tuberculosis in Modern Society" (*Bulletin of the History of Medicine*, XXVII, 1953, 301–319); on cholera, J. S. Chambers: *The Conquest of Cholera* (New York, 1938); R. Pollitzer: "Cholera Studies: History of the Disease" (*Bulletin of the World Health Organization*, X, 1954, 421–461); Norman Longmate: *King Cholera* (London, 1966); Charles E. Rosenberg: "Cholera in Nineteenth Century Europe" (*Comparative Studies in Society and History*, VIII, 1966, 452–463); on public health, George Rosen: *A History of Public Health* (New York, 1958); Colin F. Brockington: *Public Health in the Nineteenth Century* (London, 1965).

cessfully used the much stronger chloroform first in obstetrics, then in surgery (see Illustration 20). The "conquest of pain" naturally put an entirely new complexion on surgery, in as much as longer and more complicated operations became possible and humanity was spared much anguish.[63]

But of all the sciences it was geology that was most brilliantly successful and most popular in the midcentury, so much so that, according to Harriet Martineau, the educated middle-class public would buy five expensive books on the subject to every copy of current novels.[64] By 1830 the European world had for years been treated to various theories about the history of the earth's crust, reflecting the effort to explain the baffling fact that marine fossils were to be found high in the mountains. In general, scientists were adherents of either the neptunist or the vulcanist school, the first of which held that the face of the earth had been formed by one or more great floods, while the second attributed earth forms to the action of volcanoes and to other cataclysms such as earthquakes. James Hutton had argued, as early as 1795, that observation revealed no vestige of a beginning, nor any prospect of an end to the earth. The earth's crust, he was convinced, was the result of various forces operating over immense periods of time and continuing even into the present. But this doctrine made few converts. It ran counter to the Biblical story of creation, according to which God's work was performed in 4004 B.C., the birthday of man and his planet.[65]

An important departure was the publication in 1830–1833 of Charles Lyell's *Principles of Geology* in three volumes. It was a work based on wide travel and intensive study which brought together a mass of illustrative material to fortify and elaborate Hutton's thesis. Interestingly written, it made an immediate appeal to the educated public and became one of the most influential works in the history of science. Geology, or at least "gentlemanly geology," to use Henry Adams'

---

[63] Barbara M. Duncum: *The Development of Inhalation Anaesthesia* (New York, 1947); Murray: *Science and Scientists,* chap. ii; Kenneth Walker: *The Story of Medicine* (New York, 1955).

[64] Martineau: *History of England,* II, 334; Charles G. Gillispie: *Genesis and Geology* (Cambridge, 1951), xi.

[65] Frank D. Adams: *The Birth and Development of the Geological Sciences* (Baltimore, 1938), chaps. vii *et seq.;* Sir Archibald Geikie: *The Founders of Geology* (2 ed., London, 1905), chaps. viii *et seq.;* Milton Millhauser: *Just before Darwin* (Middletown, 1959), chap. ii; Gertrude Himmelfarb: *Darwin and the Darwinian Revolution* (New York, 1959), chap. viii.

phrase, became popular. Even genteel ladies could join in fossil-hunting parties and in the exploration of neighboring earth forms.[66]

Lyell's book rejected all "catastrophic" theories and advanced the doctrine of "uniformitarianism," according to which the earth's crust was the result of slow processes of erosion, deposition, elevation and depression. It was so drastic a departure from accepted ideas that most geologists, including the eminent explorers Adam Sedgwick and Roderick Murchison, who had studied the oldest fossil-bearing rocks of Wales and established the familiar geologic periods, refused to accept it. Only gradually were all its implications recognized. In the words of Charles Darwin, it altered the whole tone of one's mind.[67] Gradually but surely it was to expand immeasurably man's conception of the age of his planet and, by casting doubt upon the credibility of the Biblical account of creation, to lay the foundation for the conflict between science and religion.

Further evidence of the great age of the earth was provided in 1840 by Louis Agassiz' study of Alpine glaciers, which convinced him that in earlier ages glaciers had extended much further than at present and that in fact Europe had experienced an ice age:

The surface of Europe, adorned before by a tropical vegetation and inhabited by troops of large elephants, enormous hippopotami, and gigantic carnivora, was suddenly buried under a vast mantle of ice, covering alike plains, lakes, seas and plateaus. Upon the life and movement of a powerful creation fell the silence of death.[68]

Establishment of the antiquity of the earth and the development of geologic formations through the operation of natural forces over the ages lent support to the notion of evolution which, since the end of the eighteenth century, had increasingly preoccupied philosophers, social theorists and even biologists such as Lamarck. The word "evolution" was not in common use prior to 1850, but the principle of change was one that fascinated many minds. The public was therefore well prepared to welcome a remarkable book, *Vestiges of the Natural History*

---

[66] Geikie: *Founders of Geology*, chap. xii; Carroll L. and Mildred A. Fenton: *Giants of Geology* (New York, 1952), chap. viii; Himmelfarb: *Darwin*, 222 ff.

[67] Quoted by Francis C. Haber: "Fossils and the Idea of a Process of Time in Natural History" (in Hiram B. Glass, ed.: *Forerunners of Darwin*, Baltimore, 1959, 260).

[68] Quoted by Fenton and Fenton: *Giants of Geology*, 118; see also Geikie: *Founders of Geology*, 443 ff.; Edward Lurie: *Louis Agassiz* (Chicago, 1960).

of Creation, which appeared anonymously in 1844 and ran through four editions in six months. The author, as it turned out much later, was the Edinburgh publisher Robert Chambers, well known as a writer of popular treatises on many subjects. He had, after some years of intensive reading, undertaken to construct a comprehensive system of nature. Scientists ridiculed the effort of this brash amateur, who certainly made many mistakes and engaged in some pretty wild speculation. But the fact remains that he was the first to present a coherent theory of "development" (evolution) and a picture of the universe as controlled by unvarying law. His basic ideas foreshadowed those of Darwin, published fifteen years later, but of course he was unable to provide proof and furthermore had nothing but a superficial explanation of the causes of evolution. While he could not accept the miracle of creation or believe that God Almighty had troubled to create every little thing, he argued that the universe as revealed by science was the most eloquent testimony to His divine Majesty. According to Chambers all things had a God-given proclivity to change and advance. Organisms were subject to two impulses: to advance and to be "modified in accordance with their environment." Darwin's thought was to run much deeper, but he never treated the Chambers book with contempt. He recognized that it stimulated interest in the problem of evolution and cushioned the shock of evolutionary ideas when they were more cogently presented.[69]

In the very year of Chambers' book, Charles Darwin wrote a "sketch" of almost 200 pages in which the essentials of his theory, as published in *The Origin of Species* (1859), were already embodied. The impact of Darwinian doctrine was, of course, to come later, but it is worth noting that his thinking antedated the midcentury. Darwin served for some time as secretary of the Geological Society and was a close friend of Lyell. He returned in 1836 from his extended voyages and researches in South America and the Pacific, and not long after arrived at his theory of the evolution of species by natural selection. For the validation of the theory it was necessary to accept the great antiquity of the earth and of organic life, as it was also to under-

[69] Julius M. Drachman: *Studies in the Literature of Natural Science* (New York, 1930), chap. ix; Charles C. Gillispie: *Genesis and Geology* (Cambridge, 1951), 163 ff.; Himmelfarb: *Darwin,* 208 ff.; and especially Milton Millhauser: *Just before Darwin: Robert Chambers and the "Vestiges"* (Middletown, 1959).

stand Malthus' teaching of the struggle for existence and the survival of the fittest. If it can fairly be said that Lyell and the uniformitarian geologists established the evolution of earth forms, it can also be said that Chambers went a step further and advanced from geologic to biologic evolution. It then remained for Darwin to present scientifically sound, well-organized evidence for evolution and to present it in abundance. Only after another fifteen years was he prepared to publish the book which ushered in a new era in man's thought about his own nature and his place in the universe.[70]

---

[70] From Ernst Mayer's splendid introduction to the *Facsimile of the First Edition of Charles Darwin: On the Origin of Species* (Cambridge, 1964), but see also Arthur O. Lovejoy: "The Argument for Organic Evolution before the 'Origin of Species' " (revised form in Hiram B. Glass, ed.: *Forerunners of Darwin*, Baltimore, 1959, chap. xiii); Robert B. Stauffer: "On the 'Origin of Species': an Unpublished Version" (*Science*, CXXX, 1959, 1449–1452); Himmelfarb: *Darwin*, chaps. viii and ix.

Chapter Sixteen

LITERATURE

I. HISTORICAL WRITING

THE POPULARITY of historical writings in the mid-nineteenth century can hardly be exaggerated. The rising middle class created a new and numerous reading public, eager to learn something of its place in the development of European society. Romanticism, too, cast glamour on the past, while the champions of a new order found in history the arguments needed to buttress their cause. In any event, a sense of history was deeply ingrained in the mentality of the time. Historical works in many volumes and historical novels of almost equal length were avidly devoured, while magazines and newspapers crammed their columns with historical essays, and parliamentary debates not infrequently turned into historical disquisitions. In the days before radio and television, men relied on the printed and spoken word for instruction and entertainment. Historians were expected to provide rich fare. Macaulay took five volumes to cover fifteen years of English history; Lamartine needed eight to tell the story of the Girondists, while Thiers devoted seventeen to the history of the Consulat and Empire. These were by no means exceptional cases. The public, which had little interest in novels of less than three volumes, fully expected the historian to provide at least four.[1]

Historical writing being still regarded primarily as a form of literature, historians like novelists strove for popular appeal. Scott, according to Carlyle, had demonstrated that "the bygone ages of the world were actually filled by living men, not by protocols, state papers, controversies and abstractions of men."[2] Macaulay, too, insisted that "the

---

[1] Stanley Mellon: *The Political Uses of History* (Stanford, 1958), 1 ff.; Jerome H. Buckley: *The Triumph of Time* (Cambridge, 1966), 3–12; Olive Anderson: "The Political Uses of History in Mid-Nineteenth Century England" (*Past and Present*, April, 1967).

[2] Quoted by J. R. Hale: *The Evolution of British Historiography* (New York, 1964), 36.

noiseless and nameless revolutions of the past" should not remain unrecorded; that the historian "must see ordinary men as they appear in their ordinary desires and their ordinary pleasures. He must mingle in the crowds of the exchange and the coffee-house."[3] Ideas of equality meant a new interest in the common man. History must tell of his role in the past; it must reflect the drama and movement not merely of the upper classes but also of the populace.

Most historians of the period were men of middle-class origin, hence inclined to be liberal or even radical in their outlook. Thus the French "political" historians discussed in Chapter III reflected a wide range of opinion and purpose. Guizot preached the virtues of constitutional government as the golden mean between despotism and mob rule, while Thiers stressed the advantages of good administration under strong leadership and so contributed to the popularity of Bonapartism. Lamartine's *History of the Girondists* was more romance than history, but vindicated the French Revolution and discredited the July Monarchy. Michelet, on the other hand, was a true son of the people and a passionate democrat, all of whose work was imbued with a profound love for the common man and passionate devotion to France. Still further to the left was Louis Blanc, the advocate of social democracy, whose *History of Ten Years* was a landmark in the development of social history. If Michelet glorified the peasant and the artisan, Blanc was the champion of the worker.[4]

The most widely read English historians were Thomas Carlyle and Thomas Babington Macaulay, of whom the former defies classification. A Scot of humble background, Carlyle was out of step with his time and at odds with his society. Starting as a student of the German idealist philosophy, he became an uncompromising opponent of ra-

[3] Quoted by H. A. L. Fisher: *The Whig Historians* (London, 1928), 15–16.

[4] Basic studies are Eduard Fueter: *Geschichte der neueren Historiographie* (Munich, 1911), 505 ff.; George P. Gooch: *History and Historians in the Nineteenth Century* (new ed., Boston, 1959), 168 ff.; James W. Thompson: *A History of Historical Writing* (New York, 1942), II, chap. xliv; Harry E. Barnes: *A History of Historical Writing* (rev. ed., New York, 1962), chap. ix; Heinrich von Srbik: *Geist und Geschichte* (Munich, 1950), I, chap. xi. On specific historians, Mary C. O'Connor: *The Historical Thought of François Guizot* (Washington, 1955), 82 ff.; Douglas Johnson: *Guizot* (London, chap. vii; Jean-Marie Carré: *Michelet et son temps* (Paris, 1926); Ethel Harris: *Lamartine et le peuple* (Paris, 1932); Pieter Geyl: "Michelet and His History of the French Revolution" (in his *Debates with Historians*, New York, 1956, chap. iv.).

tionalism, which, he felt, would never suffice to explain the story and fate of mankind. History, he believed, was an expression of God's will and therefore the function of the historian should be to interpret that will. Like the poet, the historian should have imagination and the inner vision by which he could sense the soul of the people and the spirit of a period.

Carlyle became interested in the French Revolution through the events of July, 1830. Considering Thiers' history too political, he undertook to create the drama of the Revolution, to write a human history of that great event. He made an honest effort to establish the facts, but his real objective was to make the past live again. His *French Revolution,* which appeared in 1837, has been criticized as much for what it omitted as for what it included, yet stands as a supreme example of literary as distinct from professional history. In its day it probably helped to discredit revolution; in the long term it will indubitably live as literature.

Among the historians of his time Carlyle was almost unique in having personal experience of modern industry and the life of the factory workers. He regarded industrialism as an inevitable stage in historical development and admired the machine for what it could accomplish. But he feared greatly for the future of man in the industrial age, foreseeing the subordination of man to the machine and the growing isolation and alienation of the worker, which he termed "the sum total of wretchedness to men . . . the frightfullest enchantment." His insights into the social problems of modern life lends him a significance far beyond that of the historian.[5]

Macaulay, in sharp contrast to Carlyle, was a typical, conventional liberal, the perfect "Whig" historian. Of middle-class background, he had an unusually rich intellectual endowment, being a lightning reader and a man of prodigious memory, a forceful speaker and a brilliant controversialist. Having made his reputation as an essayist, Macaulay spent most of the decade following 1830 in political activity before

[5] Herbert L. Sussman: *Victorians and the Machine* (Cambridge, 1968), 17 ff.; Pieter Geyl: "Carlyle, his Reputation and Influence" (in his *Debates with Historians,* chap. iii); Louise M. Young: *Thomas Carlyle and the Art of History* (Philadelphia, 1939), chaps. i–iii; Julian Symons: *Thomas Carlyle: the Life and Ideas of a Prophet* (London, 1952); H. Ben-Israel: "Carlyle and the French Revolution" (*Historical Journal,* I, 1958, 115–135).

turning to sustained historical work. He was thoroughly versed in the ancient classics, but had no special training in history and remained throughout his career strangely provincial. His ignorance of French and German historical writing led him to complain that most historians left out what was colorful and interesting, despite the fact that this was exactly what Frenchmen such as Barante, Thierry, Sismondi and Michelet did not do.[6]

Macaulay was a practical, common-sense person. He had little use for philosophy ("German humbug") and even less for anything savoring of the mystical. Like many a successful bourgeois, he was well-satisfied with his nation and with his time. Progress, the key to history, had culminated in the modern British people, "the greatest and most highly civilized people that the world ever saw." Exulting in Britain's avoidance of the Revolution of 1848, he declared: "It is because we had freedom in the midst of servitude that we have order in the midst of anarchy." The English were fortunate in having had the Glorious Revolution of 1688, which Macaulay described with such loving care. Through the liberty which it entailed Britain was able to make the enormous (material) progress that put it in the forefront of nations.

Believing that history should be interesting as well as instructive, Macaulay labored incessantly to perfect his style, to combine color with clarity and to attain a sense of drama and movement. The result was perhaps the finest narrative style in the language—vivid, quick-paced, colloquial. The flood of entertaining detail, says H. A. L. Fisher, had none of "the deadly relevance and cold impartiality" of the academic seminar. In the effort to recapture the spirit of the time Macaulay spared himself no pains in travel and research, scouring the libraries and other repositories for pamphlet material, sermons, theater bills and other such evidence. In the sequel he was to be much criticized for his partisanship, his loose use of evidence, his failure to grasp real historical problems, his general superficiality and prolixity. But in his time he was universally acclaimed and eagerly read. The first two volumes of his *History of England since the Accession of James II* (1848) reached a fifth edition in six months and were translated at once into all European languages, including Hungarian and Russian. Macaulay became the most popular writer of history that the world had yet seen.

---

[6] J. Cotton Morison: *Macaulay* (London, 1882, 1909), 49 ff.; Richmond C. Beatty: *Lord Macaulay: Victorian Liberal* (Norman, 1938), 307 ff.

Even a century later, in the days of his neglect, there are still those who consider him the greatest of English historians.[7]

In Germany there was the same lively interest in history. Within a couple of decades some fifty historical societies sprang up, whose journals burrowed into local records and at the same time discovered the unity of national development. In 1846, at a great congress of Germanists at Frankfurt, plans were laid for an all-German historical society. At the same time the writing of political history, mostly of the liberal stripe, flourished everywhere. The most popular historian was Friedrich G. Schlosser, for forty years professor at Heidelberg, whose best-known work was his *General History for the German People,* in eighteen volumes (1844–1856). Schlosser was more the eighteenth-century moralist than the liberal theorist, but his constant harping on the misdeeds of the privileged classes, his sympathetic treatment of the French Revolution, his unshakable faith in progress and his conviction of the moral superiority of the third estate made him a valuable ally of opposition elements. He was casual in his use of sources, selecting only those that served his argument, but made a great impression on his contemporaries, including Karl Marx, who drew on him heavily for historical ammunition.

In Chapter IV the political importance of Karl von Rotteck has already been noted. His unabashedly liberal and nationalist *General History* reached its thirteenth edition in 1840 and was read in translation throughout the Continent. Friedrich C. Dahlmann, one of the prime authors of the Frankfurt constitution of 1848, wrote admiringly of the English Revolution of 1688 and sang the praises of constitutional government, while the classicist Gustav Droysen in 1846 turned to modern history, extolling the reformers of the revolutionary period and advocating Prussian leadership of a united Germany. An out-and-out activist was Georg G. Gervinus, a pioneer of the history of literature, for whom both history and literature were meant to serve the interests of moderate liberalism and especially nationalism. Gervinus in 1846

---

[7] Fundamental is Sir Charles Firth's *Commentary on Macaulay's History of England* (London, 1938), especially chaps. i–iv; but see further H. A. L. Fisher: *Whig Historians;* Robert L. Schuyler: "Macaulay and his History: a Hundred Years After" (*Political Science Quarterly,* LXIII, 1948, 161–193); Pieter Geyl: "Macaulay in his Essays" (in his *Debates with Historians,* chap. ii); David Knowles: *Lord Macaulay* (London, 1960); John R. Griffin: *The Intellectual Milieu of Lord Macaulay* (Ottawa, 1956), 93 ff.

became the editor of the newly founded *German Gazette,* which became the chief organ of the nationalists.[8]

The works of the political historians, outstanding though some of them were, are no longer read except as literature. In long-term importance they have been overshadowed by the "scientific" or professional history ("historism" or "historicism") which had its origin in this period and was eventually to put its stamp on all serious historical work.[9] This new departure hinged on the critical analysis of sources, reliance on contemporary documents and other records, objectivity in the evaluation of past events, and abstention from partisanship in the presentation of results. Criticism of the sources, taken over from the philologists, was first applied to historical problems by Barthold G. Niebuhr in his study of early Roman history. But the greatest exponent of the new school was Leopold von Ranke, for sixty years professor at the University of Berlin, who in his seminar (1833—) trained many of the leading German historians of the later nineteenth century. Ranke was a most creative scholar, a man of keen historical insight and exceptional detachment. Though not a great lecturer, he impressed his audiences by his vast erudition, skill in presentation and balance of judgment. Refusing to use history for pedagogical, moralistic or political purposes, he strove to deal with the past on its merits, that is, to understand the past in its own terms, without reference to later interpretations or objectives. The idea that he shunned opinions and generalizations is quite erroneous. Many of his generalizations and interpretations have stood the test of time. The point was that he insisted that conclusions should be derived solely from the established facts and not from the initial preconceptions of the historian.

Ranke's writings, some fifty volumes in all, deal almost exclusively with Western European history in the sixteenth to nineteenth centuries. Two of his major works, the *History of the Popes* (1834–1836)

---

[8] In addition to the standard histories of historiography, see the essay by Gustav Wolf, Dietrich Schäfer and Hans Delbrück: *Nationale Ziele in der deutschen Geschichtsschreibung seit der französischen Revolution* (Gotha, 1918); also Franz Schnabel: *Deutsche Geschichte im 19 Jahrhundert* (2 ed., Freiburg, 1950), III, 100 ff.; and the chapters by Gerhard Schilfert and Karl Obermann in the scholarly Marxist study edited by Joachim Streisand: *Die deutsche Geschichtswissenschaft vom Beginn des 19 Jahrhunderts bis zur Reichsgründung von Oben* (Berlin, 1963).

[9] The classic study of the background is Friedrich Meinecke's *Die Entstehung des Historismus* (Munich, 1936).

and the *German History in the Era of the Reformation* (1839–1843), belong to the period of the present study. In these histories Ranke was able to elaborate his concept of a Romanic-Germanic community of nations which, though having much in common, defended their individuality and independence through a balance of power. Working largely from government documents, Ranke developed an almost uncanny insight into the problems of power and international relations. His analyses of the changing balance of power remain among his chief contributions. So far as domestic affairs were concerned, he was a man of moderate conservative views and therefore does not belong with the liberal political historians of his time. Born during the French Revolution, he remained throughout his life deeply concerned with the conflict between conservative and liberal forces and frequently dealt with it in his university lectures. He considered the rise of the middle classes inevitable, but feared lest the clash of old and new forces stir up mass movements that might threaten the very fabric of European society. Like Burke and Gentz he urged that governments should take a positive line and, through constant, gradual reform, continue to adjust to changing conditions. He had no faith whatever in revolution and never overcame his dread of social upheaval and violence.

The July Revolution in France led Ranke to ask whether society could tolerate the government's being taken over by a mob of apprentices and city rowdies. The revolutions of 1848 troubled him even more, for he saw that they were basically social and in a sense were attempts by the "factory population" to subvert the social order. Of course, none of the great historians of the period showed much concern for or understanding of the masses. Macaulay might insist that the historian "must not shrink from exploring even the retreats of misery," but he himself abstained from doing so and identified himself with the Whig aristocracy. Carlyle, for all his distress over the "condition of England" question, in his historical work dealt chiefly with great men, whom he considered the chief motive forces in human development. Even Michelet, a man of the people who wrote *Of the People* (1846), referred primarily to the *petite bourgeoisie* and not to the proletarians. Ranke's attitude was therefore not exceptional, though he was more conservative than most of his fellow historians. Like most leaders of thought in the midcentury, he was ignorant of modern industry and of the drastic changes that were taking place in society. His sensing of dangerous mass movements was purely intuitive. In any case he ruled his personal views out of his historical work. Even when discussing popular forces and insurrections of the past, he never gave expression to his fears. It was this reserve and balance of judgment that won him the admiration of his contemporaries and the highest commendation of his successors. "He must be given a place beside the greatest not only in the field of historiography, but in that of general scholarship as well," declared Ernst Cassirer, the great historian of ideas. And according to those eminent historians of the nineteenth century Eduard Fueter and George P. Gooch, he came closer to the ideal of the historian than any one else; he was "the master of us all."[10]

French historians, many of whom were personally acquainted with Ranke, were loath to abandon the traditional literary history in which they excelled. Only toward the end of the century was scientific history well established in France. But Niebuhr and Ranke had a great and immediate impact in England. Niebuhr's *Roman History* was translated in 1828 by Conop Thirlwall, who applied the critical method in his eight-volume *History of Greece* (1835-1844), the first scholarly treatment of the subject in any language. He was followed by George Grote, whose twelve-volume *History of Greece* (1846-1856) was imbued with the spirit of Niebuhr and Ranke. Thomas Arnold, in his *History of Rome* (1838-1841), aimed to popularize the new method. But Carlyle and Macaulay, while expressing admiration for Ranke, chose, like their French colleagues, to stick by the more colorful traditional narrative. The critical school, which, according to Lord Acton, had more "body" but lacked "sparkle," could only gradually establish its supremacy.[11]

---

[10] Among recent contributions to the voluminous Ranke literature may be mentioned Ernst Cassirer: *The Problem of Knowledge* (New Haven, 1950), 227 ff.; Herbert Butterfield: *Man on his Past* (Cambridge, 1955), chaps. ii and iii; Heinrich von Srbik: *Geist und Geschichte*, chap. viii; Geyl: *Debates with Historians*, chap. i; Gerhard Schilfert: "Leopold von Ranke" (in Streisand: *Die deutsche Geschichtswissenschaft*, 241–270); Theodore H. von Laue: *Leopold Ranke: the Formative Years* (Princeton, 1950), especially chap. vi; Bernard Hoeft: *Rankes Stellungnahme zur französischen Revolution* (Greifswald, n.d.); Rudolf Vierhaus: *Ranke und die soziale Welt* (Münster, 1957); Wilhelm Mommsen: *Stein, Ranke, Bismarck* (Munich, 1954), chap. ii. An intimate view of Ranke in the 1830's appears in the biography of his most interesting pupil; see Werner Kaegi: *Jacob Burckhardt* (Basel, 1950), II, 54 ff.

[11] Richard A. E. Brooks: "The Development of the Historical Mind" (in Joseph E. Baker, ed.: *The Reinterpretation of Victorian Literature*, Princeton, 1950, 130–152).

2. POETRY

In literature as in the fine arts, the mid-third of the nineteenth century might equally well be described as the twilight of Romanticism or the dawn of Realism. Indeed, the term Romantic Realism has been coined to designate the amalgam of the transitional period in the field of the novel.[12] Actually, both the concepts Romanticism and Realism are so broad and vague as to be confusing rather than illuminating. Besides, the development of literature varied from country to country. In England and Germany, the homelands of Romanticism, that movement was definitely in decline by 1830, while in France, Italy, and Spain, where the classical tradition was strong, Romanticism came into its own only in the 1830's. In Northern, Central and Eastern Europe Romanticism inspired the national movements and continued to color literature and the theater. Everywhere, however, the written and spoken word continued to bear the stamp of Romanticism. It was an age of strong and colorful language, so prolix and emotional as to be almost distasteful to the twentieth-century reader.

Realism has frequently been identified with the middle classes, as was Romanticism with the aristocracy. The Germans, for example, have given the middle-class mentality the name *Biedermeier,* an untranslatable term borrowed from art history to express acceptance, resignation, sobriety, contentment with the simple, the homely existence of the average bourgeois. Something of this outlook marked the English Utilitarians or Evangelicals with their common sense, moderation and faith in progress. Even though there was a great deal of dynamism in European life, there was in literature an undeniable note of sadness and resignation, a sense of impending doom. This may have been a reflection of the letdown after the storm and stress of the revolutionary and Napoleonic period, or it may have stemmed from the ravages of disease. But to a large extent it was a reaction to the strains of rapid social change, a feeling of helplessness in the face of unknown forces threatening upheaval and misery.[13]

[12] Donald Fanger: *Dostoevsky and Romantic Realism* (Cambridge, 1965), introduction.
[13] Paul Kluckhohn: "Biedermeier als literarische Epochenbezeichnung" (*Deutsche Vierteljahrschrift für Literaturwissenschaft,* XIII, 1935, 1–43); M. J. Norst: "Biedermeier" (in J. M. Ritchie, ed.: *Periods in German Literature,* London, 1966, 147–160); Pierre Barrière: *La vie intellectuelle en France* (Paris, 1961), 465 ff.; Walter E.

A novel feature in the literature of the period was the growing interest in social problems. Writers in all countries were converted or at least influenced by the Saint-Simonians and their vision of a new society. Many were men of lower-middle-class origin, themselves alienated and concerned with their place in society.[14] Above all, they had to take account of the vastly growing reading public. The traditional literary salon was fast disappearing, its place taken by new journals and newspapers with literary *feuilletons*. In many countries novels and other forms of literature were becoming available in pamphlet installments at low price. Reading rooms and lending libraries were springing up in the cities to cater to the demand for new literature. In Germany the number of new works doubled between 1830 and 1843, while the number of periodicals and newspapers more than doubled.[15]

The role of literature in the political and social life of Europe has been discussed in various contexts throughout the preceding chapters and the emphasis in the following will therefore be on those aspects of literature not yet touched upon. Lyric poetry, for example, was not much affected by the rapid changes of the age, yet even in this branch of literature there was a tendency to deal with ideas and problems rather than with subjective matters. Poets showed more interest in longer forms such as epics, topical poems and dramatic monologues. In England the new stars, Alfred Tennyson and Robert Browning, had both risen to prominence before 1850. Tennyson was a most representative Englishman, insular, patriotic, xenophobic, a hard-working, earnest, moralistic bourgeois, given to sentimentality and pomposity. Lacking in genuine political interest, his heart and intellect were with old England as it had developed under the aegis of the landed aristocracy.[16] He felt abandoned in the modern universe and was deeply troubled by doubts and lack of faith, particularly by the impact of science on religion. His masterpiece, *In Memoriam* (1850), a huge

---

Houghton: *The Victorian Frame of Mind, 1830–1870* (New Haven, 1957), chap. iii; Gabriel Peterli: *Zerfall und Nachklang* (Zürich, 1958), 109 ff.

[14] This is the theme of Alfred de Vigny's play *Chatterton* (1835) and of several other plays. See David-Owen Evans: *Le drame moderne* (Paris, 1923), 249 ff.

[15] C. P. Magill: "The German Author and his Public in the Mid-Nineteenth Century" (*Modern Language Review*, XLIII, 1948, 492–499); Amy Cruse: *The Victorians and Their Books* (Boston, 1935); Richard D. Altick: *The English Common Reader* (London, 1957).

[16] Robert Preyer: "Alfred Tennyson: the Poetry and Politics of Conservative Vision" (*Victorian Studies*, IX, 1966, 325–352).

collection of reflective poems grappling with various problems of human existence, gave his troubled age some measure of assurance.

Of Tennyson, G. K. Chesterton once said that "he could not think up to the height of his own towering style."[17] That is, he concealed the paucity and banality of his ideas, his indecision and his fears under a brilliant and varied style, unexcelled for beauty of diction and range of thematic material. But the charm of his verse conveys no message to later generations. He is interesting to posterity chiefly as a representative of his time and society.[18]

Browning, in contrast to Tennyson, was essentially of an optimistic nature, a man of tough and adventurous mind who enjoyed to the full the thrill of struggle. Though he too was troubled by the conflict of science and religion, Browning found faith in God's working, through human imperfections, toward some end transcending human understanding. In his long and obscure as well as erudite poems and dramatic monologues, he analyzed the human soul and depicted situations affecting human psychology. More profound than Tennyson, he was less representative of his age and, indeed, more European than English in his outlook.[19]

Matthew Arnold, the intellectual poet *par excellence* and the perfect example of doubt and resignation, published his first poems in the 1840's, but became important only after the period of the present study and therefore need not be considered here. On the other hand, something may be said about early poetry dealing with industrialism. Not many poets touched on this problem, for the idea that poetry should be confined to what is noble and beautiful was still firmly held in the midcentury. Ebenezer Elliott, a Sheffield foundry worker, led the way with his *Corn-Law Rhymes* (1831), dedicated to Bentham and directed

---

[17] G. K. Chesterton: *The Victorian Age in Literature* (2 ed., London, 1966), 73.

[18] Sir Herbert Grierson and J. C. Smith: *A Critical History of English Poetry* (London, 1944), chap. xxxi; John D. Cooke and Lionel Stevenson: *English Literature of the Victorian Period* (New York, 1949), 109 ff.; Douglas Bush: *Introduction to Selected Poetry of Tennyson* (New York, 1951); Jerome H. Buckley: *Tennyson, the Growth of a Poet* (Cambridge, 1960); Valerie Pitt: *Tennyson Laureate* (London, 1962); Joanna Richardson: *The Pre-Eminent Victorian: a Study of Tennyson* (London, 1962), especially 57 ff., 275 ff.; J. B. Steane: *Tennyson* (London, 1966), 144 ff.

[19] Francis G. R. Duckworth: *Browning: Background and Conflict* (London, 1931); Ioan M. Williams: *Robert Browning* (London, 1967); and the valuable introduction to Edward Lucie-Smith: *A Choice of Browning's Verse* (London, 1967). On the religious issue, see J. Hillis Miller: *The Disappearance of God* (Cambridge, 1963).

against exploitation of the poor. In later poems Elliott celebrated "the unwearied crash and roar of iron powers that, urged by restless fire, toil ceaseless, day and night, and never tire." In his poem on Preston Mills he pictured children leaving the factory after a long day's work:

> But from their lips the rose had fled,
>   Like "death-in-life" they smiled;
> And still, as each passed by, I said,
>   Alas! Is that a child?
>
> .   .   .   .
>
> Thousands and thousands—all so white—
>   With eyes so glazed and dull;
> O God! It was indeed a sight
>   Too sadly beautiful![20]

During the 1840's the Chartist movement produced in Ernest Jones and William Linton two poets who exalted the uprisings of the workers and celebrated the revolutions of 1848, while Elizabeth Browning, far better known for her lovely *Sonnets from the Portuguese* (1847), reacted to the report of the commission on child labor with her poem "The Cry of the Children" (1843):

> For, all day, we drag our burden tiring
>   Through the coal-dark, underground,
> Or, all day, we drive the wheels of iron
>   In the factories, round and round.

She pictured two of the children weeping and longing for death, but not even God would hear them: "He is speechless as a stone." Thomas Hood, to mention one more poet, in an influential poem, "The Song of the Shirt," had a needlewoman in a London sweatshop speak as follows:

> Work—work—work!
>   My labour never flags;
> And what are its wages? A bed of straw,
>   A crust of bread, and rags.
> That shatter'd roof—and this naked floor—
>   A table—a broken chair;
> And a wall so blank, my shadow I thank
>   For something falling there!

[20] Ebenezer Elliott: *Poetical Works* (New ed., London, 1876), I, 352 ff., 379 ff.; II, 9.

"Oh God!" she exclaims, "that bread should be so dear, and flesh and blood so cheap."[21]

The German world produced in this period several fine poets, though only one, Heinrich Heine, of the first rank. Ludwig Uhland, a typical bourgeois, devout and patriotic, had all but given up the writing of poetry after 1830 and immersed himself in the political movements of the time. Adalbert von Chamisso, too, had done his most important work earlier, but Nikolaus Lenau, Eduard Mörike and Annette von Droste-Hülshoff were all active. Lenau, a Hungarian German, continued to write in the Romantic style, expressing *Welt-schmerz*, melancholy, pessimism. Mörike, an obscure Swabian pastor, treated a wide range of subject matter and employed a great variety of metrical forms, but always in an artless, graceful, harmonious way. Droste-Hülshoff, a Westphalian noblewoman, on the other hand, excelled in the realistic treatment of nature and the expression of smoldering passions. She rather defies classification.[22]

Heinrich Heine, one of the greatest German poets of all time, lived in exile in Paris during these years and wrote in prose as much as in verse. His many poems of love and nature, most of them Romantic in mood, form and rhythm, were remarkable not only for beauty of language and richness of imagery but also for simplicity, economy of thought and exceptional brevity. George Brandes, the Danish critic, once called Heine the wittiest man of modern times, yet the poet was deeply embittered and his wit was often caustic and corrosive. Many of his most moving poems end unexpectedly in an ironic punch line.

Among Heine's poetic works dating from this period were his satirical masterpieces *Atta Troll* (1843) and *Germany: a Winter's Tale* (1844), both of which deal mercilessly with the foibles of the Germans and the problems of the age. Yet for all his irony and flippancy Heine was a sincere and noble soul, a man devoted to liberty and an uncom-

21 On this early social literature, see Samuel C. Chew, in Albert C. Baugh, ed.: *A Literary History of England* (New York, 1948), 1253 ff.; Y. V. Kovalev: "The Literature of Chartism" (*Victorian Studies*, II, 1958, 117–138). Some items are included in the anthology by Jeremy Warburg: *The Industrial Muse* (Oxford, 1958).

22 Hugo Bieber: *Der Kampf um die Tradition, 1830–1880* (Stuttgart, 1928); Martin Greiner: *Zwischen Biedermeier und Bourgeoisie* (Göttingen, 1953); Franz Koch: *Idee und Wirklichkeit: Deutsche Dichtung zwischen Romantik und Naturalismus* (Düsseldorf, 1956); Paul Reimann: *Hauptströmungen der deutschen Literatur, 1750–1848* (Berlin, 1956); Fritz Martini: *Deutsche Literaturgeschichte* (2 ed., Stuttgart, 1950); J. G. Robertson: *A History of German Literature* (5 ed. by Edna Purdie, London, 1966).

promising enemy of all forms of oppression or exploitation. His last years (he died in 1856) were spent in excruciating pain, which he bore with rare fortitude.

In Paris, Heine, as a writer of world reputation, was admitted to all circles and became acquainted with many figures prominent in literature and politics. He was much impressed by the teachings of the Saint-Simonians and other socialist writers and was alert to the implications of the social problem. While highly critical of the bourgeois regime and sympathetic to the workers, he had a premonition of social upheaval and feared that this would spell the end of European culture. One of his famous poems was written after the great insurrection of the Silesian weavers in 1844. He pictured them as grinding their teeth as they wove Germany's shroud:

> Doomed be the king, the rich man's king,
> Who would not be moved by our suffering,
> Who tore the last coin out of our hands,
> And let us be shot by his blood-thirsty bands—
> We weave, we weave.[23]

During the 1840's German exiles produced a substantial body of revolutionary poetry, much of which was collected and published in an *Album of Original Poetry* edited by Hermann Puttmann in 1847. Among the more important figures were Georg Herwegh, the friend of Karl Marx, who in 1841 created a sensation with his *Poems of a Live Man,* which were full of fervor and revolutionary *élan.* A few years later came Ferdinand Freiligrath's *Confession of Faith* (1844) and his *Ça Ira* (1846), devoted to the suffering lower classes. Freiligrath, who also was associated with Marx, translated into German, Elliott's *Corn-Law Rhymes* and Hood's "Song of the Shirt." Another poet of the workers, Karl Beck, the author of *Songs of the Poor Man* (1846), was highly regarded in his day and made a deep impression with his poems depicting the horrors of the city slums. Lastly Georg Weerth, who

---

[23] Translation by Aaron Kramer, in Frederic Ewen: *The Poetry and Prose of Heinrich Heine* (New York, 1948), 244. Among recent English studies are E. M. Butler: *Heinrich Heine* (London, 1956); William Rose: *Heinrich Heine: Two Studies of his Thought and Feeling* (Oxford, 1956), which is excellent on his social views; S. S. Prawer: *Heine, the Tragic Satirist* (Cambridge, 1961); Laura Hofrichter: *Heinrich Heine* (Oxford, 1963), essentially a study of his philosophy of life. On Heine's Paris connections there is an admirable monograph by Joseph Dresch: *Heine à Paris* (Paris, 1956).

wrote his *Poems from Lancashire* (1845) from personal experience, was regarded by Engels as the most outstanding poet of the proletariat. Marx gladly published his contributions in the *New Rhenish Gazette* in 1848–1849.[24]

French literature in these years was rich in lyric poetry, almost all of it in the Romantic vein, with emphasis on the vagaries of love, the tribulations of the poet, and the insuperable sadness which Chateaubriand had long since made fashionable. Lamartine, whose *Méditations poétiques* (1820) had marked the onset of the Romantic period in French literature, published but little poetry after his *Harmonies poétiques et religieuses* (1830). Not content with being a truly great poet, he devoted himself to the study of economics and to political activity. Alfred de Musset, whose elegance and insolence irritated many of his contemporaries, was a poet of unrestrained yet unsatisfied passion, whose lyrics generally ended on a note of misery and resignation. His work has worn less well than that of Alfred de Vigny, who avoided the personal note and dealt rather with larger human problems, such as loss of religious faith and the impact of social change. Among French poets he was the most intellectual and profound.[25]

The recognized leader of French Romanticism was Victor Hugo, still considered by many critics the greatest of French poets and the only one worthy to be ranked with Dante, Shakespeare and Goethe. Hugo was a man of extraordinary energy and talent, impressive as an artist as well as a poet, novelist, dramatist and essayist. For him the poet was the voice of God and he himself a major prophet. Actually he, like Tennyson, lacked intellectual distinction. His outlook was that of a liberal, enlightened, progressive, humanitarian bourgeois. Originally a royalist, he accepted the July Monarchy, eventually turned democrat and republican, and ended as the inexorable enemy of Napoleon III. The 1830's were one of his productive poetic periods, ranging over

---

[24] Otto Rommel, ed.: *Die politische Lyrik des Vormärz* (Vienna, 1921) provides a good anthology. See further, Solomon Liptzin: *The Weavers in German Literature* (Baltimore, 1926), 28 ff., and the same author's *Lyric Pioneers of Modern Germany* (New York, 1928), chaps. iii *et seq.* On Weerth, see especially Reimann: *Hauptströmungen der deutschen Literatur*, 805 ff.

[25] Gustave Lanson and P. Tuffrau: *Manuel illustré d'histoire de la littérature française* (Paris, 1953); Louis Cazamian: *A History of French Literature* (Oxford, 1955); Pierre Moreau: *Le romantisme* (Vol. VIII of Jean Calvet, ed.: *Histoire de la littérature française*, 2 ed., Paris, 1957).

many topics and employing a large variety of forms. Hugo was much moved by the misery of the poor, which led him to beseech the rich, during their winter entertainments, to remember that under the frost and snow there was always an unemployed father, his family threatened by famine.[26]

French poets more than the English were impressed by the coming of the machine, about which they were of mixed mind. Vigny, describing an iron foundry in 1831, could not make up his mind whether it augured evil or good, but was convinced that an entirely new world was being forged in its fires. The advent of the steamboat and railway conveyed the notion of tremendous power and led Vigny, Lamartine, Hugo and others to glorify the age of steam, though Vigny, after a terrible railway accident in 1842, reversed himself and denounced these "blind and inexorable machines" which threatened to dominate mankind. Another poet, Victor Pommier, went so far as to condemn the entire industrial system for its dehumanizing tendencies: humanity, he declared, was becoming a squirrel in a cage. Particularly interesting among these poets was Auguste Barbier, who had firsthand knowledge of the English industrial scene. In his collection *Lazare* (1837) there were poems of factory and mining life, child labor, alcoholism and prostitution. While the filthy Thames with every tide was bringing to Britain the riches of the world, wrote Barbier, the cotton-mill workers labored under horrible factory conditions while the Newcastle miners had to toil like moles, six hundred feet deep in the bowels of the earth, exposed to nameless dangers.[27]

3. DRAMA

The theater was extremely popular in this period, and changed rapidly to meet the taste of the middle and even lower classes. The government-subsidized theaters, which were the preserve of the fash-

---

[26] *Feuilles d'automne* (1831), quoted by Roger Picard: *Le romantisme social* (New York, 1944), 154. Further, André Maurois' biography (1956), which is largely personal; Fernand Gregh: *L'oeuvre de Victor Hugo* (Paris, 1933), an excellent analysis of his work; Jean-Bertrand Barrère: *Hugo, l'homme et l'oeuvre* (Paris, 1952) is a serious, up-to-date biography.

[27] Auguste Barbier: *Iambes et poèmes* (35 ed., Paris, 1888), 191 ff. Elliott M. Grant: *French Poetry and Modern Industry, 1830–1870* (Cambridge, 1927), 18 ff.; Helen D. Lockwood: *Tools and the Man* (New York, 1927), chaps. vi and vii; Marc Baroli: *Le train dans la littérature française* (Paris, 1963), 25 ff.

ionable world, enjoyed the resources of many talented actors (in England William Macready, Charles Kean, Charles and Fanny Kemble), but suffered from a dearth of good dramas. The versatile Edward Bulwer Lytton provided a few good historical plays (*The Lady of Lyons,* 1838, was especially popular), but most of the dramas written by the poets were unfit for stage production. Browning composed no less than six such plays (notably *Strafford,* 1837), which were strong on psychological analysis, but weak in plot and action. Under the circumstances the legitimate stage was thrown back on Shakespeare and other classics, or obliged to resort to translations or adaptations of popular novels.[28]

The situation on the Continent was markedly better. The Viennese stage, for example, was active and prosperous despite the irritating censorship. In Franz Grillparzer it had a playwright of the first order, a Romanticist who accepted the restraints of classical forms. Grillparzer had produced a number of plays before 1830 and in fact published but little after 1838. But during the 1830's he brought out *Hero and Leander* (1831), a modern treatment of the classical Hero and Leander theme, which many critics regard as his masterpiece. It was followed by *A Dream Is Life* (1834), a tense drama of excessive ambition, and by his one comedy *Thou Shalt Not Lie* (1838), which is as live and amusing on the present-day stage as ever. Grillparzer's dramas were written in verse, much of which is lyrical poetry of the purest kind. The author was a basically unhappy man, whose psychological insight was perhaps too keen for comfort. His work was marked by pessimism, by a feeling of sadness at the thought that noble personalities usually succumb to the ignoble, or are defeated by dark and incomprehensible forces.[29]

[28] Allardyce Nicoll: *A History of Early Nineteenth Century Drama, 1800–1850* (Cambridge, 1930), I, *passim;* Thomas N. Dickinson; *The Contemporary Drama in England* (Boston, 1931), chaps. i and ii. Arthur L. Hayward: *The Days of Dickens* (London, 1925) has a good chapter on the social side of the theatrical world.

[29] Josef Nadler: *Literaturgeschichte des deutschen Volkes* (4 ed., Berlin, 1938), III, Book XVI, chap. iii, which gives an excellent account of the cultural life of Vienna, and the same author's *Franz Grillparzer* (Vienna, 1952). Gerhart Baumann: *Franz Grillparzer: Dichtung und oesterreichische Geistesverfassung* (2 ed., Frankfurt, 1966) is a basic study. In English see M. Morris: *The Social and Political Implications of the Work of Grillparzer* (London, 1948); P. Drake: *Grillparzer and Biedermeier* (Waco, 1953). The various dramas of Grillparzer have been admirably translated into English by Arthur L. Burkhard.

Another German dramatist of major importance was Friedrich Hebbel, a North German born in grim poverty, all of whose work was marked by stark realism, foreshadowing late-nineteenth-century drama. Many of Hebbel's plays were written after 1850, but the earlier ones (*Judith*, 1839; *Mary Magdalene*, 1843; *Herod and Mariamne*, 1847; *Agnes Bernauer*, 1851) were as interesting and significant as the later ones. Hebbel used classical themes, but adapted them freely and had no compunction about choosing very ordinary subjects, as in *Mary Magdalene*. Like Grillparzer, he was much impressed by the never-ending conflict of the individual with the world about him, and by the inescapable woes of human existence.[30]

Georg Büchner was an amazing figure in German literature, a man who died at the age of twenty-four (1837) whose impact on Germany and the world was to come only a century later. He was a native of Hesse and, as a student at Strasbourg, had become imbued with French revolutionary and socialist thought. Convinced that the relatively small bourgeois middle class could never hope to destroy the old regime, he argued the necessity for mobilizing the peasantry for a mass revolutionary effort. This he was engaged in doing at the time of his premature death. Meanwhile he had written a powerful drama of the French Revolution (*Danton's Death*, 1835), a highly realistic play full of disillusionment. Man there appeared as but a plaything in the hands of fate, in a world that had no place for greatness or nobility. In another play (*Woyzeck*, 1836), really a fragmentary sequence of scenes which was not published until 1879, Büchner for the first time introduced the commonest of common men, the poor devil Woyzeck against whom everyone and everything conspired. When well produced, *Woyzeck* is an extremely moving spectacle even today, either as a play or as an opera with music by Alban Berg.[31]

French poets frequently turned to drama, writing either in prose or in verse. The best of their plays were on historical themes, inspired by Shakespeare, Schiller or Scott. The first performance of Victor Hugo's *Hernani* (1830) was the occasion for the famous battle and victory of

[30] Franz Mehring: *Beiträge zur Literaturgeschichte* (Berlin, 1948), 181 ff.; G. R. Mason: *From Gottsched to Hebbel* (London, 1961), 240 ff.; and the excellent biography by Edna Purdie: *Friedrich Hebbel* (London, 1932).

[31] Karl Viëtor: *Georg Büchner* (Bern, 1949); Arthur H. J. Knight: *Georg Büchner* (Oxford, 1951); Hans Mayer: *George Büchner und seine Zeit* (Wiesbaden, 1960).

Romanticism, while his *Ruy Blas* (1838), the story of the love of a lackey for a queen, was extraordinarily successful. However, Hugo had but little dramatic sense. His plots were conventional, his action exaggerated and his language painfully extravagant. Nonetheless, the plays contain many lyrical passages. They have, in fact, been described as "collections of lyrics, linked by the thread of an intrigue."[32]

Vigny's *Chatterton* (1835) was a moving study of an artist suffering at the hands of a materialistic society. Musset's plays, on the other hand, were lively, highly colored skits intended for reading. The best are the historical drama *Lorenzaccio* (1834) and the comedy *One Does Not Trifle with Love* (1834). Henry James was to appreciate their "sentimental fragrance."[33]

Mention must be made also of Dumas and Scribe, whose popularity knew no bounds. Alexander Dumas produced no less than twenty-five plays, all of them romantic, heroic, passionate, exciting, and all of them characterized by sureness of plot and action. His *Henry III* (1829) and *The Tower of Nesle* (1832) were thought his best.

Most Romantic plays verged on melodrama, which appealed greatly to the half-educated *petite bourgeoisie*. The Paris boulevards were lined with small theaters, where the wildest and most provocative spectacles were available for a mere pittance. In these playhouses the social comedies of Eugène Scribe were staged by the dozen. Marriage, divorce, adultery, illegitimacy, prostitution, themes usually barred from respectable literature, were freely debated, while ill-disguised attacks on the monarchy and glorifications of Napoleon were regular fare. The favorite theme, it seems, was the antagonism of social classes. The evils of wealth, the exploitation of the poor and weak, the seduction of the worker's virtuous sister or daughter by the heartless aristocrat, these topics were constantly harped upon. The cumulative effect of this propaganda must have been considerable.[34]

In London there were some eighty "penny theaters," attended nightly by about 24,000 people. Since Victorian prudery forbade the presenta-

---

[32] Lanson and Tuffrau: *Manuel illustré d'histoire de la littérature française,* 592 ff.

[33] Henry James: *French Poets and Novelists* (London, 1878; New York, 1964), 27.

[34] David-Owen Evans: *Le drame moderne* (Paris, 1923), 233 ff., 260 ff., 307 ff.; F. W. M. Draper: *The Rise and Fall of the French Romantic Drama* (London, 1923), 248 ff.; Hugh A. Smith: *Main Currents of Modern French Drama* (New York, 1925), 36 ff.

tion of sex themes, the audiences were treated to every conceivable type of villainy.[35] On the other hand, in Vienna, the headquarters of political censorship, the popular playhouses were permitted to regale their audiences with the farces of Ferdinand Raimund, the sparkling satires of Johann Nestroy, and the vivid pictures of bourgeois society of Eduard von Bauernfeld.

4. FICTION

The form of literature most favored by the new reading public was the novel, which in this period reached its highest development. Sir Walter Scott through his *Waverley Novels* had made the novel form popular. He not only provided his readers with interesting stories but wrote of ordinary people as well as eminent historical figures. His careful description of local conditions stimulated interest in social analysis, and the pure morality of his work made it accessible even to young ladies. Scott's novels were translated into all European languages. The spread and depth of his influence can hardly be overstated. The period of the present study was indeed the golden age of the historical novel. Among its most distinguished examples were Victor Hugo's *Notre Dame de Paris* (1831), the wonderful yarns of Alexander Dumas (*The Three Musketeers,* 1844; *The Count of Monte Cristo,* 1844; *The Vicomte de Bragelonne,* 1848), and, on the English side, Bulwer-Lytton's *The Last Days of Pompeii* (1834), *The Last of the Barons* (1843) and *The Caxtons* (1849). They pale in literary importance, however, when compared with the social novels which emerged at this time in France and England and marked the transition to realism.[36]

The historical novel was, from its very nature, apt to be written in the romantic vein and so carried on the tradition of an earlier period, while the more realistic novel was coming to maturity. The point has been frequently made that the age was one of increasing materialism, intent above all on making money, which meant political as well as

---

[35] James Grant: *Sketches in London* (London, 1838).
[36] Bradford A. Booth: "Form and Technique of the Novel" (in Joseph E. Baker, ed.: *The Reinterpretation of Victorian Literature,* 67–96). On Scott's influence in France, see Frederick C. Green: *French Novelists from the Revolution to Proust* (new ed., New York, 1964), 108 ff.; on Germany, Lawrence M. Price: *English Literature in Germany* (Berkeley, 1953), chap. xxiii; on Russia, Ernest J. Simmons: *Introduction to Russian Realism* (Bloomington, 1965), chap. i.

social power. "Ours is a ready-money society," says one of Thackeray's characters; "we live among bankers and city big-wigs . . . and every man, as he talks to you, is jingling his guineas in his pocket."[37] But this is not to say that all novels of the time, if they were not historical, were realistic or even social. In France the short novels of Prosper Merimée (*Colomba*, 1840; *Carmen*, 1845) were distinguished chiefly by their grim and sardonic humor. Neither can the Dane, Hans Christian Andersen, be easily classified. He was a prolific writer of plays and novels which made but little mark in their day and have since been forgotten, while his *Fairy Tales* (1835, 1843) quickly gained him a world reputation and were ranked, in terms of sales, with the Bible, Shakespeare and Bunyan's *Pilgrim's Progress*.[38]

But by far the most striking case of uncommitted literature was provided by the principal novels of the three sisters, Charlotte, Emily and Anne Brontë, daughters of a Yorkshire parson with literary aspirations, brought up in isolation and therefore self-taught in the art of writing. Charlotte, the eldest, wrote several novels, of which *Jane Eyre* (1847) is the best-known and most important. Emily wrote only one, *Wuthering Heights* (1848), and Anne two, of which *The Tenant of Wildfell Hall* (1848) is the more noteworthy. These novels had nothing to do with problems of politics or society, nor did they represent any particular literary form. They were simply great and original works of the creative imagination, the expression of pent-up passions. As such they belong more properly with the novels of the late nineteenth century.

Jane Eyre is a masterpiece of self-revelation, the first novel freely expressing a woman's passion and the first to clothe the life of a plain woman in romance. *Wuthering Heights,* generally rated highest among the Brontë novels, is quite unique, "the one perfect work of art among all the vast, varied canvases of Victorian fiction." A story of basic human passions, it tells of two tragic characters dominated by feeling rather than reason and doomed to poetic disaster. It is one novel which critics agree in proclaiming a masterpiece in form as well as substance. Anne's novel, alleged to pale in comparison with the works

---

[37] George Osborne in *Vanity Fair* (Thackeray: *Works,* London, 1869, I, 219); see also on this topic Harry Levin: *The Gates of Horn* (New York, 1963), 32 ff.

[38] P. M. Mitchell: *A History of Danish Literature* (New York, 1958), chap. ix; Rumer Godden: *Hans Christian Andersen* (New York, 1955), 8.

of her sisters, is gaining increased recognition as a study of the degeneration of a human character.[39]

Most of the great novels of the period portray society realistically, but without having a primary political or social purpose. This is certainly true of the work of Stendhal (Henri Beyle), Balzac, Dickens, Thackeray, and Gogol, none of whom owes his world renown primarily to faithful reporting of conditions. In such novels as *The Red and the Black* (1831) and *Lucien Leuwen* (1835) Stendhal portrayed fascinating scenes of French society in his time, but only incidentally. His concern was chiefly with himself, and the heroes of his novels reflect various aspects of his own complicated personality. Stendhal was basically a man of the Enlightenment, a Voltairean, cool, critical and even cynical, and a fierce enemy of romantic sentimentality. His aim was uncompromising fidelity to the truth, however repulsive it might be. Politically his allegiance was to Napoleon, under whom he had served. He admired the intelligence and energy of the great emperor, foresaw the revolutionary changes coming over society, and steeped himself in the writings of the English economists, whose importance he sensed. Little regarded in his own day and rejected because of his "sinister and cold philosophy" (Balzac), Stendhal is highly esteemed by posterity as an exceptionally keen observer of his society and a master of psychological analysis.[40]

Honoré de Balzac, like Stendhal, was an admirer of Napoleon as the exponent of enlightened administration, order and authority. He was one of the first to appreciate Stendhal's work, but in contrast to Stendhal was concerned less with his own self than with others. He had what Henry James was to call a "huge, all-comprising, all-desiring, all-devouring love of reality," an intense interest in human beings and in the workings of society. A man of unbelievable energy and industry,

---

[39] Among the innumerable biographical studies of these remarkable sisters, Lawrence and E. M. Hansen's *The Four Brontës* (New York, 1949) and Phyllis Bentley: *The Brontë Sisters* (London, 1950) can be recommended. For criticism see G. K. Chesterton: *The Victorian Age in Literature*, 47 ff.; Walter Allen: *The English Novel* (New York, 1954), 124 ff.; Lord David Cecil: *Victorian Novelists* (Chicago, 1958), chaps. iv and v; Frederick R. Karl: *The Nineteenth Century British Novel* (New York, 1964), 77 ff.

[40] Green: *French Novelists*, 125 ff.; Levin: *Gates of Horn*, chap. iii. There are recent biographies by Richard Coe: *Stendhal* (London, 1963) and Armand Caraccio: *Stendhal* (New York, 1965). On contemporary opinion, see Bernard Weinberg: *French Realism: the Critical Reaction, 1830–1870* (Chicago, 1937), 10 ff.; and on the economic side, Lucien Jansse: "Stendhal et l'économie politique" (*Stendhal Club*, VII, 1965, 295–308).

Balzac undertook to depict the "human comedy" in all its aspects. In the twenty years covered by the present book he wrote twenty-four full-scale novels and numerous short stories which carried him a long way toward attainment of his goal. Among the greatest of his novels were *Eugénie Grandet* (1833), *Old Man Goriot* (1834), *The Peasants* (1844), and *Cousin Bette* (1847). They have been referred to frequently in earlier chapters for the light they shed on the conditions and problems of the period.

Balzac's novels were hastily written and poorly constructed, but were extraordinarily rich in detail and in depiction of social types. Modern studies have fully demonstrated the accuracy of his observations, with special reference to the dominant upper middle class. He had little to say of the aristocracy and next to nothing of the proletariat. Though a bourgeois himself, he detested the financial and business classes, having convinced himself from his own business failures that all business is dishonest and government corrupt. Many of his plots hinge on money problems and reflect his fascination with what men and women will do to get money. Vice, he suggests, invariably triumphs over virtue. "He had little belief in virtue and still less admiration for it," says Henry James, adding that, having probed vice and human frailty to their depths, he had a profound understanding of them. His novels, then, provided a unique documentation of a society in transformation as the old landed aristocracy was supplanted by the moneyed bourgeoisie. Widely read all over Europe, Balzac undoubtedly contributed heavily to the popular dislike of the newly influential middle class.[41]

Charles Dickens, nine of whose novels were published between 1836 and 1852, has often been compared to Balzac. Both had enormous creative energy and imagination, and both aimed at what Dickens called "the stern truth." Both disdained the aristocracy and feared the barbarous mob, yet disliked intensely the moneyed upper middle class

---

[41] Stefan Zweig: *Balzac* (New York, 1948) is an interesting psychological study. Important recent biographies are Félicien Marceau: *Balzac et son monde* (Paris, 1955) and E. J. Olivier: *Honoré de Balzac* (London, 1966). More specialized studies include Emmanuel Failletaz: *Balzac et le monde des affaires* (Paris, 1932); Bernard Guyon: *La pensée politique et sociale de Balzac* (Paris, 1947); Jean-Hervé Donnard: *Les réalités économiques et sociales dans la Comédie Humaine* (Paris, 1961); Donald Fanger: *Dostoevsky and Romantic Realism* (Cambridge, 1965), chap. ii. George Lukács' essay on *The Peasants* (reprinted in his *Studies in European Realism,* New York, 1964) is a discerning Marxist analysis.

and the political institutions of their time. But Dickens, in contrast to Balzac, believed in virtue and had warm sympathy for the suffering poor in the soul-destroying tragedy of their everyday life. It has been well said of him that he yearned for the mythical pastoral England before it was shattered by industrialism, and felt uncomfortable in the presence of the machine, whose achievements he could not help but admire. Much has been made of his social criticism, his exposure of the poor law, the debtor's prison, the schools and numerous other institutions. But he was no radical and had no specific program of reform. The institutions he criticized were meant merely as background for his stories. It was only incidentally that he exposed many evils of the day and created sentiment for reform. Not until his novel *Hard Times* (1854) did he attempt to deal with the psychological effects of industrialism.

As a writer Dickens is now valued not so much for his reporting of social conditions as for his imagination, his characterizations, and his humor. Unlike Balzac, he did not attempt to depict social types or trace the development of his characters. "He had the power of creating people, both possible and impossible, who were simply precious and priceless people," says G. K. Chesterton. Hence his characters and their vicissitudes had an immediate appeal for the common man. Dickens was universally popular in his own day and was read through the length and breadth of Europe. More than a century later he still makes good reading and is still regarded as one of the greatest novelists of all time.[42]

William M. Thackeray, Dickens' contemporary, was a novelist more akin to Stendhal than to Balzac. He had the same aversion to romantic sentimentalism and self-delusion, the same cynicism about human nature and society, the same sharp eye for character. His masterpiece, *Vanity Fair,* which appeared serially in 1847–1848, has been criticized

[42] The standard biography is Edgar Johnson: *Charles Dickens: His Tragedy and Triumph* (New York, 1953). K. J. Fielding: *Charles Dickens* (new ed., London, 1965) is an excellent combination of biography and criticism. Edmund Wilson: "Dickens, the Two Scrooges" (1941, reprinted in his *Eight Essays,* New York, 1954) was a landmark in criticism. See further, Ada Nisbet: "Charles Dickens" (in Lionel Stevenson, ed.: *Victorian Fiction,* Cambridge, 1964, 44–153); Steven Marcus: *Dickens, from Pickwick to Dombey* (New York, 1965); Edward Wagenknecht: *The Man Dickens* (rev. ed., Norman. 1966). Humphrey House: *The Dickens World* (London, 1941) is an outstanding study of Dickens' social criticism, while George H. Ford: *Dickens and His Readers* (London, 1955) is a basic study of the evolution of Dickens' reputation.

not only for the looseness of its form but for the author's paradoxical attitude toward life, the inconsistency of his political and social views, his obnoxious moralizing. But it is a wonderful story, extremely well written, and has continued to enjoy great popularity for its realistic portrayal of upper-middle-class people in varying social situations and for its trenchant criticism of men and manners. Thackeray's characters have nothing of the heroic. They are frail humans, mixtures of good and bad.[43]

The social novel proper, that is, the story designed to argue a point, became popular through the work of George Sand (Aurore Dude-vant), whose early romantic novels (*Indiana,* 1832; *Lélia,* 1833) proclaimed the rights of love and demanded greater freedom for women. Sand was a highly intelligent, generous, courageous woman, easily influenced by Utopian socialism, as reflected in several of her later novels (*Consuelo,* 1842; *The Miller of Angibault,* 1845). She was a prolific writer and an interesting and influential personality. Many advanced writers and radical thinkers throughout Europe recognized their indebtedness to her.[44]

It was in England, where social changes were most drastic, that the social novel reached its fullest development. The impetus no doubt came from Carlyle, who, before coming to London in 1834, had already become a critic of the laissez-faire economics. While recognizing the potential benefits of industrialism, he had dark forebodings of the "deep-lying struggle in the whole fabric of society," which was "strangely altering the old relations and increasing the distance between the rich and the poor." Deeply troubled by the fact that "countries are rich, prosperous in all manner of increase, beyond example; but the men of these countries are poor, needier than ever in all sustenance outward and inward," he called upon government to intervene to save human nature from the consequences of mechanization. In

---

[43] The standard biography is Gordon N. Ray: *Thackeray: the Uses of Adversity* and *Thackeray: the Age of Wisdom* (New York, 1955–1958), but the shorter biography by Lionel Stevenson: *The Showman of Vanity Fair* (New York, 1947) is still valuable. See also Geoffrey Tillotson: *Thackeray, the Novelist* (London, 1954); Lionel Stevenson: "Thackeray" (in his *Victorian Fiction,* 154–178).

[44] André Maurois: *Lélia: the Life of George Sand* (New York, 1953) is a strictly personal biography. See also Jean Larnac: *George Sand révolutionnaire* (Paris, 1948), and Jeanne Galzy: *George Sand* (Paris, 1950). Further, David-Owen Evans: *Le roman social sous le Monarchie de Juillet* (Paris, 1936); Edouard Dolléans: *Féminisme et mouvement ouvrier: George Sand* (Paris, 1951).

his own inimitable, passionate language he drove home his argument in books (*Chartism*, 1839; *Past and Present*, 1843) and in essays calling on the workers to organize and on the government to take action in behalf of those too weak to act for themselves. The real ordeal of life, he wrote, "is to live miserable, we know not why; to work sore and gain nothing; to be heart-worn, weary, yet isolated, girt-in with a cold, universal laissez-faire."[45]

Carlyle once described himself as "a bringer-back of men to reality." Like Balzac and Heine and many other thoughtful people, he was apprehensive of what the cold and hungry masses might some day do to European society. It is understandable, then, that there should have been a note of urgency in the strictly social novels that began to appear in large numbers. Only a few of them had literary merit and therefore call for nothing more than the briefest mention. Frances Trollope led the way with *Michael Armstrong: the Factory Boy* (1840) in which the horrors of child labor were exposed and the bloated exploiters of the children denounced (see Illustrations 32, 33). Charlotte Tonna followed with *Helen Fleetwood* (1841), depicting the miseries of the rural poor that drove them into the industrial cities. Benjamin Disraeli's politico-social novels *Coningsby* (1844) and *Sybil* (1845) have already been noted in another connection.[46] *Sybil* in particular was devoted to analysis of the condition of England and was based on the author's visits to the industrial North as well as on the evidence of parliamentary commissions. Disraeli's program for "Young England" was designed to forestall "a revolt against empty fireplaces and bare cupboards" through a return to the old society, a prospect that fascinated Balzac and Carlyle too and appealed greatly to many displaced workers.[47]

---

[45] Quoted by David Daiches: *Carlyle and the Victorian Dilemma* (Edinburgh, 1963). See also Hugh Walker: *The Literature of the Victorian Era* (Cambridge, 1913), chap. ii; Frederick W. Roe: *The Social Philosophy of Carlyle and Ruskin* (New York, 1921), 43 ff.; Raymond Williams: *Culture and Society, 1788–1850* (New York, 1958), 71 ff.; Herbert L. Sussman: *Victorians and the Machine* (Cambridge, 1968), 10 ff.

[46] See above, Chapter VII.

[47] Muriel Masefield: *Peacocks and Primroses* (London, 1953) is a rather light treatment of the Disraeli novels. On the other hand, Raymond Maître: *Disraeli, homme de lettres* (Paris, 1963) is exhaustive. The best general study of the social novel is still Louis Cazamian: *Le roman social en Angleterre, 1830–1850* (Paris, 1903, 1935), but see also Kathleen Tillotson: *Novels of the Eighteen-Forties* (Oxford, 1954), 150 ff.; William O. Aydelotte: "The England of Marx and Mill as Reflected in Fiction" (*Journal of*

Mrs. (Elizabeth) Gaskell's social novel *Mary Barton* (1845) was an outstanding example of the type, and has been discussed in an earlier context.[48] This brief list may, therefore, be closed by mention of the two novels of Charles Kingsley, the leader of the Christian Socialist movement. *Yeast,* written in 1848, discussed the plight of the rural workers, while the second and better one, *Alton Locke* (1850), was concerned with London sweatshops and the Chartist movement. Kingsley, who was directly inspired by Carlyle, was perhaps too ardent in his advocacy of the workers' cause, but his descriptions of London's East End and the riots of the Chartist period are nonetheless memorable.[49]

Karl Marx, writing in 1854, declared that the English novelists, through their descriptions, had "revealed more political and social truths to the world than all the politicians, publicists and moralists added together."[50] Certainly this realistic literature provided valuable contemporary evidence of the newly emerging social problem. Other countries, being less advanced economically than Britain, produced no parallels, though in Germany there was at least some rather little-known fiction of this character in the years just preceding 1848.

The background was provided by the writers of the Young Germany school, which was discussed in Chapter IV. These writers reflected the ideas of French democracy in their demands for freedom not only in politics but also in social relations. Karl Immerman, in his voluminous novel *The Epigones* (1836) went even further and tried to depict the transformation of the old, landed society. He was critical of advancing industrialism for what it was doing to the traditional peasantry, and dreamed of a return to the old social order, even though he recognized that such a return was out of the question: "With the speed of a storm the present-day world is rushing toward arid mechanization; we cannot check its course," he wrote.

Economic History, VIII, 1948, Suppl., 42–58); Christopher Hollis: "Disraeli's Political Novels" (in *Tradition and Change*, London, 1954, 98–117); Sheila M. Smith: "Truth and Propaganda in the Victorian Social Novel" (*Renaissance and Modern Studies*, VIII, 1964, 7–591).

[48] See above, Chapter VI.

[49] See Arnold Kettle: "The Early Victorian Social Problem Novel" (in Boris Ford, ed.: *From Dickens to Hardy*, Baltimore, 1958, 169–187).

[50] Quoted from the New York *Tribune* articles by Ralph Fox: *The Novel and the People* (London, 1937), 72.

Immermann and many other writers were deeply moved by the plight of the handloom weavers, especially after the Silesian insurrection had revealed the intolerable conditions under which they lived. By that time the novels of Balzac, Dickens and Sue, with their revelations of misery and crime in the growing cities, had aroused interest in this aspect of the social problem. Following Sue's *Mysteries of Paris,* similar "mysteries" of other large cities soon saw the light. Ernst Dronke, described the underworld of Berlin and wrote *Police Stories* exposing urban criminality, which he attributed to despair brought on by unemployment and hunger. At much the same time Ernst Willkomm published his novel *Iron, Money and Soul* (1843), a study of factory and slum life. He followed this with his better-known story *White Slaves* (1845), dealing with the impoverished weavers among whom he lived.

There are no more serfs in our district [he wrote]. The people are no less free than their lords to die by drowning, or hanging, or shooting, or ordinary starvation. Not a few have to take advantage of the liberty to starve, but there are many who do not want this freedom and who therefore auction themselves off for a pittance and are hired as servants of other men or of machines.

Finally, to mention one more writer, Robert Prutz, in his novel *Little Angels* (written in 1845, but not published until 1851), drew a terrible picture of the exploitation of the weavers and the impact of industrialization on a village community.[51] These novels may not have been literature of the highest order, but even as literature they were far from negligible and in any case provided ample evidence of the rapidly developing social problem and of growing class consciousness.

---

[51] On this neglected literature, see Solomon Liptzin: *The Weavers in German Literature* (Baltimore, 1926), 45 ff.; Volkmar Frobenius: *Die Behandlung von Technik und Industrie in der deutschen Dichtung von Goethe bis zur Gegenwart* (Bremen, 1935), 64 ff.

Chapter Seventeen

THE ARTS

I. ARCHITECTURE

ALTHOUGH in the field of painting this period produced a number of truly distinguished figures, in architecture and sculpture its achievement was unimpressive. The tradition of an accepted style and of systematic training for craftsmen had broken down. The architect or artist was now free to work in any style that appealed to him or attracted patrons. All was individualism and free competition in a period marked by complete fragmentation. The two predominant styles of the late eighteenth century, the Neoclassical and the Gothic, continued to hold their own until the mid-nineteenth century, but presently other historic styles were revived: the Old English or Tudor, the Renaissance or Italianate, and even the Egyptian, Hindu and Chinese. Architecture, wrote one of its leading English practitioners, was no longer "the expression of existing opinions and circumstances, but a confused jumble of styles and symbols borrowed from all nations and periods."[1]

This is not to say that no beautiful buildings were erected in these years. But there were few or no new ideas, no major innovations, no fresh approaches to artistic problems. The principles of pure Greek art were by this time well established, and Gothic became the subject of professional study in the 1840's. This means that the Gothic style was treated rather impressionistically, the emphasis being on ostentation and ornamentation. Gothic buildings were frequently quite conventional in general plan, with only a Gothic façade.

Britain continued to set the pace for European building. The successors of the great Regency architects followed in their footsteps, building in various styles as their commissions required. Palaces and government buildings were usually designed in the Neoclassical style, theaters and opera houses in the Baroque, city residences and clubs in

---

[1] Augustus W. Pugin, quoted by Kenneth Clark: *The Gothic Revival* (3 ed., London, 1967), 123.

the Renaissance, and the country "seats" of the landed classes in either Neoclassical or Gothic.[2] Among the best Neoclassical structures were the British Museum with its splendid Greek façade, built by Robert Smirke in the years 1823–1846, and the Ashmolean Museum at Oxford with its Ionic portico, a building distinguished for its balance and elegance, the work of Charles R. Cockerill (1839–1845). The Travellers Club (1830), the Reform Club (1837), and Bridgewater House were all built by Charles Barry in the style of the Italian palazzo. Barry and Anthony Salvin were much favored by the aristocracy, many members of which had their country houses remodeled in one of the fashionable styles. There was a veritable "rage for turning comfortable houses into uninhabitable castles." It is said that no less than twenty-five country seats were Gothicized in these years. Everyone, it seemed, had to have turrets, battlements, spiral staircases and other Gothic appurtenances. Salvin's reconstruction of Alnwick Castle and his work on Peckforton Castle (1846–1850) are outstanding examples of the castellated style.[3]

A landmark in the history of European architecture was the design of the new houses of Parliament, which were built between 1836 and 1852. The commission called for the Elizabethan or Gothic style, considered peculiarly English. Basically the plan, by Barry, was fairly conventional, though the proportions were impressive and the rich ornamentation, due largely to Barry's collaborator A. W. Pugin, gave the structure great distinction. Some writers describe it as "the most creditable architectural performance of Victoria's reign" and as "ranking high among the world's greatest architectural groups."[4]

Pugin, a great figure in British art history, was incredibly active and influential in the years 1836–1844. His study of medieval architecture had convinced him that the greatness of Gothic buildings derived from the virtue of their builders. Converted to Catholicism, Pugin held that the degraded state of the arts was "purely owing to the absence of

---

[2] E. H. Gombrich: *The Story of Art* (11 ed., New York, 1966), 378.

[3] H. S. Goodhart-Rendel: *English Architecture since the Regency* (London, 1953); Henry-Russell Hitchcock: *Early Victorian Architecture* (London, 1955), and *Architecture, Nineteenth and Twentieth Centuries* (in *Penguin History of Art,* London, 1958); Robert E. Jordan: *Victorian Architecture* (London, 1966); Thomas S. R. Boase: *English Art, 1800–1870* (Oxford, 1959), 23 ff.; and the essays by various authorities in Peter Ferriday, ed.: *Victorian Architecture* (London, 1963).

[4] See the essays by Goodhart-Rendel and Fleetwood-Hesketh in Ferriday: *Victorian Architecture.*

Catholic feeling." In his principal theoretical work, *The True Principles of Christian Architecture* (1841), he therefore taught that a building should express the purpose for which it was built and that "all ornament should consist of the enrichment of the essential construction of the building." Between 1839 and 1841 he built the Catholic cathedral at Birmingham and numerous parish churches throughout the Midlands and in Ireland.[5]

Parallel movements in religious architecture were inaugurated by the Camden Society of Cambridge in 1839 and the Oxford Architectural Society soon after. Their objective was to check the "eager vandalism" which marked the restoration of many Gothic cathedrals and monuments and to reform the Gothic style so as to meet the requirements of Anglican ritual. The movement was closely related to the Oxford or Tractarian movement and proved itself so influential that for fifty years almost every new Anglican church was built and furnished according to its specifications.[6]

While professional architects showed little interest in the problems of business and industry, engineers made notable contributions in design and in the utilization of new materials. By 1830 the use of cast iron in the construction of galleries, roofs and bridges was already well established. The advent of the railway created an ever greater demand. Many railway station platforms consisted of paneling resting on cast-iron columns and beams, while the station itself was usually Neoclassical, like most public buildings. Thus Euston Station in London was modeled on the Greek temples at Girgenti (Sicily), with an imposing façade. A particularly interesting case was the Clifton Suspension Bridge, begun in 1830. Two eminent engineers, Thomas Telford and Isambard K. Brunel, competed for the design. The former proposed for the piers two Gothic towers, complete with turrets and generous ornamentation. The second, the winner, called for two massive gateways in the Egyptian style, the towers of which were guarded by sphinxes.[7]

Among outstanding examples of the new construction were Joseph

[5] Clark: *Gothic Revival*, 106 ff.; Boase: *English Art*, 227 ff.; and the essay by Alexandra G. Clark in Ferriday: *Victorian Architecture*, 139–152.

[6] Clark: *Gothic Revival*, 137 ff.; Boase: *English Art*, 237 ff.

[7] Celia Brunel Noble: *The Brunels, Father and Son* (London, 1938), 108; Nikolaus Pevsner: "Victorian Prolegomena" (in Ferriday: *Victorian Architecture*, 19–37); Francis D. Klingender: *Art and the Industrial Revolution* (London, 1947), 106.

Paxton's huge conservatory at Chatsworth (1836–1840), J. B. Bunning's London Coal Exchange (1846–1849) and, on the Continent, Henri Labrouste's Bibliothèque Sainte-Geneviève, high-vaulted and forbidding (1843–1850), the Paris Gare de l'Est (1847–1852) and Saint Isaac's Cathedral in St. Petersburg (1842). But the masterpiece was the Crystal Palace, built by Paxton to house the Great Exhibition of 1851 (see Illustration 18). Designed and built in a mere nine months, the Crystal Palace was a miracle of modernity in the use of materials, and in standardization and prefabrication of parts. It was 1,848 feet long and 140 feet high, and had 2,300 cast-iron girders and 900,000 square feet of glass. No effort was made to conceal the framework. On the contrary, the girders were painted red and the columns yellow, thus lending a note of gaiety to the huge structure. Small wonder that the palace was the cynosure of all eyes.[8]

To a large extent Continental architecture followed the English example. In France a number of Napoleonic structures were completed (Arc de Triomphe de l'Etoile, 1836; Madeleine, 1842) and there was much construction of hospitals and prisons, but of noteworthy structures there were almost none in this period. As in England, various styles were employed concurrently. The great church of Saint-Vincent de Paul (1824–1844) was the most important example of the Neoclassical, the church of Sainte-Clothilde (1846) of the Gothic, and the Bibliothèque Sainte-Geneviève (1843–1850) of the Renaissance. The Gothic style became increasingly popular and, as in England, led to countless restorations. The eminent archaeologist-engineer E.-E. Viollet-le-Duc began the restoration of Notre Dame de Paris and of the citadel of Carcassonne. His frantic effort to attain pristine purity of style led him to destroy many accretions of importance or interest and some of his work is now looked upon by critics with decidedly mixed feelings.[9]

In Germany there was much monumental building in Berlin and in Munich, where King Louis was determined to make his capital

---

[8] See above, Chapter II, for the economic and social aspects of the exhibition, and on the architectural side Klingender: *Art and the Industrial Revolution*, 128 ff.; Boase: *English Art*, chap. x; and the essay on Paxton by Robert F. Jordan, in Ferriday: *Victorian Architecture*, 155–165.

[9] Henri Réau: *L'ère romantique: les arts plastiques* (Vol. LXXVI bis of Henri Berr, ed.: *L'évolution de l'humanité*, Paris, 1949), 204 ff.; Pierre Lavedan: *French Architecture* (London, 1956), 142 ff.; Marcel Brion: *Romantic Art* (New York, 1960), 29 ff.; Hitchcock: *Early Victorian Architecture*, 49 ff., 197.

a modern Athens. Much of the work in Munich was done by Leo von Klenze and Friedrich von Gärtner, and antedated 1830, but in the period of the present study Klenze, who had traveled extensively in Greece, built near Regensburg a *Walhalla* for Teutonic gods along the lines of the Parthenon at Athens (1831–1842) a strange incongruity, and at Munich a Hall of Fame modeled on the Loggia dei Lanzi at Florence (1843–1853). He designed the great Hermitage Museum at St. Petersburg in the Grecian style (1839–1849), but the Old Pinakothek at Munich in the revived Renaissance style. The same style was used by Gärtner for the National Library in Munich (1831) and later by Gottfried Semper for the Royal Theater at Dresden (1838–1841).

Karl Friedrich von Schinkel had, prior to 1830, already put his stamp on the architecture of Berlin. Though he, too, was at home in both the Gothic and the Neoclassical styles, his designs were mostly Grecian, e.g., the Church of Saint-Nicholas (1830–1837). Gothic was less popular in Germany than in England, but there was a renewed interest in it during the 1840's resulting from the rediscovery of the plans for the great cathedral at Cologne, the nave and towers of which had remained incomplete since the sixteenth century. During the next thirty years work on the cathedral was carried on as a national enterprise.[10]

2. SCULPTURE

Sculpture had little indeed to show in this period. In his novel *The Marble Faun* (1860) Hawthorne had one of his characters declare that sculpture could no longer claim a place among the living arts: "It has wrought itself out and come fairly to an end. There is never a new group nowadays; never even so much as a new attitude." The reason was that Bertel Thorvaldsen, the leading disciple of Canova (who died in 1825), so dominated the art life of Rome that departure from the Neoclassical style was all but impossible. Yet Thorvaldsen, for all his reputation and productivity, was "little more than a respectable copier of the antique." His school tended to destroy rather than encourage creativity.[11]

[10] Max von Boehn: *Biedermeier* (Berlin, n.d.), 408 ff.; Eberhard Hempel: *Geschichte der deutschen Baukunst* (Munich, 1949), 525 ff.; Hitchcock: *Early Victorian Architecture*, 24 ff., 111; Hans Weigert: *Geschichte der deutschen Kunst* (Frankfurt, 1963), II, 171 ff.

[11] Chandler R. Post: *A History of European and American Sculpture* (Cambridge, 1921), II, 88.

Despite the continuing demand for sculpture—portrait busts, funerary groups, historical monuments—neither English nor German artists were able to get beyond the severely classical style of Canova. John Gibson, who spent most of his life with Thorvaldsen in Rome and was the best-known English sculptor of the time, was an ardent protagonist of the pure, simple, classical style. Among the Germans Gottfried Schadow, Johann Dannecker, and David Rauch produced countless busts of princes and generals, all in the accepted style though with somewhat more realism. Most of Schadow's work was done before 1830. Dannecker is known chiefly for his statues of Goethe and Schiller, and Rauch's greatest achievement was his monument to Frederick the Great (1840–1852).[12]

The French, on the other hand, showed some disposition toward novelty. Not that they departed from Neoclassical standards. Even in François Rude's great relief on the Arc de Triomphe the hard-bitten French volunteers of 1792 were clothed like ancient warriors, the oldest of whom strongly resembled classical statues of Jupiter (see Illustration 68). But Rude's panel added to the traditional classical more than a dash of energy and action, in short an admixture of the Romantic. It was undoubtedly the most distinguished piece of sculpture of the period and belongs with the masterpieces of all time.[13]

Among numerous other French sculptors David d'Angers was most popular, his rather realistic portrait busts of writers, artists, statesmen and others appealing particularly to the bourgeois taste. But of greater interest was Antoine-Louis Barye, outstanding for his animal sculpture. His famous groups (e.g., *A Lion Crushing a Serpent*) are comparable to Rude's work in strength and drama.[14]

The canons of Neoclassical sculpture were sufficiently liberal to permit the portrayal of even contemporaries in the nude. In 1847 George Sand's son-in-law, the sculptor Clésinger, provoked a scandal by exhibiting a nude statue of a well-known Parisienne, to whom he

---

[12] Hans Weigert: *Geschichte der deutschen Kunst*, II, 179 ff.; Brion: *Romantic Art*, 40 ff.

[13] Joseph Calmette: *François Rude* (Paris, 1920); Bernard S. Myers: *Art and Civilization* (New York, 1957), 566; Brion: *Romantic Art*, 40 ff.; Max von Boehn: *Vom Kaiserreich zur Republik* (Munich, 1921), 221; Réau: *L'ère romantique*, 185 ff.

[14] Post: *History of European and American Sculpture*, II, 121 ff.; Réau: *L'ère romantique*, 189 ff.; Fritz Novotny: *Painting and Sculpture in Europe, 1780–1880* (Baltimore, 1960), chaps. xviii and xix.

affixed a snake in imitation of Cleopatra. This was a severe tax on the morality even of the Parisians, but everywhere in Europe there was a lively and growing demand for statues of Venus or of nymphs which, in an age of bourgeois prudery, could be admired as art if ostensibly for no other reason. It was possible, says Sir Kenneth Clark, "to fill a conservatory with nude figures in Carrara marble, although the mention of an ankle was held to be a gross indecency." "Every young sculptor," says Hawthorne's character mentioned above, "seems to think that he must give the world some specimen of indecorous womanhood and call it Eve, Venus, a Nymph or any name that may apologize for a lack of decent clothing." The Great Exhibition of 1851 included a "forest of marble nudes," which was far from the least-favored attraction, despite the disgust voiced by Anglican bishops. Easily the most popular item was the American Hiram Powers' *Captive Slave,* a classical nude of the purest type, particularly appealing because of the shackles hanging from her wrists. It seems more than likely that these smooth, white females answered more than merely aesthetic needs.[15]

3. PAINTING

Painting was by far the most important of the visual arts in the midcentury and most interesting for the changes and new departures resulting from the greater liberty enjoyed by the artist. There seemed at the time to be no end to the demand for paintings and engravings. The upper classes continued to commission portraits and mythological or historical scenes, while governments opened competitions for the decoration of public buildings and purchased paintings exhibited in the salons for the museums of the large cities, which by 1830 were mostly opened to the public. The prosperous middle class followed the lead of the aristocracy and before long joined the ranks of the collectors, while the common man found satisfaction in the engravings which could be had for a few cents. Under these circumstances it is not surprising that the number of painters and sculptors increased notably. In France there were only 354 in 1789, as against 1,375 in 1830 and 2,159 in 1838.[16] Favorite artists were well rewarded for their work. They could obtain

---

[15] Kenneth Clark: *The Nude* (New York, 1959), 130 ff.; 221 ff.

[16] Statistics published by the *Journal des artistes* in 1838, quoted in Léon Rosenthal: *Du romantisme au réalisme* (Paris, 1914), 77.

from one to three thousand francs for a picture and in some cases far more. Czar Nicholas of Russia, who doted on the great battle pictures of Horace Vernet, paid 25,000 francs for the painting of Napoleon reviewing the Imperial Guard, and later 100,000 francs for *The Battle of Wola*. In England, Turner on his death bequeathed several hundred of his works to the nation, yet left an estate valued at £140,000.[17] These were certainly exceptional cases, but the fact remains that the average painter, no longer dependent on a wealthy patron, could usually eke out a living by doing portraits in oil, aquarelle or lithograph. In the days before photography, portrait work, despised by many artists, was at least a dependable source of income.

The academies of art, which controlled the annual Salon exhibitions, naturally tended to be conservative, yet within certain limits they were amazingly tolerant. Over the years they would accept works of widely varying tendency, just as they would, on occasion, reject a painting submitted by a recognized master.[18] In painting as in the other arts there was no single accepted style, nor is it possible to classify the painting of the period as either Neoclassical or Romantic. In the words of one present-day critic, Romanticism is now seen as a mode of feeling, "a flavour that can occur in any classic dish in any proportion."[19] Great artists such as Delacroix and Ingres, representing different ideals and objectives, treated classical and romantic themes indiscriminately. Delacroix, generally regarded as the greatest of the Romantic painters, actually resented being so called and insisted that he was a classicist. It is not surprising, then, to find critics referring to his work as classic Romanticism, while his opposite, Ingres, is put down as a romantic Classicist. About all one can say is that in this period of political and social upheaval, painting, like literature, felt the impact of new forces. Painters took many of their themes from contemporary literature (Goethe, Byron, Scott) and in their work revealed the same restlessness, yearning, sadness found in their sources. On the one hand, classical themes and classical treatments enjoyed the sanction of tradition and respectability. On the other, even the common

[17] R. H. Wilenski: *English Painting* (2 ed., London, 1943), 185 ff.; Réau: *L'ère romantique,* 129.

[18] Nikolaus Pevsner: *Academies of Art, Past and Present* (Cambridge, 1940); Bernard S. Myers: *Art and Civilization* (New York, 1957), 564.

[19] Sir Eric Newton: *The Romantic Rebellion* (New York, 1964), 11 ff., 29.

man was intrigued by the drama and color of the Romantic picture. When one of John Martin's extravagantly Romantic paintings was exhibited in London, madly enthusiastic spectators had to be held off by barriers erected for the purpose. Similar scenes were enacted in Paris.[20]

In the art of painting the primacy of France throughout the nineteenth century is beyond dispute, but as a matter of convenience the achievement of England and Germany, which was less diverse or complicated than the French, will be considered first. In England the age of the great portraitists came to an end with the demise of Sir Henry Raeburn (1823) and Sir Thomas Lawrence (1830). The Romantic, visionary artists Henry Fuseli and William Blake had also passed from the scene in 1825 and 1827. But the highly Romantic and dramatic style was carried on by John Martin and Francis Danby, who loved cataclysmic themes from the Old Testament, such as the Deluge and the Last Judgment. Martin's visions of cosmic doom usually contained huge mountain masses, terrifying cloud formations rent by lightning, and diminutive human figures about to be engulfed in torrents of water. Those who were religiously inclined found in these works the appropriate expression of God's wrath and were duly terrified. Bulwer Lytton saw in Martin "the divine intoxication of a great soul, lapped in majestic and unearthly dreams," and declared him "the greatest, the most lofty, the most permanent, the most original genius of his age." This judgment, if it has no other value, provides a measure of the interest and taste of the period.[21]

In great demand also were the works of the genre painters, which appealed strongly to the middle classes. While Benjamin Haydon tried desperately to revive interest in the heroic historical canvas, David Wilkie made a great reputation from faithful depictions of village life.

[20] Newton: *Romantic Rebellion;* Quentin Bell: *Victorian Artists* (Cambridge, 1967), 8 ff.; Sir Kenneth Clark's introduction to *The Romantic Movement* (Arts Council of Great Britain Exhibition, London, 1959); Michel Florisoone: "The Romantic and Neo-Classical Conflict" (*ibid.,* 21–26); Novotny: *Painting and Sculpture in Europe,* 1; Eric G. Underwood: *A Short History of French Painting* (London, 1931), chap. xii; Geraldine Pelles: *Art, Artists and Society: Painting in England and France, 1750–1850* (New York, 1963), 11, 15; Brion: *Romantic Art,* 7 ff.

[21] Edward L. Bulwer: *England and the English* (London, 1833), quoted by Thomas Ralston: *John Martin, His Life and Works* (London, 1947), 148; Klingender: *Art and the Industrial Revolution,* 104 ff.; Boase: *English Art,* 105 ff.; Graham Reynolds: *Victorian Painting* (New York, 1967), 15.

Edwin Landseer, though he painted some excellent landscapes (e.g., *Lake Scene*, 1836), endeared himself mostly by his sentimental animal scenes (e.g., *The Stag at Bay; The Old Shepherd's Chief Mourner*, 1837), while William Etty applied real talent to satisfying the popular interest in the female nude (e.g., *A Bivouac of Cupid and His Company*, 1838).[22]

In terms of significance for art history, these painters were not in a class with John Constable and Joseph M. W. Turner, both of them among the greatest landscapists of all time. Both had made their mark well before 1830. Ever since 1824 Constable had been exercising an international influence, while Turner had made an impressive fortune from his paintings. Constable broke with the Classical tradition, according to which landscape served only as background for the main theme or at best provided an imaginary vista. Instead he devoted himself to intensive study of certain scenes, which he sketched in the open and then completed in his studio. Painstaking in his observations, his one aim was to paint exactly what he saw. His depiction of seasonal changes, of weather and of differing lights on the same object were nothing less than revolutionary. His rendering of the freshness of the atmosphere and the incidence of light made him perhaps the best-loved English painter. However, he suffered much from depression after the death of his wife in 1829 and the paintings of his last years (he died in 1837) tended to be somber and stormy.[23]

Turner, like many great artists, went through various phases. Of peasant origin, undersized, uncouth and taciturn, he was so precocious that his work was at once recognized and supported by the Royal Academy. Starting as a water-colorist, he soon began to work in oil and during the early decades of the century built for himself an enviable reputation. Turner was constitutionally experimental and adventurous. In the 1830's he finally arrived at the complete mastery of color which characterized his later paintings. No longer dependent on the sale of his pictures, he painted in an entirely personal style and employed

[22] These artists are well discussed in Reynolds: *Victorian Painting*, where many of their works are reproduced.

[23] Phoebe Pool: *John Constable* (New York, 1964), an excellent biographical and analytical survey; Carlos Peacock: *John Constable, the Man and His Work* (New York, 1965), another serious study; Graham Reynolds: *Constable, the Natural Painter* (New York, 1965), an authoritative treatise.

techniques all his own. He no longer attempted a naturalistic reconstruction of nature, but aimed at conveying impressions and memories of things seen, experiences intensively felt, or even imaginary natural forces, using color to express form and space, and to blend the world of reality with the world of human experience. His later paintings were so far out of the ordinary that they held no appeal for his former public, though they greatly impressed the young Ruskin. Even *The Times,* in discussing one of his pictures, declared that it represented nothing in nature beyond eggs and spinach.[24] But recognition of their greatness was to come a century later, when his important contribution to the development of modern painting was fully realized.[25]

Modern critics, groping to convey something of the magic of Turner's late paintings, take refuge in phrases such as "golden visions," "mirage of light and color," "iridescent mist," "overwhelming luminosity." Most of these late canvases deal with the destructive forces of nature: catastrophic fires, storms at sea, and so on. Among the most impressive are *The Burning of the Houses of Lords and Commons* (1835), with the Thames reflecting the monstrous conflagration as a sea of fire; *Fire at Sea* (1835), "the greatest cascade of flame, blazing out against a turbulent sea"; *The Fighting 'Téméraire' Tugged to Her Last Berth to Be Broken Up* (1839), a deeply moving picture of the valiant frigate on the way to the wrecking yard and "the most popular and perhaps the finest of Turner's late, highly finished paintings"; *Slavers Throwing Overboard the Dead and the Dying—Typhoon Coming On* (1840), an unforgettable picture of brutality and horror, technically a most advanced work and one highly praised by Ruskin; *Snowstorm: Steamboat Off a Harbour's Mouth* (1842), "outlines seen in varying lights and dissolution of shape into atmosphere; all forms, whether of sea, sky or smoke come near to losing their identities in the flailing whirlpool"; *Rain, Steam and Speed: The Great Western Railway* (1844), "the steam fuses with the mist, the forms dissolve in it as

[24] *The Times,* May 4, 1841, quoted by Yvonne Ffrench: *News from the Past, 1805–1887* (London, 1935), 308.
[25] Hilton Kramer: "A True Father of Modern Painting" (*New York Times Magazine,* March 20, 1966) and the review of the exhibition of Turner paintings at the Museum of Modern Art, in New York, by John Canaday (*New York Times,* March 23, 1966).

in some 'Götterdämmerung,' the end of an epoch: a salute to the new railway age."[26]

Just before the midcentury was reached a new departure in English painting was inaugurated by the Pre-Raphaelite Brotherhood, a loose association of young artists of whom William Holman Hunt was the leader and John E. Millais and Dante Gabriel Rossetti the most significant figures. Hunt, as theorist of the movement, was in revolt against the conventional art of the day, against materialism and also against sentimentalism. There was to be a return to the supposed purity of pre-Raphaelite painting, to the age of faith, to the careful craftsmanship of the Middle Ages. Emphasis was to be on serious themes, depicted with inexorable truth and scrupulous attention to detail; light colors on luminous backgrounds were to replace the somber browns theretofore popular. Millais' *Christ in the House of His Parents* (1850) is one of the best-known and most representative works of this short-lived association.[27]

German art was an important influence on the Pre-Raphaelites through the work of the Nazarene School, a group of German painters resident in Rome who aspired to revive the Christian art of the later Middle Ages. One of its members, Peter von Cornelius, came to have a dominant position in German painting and in his later years produced colossal murals such as *The Last Judgment* (1836–1839) and the *Four Horsemen* (1850), works which earned him a European reputation (see Illustration 49). In general, German painting was more Romantic than was architecture. The greatest of the Romantic painters, Caspar David Friedrich, though he lived until 1840, was too ill to be productive in his later years. His impressive landscapes reflected a visionary pantheism and an effort to depict the superhuman elements in nature. Of the members of his circle the Norwegian Johann C. Dahl was particularly successful in his mountain views and cloud studies. Alfred Rethel stood somewhat apart, a sad, consumptive figure who died at

---

[26] The quotations are from Boase: *English Art,* 120 ff., and from the splendid monograph by John Rothenstein and Martin Butlin: *Turner* (New York, 1964), 58 ff.; A. J. Finberg: *The Life of J. M. W. Turner* (rev. ed., London, 1961) is a standard biography. See further Wilenski: *English Painting* 185 ff.; Newton: *Romantic Rebellion,* 110; and the short study by Michael Kitson: *Joseph M. W. Turner* (New York, 1964).

[27] Boase: *English Art,* chap. xi; Reynolds: *Victorian Painting,* chap. iii; Quentin Bell: *Victorian Artists* (Cambridge, 1967), 28 ff.; G. H. Fleming: *Rossetti and the Pre-Raphaelite Brotherhood* (London, 1967).

an early age, haunted by ghosts and skeletons. He left but few easel pictures, one of which ranks as an early picture of a German foundry (see Illustration 15), but during the 1840's painted the frescoes on the life of Charlemagne in the town hall at Aachen, and also completed a series of *Dance of Death* woodcuts not unworthy of his sixteenth century predecessors in this genre.

Most numerous among the German painters, however, were the realist or naturalist artists, of whom the greatest was Adolf von Menzel. Menzel made his reputation by the four hundred illustrations to Franz Kugler's *History of Frederick the Great* (1840–1842), which have fixed the popular conception of the Prussian king for all time. These illustrations reveal the utmost attention to detail and were, in a sense, the very epitome of naturalism. Another realist, Karl Blechen, painted not only clearly lighted and beautifully colored landscapes but also the earliest German industrial scene, the *Rolling Mill at Eberswalde* (1835). Other artists belonged to the Biedermeier school, treating homely subjects in a kindly way and thereby winning the affection of the middle classes. Ferdinand Waldmüller was superior to most of them, specializing in pictures of Viennese life. Adalbert Stifter caught the quiet charm of the Vienna woods, while Moritz von Schwind peopled them with sprites and knights-errant in whose existence he seemed firmly to believe. Yet another popular artist, Ludwig Richter, "conjured up unforgettable pictures of an ideal Germany, with its cosy, half-timbered houses and forests haunted by eerie gnomes and unicorns (see Illustration 71)."[28] None of these men could be even remotely compared with the great English and French artists of their time, but their work is interesting as a reflection of the placid, easygoing, sober life of the German *bourgeoisie* in the preindustrial age.[29]

Paris in this period was the undisputed art capital of the world and among its many artists the painters and engravers were pre-eminent. Neoclassicism, which had been brought to perfection by Jacques Louis David, continued to have a deep and lasting influence. Traditionally the large panel treating mythological, Biblical or historical subjects was

[28] Brion: *Romantic Art*, 99.

[29] R. Hamann: *Die deutsche Malerei im 19 Jahrhundert* (Leipzig, 1914); Weigert: *Geschichte der deutschen Kunst*, II, 188 ff., 228 ff.; Novotny: *Painting and Sculpture in Europe*, chaps. ix and x; Herbert von Einem: *Caspar David Friedrich* (Berlin, 1938); Josef Ponten: *Alfred Rethel* (Stuttgart, 1911).

still regarded as the highest art, with portrait painting and landscape falling into lower categories. Consequently all painters applied themselves to the heroic canvas, the type of painting most likely to be accepted for the Salon. This does not mean, of course, that French painting all came under the same rubric. Individual artists could and did work in their own style and influenced the development of painting in their own way.

Among the greatest and most influential painters of the period was Jacques Dominique Ingres, the disciple of David and an uncompromising proponent of Neoclassicism, who lived by preference in Italy and was a devoted student of the Renaissance painters. Ingres was an earnest, hard-working, humorless person, who took no interest in politics and who in his social relations was intolerant and irritable. As an artist he remained throughout his life an enemy of Romanticism and revolt, and a champion of order and discipline. In his view the essentials of great painting were beauty of contour and line, and of these he was a past master, as shown by his superb portrait studies. His remarkable portrait of M. Bertin, the publisher of the *Journal des débats* (1832), is a rare example of fine character analysis and brilliantly reflects the self-assurance and pride of the successful bourgeois (see Illustration 67). Ingres' portraits of the opposite sex called forth his best efforts. Thus the portrait of Countess d'Haussonville (1842) is a wonderful example of what has been called Ingres' "static rhythm," his "adorable sinuosity of line," comparable to that of Botticelli (see Illustration 66).[30] The female nude held for him an irresistible attraction, reflecting perhaps a firmly repressed sexuality finding an outlet in art. Among the most beautiful were the *Odalisque and Slave* (1839) and the *Venus Anadyomene* (1848). Even in advanced age Ingres seemed hypnotized by the female body and loved to portray Oriental scenes such as *The Turkish Bath* (1862), which has been described as "a whirlpool of carnality."[31]

The prestige enjoyed by Ingres was such that many students flocked

---

[30] Jean Alazard: *Ingres et l'ingrisme* (Paris, 1950); Georges Wildenstein: *Ingres* (London, 1954).

[31] Clark: *The Nude*, 212; Michael Levy: *A Concise History of Painting* (New York, 1962), 276; Réau: *L'ère romantique*, 108 ff.; Georges Peillex: *Nineteenth Century Painting* (New York, 1964), 6.

to his studio. His influence, great in its day, made itself felt in French painting even into the twentieth century. Among his pupils Theodore Chassériau, who died at the age of thirty-seven, was highly talented, as demonstrated by his sensitive portrait of Lacordaire (1848), his splendid scenes of North African life (*The Caid of Constantine,* 1845), and his beautiful treatment of the female nude (*Susanna in the Bath; Esther's Toilette,* 1842). Thomas Couture, another pupil of Ingres, is known chiefly for his huge panel *Romans of the Decadence* (1847), which was greeted, so it is said, with more enthusiastic criticism than any painting of the century. To the present-day observer it seems to depict a most implausible orgy, with men carousing at the base of immense pillars while nude women stand about in alluring poses. Among other painters rated highly in their day were Paul Delaroche, whose many historical scenes enjoyed a European reputation; Horace Vernet, painter *par excellence* of vast battle scenes; and Ary Scheffer, praised for the sentimental pensiveness of his pictures and a great favorite at the royal court.[32]

Delacroix, however, was the only French painter to be rated with Ingres. Despite his aversion to dreamy sentimentalism and his dislike of being called a Romantic, he is invariably identified as the leader of the Romantic school. A man of aristocratic birth, he could be brilliant and witty in conversation, but was generally reserved and lonely. His great interests, in addition to his profession, were in literature, music and the theater, and his dearest friend was the composer Frédéric Chopin, of whom he did a profound portrait study.[33]

Delacroix, like his rival Ingres, painted chiefly themes of the traditional type, that is, mythological, historical and Biblical topics. Ingres was more of a portrait painter, while Delacroix was inclined to choose subjects from literature, notably from Shakespeare, Goethe, Byron and Scott. Both men were greatly attracted, too, by the Orient. Delacroix, during a visit to Morocco, made enough sketches to keep

32 Novotny: *Painting and Sculpture in Europe,* 95 ff.; Réau: *L'ère romantique,* 112 ff., 126 ff.
33 The basic work on Delacroix is still Raymond Escholier: *Delacroix, peintre, écrivain, graveur* (3 vols., Paris, 1926–1929), while René Huyghe: *Delacroix* (New York, 1963) is the most complete biography in English. Other recent studies are Jacques Lasaigne: *Eugène Delacroix* (New York, 1950); Lee Johnson, *Delacroix* (New York, 1963); Maximilien Gauthier: *Delacroix* (Paris, 1964).

him busy throughout his life. Among his outstanding Oriental paintings of the period 1830 to 1850 were *Algerian Women in Their Apart-
ment* (1834); *Giaour and Slave* (1835) (see Illustration 69); and
Odalisque (1847). Scenes from literature were *Medea* (1838), one of
his masterpieces; *The Prisoner of Chillon* (1834); *The Abduction of
Rebecca,* from *Ivanhoe* (1846); *Crusaders Entering Constantinople
in 1204* (1840), along with the striking *Shipwreck* (1841) and *The
Entombment of Christ* (1848). Highly rated are also Delacroix's great
murals in the church of Saint-Sulpice, the Hôtel de Ville, the Palais
Luxembourg, the Palais Bourbon and other public buildings, mostly on
mythological or classical themes.

What distinguished Delacroix was his dramatic imagination, his
dynamism and above all his use of color. Where Ingres worshiped
Raphael, Delacroix was devoted to Rubens and was much impressed
by the treatment of light and color by Constable and other English
artists. He never tired in his study of the effect of lights and shadows
on colors and strove continually for color harmonies: "When the tones
are right, the lines draw themselves," he declared. Or again: "Certain
color-harmonies produce sensations which even music cannot rival."
His paintings, then, were "a feast for the eyes," bold, dramatic, vivid
and colorful. While he had no school or disciples and his immediate
influence was less than that of Ingres or even Delaroche, his reputation
continued to grow and his treatment of color profoundly affected the
further development of painting.[34]

Landscape painting came into its own in the early nineteenth century
and reached its highest development in the period of the present study.
The work of Constable and Turner was unequaled elsewhere, but
France, like Germany, made important contributions. Jean-Baptiste
Corot, for instance, spent a long life traveling in Italy and all over
France, sketching and painting scenes and people. Like Delacroix, he
was fascinated by problems of light, and in his earlier work strove
for clarity and precision (see Illustration 14). But in his later years,
beginning about 1845, he painted landscapes more impressionistically, making much use of the soft, silvery light of dawn or twilight.

    34 Walter Friedländer: *David to Delacroix* (Cambridge, 1963), 114 ff.; Novotny:
Painting and Sculpture in Europe, 88 ff.; Brion: *Romantic Art,* 134 ff.; Réau: *L'ère
romantique,* 99 ff.

Though Corot is often called the greatest of the Romantic landscapists, he was in some respects quite unromantic, for he was serene and well-balanced, with not a trace of the demonic. His goodness and generosity were well reflected in his work.[35]

The so-called Barbizon School of landscape painters is generally dated from 1848, when Theodore Rousseau, already a well-known painter, settled at the village of Barbizon in the forest of Fontainebleau. There he was joined by Charles Daubigny, Jean F. Millet and others, mostly poor artists disgusted with the conditions of life in Paris and yearning for closer contact with nature. They frequently painted out of doors and in the more realistic fashion of the seventeenth-century Dutch painters and of Constable, whose influence on them was direct. Millet, who was a radical and republican, in 1848 exhibited the first of his peasant pictures, *The Winnower,* soon to be followed by his famous canvases *The Sower, The Gleaners* and *The Angelus* (see also Illustrations 9, 10). These pictures first represented the common man and his labor, not in terms of genre, but in terms of human dignity. They were violently denounced at the time as being unworthy art, and Millet was accused of being a socialist, intent on instigating a *Jacquerie.* But he made a deep impression on some American visitors, who bought many of his works. Though in eclipse for some time, Millet and other Barbizon painters were, a century later, to be held in high esteem and much appreciated.[36]

At least brief mention must be made of the great French engravers of this period, during which lithography was perfected. The process of engraving on stone had been discovered by the Bavarian Aloysius Senefelder in 1796, but had come into its own only after 1815, when the French engraver, Nicolas Charlet, followed by Auguste Raffet, Horace Vernet and others, popularized the process through their prints of

---

[35] Pierre Francastel: *Histoire de la peinture française* (Paris, 1955), 48; Novotny: *Painting and Sculpture in Europe,* 105 ff.; Réau: *L'ère romantique,* 137 ff.; Peillex: *Nineteenth Century Painting,* 19 ff.; Maurice Serullaz: *Corot* (Paris, 1951); G. Bazin: *Corot* (rev. ed., Paris, 1951); Jean Alazard: *Corot* (Milan, 1952); Jean Leymarie: *Corot* (Lausanne, 1966).

[36] See the excellent introduction by Robert L. Herbert to the catalogue of the exhibition Barbizon Revisited (1962); further, Underwood: *Short History of French Painting,* chaps. xiv and xv; Novotny: *Painting and Sculpture in Europe;* Réau: *L'ère romantique,* 147 ff.

Napoleon and his soldiers (see Illustrations 47, 48). Thereafter most French artists made use of it, especially in book illustration (e.g., Delacroix's impressive illustrations for Goethe's *Faust*).[37]

Almost half of the innumerable prints produced in France in these years were caricatures, which appealed tremendously to the common people, from whom most of the artists came. Charles Philipon and the group supplying the magazines *Caricature* and *Charivari* played an important part in whipping up popular sentiment against Louis Philippe and the July Monarchy and when political satire was prohibited in 1835 turned to lampooning Parisian society at all levels. Paul Gavarni, an important illustrator, was a roué who delighted in ridiculing the foibles of high society (*Les Français peints par eux-mêmes,* 1840–1842), while Achille Devéria excelled in portraying the feminine world (*Histoire d'un mariage*).[38]

The members of this brilliant group were all competent artists and one of them, Honoré Daumier, perhaps the greatest caricaturist of all time, was also a sculptor and painter of the highest rank. The son of poor parents, Daumier was deeply concerned throughout his life with the problems of inequality and injustice. The great political caricatures of his early career have been discussed in Chapter III, above, and need not be further considered here. After 1835 he was obliged to confine himself to social criticism, represented by various series of prints: *French Types, Paris Bohemians, Worthy Citizens, Married Manners, Men of the Law,* and so on. Daumier was a prodigious worker who, in the course of his career, produced over three thousand lithographs and in addition a thousand woodcuts and numerous drawings. His work has been compared to that of Michelangelo, Rembrandt and Goya, and in point of design he has been put on a par with Ingres and Dalacroix. His work is elemental and powerful, searching and realistic, yet always sane, just and humane. In the words of the late Paul Sachs, "no other draughtsman had ever left for the student of human nature so many priceless records of a passing epoch; no novelist had ever mirrored for posterity a more throbbing, varied world."[39] Like his contemporary

37 Wilhelm Weber: *The History of Lithography* (New York, 1966) is an authoritative study, but see also Jean Adhémar: *La lithographie en France* (Paris, 1842), and Claude Roger-Marx: *Graphic Art of the Nineteenth Century* (London, 1962).

38 Armand Dayot: *Les maîtres de la caricature française au XIXe siècle* (Paris, n.d.); Jean Adhémar: *Gavarni: Exposition* (Paris, 1954); Réau: *L'ère romantique,* 163 ff.

39 Paul J. Sachs: *Great Drawings* (New York, 1951), 101 ff.

Balzac, Daumier portrayed the society of his time and left a record both lively and amusing, yet of the highest artistic distinction. A number of his prints are included in the illustrations of the present volume.[40]

4. PHOTOGRAPHY

The period of the July Monarchy saw the completion of one of the great inventions of modern times, one which was to affect the position of the artist in a very fundamental way. On January 7, 1839, the eminent physicist François Arago announced to the Academy of Sciences the discovery of a technique (photography) by which familiar images produced in the camera obscura could be fixed in black, white and gray. The inventor was a painter and promoter, Louis Daguerre, who had worked with Nicéphore Niepce, a learned gentleman who had in 1826 produced the first genuine, though unsatisfactory, photograph, but had died before being able to perfect the process. Daguerre had carried the work to conclusion and had interested several prominent scientists such as Arago, Biot, Humboldt and Gay-Lussac, all of whom were impressed by the clarity and exactness of Daguerre's photographs of Notre Dame, the Louvre and the Seine bridges (see Illustration 70). These men at once recognized the potential value of the discovery for scientific work. Arago persuaded the French government to purchase Daguerre's specifications and then make them available for the benefit of the entire world. An agreement was signed with Daguerre by which he and the Niepce family were each to receive an annuity of 4,000 francs. On August 19, 1839, the official birthday of photography, Arago was able to reveal the details of Daguerre's process. Daguerre had, in the meantime, written a brief book of instructions, which was published at once in French, English and German. He had also made a deal with Giroux, an instrument maker, calling for the production of appropriate cameras and the

---

[40] Jean Adhémar: *Honoré Daumier* (Paris, 1954) is an authoritative biographical study, but see also the excellent work of Oliver Larkin: *Daumier, the Man and His Time* (New York, 1966). Among innumerable monographs and collections of prints may be mentioned E. Bouvy: *Daumier: l'oeuvre du maître* (Paris, 1933); Jacques Lasaigne: *Daumier* (New York, 1938); Gerhard Ziller: *Honoré Daumier* (Dresden, 1957); Robert Rey: *Honoré Daumier* (New York, 1966); and Wolfgang Balzer: *Der junge Daumier und seine Kampfgefährten, 1830–1835* (Dresden, 1965), an admirable contribution.

preparation of the chemicals needed for development of the plate. In this way Daguerre was able to make the most of his discovery.[41]

News of Daguerre's invention aroused lively interest everywhere, for the demand for pictorial material was so great that even the army of painters and engravers could not satisfy it. The inventor's book of instructions reached New York before the end of September, 1839 and specimens of his work, the so-called daguerreotypes, were admired for their beauty, accuracy and detail, which went beyond anything an engraver could hope to attain. Samuel F. B. Morse, the American inventor of the telegraph, had been shown specimens of photography by Daguerre himself while in Paris in the spring of 1839. When the details of the process became known, he, like several others, opened a studio and made a business of daguerreotype portraits. Morse took what was probably the first group picture, the reunion of the Yale College class of 1810.[42]

The implications of the new device were recognized at once. "The draughtsman must lay down his pencil, the engraver his tool, and confess that he cannot now or ever equal this result," wrote a Vienna newspaper, while the painter Delaroche exclaimed: "From today, painting is dead." But there was no turning back. A veritable daguerreomania seized society and everywhere "sun artists" did a thriving business. The English almost at once added substantially to Daguerre's achievement through the work of the gentleman-scientist W. H. Fox Talbot, which he revealed immediately after the first announcement of the French discovery. Instead of using a silvered copperplate for his impression, Talbot had devised a chemically treated paper which produced a softer, less precise image, susceptible of greater artistry, as shown by the portraits made by David Hill in the 1840's. More important yet, Talbot's "calotypes" or "talbotypes" could be printed in

[41] On Niepce's role, see Victor Fouqué: *The Truth Concerning the Invention of the Photograph: Nicéphore Niepce* (Paris, 1867, English translation by Edward Epstean, New York, 1935). See further, Joseph M. Eder: *History of Photography* (New York, 1945); Helmut and Alison Gernsheim: *History of Photography* (New York, 1955); Beaumont Newhall: *The History of Photography* (rev. ed., New York, 1964). Important texts are reprinted in Wolfgang Baier: *Quellendarstellungen zur Geschichte der Fotografie* (Halle, 1964).

[42] Robert Taft: *Photography and the American Scene: a Social History, 1839–1889* (New York, 1942); Carleton Mabee: *The American Leonardo: a Life of Samuel F. B. Morse* (New York, 1943); 229 ff.; Helmut and Alison Gernsheim: *L. J. M. Daguerre* (New York, 1956), chap. v.

numerous positives, whereas the daguerreotype returned but a single, nonreproducible picture. The importance of Talbot's contribution requires no emphasis.[43]

Photography was from the outset regarded as an art, closely related to engraving. It was so attractive and important that much effort was devoted to its perfection. In 1840 the Austrian physicist Josef Petzval brought out a portrait lens which reduced the required exposure time from five or more minutes to a matter of seconds. Only then did portrait work become really practicable, thus meeting the needs of the middle classes.[44] Another significant advance was the use of photography for book illustration, of which Talbot's *The Pencil of Nature* (1844) was the pioneer. By the mid-forties travelers equipped with camera and laboratory were photographing not only in Europe and America but in the Near East and Asia as well. Daguerre, at Arago's request, had taken the first faint image of the moon, after which the American astronomer William C. Bond in 1850 first photographed a star (Vega). Bond's excellent picture of the moon was much admired at the Great Exhibition in 1851.

The introduction of the wet plate (collodion process) in 1851 marked the beginning of the second stage in the history of the new process, during which the daguerreotype and talbotype gradually gave way to other techniques. But the 1840's remain memorable as the art's bright infancy, when an age-old human dream was realized and the deep-seated human desire to capture the fleeting features of nature for a permanent record was at last satisfied.

5. INSTRUMENTAL MUSIC

Music, like other arts, felt the winds of change in this period. Though princely courts and aristocratic salons still played a significant role in musical life, patronage was becoming less important as the emergence of the middle classes broadened the social base of music. The training and control formerly provided by guilds were being taken over by music schools, while public concerts were supplanting private soirées. The Paris Conservatoire, for example, perfected the study of music beyond anything known before. Eminent leaders such as Fran-

---

[43] Alexander Strasse: *Victorian Photography* (London, 1942), 29 ff.

[44] On the social aspects of photography, see Gisèle Freund: *La photographie en France au XIXe siècle* (Paris, 1936), chap. i.

çois Habeneck, Ludwig Spohr and Felix Mendelssohn raised the standards of Paris and London concerts to new levels by their insistence on accuracy in performance and on the conductor as the interpreter of the music. Naturally, lesser organizations still fell short of the ideal. In Germany there were important musical centers in Vienna, Munich, Cassel, Berlin and Weimar, but there, and even more in England and Italy, provincial orchestras tended to be of low grade. The players were frightfully underpaid and shockingly overworked, since they were obliged to supplement their salaries through teaching, copying of music and other tasks. It was not without cause that Liszt protested against the low social standing of the musician, or that Wagner, who suffered real privation during his Paris stay, turned socially as well as politically revolutionary. As for the conductors, they usually lacked even basic funds, having to perform as many as a hundred different works in the course of a year, with no more than one rehearsal for a symphony. Mendelssohn, Berlioz, and later Wagner were all driven to distraction by the inadequacies of the average orchestra. No doubt their standards were all but humanly unattainable, but there can be little doubt that ensemble playing in the midcentury was greatly inferior to what it was to be a century later.[45]

The virtuosi of the violin or piano, and the leading operatic singers, to be sure, were highly regarded and well rewarded, for they could command admission prices of a guinea in London or twenty francs in Paris. Paganini, who well knew how to drive a bargain, was paid 22,000 francs for a single concert in Paris in 1831, and netted about £7500 for fifteen London concerts between June and August of the same year.[46] Composers of serious music, on the other hand, fared hardly better than the ordinary musician. They often sold compositions that were masterpieces for a few hundred francs. Most of them had to

[45] Richard Wagner: *Letters from Paris, 1841* (in W. A. Ellis, ed.: *Richard Wagner's Prose Works*, London, 1895, VIII, 129); Henry F. Chorley: *Music and Manners in France and Germany* (London, 1844), III, 65–66. See also Paul Bekker: *The Story of the Orchestra* (New York, 1936); Edward J. Dent: "Music" (in *Early Victorian England, 1830–1865*, London, 1934, II, 249–264) E. D. Mackerness: *A Social History of English Music* (Toronto, 1964), 177 ff.; Ernest Newman: *Life of Richard Wagner* (London, 1933), I, chap. viii.

[46] *Biographical Sketch of Nicolò Paganini*, by the Paris Correspondent of the late *Foreign Literary Gazette*, London, 1831, 22; Stephen S. Stratton: *Nicolò Paganini* (London, 1907), 43–57; Harold Spivacke: "Paganiniana," (Library of Congress: *Quarterly Journal of Current Acquisitions*, II, 1945, 1-19).

fortify their income by concert performances or by serving as conductors or music critics.[47]

Music is said to be the Romantic art *par excellence,* since it strives to express feelings and ideas beyond the reach of reason or language, and the decades following 1830 are generally described as the very apogee of Romanticism, in music as in literature and painting. This does not mean that there was an actual revolt against the eighteenth century or a clean break from Classicism. On the contrary, the great composers of the Romantic period worshiped Bach, Mozart and Beethoven. Mendelssohn's revival of Bach's *Passion according to St. Matthew* (1829) and Habeneck's performances of the Beethoven symphonies by the Conservatory orchestra (1828) were major events in musical history, after which the symphonies were regularly played, despite complaints that the later ones were incomprehensible.[48]

Beethoven, of course, had more than a grain of Romanticism in his music. He appealed to later composers also because he was the first completely independent composer, who wrote not to order, but in response to his own inspiration. His successors therefore resented all fetters, consulted only their own feelings, indulged freely in fantasy, worshiped nature, and reveled in all that was strange and terrifying. It was not mere chance that so many of them (Spohr, Berlioz, Liszt, Schumann, Wagner) were attracted by the *Faust* theme.[49]

Many artists regarded music as the ultimate art, the only art able to express the ineffable.[50] One might almost say that musicians were encouraged to seek for new forms and effects. And so, while retaining the classical forms of the symphony, concerto, quartet and sonata, they loosened the structure, so that in Berlioz' *Symphonie fantastique* or Liszt's *Années de pèlerinage* one is confronted with a series of episodes rather than a strict development. In orchestration, too, the Romantic composers were innovators, introducing daring rhythms and harmonies, employing instruments (notably horns) to attain colorful effects, and treating themes in a dramatic fashion. Their relationship to literature was at this time peculiarly close and they drew heavily on all of

---

[47] Franz Liszt: "The Situation of Artists" (*Gazette musicale,* 1835), cited in Newman: *Life of Richard Wagner,* I, chap. ix, where this topic is discussed at length.

[48] On Beethoven in Paris, see Andreas Liess: *Deutsche und französische Musik in der Geistesgeschichte des 19 Jahrhunderts* (Vienna, 1950), chap. i.

[49] Guy Ferchault: *Faust: une légende et ses musiciens* (Paris, 1948).

[50] Ernst Glöckner: *Studien zur romantischen Psychologie der Musik* (Munich, 1909).

European literature for their musical themes. Much of the "new" music was in fact "program music," which attempted to tell a story in musical language, often with an explanatory text (e.g., Berlioz' *Harold in Italy* or Liszt's *Mazeppa*). Many Romantics dreamed of an eventual reunion of all the arts and the creation of a new all-inclusive art form, of which music should be the keystone. Mazzini and Lamennais envisioned something of this kind as an integral part of their new society, and Wagner, the archchampion of the *Gesamtkunstwerk,* insisted in 1849 that the new revolutionary art "must embrace the spirit of a free mankind, delivered from every shackle of hampering nationality; its racial imprint must be no more than an embellishment, the individual charm of manifold diversity, and not a cramping barrier."[51]

To express their lyric inspiration, their personal moods and reactions, the Romantic composers preferred small forms, that is, short, intimate pieces. It was the time of romances, rhapsodies, impromptus, moments musicaux, preludes, ballades, fantasias, nocturnes, mazurkas and polonaises. Symphonic and chamber music were thought by many to be incapable of expressing the deepest personal feelings and were left to the enjoyment of aristocratic cognoscenti.[52]

The Romantics found the pianoforte the perfect instrument for their purpose. That instrument had by this time been mechanically perfected and the technique of playing was now brought to a new high point.[53] It was the great violin virtuoso, Nicolò Paganini, who inspired his contemporaries to explore further the possibilities of the piano (see Illustration 46). He had first appeared in Vienna in 1828 and three years later began to give concerts of his own compositions in Paris and London. Musicians and laymen were alike dumfounded both by his personality and by his performance. A gaunt, spiderlike apparition with flashing eyes, he displayed an agility and technique far beyond any-

---

51 Wagner: "Art and Revolution" (in *Prose Works,* I, 53–54); see also Jack M. Stein: *Richard Wagner and the Synthesis of the Arts* (Detroit, 1960); Alfred Einstein: *Music in the Romantic Era* (New York, 1947), 31 ff.; Jean Chantavoine and Jean Gaudefroy-Desmombynes: *Le romantisme dans la musique européenne* (Paris, 1955), 7; Hans Eckardt: *Die Musikanschauung der französischen Romantik* (Cassel, 1935), chaps. ii and iv; W. H. Hadow: *Studies in Modern Music* (10 ed., London, 1921), 201 ff.

52 Jules Combarieu: *Histoire de la musique* (3 ed., Paris, 1920), III, 226 ff.; Edward Dannreuther: *The Romantic Period* (2 ed., London, 1931), 361; Paul H. Lang: *Music in Western Civilization* (New York, 1941), 816 ff.; Einstein: *Music in the Romantic Era,* chap. vii.

53 Rosamund Harding: *The Piano-forte* (Cambridge, 1939) traces the evolution of the piano to 1851.

thing hitherto seen. "The violin, in his hands, is a new instrument," wrote the *Foreign Literary Gazette;* "its original powers and supposed extent, even as displayed by the most eminent professors, are more than doubled under the touch of Paganini."[54] The audience gasped when he removed three of the four strings from his violin and, tuning the G string up to B flat, performed on this one string. Hardly less impressive was his use of double notes and double trills in harmonics, and his playing a pizzicato with the left hand while bowing with the right. Without a doubt he advanced violin technique beyond any of his predecessors. But he was also a competent composer and a consummate musician, the beauty of whose playing was as impressive as his dexterity. Heine, who heard him in Paris, was only one of many auditors who were transported:

A holy, ineffable ardor dwelt in the sounds, which often trembled, scarce audibly, in mysterious whisper on the water, then swelled out again in shuddering sweetness, like a bugle's notes heard by moonlight, and then finally poured forth in unrestrained jubilee, as if a thousand bards had struck their harps and raised their voices in a song of victory.[55]

Schumann, Berlioz, Liszt and Chopin all heard Paganini in concert and were inspired by his playing to examine the possibilities of the piano in terms of brilliancy and sonority. Schumann and Liszt both transcribed Paganini's *Caprices* for the piano, which instrument became the vehicle for making much music readily available. Among Liszt's innumerable transcriptions were the nine symphonies of Beethoven. All in all, it was a great period of piano playing as well as of piano composition. Among the many virtuosi were Ignaz Moscheles, much beloved in England; John Field, whose playing and compositions were an inspiration to Chopin; William Sterndale Bennett, the friend of Mendelssohn and Schumann and the founder of the Bach Society; Clara Wieck, who became Schumann's wife in 1840; Friedrich Kalkbrenner, considered by some to be superior to Liszt; and Sigismund Thalberg, who was much admired for his beautiful legato.[56]

---

[54] *Biographical Sketch of Nicolò Paganini,* 27 ff.

[55] Stratton: *Nicolò Paganini,* 44. There is an exhaustive study of Paganini by Geraldine de Courcy: *Paganini, the Genoese* (Norman, 1957), and a beautiful appreciation by Mario Codignola: *Arte e magia di Nicolò Paganini* (Milan, 1960). I have not seen Lillian Day: *Paganini of Genoa* (London, 1966).

[56] Hugo Leichtentritt: *Music, History and Ideas* (Cambridge, 1939), 212 ff.; Einstein: *Music in the Romantic Era,* 240 ff.

Of the German non-operatic composers both Felix Mendelssohn and Robert Schumann attained lasting fame. The former was perhaps the least Romantic as Schumann was possibly the most Romantic composer of his time. Mendelssohn, scion of a wealthy and cultured banker family, was highly sensitive and reserved. Unlike most Romantics, he was unwilling to lay bare his soul or parade his intimate feelings.[57] Decidedly a follower of Beethoven, Mendelssohn composed a number of orchestral works (*Midsummer Night's Dream,* overture, 1826; the *Italian Symphony,* 1845; the *Elijah* oratorio, 1846) as well as quartets in the traditional form. All his works were distinguished for consummate craftsmanship, classical restraint and unusual clarity. His Romanticism, such as it was, was reflected chiefly in his love of the picturesque and the colorful: the *Fingal's Cave* overture is indeed a landscape painting in sound.

Schumann is considered by some to have been the greatest of the purely Romantic composers.[58] Unlike Mendelssohn, he was a warm and tender personality, at times fiery, but always imaginative, original and even problematical. His music was an expression of the eternal spirit of youth (e.g., his *Scenes of Childhood,* 1838) and of poetic lyricism. In the years after his marriage (1840) he composed over a hundred lieder based on the poems of Heine, Chamisso, Eichendorff and other Romantics. Nonetheless, he like Mendelssohn devoted himself also to ensemble music, symphonies and chamber music. Though his music is generally more difficult to understand than Mendelssohn's, it is always rich, stimulating and intriguing. One French critic has compared it to the landscapes of Corot, a comparison to which one can readily subscribe.[59]

---

[57] Schima Kaufman: *Mendelssohn, a Second Elijah* (New York, 1934) is a serious biography. Heinrich A. Jacob: *Felix Mendelssohn and His Times* (New York, 1963) is an interesting discussion of the composer's career and personality. Eric Werner: *Mendelssohn, a New Image of the Composer and His Age* (Glencoe, 1963) is the translation of a basic German study.

[58] Leichtentritt: *Music, History and Ideas,* 213; George Szell, in his essay on Schumann in the *New York Times,* March 13, 1960.

[59] Combarieu: *Histoire de la musique,* III, 277. Schumann's career and more particularly his love affair and marriage to Clara Wieck have been a perennial inspiration to biographers. Wolfgang Boetticher: *Robert Schumann: Einführung in Persönlichkeit und Werk* (Berlin, 1941) is a basic treatment. Other worthwhile biographical and musical studies are Robert H. Schauffler: *"Florestan": the Life and Work of Robert Schumann* (New York, 1945); Paula and Walter Rehberg: *Robert Schumann, sein Leben und sein Werk* (Zürich, 1954); Marcel Brion: *Schumann and the Romantic Age* (London,

Schumann greatly admired the French composer Frédéric Chopin, whom he characterized as "the most audacious poetic genius of his time." Chopin, though born and educated in Poland and at all times deeply moved by the sufferings of that country, was the son of a French father and spent his mature years in Paris. He was universally recognized as one of the greatest of the piano virtuosi even though, because of illness, he played but rarely in public. He generally played a few Bach preludes or fugues before appearing in concert and also drew inspiration from Mozart, who was his favorite composer. It has been said of him that he was a Romantic who detested Romanticism, that is, whatever was extravagant or even undisciplined.[60] He played quietly and avoided sentimentalism, but always with the utmost good taste and musical understanding. Heine once called him "the Raphael of the pianoforte."

Chopin, a victim of tuberculosis, was afflicted with chronic weakness. Personally reserved, fastidious and exacting, he lived a lonely life, plagued by death fears and premonitions. His intimate friends were few—really only the composer Bellini and the painter Delacroix, whose work he appears not to have appreciated (see Illustration 72). Perhaps the most fortunate episode in his short life was his love affair with the novelist George Sand, who for ten years protected and cared for him. Yet for all his debility, Chopin was a highly productive composer, who went about his work with the businesslike precision of a Bach. Resisting the importunities of friends, he refused to undertake a symphony or opera, even the Polish national opera so dear to the Polish *émigrés*. He composed almost exclusively for the piano and chiefly in the smaller forms best suited to his nature and inspiration. All his work was characterized by magnificent melodies and harmonies, by extraordinary range of sentiment, musical color, striking modulations, and fascinating ornamentation. His compositions are as much played now as they were in his own time. Piano concerts without one or more Chopin numbers are rare and piano virtuosi strive above all to play Chopin well. The musical public apparently never tires of Chopin music, every last item

---

1956); Percy M. Young: *Tragic Muse: the Life and Works of Robert Schumann* (London, 1957).

[60] Harold C. Schonberg: "Chopin" in the *New York Times Sunday Magazine,* February 14, 1960.

of which is now available on records, usually in many different renderings.[61]

Hector Berlioz, rated by some as the greatest of French composers, was the very antithesis of Chopin, who, incidentally, detested his work. Berlioz had the real Romantic temperament, exuberant and unrestrained. He reveled in the new freedom of the artist, followed his inspiration without regard for success or failure, and boldly injected his personality and private affairs into his music. A man of extravagant imagination and grandiose conceptions, he looked upon music as another language, particularly suited to the expression of profound, poetic ideas. Full of admiration for Beethoven, he attempted to use the orchestra to express great human tragedies, such as those of Shakespeare or Goethe. Going beyond the traditional symphonic form, he introduced program music, for which he supplied an explanatory text. These instrumental dramas (the "concerto-symphony" *Harold in Italy,* 1834; the "dramatic symphony" *Romeo and Juliet,* 1839; the "concert-opera" *The Damnation of Faust,* 1846) were loosely constructed but full of original, striking ideas and effects. Berlioz thought always in grandiose terms. His *Requiem* (1837) called for a large orchestra, a chorus of two hundred voices and, in one movement, four brass choirs sounding from different parts of the concert hall. His *Te Deum* (1849) went even further, requiring an orchestra of two hundred, an organ, two choirs of two hundred voices, and a third choir of six hundred children. Naturally such works can be produced only very rarely. But to hear them is a thrilling experience, which alone can convey the effectiveness of the composer's conceptions.

Berlioz has been criticized for the weakness of his harmony and the general disorderliness of his compositions. But his originality and especially the magic of his orchestration are not in dispute. Indeed, he was the father of modern orchestration, on which he wrote a basic treatise (1844). More than anyone else he developed the personality of the different instruments and brought out the full tone color of the ensemble. The recurrent use of a specific theme (*idée fixe* or *Leitmotif*) to identify a certain character or situation has also been attributed to

---

[61] André Maurois: *Frédéric Chopin* (New York, 1942) is colorful biography. More intensive, A. E. Cherbuliez: *Frederyk Chopin: Leben und Werk* (Zürich, 1948) and Casimir Wierzynski: *The Life and Death of Chopin* (New York, 1949). Victor I. Seroff: *Chopin* (New York, 1964) is a competent biographical sketch, while Herbert Weinstock: *Chopin, the Man and His Music* (New York, 1959) is an authoritative critical study.

him, as have many daring rhythms and syncopations. His work was at the time so out of the ordinary that he won but few disciples, though Schumann, Liszt and Wagner were all impressed and the German public gave him a warmer reception than did the French. A century later his extraordinary achievement is fully recognized and a number of his major works are regularly performed.[62]

The career of Franz Liszt as virtuoso, conductor and composer extended over six decades and made him the most prominent musical figure of the century, with the possible exception of Wagner. As a master of the pianoforte he was almost legendary, constantly on tour from Portugal to Russia, and adding substantially to the development of piano technique. Liszt's was an attractive personality, sincere, unconventional, generous. He wrote hundreds of works for orchestra, piano and voice, but they have not worn well and are now but rarely heard. He is now regarded more as a developer of ideas stemming from others than a contributor of importance. Certainly his compositions, while they show inventiveness, dramatic fervor and even occasional reflectiveness, leave the impression of cleverness rather than depth. His was a vibrant personality that conquered the public. But his great generosity to other musicians, his readiness to consider innovations, and his sense of the social mission of music should not be forgotten.[63]

6. SONG, OPERA AND MUSIC DRAMA

In the days before radio and television, song was one of the chief sources of entertainment. In terms of popular interest and response vocal music was more important than instrumental. Every town of any note had an opera house, which was a social center as well as an arena for the conflict of musical factions. The upper classes as well as the governments supported the opera as well as vocal concerts. At lower

[62] Recent biographies and studies are Adolphe Boschot: *Hector Berlioz, une vie romantique* (Paris, 1951); Henry Barraud: *Hector Berlioz* (Paris, 1955); and the excellent work of Jacques Barzun: *Berlioz and the Romantic Century* (Boston, 1950), of which the same author's *Berlioz and His Century* (New York, 1956) is a shorter version.

[63] Liszt's Bohemian life continues to lure biographers. Among recent books, Peter Raabe's *Liszts Leben* (Stuttgart, 1931) is important, and both Sachverell Sitwell's *Liszt* (London, 1934) and Ernest Newman's *The Man Liszt* (London, 1934) stimulating. Still more recent studies of importance are Jean Chantavoine: *Franz Liszt* (Paris, 1950); Humphrey Searle: *The Music of Liszt* (London, 1954); Walter G. Armando: *Franz Liszt* (Hamburg, 1961); and Paula Rehberg: *Franz Liszt, die Geschichte seines Lebens, Schaffens und Wirkens* (Zürich, 1961).

levels of society song hits ("romances") were heard in the music halls as well as in bourgeois homes, where young ladies were gradually abandoning the harp in favor of the piano. Singing was, in fact, reaching down to the lowest classes. In Paris Guillaume Wilhem, later director general of music in the schools, had in 1815 inaugurated musical instruction by the monitorial method, which in 1835 was made obligatory in the elementary schools. In 1836 Wilhem founded a choral society, the Orphéon, to provide instruction in part singing for workmen after hours. This institution was so popular that foremen and even employers enrolled in it. Presently there were several hundred Orphéons scattered throughout France, some with choruses numbering a thousand voices, which must have delighted Berlioz.[64]

In Germany singing societies were well established and extremely popular. The great annual festival at Düsseldorf attracted the leading conductors, such as Mendelssohn. In 1852 twenty different societies competed there, while another thirty sent delegations.[65] Oratorios were much favored in both Germany and England, where Handel's *Messiah*, Haydn's *Creation*, Spohr's *Calvary*, and especially Mendelssohn's *St. Paul*, *Elijah*, and *Hymn of Praise* were constantly performed. In England amateur choral societies were organized. There were three in London alone, beginning with the Sacred Harmonic Society in 1832. Each of these organizations would have six to eight hundred singers, would have weekly rehearsals and would engage professional orchestras and soloists for their public concerts. The movement spread rapidly to other cities. In Birmingham, for instance, a four-day festival was regularly staged.[66]

The modern music hall developed in this period from the "caves of harmony" and "supper rooms" where men about town met for talk and song, often after the theater.[67] Furthermore, the first steps were taken to bring music into schools and factories, if only in the hope that music "would wean the mind from vicious and sensual indulgences,"

[64] Wilhem wrote a well-known textbook of singing, as did the eminent music critic F. J. Fétis: *La musique mise à la portée de tout le monde* (2 ed., Paris, 1834). See also Henry F. Chorley: *Music and Manners in France and Germany* (London, 1844), III, 281 ff.; Hans Eckardt: *Die Musikanschauung der französischen Romantik* (Cassel, 1935), chap. iv.

[65] Lowell Mason: *Musical Letters from Abroad* (New York, 1854), 164.

[66] *Ibid.*, 252 ff.; George Hogarth: *Musical History, Biography and Criticism* (London, 1838), 270, 275. On Spohr, who is now neglected but whose oratorios were highly esteemed, see Dorothy M. Mayer: *The Forgotten Master* (London, 1958).

[67] Archibald Haddon: *The Story of the Music-Hall* (London, 1935).

and "incline the heart to kindly feelings and just and generous emotions."[68] In 1839 John Hullah went to Paris to study Wilhem's methods. Two years later he began training music teachers at Exeter Hall. His efforts were soon supported by the Reverend John Curwen, who published a basic *Grammar of Vocal Music* (1843), and by Joseph Mainzer, whose lectures on *Singing for the Million* were much prized. By 1850 the monitorial system of singing was well established in schools and factories, where employers found it a paying proposition to provide instruction and even to supply the instruments for brass bands.[69]

It stands to reason that so lively a public interest should have called forth much vocal talent. It was one of the very greatest ages of song and singers, most of whom were Italian-born or trained. Many were vivid personalities and good actors as well as singers. Audiences went simply mad over them, and every kind of trinket or souvenir was named in their honor. More importantly, they brought fantastic box-office receipts and consequently received fabulous salaries. Among the women Henrietta Sontag has been called the first darling of the new *bourgeoisie*. Neither a singer nor an actress of the highest rank, she captivated Goethe, Chopin and many other artists by her charm, by what Chopin called her "supernatural amiability." Of far greater artistic importance were Wilhelmina Schröder-Devrient and Giuditta Pasta. The former was the greatest of dramatic singers, whose performance of *Fidelio* was admired by Beethoven himself, while Wagner declared that even the remotest contact with her electrified and inspired him. Pasta, too, was renowned for her dramatic acting as well as for her fine voice. Among her contemporaries were Giulia Grisi and, briefly, Cornelia Falcon, a Spanish beauty who made her mark as a tragedian in Meyerbeer's operas. But the greatest of the women singers of the period were undoubtedly Marie Malibran and Jenny Lind. The former was recognized as a genius long before her early death at the age of twenty-eight. She sang successfully in every type of opera and in every operatic language, and in addition was a composer of some note and an admirable athlete. Malibran's voice extended over three octaves and was exceptionally flexible, but even more striking was her tem-

[68] Quoted from W. E. Hickson, by E. D. Mackerness: *A Social History of English Music* (Toronto, 1964), 154.

[69] Francis Hueffer: *Half a Century of Music in England, 1837–1887* (London, 1889), 19; J. W. Davison: *From Mendelssohn to Wagner* (London, 1912); Mackerness: *Social History of English Music*, 154 ff.

perament—impulsive, passionate, audacious. It was said of her that she rose to her role as the opera progressed and that she never sang the same part in exactly the same way. Her reputation was such that in 1834–1835 she was paid $15,000 for the season, which was more than her great admirer, the composer Bellini, received for three new operas. At La Scala Opera in Milan it took the mayor of the city to clear the house lest it collapse under the weight of the crowd eager to hear her. So great an artist was she that her name has become legendary.[70]

Jenny Lind, "the Swedish Nightingale," first appeared in London in 1847 and quickly created a furor on both sides of the Atlantic. At the very outset she commanded a salary of 120,000 francs for the season, in addition to a furnished house and a carriage. It was reported at the time that when the doors of the opera house opened, a tumultuous crowd surged in: "Ladies' ornaments were forced into their heads and their dresses torn from their backs. Gentlemen's coattails were wrenched off, and their hats smashed to atoms; in one moment every seat in the house was filled and every piece of ground occupied."[71] To a certain extent, no doubt, these ovations were a tribute as much to her personality as to her singing. She had, of course, a fine voice and her singing, notable for an indescribably soft and seraphic pianissimo, enchanted both Mendelssohn and Chopin. But contemporaries kept harping on the force of her personality. She seemed to them the very embodiment of bourgeois ideals: she was simple, modest, kind and charitable. During her fantastic success in Boston in 1850, she could write: "Herrings and potatoes—a clean wooden chair and a wooden spoon to eat milk-soup with, that would make me skip like a child for joy."[72]

The men singers, though they were equally distinguished, have not

---

[70] Countess de Merlin: *Memoirs of Madame Malibran* (London, 1840); Arthur Pougin: *Marie Malibran* (London, 1911); Henri Malherbe: *La passion de Malibran* (Paris, 1937). Other singers as well as Malibran are discussed in Ellen C. Clayton: *Queens of Song* (London, 1863) and in H. Sutherland Edwards: *The Prima Donna* (London, 1888).

[71] *A Review of the Performances of Mademoiselle Jenny Lind . . . and Their Influence and Effect upon Our National Drama* (London, 1847), 22.

[72] Henry S. Holland and W. S. Rockstro: *Memoir of Jenny Lind-Goldschmidt* (London, 1891), II, 421. See also the biography by her daughter, Mrs. Raymond Maude: *The Life of Jenny Lind* (London, 1926); Edward Wagenknecht: *Jenny Lind* (Boston, 1931); and Helen Headland: *The Swedish Nightingale: a Biography of Jenny Lind* (Rock Island, 1940).

attracted as much attention from biographers as the women. Among the leading figures were Giovanni Rubini, Luigi Lablache, Antonio Tamburini, Adolphe Nourrit and Giuseppe Mario. Rubini was the first of the great tenors and several famous operas were written for him. Though an indifferent actor, he won acclaim for his florid singing, especially for his trills and vibrato. Lablache and Tamburini were both bassos, men of fine presence who could act as well as sing. As much as any woman they gave distinction to the Italian operas.

If we are to believe contemporaries, the loose living of opera stars was proverbial, so much so that they could not be received in society. When they appeared in salon concerts, they were separated from their auditors by a silken rope. Gradually, however, the weight of bourgeois morality made itself felt. Taglioni, the great dancer, was forbidden by her father to assume any voluptuous or indecent pose and even Malibran, who lived "in sin" with the violinist De Beriot simply because her husband denied her a divorce, was ostracized by her family and so cooly received in Paris, when it became known that she was expecting a child, that she had to retire temporarily from the stage. Both she and Jenny Lind scored their greatest successes in the role of Amina in Bellini's *La Sonnambula,* the story of innocence unjustly suspected but ultimately triumphant, as it should be. Of Jenny Lind it was said again and again that it was her goodness, her virtue, her piety and her charity that won all hearts. "She was a woman," remarked Phineas Barnum, the American showman, "who would have been adored if she had had the voice of a crow" or, to quote *Punch:*

> . . . . Why thou charmest this heart of wood,
> Delightful Jenny, would'st thou know?
> Because thou look'st so gentle and so good,
> And all accounts declare thee so;
>   Thy acting shows a sense of duty,
>   An earnest love of truth and beauty,
> An aim to make thine author understood.[73]

By 1830 the Italian opera form had been brought to perfection in Gioacchino Rossini's *William Tell.* It was at that time the predominant form, played in every opera house in every country. Italian opera

---

[73] *Punch,* 1847, quoted by Mrs. Maude: *Life of Jenny Lind,* 116 ff. See also the *Review of the Performances of Jenny Lind,* cited above, and Wagenknecht: *Jenny Lind,* 25, chap. iv.

was meant for entertainment and depended entirely on singing. The plot was usually simple, often implausible and not infrequently silly. The orchestra, too, played an altogether subordinate part, ordinarily an elementary accompaniment. The show was therefore left to the singers, relieved from time to time by the chorus or ballet, the latter coming more and more to consist of girls in increasingly scanty attire. The demands made on the singer by the so-called *bel canto* style were nothing less than terrific: a huge technique, exceedingly high notes, astounding cadenzas, and fantastic ornamentation. Operas were frequently written for particular singers, and might well consist of a carefully planned series of melodic arias and cabalettas, occasionally relieved by ensemble. The singers then outdid each other in their vocal achievement, the level of which is but rarely attained in our day. They would often omit substantial sections of the opera to make room for their improvisations or, if they were sufficiently eminent, would appropriate the arias of other characters. They might even interpolate favorite arias from entirely different works. It is reported of Mme. Catalani that in a London performance she made no attempt to play a part, "but walked on and off and went through her songs as if she were alone, hardly appearing to acknowledge the presence of the 'puppets' about her." In short, the whole point of Italian opera was to have great singers sing beautiful music.[74]

It must be said that some of the leading composers tried to curb such excesses. Rossini, for example, usually wrote out the ornamentation of his arias, though he did not object to the great singers substituting their own if they did it well. His two eminent successors, Vincenzo Bellini and Gaetano Donizetti, both tried to get good, dramatic librettos. They also restricted the arias to reasonable proportions and refused to write extravagant embellishments simply to please individual singers. Bellini, a gentle, well-loved young revolutionary, died at the age of thirty-four (1835), after writing several operas perfectly suited to bring out the beauties of the human voice. His superb melodies impressed men as different as Chopin and Wagner. Some of his works, such as *La Son-*

---

[74] The quotation is from George Hogarth: *Memoirs of the Opera* (London, 1851), 293. See also Anon.: *The Italian Opera in 1839* (London, 1840), 33 ff.; Castil-Blaze: *L'Académie Impériale de Musique* (Paris, 1855), II, 182. For the development of coloratura singing, see Lotte Medicus: *Die Koloratura in der italienischen Oper des 19 Jahrhunderts* (Zürich, 1939), 37 ff.

nambula (1831), a sentimental story of village life, and *Norma* (1831), a grand Druid tragedy, are still performed, despite the difficulties presented by the *bel canto* style. His last opera, *I Puritani,* a story of the English civil war, was naturally a favorite in England, where Rubini, Lablache, Grisi and Tamburini were obliged to sing their parts *ad nauseam.*[75]

Donizetti, who wrote dozens of operas, excelled in the treatment of lighter themes, as in *L'elisir d'amore* (1832), and *Don Pasquale* (1840), but he earned lasting fame by his tragic *Lucia di Lammermoor* (1835), famous for its sextet and for its mad scene. These operas continue to appear on the operatic repertories, though other works of Donizetti, popular in their day (*Anna Bolena,* 1830; *La fille du régiment,* 1840; *La favorita* (1840), are but rarely heard.[76]

Italian opera was to attain new heights through the work of Giuseppe Verdi, the Italian patriot, who was to be the most formidable competitor of Wagner. Only his early and less-known operas (*Nabucco,* 1842; *I Lombardi,* 1843; *Ernani,* 1844; *Macbeth,* 1847) fall within this period, but they were considerable successes in their day and *Ernani* secured the young composer an international reputation. Verdi laid great store by the quality of the libretto and, while continuing to write for the voice, dealt with elemental human passions in a highly dynamic way. His first major work, *Rigoletto* (1851), is an unexcelled study in tragic character and has rightly remained one of the most popular of all operas.[77]

Toward the midcentury there grew up several schools of mildly national opera, namely the French or Grand Opera, the German or Romantic Opera, and the Russian or National Opera. The first of these was really an offshoot of the traditional Italian Opera, with greater emphasis on romantic and dramatic elements, and on grandiose production. Many of the librettos, written by Eugène Scribe, were theatri-

[75] William A. C. Lloyd: *Vincenzo Bellini* (London, n.d.); Francesco Pastura: *Bellini, secondo la storia* (Turin, 1959).

[76] There are two excellent recent studies: Herbert Weinstock: *Donizetti and the World of Opera in Italy, Paris and Vienna in the First Half of the Nineteenth Century* (New York, 1963); William Ashbrook: *Donizetti* (New York, 1965).

[77] A. E. A. Cherbuliez: *Giuseppe Verdi, Leben und Werk* (Zürich, 1949) and the exhaustive work of Franco Abbiati: *Giuseppe Verdi* (Milan, 1959). In English there are two substantial recent books: Frank Walker: *The Man Verdi: a Critical and Biographical Study* (London, 1962) and George Martin: *Verdi, His Music, His Life and Times* (New York, 1963).

cally effective and even brilliant. Leaving aside the lesser exponents of this opera type, such as Jacques Halévy (*La juive,* 1835), Adolphe Adam (*Le postillon de Longjumeau,* 1836), and Ferdinand Hérold (*Zampa,* 1831; *Le pré aux clercs,* 1832), a few words may be said about Daniel Auber and Giacomo Meyerbeer. Auber was highly regarded by his contemporaries as the pioneer of the picturesque, Romantic Opera with his *La muette de Portici* (known in English as *Masaniello,* 1829), a stirring story which contributed to the revolutionary fervor of 1830. It was followed by *Fra Diavolo* and other lively and appealing works, but Auber was soon overshadowed by Meyerbeer, who created a sensation in 1831 with his *Robert le Diable.* According to Wagner, Meyerbeer was musically "an absolute zero," a judgment with which many critics have sympathized. But no one questioned his dramatic craftsmanship or his ability to sense and satisfy public taste. To quote Wagner again: "He became the weathercock of European opera-music, the vane that always veers at first uncertain with the shift of wind, and only comes to a standstill when the wind itself has settled on its quarter."[78]

Meyerbeer decided that what was wanted was the grandiose spectacle, with dramatic vigor even if without plausibility. His *Robert le Diable* provides a full dose of black magic and has dissolute nuns dancing the ballet (see Illustration 73). In his other two masterpieces, *Les Huguenots* (1836), with its massacre of St. Bartholomew, and *Le prophète* (1843), with its fanatical Anabaptists, there are huge mob scenes, endless processions, choirs of demons and corteges of phantoms. Opera thus became truly "grand," pretentious and expensive, "a conglomeration of monstrosities," and "a pompous spectacle enhanced by music" (Schumann). But its appeal to the public was without limit.[79]

German Romantic Opera was unable, at the time, to compete with either Italian or French opera, even on its own grounds. The German national form goes back to Carl Maria von Weber's *Freischütz* (1821), with its ultra-Romantic subject matter, its spooks and fairies. It has been estimated that between the Weber opera and Wagner's *Lohengrin* (1848), some five hundred operas were composed by Germans, many

---

[78] Wagner: *Opera and Drama* (1851), in his *Prose Works,* II, 88 ff.

[79] Donald J. Grout: *A Short History of Opera* (2 ed., New York, 1965), 315 ff.; William L. Crosten: *French Grand Opera: an Art and a Business* (New York, 1948); Lang: *Music in Western Civilization,* 825 ff. For biography, see the popular account by Julius Kapp: *Meyerbeer* (8 ed., Berlin, 1930); L. Dauriac: *Meyerbeer* (new ed., Paris, 1930).

of them stories of demons, ghosts and elves. Almost all of them are now forgotten, even those of Ludwig Spohr, a musician of real stature. At the time, however, many of them were highly regarded. Heinrich Marschner's *Der Vampyr* (1828) ran for sixty nights in London, and his *Der Templar und die Jüdin,* on the *Ivanhoe* theme, as well as his *Hans Heilung* (1831) was extremely popular. The same was true of Friedrich von Flotow's *Martha* (1847) and Gustav Lortzing's *Zar und Zimmermann* (1837), which have continued to appear on the present-day German stage.[80]

Russian National Opera, strictly patriotic in inspiration, was represented by the single figure of Michael I. Glinka, who had heard many operas in Italy during a prolonged stay in 1830–1834. On his return to Russia he associated with writers such as Pushkin, Joukovsky and Odoevsky, who inspired him to attempt a truly national opera. The result was *A Life for the Czar* (1836), which dealt with the Russian-Polish conflict of the seventeenth century and made liberal use of folk themes. In a later opera, *Russlan and Liudmilla* (1842), Glinka introduced Oriental dances which were to influence his successors, Moussorgsky and Rimsky-Korsakov. These operas, however, were quite overshadowed, even in Russia, by the Italian operas which brought even the greatest singers to Russia on tour.[81]

Toward the end of the period Richard Wagner gave the history of opera a fundamental turn and initiated the greatest musical controversy of modern times. For Wagner the years prior to 1848 were a preparatory period, during which he formulated his doctrine. His ideas were not strictly new, but like Karl Marx in another field he succeeded in assimilating and consolidating many notions and aspirations current at the time, and then translating them into practice. Although there is still much disagreement about Wagner and his achievement, certain features are clear enough. He was a restless, ambitious young man,

---

[80] J. Cornet: *Die Oper in Deutschland* (Hamburg, 1949). See also Lang: *Music in Western Civilization,* 839 ff.; Einstein: *Music in the Romantic Era,* 141 ff.; Rudolf Bauer: *Die Oper* (Berlin, 1959), 69 ff.; Helmut Schmidt-Garré: *Oper: eine Kulturgeschichte* (Cologne, 1963), 175 ff., 202 ff.; Grout: *Short History of Opera,* 375 ff.

[81] Iurii V. Keldysh: *Istoriia russkoi muzyki* (Moscow, 1947), Vol. II; Richard A. Leonard: *A History of Russian Music* (London, 1956); Martin Cooper: *Russian Opera* (London, 1951); and on Glinka, W. D. Calvocoressi and Gerald Abraham: "Glinka" (in *Masters of Russian Music,* London, 1936, 13–64); Vladimir V. Stasov: *Mikhail Ivanovich Glinka* (Moscow, 1953).

born into a theatrical family and in many ways unstable and irresponsible, especially in money matters. Financial stringency seems to have bred in him a deep dissatisfaction which in turn led him to socialist thought.[82] His general attitude of rebellion derived, however, from the study of philosophy, notably from the writings of the Young Hegelians,[83] In any event, he suffered from a growing sense of estrangement and freely admitted that he composed his early operas (*Rienzi; Der Fliegende Holländer*) in order to escape from everyday relations. In a sense all his work aimed at escape from the real world into another realm of mythology.

Prior to his arrival in Paris in 1839, Wagner had read deeply in the history and theory of music and opera, and had already embarked upon literary work, for which he proved himself highly gifted. In his musical thought he was much influenced by Beethoven and Weber, but also by Rossini, Bellini and other exponents of the Italian opera. During his two-year stay in Paris, a period of privation and disappointment, he became acquainted with Berlioz and Meyerbeer, from whom he gladly accepted financial aid, though he came to despise the commercialism of the operatic world, designed as he thought solely to provide entertainment for the rich whose time hung heavily on their hands.[84] It is strange that, nonetheless, his own opera, *Rienzi,* composed at this time, not only emulated Auber and Meyerbeer, but tried to outdo them in grandiose effects and noisy music. No doubt this helps to explain the immediate and continued success of this opera after its first performance at Dresden in 1842. *Der Fliegende Holländer* (1843), rated as the first genuinely Wagnerian opera and a vigorous, dramatic piece, was somewhat mystifying and held less appeal. There followed *Tannhäuser* (1845) and *Lohengrin* (1848, but first performed under Liszt's direction in 1850). These operas, which have been called "the consummation of German Romantic opera,"[85] were succeeded by a major break, during which Wagner became involved in the Dresden insurrection of 1849 and was obliged to flee to Switzerland.[86] During

[82] See, e.g., his *Art and Revolution* (1849), in *Prose Works,* I, 42, 57.

[83] Hugo Dinger: *Richard Wagners geistige Entwicklung* (Leipzig, 1892); Maurice Boucher: *The Political Concepts of Richard Wagner* (New York, 1950).

[84] *Art and Revolution,* 42, 44; Ernest Newman: *The Life of Richard Wagner* (New York, 1933–1946), I, 253 ff.

[85] Grout: *Short History of Opera,* chap. xxiii.

[86] See Chapter XIV.

the ensuing five years he published a number of theoretical writings, notably his programmatic essay *Opera and Drama* (1851), but also worked on the *Ring der Nibelungen,* which ushered in the great years of his career.

Wagner's theoretical essays are repetitious and argumentative, so that they now make rather dull reading. His basic idea was the fusion of the arts in one supreme art, the music drama, to which reference has already been made. Though composers such as Gluck and Beethoven had already pointed the way toward a better balance of music and drama in the opera, Wagner made the notion of the *Gesamtkunstwerk* his own. Increasingly he attempted to break the predominance of the singer, to reduce the importance of the aria, and to stress the dramatic and orchestral sides. Though he had a marked aptitude for stage management, he was actually not very successful as a dramatist. Many parts of his greatest operas are dramatically tedious and dull. His reputation, therefore, rests chiefly on his music, on his extraordinary power to evoke and express feelings. But the apogee of Wagner's career fell in the years after the midcentury, when *Lohengrin* notified the world of an important new departure in operatic and indeed in general musical history.[87]

---

[87] In addition to Newman's standard biography, the following recent books are of value: Othmar Fries: *Richard Wagner und die deutsche Romantik* (Zürich, 1952); Curt von Westernhagen: *Richard Wagner, sein Werk, sein Wesen, und seine Welt* (Zürich, 1956); Jacques Bourgeois: *Richard Wagner* (Paris, 1959); Walter G. Amando: *Richard Wagner* (Hamburg, 1962); and the admirable critical appreciation of Hans Gal: *Richard Wagner: Versuch einer Würdigung* (Frankfurt, 1963).

BIBLIOGRAPHICAL ESSAY

A great deal of specialized literature has been cited in the footnotes and need not be repeated here. For general guidance see the American Historical Association's *Guide to Historical Literature* (New York, 1961) and Jacques Droz, L. Genet, and J. Vidalenc: *L'époque contemporaine. I: Restaurations et révolutions, 1815–1871* (Vol. I of the collection "Clio," Paris, 1953), which lists the sources as well as the literature. William L. Langer, ed.: *An Encyclopedia of World History* (4 rev. ed., Boston, 1968) is useful for chronology and genealogy.

General Accounts

Still the most extensive and comprehensive history is Alfred Stern's *Geschichte Europas, 1815–1871* (10 vols., Stuttgart, 1894–1924), of which Vols. IV–VII cover the years 1830–1852. Of recent universal histories, mostly collaborative, may be mentioned Louis Halphen and Philippe Sagnac, eds.: *Peuples et civilisations,* Vol. XV by Georges Weill entitled *L'éveil des nationalités et le mouvement libéral, 1815–1848* (2 ed., Paris, 1960) and Vol. XVI by Charles H. Pouthas entitled *Démocratie et capitalisme, 1848–1860* (Paris, 1941). More recent is Edouard Crouzet, ed.: *Histoire générale des civilisations,* of which Vol. VI, by Robert Schnerb, is entitled *Le XIXe siècle: l'apogée de l'expansion européenen, 1815–1914* (Paris, 1955). The *New Cambridge Modern History,* ed. by J. P. T. Bury, consists of chapters on various topics by various authors. Vol. X (Cambridge, 1960) is entitled *The Zenith of European Power, 1830–1870.* Vol. VIII of the *Propyläen Weltgeschichte,* ed. by Golo Mann (Frankfurt, 1960), covers the nineteenth century. For a comparable Marxist study, see the Soviet Academy of Sciences' *Vsemupnaiia Istoriia,* Vol. VI of which deals with 1789–1871 (Moscow, 1959).

A truly international survey of recent history is the four-volume work edited by Max Beloff, Pierre Renouvin, Franz Schnabel and Franco Valsecchi entitled *L'Europe du XIXe et du XXe siècle* (Milan, 1959), of which the first two volumes contain varied essays by recognized authorities. Unusual also is Carlo Curcio's *Europa: storia di un'idea* (2 vols., Florence, 1958), analyzing the concept of the European community. Friedrich Heer: *Europa, Mutter der Revolutionen* (Stuttgart, 1964) reviews the main intellectual and religious currents of the nineteenth century, while Feliks Gross: *The Seizure of Political Power in a Century of Revolutions* (New York,

1958) surveys the upheavals since 1825. Charles Morazé, in his *The Triumph of the Middle Classes* (London, 1966) discusses the bourgeois world, with special reference to France. George Rude's *The Crowd in History, 1700–1840* (London, 1965) is a pioneer attempt to analyze the urban mass movements.

Political Theory

Fundamental is still W. A. Dunning: *A History of Political Theories,* Vol. III, *From Rousseau to Spencer* (New York, 1936). Briefer but equally competent are George H. Sabine: *A History of Political Theory* (rev. ed., New York, 1950); Walter Theimer: *Geschichte der politischen Ideen* (Berne, 1955); and Marcel Prélot: *Histoire des idées politiques* (Paris, 1959). The various chapters of Jean Touchard, ed.: *Histoire des idées politiques* (2 vols., Paris, 1959) are written by specialists.

Guido de Ruggiero: *The History of European Liberalism* (London, 1927) is a classic. Jacob S. Shapiro: *Liberalism, Its Meaning and History* (Princeton, 1958 is valuable for its introduction to selected sources. David Caute: *The Left in Europe since 1789* (London, 1965) attempts a synthesis of radical movements, while J. L. Talmon: *Political Messianism: the Romantic Phase, 1815–1848* (London, 1960) is a learned and altogether original analysis of intellectual currents.

The Historical Evolution of Nationalism, by Carlton J. H. Hayes (New York, 1931), is still the most satisfactory survey. Hans Cohn's *Prophets and Peoples: Studies in 19th Century Nationalism* (New York, 1946) is a collection of vivid biographical sketches. Eugen Lambert: *Geschichte des Nationalismus in Europa* (Stuttgart, 1950) is an excellent account going back to the Renaissance. Boyd O. Shafer: *Nationalism: Myth and Reality* (New York, 1955) is essentially a critical analysis.

Economic History

The classic account of economic theories is still Charles Gide and Charles Rist: *A History of Economic Doctrines* (7 ed., 3 vols., London, 1948). Shorter competent surveys are Eric Roll: *A History of Economic Thought* (rev. ed., London, 1954) and Overton H. Taylor: *A History of Economic Thought* (New York, 1960). René Gonnard: *Histoire des doctrines économiques depuis les physiocrates* is a well-known French survey (5 ed., Paris, 1947).

Of many textbooks of economic history Shepard B. Clough and Charles W. Cole: *Economic History of Europe* (3 ed., Boston, 1952) can be recommended. Part II of Gino Luzzatto: *Storia economica dell'età moderna e contemporanea* (4 ed., Padua, 1955–1958) is one of the best treatments of economic development. Indispensable, however, is now Vol. VI of the

Cambridge Economic History of Europe (Cambridge, 1965), in which David S. Landes and Folke Dovring treat respectively the Industrial and Agricultural Revolutions. Most studies of the Industrial Revolution deal exclusively with Great Britain. Among recent ones are T. S. Ashton: *The Industrial Revolution, 1760–1830* (London, 1948); H. L. Beales: *The Industrial Revolution* (rev. ed., London, 1958); Phyllis Deane: *The First Industrial Revolution* (London, 1965), which is excellent; Paul Bairoch: *Révolution industrielle et sous-développement* (Paris, 1963) is a detailed, scholarly study of the origins of industrialism, while Rondo Cameron: *Banking in the Early Stages of Industrialization* (New York, 1967) fills an important gap. Corrado Barbagallo: *Le origini della grande industria contemporanea, 1750–1850* (new ed., Florence, 1951), is an authoritative work of a technical nature.

Population

Population in History, ed. by D. V. Glass and D. E. C. Eversley (London, 1965) is a valuable collection of key articles, many of which touch the early nineteenth century. E. A. Wrigley: *Industrial Growth and Population Change* (Cambridge, 1962) is also important. Charles H. Pouthas: *La population française pendant la première moitié du XIXe siècle* (Paris, 1956) is an exemplary study. For Germany Paul Mombert: *Studien zur Bevölkerungsbewegung in Deutschland* (Karlsruhe, 1907) is still valuable for data on the early nineteenth century. Erich Keyser: *Bevölkerungsgeschichte Deutschlands* (3 ed., Leipzig, 1943), is first rate. A well-known pioneer work was G. T. Griffith: *Population Problems in the Age of Malthus* (Cambridge, 1926), but this now needs revision (see William L. Langer: "Europe's Initial Population Explosion," in *American Historical Review,* LXIX, 1963, 1–17).

The Agrarian Problem

Henri Sée: *Esquisse d'une histoire du régime agraire en Europe au XVIIIe et XIXe siècle* (Paris, 1921) is still worth consulting. Excellent recent surveys are Bernard E. Slicher van Bath: *The Agrarian History of Western Europe, 1500–1850* (London, 1963) and Robert Trow-Smith: *Life from the Land: the Growth of Farming in Western Europe* (London, 1967). Wilhelm Abel: *Agrarkrisen und Agrarkonjunktur; eine Geschichte der Land—und Ernährungswirtschaft Mitteleuropas seit dem hohen Mittelalter* (Hamburg, 1966) is the work of an eminent authority.

Education

As a general introduction there is William Boyd: *The History of Western Education* (7 ed. by Edmund J. King, London, 1964) and the stimulating comparative essay by Robert Ulich: *The Education of Nations* (rev. ed., Cambridge, 1967). For Britain there is John W. Adamson: *English Education, 1789–1902* (London, 1930) and G. Birchenough: *History of Elementary Education in England and Wales from 1800 to the Present Day* (London, 1938). Two excellent recent works are Hugh M. Pollard: *Pioneers of Popular Education, 1760–1850* (Cambridge, 1957) and Brian Simon: *Studies in the History of Education, 1789–1870* (London, 1960). For France Vol. VI of Louis Grimaud: *Histoire de la liberté d'enseignement en France* (Paris, 1954) is devoted to the July Monarchy. An excellent institutional study is Félix Ponteil: *Histoire de l'enseignement en France, 1789–1964* (Paris, 1966). Maurice Gontard: *L'enseignement primaire en France de la Révolution à la loi Guizot* (Paris, 1959) is first rate. German education is dealt with in detail in Richard Müller-Freienfels: *Bildungs und Erziehungsgeschichte* (3 vols., Leipzig, 1932); Johann von den Driesch: *Geschichte der Erziehung* (2 vols., Paderborn, 1953).

Public Health

Colin F. Brockington: *Public Health in the 19th Century* (London, 1965) and William M. Frazer: *A History of English Public Health, 1834–1939* (London, 1950) are both good, while Alfons Fischer: *Geschichte des deutschen Gesundheitswesens* (2 vols. Berlin, 1933) is an authoritative, exhaustive study. Samuel E. Finer: *The Life and Times of Sir Edwin Chadwick* (London, 1952) puts the life of that great reformer into a larger setting. Detailed literature on the cholera epidemics of the period is cited in the text. R. Pollitzer: "Cholera Studies: History of the Disease" (*Bulletin of the World Health Organization*, X, 1954, 421–461) is an excellent summary treatment by an outstanding epidemiologist.

Social Structure and Social Thought

Jean Lhomme: *Le problème des classes: doctrines et faits* (Paris, 1938); Goetz Briefs: *The Proletariat* (New York, 1937); G. D. H. Cole: *Studies in Class Structure* (London, 1955) all deal with the knotty problem of social classes. See also the valuable survey by Armand Cuvillier: "Les antagonismes des classes dans la littérature sociale française de Saint-Simon à 1848" (*International Review of Social History*, I, 1956, 433–663). Max Beer: *Allgemeine Geschichte des Sozialismus und der sozialen Kämpfe* (Berlin, 1924) is still one of the best general accounts. Alexander Gray: *The Socialist Tradition* (London, 1946) is one of the best brief surveys. G. D. H. Cole: *Socialist Thought: the Fore-runners, 1789–1850* (London, 1954) is a conventional treatment, while Thilo Ramm: *Die grossen Sozialisten als Rechts- und Sozialphilosophen* (Stuttgart, 1955) is an exceptional, original evaluation. Werner Hofmann: *Ideengeschichte der sozialen Bewegung des 19 und 20 Jahrhunderts* (Berlin, 1962) is a compact review of doctrines. Among national histories, Max Beer: *History of British Socialism* (2 vols., London, 1919–1920) is outstanding. For Germany, Franz Mehring's *Geschichte der deutschen Sozialdemokratie* (latest ed., Berlin, 1960) remains fundamental. Among many histories of French socialism, Paul Louis: *Histoire du socialisme en France* (5 ed., Paris, 1950) and Maxime Leroy: *Histoire des idées sociales en France* (2 vols., Paris, 1951) can be recommended. Illuminating ancillary studies are David-Owen Evans: *Social Romanticism in France, 1830–1848* (Oxford, 1951) and Donald G. Charlton: *Secular Religions in France, 1815–1870* (New York, 1963). The Saint-Simonian movement has been admirably treated in Sebastien Charléty: *Histoire du Saint-Simonisme* (latest ed., Paris, 1931) and in Henri d'Allemagne: *Les Saint-Simoniens* (Paris, 1930), which is lavishly illustrated.

The early history of Marxian socialism is dealt with in Paul Kägi: *Genesis des historischen Materialismus* (Berlin, 1965) and in T. I. Oisermann: *Die Entwicklung der marxistischen Philosophie* (Berlin, 1965), the latter a systematic Communist account. Auguste Cornu's *Karl Marx et Friedrich Engels: leur vie et leur oeuvre* (2 vols., Paris, 1955–1958) promises to be a definitive biographical study when completed. Important also is Jean-Yves Calvez: *La pensée de Karl Marx* (Paris, 1956), which has a valuable bibliography. George Lichtheim's *Marxism: a Historical and Critical Study* (New York, 1961) is excellent. The Hegelian background of Marxian thought is treated in Sidney Hook: *From Hegel to Marx* (New York, 1935) and Herbert Marcuse: *Reason and Revolution: Hegel and the Rise of Social Theory* (2 ed., New York, 1955). David McLellan: *The Young Hegelians and Karl Marx* (London, 1968) appeared too late to be used in the present study. Mandell M. Bober: *Karl Marx's Interpretation of History* (Cambridge, 1950) is a fundamental study.

The beginnings of communism are traced in Werner Kowalski's scholarlv Communist monograph: *Vorgeschichte und Entstehung des Bundes der Gerechten* (Berlin, 1962) and in Herwig Foerder: *Marx und Engels am Vorabend der Revolution* (Berlin, 1960). Charles Andler's *Le manifeste communiste* (Paris, 1922) analyzes the contribution of French social thought.

Many biographies of early socialists have been cited in the text. Among the more important recent studies may be mentioned Rowland H. Harvey: *Robert Owen: Social Idealist* (Berkeley, 1949) and Asa Briggs: *Robert Owen in Retrospect* (Loughborough, 1959). Armand Saitta's *Filippo Buonarroti* (Rome, 1950) is a major contribution, to which Elizabeth

Eisenstein's *The First Professional Revolutionary, Filippo Michele Buonarrotti* (Cambridge, 1959) is a welcome English supplement. *Etienne Cabet and the "Voyage en Icarie,"* by Sylvester A. Piotrowski (Washington, 1935), is a systematic account. The classic biography of Fourier is by Charles Gide: *Fourier, précurseur de la coöpération* (Paris, 1923). Leo R. Loubère: *Louis Blanc* (Evanston, 1960) and Jean Vidalenc: *Louis Blanc* (Paris, 1948) do full justice to their subject. Denis W. Brogan: *Proudhon* (London, 1934) is a rather personal appreciation. Edouard Dolléans: *Proudhon* (Paris, 1948) is the work of an authority on labor history. George Woodcock: *Pierre-Joseph Proudhon* (New York, 1956) can also be recommended. On Weitling, the biography by Carl Wittke: *The Utopian Communist: a Biography of Wilhelm Weitling* (Baton Rouge, 1950) is scholarly and broad in scope.

Biographies of Marx are legion. Among them Boris Nicolaievski and C. Maenchen Helfen: *Karl Marx* (Philadelphia, 1936) is well-informed and strong on the earlier period. Franz Mehring: *Karl Marx* (Berlin, 1918, now available in English, Ann Arbor, 1962) remains a classic. Georg Mende: *Karl Marx' Entwicklung vom revolutionären Demokraten zum Kommunisten* (3 ed., Berlin, 1960) is a valuable analysis of the early writings. Isaiah Berlin: *Karl Marx* (3 ed., London, 1963) is a little masterpiece, stimulating and readable. The Cornu biography has been noted above. On Engels the magistral study by Gustav Mayer: *Friedrich Engels* is available in an English translation of the second German edition (London, 1936).

INTERNATIONAL RELATIONS

By far the best general survey is Vol. V of the *Histoire des relations internationales,* ed. by Pierre Renouvin (Paris, 1953–1958). Vol. I of the *Histoire de la diplomatie,* ed. by Vladimir P. Potemkin (2 ed., Paris, 1959) is an official Soviet treatment of the period prior to 1871. Robert W. Seton-Watson's *Britain in Europe, 1789–1914* (New York, 1937) is a highly competent survey of British policy, while Donald Southgate's *"The Most English Minister": the Policies and Politics of Palmerston* (New York, 1966) summarizes and supplements the basic studies of Sir Charles K. Webster: *The Foreign Policy of Palmerston, 1830–1841* (2 vols., London, 1951). Anglo-French relations are studied in John R. Hall: *England and the Orleans Monarchy* (London, 1912), which is still useful; Raymond Guyot: *La première Entente Cordiale* (Paris, 1926); and Jean Duhamel: *Louis Philippe et la première Entente Cordiale* (Paris, 1951), which deals chiefly with personal relations. Paul Henry: *La France devant le monde* (Paris, 1945) is a sound account of French foreign policy in the nineteenth century, which should be supplemented by Charles H. Pouthas: *La politique étran-*

gère de la France pendant la Monarchie Constitutionnelle (Paris, 1948). *La politica estera del Guizot, 1840–1847* (Florence, 1957), by S. Mastellone, adduces much unpublished material. The later stages of the Belgian problem are traced in F. de Lannoy's *Histoire diplomatique de l'indépendance belge* (Brussels, 1930). *La Belgique devant la France de Juillet, 1839–1848* (Paris, 1956), by Henry-Thierry Deschamps, is a highly detailed analysis of a critical period.

The first two volumes of Jeronimo Becker's *Historia de las relaciones de España durante el siglo XIX* (Madrid, 1924–1926) cover the years 1800–1868. Philip E. Mosely's "Intervention and Non-Intervention in Spain, 1838, 1839" (*Journal of Modern History*, XIII, 1941, 195–217) is a fundamental contribution which rests on Russian as well as other archival material. Federico Suarez: "La intervencion extranjera en los comienzos del regimen liberal español" (*Revista de estudios politicos*, VII, 1944, 409–471) is the best general treatment of the intervention. *The Spanish Marriages, 1841–1846* (London, 1936), by Ernest J. Parry, is an admirable study of a most complicated problem.

On the Swiss problem, the reader may consult Jean-Charles Biaudet: *La Suisse et la Monarchie de Juillet, 1830–1838* (Lausanne, 1941); Karl Eckinger: *Lord Palmerston und der schweizer Sonderbundskrieg* (Berlin, 1938); A. G. Imlah: *Britain and Switzerland, 1845–1860* (London, 1966).

General studies of Russian policy are mostly brief. Among them may be mentioned Andrei Lobanov-Rostovsky: *Russia and Europe, 1825–1878* (Ann Arbor, 1954); Constantin de Grunwald: *Trois siècles de diplomatie russe* (Paris, 1945); Barbara Jelavich: *A Century of Russian Foreign Policy* (New York, 1964). Ersebet Andiés: *Das Bündnis Habsburg-Romanov* (*Studia Historica*, LII, Budapest, 1963) is a valuable Marxist monograph which adduces much new material.

The literature on the Near Eastern question is voluminous. Harold Temperley's *The Crimea* (London, 1936) provides an excellent general account, with special reference to British policy. M. S. Anderson: *The Eastern Question, 1774–1923* (London, 1966) can be warmly recommended as a competent, up-to-date review. Frederick S. Rodkey: *The Turco-Egyptian Question in the Relations of England, France and Russia, 1832–1841* (Urbana, 1921), though old, is still a useful account of the Turco-Egyptian conflict. Vernon J. Puryear's studies *England, Russia, and the Straits Question, 1844–1856* (Berkeley, 1932) and *International Politics and Diplomacy in the Near East: a Study of British Commercial Policy in the Levant, 1834–1853* (Stanford, 1935) are detailed archival monographs. An interesting and illuminating analysis of British public opinion is John H. Gleason's *The Genesis of Russophobia in Great Britain* (Cambridge, 1950).

Philip E. Mosely's *Russian Diplomacy and the Opening of the Eastern Question in 1838 and 1839* (Cambridge, 1934) is an indispensable corrective to the official Russian version as presented in Serge Goriainov: *La Bosphore et les Dardanelles* (Paris, 1910). Eugène de Guichen's *La crise d'Orient de 1839 à 1841 et l'Europe* is valuable for domestic aspects of the crisis.

There is no single satisfactory treatment of the Polish question in this period, but the following studies make valuable contributions: Marian Kukiel: *Czartoryski and European Unity* (Princeton, 1953); Gunter Weber: *Die polnische Emigration im 19 Jahrhundert* (Essen, 1937); Wolfgang Hallgarten: *Studien über die deutsche Polenfreundschaft in der Periode der Märzrevolution* (Munich, 1928); L. Cukierman: *Die polenfreundliche Bewegung in Frankreich im Jahre 1830–1831* (Warsaw, 1926); Stefan Kieniewicz: "The Free State of Cracow, 1815–1846" (*Slavonic and East European Review,* XXVI, 1947–1948, 69–89).

NATIONAL HISTORIES

The British Isles

Sir Llewelyn Woodward's *The Age of Reform, 1815–1870* (rev. ed., London, 1962) is still the outstanding account of Britain in the midcentury. Elie Halévy's *History of the English People in the 19th Century* (rev. ed., 6 vols., London, 1949–1952) is something of a classic, being stimulating and original in approach and conclusions. Asa Briggs: *The Age of Improvement* (Vol. VIII of *A History of England,* London, 1959) is an excellent survey, by a specialist. George M. Young's *Victorian England: Portrait of an Age* (London, 1959) is a brilliant and suggestive essay. *Early Victorian England* (2 vols., ed. by George M. Young, London, 1934) is a valuable collection of essays by different scholars. John W. Dodds: *The Age of Paradox: a Biography of England, 1841–1851* (New York, 1952) is rather anecdotal but rich in information. George K. Kitson Clark: *The Making of Victorian England* (London, 1961) is a most stimulating review. In *English Historical Documents, XII (1), 1833–1871* (London, 1956), George M. Young and W. D. Hancock print most of the key documents, with valuable comment and bibliography.

Elizabeth Longford's *Queen Victoria* (New York, 1964) attempts a critical study of the queen's personality, as does Roger Fulford for her husband in his *The Prince Consort* (London, 1949). Of interest also are the books of Algernon Cecil: *Queen Victoria and Her Prime Ministers* (New York, 1953) and of Lord David Cecil: *"Lord M." The Later Life of Lord Melbourne* (London, 1954).

For political thought the reader should consult Crane Brinton: *English Political Thought in the 19th Century* (Oxford, 1949); George K. Kitson

Clark: *Peel and the Conservative Party, 1832–1841* (London, 1929), a basic study; R. B. McDowell: *British Conservatism, 1832–1914* (London, 1959); Arthur S. Turberville: *The House of Lords in the Age of Reform, 1784–1837* (London, 1958), a fundamental monograph; John A. Thomas: *The House of Commons, 1832–1901* (Cardiff, 1939), an interesting analysis; Norman Gash: *Politics in the Age of Peel, 1830–1850* (London, 1953) and the same author's *Reaction and Reconstruction in English Politics, 1832–1852* (New York, 1965), both basic studies by a specialist; Donald Southgate: *The Passing of the Whigs, 1832–1886* (London, 1962); Raymond G. Cowherd: *The Politics of English Dissent, 1815–1848* (London, 1959); S. Maccoby: *English Radicalism, 1832–1852* (London, 1935), a highly detailed, authoritative treatment; John Plamenatz: *The English Utilitarians* (2 ed., Oxford, 1958); W. L. Guttsman: *The British Political Elite, 1832–1935* (London, 1963), a stimulating essay; Joseph Hamburger: *Intellectuals in Politics: John Stuart Mill and the Philosophical Radicals* (New Haven, 1965). The Anti-Corn Law movement has spawned a large literature, of which only Donald G. Barnes: *A History of the English Corn Laws, 1660–1846* (New York, 1930) and Norman McCord: *The Anti-Corn Law League, 1838–1846* (London, 1958) can be listed here.

John H. Clapham's *An Economic History of Modern Britain*, Vol. I (2 ed., Cambridge, 1930) remains an impressive, indispensable work of scholarship. Among many briefer treatments, H. B. Court: *A Concise Economic History of Britain from 1750 to Recent Times* (New York, 1954) can be recommended. *British Economy in the 19th Century*, by Walt W. Rostow (Oxford, 1948), is a stimulating pioneer study, the argument of which is carried further in Arthur D. Gayer, Walt W. Rostow and A. J. Schwartz: *The Growth and Fluctuation of the British Economy, 1790–1850* (Oxford, 1953).

For the history of British agriculture, see the authoritative treatment by J. D. Chambers and G. E. Mingay: *The Agricultural Revolution, 1750–1880* (London, 1966). The classic account of farming by Rowland E. P. Ernle: *English Farming Past and Present* (6 ed. by G. E. Fussell and O. R. McGregor, Chicago, 1961) should be supplemented by Robert Trow-Smith: *English Husbandry from the Earliest Times to the Present Day* (London, 1951). G. E. Fussell: *The English Rural Labourer* (London, 1949) supersedes earlier works on the subject. F. M. L. Thompson: *English Landed Society in the 19th Century* (London, 1963) is of interest and value. David Williams: *The Rebecca Riots* (Cardiff, 1955) is one of the few scholarly studies of rural unrest. On emigration see W. A. Carruthers: *Emigration from the British Isles* (London, 1929); William S. Shepperson: *British Emigration to North America* (Minneapolis, 1957); and the exhaustive

Soviet inquiry: *Narodnaiia Emigratsiia i Klassovaiia Borba v Anglii v 1825–1850* by N. A. Erofeev (Moscow, 1962).

On industrial development there is an authoritative review by S. G. Checkland: *The Rise of Industrial Society in England, 1815–1885* (London, 1965) and a shorter survey by Thomas K. Derry and T. L. Jarman: *The Making of Modern Britain* (London, 1955). E. J. Hobsbawm: *Industry and Empire* (London, 1967) is an original, stimulating treatment. L. G. Johnson: *The Social Evolution of Industrial Britain* (Liverpool, 1959) is thoughtful and scholarly, and Neil J. Smelser: *Social Change in the Industrial Revolution* (Chicago, 1959), while dealing chiefly with the cotton industry, is of larger sociological import. Phyllis Deane and W. A. Cole: *British Economic Growth, 1688–1959* (2 ed., London, 1967) is an authoritative analysis and unique in covering a long period. Jonathan D. Chambers: *The Workshop of the World* (Oxford, 1961), though popular, is a reliable survey covering the years 1820 to 1880. *The Railway Age,* by Cyril B. Andrews (London, 1938) is richly illustrated and quotes much from the sources. Further literature on railway development includes Cuthbert H. Ellis: *British Railway History, 1830–1947* (2 vols., London, 1954, 1959), highly competent but poorly organized; Henry G. Lewin: *Early British Railways, 1801–1844* (London, 1925), still the best factual account; and Michael Robbins: *The Railway Age* (London, 1962), which relates the railway to the social setting and has an excellent bibliography.

William D. Grampp: *The Manchester School of Economics* (Stanford, 1960) is a valuable reconsideration of the free-trade movement, and David Roberts: *Victorian Origins of the British Welfare State* (New Haven, 1960) analyzes administrative developments. J. T. Ward: *The Factory Movement, 1830–1855* (London, 1962) is a highly detailed analysis. Elizabeth L. and Amy Harrison: *A History of Factory Legislation* (3 ed., London, 1936) is still useful, but should now be supplemented by Maurice W. Thomas: *The Early Factory Legislation* (London, 1948), which concentrates on the years 1834–1844. C. R. Fay: *Life and Labour in the 19th Century* (4 ed., London, 1947) is still unexcelled. On the labor movement the following are important: G. D. H. Cole: *British Working Class Politics, 1832–1914* (London, 1941); Henry Pelling: *A History of British Trade Unionism* (New York, 1963), a competent brief survey; E. P. Thompson: *The Making of the English Working Class, 1790–1840* (London, 1963), a fundamental though controversial study. A. L. Morton and G. Tate: *The British Labour Movement, 1770–1920* (London, 1956) and Jürgen Kuczynski: *Darstellung der Lage der Arbeiter in England von 1832 bis 1900* (Vol. XXIV of his exhaustive *Geschichte der Arbeiter unter dem Kapitalismus,* Berlin, 1965) are both written from the Marxist standpoint. Richard D.

Altick: *The English Common Reader* (London, 1967) is a superb analysis of the reading of the English working classes. Arthur Redford's *Labour Migration in England, 1800–1850* (Manchester, 1926) is still the basic study of the subject. John A. Jackson: *The Irish in Britain* (London, 1963) is also important.

On Chartism the book by L. B. and B. Hammond: *The Age of the Chartists, 1832–1854* (London, 1930) is one of the best-informed and readable accounts. A recent volume of importance is R. Schoyen: *The Chartist Challenge* (New York, 1958), a biography of Harney with special reference to the international contacts of the Chartists.

Among specialized studies are Robert L. Schuyler: *The Fall of the Old Colonial System: a Study in British Free Trade* (New York, 1945); William L. Mathiesen: *Great Britain and the Slave Trade, 1839–1865* (London, 1929), and the same author's *British Slavery and Its Abolition, 1823–1838* (London, 1926).

Modern Scotland has been well studied in R. H. Campbell: *Scotland since 1707; the Rise of an Industrial Society* (New York, 1965); Laurence J. Saunders: *Scottish Democracy, 1815–1840* (Edinburgh, 1950); Henry Hamilton: *The Industrial Revolution in Scotland* (London, 1932). For Wales, see David William: *A History of Modern Wales* (London, 1950, 1962).

Ireland

Sir James O'Connor: *History of Ireland, 1798–1924* (2 vols., New York, 1925), a general, critical account; Patrick S. O'Hegarty: *A History of Ireland under the Union, 1801–1922* (London, 1952), valuable for extensive quotations from sources; Eleanor Hull: *A History of Ireland* (2 vols., London, n.d.) an excellent treatment; Edmond Curtis: *A History of Ireland* (6 ed., London, 1957), perhaps the best short account; J. C. Beckett: *The Making of Modern Ireland, 1603–1923* (London, 1966), an up-to-date survey. Robert B. McDowell: *Public Opinion and Government in Ireland, 1801–1846* (London, 1952) rests on unpublished materials; Nicholas Mansergh: *The Irish Question, 1840–1921* (London, 1965) is an enlarged version of an earlier work; Denis R. Gwynn: *Daniel O'Connell, the Irish Liberator* (rev. ed., Cork, 1947) is first rate; Angus Macintyre: *The Liberator, Daniel O'Connell and the Irish Party, 1830–1847* (London, 1965) is essentially parliamentary history; Kevin B. Nowlan: *The Politics of Repeal, 1841–1850* (London, 1964) is a highly detailed archival study.

The Population of Ireland, 1750–1845, by Kenneth H. Connell (London, 1950), is a basic study. R. B. McDowell, ed.: *Social Life in Ireland, 1800–1845* (Dublin, 1957) is a valuable collection of essays by various authors. John B. Pomfret's *The Struggle for Land in Ireland, 1800–1923* (Princeton,

1930) is a comprehensive study of lasting value, but may be supplemented by Thomas W. Freeman's *Pre-Famine Ireland* (Manchester, 1957). The history of the great famine is thoroughly reviewed in Robert D. Edwards and T. Desmond Williams, eds.: *The Great Famine, 1845–1852* (New York, 1956), a collection of essays by authorities, with an excellent bibliography. Cecil Woodham-Smith's *The Great Hunger* (London, 1962) is designed for a large public, but is well-informed and highly readable. William F. Adams: *Ireland and Irish Emigration to the New World, from 1815 to the Famine* (New Haven, 1932) is exhaustive, while Oliver Mac-Donagh: *The Pattern of Government Growth, 1800–1860* (London, 1961) is largely a study of the modalities of Irish emigration.

France

For general coverage, several recent books can be recommended: J. P. T. Bury: *France, 1814–1870* (Philadelphia, 1949); Gordon Wright: *France in Modern Times* (Chicago, 1960); Alfred Cobban: *A History of Modern France,* Vol. II (rev. ed., London, 1963); Felix Ponteil: *La monarchie parlementaire, 1815–1848* (Paris, 1949), which is excellent. Still of great value are the larger-scale studies of Eugène Fournière: *Le règne de Louis Philippe* (Vol. VIII of Jean Jaurès, ed.: *Histoire socialiste,* Paris, 1906) and Sébastien Charléty: *La Monarchie de Juillet* (Vol. V of Ernest Lavisse, ed.: *Histoire de la France contemporaine,* Paris, 1921) an exemplary study. Catherine I. Gavin: *Louis Philippe* (London, 1933) is competent but deals largely with foreign affairs. T. E. B. Howarth: *Citizen King: the Life of Louis Philippe* (London, 1961) is a serious biography.

On the middle classes and their political role there are Emmanuel Beau de Loménie: *Les responsabilités des dynasties bourgeoises* (Paris, 1943), a suggestive pioneer study; Jean Lhomme: *La grande bourgeoisie au pouvoir, 1830–1880* (Paris, 1960) is also valuable; Régine Pernoud: *Histoire de la bourgeoisie en France* (2 vols., Paris, 1960–1962) is well-informed and readable; Adeline Daumard: *La bourgeoisie parisienne de 1815 à 1848* (Paris, 1963) is an exhaustive descriptive and statistical study.

For political theory there are Roger Soltau: *French Political Thought in the 19th Century* (New Haven, 1931), still the best general survey. More detailed and recent is Vincent E. Starzinger: *Middlingness: 'Juste Milieu' Political Theory in France and England, 1815–1848* (Charlottesville, 1965). Jean-Jacques Chevallier: *Histoire des institutions politiques de la France de 1789 à nos jours* (Paris, 1952) is much broader in scope than the title suggests. Paul Bastid: *Les institutions politiques de la monarchie parlementaire française, 1814–1848* (Paris, 1954) is a first-class treatment, and Félix Ponteil: *Les institutions de la France de 1814 à 1871* (Paris, 1966) is equally good as a topical analysis. René Rémond: *La vie politique en France depuis 1789* (Vol. I, Paris, 1965) is really an advanced text.

Electoral procedures have been studied by Sherman Kent: *Electoral Procedure under Louis Philippe* (New Haven, 1937) and more summarily by Peter Campbell: *French Electoral Systems and Elections, 1789–1957* (New York, 1958). On the press there is a solid monograph by Irene Collins: *The Government and the Newspaper Press in France, 1814–1881* (Oxford, 1959) and a more sketchy survey by Charles Ledré: *La presse à l'assaut de la monarchie, 1815–1848* (Paris, 1960). Louis Girard's *La garde nationale, 1814–1871* (Paris, 1964) is a much-needed, scholarly study of a key institution.

La Droite en France de 1815 à nos jours (Paris, 1954), by René Rémond, is a stimulating analysis of conservative forces. Of equal interest and value is André-Jean Tudesq's exhaustive study *Les grands notables de France, 1840–1849* (2 vols., Paris, 1964). Of political biographies, only a few can be listed: J. M. S. Allison: *Thiers and the French Monarchy, 1797–1848* (London, 1926); Henri Malo: *Monsieur Thiers* (Paris, 1932); Elizabeth P. Brush: *Guizot in the Early Years of the Orleanist Monarchy* (Urbana, 1929); Douglas Johnson: *Guizot: Aspects of French History, 1787–1874* (Toronto, 1963), a really substantial contribution.

On the revolutionary movement, John Plamenatz: *The Revolutionary Movement in France, 1815–1871* (London, 1952) is competent but slight. Gabriel Perreux: *Aux temps des sociétés secrètes: la propagande républicaine au début de la Monarchie de Juillet, 1832–1835* (Paris, 1931) is a basic, archival study. *Histoire du parti républicain en France de 1814 à 1870*, by Georges Weill (rev. ed., Paris, 1928) is a classic in this field, while Alessandro Galante Garrone's *Filippo Buonarroti e i revoluzionari dell'ottocento* (Turin, 1951) is a significant contribution.

Michel Augé-Laribe's *La révolution agricole* (Paris, 1955) is the best general treatment of the French agrarian problem, but the following are also valuable: Louis Chevalier: *Les paysans: étude historique et d'économie rurale* (Paris, 1947); Gérard Walter: *Histoire des paysans en France* (Paris, 1963); Marcel Faure: *Les paysans dans la société française* (Paris, 1966).

For French industry, see Henri Sée: *Histoire économique de la France* (2 ed., 2 vols., Paris, 1951); Arthur L. Dunham: *The Industrial Revolution in France, 1815–1848* (New York, 1955); Shepard S. Clough: *France: a History of National Economics, 1789–1939* (New York, 1939). Rondo E. Cameron: *France and the Economic Development of Europe, 1800–1914* (Princeton, 1961) analyzes French investments. John H. Clapham's *The Economic Development of France and Germany, 1800–1914* (4 ed., Cambridge, 1951) is still an excellent introduction.

Pierre Dauzet: *Le siècle des chemins de fer en France, 1831–1914* (Paris, 1948) is fundamental on railway development. On business and finance, the lavishly illustrated collection of essays edited by J. Boudet, entitled *Le monde des affaires en France de 1830 à nos jours* (Paris, 1952), is extremely interesting. Guy P. Palmade: *Capitalisme et capitalistes français au XIXe siècle* (Paris, 1961) provides a compact review, while Bertrand Gille: *La banque et le crédit en France de 1815 à 1848* (Paris, 1959) and his *Histoire de la maison de Rothschild* (Vol. I, to 1848, Geneva, 1965) are invaluable contributions. Paul Leuillet: *L'Alsace au début du XIXe siècle* (3 vols., Paris, 1959–1960) is a unique detailed study of an important industrial area.

The labor movement has been surveyed by Edouard Dolléans: *Histoire du mouvement ouvrier* (5 ed., 3 vols., Paris, 1953) and, more briefly, by Jean Montreuil: *Histoire du mouvement ouvrier en France des origines à nos jours* (Paris, 1947). Jean Bruhat: *Histoire du mouvement ouvrier français* (Paris, 1952) is a competent Marxist account, while Ernest Labrousse: *Le mouvement ouvrier et les idées sociales en France de 1815 à la fin du XIXe siècle* (Paris, 1948) consists of the Sorbonne lectures of an eminent authority. The same author's *Aspects de la crise et de la depression de l'économie française au milieu du XIXe siècle, 1846–1848* (Paris, 1956) is a collection of studies and perhaps the most important analysis of the eco-collection of studies and perhaps the most important single analysis of the economic crisis.

Hilde Rigaudias-Weiss: *Les enquêtes ouvrières en France entre 1830 et 1848* (Paris, 1936) is an excellent analysis of the official and unofficial investigations of labor conditions. On the same subject, André Lasserre: *La situation des ouvriers de l'industrie textile dans la region lilloise sous la Monarchie de Juillet* (Paris, 1953) is a model monographic study, as is also Octave Festy's *Le mouvement ouvrier au début de la Monarchie de Juillet, 1830–1834* (Paris, 1908). The Lyons insurrections have been studied exhaustively by the Marxist historian F. Potemkin: *Lionskie Vosstaniia 1831 i 1834* (Moscow, 1937).

Special mention must be made of the pioneer studies in historical sociology by Louis Chevalier: *La formation de la population parisienne au XIXe siècle* (Paris, 1950) and *Classes laborieuses et classes dangereuses à Paris pendant la premiere moitié du XIXe siècle* (Paris, 1958).

The Low Countries

The *Algemene Geschiedenis der Nederlanden,* ed. by J. A. van Houtte and others (Utrecht, 1955–1956) is a splendid illustrated history of both the Netherlands and Belgium, the various chapters written by different experts. Henri Pirenne: *Histoire de Belgique* (7 vols., Brussels, 1932) is the work of a great historian, while the *Histoire de la Belgique contemporaine,* ed. by Jean Deharveng (3 vols., Brussels, 1928–1930) is an excellent collaborative work. Two first-rate short accounts are Franz van Kalken: *Histoire de la Belgique* (Brussels, 1954) and Adrien de Meeüs: *Histoire des Belges* (Paris, 1958). In English the best brief treatment is Emile Cammaerts: *The Keystone of Europe: History of the Belgian Dynasty, 1830–1939* (London, 1939). Social aspects are examined in the compact volume *Cent ans d'histoire sociale en Belgique,* by B. S. Chlepner (Brussels, 1959), and in Armand Julin's "La condition des classes laborieuses en Belgique, 1830–1930" (*Annales de la Société Scientifique de Bruxelles,* Sr. D, LV, 1935, 247–302).

The best history of the Netherlands is by L. G. J. Verberne in Vol. VII of Hajo Brugmans, ed.: *Geschiedenis van Nederland* (Amsterdam, 1935–1938). Izaak H. Gosses and N. Japikse: *Handboek tot de staatskundige Geschiedenis van Nederland* (3 ed., The Hague, 1947) is an admirable guide and bibliography. Among special studies may be mentioned Karel E. van der Mandele: *Het liberalisme in Nederland* (Arnhem, 1933); Izaak J. Brugmans: *Paardenkracht en Mensenmacht: sociaal-economische Geschiedenis van Nederland, 1795–1940* (The Hague, 1961); Ernst Baasch: *Holländische Wirtschaftsgeschichte* (Jena, 1927).

The Iberian Countries

The well-known *History of Spain from the Beginnings to the Present Day,* by Rafael Altamira y Crevea (New York, 1949), is too brief on the modern period to be of much use. It should be supplemented by Vol. VII of Antonio Ballesteros y Beretta: *Historia de España i su influencia en la historia universal* (Barcelona, 1934) and by Vol. VII of F. Soldevila's *Historia de España* (Barcelona, 1959). Of histories in English may be mentioned Salvador de Madariaga: *A History of Modern Spain* (New York, 1958) and Rhea M. Smith: *Spain: a Modern History* (Ann Arbor, 1965). Ivan M. Maiski: *Neuere Geschichte Spaniens, 1808–1917* (Berlin, 1961) is a translation of a stimulating survey by an eminent Soviet diplomat. Raymond Carr: *Spain, 1808–1939* (New York, 1966) is easily the best general account in English. Antonio Ramos Oliviera: *Politics, Economics and Men of Modern Spain, 1808–1946* (London, 1947) is a keen, topical analysis, while Luis Sanchez Agesta: *Historia del constitucionalismo español* (Madrid, 1955) is unique in the constitutional field. Federico Suarez: *Le crisis politica del antiguo regimen en España, 1800–1840* (Madrid, 1940) is one of the rare analytical studies. *Politics and the Military in Modern Spain,* by Stanley G. Payne (Stanford, 1967), deals largely with the later nineteenth century, but is valuable also for the earlier years. Roman de Oyarzun: *Historia del Carlismo* (2 ed., Madrid, 1944) is written from the Carlist standpoint, while Gaston Capadupuy: *Don Carlos: la guerre civile en Espagne, 1833-1840* (Paris, 1938) is a good popular narrative. Edgar Holt: *The Carlist Wars in Spain* (London, 1966) is excellent, but deals largely with the military side. E. Allison Peers' *The Church in Spain, 1737-1937* (London, 1938) is an authoritative book, and Jules Chaix Ruy's *Donoso Cortes, théologien de l'histoire et prophète* (Paris, 1956) is one of the best studies of the Spanish philosopher. The economic history of Spain is analyzed in detail in Jaime Carrera Pujal: *Historia de la economia española* (5 vols., Barcelona, 1943-1947) and in the five-volume work of Jaime Vicens Vives (Barcelona, 1957-1959), of which a shorter version is available in English translation: *An Economic History of Spain* (Princeton, 1969).

The most comprehensive modern history of Portugal is by Damiao Peres and others: *Historia de Portugal* (8 vols., Barcelos, 1928-1938), which is beautifully illustrated. In English there is Charles E. Newell: *A History of Portugal* (New York, 1952) and H. V. Livermore: *A New History of Portugal* (New York, 1966), which is a revamped edition of an earlier book, with much greater emphasis on the nineteenth century.

The Italian States

George F. H. Berkeley: *Italy in the Making, 1815-1848* (3 vols., Cambridge, 1932-1940) is a solid if somewhat repetitious account. Cesare Spellanzon's *Storia del Risorgimento e dell'unità d'Italia* (5 vols., Milan, 1933-1950) is an outstanding, original piece of work, and Giorgio Candeloro's *Storia dell'Italia moderna* (4 vols., 2 ed., Milan, 1959-1960) is a first-rate Marxist study. *L'Italia nel Risorgimento dal 1789 al 1870,* by F. Catalano, R. Moscati and F. Valsecchi (Verona, 1964) is Vol. VIII of the new *Storia d'Italia,* scholarly, lavishly illustrated and equipped with valuable bibliographies. Good short accounts of the Risorgimento are Antonio Monti: *Il Risorgimento* (3 ed., 2 vols., Milan, 1948); Adolfo Omodeo: *L'età del Risorgimento italiano* (9 ed., Naples, 1960). Maurice Vaussard: *De Pétrarque à Mussolini: évolution du sentiment nationaliste italien* (Paris, 1961) is a stimulating essay by a foreigner.

Shepherd B. Clough: *The Economic History of Modern Italy* (New York, 1964) is excellent but rather slight on the early nineteenth century. Roberto Tremollini: *Storia dell' industria italiana contemporanea* (Turin, 1947) is a basic account. Antonio Fossati: *Lavoro e produzione in Italia della metà del secole XVIII alla secondo guerra mondiale* (Turin, 1951) is important for labor history

Luigi Salvatorelli: *Il pensiero politico italiano dal 1700 al 1870* (5 ed.,

Turin, 1949) is a standard account. Nello Quilici: *Origine, sviluppo e insufficienza della borghesia italiana* (Ferrara, 1932) stresses the peculiar character of the Italian middle class, while Guido Quazza, in *La lotta sociale nel Risorgimento, 1815–1871,* traces the development of the class struggle. The history of Piedmont is covered in the three volumes of Niccolò Rodolico's *Carlo Alberto* (Florence, 1936–1948), but these should be supplemented by the excellent recent studies of Rosario Romeo: *Dal Piemonte sabaudo all'Italia liberale* (Turin, 1963) and of Luigi Bulferetti and Raimondo Luraghi: *Agricoltura, industria e commercio in Piemonte dal 1814 al 1848* (Turin, 1966). For Lombardy, Raffaele Ciasca's *Le origini del programma per l'opinione nazionale italiana del 1847–1848* (Milan, 1916) remains fundamental, while Kent R. Greenfield's *Economics and Liberalism in the Risorgimento, 1815–1848* (rev. ed., Baltimore, 1965) is devoted primarily to analysis of the economic forces in Lombard nationalism. For the States of the Church, Guillaume Mollat's *La question romaine de Pie VI à Pie IX* (Paris, 1932) remains the best general review. For economic and social history, however, Domenico Demarco's *Il tramonto dello Stato Ponteficio* (Turin, 1949) is indispensable. Among many studies of the Papacy, Josef Schmidlin: *Papstgeschichte der neuesten Zeit* (2 ed., Munich, 1833) remains basic, but there are excellent treatments also by Roger Aubert: *Le pontificat de Pie IX* (Paris, 1952) and Charles H. Pouthas: *L'église catholique de l'avènement de Pie VII à l'avènement de Pie IX* (Paris, 1945) and *Le pontificat de Pie IX* (Paris, 1962). Edward E. Y. Hales: *Pio Nono* (New York, 1954) is a well-informed, short account. For Naples there is Harold Acton: *The Last Bourbons of Naples, 1825–1861* (New York, 1961), but this is undocumented and anecdotal. Pasquale Villani: *Mezzogiorno tra riforme e rivoluzione* (Bari, 1962) is valuable for economic conditions, as is also Vol. I of Domenico Demarco's *Il crollo del Regno delle Due Sicilie* (Naples, 1960).

Among the many studies of Mazzini and Young Italy, Gwilyn O. Griffith: *Mazzini* (New York, 1932) stands up remarkably well. The biographies, in Italian, by Arturo Codignola (Turin, 1946) and Alessandro Levi (Florence, 1955) are both by competent scholars. Otto Vossler's *Mazzinis politisches Denken und Wollen* (Berlin, 1927) remains interesting as an analysis of doctrine, though Gaetano Salvemini's *Mazzini* (Stanford, 1957) is a classic in that field. On Mazzini's activities there are Alberto Falcionelli: *Les sociétés secrètes italiennes* (Paris, 1936); Edward E. Y. Hales: *Mazzini and the Secret Societies* (New York, 1956); S. Mastellone: *Mazzini e la 'Giovine Italia,' 1831–1834* (2 vols., Pisa, 1960); Cesare Vidal: *Mazzini et les tentatives révolutionnaires de la Jeune Italie dans les Etats*

Sardes (Paris, 1928). Anzilotti's *Gioberti* (Florence, 1922) is largely an exposition of the federalist doctrine, to which Adolfo Omodeo's *Vincenzo Gioberti e la sua evoluzione politica* (Turin, 1941) is an important rejoinder.

The Swiss Confederation

A Short History of Switzerland (Oxford, 1952), by Edgar Bonjour, H. S. Offler, and G. R. Potter, is the work of experts in Swiss history, and *Histoire de la Suisse* (Paris, 1946) by Ernest Fischer is also a clear, succinct review. The basic work is Ernst Gagliardi: *Geschichte der Schweiz von den Anfängen bis zur Gegenwart* (3 ed., 3 vols., Zürich, 1938). Edgar Bonjour: *Die Gründung des schweizerischen Bundesstaates* (Basel, 1948) is an authoritative constitutional study, supplementing Eduard His: *Geschichte des neueren schweizersichen Staatsrecht* (3 vols., Basel, 1920–1938). An admirable account of the revision of the constitution in 1848 may be found in William E. Rappard: *La constitution fédérale de la Suisse, 1848–1948* (Neuchâtel, 1948). Ferdinand Strobel: *Die Jesuiten und die Schweiz im 19 Jahrhundert* (Olten, 1954) is a detailed review of the Jesuit issue. *Der Sonderbundskrieg* (Zürich, 1948), by Fritz Rieter, is short but well-informed and beautifully illustrated. For economic developments, William E. Rappard: *La révolution industrielle en Suisse* (Berne, 1914) is indispensable.

The Austrian Empire

Karl and Mathilde Uhlirz: *Handbuch der Geschichte Oesterreichs und seiner Nachbarländer* (2 ed., Graz, 1963) is a useful guide. A. J. P. Taylor: *The Habsburg Monarchy, 1809–1918* (new ed., London, 1948) is a competent critical review, while Hugo Hantsch: *Die Geschichte Oesterreichs* (2 vols., 2 ed., Vienna, 1955) is the best general account. Robert A. Kann: *The Multinational Empire* (2 vols., New York, 1950) is learned and suggestive though poorly arranged. Viktor Bibl: *Die Tragödie Oesterreichs* (Vienna, 1937) is a vigorous indictment of the Metternich system. *Der Josefinismus*, by Fritz Valjavec (2 ed., Munich, 1945), is valuable for the evolution of the bureaucracy. Heinrich Ritter von Srbiks *Metternich, der Staatsmann und der Mensch* (2 vols. and Suppl., Munich, 1925, 1954) is one of the chief revisionary works of recent times. G. Bertier de Sauvigny: *Metternich et son temps* (Paris, 1959) is a sympathetic study of the Metternich system. K. Eder: *Der Liberalismus in Altoesterreich* (Vienna, 1955) is a valuable study, more so than Georg Franz: *Liberalismus: die deutschliberale Bewegung in der habsburgischen Monarchie* (Munich, 1955). Hanns Schlitter: *Aus Oesterreichs Vormärz* (Vienna, 1920) cannot be too highly recommended for its critical analysis of affairs in Austria, Bohemia,

Hungary and Galicia. Werner Meyer: *Vormärz: die Ära Metternich* (Potsdam, 1948) is a Marxist study, while Heinz Rieder: *Wiener Vormärz* (Vienna, 1959) is good on Viennese cultural life.

Jerome Blum: *Noble Landowners and Agriculture in Austria, 1815–1848* (Baltimore, 1948) is a basic study, but may be supplemented by Alois Brusatti: "Die Stellung der herrschaftlichen Bauern in Oesterreich in der Zeit von 1780 bis 1848" (*Vierteljahrschrift für Sozial- und Wirstschaftsgeschichte*, XLV, 1958).

There are several good general accounts of Bohemian history, among them Kamil Krofta: *A Short History of Czechoslovakia* (London, 1935); Robert W. Seton-Watson: *A History of the Czechs and Slovaks* (London, 1943); and S. Harrison Thomson: *Czechoslovakia in European History* (Princeton, 1953). Bertold Bretholz: *Geschichte Böhmens und Mährens* (4 vols., Reichenberg, 1924) is excellent from the German standpoint. *The Czech National Revival* (Chicago, 1934), by Joseph Chada, draws on much Czech literature. For the same subject as seen by the Germans, see Hans Raupach: *Der tschechische Frühnationalismus* (Essen, 1939). Karl Obermann and J. Polišensky: *Aus 500 Hundert Jahren deutsch-tschechoslovakischer Geschichte* (Berlin, 1958) is a Marxist study of economic and social problems. Theodor J. G. Locher: *Die nationale Differenzierung und Integrierung der Slovaken und Tschechen in ihrem geschichtlichen Verlauf bis 1848* (Haarlem, 1931) is a valuable detailed analysis of the Czech-Slovak relationship. Hélène Tourtzer: *Louis Štur et l'idée de l'indépendance slovaque, 1815–1856* (Paris, 113) is based on much unpublished material.

A good brief history of Hungary is Dominic G. Kósary: *A History of Hungary* (New York, 1941). Julius Miskolczy: *Ungarn in der Habsburger-Monarchie* (Vienna, 1959) is an admirable monograph. The agrarian problem is studied in Julius Varga: *Typhen und Probleme des bäuerlichen Grundbesitzes in Ungarn, 1767–1849* (Budapest, 1965). On the nationality question there is Robert W. Seton-Watson's *Racial Problems in Hungary* (London, 1908), a biased but highly influential book, which should be read in conjunction with Friedrich Walter and Harold Steinacker: *Die Nationalitätenfrage im alten Ungarn und die Südpolitik Wiens* (Munich, 1959). George Barany: *Stephen Széchenyi and the Awakening of Hungarian Nationalism, 1791–1841* (Princeton, 1968) brings together various monographic studies by the author. Otto Zarek's *Kossuth* (London, 1937) is an adequate biography, while René Schwachhofer: *Bettelsack und Freiheit: Leben und Werk Alexander Petöfis* (Weimar, 1954) is easily the best biography of the poet in a western language.

On Croatia there is Z. Kostelski: *The Yugoslavs* (New York, 1952) and Gilbert in der Maur: *Die Jugoslawen einst und jetzt* (2 vols., Leipzig, 1936), which is excellent on the Illyrian movement. Emile Haumant: *La formation de la Yougoslavie* (Paris, 1930) is an authoritative work, while *A Short History of Yugoslavia,* ed. by Stephen Clissold (Cambridge, 1967), consists of chapters by various authors dealing with the constituent parts of the state. Jozo Tomasevich: *Peasants, Politics and Economic Change in Yugoslavia* (Stanford, 1955) is an excellent analysis of the agrarian problem.

The German States

Heinrich von Treitschke's *History of Germany in the 19th Century* (trans. by Eden and Cedar Paul, 7 vols., New York, 1915–1919) remains the basic account for the period prior to 1848. Despite its Prussian bias, it is a broad-gauged and interestingly written book, a real classic of historical writing. Friedrich Meinecke's *Weltbürgertum und Nationalstaat* (3 ed., Munich, 1915; reprinted in his *Werke,* 1963) is no less a classic. Among the many histories of German unification may be mentioned, for the Prussian side, Erich Marcks: *Der Aufsteig des Reiches* (2 vols., Stuttgart, 1936); and on the Austrian, Heinrich Ritter von Srbik: *Deutsche Einheit* (4 vols., Munich, 1935–1942). Egmont Zechlin: *Die deutsche Einheitsbewegung* (Frankfurt, 1967) can be highly recommended as a reliable, readable survey.

Among more recent histories of modern Germany is Johannes Bühler: *Deutsche Geschichte* (6 vols., Berlin, 1934–1960). Hajo Holborn's *A History of Modern Germany* (2 vols., New York, 1959–1964) now reaches to 1840 and when complete will be one of the best histories of Germany in any language. Both Golo Mann: *The History of Germany in the 19th and 20th Centuries* (London, 1966) and Koppel S. Pinson: *Modern Germany* (2 ed., New York, 1966) are both superior shorter accounts.

More specialized studies are Theodore S. Hamerow: *Restoration, Revolution, Reaction* (Princeton, 1958), a most competent work which emphasizes economic aspects; Karl Obermann: *Deutschland von 1815 bis 1849* (Berlin, 1961), the best Marxist history; Fritz Hartung: *Deutsche Verfassungsgeschichte* (8 ed., Stuttgart, 1950), an admirable brief constitutional survey; and Enrst R. Huber: *Deutsche Verfassungsgeschichte seit 1789* (2 vols., Stuttgart, 1950), which is really an excellent political history, with extensive bibliographies.

Leonard Krieger: *The German Idea of Freedom* (Boston, 1958) deals with political theory, while Sigmund Neumann: *Die Stufen des preussischen Konservatismus* (Berlin, 1930) traces the origins of conservative thought. On the liberal side there are a number of solid studies, such as Kurt Baumann, ed.: *Das Hambacher Fest: Männer und Ideen* (Speyer, 1957); Friedrich Sell: *Die Tragödie des deutschen Liberalismus* (Stuttgart,

1953); Wolfgang Hock: *Liberales Denken im Zeitalter der Paulskirche* (Münster, 1957); Jacques Droz: *Le libéralisme rhénan* (Paris, 1940). Donald G. Rohr: *The Origins of Social Liberalism in Germany* (Chicago, 1963) traces the growing concern with the social problem.

A key study of the agrarian problem is Friedrich Lütge: "Ueber die Auswirkungen der Bauernbefreiung in Deutschland" (*Jahrbücher für Nationalökonomie und Statistik*, CLVII, 1943, 353–404). On agricultural development, see Hans Graf Finck von Finckenstein: *Entwicklung der Landwirtschaft in Preussen und Deutschland* (Göttingen, 1960); Heinz Haushofer: *Die deutsche Landwirtschaft im technischen Zeitalter* (Vol. V of *Die deutsche Agrargeschichte*, Stuttgart, 1963); Sigmund von Frauendorfer: *Ideengeschichte der Agrarwirtschaft und Agrarpolitik im deutschen Sprachgebiet* (2 vols., Munich, 1957–1958). Walter Görlitz: *Die Junker: Adel und Bauer im deutschen Osten* (Glücksburg, 1956) studies the political role of the eastern landowners. Johannes Ziekursch: *Hundert Jahre schlesischer Agrargeschichte, 1748–1848* (Breslau, 1915) is a model regional study. *Die deutsche überseeische Auswanderung* (Jena, 1912), by Wilhelm Monckmeier, is a mine of information on emigration. Mack Walker: *Germany and the Emigration, 1816–1885* (Cambridge, 1964) is a valuable contribution.

Friedrich Lütge: *Deutsche Sozial- und Wirtschaftsgeschichte* (Berlin, 1952) is a standard work, as is the more detailed study by Heinrich Bechtel: *Wirtschaftsgeschichte Deutschlands* (3 vols., Munich, 1951–1956). On industrial development, Hans Linde: "Die Bedeutung der deutschen Agrarstruktur für die Anfänge der industriellen Entwicklung" (*Jahrbuch für Sozialwissenschaft*, XIII, 1962, 179–195) is valuable. A basic study is Pierre Benaerts: *Les origines de la grande industrie allemande* (Paris, 1933). *Studien zur Geschichte der industriellen Revolution in Deutschland* (Berlin, 1960), by Hans Mottek and others, is a collection of specialized studies by Marxist historians.

W. O. Henderson: *The State and the Industrial Revolution in Prussia, 1740–1870* (Liverpool, 1958) analyzes a basic problem. Particularly illuminating is the study by Wolfram Fischer: *Der Staat und die Anfänge der Industrialisierung in Baden, 1800–1850* (Berlin, 1962). Jürgen Kuczynski: *Die Bewegung der deutschen Wirtschaft von 1800 bis 1946* (2 ed., Berlin, 1947) is a collection of lectures by a prominent Marxist historian. On Friedrich List the best general biography is Carl Brinkmann's (Berlin, 1949), but Hans Gehrig's *Friedrich List und Deutschlands politischökonomische Einheit* (Leipzig, 1956) is also valuable. W. von Eisenhart-Rothe and A. Ritthaler: *Vorgeschichte und Würdigung des deutschen Zollvereins, 1815–1834* (3 vols., Berlin, 1933) is an indispensable monograph. Admirable studies are also W. O. Henderson: *The Zollverein* (Cambridge, 1939) and Arnold H. Price's *The Evolution of the Zollverein* (Ann Arbor, 1949).

The beginnings of the German labor movement are traced in Wolfgang Schieder: *Anfänge der deutsche Arbeiterbewegung: die Auslandsvereine im Jahrzehnt nach der Juli-Revolution* (Stuttgart, 1963). Werner Conze and Dieter Groh: *Die Arbeiterbewegung in der nationalen Bewegung* (Stuttgart, 1966) stresses the nationalism of German labor. On working conditions there is a translation of Jürgen Kuczynski: *A Short History of Labour Conditions under Industrial Capitalism: Germany, 1800 to the Present Day* (London, 1945). The same author has published also a *Geschichte der Kinderarbeit in Deutschland, 1750–1939* (2 vols., Berlin, 1958).

The Scandinavian Countries

B. J. Hovde: *The Scandinavian Countries, 1720–1865* (2 vols., Boston, 1943) is comprehensive, informative, but poorly organized. On the Pan-Scandinavian movement there is Theodore Jorgenson: *Norway's Relation to Scandinavian Unionism, 1815–1871* (Northfield, 1935), and the more detailed work by John Sanness: *Patrioter Intelligens og Skandinaver* (Oslo, 1959).

Ludwig Krabbe: *Histoire de Danemark* (Copenhagen, 1950) is one of the best short histories. For the rise of the Schleswig-Holstein problem, see Otto Brandt: *Geschichte Schleswig-Holsteins* (5 ed., Kiel, 1957) and especially W. Carr: *Schleswig-Holstein, 1815–1848* (Manchester, 1963). Christian Dega: *Orla Lehmann und der nationale Gedanke* (Neumünster, 1936) is valuable, though long-winded.

Karen Larsen: *A History of Norway* (New York, 1948) is a good survey, more detailed than Kingston Derry's *A Short History of Norway* (London, 1957). Andreas Elviken: *Die Entwicklung des norwegischen Nationalismus* (Berlin, 1930), while comprehensive, is not as good as Oscar Falnes' *National Romanticism in Norway* (New York, 1933).

Ingvar Andersson: *A History of Sweden* (New York, 1956) is not well organized but is the best general text in English. A fundamental work on the period is the magistral study by Torvald T. Höjer: *Carl XIV Johan* (3 vols., Stockholm, 1939–1960). On the background of Swedish emigration there are two special studies: John S. Lindberg: *The Background of Swedish Emigration to the United States* (Minneapolis, 1930) and Florence E. Janson: *The Background of Swedish Emigration, 1840–1930* (Chicago, 1931).

John H. Wuorinen: *A History of Finland* (New York, 1965) is a superior work. The same author has published a monograph on *Nationalism in Modern Finland* (New York, 1931), a subject that has been exhaustively studied also by Peter Scheibert: *Volk und Staat in Finland in der ersten Hälfte des vorigen Jahrhunderts* (Breslau, 1941).

The Russian Empire

Michael T. Florinsky: *Russia: a History and an Interpretation* (2 vols., New York, 1953) is a solid but possibly hypercritical account. There are two major German histories of Russia: Karl Stählin: *Geschichte Russlands* (5 vols., Berlin, 1923–1939) and Valentin Gitermann: *Geschichte Russlands* (3 vols., Zürich, 1944–1949), richly illustrated. Ettore Lo Gatto: *Storia della Russia* (2 vols., Florence, 1946) is also outstanding. On the nineteenth century M. V. Nechkina: *Russia in the 19th Century* (2 vols., Ann Arbor, 1953) is the translation of a standard Soviet treatment. In English there are substantial accounts by Sergei Pushkarev: *The Emergence of Modern Russia, 1801–1917* (New York, 1963) and especially Hugh Seton-Watson: *The Russian Empire, 1801–1917* (Oxford, 1967). The early nineteenth century is covered in Semen B. Okum: *Ocherki istorii S.S.S.R. vtoraiia chetvert XIX veka* (Leningrad, 1957), which summarizes recent Russian studies.

Theodor Schiemann: *Geschichte Russlands unter Kaiser Nikolaus I* (4 vols., Berlin, 1904–1919) is far more than a biography of the czar; it is actually one of the best histories of the period. Mikhail Polievktov: *Nikolai I* (Moscow, 1918) is especially strong on domestic affairs. Constantin Grunwald: *Tsar Nicholas I* (New York, 1955), though not profound, is well-informed and judicious. Nicholas V. Riasanovsky: *Nicholas I and Official Nationality in Russia* (Berkeley, 1959) is broader in scope than the title suggests.

Peter I. Lyashchenko: *History of the National Economy of Russia to the 1917 Revolution* (New York, 1949) is the translation of a standard Soviet treatise. Somewhat later and restricted to the nineteenth and twentieth centuries is Pavel A. Khromov: *Ekonomicheskoye razvitiye Rossii v XIX–XX vekakh* (Moscow, 1950). Bertrand Gille: *Histoire économique et sociale de la Russie du Moyen Age au vingtième siècle* (Paris, 1949) is a mere sketch, but highly stimulating. A study too recent to be used in the present book is William L. Blackwell: *The Beginnings of Russian Industrialization, 1800–1860* (Princeton, 1968). The agrarian situation is well surveyed in Geroid T. Robinson's *Rural Russia under the Old Regime* (New York, 1932). Jerome Blum's *Lord and Peasant in Russia* (Princeton, 1961) is a first-rate recent study and Wayne Vuchinich, ed.: *The Peasant in Nineteenth Century Russia* (Stamford, 1968) is a collection of special studies by various experts. The latest literature is surveyed in Michel Laran:

"Nobles et paysans en Russie, 1762–1861" (*Annales*, XXI, 1966, 111–140). In Russian there is an extensive literature, of which only a sampling can be given. *Velikaiia Reforma*, ed. by A. K. Dzhivelegov and others (6 vols., Moscow, 1911) remains a mine of information on the serf problem. Restricted to the early nineteenth century are Konstantin V. Sivkov: *Ocherki po istorii krepostnova khozianstvo* (Moscow, 1951) and I.-A. Linkov: *Ocherki istorii krestianskogo dvisheniia v Rossii v 1825–1861 gg.* (Moscow, 1952). Nikolai M. Druzhinin: *Gosudartvennye krestiane i reforma P.D. Kiseleva* (2 vols., Moscow, 1946–1958) provides an authoritative account of the reforms of the crown serfs.

In the field of intellectual and cultural history there is the general treatment by James H. Billington: *The Icon and the Axe* (New York, 1966). Further, Nicholas V. Riazanovsky: *Russia and the West in the Teaching of the Slavophiles* (Cambridge, 1952); Alexander von Schelting: *Russland und Europa* (Berne, 1948); Edward C. Thaden: *Conservative Nationalism in 19th Century Russia* (Seattle, 1964); and the excellent monograph by Peter K. Christoff: *An Introduction to 19th Century Russian Slavophilism: A. S. Xomjakov* (The Hague, 1961). On Panslavism, Alfred Fischel: *Der Panslawismus bis zum Weltkrieg* (Stuttgart, 1919) is still valuable, but should be supplemented by Karl Stählin: "Die Entstehung des Panslawismus" (*Germanoslavica*, IV, 1936, 1–25, 237–262). Waclaw Lednicki: "Panslavism" (in Feliks Gross, ed.: *European Ideologies*, New York, 1948) is an independent study of genuine value. Hans Kohn: *Panslavism, Its History and Ideology* (Notre Dame, 1953) is a good up-to-date review by a well-known scholar.

The early revolutionary movement is analyzed in the classic account of Mikhail O. Gershenzon: *Istoriia Molodoi Rossii* (Moscow, 1923). Among recent works in western languages may be mentioned Richard Hare: *Pioneers of Russian Social Thought* (New York, 1951); Peter Scheibert: *Von Bakunin zu Lenin: Geschichte der russischen revolutionären Ideologien, 1840–1895* (Leiden, 1956); Avrahm Yarmolinsky: *Road to Revolution: a Century of Russian Radicalism* (London, 1957); E. Lampert: *Studies in Rebellion* (New York, 1959); and Franco Venturi: *Roots of Revolution* (New York, 1959), the translation of an outstanding Italian study.

Victor Leontovitsch: *Geschichte des Liberalismus in Russland* (Frankfurt, 1957) is an admirable pioneer study. More specialized are the following: Edward J. Brown: *Stankevich and his Moscow Circle* (Stanford, 1966); Charles Quénet: *Tchadaaev et les lettres philosophiques* (Paris, 1932), an exhaustive study which should be supplemented by Heinrich S. J. Falk: *Das Weltbild Peter J. Tschaadajews nach seinen acht "Philosophische Briefe"* (Munich, 1954); Martin E. Malia: *Alexander Herzen and the Birth of Russian Socialism* (Cambridge, 1961), a splendid biographical analysis; Benoît P. Hepner: *Bakounine et le panslavisme révolutionnaire* (Paris, 1950), an impressive scholarly work.

A History of the Ukraine, by Michael Hrushevsky (New Haven, 1941) is the translation of a classic account. Clarence A. Manning's *A History of Ukraine* (New York, 1947) is a competent modern work. D. Dorochenko: *Chevchenko, le poète national de l'Ukraine* (Prague, 1931) is a satisfactory biography of the Ukrainian national leader.

Poland

The *Cambridge History of Poland,* ed. by W. F. Reddaway and others (Cambridge, 1941) covers the modern period in Vol. II. Oscar Halecki: *A History of Poland* (New York, 1943) is strongly nationalist. The best treatment of Russian rule is J. Kucharzewski: *Epoka Paskiewiczowska* (Cracow, 1914). Marcel Handelsmann: *Adam Czartoryski* (3 vols., Warsaw, 1948–1950) is an authoritative biography. W. Feldman's *Geschichte der politischen Ideen in Polen seit dessen Teilungen, 1795–1914* (Munich, 1917) is the translation of a valuable Polish study. Two articles by R. F. Leslie are excellent analyses of Polish political history: "Politics and Economics in Congress Poland, 1815–1864" (*Past and Present,* No. 8, 1955, 43–63) and "Polish Left-Wing Political Tactics, 1831–1846" (*Slavonic and East European Review,* XXXIII, 1954, 120–139). For Polish Messianism there are N. O. Lossky: *Three Chapters from the History of Polish Messianism* (Prague, 1936), lectures by an eminent philosopher; Edouard Krakowski: *Adam Mickiewicz, philosophe mystique* (2 ed., Paris, 1935); Wiktor Weintraub: *Literature as Prophecy* (The Hague, 1959); and Henri Desmettre: *Towianski et le messianisme* (2 vols., Lille, 1947), an exhaustive monograph.

The Poles in Prussia are studied in Friedrich Schinkel: *Polen, Preussen, und Deutschland* (Berlin, 1932) and Manfred Laubert: *Die preussische Polenpolitik von 1772 bis 1914* (3 ed., Cracow, 1944).

The Balkan States

L. S. Stavrianos: *The Balkans since 1453* (New York, 1958) is an excellent up-to-date text with rich bibliographies. It supersedes older surveys by Robert W. Seton-Watson, Ferdinand Schevill and Nicholas Iorga.

Iorga's *Geschichte des rumänischen Volkes* (2 vols., Gotha, 1905) is still fundamental, but there are briefer and more recent treatments, such as Robert W. Seton-Watson: *A History of the Roumanians* (Cambridge, 1934), which is excellent; and L. Galdi and L. Makkai: *Geschichte der*

Rumänen (Budapest, 1942), a collaborative work which is useful despite a mild pro-Magyar bias. Pompiliu Eliade: *Histoire de l'esprit publique en Roumanie* (2 vols., Paris, 1905, 1914) is a pioneer cultural history. Crisan T. Axente: *Essai sur le régime représentatif en Roumanie* (Paris, 1937) is based largely on Rumanian records. *The Struggle against Russia in the Roumanian Principalities, 1821–1854,* by Radu R. N. Florescu (Munich, 1962) is a collection of essays based on British archive materials. On the economic side there are several excellent studies of the agrarian problem: Ifor L. Evans: *The Agrarian Revolution in Roumania* (Cambridge, 1924); David Mitrany: *The Land and the Peasant in Roumania* (New Haven, 1930); Marcel Emérit: *Les paysans roumains depuis le traité d'Andrinople jusqu'à la libération des terres, 1829–1864* (Paris, 1937) is definitive. The Rumanian renaissance in Transylvania may be studied in L. Makkai: *Histoire de Transylvanie* (Paris, 1946) and in Erich Prokopowitsch: *Die rumänischne Nationalbewegung in der Bukowina und der Dako-Romanismus* (Graz, 1965).

The histories of Yugoslavia listed above under Austrian Empire include the history of Serbia and supersede older books such as Harold Temperley: *History of Serbia* (New York, 1917). Basic Serbian works are Slobodan Jovanović: *Vlada Aleksandra Obrenovica* (3 vols., Belgrade, 1934–1936), the latest edition of a classic; and Dragoslav Stranjaković: *Vlada Ustavobranitelja, 1842–1853* (Belgrade, 1932), a basic study of the constitutional struggle. Jean Mousset: *La Serbie et son église* (Paris, 1938) is an authoritative work going far beyond mere church history.

N. Staneff: *Geschichte der Bulgaren* (2 vols., Leipzig, 1917) is a standard history, but should be supplemented by the excellent monograph by Alois Hajek: *Bulgarien unter der Türkenherrschaft* (Stuttgart, 1925). James F. Clarke: "Serbia and the Bulgarian Revival, 1762–1872" (*American Slavic and East European Review,* IV, 1945, 141–162) actually reviews the entire Bulgarian renaissance.

Nicolas Svoronos: *Histoire de la Grèce moderne* (Paris, 1953) is a brief but reliable survey. Important special studies are Nicholas Kaltchas: *Introduction to the Constitutional History of Modern Greece* (New York, 1940) and the scholarly analysis by John A. Petropulos: *Politics and Statecraft in the Kingdom of Greece, 1833–1843* (Princeton, 1968), which appeared too late to be used in the present work.

THE REVOLUTIONS OF 1848 AND AFTER

The centenary of the revolutions, in 1948, produced a spate of writings, many of which have no permanent significance. Only the merest selection of titles can be given here.

General Accounts

The *Actes du Congrès Historique du Centenaire de la Révolution de 1848* (Paris, 1948) include many essays by experts, dealing with various countries. A similar Italian collection is *Il 1848 nella storia d'Europa* (*Accademia Nazionale dei Lincei: Atti dei Convegni,* X, 1949). Very useful is François Fejtö, ed.: *The Opening of an Era, 1848* (2 vols., London, 1948), the translation of a French symposium treating of all countries. *Revoliutsii, 1848–1849* (2 vols., Moscow, 1952) is a collection of Marxist essays. Relatively few books survey the European revolutions as a whole. One of them is Priscilla Robertson: *Revolutions of 1848: a Social Study* (Princeton, 1952). Arnold Whitridge: *Men in Crisis: the Revolutions of 1848* (New York, 1949) traces the revolutions through the careers of the leaders. Lewis B. Namier: *1848: the Revolution of the Intellectuals* (London, 1944) is a provocative and somewhat overrated essay by an eminent historian. In William L. Langer: "The Pattern of Urban Revolution in 1848" (in *French Society and Culture since the Old Regime,* ed. by Evelyn M. Accomb and Marvin L. Brown, Jr., New York, 1966) the attempt is made at a comparative study.

France

Pierre Quentin-Bauchart: *La crise sociale de 1848* (Paris, 1920) is still valuable for background. Charles Moulin, ed.: *1848: le livre du centenaire* (Paris, 1948) is an impressive collection of articles and illustrations, while *1848,* ed. by Georges Bourgin and Max Terrier (Paris, 1948) presents a unique body of pictorial material. Albert Crémieux: *La révolution de février* (Paris, 1912) is still basic, while Jean Bruhat: *Les journées de février, 1848* (Paris, 1948) is a much briefer and more readable account, by a Marxist historian. Georges Duveau: *1848: the Making of a Revolution* (New York, 1966) is a translation of what is perhaps the best single study of the French revolution from February to June. Henri Guillemin: *La première résurrection de la République: 24 février, 1848* (Paris, 1967) is lively and provocative. Among other monographs may be mentioned Gaston Martin: *La révolution de 1848* (2 ed., Paris, 1959), good on the social side; Emile Tersen: *Quarante-huit* (Paris, 1958), a moderate Marxist account; Jean Dautry: *1848 et la Deuxième République* (Paris, 1957), one of the best general surveys; Adrien Dansette: *Deuxième République et Second Empire* (Paris, 1942), an introduction by a well-known writer. Paul Bastid: *Les doctrines et institutions politiques de la Seconde République* (2 vols., Paris, 1945) is indispensable. Donald C. McKay: *The National Workshops* (Cambridge, 1933, 1965) is still the standard study of that institution. Among biographies H. Remsen Whitehouse: *The Life of Lamartine* (2 vols., Boston, 1918) is strong of the poet's political role. Paul Keller: *Louis Blanc und die Revolution von 1848* (Zürich, 1926) is marked by breadth of treatment. Alvin R. Calman: *Ledru-Rollin and the Second French Republic* (New York, 1922) is a sound analysis, while Robert Schnerb: *Ledru-Rollin* (Paris, 1948) is less detailed but more up to date.

Among innumerable studies of Louis Napoleon, F. A. Simpson: *Louis Napoleon and the Recovery of France* (3 ed., London, 1951) is still as good as any. Competent biographical narratives are James E. Thompson: *Louis Napoleon and the Second Empire* (New York, 1955) and J. P. T. Bury: *Napoleon III and the Second Empire* (London, 1964). T. A. B. Corley: *Democratic Despot: a Life of Napoleon III* (London, 1961), though popular, is well-informed, while Heinrich Euler: *Napoleon III in seiner Zeit* (Würzburg, 1961) is the first volume of an exhaustive, original study. More specialized are Maurice La Fuye and Emile A. Babeau: *Louis-Napoléon Bonaparte avant l'Empire* (Paris, 1951), a substantial but conventional account; Adrien Dansette: *Louis-Napoléon à la conquête du pouvoir, 1808–1851* (2 vols., Paris, 1961), exceptionally well-written; Pierre Dominique: *Louis-Napoléon et le coup d'état du 2 décembre* (Paris, 1957), which actually covers the entire presidency; Henri Guillemin: *Le coup d'état du 2 décembre* (Paris, 1951) is perhaps the best single volume on the presidency and the coup. Gisela Geywitz: *Das Plebiszit von 1851 in Frankreich* (Tübingen, 1965) is an invaluable analysis.

Belgium

The short but acute crisis of 1848 in Belgium is treated by G. H. Dumont: *Le miracle de 1848* (Brussels, 1948) and by Brison D. Gooch: *Belgium and the February Revolution* (The Hague, 1963).

Germany

Still the classic account, based on extensive archival study, is Veit Valentin: *Geschichte der deutschen Revolution, 1848–1949* (2 vols., Berlin, 1930), but there is an excellent more recent study by Jacques Droz: *Les révolutions allemandes de 1848* (Paris, 1957). Friedrich Meinecke: *1848, eine Säkulärbetrachtung* (Bonn, 1948) embodies the reflections of a leading German historian. The same author's *Radowitz und die deutsche Revolution* (2 vols., Berlin, 1913) is basic for the conservative side. Paul Wentzke: *1848: die unvollendete deutsche Revolution* (Munich, 1938) presents a liberal interpretation, as does also Wilhelm Mommsen: *Grösse und Versagen des deutschen Bürgertums* (Stuttgart, 1949), a most stimulating essay.

Rudolf Stadelmann: *Soziale und politische Geschichte der Revolution von 1848* (Munich, 1956) is one of the most comprehensive and satisfactory of the briefer treatments. Hermann Meyer: *1848: Studien zur Geschichte der deutschen Revolution* (Darmstadt, 1949) is a valuable study of radicalism in Berlin and Vienna. The standard Soviet account has been translated under the title *Die Revolution in Deutschland, 1848–1849,* ed. by Fedor V. Potemkin and A. I. Molok (Berlin, 1956). The well-documented monograph by Frank Eyck. *The Frankfurt Parliament, 1848–1849* (New York, 1968) appeared too late to be used in the present study.

Ernst Kaeber: *Berlin, 1848* (Berlin, 1948) provides a reliable though undocumented narrative of events in Berlin. More specialized but exceedingly valuable is Gerhard Schilfert: *Sieg und Niederlage des demokratischen Wahlrechts in der deutschen Revolution* (Berlin, 1952). There are a number of important studies of the labor movement in the revolution. Karl Obermann's *Die deutschen Arbeiter in der Revolution von 1848* (2 ed., Berlin, 1953) is an excellent Marxist study, but should be read in conjunction with Paul Noyes: *Organization and Revolution: Working-Class Associations in the German Revolution of 1848–1849* (Princeton, 1966), an admirable monograph. Of significance are also Hans Stein: *Der Kölner Arbeiterverein, 1848–1849* (Cologne, 1921); Frohilde Balser: *Sozial-Demokratie, 1848–1849–1963* (Stuttgart, 1962); and Gerhard Becker: *Karl Marx und Friedrich Engels in Köln, 1848–1849* (Berlin, 1963).

The Austrian Empire

In addition to the general histories of the German revolutions, the following are of importance: Rudolf Kiszling and others: *Die Revolution im Kaisertum Oesterreich, 1848–1849* (2 vols., Vienna, 1948, 1952), an excellent comprehensive account, strong on the military side. R. John Rath: *The Viennese Revolution of 1848* (Austin, 1957) is a solid systematic treatment, with much quotation of sources. Josef Redlich: *Das oesterreichische Staats- und Reichsproblem* (2 vols., Leipzig, 1920, 1926) is indispensable for the constitutional issues, while Hanns Schlitter: *Versäumte Gelegenheiten: die oktroyierte Verfassung vom 4 März, 1849* (Vienna, 1920) is a judicious analysis. The biographies of Schwarzenberg by Adolph Schwarzenberg and by Rudolf Kiszling are both valuable. Jacques Droz: *L'Europe centrale: évolution historique de l'idée de "Mitteleuropa"* (Paris, 1960) reviews the broader Austrian program.

I. I. Udalzov: *Aufzeichnungen über die Geschichte des nationenalen und politischen Kampfes in Böhmen im Jahre 1848* (Berlin, 1953) is a scholarly Marxist study. *Slovansky Sjezd v Praze, 1848,* ed. by Vaclav Zacek (Prague, 1958), is an invaluable collection of source material on the Slavic

Congress. On the Hungarian side, I. Barta: "Die Anführer des ungarischen Freiheitskampfes und die Wiener Oktoberrevolution" (*Acta Historica*, I, 1952, 325–386) is based largely on unpublished correspondence of Kossuth. Erzsebet Andiés: "Kossuth en lutte contre les ennemis des réformes et de la révolution" (*Studia Historica*, XII, 1954, 1–169) is important for the history of internal struggles. Revekka A. Averbukh: *Revoliutsiia i Nationalno-Osvoboditelnaiia Borba v Vengrii, 1848–1849* (Moscow, 1965) is a documented Marxist study of the Hungarian revolution.

The Italian Revolution

Pietro Silva: *Il 1848* (Rome, 1948) is a reliable, succinct review. For military operations, the Austrian side is well handled in Oskar Regele: *Feldmarschall Radetzky* (Vienna, 1957) and the Italian in Guido Porzio: *La guerra regia in Italia nel 1848–1849* (Rome, 1955) and Pietro Pieri: *Storia militare del Risorgimento* (Turin, 1962). On the events in Milan, the account by Antonio Monti: *Il 1848 e le cinque giornate di Milano* (Milan, 1948) is excellent. On Rome and the Republic, see the titles listed under Papal States in a previous section. To these may be added Antonio Monti: *Pio IX nel Risorgimento* (Bari, 1928), which is basic. Domenico Demarco: *Pio IX e la rivoluzione romana del 1848* (Modena, 1947) is strong on economic and social aspects. Guido Quazza: *La questione romana nel 1848–1849* (Modena, 1947) is valuable on international relations. Luigi Rodelli: *La Repubblica Romana del 1849* (Pisa, 1955) is the best general study of the republic. Emile Bourgeois and Emile Clermont: *Rome et Napoleon III, 1849–1870* (Paris, 1907) is still basic for the French policy. George M. Trevelyan: *Garibaldi's Defence of the Roman Republic* (new ed., London, 1908) is vivid, yet reliable. Denis Mack Smith: *Garibaldi* (New York, 1956) and Christopher Hibbert: *Garibaldi and His Enemies* (London, 1965) are both valuable. On the events in Sicily, Federico Curato: *La rivoluzione siciliana del 1848–1849* (Milan, 1940) is highly satisfactory. The basic treatment of the Venetian Republic is still Vincenzo Marchesi: *Storia documentata della rivoluzione e della difesa di Venezia negli anni 1848–1849* (Venice, 1913), but this may well be supplemented by George M. Trevelyan: *Manin and the Venetian Republic of 1848* (New York, 1923) and Alessandro Levi: *La politica di Daniele Manin* (Milan, 1933).

Diplomatic Aspects of the Revolutions

Eugene de Guichen: *Les grandes questions européennes et la diplomatie des puissances sous la Seconde République* (2 vols., Paris, 1925, 1929), contains a wealth of material culled from many archives. Donald M. Greer:

L'Angleterre, la France et la Révolution de 1848 (Paris, 1925) is an archival study of lasting value, while E. Tersen: *Le gouvernement provisoire et l'Europe* (Paris, 1948) does for French policy what Greer does for the British. *The European Powers and the German Question, 1848–1871*, by W. E. Mosse (Cambridge, 1958), is a first-rate work and an important supplement to the earlier studies of Alexander Scharff: *Die europäischen Grossmächte und die deutsche Revolution, 1848–1851* (Leipzig, 1942) and Hans Precht: *Englands Stellung zur deutschen Einheit, 1848–1850* (Berlin, 1925). G. Gillesen: *Lord Palmerston und die Einigung Deutschlands, 1848–1851* (Berlin, 1961) does not add materially to earlier works. Holger Hjelholt: *British Mediation in the Danish-German Conflict, 1848–1850* (2 vols., Copenhagen, 1965) is an exceedingly detailed diplomatic study. A. J. P. Taylor: *The Italian Problem in European Diplomacy, 1847–1849* (Manchester, 1934) is confined largely to the Piedmontese-Austrian conflict. Ruggero Moscati: *La diplomazia europea e il problema italiano nel 1848* (Florence, 1947) is an admirable recent analysis. Charles Sproxton: *Palmerston and the Hungarian Revolution* (Cambridge, 1919) has not yet been superseded. On the Russian intervention in Hungary there are two basic archival studies: Revekka Averbukh: *Tsarskaiia Interventsiia v Borba c Venerskoi Revoliutsiei, 1848–1849* (Moscow, 1935) and Erzsebet Andics: "Das Bündnis Habsburg-Romanow: Vorgeschichte der zaristischen Intervention in Ungarn im Jahre 1848" (*Studia Historica*, LII, Budapest, 1963).

PHILOSOPHY, RELIGION AND SCIENCE

Philosophy

Karl Löwith: *From Hegel to Nietzsche* (New York, 1964) is the translation of the third edition of an important German analysis of post-Hegelian thought. Herbert Marcuse: *Reason and Revolution: Hegel and the Rise of Social Theory* (2 ed., New York, 1954) covers some of the same ground in an authoritative treatment. Jürgen Gebhardt: *Politik und Eschatologie* (Munich, 1963) studies the Hegelian School in the 1830's, while the eminent Marxist critic Georg Lukács, in *Die Zerstörung der Vernunft* (Berlin, 1962), analyzes the irrationalist movements of the period. George Boas' *French Philosophies of the Romantic Period* (Baltimore, 1925) remains valuable for the eclectic and positivist movements. W. M. Simon: *European Positivism in the 19th Century* (Ithaca, 1963) deals chiefly with the later history of the school.

Religion

Heinrich Hermelink: *Das Christentum in der Menschheitsgeschichte* (3 vols. Stuttgart, 1951–1955) reviews the history of Christianity since the

French Revolution and attempts to integrate religious and other social developments. The first two volumes of Kenneth S. Latourette: *Christianity in a Revolutionary Age* (New York, 1958–1959) provide an authoritative, well-documented history of the Catholic and Protestant churches respectively. James H. Nichols: *History of Christianity, 1650–1950* (New York, 1956) is a competent survey.

All the major histories of the Catholic Church deal with this period at length. Josef Schmidlin: *Papstgeschichte der Neuzeit* (4 vols., 2 ed., Munich, 1933) is basic; Jean Leflon: *La crise révolutionnaire, 1789–1846* (Vol. XX of *L'histoire de l'église*, ed. by A. Fliche and V. Martin, Paris, 1951); Roger Aubert: *Le pontificat de Pie IX* (Vol. XXI of the same series, Paris, 1952); Charles H. Pouthas: *L'église catholique de l'avènement de Pie VII à l'avènement de Pie IX* (Paris, 1945) and the same author's *Le pontificat de Pie IX* (Paris, 1962); Henri Daniel-Rops: *The Church in an Age of Revolution, 1789–1870* (New York, 1965) are among the best scholarly accounts. Hubert Becher: *Die Jesuiten* (Münster, 1951) is a brief, factual history. Special aspects of church history are dealt with by Michael P. Fogarty: *Christian Democracy in Europe, 1820–1953* (Notre Dame, 1958) and Alec R. Vidler: *A Century of Social Catholicism, 1820–1920* (London, 1964).

Catholicism in France is reviewed by Henri Guillemin in his *Histoire des catholiques français au XXe siècle* (Geneva, 1947), a collection of stimulating but controversial lectures, and in the more recent *Histoire du catholicisme en France* (3 vols., Paris, 1957–1962). Adrien Dansette: *Religious History of Modern France* (2 vols., New York, 1962) is both competent and readable, while Charles H. Pouthas: *L'église et les questions religieuses sous la Monarchie Constitutionnelle, 1814–1848* (Paris, 1961) consists of lectures by an authority. Maurice Vaussard: *Histoire de la démocratie chrétienne* (2 vols., Paris, 1956) reviews liberal Catholicism in France and other countries. Jean-Baptiste Duroselle: *Les débuts du catholicisme social en France, 1822–1870* (Paris, 1951) is a magistral study. In *Christianisme et classe ouvrière* (Tournai, 1961) François A. Isambert traces the growing concern of the church with the social question.

On Belgium there are two valuable studies: Henri Haag: *Les origines du catholicisme libéral en Belgique, 1789–1839* (Louvain, 1950) and Rudolf Rezsohazy: *Origines et formation du catholicisme social en Belgique* (Louvain, 1958).

George Kitson Clark's *The English Inheritance* (London, 1950) includes an excellent discussion of the religious situation in England. Alfred W. Benn: *History of English Rationalism in the 19th Century* (2 vols., New York, 1906, 1962) and Anthony O. J. Cockshut: *The Unbelievers: English*

Agnostic Thought, 1840–1890 (New York, 1966) deal with irreligious thought. John R. H. Moorman: *A History of the Church in England* (London, 1953) is excellent but brief on this period. Owen Chadwick: *The Victorian Church: Part I, 1829–1860* (New York, 1966) is more detailed and systematic. G. F. A. Best: *Temporal Pillars* (London, 1964) is the most recent of several histories of the reform of the Established Church. *The Churches and the Working Classes in Victorian England,* by Kenneth S. Inglis (London, 1963) deals chiefly with a later period, but has a valuable introduction. Torben Christensen: *Origin and History of Christian Socialism, 1848–1854* (Aarhus, 1962) is a thorough scholarly monograph.

The Oxford Movement has spawned a vast literature. Sidney L. Ollard: *A Short History of the Oxford Movement* (3 ed., London, 1963) is one of the best general surveys. Edmund A. Knox: *The Tractarian Movement, 1833–1845* (London, 1933) is definitely critical, while Charles S. Church: *The Oxford Movement and After* (London, 1932) carries the story much further than others. Too recent for use in the present book is the scholarly account from the Catholic standpoint by Father Marvin R. O'Connell: *The Oxford Conspirators: a History of the Oxford Movement, 1833–1845* (New York, 1969). Owen Chawick, ed.: *The Mind of the Oxford Movement* (London, 1960) and Eugene R. Fairweather, ed.: *The Oxford Movement* (New York, 1964) are useful selections from the sources.

On the Protestant churches of the Continent, Karl Barth: *Protestant Thought from Rousseau to Ritschl* (New York, 1959) is the translation of selected parts of a larger German study (3 ed., Zürich, 1946) by an eminent German theologian. Walter Nigg: *Geschichte des religiösen Liberalismus* (Zürich, 1937) can hardly be praised too highly. The same remark applies to Albert Schweitzer: *The Quest of the Historical Jesus* (London, 1954), which is the translation of the third edition of a German classic. William O. Shanahan: *German Protestants Face the Social Question* (Notre Dame, 1954) is valuable for early social thought.

On the Greek Orthodox Church and Russian religious thought the reader may consult George F. Fedotov: *The Russian Religious Mind* (2 vols., Cambridge, 1946–1947).

Science

Charles Singer: *A Short History of Scientific Ideas to 1900* (Oxford, 1959) is the revised edition of a survey by an outstanding authority. Charles G. Gillispie: *The Edge of Objectivity* (Princeton, 1960) is a first-rate review of the evolution of scientific thought, while Robert J. Forbes and E. J. Dijksterhuis: *A History of Science and Technology* (London, 1963) is a popular survey, mostly of science. The French *Histoire de la science,* ed. by Maurice Daumas (Paris, 1957), is a comprehensive work, each section of which is written by an expert. Sir William C. Dampier: *A History of Science* (4 ed., Cambridge, 1948) is too technical for most laymen, but contains an admirable bibliographical essay by I. Bernard Cohen. *Fore-runners of Darwin, 1745–1859,* ed. by Hiram B. Glass, Owsei Temkin and William Strauss (Baltimore, 1959), is a collection of basic essays on evolution, while Gertrude Himmelfarb: *Darwin and the Darwinian Revolution* (New York, 1959) provides an admirable study of the origins of the theory. René Taton, ed.: *Science in the 19th Century* (London, 1965) is another useful collection of essays, while John D. Bernal: *Science and Industry in the 19th Century* (London, 1953) is a stimulating analysis. Alexander Vucinich: *Science in Russian Culture* (Stanford, 1963) is a pioneer study in a rather neglected field.

On astronomy there are good short histories by Reginald L. Waterfield: *A Hundred Years of Astronomy* (London, 1938) and Giorgio Abetti: *The History of Astronomy* (trans. by Betty Burr Abetti, New York, 1952). For chemistry there are Aaron J. Ihde: *The Development of Modern Chemistry* (New York, 1964), and for physics Henry Crew: *The Rise of Modern Physics* (2 ed., Baltimore, 1935). Sir Archibald Geikie: *The Founders of Geology* (2 ed., London, 1905) still makes excellent reading, while Charles C. Gillispie: *Genesis and Geology* (Cambridge, 1951) is a fascinating study of the impact of geological discovery on religious thought. Illuminating is also Milton Millhauser: *Just before Darwin: Robert Chambers and "Vestiges"* (Middletown, 1959).

Richard H. Shryock: *The Development of Modern Medicine* (2 ed., New York, 1947) is excellent and broad-gauge, while Charles Singer and E. Ashworth Underwood: *A Short History of Medicine* (2 ed., Oxford, 1962) leaves nothing to be desired. Important books on the life sciences are Erik Nordenskiöld: *The History of Biology* (New York, 1949) and Charles Singer: *A History of Biology* (3 ed., London, 1959). Esmond R. Long: *A History of Pathology* (new ed., New York, 1965) is an admirable survey.

Technology

The standard treatment is the five-volume work by Charles Singer, E. J. Holmgard, A. R. Hall and T. I. Williams: *A History of Technology* (Oxford, 1954–1958), but this covers so huge a field that the treatment is often summary. Pierre Rousseau: *Histoire des techniques* (10 ed., Paris, 1956) is a first-rate short account. The same can be said of T. Kingston Derry and Trevor I. Williams: *A Short History of Technology* (New York,

1961). Melvin Kranzberg and Carroll W. Pursell, Jr.: *Technology in Western Civilization* (Vol. I, to 1900, New York, 1967) bids well to be a standard work.

LITERATURE AND THE ARTS

Historical Writing

Eduard Fueter: *Geschichte der neueren Historiographie* (Munich, 1911; French trans., Paris, 1914) is still the basic treatment. George P. Gooch: *History and Historians in the 19th Century* (new ed., Boston, 1959) is vivid and readable. Vol. II of James W. Thomspon's *A History of Historical Writing* (New York, 1942) covers the nineteenth century. An important re-evaluation is Heinrich Ritter von Srbik: *Geist und Geschichte vom deutschen Humanismus bis zur Gegenwart* (2 vols., Munich, 1950–1951). Herbert Butterfield: *Man on His Past* (Cambridge, 1955) consists of stimulating lectures. *The Evolution of British Historiography,* ed. by J. R. Hale (New York, 1964), is a collection of readings, with a lengthy introduction. Heinz-Otto Sieburg: *Deutschland und Frankreich in der Geschichtsschreibung des 19 Jahrhunderts* (2 vols., Wiesbaden, 1954–1958) is a provocative comparative study. Antoine Guilland: *Modern Germany and Her Historians* (new ed., New York, 1915) is old but still useful. Later works are Georg von Below: *Die deutsche Geschichtsschreibung von den Befreiungskriegen bis zu unseren Tagen* (2 ed., Munich, 1924) and Friedrich Engel-Janosi: *The Growth of German Historicism* (Baltimore, 1944). Joachim Streisand, ed.: *Die deutsche Geschichtswissenschaft vom Beginn des 19 Jahrhunderts bis zur Reichsgründung von Oben* (Berlin, 1963) consists of critical essays by various Marxist historians. On the French side may be mentioned Pierre Moreau: *L'histoire en France au XIXe siècle* (Paris, 1935) and Peter Stadler: *Geschichtsschreibung und historisches Denken in Frankreich, 1789–1871* (Zürich, 1958). For Italy there is the classic account by Benedetto Croce: *Storia della storiografia italiana nel secolo decimonono* (Bari, 1921) and for Russia Anatole Mazour: *Modern Russian Historiography* (2 ed., Princeton, 1958).

Only a few specialized studies can be listed here: Louise M. Young: *Thomas Carlyle and the Art of History* (Philadelphia, 1939); Mary C. O'Connor: *The Historical Thought of François Guizot* (Washington, 1955); Gabriel Monod: *La vie et la pensée de Jules Michelet* (2 vols., Paris, 1923); Pieter Geyl: *From Ranke to Toynbee* (Northampton, 1952), brilliant lectures; Theodore von Laue: *Leopold von Ranke: the Formative Years* (Princeton, 1950); Werner Kaegi: *Jacob Burckhardt* (3 vols., Basel, 1947).

Literature

Paul Van Tieghem: *Le romantisme dans la littérature européenne* (Paris, 1948) is one of the few books dealing with European literature on a comparative basis. The *Cambridge History of English Literature,* Vol. XIII, ed. by Sir A. W. Ward and A. R. Waller (New York, 1917), is a fundamental work, and *A Literary History of England,* ed. by Albert C. Baugh (2 ed., New York, 1967), is an excellent handbook. John D. Cooke and Lionel Stevenson: *English Literature of the Victorian Age* (New York, 1949) is also a useful survey. Other general works are *A Critical History of English Literature,* by David A. Daiches (2 vols., New York, 1960), with numerous quotations; *A History of English Literature,* by Louis Legouis and Louis Cazamian (rev. ed., New York, 1964), by two distinguished French scholars. More specialized studies include Jerome H. Buckley: *The Victorian Temper* (Cambridge, 1951); Walter E. Houghton: *The Victorian Frame of Mind* (New Haven, 1957); Raymond Williams: *Culture and Society, 1780–1950* (London, 1958).

In the field of English poetry there is an excellent critical study by Sir Herbert J. C. Grierson and J. C. Smith: *A Critical History of English Poetry* (London, 1944). Allardyce Nicoll: *A History of Early 19th Century Drama, 1800–1850* (Cambridge, 1930) is basic. Ernest A. Baker's *The History of the English Novel* (London, 1935) is an exhaustive study, of which Vol. VII covers the period of Dickens and Thackeray. Walter E. Allen: *The English Novel* (New York, 1954) is one of the best brief studies. Frederick R. Karl: *The 19th Century British Novel* (New York, 1964) can also be recommended. *Victorian Novelists,* by Lord David Cecil (Chicago, 1958), is the latest edition of well-known essays on structure and style, which are dealt with also by the eminent critic F. R. Leavis in his *The Great Tradition* (London, 1948). A highly competent recent survey is Lionel Stevenson's *The English Novel: a Panorama* (New York, 1960). Louis Cazamian: *Le roman social en Angleterre, 1830–1850* (Paris, 1903, 1935) remains the basic work on the social novel, but Kathleen Tillotson: *Novels of the Eighteen-Forties* (Oxford, 1954) is a distinguished critical contribution. Of the immense literature on Dickens and Thackeray, only the splendid biographies of Edgar Johnson and Gordon N. Ray can be mentioned here, along with a few outstanding recent special studies: Humphrey House: *The Dickens World* (London, 1941), on the sociological side of the novels; K. J. Fielding: *Charles Dickens: a Critical Introduction* (new enlarged ed., London, 1966); Marcus Steven: *Dickens, from Pickwick to*

Dombey (New York, 1965); Geoffrey Tillotson: *Thackeray, the Novelist* (London, 1954).

On French literature, Joseph Bédier and Paul Hazard: *Histoire de la littérature française illustrée* (2 vols., Paris, 1949) is excellent. Gustave Lanson and P. Tuffrau: *Manuel illustré d'histoire de la littérature française* (Paris, 1953) is the latest edition of a well-known handbook. Albert Thibaudet: *Histoire de la littérature française de 1789 à nos jours* (Paris, 1936) aims to integrate literature with political developments. Pierre Köhler: *Histoire de la littérature française* (3 vols., Lausanne, 1948–1955) is an independent work by a Swiss scholar. More restricted are Jules Bertaut: *L'époque romantique* (Paris, 1947), a vivid cultural history; Pierre Moreau: *Le romantisme* (2 ed., Paris, 1957), which is Vol. VIII of Jean Calvet: *Histoire de la littérature française;* Fred Berence: *Grandeur spirituelle du XIXe siècle français* (2 vols., Paris, 1958), which consists of biographical appreciations. Specialized works include David-Owen Evans: *Le drame moderne à l'époque romantique 1827–1850* (Paris, 1923) and the same author's *Le roman social sous la Monarchie de Juillet* (Paris, 1936); Frederick C. Green: *French Novelists from the Revolution to Proust* (new ed., New York, 1964), a splendid critical study. There are recent biographies of Hugo by Elliott M. Grant (Cambridge, 1945), Jean B. Barrère (Paris, 1952), and André Maurois (London, 1956); of Stendhal by Richard Coe (London, 1963) and Armand Caraccio (New York, 1965); of Balzac by André Billy (rev. ed., Paris, 1944–1947), Abbé Philippe Bertault (Paris, 1946), Félicien Marceau (London, 1967), Herbert J. Hunt (London, 1957), André Maurois (New York, 1966) and E. J. Oliver (London, 1966).

A History of German Literature, by J. G. Robertson (5 ed., by Edna Purdie, London, 1966) leaves little to be desired. Fritz Martini: *Deutsche Literaturgeschichte* (2 ed., Stuttgart, 1950) is first rate. Covering a more limited period are G. R. Mason: *From Gottsched to Hebbel* (London, 1961); Paul Reimann: *Hauptströmungen der deutschen Literatur, 1750–1848* (Berlin, 1956), a scholarly Marxist study; Hugo Bieber: *Der Kampf um die Tradition: die deutsche Dichtung im europäischen Geistesleben, 1830–1880* (Stuttgart, 1928), a basic work on German intellectual history; Karl Viëtor: *Deutsches Dichten und Denken von der Aufklärung bis zum Realismus* (Berlin, 1936), a semipopular book by an authoritative writer; Martin Greiner: *Zwischen Biedermeier und Bourgeoisie* (Göttingen, 1953), a rather pretentious account of the early nineteenth century; Ernst Alker: *Die deutsche Literatur im 19 Jahrhundert, 1832–1914* (2 ed., Stuttgart, 1962), a solid, systematic account; Franz Koch: *Idee und Wirklichkeit: Deutsche Dichtung zwischen Romantik und Naturalismus* (2 vols., Düsseldorf, 1956), a highly detailed study of the emergence of realism; Georg

Luckaćs: *Deutsche Realisten des 19 Jahrhunderts* (Berlin, 1952), essays by an eminent Marxist critic; Jost Hermand, ed.: *Das Junge Deutschland* (Stuttgart, 1966), a collection of texts with a valuable analytical essay. Recent biographies and studies of Heine are by E. M. Butler (London, 1956), Laura Hofrichter (Oxford, 1963), and William Rose: *Heinrich Heine: Two Studies of his Thought and Feeling* (Oxford, 1956). There is also a perceptive essay by Hans Kaufmann in Vol. X of Heine: *Werke und Briefe* (Berlin, 1964) and a stimulating Marxist biography by Hans Kaufmann (Berlin, 1968). The biographies of Grillparzer by Josef Nadler (Vienna, 1952) and Gerhart Baumann (Frankfurt, 1966) are outstanding. Hans Meyer: *Georg Büchner und seine Zeit* (2 ed., Wiesbaden, 1960) is an important Marxist work.

On other literatures the following titles will prove useful: Ernest H. Wilkens: *A History of Italian Literature* (Cambridge, 1954); E. Allison Peers: *The Romantic Movement in Spain* (2 vols., Cambridge, 1940); Hanus Jelinek: *Histoire de la littérature tchèque* (3 vols., Paris, 1932–1935); Julius von Farkas: *Die Entwicklung der ungarischen Literatur* (Berlin, 1941); D. Mervyn Jones: *Five Hungarian Writers* (London, 1966); Giovanni Bach: *The History of the Scandinavian Literatures* (New York, 1938); P. M. Mitchell: *A History of Danish Literature* (New York, 1958); Theodore Jorgenson: *A History of Norwegian Literature* (New York, 1933); Harald Beyer: *A History of Norwegian Literature* (New York, 1956); Alrik Gustafson: *A History of Swedish Literature* (Minneapolis, 1961); Hans Grellmann: *Finnische Literatur* (Breslau, 1936); Julian Krzyzanowski: *Polish Romantic Literature* (New York, 1931); K. Karel: *Geschichte der polnischen Literatur* (Halle, 1956); Manfred Kridl: *A Survey of Polish Literature and Culture* (New York, 1956); Wiktor Weintraub: *The Poetry of Adam Mickiewicz* (Leiden, 1955); Ettore Lo Gatto: *Histoire de la littérature russe* (5 ed., Bruges, 1964); Adolf Stender-Petersen: *Geschichte der russischen Literatur* (2 vols., Munich, 1957); Thais S. Lindstrom: *A Concise History of Russian Literature* (New York, 1966); Ernest J. Simmons: *Introduction to Russian Realism* (Bloomington, 1965); Donald L. Fanger: *Dostoevsky and Romantic Realism* (Cambridge, 1965); Clarence A. Manning: *Ukrainian Literature;* Miloš Savković: *La littérature yougoslave moderne* (Belgrade, 1936); Petra V. Hanes: *Histoire de la littérature roumaine* (Paris, 1934).

The Arts

E. H. Gombrich: *The Story of Art* (rev. ed., London, 1966) is an ideal survey, by a leading authority. Louis Réau: *L'ère romantique: les arts plastiques* (Paris, 1949), which is Vol. LXXVI of the series *Evolution de l'humanité,* is an excellent synthesis of the arts of all countries. Francis D. Klingender: *Art and the Industrial Revolution* (rev. ed., London, 1968) is a most interesting essay on the impact of economic change on the arts. *Romantic Art,* by Marcel Brion (New York, 1960), is primarily a beautiful album. Thomas S. R. Boase: *English Art, 1800–1870* (Oxford, 1959) is a comprehensive, factual survey. The same holds for Hans Weigert: *Geschichte der deutschen Kunst* (Frankfurt, 1963).

Nikolaus Pevsner: *An Outline of European Architecture* (7 ed., London, 1963) is by an eminent authority. *The Gothic Revival,* by Kenneth Clark (3 ed., London, 1962), is stimulating and readable. Peter Ferriday has edited a collection of essays on Victorian architecture (London, 1963), and there are other works on the same subject by Henry R. Hitchcock (2 vols., London, 1955) and by R. Furneaux Jordan (London, 1966).

Fritz Novotny: *Painting and Sculpture in Europe, 1780–1880* (Baltimore, 1960) is a fine comprehensive study. *The Romantic West, 1789–1850,* ed. by Eugènie de Keyser (New York, 1965), is a splendid collection of plates. Important as a critical study is Walter Friedländer: *David to Delacroix* (Cambridge, 1952), and still valuable is Léon Rosenthal: *Du romantisme au réalisme* (Paris, 1914). Reginald H. Wilenski: *French Painting* (rev. ed., Boston, 1949) is stimulating, and Pierre Francastel: *Histoire de la peinture française* (2 vols., Paris, 1955) is authoritative but rather technical. Jean Marie: *French Painting* (London, 1962) is competent and systematic. On the English side there is Graham Reynolds: *Victorian Painting* (London, 1966), and the special studies of William E. Fredeman: *Pre-Raphaelitism* (Cambridge, 1965) and G. H. Fleming: *Rossetti and the Pre-Raphaelite Brotherhood* (Vol. I, London, 1967).

Studies of particular artists include Jean Alazard: *Ingres et l'ingrisme* (Paris, 1950); Jacques Lasaigne: *Eugène Delacroix* (New York, 1950); Lee Johnson: *Delacroix* (New York, 1963); René Huyghe: *Delacroix* (London, 1964), a full-length biography. *Honoré Daumier,* by Jean Adhémar (Paris, 1954) is a standard biography, but should be supplemented by the excellent book by Oliver W. Larkin: *Daumier, Man of His Time* (New York, 1966) and Wolfgang Balzer: *Der junge Daumier und seine Kampfgefährten* (Dresden, 1965), an excellent monograph on the political satire of the years 1830–1835. For English painters there are recent studies of Constable by Carlos Peacock (London, 1965) and Graham Reynolds (London, 1965). A. J. Finberg: *The Life of J. M. W. Turner* (rev. ed., London, 1961) is a standard work, and John Rothenstein and Martin Butlin: *Turner* (New York, 1964) is an important critical work.

Wilhelm Weber: *A History of Lithography* (New York, 1966) is an exhaustive scholarly history. Georges Potonniée: *History of the Discovery of Photography* (New York, 1936) is basic for the early years. Josef M. Eder: *History of Photography* (New York, 1945) is a mine of information, and Beaumont Newhall: *The History of Photography* (4 ed., New York, 1964) is admirable both in text and plates. Helmut and Alison Gernsheim: *A Concise History of Photography* (New York, 1965) is easily one of the best books. The same authors have published a biography of Daguerre (New York, 1956).

Music

Jules Combarieu: *Histoire de la musique* (3 vols., Paris, 1919) holds its own as perhaps the best single systematic account. Hugo Leichtentritt: *Music, History and Ideas* (Cambridge, 1939) is a stimulating essay, but Paul H. Lang: *Music in Western Civilization* (New York, 1941) is rather difficult. Donald J. Grout: *A History of Western Music* (New York, 1960) is a substantial general text. Georg Knepler: *Musikgeschichte des 19 Jahrhunderts* (2 vols., Berlin, 1961) stresses the social aspects. Alfred Einstein: *Music in the Romantic Era* (New York, 1947) is a reliable German treatment, while Jean Chantavoine and Jean Gaudefroy-Desmombynes: *Le romantisme dans la musique européenne* (Paris, 1955) is very satisfactory. Eric D. Mackerness: *A Social History of English Music* (Toronto, 1965) is concerned chiefly with the spread of popular interest. Donald J. Grout: *A Short History of Opera* (rev. ed., 2 vols., New York, 1966) is a solid systematic survey, with superb bibliographies. The two books by Ivor Guest: *The Romantic Ballet in England* (London, 1954) and *The Romantic Ballet in Paris* (London, 1966) are serious, beautifully illustrated works.

Biographies and critical studies of individual artists are legion. Among the more recent are Herbert Weinstock: *Chopin, the Man and His Music* (New York, 1959); Alan Walker: *Frédéric Chopin* (London, 1966), both excellent; Paula Rehberg: *Franz Liszt* (Zürich, 1961), exhaustive; Jacques Barzun: *Berlioz and His Century* (New York, 1956), competent and readable; Eric Werner: *Mendelssohn* (Glencoe, 1963), perhaps the best general biography; Heinrich E. Jacob: *Felix Mendelssohn and his Times* (New York, 1963), essays by a leading authority; Robert H. Schauffler: *"Florestan": the Life and Work of Robert Schumann* (New York, 1945), well-informed and readable, as is also Marcel Brion: *Schumann and the Romantic Age* (London, 1956).

Ernest Newman's *Life of Richard Wagner* (4 vols., New York, 1933–1941) is almost in a class by itself, being much broader in scope than the usual biography. Hans Gal's *Richard Wagner: Versuch einer Würdigung* (Frankfurt, 1963) is a most rewarding essay and Robert W. Gutman: *Richard Wagner, His Mind and His Music* (London, 1968) is an important critical study. There are two excellent recent studies of Verdi: Frank Walker: *The Man Verdi* (London, 1962) and George Martin: *Verdi: His Music, His Life and Times* (New York, 1963). Herbert Weinstock's *Donizetti and the World of Opera in Italy, Paris and Vienna* (New York, 1963) is an indispensable study.

INDEX

Messenhauser, Wenzel, 475 f.
Messianism, Polish, 248; Italian, 252 ff.
Metternich, Prince Klemens von, 6, 111, 119, 526; and Switzerland, 133 ff., 136; and Belgium, 283–284; and Near East, 300–301; and Galician insurrection, 316; and Cracow, 316; and French advances, 316–317; and Russia, 292, 306, 489; dismissal of, 320–321, 354; and 1848 revolution, 352 ff.
Mevissen, Gustav, 127, 205
Meyerbeer, Giacomo, 610
Meyerskappel, battle of, 135
Michelet, Jules, 90, 171, 249, 281; as an historian, 90, 548, 553; quoted, 46, 216, 218, 252, 308
Mickiewicz, Adam, 171, 247 ff., 277, 281
middle class, see bourgeoisie
Mieroslawski, Louis, 401 ff., 504
Miguel, Dom, 95 ff.
Milan, revolution in, 371 ff.; peace treaty of, 439
Mill, James, 58, 203, 207, 514
Mill, John Stuart, 21, 206 f., 225, 515, 522
Millais, John E., 586
Millet, Jean F., 591
Milman, Henry H., 522, 529
Milutinovich, Sima, 278
Minto, Elliot Lord, 318
Mirari vos, encyclical, 526
missions, foreign, 311, 519, 522
Mitchel, John, 244
Mitteleuropa, projects for, 259, 506 f., 511
Modena, fusion of, with Piedmont, 377
Moderados, in Spain, 95 ff.
Moga, Field Marshal Franz, 473 ff.
Mohl, Robert von, 198, 205
Moldavia, see Danubian Principalities
Moltke, Captain Helmuth von, in Turkey, 299, 300
Mommsen, Wilhelm, quoted, 411
Monitorial Schools, in France, 84; in Britain, 208
Montalembert, Count Charles de, 425, 454, 525 f.
Montanelli, Guiseppe, 432 f., 449
Montemolín, Carlos Luis, Count of, 312–313
Montpensier, Duke of, 314 t.
Morea, Egyptian claim to, 286

Mörike, Edward, 559
Morley, John, quoted, 61
Morny, Count Auguste de, and the coup d'état, 458 ff.
Morocco, French operations in, 310
Morrison, James, 201
Morse, Samuel F. B., 31, 594
mortality, rates of, 193 f.
Morton, W. G. T., 542
Moscheles, Ignaz, 599
"Mountain," the, in French politics, 451 f.
Muhammad Ali, see Mehemet Ali
Müller, Johannes, 540 f.
Munch, Peder A., 261
Münchengrätz Agreement, 99, 292 f., 489
Municipal Guard (garde municipale), 81, 327 f., 335
Muraviev, General Nicholas, 289
Murchison, Roderick, 544
music, 595 ff.
Musset, Alfred de, 77, 561, 565

Napier, Sir Charles, 69, 96, 303–304
Naples, revolution in, 379 f.; and The Roman Republic, 441, 444
Napoleon I, cult of, 76 ff., 85, 247, 425
Nappist Party, in Greece, 178 f.
Narváez, General Ramón, 104 ff.
National Assembly (Austrian), 470 ff.
National Assembly (French), 344 ff., 421 ff., 442, 450 ff.
National Association for the Protection of Labour, 201
National Charter Association, 70
National Congress (Serbian), 363
National Guards, Austrian, 354, 469, 475–476; French, 82, 88, 320, 327 ff., 335, 340–341, 345, 348–349, 452; Hungarian, 358; Neapolitan, 379; Spanish, 101
nationalism, chap. VIII, passim; Irish, 239; Polish, 245 ff.; Italian, 251 ff.; German, 256 ff., 404 ff.; Scandinavian, 260 ff.; Russian, 268 ff.; Austrian, 270 ff.; and revolutions of 1848, 351
nationality, principle of, 115; problems of, in Hungary, 145; official, in Russia, 153
National Liberal Party, in Denmark, 133
National Mobile Guard (French), 332 ff.
National Society for the Education of the Poor, 208

69 70 71 72 73   8 7 6 5 4 3 2 1